D1278268

COMICS COLLECTIBLES AND THEIR VALUES

Stuart W. Wells III
and
Alex G. Malloy

Wallace-Homestead Book Company
Radnor, Pennsylvania

Published in Radnor, Pennsylvania 19089
by Wallace-Homestead,
a division of Chilton Book Company

Designed by Stuart Wells III
Manufactured in the United States of America

Wallace-Homestead ISBN: 0-87069-724-2

1 2 3 4 5 6 7 8 9   5 4 3 2 1 0 9 8 7 6

CONTENTS

ACKNOWLEDGMENTS

The authors would especially like to thank: Claude Held, Paul Fink, Robert J. Sodaro, Neil Hansen, Pat and Mat at Cave Comics, Tim and Steve at T & S Comics and Cards, John DiCicco, Jim Main, Bruce Whitehill, Debby and Marty Krim, Harry Rinker, DC Comics, Marvel Comics, Todd McFarlane and Troy Vozzella of Chilton Book Company.

Photos: Most of the photos in the "Figures" sections are by Evan Wells. Others are promotional photos by Kenner, Toy Biz, Tyco, Playmates, Ertl and Horizon. Most of the photos in the "Toys" sections are by Debby and Marty Krim. Others are by Evan Wells, Stuart Wells, Alex Maurizio or Alex Malloy. Most of the illustrations in the "Paper" sections, plus some illustrations of pins and buttons, are direct computer scans of the objects. Additional photos in these sections are by Evan Wells or Stuart Wells. A number of the photos in this book are from the archives of *Collectible Toys and Values* magazine and the name of the photographer is, unfortunately, no longer known to the authors.

INTRODUCTION

W e live in a throwaway society, but you may be one of the people who fights this trend and can't bring yourself to throw everything out. Consequently, when the stuff you like fills up the house you face terrible choices—admit that you need counseling and call the local trash hauling company or convince your friends and family that the stuff is your collection! If you are one of this group — the few, the strange, the collectors — take heart; this book may be for you!

We have assembled here an incredible list of comic book and comic strip collectibles, described them in detail, and determined their current market value. We have added our collecting tips and other information and squeezed in almost 500 photos to go with the over 10,000 collectibles listed.

What characters? All the great heroes and superheroes from the last 75 years who started out their life as a picture on a page: Batman, Buck Rogers, Dick Tracy, Flash Gordon, Peanuts, Popeye, Spawn, Spider-Man, Superman, X-Men and everyone in between.

What collectibles? Action figures, dolls, model kits, vehicles, games, pins, buttons, rings, posters, books, magazines and trading cards—they're all here.

There is only so much that can be listed in one book: Comic books are listed in *Comics Values Annual: 1995 Edition* by Alex G. Malloy; a detailed list of comic and cartoon trading cards is contained in *Comic Cards and Their Prices* by Stuart Wells III and profiles of 150 major comic book artists (together with the values of their comics) are covered in *Comic Book Artists*, edited by Alex G. Malloy (with Brian Kelly and Kevin Ohlandt).

W e have tried to organize this book to serve the needs of collectors of particular types of items (e.g. action figures, games, trading cards) as well as the needs of collectors who specialize in one, or just a few characters.

Where to Find Things

This book leads off with action figures, listed by series. However, many popular comic book super heroes, such as Batman, Spider-Man and Superman, appeared in several action figure series, and so they are listed again, with more detail, by character. This double listing means that you can compare a given figure with others in the same series, which is often the most important factor in determining value, and also compare it with earlier and later versions of the same character from other series. Other comic book heroes, such as the Teenage Mutant Ninja Turtles, are listed only by series because they have appeared only in a single series.

Other figural representations of comic book (and comic strip) characters, such as Bendable, Die-Cast and PVC Figures are listed next, along with Dolls and Model Kits & Sculptures, and finally, Vehicles.

Only a few comic strip characters have appeared in these kinds of figures. Most comic strip collectibles are listed under Comic Strip Toys, which comes next. This section contains large listings of the many toys based on such early heroes as Buck Rogers, Dick Tracy, Flash Gordon and Popeye, and the more recent comic strip characters such as Garfield and Peanuts. Similar types of miscellaneous toys based on comic book characters follow in Superhero Toys.

Next come sections on Games, Pins, Buttons, and Rings, which are often collected as categories in themselves.

The final sections of this book cover paper collectibles such as Sunday comics pages, original art, posters, books, magazines and trading cards. If you need help finding information on a particular character, please check the extensive index in the back.

About Prices...

We have tried to give a single price for each item listed in this book — the **retail** value of an example of the item in **near mint** condition. This works well for toys from the 1960s to the 1980s, which constitute the vast bulk of available toys. Toys from the 1930s to the 1950s are much harder to find in near mint condition, so the buyer should examine each potential purchase carefully. Defects greatly reduce the value of an older toy collectible. However, less than perfect older toys are still collectible. Recent toys which are out of package or damaged should probably not be purchased at all. A near mint toy can be stored carefully and will appreciate as other toys deteriorate in condition. A toy which is not in top condition will never fetch a top price (or, at least, not until it's the only surviving example).

The value of some recent toys is listed as "CRP" which means "Current Retail Price." These items have not appreciated in value beyond the original retail price, and you may be able to find it at a substantial discount. In the 1990s, popular characters, such as Batman and the Teenage Mutant Ninja Turtles have been licensed to manufacturers of every conceivable type of children's product. In a few years, the manufacturers move on to other characters (such as the Mighty Morphin' Power Rangers). Normally, this would be a good thing for collectors, because prices would rise once a given series was no longer being made.

The problem for collectors is that millions of each potential collectible item were made and hundreds and hundreds of different items were produced. In addition, excess items can still be found at secondary and tertiary toy outlets, such as discount stores, grocery and drugstores, and surplus stores. Our listing of *Batman Returns* toys is meant as an example of this phenomena. Most of the hundreds of items listed there were recycled, with different graphics, as *Batman: The Animated Series* toys, and will be recycled again with *Batman Forever* artwork. However, Batman villains, such as Catwoman, The Joker, The Penguin and The Riddler still have potential.

Information...

Each listing includes a description of the item, and, where known, manufacturer, product code number, and year. Titles correspond, as nearly as possible, to the name on the product itself. Our goal, and our hope, is that the reader will not be in doubt about matching a given toy with our listing. Unfortunately, many classified and dealer ads abbreviate toy names in an attempt to squeeze in as many items as possible. If in doubt when reading an advertisement, make the dealer give you more complete information.

ACTION FIGURE—SERIES

- Marvel and DC superheroes are also listed alphabetically in the next section.
- Figures listed are for in-box or original blister card values; out of blister pack reduces values by 50%. Missing box reduces value by 50%; figures with box never opened increase value by 10%.

This section covers comics-based Action Figure toys, such as the Teenage Mutant Ninja Turtles and especially Superheroes like Batman and X-Men by **series**. Superhero action figures are also listed by character, starting on page 76. Vehicles associated with these series of figures are listed here and also alphabetically in the Vehicles section.

See the Comic Strip Toys section for Dick Tracy, Buck Rogers, Flash Gordon and similar figures.

We have included the product code for just about every action figure, vehicle and collectible that has one. This is the number in the bar code on the back of the toy package and its listing is a unique feature of this book. Different versions of an action figure generally have different product code numbers and so this number can be used to provide certainty that the toy (when you find it) is the one described in our listing and not a later one with a similar name and features.

Variations sometimes occur during the production run of a figure. Scarce variations are highly sought by collectors and command a premium price from dealers. Many variations are covered in this book, but new ones are discovered (or claimed to be discovered) regularly. Different variations of older toys have reasonably well established prices, but on recent toys the number and relative scarcity of variations cannot yet be known with certainty and so prices are very speculative.

Our advice is not to pay a large premium price for a recent variation without first looking for the item in toy stores and secondary outlets like drug stores. You can always pay a premium price later if you wish. By then, collector interest may well have moved on to the next hot item and you can get the one you want for a better price. In the long run you will save a lot of money this way.

ARCHIES

They're not exactly superheroes, nor are they ninja experts and I don't think they qualify as mutants (although I'm not sure), but they are teenagers (and have been for over 50 years). They are also comic book characters and in 1975 Marx Toys made them into action figures.

Betty (Marx Toys 1975)

ARCHIES
(Marx Toys 1975)

Archie	40.00
Betty	45.00
Jughead	40.00
Veronica	40.00
Archie's Jalopy Car	75.00
Carrying Case	25.00

BATMAN

Until 1989, Batman action figures were included in other series, such as (DC) Super Powers and the World's Greatest Super Heroes. Those series are covered below, and, of course, all the Batman action figures are also listed in the next section. The first Batman series (with companions and villains) dates from the 1989 Batman movie. Subsequent series were based on the 1992 and 1995 movie sequels plus the animated TV show and movie. All are from Kenner, except the first one.

When the Super Powers collection came and went, there wasn't much in the way of DC comic character–based action figures for roughly three years. You can just imagine what that was like for the die-hard collectors out there. Why, it brings a tear to the eye just thinking about those days. Then came the year 1989, the year of the Batman movie. Suddenly, superheroes, especially the DC ones, were back in style again. It was like 1966 all over again.

A new company called Toy Biz entered the picture and began producing a line of action figures based on characters that appeared in this new Batman picture, along with some older, more familiar faces as well. The new black-costumed **Batman** showed up in four different variations during its production. There were what collectors call the Keaton Face, Square Jaw, Round Face and Big Lip. If that wasn't enough, variations also showed up with the **Joker**. There was one issue that had a small curl of hair on his forehead and the more common Joker without the curl. Bob the Goon was the only other figure in this series.

Accessories that sported the Batman movie logo on its packaging included the Batmobile and Batwing, both of which came in two different versions. The Batmobile could be bought with or without the cocoon/shroud protective covering. The Batwing could be found with either a plain white box back or one not so plain with black line art of the vehicle and a purple ink pattern. This series was quite similar to, and sold with, the DC Comics Super Heroes series listed later. Other Batman characters, including **Robin**, **The Penguin** and the **Riddler**, were packaged in that series.

Batman and Robin (flanked by Superman and Green Lantern), Super Powers (Kenner 1984)

Joker figure (Toy Biz 1990)

Bob the Goon drawing (Toy Biz 1990)

BATMAN
Toy Biz (1989–90)
4¾" Action Figures

Batman (#4401, 1989)

Keaton Face	10.00
Round Face	10.00
Square Jaw	12.00
Big Lip	10.00

Joker (#4406, 1990), no curl 10.00

with curl	15.00
Bob, the Goon (#4407, 1990)	12.00

Vehicles

Batmobile (#4416, 1989)	30.00
with Cocoon (1989)	40.00
Batmobile "Turbine Sound" (#4432, 1989)	15.00
Batwing (#4418, 1989)	35.00
with white back package	40.00
Batcycle (#4436, 1990)	10.00
Electronic Batmobile (#4435, 1990)	11.00
Radio control Batmobile (#4429, 1990)	20.00
Remote control Batmobile (#4431, 1990)	9.00
Speed Sound Batmobile (1990)	6.00
Joker Cycle & Side Car (#4437, 1989)	10.00
Joker Van (#4438, 1990)	35.00

Batwing vehicle drawing (Toy Biz 1989)

All prices listed are for *Near Mint* condition.

Thunderwhip Batman (Kenner 1991)

BATMAN, THE DARK KNIGHT

T he Batman, The Dark Knight collection from Kenner is nothing short of a wonderful series of toys. It almost harkens back to the glory days of their great Super Powers collection, except these figures don't move as well. But they are, still, wonderfully detailed and well-done figures. The series began in 1990 and was available until about 1992, when it was superseded by the Batman Returns series. The most desired, and hardest to find, **Batman** figures are the Thunderwhip and Power-wing figures which came out late in 1991.

Batman's archenemy, **The Joker**, comes in two variations, with Knock-Out or with Sky Escape features. The Knock-Out Joker is by far the scarcest figure in the whole series and commands the high-

est price. The three "Crime Master" figures are boxed rather than carded and were originally priced higher than the other figures.

The Batcave Command Center Playset is a combination Wayne Manor and Batcave rolled into one. It didn't come out until 1992.

Look for three Dark Knight collection figures: **Thunderwhip Batman, Powerwing Batman and Knock-Out Joker**. These were the last figures produced for this line and are very scarce, particularly the Knock-Out Joker. **Note: There are also Thunderwhip Batman and Powerwing Batman in the Batman Returns series which are not scarce.**

Sky Escape Joker (Kenner 1990)

Batcopter vehicle (Kenner 1990)

BATMAN, THE DARK KNIGHT
Kenner (1990–91)
4¾" Action Figures

Crime Attack Batman (#63110) 18.00
Tec-Shield Batman (#63120)
    Black pull (scarce) 25.00
    Gold Pull 15.00
Wall Scaler Batman (#63130) 15.00
Sky Escape Joker (#63140) 25.00
Iron Winch Batman (#63160) 18.00
Shadow Wing Batman (#63170) 15.00
Bruce Wayne (#63180) 15.00
Powerwing Batman (#63380, 1991) 30.00
Thunderwhip Batman (#63390, 1991) 30.00
Knock-Out Joker (#63450, 1991) 50.00
Boxed, "Deluxe Crime Master Edition" (1991)
Batman with Claw Climber (#63540) 30.00
Batman with Blast Shield (#63460) 30.00
Batman with Night Glider (#63470) 40.00
Batman, The Dark Knight Vehicles
Batcycle (#63190) 15.00
Joker Cycle (#63200) 15.00
Batjet (#63210) 35.00
Batcopter (#63220) 30.00
Turbojet Batwing (#63230) 40.00
Batmobile (#63240) 60.00
Batman Bola Bullet (#63340, 1991) 12.50
Batman Strikewing (#63350, 1991) 12.50

BATMAN RETURNS

The first batch of Batman Returns action figures included **Arctic Batman**; **Air Attack Batman**; Deep Dive Batman; Powerwing Batman; Thunderwhip Batman; Laser Batman and The Penguin as well as a couple of the vehicles. The second batch of figures appeared about a week before the movie opened. The **Robin** and **Penguin Commandos** figures were previously announced, along with **Robin's Jet Foil**, but the big news was the inclusion of the **Catwoman** and **Bruce Wayne** figures! These figures were not previously announced. The assortments contained two of each new figure, but Catwoman

Polar Blast Batman (Kenner 1992)

Firebolt Batman (Kenner 1992)

sold fast to collectors!

The **Bruce Wayne Custom Coupe** vehicle is a 13" black car packaged with the Bruce Wayne figure. The package promises that it "Converts to Crime Fighting Car! Bruce Wayne figure 'becomes' Batman figure!" The conversion is accomplished by replacement as the car will hold any of the Batman figures along with Bruce.

Three other new figures to look for are the **Claw Climber Batman, Bola Strike Batman and Polar Blast Batman**. They are packaged in the same manner as the Deluxe Crime Master Edition figures from the first movie, in a box indicating

that they are Limited Edition Toys "Я" Us figures. These figures should be collectible, as are the three Crime Master figures, which were never produced in great quantity to begin with.

Long after the other figures in this series had appeared, Kenner has produced an additional figure: **Aero Strike Batman**. This figure is a lot like the previous figures, but the point is, it wasn't produced in the same quantity as the earlier figures. The tail-end figures from the earlier Batman series have all been good investments. It's cheap at the moment.

BATMAN RETURNS
Kenner (1992–93)
4¾" Action Figures

Air Attack Batman (#63610) 11.00
Deep Dive Batman (#63790) 10.00
Laser Batman (#63810) 10.00
Arctic Batman (#63820) 11.00
Powerwing Batman (#63880) 12.00
Thunderwhip Batman (#63890) 10.00
Penguin (#63640) 25.00

Penguin (Kenner 1992)

Second batch

Bruce Wayne (#63970) 15.00
Robin (#63630) 15.00
Catwoman (#63870) 20.00
Penguin Commandos (#63860) 15.00
Crime Attack Batman 20.00
Shadow-Wing Batman 20.00
Sky Winch Batman 25.00

1993 Figure

Aero Strike Batman (#63649, 1993) 8.00

Boxed, Deluxe Toys "R" Us Limited Edition

Bola Strike Batman (#63102) 20.00
Polar Blast Batman (#63103) 20.00

Aero Strike Batman (Kenner 1993)

Claw Climber Batman (#63104) 20.00
Boxed, Deluxe Electronic
Firebolt Batman (#63930) 40.00
Rocket Blast Batman (#63940) 40.00
Large Figure
Batman Deluxe 15" (Kenner #63990) 30.00
Vehicles
All-Terrain Batskiboat (#63920) 20.00
Laser Blade Cycle (#63740) 10.00
Skyblade Vehicle (#63400) 12.50
Batman Sky Drop Airship (#63680) 20.00
Batmissile Batmobile (#63910) 40.00
Bruce Wayne Custom Coupe and figure
(#63550) 20.00
  with blue shirted figure, rare 30.00
Robin Jet Foil (#63730) 10.00
Penguin Umbrella Jet (#63690) 6.00

BATMAN RETURNS II

T his series doesn't want to die! Kenner issued three new Batmen in what is now called Batman Returns II: **Hydro Charge Batman, Night Climb-**

---

er **Batman** and **Jungle Tracker Batman.** Each Batman has a different gadget plus different colored and patterned costumes. Bruce Wayne is rich so I guess he can afford all these clothes. In the movie, he had a whole wardrobe full of his basic black outfits, and if he has similar quantities of these and his other specialized outfits, his closet space requirements at stately Wayne Manor must be the envy of Gotham's social set. Maybe that's why Catwoman had to die in the movie. If she had lived, she would have moved in with Bruce and the battle over closet space for her outfits would have made their fights in the movie look like foreplay.

Night Climber Batman, Batman Returns Series II (Kenner 1994)

BATMAN RETURNS II
Kenner (1994)
4¾" Action Figures

Hydro Charge Batman (#64046)	7.00
Jungle Tracker Batman (#64047)	7.00
Night Climber Batman (#64048)	7.00

Vehicle

Camo Attack Batmobile (#63919)	25.00

BATMAN: THE ANIMATED SERIES

The first group of **Batman: The Animated Series** action figures included two **Batman** figures, **Combat Belt Batman** and **Turbojet Batman** plus **Robin, Riddler, Two-Face** and **Penguin.** The only collecting news is that the Penguin figure is scarcer than the others.

There have been so many Batman figures available in the last few years that it's hard to believe that anyone would care about these new ones. But they do! The incredible popularity of the Batman animated TV series has made this an eagerly awaited set of figures. Comic stores in the area bought most of the first ones to appear, and the only complaint was that Catwoman wasn't among the first six figures released. Are any of you toy manufacturers listening? You may have a hard time selling female figures to boys but everyone over 12 buying these figures loves them. The next month Ken-

Clayface (Kenner 1994)

MAN BAT™

SCARECROW™

BRUCE WAYNE SKY DIVE BATMAN THE JOKER CATWOMAN

Six figures from Batman: The Animated Series (Kenner 1993)

ner shipped the **Hoverbat** vehicle to supplement the line.

The next batch included **Bruce Wayne, Sky Dive Batman** and **The Joker**. The package back announces these figures along with **Man-Bat**, but that figure was not included in the initial shipment. When we finally saw **Man-Bat** we thought it was definitely the most collectible of the figures released to that date. Unfortunately, either it didn't sell well or was overproduced because it was available in massive quantities for months.

Next appeared **Scarecrow** and **Ninja Robin**. The new package backs list **Infrared Batman**, but it didn't appear until later. Scarecrow is by far the more interesting figure and this is the first appearance of this villain as a collectible.

The movie opened on Christmas Day to somewhat less fanfare than we expected. Mark Hamill was the voice of the Joker. There were no new figures released to tie into the movie opening, but McDonald's

had an excellent series of eight Happy Meal premiums, including Batman, Catwoman, Batgirl and Poison Ivy and the usual villains.

A number of new figures were on display during Toy Fair 1994 and several hit the stores the week after. These included **Clayface, Mr. Freeze, Knight Star Batman** and **Lightning Strike Batman**, along with **Phantasm** and **Jet Pack Joker** from the "Mask of the Phantasm" movie. The best figure is Phantasm and you should have one in your collection.

There are also a couple of new, deluxe figures: **Ground Assault Batman** is packaged a lot like the deluxe Batman and Batcycle and comes with a motorized turbo-powered ground jet, which has wheels and a spring flywheel. Batman carries a double-bladed axe, which looks like it was stolen from Conan. There is also a deluxe **Power Vision Batman**, which is packaged the same way.

This series was continued in 1995 with

All prices listed are for *Near Mint* condition.

Man-Bat (Kenner 1993)

Poison Ivy (Kenner 1994)

an additional seven figures. **Rapid Attack Batman** and **Tornado Batman** are repackaged from the "Mask of the Phantasm" set. The two Robin figures and the other two Batmen are quite common, but the villain **Bane** has been next to impossible to locate! All of these five figures come on cards with the figure in a plastic bubble rather than the plastic box of previous figures. The recent "Crime Squad" figures are on similar packages.

BATMAN: THE ANIMATED SERIES
Kenner (1993–95)

4¾" Action Figures (1993)

Turbojet Batman (#64660)	10.00
Combat Belt Batman (#64670)	10.00
Robin (#64680)	15.00
The Penguin (#64690)	25.00
The Riddler (#64700)	20.00
Two-Face (#64710)	18.00

Second batch (1993)

Skydive Batman	8.00

The Joker	12.00
Bruce Wayne (#64664)	10.00
Man-Bat (#64666)	10.00
Scarecrow	12.00
Ninja Robin	10.00
Catwoman (#63652)	20.00
Infrared Batman (#63997, 1994)	8.00

Third batch (1994)

Lightning Strike Batman (#64002)	8.00
Knight Star Batman (#64003)	8.00
Mr. Freeze (#64004)	12.00
Clayface (#64005)	15.00
Killer Croc (#64009)	15.00
Poison Ivy (#64012)	25.00
Dick Grayson/Robin (#64016)	8.00
Anti-Freeze Batman (#64018)	8.00
Ninja Power Pack Batman and	
Robin (#64110)	15.00

Fourth batch (1995)

Tornado Batman (#63982)	6.00
Rapid Attack Batman (#63984)	6.00
Cyber Gear Batman (#64119)	7.00
Bane (#64124)	25.00

Bane (Kenner 1995)

Glider Robin (#64133) 7.00
Bola Trap Robin (#64134) 7.00
Radar Scope Batman (#64136) 7.00
Deluxe "Crime Fighter" figures (1994)
High Wire Batman (#63998) 10.00
Mech-Wing Batman (#63653) 10.00
Ground Assault Batman (#63657) 10.00

Power Vision Batman (#63656) 10.00
Oversize Figure
Ultimate Batman, 15" (#64019) 25.00
Vehicles
Batcycle with Batman figure (#63981) . . . 12.00
Jokermobile (#63530) 18.00
Batmobile (#64730) 20.00
Turbo Batplane (#64740) 20.00
Robin Dragster (#63995) scarce 150.00
B.A.T.V. mini vehicle (#63983) 8.00
Hoverbat mini vehicle (1993) 8.00
Bat Signal Jet mini vehicle (1993) 8.00
Aero Bat mini vehicle (#64031, 1994) 8.00
Hydro Bat mini vehicle (#64032, 1994) 8.00
Ice Hammer (#64039, 1994) 12.50
Electronic Crime Stalker (#64023, 1994) . 15.00
Bruce Wayne Street Jet (#63551, 1994) . . 20.00

BATMAN:
MASK OF THE PHANTASM

The Batman: The Animated Series movie figures from Kenner come on a light reddish brown display card. They were shipped to toy stores during 1994, arriving about two months after the movie's Christmas 1993 release. **Total Armor Batman**, **Retro Batman** and the other Batman figures were always available in quantity and could still be found in late 1995. **Jet Pack Joker** and **Phantasm** were always difficult to locate. Those two figures, especially Phantasm, are expensive and highly desirable!

Bruce Wayne Street Jet vehicle with Batman figure (Kenner 1994)

All prices listed are for *Near Mint* condition.

Batman: The Animated Series Mask of the Phantasm figures: Phantasm and Jet Pack Joker (Kenner 1994)

MASK OF THE PHANTASM
Kenner (1994)
4¾" Action Figures

Tornado Batman (#63978)	7.00
Decoy Batman (#64017)	8.00
Rapid Attack Batman (#63965)	7.00
Retro Batman (#63977)	7.00
Total Armor Batman (#64001)	7.00
Phantasm (#64006)	25.00
Jet Pack Joker (#64007)	
Green face	20.00
White face	15.00

BATMAN: CRIME SQUAD

T he final Batman: The Animated Series figures have the "Crime Squad" logo. All come with the figures in a plastic bubble on the card rather than the more common box shape.

I imagine this is cheaper to make, or to ship, or both. None of the figures seem to be scarce, and the first two batches don't contain any villains. So far none of them have acquired any significant collector interest.

CRIME SQUAD
Kenner (1995)
4¾" Action Figures

Air Assault Batman (#64120)	6.00
Land Strike Batman (#64121)	6.00
Torpedo Batman (#64122)	6.00
Ski Blast Robin (#64123)	6.00
Piranha Blade Batman (#64116)	6.00
Sea Claw Batman (#64117)	6.00
Stealth Wing Batman (#64118)	6.00

Vehicles

Triple Attack Jet (#64662)	15.00
Batcycle, with Batman figure (#64672)	9.00

Torpedo Batman (Kenner 1995)

LEGENDS OF BATMAN

The Legends of Batman series came out in the fall of 1994. **Catwoman, The Riddler** and **The Joker** have been the most valuable figures to date. The other figures are all easy to find. All of the figures come with an exclusive trading card from SkyBox which is not related to any other trading card series.

LEGENDS OF BATMAN
Kenner (1994–95)
4¾" Action figures with trading card

Crusader Batman (#64026)	8.00
Power Guardian Batman (#64027)	8.00
Cyborg Batman (#64028)	8.00
Nightwing (Robin) (#64029)	8.00
Catwoman (#64033)	15.00
The Joker (#64034)	12.00
Future Batman (#64037)	8.00
Knightquest Batman (#64041)	8.00

Second batch (Spring 1995)

Samurai Batman (#64126)	6.00
Knightsend Batman (#64127)	6.00
Viking Batman (#64128)	6.00
The Riddler (#64130)	15.00

Third batch (Fall 1995)

Dark Warrior Batman (#64038)	6.00
Long Bow Batman (#64043)	6.00
Crusader Robin (#64057)	6.00
Deluxe Flightpak Batman (#64131)	12.00
Deluxe Silver Knight Batman (#64132) ...	12.00
Deluxe Desert Knight Batman (#64058) ..	12.00

Vehicles

Batcycle (#64981)	10.00
Dark Rider Batman (on Stallion) (#64042)	20.00
Batmobile (#64025)	20.00

Oversize Figure

Ultimate Batman, 15" electronic (#64019) .	25.00

Legends of Batman: Catwoman (Kenner 1994)

Cyborg Batman (Warner Bros./Kenner 1995)

BATMAN (SPECIAL EDITION)

S ix of the original Legends of Batman figures were repackaged with
special display cards and color
variations and sold exclusively at Warner
Bros. stores. Warner Bros. owns DC
Comics so more figures are certainly
possible. Warner Bros. has opened a lot
of stores in the last few years and also
sells by catalog. Consequently, the figures
may be hard to find in some areas, but
they should not be impossible to locate.
They are probably the best versions of
these particular figures to collect.

ToyBiz (1995)

Crusader Batman	10.00
Power Guardian Batman	10.00
Cyborg Batman (#64781)	10.00
Nightwing (Robin)	10.00
Future Batman	10.00
Knightquest Batman (#64785)	10.00

T he last series of Batman figures is
based on the *Batman Forever*
movie staring Val Kilmer and
Chris O'Donnell as the "Dynamic Duo"
plus Jim Carrey and Tommy Lee Jones as
The Riddler and **Two-Face**. These four
characters have been featured on all of
the merchandise from the movie. Unfortunately there have been no figures of
Chase Meridian, Sugar or Spice. Only the
two villians have garnered any collector
interest to date. We recommend these two
figures plus the **Guardians of Gotham
City** two-pack for the discriminating
collector. It's too early to tell about any
of the other figures. There will be more
of them in 1996.

BATMAN FOREVER
Kenner (1995)
4¾" Action Figures

Street Biker Robin (#64144)	6.00

The Riddler (Kenner 1995)

Hydroclaw Robin (#64145) 6.00
Transforming Dick Grayson (#64146) 6.00
Two-Face (#64147) 10.00
The Riddler (#64148) 10.00
Blast Cape Batman (#64149) 6.00
Fireguard Batman (#64150) 6.00
Sonar Sensor Batman (#64151) 6.00
Transforming Bruce Wayne (#64152) 6.00
Manta Ray Batman (#64153) 6.00
Night Hunter Batman (#64154) 6.00
Second batch (late 1995)
Ice Blade Batman (#64164) 6.00
Power Beacon Batman (#64165?) 6.00
Batarang Batman (#64166) 6.00
Deluxe figures (1995)
Deluxe Attack Wing Batman (#64161) ... 12.00
Deluxe Martial Arts Robin (#64162) 10.00
Guardians of Gotham City
    two-pack (#64171) 12.00
Vehicles & Accessories
Robin Cycle (#64156) 6.00
Batwing vehicle (#64157) 25.00
Electronic Batmobile (#64158) 25.00
Wayne Manor/Batcave (#63360) 50.00
Oversize Figures
Ultimate Batman, 15" electronic
    (#64177, 1995) 22.50
Electronic Talking Batman, soft (#29427) . 20.00
Robin, 16" soft (#29417) 15.00

CADILLACS & DINOSAURS

C adillacs and Dinosaurs has been around for a while as a comic book, but now that it's on Saturday morning TV there's a toy series from Tyco. The first eight figures listed below are already out and the rest, mostly dinosaurs and accessories, are listed on the package back, but we haven't seen them. We also got a free "Special Tyco Toys edition" #1 comic book with our purchase. They are nice, but not exceptional, figures and haven't drawn much collector interest so far.

Hannah Dundee, is the only female figure in the line and seems to be somewhat scarce. It's the only one that has increased in value.

CADILLACS & DINOSAURS
Tyco (1994)
5" Action Figures
Jack Cadillac Tenrec (#13021) 5.00
Mustapha Cairo (#13022) 5.00
Hannah Dundee (#13023) 9.00

Hannah Dundee (Tyco 1994)

Jungle Fighting Jack Tenrec (#13024) 5.00
Hammer Terhune (#13025) 5.00
Vice Terhune (#13026) 5.00
Dinosaurs, Vehicles and Accessories
Hermes (Deinonychus) (#13027) 5.00
Zeke (Quetzalcoatlus) (#13028) 5.00
Kentrosaurus 8.00
Triceratops 8.00
Jack Tenrec's Cadillac 12.50
Jack Tenrec's Glider 6.00
Hammer's Tribike (#13072) 6.00
Jack's Garage .... not released

The Original Captain Action (Ideal 1966)

CAPTAIN ACTION

T he closest Marvel and DC Comics ever came to having actual "action figures" in the 1960s was with the Captain Action series by Ideal Toys. This line featured the main character, Captain Action, which was a fully posable, 12" figure, much in the same vein as the popular G.I. Joes of that period were. He also, as with the aforementioned series by Hasbro, had an array of outfits you could purchase separately. However, unlike the Joes, all the costume outfits for Captain Action were that of an adventure hero nature. With these outfits at his disposal, a boy could change his Captain Action figure into 13 other different characters. Three of these were Marvel Comics characters: Sgt. Fury, Spider-Man and Captain America. The **Captain America** set was issued twice by Ideal: once in 1966 and again in 1967 when four new

costumes along with eight of the original nine outfits were re-issued. The reissued character outfits all came with a flasher or, as they called it, "videotronic" ring. This ring changed from Captain Action to the character that was in the outfit box by way of a simple movement of the hand. **Sgt. Fury** was the outfit that was issued but once in 1966. Rumors have it that this was possibly due to slow sales from competition with the similar-looking G.I. Joes of that period. **Spider-Man**, issued in 1967 with a flasher ring, is one of the most looked for of these costume outfits.

Ideal's claim to fame, figurewise, was, of course, the 12" posable (1,001 poses in all, the ads claim) Captain Action toy line.

Aquaman: This set had some nice accessory pieces for the "swift and powerful monarch of the ocean," including a swordfish sword, trident-tipped spear and shell-like horn. But, somebody please tell me what Aquaman needs with a pair of swim fins!?!

Superman: The Man of Steel's outfit came with notable extras like shackles, a piece of green kryptonite, as well as his pet dog Krypto. It's a pity that Dr. Evil, the villain of the Captain Action figure line, never had any comic villain character outfits to change into. If that was the case, he could've used some of these pieces as part of a Luthor outfit. And, don't you think that Krypto would have made a better accessory piece with the Superboy outfit made for the Action Boy figure of this series?

Batman: No complaints here except that with all character costumes that have capes, the plastic used tends to rip and tear a great deal. Otherwise, this is a fine costume, with a great load of utility belt pieces, such as a flashlight, drill, batarang

---

and grappling hook.

Each one of these kits was reissued, as every Captain Action collector knows, with a flicker ring.

Action Boy was the youthful sidekick of the C.A. posable figure line. Standing 9" tall in his boot-covered feet, he could change into three different comic book characters, all of which were from the DC Comics universe.

Superboy: Some pretty exotic stuff here for the Kid from Krypton, including a "telepathic scrambler helmet," minilab and a space language translator. Again, I think Krypto would have made a better piece in this set.

Aqualad: This founding member of the original Teen Titans had some truly fine pieces accompanying his costume. The sea horse knife, seashell axe, swordfish

Action Boy: Superboy outfit (Ideal 1967)

spear and his pet octopus, Octo, almost make up for his adult partner's swim fins.

Robin: Kudos for an excellent costume and equally impressive array of accessories that range from Bat Grenade to Bat-arang launcher (with two batarangs) and climbing suction cups. The only truly bad pieces in this set are his green gloves that closely resemble oven mitts.

As a side note, the vast majority of the

Batman Captain Action outfit; Robin Action Boy outfit; Captain Action figure (Ideal 1966)

---

collectors with whom we've corresponded, find it rather odd that Action Boy only had outfits based on DC Comics characters. Although it's a well-known fact that there weren't too many boy sidekicks at Marvel at the time, while the Captain Action line was in production, a costume of Bucky, Captain America's youthful partner, would have been a welcomed addition.

The **Videomatic Rings** from the 1967 series figures are collectible in their own right. See the section on "Rings" later in this volume.

We have included **all** the costumes from this series, even though The Lone Ranger and Tonto are Western heroes, not comics characters, and are not otherwise covered in this book.

CAPTAIN ACTION
Ideal (1966–68)
12" Action Figures

Action Boy (1st issue, #3420, 1967) 800.00
Action Boy (photo box/space suit) 1,100.00
Captain Action (1st issue) 500.00
Captain Action (2nd issue, #3400, 1967) . 600.00
Captain Action (free parachute) 750.00
Captain Action (photo box) 800.00
Dr. Evil (photo box) 800.00
Dr. Evil Doll and Lab Set (1968) 1,400.00
Costumes
Aquaman (1966) 400.00

Batman (1966) 500.00
Captain America (1966) 400.00
Flash Gordon (1966) 475.00
Lone Ranger (red shirt) (1966) 550.00
Phantom (1966) 450.00
Sgt. Fury (1966) 450.00
Steve Canyon (1966) 475.00
Superman with Krypto (1966) 550.00
Aqualad (Action Boy outfit) with Octo the
    octopus (#3423, 1967) 600.00
Aquaman with ring (#3408, 1967) 550.00
Batman with ring (#3402, 1967) 600.00
Buck Rogers with ring (#3416, 1967) . . 1,600.00
Captain America with ring (#3409, 1967) . 500.00
Flash Gordon with ring (#3403, 1967) . . . 750.00
Green Hornet with ring (#3413, 1967) . 3,750.00
Lone Ranger (Blue Shirt, with ring)
    (#3406, 1967) 900.00
Phantom with ring (#3407, 1967) 750.00
Phantom with .45 automatic (1967) 750.00
Robin (Action Boy outfit) (#3421, 1967) . . 750.00
Spider-Man with ring (#3414, 1967) . . . 2,000.00
Steve Canyon with ring (#3405, 1967) . . . 350.00
Superboy (Action Boy outfit) (#3422, 1967) 700.00
Superman with ring (#3401, 1967) 700.00
Tonto with ring (#3415, 1967) 1,200.00
Vehicles and playsets
Headquarters carry case (Sears 1967) . . . 500.00
Action Cave carry case (Wards 1967) . . . 650.00
Quick Change Chamber (Sears 1967) . . . 750.00
Silver Streak Amphibian Car (1967) 900.00
Silver Streak Garage (Sears 1967) . . . 1,200.00
Dr. Evil Sanctuary carry case (1967) . . 1,000.00
Accessories: see Superhero Toys section

Buck Rogers, Captain America and Steve Canyon outfits (Ideal 1966–67)

The Batmobile in peril on the Exploding Bridge playset (Mego 1975)

COMIC ACTION HEROES

Mego's Comic Action Heroes was a series of 3¾" superheroes and villains made of a soft plastic. All of these figures were bent at the knees and lacked the posability of the larger figures. The main interest here is in the deluxe accessory sets.

One was a Fortress of Solitude playset that would fall apart (on purpose, of course). There is also a Wonder Woman Collapsing Tower playset that came with an invisible jet. Also available was the Batman and Robin Exploding Bridge playset that came with a Batmobile as well. This last set was repackaged and included the Joker and Penguin figures the second time around.

COMIC ACTION HEROES
Mego (1975–78)

3¾" Figures

Aquaman (#62101-5) 75.00
Batman (#62101-2) 75.00
Captain America (#62102-4) 90.00
Green Goblin (#62102-3) 90.00
Hulk (#62102-1) 75.00
Joker (#62101-8) 75.00
Penguin (#62101-7) 75.00
Robin (#62101-3) 75.00
Shazam (#62101-4) 75.00
Spider-Man (#62102-2) 75.00
Superman (#62101-1) 75.00
Wonder Woman (#62101-6) 75.00

Accessories

Collapsing Tower/Invisible Airplane playset
   with Wonder Woman 3¾" figure 120.00
Exploding Bridge/Batmobile playset
   with Batman & Robin 3¾" figures . . . 150.00
Exploding Bridge playset with Batman and
   Robin, Joker and Penguin (1975) . . . 200.00
Fortress of Solitude playset
   with Superman 3¾" figure 200.00
Mangler 250.00

All prices listed are for *Near Mint* condition.

19

DC COMICS SUPER HEROES

In addition to the Batman film series of figures and accessories covered above, Toy Biz produced a companion line of toys under the DC Comics Super Heroes banner logo. Superman, Robin, Wonder Woman, Mr. Freeze, Penguin, Lex Luthor and The Riddler appeared first. Superman disappeared first and is now very scarce. Roughly a year later, Aquaman, Green Lantern, Flash, Hawkman and Two Face were produced.

The Penguin figure was first equipped with an umbrella that shot small missiles. However, they shot out too powerfully and were small enough for a child to swallow. Collectors loved it, but it was soon replaced with a larger missile and, fairly quickly, by a third Penguin figure, whose entire umbrella top shot off.

Another variation was to be found in the packaging of The Flash, who came with the usual-sized DC Comics Super Heroes logo as well as a smaller one on his package. The Flash was also reissued with a speed-simulating Turbo Board. Unfortunately, by the time this new figure was available, his TV series was canceled. This was the last DC characters which Toy Biz produced. They went on to Marvel and X-Men figures and were eventually bought out by Marvel.

DC COMICS SUPER HEROES
Toy Biz (1989–91)

5" Action Figures

Aquaman (#4415, 1990)	20.00
The Flash (#4414, 1990), regular-sized logo	5.00
Smaller logo (#4414, 1991)	8.00
The Flash (#4441, 1991)	15.00
Green Lantern (#4413, 1990)	25.00
Hawkman (#4421, 1990)	20.00
Lex Luthor (#4408, 1989)	8.00
Mr. Freeze (#4412, 1990)	10.00
The Penguin (#4409, 1989)	
Small Missile	35.00
Large Missile	25.00
"Missile Firing Umbrella"	8.00
The Riddler (#4411, 1989)	15.00
Robin (#4402, 1989) with grappling hook	10.00
with gun	25.00
Superman (#4403, 1989)	35.00
Two Face (#4427, 1990)	15.00
Wonder Woman (#4404, 1989)	8.00

Lex Luthor (Toy Biz 1989) and The Flash (Toy Biz 1990)

The Thing and Mr. Fantastic (Toy Biz 1994)

FANTASTIC FOUR

T he first few figures in this line of action figures appeared at Christmas 1994 and the rest showed up in January. Two batches followed in 1995. There are two versions of the Invisible Woman, clear and in blue costume and both are highly collectible. The Human Torch with Glow-in-the-Dark Flames is quite scarce. It was replaced quickly by the Human Torch with Flame-On Sparking Action.

FANTASTIC FOUR
Toy Biz (1994–95)

5" Action Figures

The Thing (#45101)	7.00
Black Bolt (#45102)	7.00
Silver Surfer (#45103)	8.00
Mole Man (#45104)	7.00
Terrax (#45105)	7.00
Dr. Doom (#45106)	7.00
Mr. Fantastic (#45107)	7.00

Second batch (1995)

Invisible Woman (blue costume) (#45108)	25.00
Human Torch (Glow-in-the-Dark Flames) (#45109)	20.00
Human Torch (Flame-On Sparking Action) (#45111)	6.00
Invisible Woman (clear) (#45112)	12.00
Gorgon (#45113)	6.00
Firelord (#45114)	6.00
Thanos (#45115)	6.00
Dragon Man (#45116)	6.00
Blastaar (#45117)	6.00

Third batch (1995)

The Thing II (#45121)	6.00
Namor (#45122)	6.00
Annihilus (#45123)	6.00
Attuma (#45125)	6.00
Super Skrull (#45126)	6.00
Triton (#45127)	6.00

Vehicles and Accessories

Thing Sky Cycle (#45325)	10.00
Galactus 14" electronic figure (#45310)	18.00
Cosmic Modular Space Vehicle (#45320)	30.00

10" "Fantastic Four" figures

Silver Surfer (#45501)	10.00
Human Torch (#45502)	10.00
Dr. Doom (#45503)	10.00
The Thing (#48125)	10.00
Johnny Storm (#48406)	10.00

All prices listed are for *Near Mint* condition.

GENERATION X

T he Generation X figures appeared just before Christmas 1995, making them the last group of figures included in this book. There are two female figures in the group, **Jubilee** and **Penance**, which is extraordinary. The entire rest of the Marvel, X-Men, and Spider-Man line of figures, about 350 strong, only has a total of 12 versions of 7 other female figures. Give up? The others are Domino, Invisible Woman, Phoenix, Rogue, Spider-Woman, Spiral and Storm.

GENERATION X
Toy Biz (1995)
5" Action figures

Chamber (#43117)	6.00
Penance (#43118)	7.50
Skin (#43119)	6.00
Jubilee (#43120)	7.50
Emplate (#43121)	6.00
Phalanx (#43122)	6.00

Jubilee (Toy Biz 1995)

Ghost Rider II (Toy Biz 1995)

GHOST RIDER

T his set appeared in November 1995. The 10" figures actually appeared before the 5" figures. Skinner didn't arrive until early 1996.

GHOST RIDER
Toy Biz (1995)
5" Action Figures, with mini-comic

Ghost Rider (#52301)	6.00
Blaze (#52302)	6.00
Vengeance (#52303)	6.00
Skinner (#52305, 1996)	6.00
Blackout (#52306)	6.00
Ghost Rider II (#52307)	6.00

10" "Ghost Rider" Figures

Ghost Rider (#52401)	10.00
Blaze (#52402)	10.00
Vengeance (#52403)	10.00

Stunt Cycle vehicles with figure

Ghost Rider's Ghost Fire Cycle (#52436)	10.00
Blaze's Dark Cycle (#52437)	10.00
Vengeance's Steel Skeleton Cycle (#52438)	10.00

Spirits of Vengeance cycle and 5" rider, boxed

Ghost Rider (#52431)	10.00
Blaze (#52432)	10.00
Vengeance (#52433)	10.00

IRON MAN

T his set of action figures appeared in early March 1995. Most of the early collector interest centered on **Spider-Woman**, the only female figure. However, she turned out to be fairly common and has not begun to appreciate until recently. The second and third batches appeared later, with different Iron Men depicted on the package. It's too early to determine if any of them will draw any substantial collector interest.

IRON MAN
Toy Biz (1995)
5" Action Figures

Iron Man (#46101)	8.00
Iron Man Hydro-Armor (#46102)	8.00
War Machine (#46103)	9.00
Spider-Woman (#46104)	10.00
Mandarin (#46105)	7.00
Blacklash (#46016)	7.00
Grey Gargoyle (#46107)	7.00

Second batch

Iron Man Space Armor (#46111)	6.00
Iron Man Stealth Armor (#46112)	6.00
Iron Man Hologram Armor (#46113)	6.00
Hawkeye (#46114)	6.00
Modok (#46115)	6.00
Blizzard (#46116)	6.00
Whirlwind (#46117)	6.00

Third batch

Tony Stark (#46121)	6.00
Iron Man Arctic Armor (#46122)	6.00
Hulk Buster Iron Man (#46123)	6.00
Century (#46124)	6.00
Dreadknight (#46125)	6.00
Titanium Man (#46127)	6.00

10" "Iron Man" figures

Iron Man (#46601)	10.00
Mandarin (#46602)	10.00
War Machine (#46603)	10.00
Iron Man Space Armor (#48126)	11.00
Tony Stark Techno Suit (#48407)	11.00

"Iron Man" dragons

Fin Fang Foom (#46131)	10.00
Aureus Gold Dragon (#46132)	10.00
Argent Silver Dragon (#46133)	10.00

Spider-Woman (Toy Biz 1995)

Dreadknight (Toy Biz 1995)

JUSTICE LEAGUE OF AMERICA

T he Ideal Toy Company had a stranglehold on the DC characters during the 1960s. They first produced a three-piece figure set consisting of Batman, Robin and The Joker. These figures, each 3" in size (as were all other figures of this series), came packaged both painted and unpainted. However, The Joker, and all the other villains to follow, always came unpainted. This set was called the "Official Batman Figure Set."

Also available during the same time were three other figure sets of this type, with four figures to a package. These particular sets featured two painted superheroes as well as two unpainted villains and have been referred to, by collectors, as the Justice League of America figure sets. One set contains Batman, Robin, Joker and Brainstorm while another features Aquaman, Superman, Mouseman and Koltar. The third and last issue is comprised of Wonder Woman, Flash, Thunderbolt and Keyman. The set that includes Batman and Robin is the highest priced of the three. All the figures were very nicely detailed, and the painted ones, especially, were very nicely rendered. However, these are really just plastic figures, not *action* figures. They are included here because they are precursors of the modern action figure series.

Ideal also produced playsets that included these figures as well as some made just for the occasion. First up was a six-piece Batman playset. Made exclusively for Sears, this set included the nonpainted Joker figure plus another

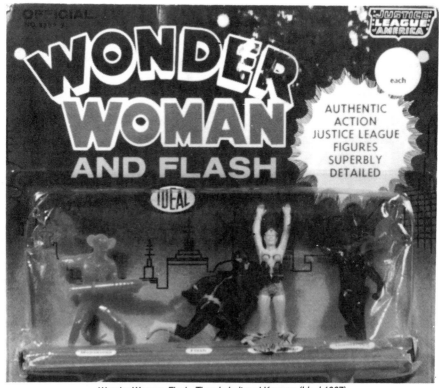

Wonder Woman, Flash, Thunderbolt and Keyman (Ideal 1967)

villain, a color cardboard backdrop of Gotham City, and figures of Batman and Robin seated in a Batmobile. A deluxe 23-piece version of this set by Ideal was also produced exclusively for Sears. This wonderfully extravagant set came with all the items from the first set plus much more. Additional items included a villainous towering robot figure, a Batplane, a Batcave with assorted equipment, and a Bat Signal device.

Ideal made a Batcave carrying case for Sears stores that comes either with or without the playset pieces for the 23-piece set. Even though the 23-piece Batman playset is larger in scope, the smaller six-piece set is the rarer of the two.

Doctor Doom, Secret Wars (Mattel 1984)

JUSTICE LEAGUE OF AMERICA
Ideal (1966–67)
3" plastic figures

Four-pack of 3" plastic figures (1966–67) depending on assortment, per pack	150.00
Batman Official Figures Set (with Robin and Joker) (1966)	125.00
Aquaman	60.00
Batman	50.00
Robin	75.00
Joker	75.00
Brainstorm	50.00
Flash	80.00
Keyman	50.00
Koltar	50.00
Mouserman	50.00
Superman	75.00
Thunderbolt	50.00
Wonder Woman	75.00

Playsets

Batman 6-piece Play Set in plain box (Ideal/Sears 1966)	150.00
Batman Playset (6 piece) (Ideal, 1966)	1,700.00
Batman Playset (23 pieces, with Batcave carrying case) (Ideal/Sears, 1966)	1,500.00
Set in plain box (Ideal/Sears 1966)	500.00
Carrying Case (Ideal/Sears 1966)	300.00
Batman Playset (11 piece) (Ideal #3305, 1966)	1,100.00
Set in plain box (Ideal/Sears 1966)	350.00
Superman Metropolis Play Set (Ideal #3323) (Advertised but never found)	Not determined

A period of three years came and went before another series of Marvel-based action figures showed up. These were the Marvel Super Hero Secret Wars figures by Mattel. They were produced to compete with the DC Comics–derived Super Powers collection of the same year by Kenner. These posable 4½" figures, all came with a secret flasher shield. This toy line got its inspiration, in part, from the Marvel Comics limited 12-issue series of the same name. The figures that were produced for this line are: Iron Man, Captain America, Baron Zemo, Doctor Doom, Dr. Octopus, Kang, The Falcon, Hobgoblin, Magneto and Daredevil. Wolverine was issued twice, as was Spider-Man. The difference that separates the two versions of Wolverine is in the claws. There is the first issue with black claws and the silver-clawed later issue.

Spider-Man was issued first with his regular red-and-blue costume and again in an all-black outfit. The reason for this color change was to, again, form a bond between the toy line and the comic series it was based on. In that self-same series, Spidey is given a new black costume while on an alien world. There are three other figures available that make this set complete, but if you were trying to add them to your set when they first came out, you and countless others had a difficult time doing so. You see, they were only available in Spain and France. The figures I'm referring to were Iceman, Electro and The Constrictor. At the time they first were available, they were probably going for less than $5.00 in United States currency.

There were also two special figure sets you could find: one featured Captain America and Doctor Doom while the other came with the trio of Captain America, Daredevil and the black-suited Spider-Man. The foreign figures and the later set are highly sought.

Vehicles aplenty were made available for this toy line by Mattel. There were two gliders: the Dark Star, which came with a Kang figure, and the Star Dart, which came with a figure of Kang, the black-suited Spider-Man. The Doom Cycle came either with or without the Dr. Doom figure, as did the Doom Copter, while the Turbo Copter came with or without a figure of Captain America.

Magneto, Secret Wars (Mattel 1984)

Wolverine, Secret Wars (Mattel 1984)

MARVEL — SECRET WARS
Mattel (1984)
4¼" Action Figures with Secret Shields

Baron Zemo (#0139)	30.00
Captain America (#7205)	20.00
Constrictor (#9631)	55.00
Daredevil (#914)	32.00
Doctor Doom (#7210)	15.00
Doctor Octopus (#7213)	18.00
Electro (#9569)	65.00
Falcon (#9141)	40.00
HobGoblin with flying bat (#9138)	50.00
Iceman (European issue #9561)	50.00
Iron Man (#7206)	20.00

Kang (#7212) 13.00
Magneto (#7211) 15.00
Spider-Man, Black outfit (#9153) 48.00
Spider-Man, Red outfit (#7207) 30.00
Wolverine (#7208) Silver claws 60.00
    Black claws 90.00
Captain America vs Dr. Doom Set 50.00
Doctor Doom, Magneto, Kang set 100.00
Spider-Man (black outfit), Captain America and
    Daredevil gift set (#9482) 85.00
Vehicles and Accessories
Dark Star flying wing with Kang figure
    (#9692) 30.00
Doom Copter 16" (#9572) 45.00
    with Doom figure 55.00
Doom Cycle 8" (#7600) 15.00
    with Doom figure 25.00
Doom Roller Command Unit (#7474) 20.00
Freedom Fighter 16" (#9392) 25.00
Marvel Super Heroes Machine (#9877) . . 30.00
Marvel Super Villains Machine (#9880) . . 30.00
Secret Messages Pack (#7599) 25.00
Star Dart flying wing with black-suited
    Spider-Man figure (#9693) 45.00
Tower of Doom 15" (#7472) 30.00
Turbo Copter (#9246) 40.00
    with Captain America figure 55.00
Turbo Cycle (#7473) 13.00
    with Figure 25.00

MARVEL SUPERHEROES

T he super hero action figure was abandoned yet again, shortly after Kenner and Mattel dropped their toy lines, and still another dry spell began. And this time it lasted until 1989, the year of the Batman movie. Due to this film, merchandising of superheroes finally hit a high note. A relatively new company, Toy Biz, was the new action figure manufacturer on the block, and with licenses from both DC and Marvel, it was the first to do so since Mego. Beginning with action figures based solely on the Batman movie, they quickly added more from the DC Comics universe and the Marvel universe as well.

In 1990 they introduced a series of Marvel Super Heroes, in a toy line called,

Silver Surfer (Toy Biz 1990)

appropriately enough, Marvel Superheroes. The first batch included Captain America, The Hulk, Spider-Man, Daredevil, The Punisher, Silver Surfer, Dr. Doom and Dr. Octopus.

The first batch of Marvel Superhero figures must have done well for Toy Biz as they added Thor, Iron Man (with removable armor), Venom, The Green Goblin, The Punisher (with Real Machine Gun sounds) and Spider-Man (now with Web Climbing Action) to the line. Also, look for The Punisher Van, the Spider-Man Attack Tower and the Hulk Rage Cage. All these figures are very good looking and all have done very well for Toy Biz. Their next new series was The X-Men, covered below.

MARVEL SUPERHEROES
Toy Biz (1990–91)
5" Action Figures (1990)
Captain America (#4801) 15.00
Spider-Man (Web-Suction Hands) (#4802) 20.00
Dr. Doom (#4803) 15.00
Dr. Octopus (#4804) 15.00
Punisher (Cap Firing Weapons) (#4806) . . 15.00

All prices listed are for *Near Mint* condition.

Silver Surfer (#4807) 30.00
Daredevil (#4808) 50.00
Incredible Hulk (#4809) 15.00

Venom (Toy Biz 1991)

Second batch (1991)
Incredible Hulk (small logo)
  (#4809) 10.00
Amazing Spider-Man (Web-Shooting)
  (#4811) 20.00
  With "New Action" sticker (#4811) . . 20.00
Amazing Spider-Man (Web-Climbing)
  (#4812) 25.00
  With "New Action" sticker (#4812) . . 25.00
Punisher (Machine Gun Sounds) (#4813) . 15.00
  With "New Action" sticker (#4813) . . 10.00
Iron Man (#4814) 20.00
Green Goblin with lever (#4815) 35.00
Green Goblin without lever (#4815) 15.00
Venom (Living Skin Slime Pores) (#4816)   20.00
Thor with lever (#4817) 35.00
Thor without lever (#4817) 20.00
Thor with short hammer (#4817) 30.00
Vehicles and Accessories
Captain America Turbo Coupe 25.00
Spider-Man Dragster 20.00
Marvel Super Heroes Training Center . . . 40.00
Punisher Van (#4863, 1991) 30.00
Spider-Man Attack Tower (#4874, 1991) . 25.00
Hulk Rage Cage + Hulk (#4872, 1991) . . . 15.00

MARVEL SUPERHEROES (1992–93)

Eleven (count 'em E-l-e-v-e-n) new Marvel and X-Men figures appeared from Toy Biz all at the same time! The Human Torch was our early pick for the hottest figure in the lineup! The chrome-colored Silver Surfer is pretty cool too, but it looks like it's just last year's figure with a shiny surface. Gambit (X-Men) was the only one that disappointed us. The Invisible Woman was released at this time, but in very small quantities. Most of the original ones disappeared before they ever appeared on store shelves — they were sold directly to collectors, by store employees, for a hefty price. If you find one for sale cheap, it's probably the second version which was released in late 1994.

MARVEL SUPERHEROES (Cont.)
Toy Biz (1992)
5" **Action Figures** ("Cosmic Defenders")
Mr. Fantastic (#4831) 18.00
Thing (#4832) 15.00
Spider-Man (Multi-Jointed) (#4833) 10.00

Thing (Toy Biz 1992)

Deathlok (#4834) 12.00
The Silver Surfer (chrome) (#4835) 12.00
Invisible Woman (Vanishing Color) (#4836) 150.00
Human Torch (#4837) 15.00
Amazing Spider-Man (Enemy Tracking
    Tracer) (#4838) 12.00
Venom (Flicking Tongue) (#4839) 20.00
Annihilus (#4840) 12.00
Reissue batch (1993)
Captain America (#48001), reissue 6.00
Dr. Doom (#48003), reissue 6.00
Doctor Octopus (#48004), reissue 6.00
Venom (Squirts "Alien Liquid") (#48005) ... 8.00
Incredible Hulk (small logo) (#48007), reissue 6.00

MARVEL SUPERHEROES (1994)

T he hottest news in 1994 was that **Invisible Woman** reappeared. Of course, it wasn't the original version — this one doesn't become invisible — but it's still a nice figure. At least you could actually find one on store shelves. There was also a new **Daredevil** figure in his black-and-red costume and the first-ever appearance of **U.S. Agent**.

Invisible Woman (Toy Biz 1994)

U.S. Agent (Toy Biz 1994)

MARVEL SUPERHEROES (Cont.)
Toy Biz (1994)
5" Action Figures ("Cosmic Defenders")
Invisible Woman (Catapult Power
    Launcher) (#48101) 9.00
Daredevil (Grapple Hook) (#48102) 7.00
U.S. Agent (#48103) 7.00
Punisher (Full Weapon Arsenal) (#48104) . 7.00
Spider-Man (Multi Jointed) (#48105), reissue 7.00

MARVEL SUPER SIZE FIGURES

A bout June of 1991 Toy Biz greeted us with the first 15" Marvel Super Size figures. This features The Incredible Hulk, Spider-Man, Venom and The Punisher in a larger-sized series of action figures. The Hulk and Spider-Man figures were the easiest to get while Venom was initially very scarce. It quickly sold at prices of $30.00 or more, even though it became generally available later. The figure to get was **The Punisher**, but you had to buy Venom, Spider-Man and Hulk and mail in the proof of purchase seals on the back of each package. When you got The Punisher, he came without his trademark machine gun.

Super Size Punisher (Toy Biz 1991)

Super Size 15" Super Heroes (1991)
Spider-Man (#4823) 20.00
Venom (#4825) 35.00
The Incredible Hulk (#4826) 18.00
The Punisher (Mail-in, no box) 60.00
See below under "X-Men" for Super Size Magneto and Wolverine.

MARVEL ELECTRONIC TALKING SUPERHEROES

T hese figures are the same as the regular 5" Marvel and X-Men figures from 1991, with the addition of a three-phrase voice pack. The card is a little bigger, as was the price. Venom was the hit of the group as it said to Spider-Man: "I want to eat your brains!" The kids loved it, but the moms didn't. Collectors, motivated as usual by public spirit, grabbed them quickly to protect the innocent ears of the nation's youth. We got several ourselves. Too bad they didn't go up more in value.

Toy Biz (1991)
5" Action Figures
Spider-Man (#4891) 12.00
Punisher (#4892) 10.00

Electronic Hulk (Toy Biz 1991)

Hulk (#4893) 10.00
Wolverine (#4894) 15.00
Magneto (#4895) 10.00
Cyclops (#4896) 12.00
Venom (#4897) 20.00

MARVEL TEAM-UP
ToyBiz (1995)
Kmart Exclusive
The Thing and Spider-Man (#45521) 11.00
Human Torch and Spider-Man (#45522) . . . 11.00

Marvel Team-Up (Toy Biz 1995)

MAXIMUM CARNAGE

C arnage became part of the Spider-Man line, when it appeared in late 1994, but earlier in 1994 these packs appeared with their own logo and design, so they are listed separately.

MAXIMUM CARNAGE
Toy Biz (1994)
5" Action Figures
Carnage (#44100) 10.00
Multi packs
Triple Threat: Spider-Man, Carnage,
    Venom (#44300) 20.00
Carnage & Spider-Man Battle Pack
    (#44401) 12.50
Carnage & Venom Battle Pack (#44402) . 12.50
Deluxe 10" figure
Carnage, Deluxe Edition (#44200) 20.00

POCKET SUPER HEROES

A nother 3¾" series, the Pocket Super Heroes, was offered from Mego in 1979. Mego's Pocket Super Heroes were the same 3¾" size as the Comic Action Heroes, but the difference here was that these *did* move. The same four characters from the Comic Action Heroes made up the Marvel portion of this series.

There are also two vehicles made for this line of figures, both specifically created for Spider-Man: the Spider-Machine and the Spider-Car. Oddly enough, there have been two different versions of this particular vehicle. One set comes with figures of Spider-Man and the Hulk while the other variation has the Spider-Man and Green Goblin figures.

POCKET SUPER HEROES
Mego (1979)
3¾" Figures
Aquaman 90.00
Batman 40.00
Captain America 90.00
Captain Marvel 40.00
General Zod 15.00
Green Goblin 90.00

Hulk 40.00
Joker 40.00
Jor-El 15.00
Lex Luthor 15.00
Penguin 40.00
Robin 40.00
Spider-Man 40.00
Superman 40.00
Wonder Woman 40.00
Accessories
Batmobile (with Batman & Robin Figures) 200.00
Batcave 300.00
Spider-Car (with Spider-Man and Hulk) . . 75.00
Spider-Car (with Spider-Man and
    Green Goblin) 150.00
Batmachine 100.00
Spider-Machine 100.00
Invisible Jet 125.00

THE SAVAGE DRAGON

T he Savage Dragon is the comic book creation of Erik Larsen. Now there is a cartoon, so Playmates has produced a series of action figures. They came out just prior to Christmas 1995 and we had to kill a picture on this page to fit them in. The package also has a logo for the Teenage Mutant Ninja Turtles, but this seems to be for the Jim Lee series of turtle figures. These figures were available in some parts of the country by the end of 1995, but they had not reached the Northeast.

THE SAVAGE DRAGON
Playmates (1995)
6" Action figures with special comic
The Savage Dragon (#03045) 7.00
Battle Damage Dragon (#03046) 7.00
She-Dragon (#03047) 7.00
Barbaric (#03048) 7.00

Overtkill (Todd's Toys 1994)

SPAWN

T he Spawn line of action figures was the talk of Toy Fair 1994. Spawn's creator, Todd McFarlane, was starting his own line of toys! If they are half as popular as his comic books they will be a great success.

They arrived on schedule in late 1994 and received considerable attention from collectors. The original six figures come with a comic in an all-plastic pack which depicts six figures and three vehicles on the back. In the spring, a second batch of figures appeared on a blue lightning bolt display card, with no comic. The original figures were repackaged, with the same blue lightning bolt design on a sheet on top of the comic, providing a convenient way to tell the originals from the reissues. Both packs picture the second batch of figures on the back.

Variation hunters had a field day with these figures as a new variation turned up (or was rumored to have turned up) practically every day. For instance, Violator can be found with an orange border or a green border trading card, or with no card, or, reportedly, with a chromium trading card. Even Malebolgia, an oversize figure which was practically impossible to find in toy stores, had variations.

Angela (Todd Toys 1995)

Angela has been reported with two different kinds of spear shafts, with and without a ribbon painted on her staff and with and without panties. These features, particularly the latter, got her ranked in first place, along with Cosmic Angela and Mother-One from the Wetworks series, on the annual "Top 10 Warped Toy List" by Episcopal Reverend Christopher Rose, of Hartford, Connecticut.

In late 1995, new figures appeared and the original figures were reissued with new paint jobs, but the company is now McFarlane Toys, which again provides a convenient way to tell the original versions from these reissues. More figures are scheduled for 1996 and everyone expects the variations to continue to appear.

Every toy store and discount store seems to have a lot of Spawn figures (except WalMart, which reportedly won't sell them because of their demonic theme). This all means that it is too early to tell which of the variations will turn out to be the most valuable. Don't pay extra for a "scarce" variation unless you have checked a lot of sources to see if it is really scarce!

Medieval Spawn vs. Malebolgia (McFarlane Toys 1995)

SPAWN
Todd Toys (1994–95)
6" Action Figures, with comic in plastic pack

Spawn (#10101)	8.00
Spawn, Unmasked (#10101)	25.00
Spawn, blue, limited promo figure	85.00
Tremor (#10102)	12.00
Medieval Spawn (#10103)	10.00
Violator (#10104), with Green-border or Orange-border trading card, or no card	8.00
Chrome card	15.00
Clown (#10105), Alien head	12.00
Clown head showing	15.00
Overtkill (#10106) 5¢/10¢ on meter, turquoise or dark green	12.00
With 5¢ on meter, (scarce, if true)	spec.

Reissues (1995), lightning bolt plastic package

Spawn (#10101)	8.00
Spawn, Unmasked (#10101)	20.00
Tremor (#10102)	12.00
Medieval Spawn (#10103)	12.00
Violator (#10104)	7.00
Clown (#10105)	10.00
Overtkill (#10106)	12.00

Second batch (1995), with lightning bolt package

Commando Spawn, speckled gun (#10111)	9.00
Plain silver gun variation	17.50
Chapel (#10112), any variation	9.00
Angela (#10113), most variations	15.00

Unnotched spear shaft, and other variations

(if actually scarce)	up to 25.00
Badrock (#10114)	9.00
Malebolgia, deluxe figure, any variation (#10115)	35.00
Pilot Spawn, deluxe figure (#10116)	15.00

McFarlane Toys (1995)
Second batch repaints

Commando Spawn, gold guns (#10111)	8.00
Chapel, olive drab (#10112)	8.00
Angela, navy and silver (#10113)	9.00
Badrock, brown chest (#10114)	8.00
Pilot Spawn, white outfit (#10116)	12.00
Violator, red, mail-in	12.50

Third batch

Spawn II (#10121)	8.00
Violator II (#10122)	15.00
Vertebreaker (#10123)	15.00
The Curse (#10124)	8.00
Ninja Spawn (#10125)	8.00
Cosmic Angela (#10126)	9.00
Redeemer (#10127)	8.00

Special figures

Future Spawn, boxed (#10161)	10.00
Spawn, gold, numbered (#90109)	10.00
Medieval Spawn vs. Malebolgia (#90119)	25.00
F.A.O. Schwartz exclusive two-pack	15.00

Vehicles

Spawn Mobile (#10201)	20.00

All prices listed are for *Near Mint* condition.

Violator Monster Rig (#10202) 15.00
Spawn Alley playset (#10300) 30.00
Violator Chopper (#10212) 25.00
   reissue, with figure (McFarlane Toys) . 20.00
Pilot Spawn Air Cycle (#10211) 25.00
   reissue, with figure (McFarlane Toys) . 20.00
Spawn Battle Horse with figure (McFarlane
   Toys #10220) 20.00

SPIDER-MAN

T his is a new series based on the characters from the Spider-Man animated TV show. The characters made very popular toys when they were part of the Marvel Superheroes line and should do well. The first batch of figures arrived in the fall of 1994 and the second batch appeared a little before Christmas. Initial collector interest focused on the Alien Spider Slayer figure, but it has not turned out to be scarce.

When the third batch of figures appeared in the spring of 1995, Rhino could not be found and so the great Rhino hunt of 1995 was on! A few were reported at one store chain, then a few at another. It did seem to exist, which kept the hunt going. As more appeared late in 1995, the collector price dropped and everyone who paid a premium for the figure got burned.

SPIDER-MAN
Toy Biz (1994–95)

5" Action Figures
Spider-Man Web Racer (#47101) 5.00
Spider-Man Web Shooter (#47102) 5.00
Smythe (#47103) 5.00
Venom (#47104) 5.00
Carnage (#47105) 5.00
Dr. Octopus (#47106) 5.00
Hobgoblin (#47107) 5.00
Second batch (1994)
Spider-Man Web Parachute (#47111) 5.00
Peter Parker (#47112) 5.00
Alien Spider-Slayer (#47113) 5.00
KingPin (#47114) 5.00
Kraven (#47115) 5.00
The Lizard (#47116) 5.00
Vulture (#47117) 5.00
Third batch (1995)
Spider-Man Multi-Jointed (#47121) 5.00
Spider-Man Spider Armor (#47122) 5.00
Shocker (#47124) 5.00
Green Goblin (#47125) 5.00
Scorpion (#47126) 5.00
Rhino (#47127), scarce 25.00
Fourth batch, with pin (1995)
Spider-Man Black Costume (#47131) 5.00
Spider-Man Web Glider (#47132) 5.00
Mysterio (#47133) 5.00
The Chameleon (#47134) 5.00
The Prowler (#47135) 5.00
Venom II (#47136) 5.00
Spider-Man Night Shadow (#47137) 5.00
Fifth batch, with pin (1995)
Six Arm Spider-Man (#47141) 5.00
Battle Ravaged Spider-Man (#47142) 5.00
Nick Fury (#47143) 5.00
Morbius (#47144) 5.00
Punisher (#47146) 5.00
Super-Sense Spider-Man (#47147) 5.00
KayBee exclusives (1995)
Spider-Man Web Trap (#47046) 6.00
Spdier-Man Web Lair (#47047) 6.00
Vehicles
Tri-Spider Slayer (#47330, 1994) 25.00
Smythe Battle Chair (#47310, 1994) 17.00
Hobgoblin Wing Bomber (#47410, 1994) . . 15.00

Rhino (Toy Biz 1994)

Hobgoblin Pumpkin Bomber (#47457, 1995) 12.00
Spider-Man Wheelie Cycle,
    Motorized (#47456, 1995) 15.00
Spider-Man Radio Control Spider Cycle
    (#47460, 1995) 30.00
Venom Assault Racer (#47458, 1995) 12.00
Plush Spider-Man doll (#47320, 1994) 30.00
Daily Bugle Playset (#47400, 1994) 30.00
10" "Spider-Man" Figures, boxed
Spider-Man (Wall Hanging, black
    chest) (#47711, 1994) 10.00
Dr. Octopus (#47712, 1994) 10.00
The Lizard (#47713, 1994) 10.00
Spider-Man (red chest) (#47701, 1994) . . . 10.00
Venom (#47702, 1994) 10.00
Hobgoblin (#47703, 1994) 10.00
Carnage (#47721, 1995) 10.00
Kraven (#47722, 1995) 10.00
Vulture (#47723, 1995) 10.00
Super Posable Spider-Man (#48408, 1995) 10.00
The Punisher (#48411, 1995) 10.00
Spider-Man Spider Armor (#48123, 1995) . 10.00
Mysterio (#48124, 1995) 10.00
14" Electronic Talking Figures (1994)
Spider-Man (#47361) 20.00
Venom (#47362) 20.00
Spider-Man Projectors . see **X-Men Projectors**

Nick Fury (Toy Biz 1995)

Power Flight Superman (Kenner 1995)

SUPERMAN: MAN OF STEEL

T hese Superman action figures, the first in over five years, appeared in early November 1995. The figures are nicely sculpted and come on a clean blister card decorated with a large Superman "S" and little else. Initial shipments included all five figures and none appear to be scarce at the moment. Each figure comes with a trading card by Joe Jusko.

SUPERMAN: MAN OF STEEL
Kenner (1995)
5" Action Figures
Power Flight Superman (#62901) 7.00
Laser Superman (#62902) 7.00
Superboy (#62903) 7.00
Steel (a.k.a. John Henry Irons) (#62904) . . 7.00
Conduit (#62906) 7.00
Vehicles
Superboy VOTL Cycle (#62921) 11.00
Matrix Conversion Coupe with
    Clark Kent (#62923) 25.00

All prices listed are for *Near Mint* condition.   **35**

Lex Luthor, Brainiac, Joker and Penguin (Kenner 1984)

SUPER POWERS

W hile the Mego figures of the super-endowed DC characters were all well and good, one of the best, if not *the* best, toy lines to ever come out was the Super Powers collection. This wonderful series of 4" to 5¾" action figures came from Kenner in 1984. The figures, as well as the accompanying vehicles and accessories, were of the utmost quality, design and detail. Each figure had a special "action," such as a "Power Action Deep Sea Kick" for Aquaman or "Power Action Flight Wings" for Hawkman. This is common now but was an innovation in 1994. Inside the blister pack, behind the figure itself, was a mini-comic with an adventure spotlighting the packaged figure. For toy collectors like myself, it was very much appreciated. The more the folks at Kenner gave us, the more we wanted. It was a sad day when the news came about its cancellation after what we all thought was a successful three years for the series. What put an end to this well-loved toy line can

only be guessed.

1984 brought the first series of Super Powers figures to the stores with Batman, Superman, Robin, Aquaman, Flash, Green Lantern, Hawkman, Wonder Woman, The Joker, Brainiac, Lex Luthor and The Penguin making up the list.

A year later, Green Arrow, Martian Manhunter, Firestorm, Red Tornado, Dr. Fate, Darkseid, Parademon, Kalibak, Mantis and Steppenwolf were added to the growing list of heroes and villains. Steppenwolf was first available, by the way, as part of a mail-in offer. If you mailed in five proof of purchase seals from the packages, you received the figure of Steppenwolf along with a Darkseid record plus coupons worth three dollars to use for other Super Powers collection merchandise.

The last of the line gave us the likes of Plasticman, Mister Miracle, Captain Marvel, Orion, Cyborg, Tyr, Mr. Freeze, Desaad, Samari, Golden Pharoah and Cyclotron. Before you go off screaming as you try to figure out what comics those last three named characters appeared in, don't bother; they were specially made-up figures for the line only. Clark Kent also appeared as an action figure during this year, available as a mail-in offer. He came shipped in a plain white box or from Sears with a companion figure of Superman.

A great assortment of vehicles were also available for this figure line. The Batmobile, Batcopter, Supermobile, Delta Probe One, Justice Jogger, Lex-Soar 7, Kalibak Boulder Bomber and Darkseid Destroyer, along with the Hall of Justice playset, were all very well constructed and highly imaginative toys for kids as well as collectors.

Dr. Fate (Kenner 1985)

[DC] SUPER POWERS
Kenner (1984–86)

5" Action Figures

Aquaman with mini comic #8 (1984)	37.00
Batman with mini comic (1984)	50.00
Small card (1984)	30.00
Braniac with mini comic #5 (1984)	30.00
Cyborg (1986)	175.00
Cyclotron (1986)	40.00
Darkseid 5¾" w/mini comic #19 (1985) ...	20.00
Desaad with mini comic (1985)	18.00

Dr. Fate with mini comic (1985)	35.00
Firestorm with mini comic #16 (1985)	30.00
Small card	20.00
Flash with mini comic #4 (1984)	13.00

Mr. Freeze (Kenner 1986)

Golden Pharoah (1986)	75.00
Green Arrow with mini comic (1985)	35.00
Green Lantern with mini comic (1984) ...	50.00
Small card	25.00
Hawkman with mini comic #13 (1984) ...	50.00
Joker with mini comic #7 (1984)	30.00
Kalibak with mini comic #10 (1985)	15.00
Lex Luthor with mini comic #10 (1984) ...	13.00
Mantis with mini comic (1985)	30.00
Martian Manhunter with mini comic #14 (1985)	30.00
Small card	18.00
Mister Miracle (1986)	160.00
Mr. Freeze (1986)	35.00
Orion (1986)	30.00
Parademon with mini comic (1985)	28.00
Penguin 4" with mini comic (1984)	38.00
Plastic Man (1986)	70.00
Red Tornado with mini comic (1985)	32.00
Small card	20.00
Robin with mini comic #9 (1984)	30.00
Small card (1986)	20.00
Samurai (1986)	60.00
Shazam (1986)	35.00

All prices listed are for *Near Mint* condition.   **37**

Steppenwolf mail-in (1984) 10.00
Steppenwolf with mini comic (1985) 80.00
Superman with mini comic #1 (1984) 25.00
    Small card 15.00
Clark Kent (mail-in offer or free with
    Superman figure from Sears) (1986) 60.00
Tyr (1986) 45.00
Wonder Woman with mini comic #3 (1984) 20.00
    Small card 10.00
Note: Super Powers figures on Canadian blister cards are worth 25% less than on American blister cards.

Vehicles
Darkseid Destroyer (#67040) 25.00
Delta Probe One 8" (#99850) 20.00
Justice Jogger wind-up (#67280, 1986) . . 25.00
Kalibak Boulder Bomber (#67020) 20.00
Lex-Soar 7 (1984) 15.00
Supermobile (1984) 25.00
Batmobile (#99780, 1984) 83.00
Batcopter (#67270, 1986) 90.00
Hall of Justice plastic playset, 34"x10½"
    (#99830, 1984) 100.00
Darkseid Tower of Darkness playset . Not issued
Color poster of the 12 first-year
    characters, 18"x24" (Kenner) 10.00
Collector's Case 11" (Kenner) 20.00

SWAMP THING

T he Swamp Thing line is based primarily on the animated cartoon series about environmental issues as much as characters, and it tried to find a home for a year or more. A good amount, if not all, of the figures from this series that began in 1990 were still available in 1993, and you can probably still find some of them in the bargain bins somewhere.

The final two figures in this series, **Capture Swamp Thing** and **Climbing Swamp Thing**, were hard to find for a long time because the series wasn't selling well so no one ordered them. Of course, when the series was cancelled, they came out of the warehouse and were available everywhere at discount.

Anton Arcane (Kenner 1991)

SWAMP THING
Kenner (1990–91)
4½" Swamp Thing action figures
Snare Arm Swamp Thing with "Vine Winch
    Arm & Monster Trap" (#41480) 5.00
Camouflage Swamp Thing with "Vine
    Snare" (#41430) 5.00
    With paint on arm (#41430) 15.00
Bio-Glow Swamp Thing (#41490) 5.00
Snap Up Swamp Thing with "Log
    Bazooka" (#41470) 5.00
Climbing Swamp Thing with "Bayou Staff
    & Shield of Reeds" (#41690, 1991) . 10.00
Capture Swamp Thing with "Organic Net
    and Cypress Club" (#41680, 1991) . 10.00
Evil Un-Men Villains
Anton Arcane with "Spidery
    BioMask" (#41340) 6.00
Dr. Deemo with "Serpent BioMask" (#41310) 6.00
Weed Killer with "Bogsucker
    BioMask" (#41320) 6.00
Skinman with "Fangbat BioMask" (#41330) . 6.00
Heroes
Bayou Jack with "Swamp Water
    Blaster" (#41440) 6.00
Tomahawk with "Swift Shot

Crossbow" (#41450) 6.00
Vehicles
Bog Rover vehicle (#41350) 10.00
Marsh Buggy vehicle (#41370) 10.00
Bayou Blaster (#41390) 10.00
Transducer Playset (#41350) 15.00
Swamp Trap Playset (#41410) 10.00

TEENAGE MUTANT NINJA TURTLES

The Teenage Mutant Ninja Turtles action figures are among the most imaginative and best detailed figures being produced. Early TMNT figures are good bets for collecting.

The earliest turtle figures came with the "Turtle Force" fan club flyer and had soft heads. These are highly desireable figures and you will have to go to a show or a dealer if you want any of these figures. Look for advertisements in toy collector magazines.

When collecting any other TMNT figures, please remember that figures of the four turtles are much more plentiful than the other characters, so don't pay a premium price for them. Furthermore, the relatively scarce nonturtle characters are much more likely to increase in value in the future. If you are interested in future value, **don't open the blister pack!** A figure out of the original package is worth only 25% of one in the package.

The current figures date back to 1988, and the best collecting values will generally be in the earliest figures. The vintage of a TMNT character can be determined from the package back. The earliest packages (Type A) depict 10 characters (the four Turtles plus April O'Neil and Splinter along with Foot-Clan members Bebop, Shredder, Foot Soldier and Rocksteady) and have a 1988 copyright date. We were able to obtain all of them in local stores in 1991 and early 1992. **Splinter** and **Bebop** and **Rocksteady** were reissued in

Eight TMNT characters: Baxter Stockman, Leatherhead, Metalhead, Usagi Yojimbo, Krang, Casey Jones, Genghis Frog and Ace Duck (Playmates 1989)

> **Description of early TMNT package types:**
> (Also see photos)
> Type A Pack: (1988) 6 Turtle & 4 Foot in 2 rows
> Type B Pack: (1989) 8 Turtle & 6 Foot in 2 rows
> Type C Pack: (1989) 10 Turtle & 9 Foot in 2 rows
> *Type D Packs (1990) all have 4 Wacky Action figures in one row at the top:*
> Type D1 Pack: 13 Turtles & 11 Foot each in 2 rows
> Type D2 Pack: 15 Turtles & 12 Foot each in 2 rows
> *Type E Packs (1990) all have 7 Wacky Action figures, 4 in the first row & 3 in the second row:*
> Type E1 Pack: 16 Turtles & 14 Foot each in 2 rows
> Type E2 Pack: 17 Turtles & 15 Foot each in 2 rows
> Type F Pack (1990) has 7 Wacky Action figures, 2 in the first row & 5 in the second row, 22 Turtles in 3 rows starting with Mondo Gecko & 15 Foot in 2 rows.
> *Type F packs were used for reissues of many early characters & are common.*
> There are many package types for the later figures. The most recent package is a **"Pizza Back"** with all of the figures on their own pepperoni slice. Many early figures (and 1992 figures) have been rereleased on these packages.

1990 packages so the Type A pack version is scarce.

The first additions to the line were **Ace Duck, Genghis Frog, Baxter Stockman** and **Krang**. These figures were produced for several years in their original packages (Type B), which have 14 characters depicted and are dated 1989. The next additions were **Casey Jones, Usagi Yojimbo, Metalhead, Leatherhead, General Traag,** and **Rat King.** Their packages (Type C) have 19 characters (April is omitted) and are dated 1989. (All the package "Types" are our own notation.) The Leath-erhead figure is scarce and valuable because it was not distributed after 1990 even though the figure was included in the Playmates 1992 catalog.

The original **April O'Neil** figure was always in short supply as she was dropped from the line for a while. When she reappeared she went through several variations and package changes. The very earliest (and most valuable) April has no stripes on the side or front of her outfit and a Type A package with a turtle shell

The earliest TMNT blister card backs: Type A–10 figures (1988); Type B–14 figures (1989)

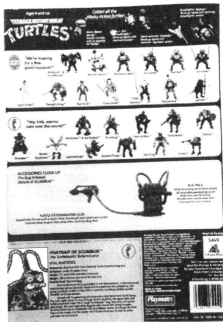

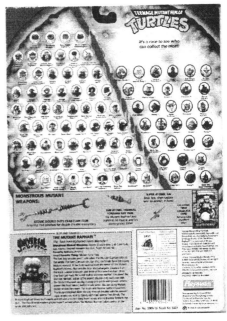

Later TMNT blister card backs: Type C–19 figures (1989); Type D1–24 figures (1989);
Type F (1990) and Pizza Back (1994)

and character name imprint (on the left) which covers the top of her head in the picture below. On later Type A cards the imprint was moved up, closer to the "T" in Turtles. Second version April figures had a blue stripe on the side (but still none on the front). Just to confuse you further, original Aprils can be found on second version cards and second version Aprils can be found on original cards.

The first "Wacky Action" Turtles were introduced in late 1989 in bigger packages (Type W1) that have four figures at the top. The **Wacky Walkin' Mouser** is by far the scarcest. April O'Neil with blue side stripes came back, this time with orange boots and breast pockets and a small blue stripe on the pockets. Most of them say "Press" over the pocket, but a (scarce and valuable) few omit the word "Press."

In early 1990, **Wingnut and Screwloose**, **Mondo Gecko**, **Muckman and Joe Eyeball** and **Scumbug** were added. Their packages (Type D) depict 24 characters (April is back) plus the four Wacky

Wacky Walkin' Mouser (Playmates 1989)

Original April O'Neil, no stripes, on second version card (Playmates 1989)

Action Turtles at the top. These new figures were all produced in great quantity because by then the TMNT figures were very popular. Later in 1990, three more Wacky Action figures were added along with **Panda Khan**, **Napoleon Bonafrog**, **Fugitoid**, **Mutagen Man**, **Slash** and **Triceraton**. **Mutagen Man** (and others) were released in packages (Type E) that have 7 Wacky Action figures at the top, 4 in the first row and 3 in the second row. **Slice 'n' Dice Shredder** and **Creepy Crawlin' Splinter** come in large packages (Type W2) with 7 Wacky Action figures and are scarce. Still later in 1990, Mike the Sewer Surfer, Leo the Sewer Samurai, Don the Undercover Agent, **Ray Fillet**, Donatello with Storage Shell, Raph the Space Cadet and **Pizzaface** were introduced. The four Turtles in this batch were shipped in exceptional quantity, and were the ones most frequently discounted. Several of the early characters were reissued in 1990 packages and these versions are fairly common (except for April). The seven Wacky Action figures are depicted at the top of these packages (Type F), two in the first row and 5 in the second. Ray Fillet was notoriously hard to find in the earlier, color changing versions.

1991

Many "Type F" packages say "NEW!" on the left side, in the middle. In 1991 and early 1992, even a casual inspection of a rack of TMNT figures in a toy store revealed how plentiful figures in these packages were. During the same period Ray Fillet went through several figure and package changes as the original color-changing version was hard to produce. Variations like this always draw collector interest. The earliest package (type E2) says "Awesome Mutant Color Change" and is the one to get, but all versions are collectible.

Late 1990/early 1991 additions to the TMNT line were the four Turtles with "Storage Shells," **Walkabout, Wyrm, Groundchuck, Dirtbag** and **Chrome Dome.** These come in a package (Type G) with Walkabout as the first listed figure. **Tattoo** was also added at this time

in a package (Type G1) that lists him first. Also added at this time (more or less) were the Wacky Action figures of **Machine Gunnin' Rocksteady** and **Headspinnin' Bebop.** They, along with the Headdroppin' Turtles, and the four Talkin' Turtles, come in the larger-size package, which generally cost about $1.50 more than the regular figures.

Most of the figures in the "larger package" lines (Wacky Action, Head Droppin', Talkin', etc.) are Turtles and were quite common on the toy store racks for a long time since they were produced in huge quantity. However, the nonturtle figures: Slice 'n' Dice Shredder, Creepy Crawlin' Splinter, Machine Gunnin' Rocksteady and Headspinnin' Bebop (all Wacky Action figures) were fairly scarce.

1992

In 1992, all new releases were produced in large quantities and were easy to obtain with a little looking. 1992 packages say "New for '92, 5th Anniversary Figure Series" in a manhole cover design. A particular figure may be hard to locate, but this is primarily due to

Channel 6 News Van with April figure (Playmates 1992)

the more than 200 different figures produced to date. 1993 continued this pattern. The only figures from this era that will ever be scarce are the Mutatin' (non-turtle) figures. However, there are some other items worthy of collector interest. A few of the vehicles, such as the **Movie III Warhorses**, the **Cave Turtles** and the **Channel 6 News Van**, came with special edition figures. The News Van, for instance, came with a green-suited April O'Neil figure available nowhere else. These are more expensive items and are not produced in anything like the massive quantity of regular figures, so they may draw more collector interest in the future.

The "Movie Star Turtles" are "modeled after the featured performers in the two hit motion pictures" and feature "a real rubbery reptilian feel." We also noted a number of the early (1989 and 1990) figures rereleased on the original cards. These include Genghis Frog, Usagi Yojimbo, Casey Jones, Ace Duck, Metalhead, Krang, Rat King and April O'Neil (1990 editon figure and card).

1992 also brought **Monty Moose** and **Doctor El**, joining **King Lionheart** and **Antrax**. These figures continued the high standard of attractiveness and detail which Playmates has maintained throughout this series. Since the series continued to be very popular, Playmates could afford to invest in highly detailed figures, which helps to keep the series popular.

Next came **Merdude, April (II), Hothead** and **Scale Tail**. There were two more **April** figures which appeared later: **April, The Ninja Newscaster** and **April, The Ravishing Reporter**. The first of these is wearing a one-piece leopard-skin bathing suit and looks like the sexiest action figure we've seen in years, even hotter than Catwoman.

1993

Also appearing are three recommended additions to this line: **Mutatin' Rocksteady, Mutatin' Bebop** and **Mutatin' Splinter**. The mutating figures come in a window box with a lid as did the "Mutatin' " turtles. The mutating figures have never been plentiful, and if the usual practice continues, Rocksteady, Bebop and Splinter will be relatively scarce. Note that the figures are sealed in a plastic bubble inside the box and cannot be removed and repackaged without damage to the bubble. However, the damage to the bubble would not be visible through the window in the box. You should check any "Mutatin' " figure bought at a show or fleamarket to make sure the inside bubble is still sealed.

We don't normally recommend collecting any of the four Turtles because they are produced in such quantity that we don't believe they will increase in value in the foreseeable future. One exception is **Cave-Turtle Leo with Dingy Dino**. The two figures come in a window box, but the inside plastic is not a sealed bubble so the figures can be removed and later repackaged. The cardboard inside package has a prehistoric scene drawing which forms a diorama.

The next big batch to be released was the **Toon Turtles** "As Seen in The Turtle Cartoon Show!" These figures all have "Real Toon Texture Feel." There are "Toon" version of all four Turtles, **Shredder** and **Zak** (formerly the Neutrino) plus five new characters. **Toon Dask** is a "Dude from Another Dimension" and **Toon Kala** is a "Cool Cruisin' Cosmic Chick." **Toons Burne, Vernon** and **Irma** are humans, the only ones in the whole TMNT series in addition to April O'Neil.

What would a new TMNT movie be without a new set of Turtles figures from Playmates? Unthinkable! About a month before the movie premiered, the new figures arrived in quantity at local stores. They have new packaging, with pictures from the movie (which was set in Japan).

Late 1993 additions to the TMNT line included **Sandstorm**, **Halfcourt**, and **Mona Lisa**. Sandstorm looks a little like Joe Camel, but he's not smoking a cigarette, so he's politically correct. Halfcourt is a giraffe with a basketball net around his neck and Mona Lisa is a cute (if you like green skin) lizard lady with a figure like April's. **Scratch** (a cat) and **Hot Spot** (a dog) were also part of this batch, but they are very scarce.

Just in time for Halloween (1993), Playmates dressed up the four Turtles as your favorite Universal Studios monsters! The four are **Mike as Frankenstein**, **Raph as the Mummy**, **Don as Dracula** and **Leo as the Wolfman**. The package comes with a certificate for $3.00 off at the Universal Studios theme park in Florida, but it won't help you any because it's inside the plastic blister and no true col-

lector will open the package.

The Sewer Heroes series of Turtle figures appeared before Christmas. This batch included **Super Don, Super Mike, Mighty Bebop** and **Rhinoman**. Basically, Playmates has put superhero costumes on your favorite characters, but they are nice-looking figures, as usual. **Rhinoman** is a new character, and there are two versions of the figure, one with red accessories and one with yellow accessories. It's unusual to find toy variations so soon after a figure is introduced. Unfortunately, neither version is scarce (or valuable).

1994-95

Most stores have slowly reduced the shelf space for this series, so their incredibly long toy life may finally be nearing an end.

One notable addition to the line was the **Shogun Ninja Turtles** with special trading cards. This was the first batch of Turtle figures to come with trading cards.

Spring brought "Warriors of the Forgot-

Mutatin' Bebop figure (mutated and unmutated) (1992)

ten Sewer" Turtles. These come with a comic book and sport a medieval theme.

Rhinoman (Playmates 1993)

During the summer, Playmates introduced "Cyber Samurai Turtles" using the fabulous four plus Shredder and Bebop from their regular cast of characters. This is a deluxe TMNT product and costs about $8.00 versus about $5.00 for a regular figure.

The second batch of Universal Monsters with trading card came out in the fall of 1994. We loved these movies and the figures, too: **Invisible Man Mike; The Mutant Raphael; Creature from the Black Lagoon Leonardo** and **Brides of Frankenstein April.** The later figure is scarce and all four are harder to find than the 1993 Universal Monster turtles.

The TMNT **Star Trek** Turtles came out in the fall, a month or two before the Star Trek: Generations movie. They came with a trading card as well.

The last batch scheduled for 1994 was the Apollo Astronaut Turtles, featuring the four Turtles, but they did not appear

until after Christmas.

Many of the new and old figures in the basic assortment got trading cards in 1994. There are about 90 such figures listed in the 1994 catalog, but we have only seen about half of them. In 1995 this was switched to a coin and some transitional figures had both. If you are looking to own some of the TMNT figures with trading cards, look for the Star Trek Turtles, Shogun April and Bride of Frankenstein April.

Major toy store chains are not ordering turtles in quantity any more and so the figures from the end of the line are much scarcer than the earlier figures. Collectors were just beginning to take notice of this at the end of 1995. If you don't want to pay dealer's prices, look for them in red tag sale sections and in secondary outlets like drug stores and smaller discount stores, but keep in mind that there may be quantities in some warehouse which could flood the market unexpectedly.

1995 also saw various mini mutant TMNT playsets with mini trading cards and other odd items. They are not included in the action figure lists.

A distinguished denizen of the sewer...
(Playmates 1992)

THE FOUR TURTLES
Playmates (1988–95)
Donatello

4½" Action Figures

Donatello (1988), with fan club flyer 40.00
Donatello (#5002, 1988) in type A pack,
 without flyer 20.00
Sewer-swimmin' Donatello (Wacky Action)
 + joke book (#5612, 1989) in type
 W1 pack 15.00
Headdroppin' Don (#5174, 1991) 4.50
Donatello, with Storage Shell
 (#5122, 1991) 4.50
Don, the Undercover Turtle (#5114, 1991) . 3.50
Talkin' Donatello (#5182, 1991) 6.00
Slam Dunkin' Don (Sewer Sports All-Stars)
 (#5145, 1991) 4.50
 Reissue (#5339, 1993) 4.00
Hose 'em Down Don (#5154, 1991) 4.50
 Reissue, with card (#5168, 1994) 4.00
Pro Pilot Don (#5151, 1991) 4.50
Punker Don (Rock 'n' Rollin') (#5156, 1991) 4.50
Movie Star Don (#5202, 1992) 4.50
Powerliftin' Don (#5212, 1992) 4.50
Delta Team Don (#5272, 1992) 4.50
Spike 'n' Volley Don (Sewer Spittin')
 (#5251, 1992) 4.50
Crazy Cowboy Don (Wacky Wild West)
 (#5300, 1992) 4.50
Super Don "Sewer Heroes" (#5422, 1993) . 5.00
 With trading card (#5422, 1994) 5.00
Cartwheelin' Karate Don "Ninja Action"
 (#5448, 1993) 6.00

Movie Star Don, rubbery (#5366, 1993) ... 6.00
Night Ninja Don (#5463, 1993) 6.00
Movie III Samurai Don (#5473, 1993) 4.50
Road Ready Don (#5372, 1993) 7.50
Don as Dracula "Universal Monsters"
 (#5453, 1993) 7.50
Toon Don with Spinnin' Bandana Action
 (#5406, 1993) 4.50
Mutatin' Donatello (#5222, 1992) 6.00
Turtle Troll Don (#5487, 1993) 4.50
Storage Shell Don + card (#5165, 1994) .. 4.00
Undercover Don + card (#5177, 1994) 4.00
Touchdown Don (#5257, 1994) 4.00
Pizza Tossin' Don (#3070, 1994) 4.00
Kung Fu Don (#3023, 1994) 5.00
Dwarf Don + comic book "Warriors of
 the Forgotten Sewer" (#5265, 1994) .. 5.00
Kowabunga Crackin' Turtle
 Egg Don (#3481, 1994) 10.00
Cyber Samurai Don (#3004, 1994) 6.00
Shogun Turtle Don with card (#5432, 1994) 5.00
Construction Mutation Don (#3083, 1994) . 10.00
Airforce Mutation Don (#3085, 1994) 10.00
"Star Trek" First Officer Donatello
 + card (#3454, 1994) 6.00
Supermutant Donatello (#3011, 1995) 5.00
Sumo Donatello "Sumo" (#5128?, 1995)
 with coin 4.50
Metal Mutant Donatello with Lion
 Spirit Armor (#3031, 1995) 6.00
Warrior Winged Donatello + coin (#5249,
 1995) 5.00

...and his three pizza-eating pals (Playmates 1992)

All prices listed are for *Near Mint* condition.   **47**

Leonardo

Leonardo (1988), with fan club flyer 40.00
Leonardo (#5001, 1988) in type A pack,
  without flyer 20.00
Headdroppin' Leo (#5171, 1991) 5.00
Leo, the Sewer Samurai (#5112, 1990) . . . 4.50
Sword Slicin' Leonardo (Wacky Action) + joke
  book (#5611, 1989) in type W2 pack 15.00
Leonardo with Storage Shell (#5124, 1991) 4.50
Talkin' Leonardo (#5181, 1991) 4.50
Classic Rocker Leo (Rock 'n' Rollin')
  (#5158, 1991) 4.50
Slap Shot Leo (Sewer Sports All-Stars)
  (#5147, 1991) 4.50
  Reissue (#5443, 1993) 4.00
T.D. Tossin' Leo (Sewer Sports All-Stars)
  (#5143, 1991) 4.50
  Reissue (#5338, 1993) 4.00
Make My Day Leo (#5153, 1991) 4.50
  Reissue, with card (#5169, 1994) 4.50
Lieutenant Leo (#5149, 1991) 4.50
Movie Star Leo (#5201, 1992) 4.50
Track 'n' Field Leo (#5211, 1992) 4.50
Kowabunga Kickboxin' Leo (#5241, 1992) . 4.50
Kookie Kavalry Leo (#5271, 1992) 4.50
Road Ready Leo (#5371, 1993) 7.50
Somersault Samurai Leo "Ninja Action"
  (#5446, 1993) 6.00
Night Ninja Leo (#5461, 1993) 6.00
Movie III Samurai Leo (#5471, 1993) 4.50
Turtle Troll Leo (#5486, 1993) 4.50
Classic Party-Reptile Leo (Bodacious
  Birthday) (#5261, 1992) 4.50
Lifeguard Leo (Sewer Spittin')
  (#5254, 1992) 4.50
Chief Leo (Wacky Wild West)
  (#5298, 1992) 4.50
Leo 5th Anniversary limited edition
  Collector Turtle (#5231, 1992) 4.50
Leo as The Wolfman "Universal
  Monsters" (#5451, 1993) 8.00
Toon Leo with Bulgin' Eye Action
  (#5404, 1993) 4.50
Mutatin' Leonardo (#5221, 1992) 6.00
Storage Shell Leo + card (#5167) 4.50
Undercover Leo (#5176, 1994) 4.50
Creature from the Black Lagoon
  Leonardo + card "Universal Monsters"
  (#5426, 1994) 7.50
Savage Leo + comic book "Warriors of
  the Forgotten Sewer" (#5264, 1994) . . 5.00
Lunar Leo (#5256, 1994) 4.50

Pizza Tossin' Leo (#3071, 1994) 4.50
Kung Fu Leo (#3021, 1994) 4.50
Kowabunga Crackin' Turtle
  Egg Leo (#3483, 1994) 4.50
Cyber Samurai Leo (#3001, 1994) 6.00
Shogun Turtle Leo + card (#5431, 1994) . . 4.50
Construction Mutation Leo (#3081, 1994) . 10.00
"Star Trek" Captain Leonardo + card
  (#3451, 1994) 6.00
Supermutant Leonardo (#3013, 1995) 5.00
Deep Sea Diver Leonardo "Adventuers"
  with coin (#5119, 1995) 4.50
Metal Mutant Leonardo with Dragon
  Spirit Armor (#3032, 1995) 6.00
Warrior Winged Leonardo + coin (#5249,
  1995) 5.00

Super Mike (Playmates 1994)

Michaelangelo

Michaelangelo (1988), with fan club flyer . 40.00
Michaelangelo (#5004, 1988) in type A pack,
  without flyer 20.00
Rock 'n' Roll Michaelangelo (Wacky Action)
  + joke book (#5614, 1990), W1 pack 15.00
Rappin' Mike (Rock 'n' Rollin')
  (#5155, 1991) 4.50
Headdroppin' Mike (#5172, 1991) 4.50
Mike, the Sewer Surfer (#5115, 1990) 4.50
Michaelangelo with Storage Shell
  (#5125, 1991) 4.50

Talkin' Michaelangelo (#5180, 1991) 4.50
Shell Slammin' Mike (Sewer Sports
  All-Stars) (#5146, 1991) 4.50
  Reissue (#5444, 1993) 4.00
Midshipman Mike (#5150, 1991) 4.50
Skateboardin' Mike (Sewer Sports
  All-Stars) (#5142, 1991) 4.50
  Reissue (#5441, 1993) 4.00
Mutatin' Michaelangelo (#5224, 1992) 6.00
Movie Star Mike (#5204, 1992) 4.50
Hot Doggin' Mike (#5214, 1992) 4.50
  Reissue (#5336, 1993) 4.00
Karate Choppin' Mike (#5242, 1992) 4.50
Navy Seal Mike (#5274, 1992) 4.50
Super Mike "Sewer Heroes" (#5421, 1993) . 5.00
  reissue + card (#5421, 1994) 4.50
  reissue + card and coin (#5421, 1995) 4.50
Battle Ready Boxer Mike (#5447, 1993) ... 4.50
Movie Star Mike, rubbery (#5368, 1993) ... 6.00
Night Ninja Mike (#5462, 1993) 6.00
Movie III Samurai Mike (#5472, 1993) 4.50
Turtle Troll Mike (#5489, 1993) 4.50
Crazy Clownin' Mike (Bodacious Birthday)
  (#5262, 1992) 4.50
Beachcombin' Mike (Sewer Spittin')
  (#5252, 1992) 4.50
Bandito-Bashin' Mike (Wacky Wild West)
  (#5299, 1992) 4.50
Mike as Frankenstein "Universal
  Monsters" (#5452, 1993) 6.00
Toon Mike with Tacky Tongue Action
  (#5405, 1993) 4.50
Storage Shell Mike, + card (#5164, 1994) .. 4.50
Undercover Mike + card (#5178, 1994) ... 4.50
Knight Mike + comic book "Warriors of
  the Forgotten Sewer" (#5266, 1994) .. 5.00
Moon Landin' Mike (#5259, 1994) 4.50
Invisible Man Michaelangelo + card
  "Universal Monsters" (#5425, 1994) .. 7.50
Pizza Tossin' Mike (#3072, 1994) 4.50
Kowabunga Crackin' Turtle
  Egg Mike (#3482, 1994) 10.00
Cyber Samurai Mike (#3003, 1994) 6.00
Shogun Turtle Mike + card (#5433, 1994) .. 4.50
Construction Mutation Mike (#3082, 1994) 10.00
"Star Trek" Chief Engineer Michaelangelo
  + card (#3452, 1994) 6.00
Supermutant Michaelangelo (#3012, 1995) . 5.00
Safari Michaelangelo "Adventuers"
  with coin (#5118, 1995) 4.50
Sumo Michaelangelo "Sumo"
  with coin (#5138, 1995) 4.50

Metal Mutant Michaelangelo with Beetle
  Spirit Armor (#3034, 1995) 6.00
Warrior Metalhead Michaelangelo + coin
  (#5206, 1995) 5.00

The Mutant Raphael (Playmates 1994)

Raphael

Raphael (1988), with fan club flyer 40.00
Raphael (#5003, 1988) in type A pack,
  without flyer 20.00
Breakfightin' Raphael (Wacky Action) + joke
  book (#5613, 1989) type W1 pack .. 15.00
Headdroppin' Raph (#5173, 1991) 4.50
Raph, the Space Cadet (#5116, 1991) 3.50
Raphael with Storage Shell (#5123, 1991) . 4.50
Talkin' Raphael (#5183, 1991) 4.50
Grand Slammin' Raph (Sewer Sports
  All-Stars) (#5144, 1991) 4.50
  Reissue (#5337, 1993) 4.00
Shell Kickin' Raph (Sewer Sports All-Stars)
  (#5148, 1991) 4.50
  Reissue (#5442, 1993) 4.00
  Reissue + card (#5442, 1994) 4.00
Raph, the Green Teen Beret (#5152, 1991) 4.50
Heavy Metal Raph (Rock ' n Rollin')
  (#5157, 1991) 4.50
Movie Star Raph (#5203, 1992) 4.50
Super-Swimmin' Raph (#5213, 1992) 4.50

*Four great April O'Neil figures: April with stripe and "Press" (1990); April (II) (1992);
April, The Ravishing Reporter (1992); Movie III April (1993)*

Yankee Doodle Raph (#5273, 1992) 4.50
Jump Attack Jujitsu Raph "Ninja Action"
(#5449, 1993) 6.00
Night Ninja Raph (#5464, 1993) 6.00
Movie III Samurai Raph (#5474, 1993) 4.50
Turtle Troll Raph (#5488, 1993) 4.50
Sewer-Cyclin' Raph (Sewer Spittin')
(#5253, 1992) 4.50
Sewer Scout Raph (Wacky Wild West)
(#5297, 1992) 4.50
Raph, The Magnificent (Bodacious
Birthday) (#5263, 1992) 4.50
Toon Raph with Head Spinnin' Action
(#5407, 1993) 4.50
Mutatin' Raphael (#5223, 1992) 6.00
Storage Shell Raph + card (#5166) 4.00
Raph as The Mummy "Universal
Monsters" (#5454, 1993) 6.00
The Mutant Raphael + card "Universal
Monsters" (#5427, 1994) 6.00
Undercover Raph (#5179, 1994) 4.00
Retro Rocket Raph (#5258, 1994) 4.00
Grand Slammin' Raph + card (#05337) ... 5.00
Pizza Tossin' Raph (#3074, 1994) 4.00
Kung Fu Raph (#3024, 1994) 5.00
Kowabunga Crackin' Turtle
Egg Raph (#3484, 1994) 10.00
Cyber Samurai Raph (#3002, 1994) 6.00
Shogun Turtle Raph + card (#5434, 1994) . 5.00
Airforce Mutation Raph (#3084, 1994) ... 10.00
"Star Trek" Chief Medical Officer
+ card (Raphael) (#3453, 1994) 6.00
Supermutant Raphael (#3010, 1995) 5.00
Sumo Raphael "Sumo" with coin
(#5127, 1995) 4.50
Metal Mutant Raphael with Phoenix
Spirit Armor (#3033, 1995) 6.00

Other figures
Playmates (1988–95)
4½" to 5" Action Figures
Ace Duck (#5055, 1989) in type B pack . 12.50
With hat off in type B pack 40.00
on Pizza Back card (#5381, 1993) ... 4.50
Antrax (#5286, 1992) 5.00
on Pizza Back card (#5286, 1993) ... 4.50
April O'Neil (#5005, 1988) no stripes
in earliest type A pack 150.00
April with orange pockets, blue stripes,
but no "Press" (#5005, 1990) 125.00
April with orange pockets, blue stripe,
says "Press" and all other versions
in type A pack (#5005, 1989) 20.00

*April, The Ninja Newscaster (and our
favorite April figure!) (Playmates 1992)*

In later packs (#5005, 1990) 15.00
On Pizza Back card + trading card
(#5378, 1993) 6.00
April (II) (#5283, 1992) 15.00
On Pizza Back card (#5283, 1993) . 12.00
April, The Ninja Newscaster (#5282, 1992) 16.00
On Pizza Back card (#5282, 1993) . 12.00
April, The Ravishing Reporter
(#5281, 1992) 15.00
On Pizza Back card (#5281, 1993) . 10.00
Mutatin' April (#5235, 1993) 12.00
Movie III April (#5479, 1993) 6.00
Bride of Frankenstein April + card
"Universal Monsters" (#5428, 1994) . 10.00
Shogun April with card (#5437, 1994) 8.00
Baxter Stockman (#5057, 1988) in
type B pack 35.00
With pink swatter 20.00
With blue swatter 20.00
On Pizza Back card (#5394, 1993) . 10.00
On new card, + trading card
(#05394, 1994) 6.00
Bebop (#5010, 1988) in type A pack 25.00
reissue (#5010, 1990) 10.00
On Pizza Back card (#5390, 1993) .. 4.50
Headspinnin' Bebop (Wacky Action) + joke
book (#5618, 1991) in type W4 pack 12.00
Mutatin' Bebop (#5226, 1992) 10.00

Ninja Knockin' Bebop (#5243, 1992) 4.50
Private Porknose Bebop (#5275, 1992) . . . 4.50
Mighty Bebop "Sewer Heroes" (#5423, 1993) 6.00
Night Ninja Bebop (#5466, 1993) 7.00
Robotic Bebop (#5496, 1993) 6.00
   With trading card (#05496, 1994) 4.50
   With coin (#05496, 1995) 4.50
Warrior Bebop + comic book "Warriors of
   the Forgotten Sewer" (#5267, 1994) . . 5.00
Cyber Samurai Bebop (#3006, 1994) 6.00
Super Mutant Bebop (#3017, 1995) 6.00

On Pizz Back card (#5296, 1993) . . . 4.50
With trading card (#05296, 1994) 4.50
With card and coin (#05296, 1995) . . 4.50
Robotic Foot Soldier with card
   (#05161, 1994) 5.00

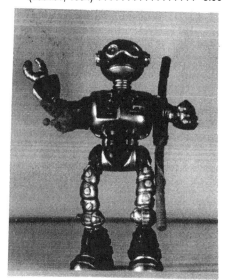

Casey Jones (Playmates 1989)

Casey Jones (#5058, 1989) in type C pack 15.00
   On Pizza Back card (#5377, 1993) . . 5.00
   On new card + trading card (#05377) . 5.00
   With card & gold coin (#05377, 1995) 5.00
Chrome Dome (#5136, 1991) 7.50
   On Pizza Back card (#5136, 1993) . . 4.50
   With trading card (#05136, 1994) 4.50
Warrior Chrome Dome + coin (#5207, 1995) 5.00
Dirtbag (#5132, 1991) 7.50
   On Pizza Back card (#5132, 1993) . . 4.50
Doctor El (#5288, 1992) 5.00
   On Pizza Back card (#5288, 1993) . . 4.50
Foot Soldier (#5008, 1988) in type A pack 25.00
   On Pizza Back card (#5393, 1993) . . 4.50
   With trading card (#05393, 1994) 4.50
   With card and coin (#05393, 1995) . . 4.50
Mutatin' Foot Soldier (#5237, 1993) 10.00
Movie Star Foot Soldier (#5296, 1992) 5.00

Fugitoid (Playmates 1990)

Fugitoid (#5109, 1990) 10.00
General Traag (#5061, 1989) in C pack . 10.00
   On Pizza Back card (#5395, 1993) . . 4.50
   With trading card (#05395, 1994) 4.50
Genghis Frog (#5051, 1989) in B pack and
   black belt 12.50
   With weapons bagged 30.00
   With yellow belt 75.00
Groundchuck (#5133, 1991) 7.50
Halfcourt (#5492, 1993) 4.50
Hot Spot (#5493, 1993), scarce 25.00
Hothead (#5285, 1992) 5.00
   On Pizza Back card (#5285, 1993) . . 4.50
   With trading card (#05285, 1994) 5.00
Movie III Kenshin (#5482, 1993) 4.50
King Lionheart (#5291, 1992) 5.00
   On Pizza Back card (#5291, 1993) . . 4.50
Krang (#5056, 1989) in type B pack 12.50
   On Pizza Back card (#5392, 1993) . . 4.50
   With trading card (#05392, 1994) 5.00
Krang's Adroid Body with card
   (#5160, 1994) 7.50
   With card and coin (#5160, 1995) . . . 5.00
   With coin (#05160, 1995) 4.50
Leatherhead (#5052, 1989) in type C pack 60.00

All prices listed are for *Near Mint* condition.

King Lionheart (Playmates 1992)

Merdude (#5290, 1992) 5.00
   On Pizza Back card (#5290, 1993) . . 4.50
Metalhead (#5053, 1989) in type C pack . 10.00
   On Pizza Back card (#5385, 1993) . . 4.50
Movie III Princess Mitsu (#5475, 1993) . . 5.00
Mona Lisa (#5495, 1993) 4.50
Mondo Gecko (#5106, 1990) blue eyebrow 10.00
   With green eyebrow 25.00
   On Pizza Back card (#5382, 1993) . . 4.50
   With trading card (#05382, 1994) 4.50
   Rock 'n' Roll Mondo Gecko (#5293, 1992) . 5.00
   On Pizza Back card (#5293, 1993) . . 4.50
Monty Moose of the Royal Mutant
   Mounted Police (#5289, 1992) 5.00
   On Pizza Back card (#5289, 1993) . . 4.50
Muckman and Joe Eyeball (#5101, 1990) 10.00
   On Pizza Back card (#5387, 1993) . . 4.50
Mutagen Man (#5107, 1990) in E1 pack . 10.00
   On Pizza Back card (#5396, 1993) . . 4.50
Napoleon Bonafrog (#5113, 1990) 10.00
   On Pizza Back card (#5386, 1993) . . 4.50
Panda Khan (#5108, 1989) 12.00
   Reissue (#5108, 1991) 4.50
Pizzaface (#5111, 1990) 10.00
   On Pizza Back card (#5398, 1993) . . 4.50
Rahzar (#5129, 1991) 10.00
   On Pizza Back card (#5129, 1993) . . 4.50
   On new card + card (#05129) 5.00
Mutatin Rahzar (#5238, 1993) 10.00

Rat King (#5059, 1989) in type C pack . . 12.50
   On Pizza Back card (#5388, 1993) . . 4.50
Ray Fillet (#5110, 1990)
   Purple torso, red V or Red torso,
   maroon V with "Awesome Mutant Color
   Change" on E2 package 30.00
   Purple torso, red V or Red torso,
   maroon V with color-change
   drawings on package 25.00
   Yellow torso, blue V, color-change
   drawings on package, (does not
   change color) 20.00
   Yellow torso, blue V, no color-
   change drawings on package 12.50
   On Pizza Back card (#5384, 1993) . 10.00

Ray Fillet (Playmates 1990)

Rhinoman "Sewer Heroes" (#5424, 1993) . 5.00
   With trading card (#05424, 1994) 4.50
   With card and coin (#05424, 1995) . . 4.50
Rocksteady (#5009, 1988) in type A pack 25.00
   Reissue in type F pack (#5009, 1990) 12.00
   On Pizza Back card (#5391, 1993) . . 4.50
   With trading card (#05391, 1994) 4.50
   With card and coin (#05391, 1995) . . 4.50
Machine Gunnin' Rocksteady (Wacky
   Action) + joke book (#5619, 1991)
   in type W4 pack 12.00
Mutatin' Rocksteady (#5227, 1992) 10.00
Power-Punchin' Rocksteady (#5244, 1992) . 6.00
Dim Wit Doughboy Rocksteady

(#5276, 1992) 4.50
Night Ninja Rocksteady (#5465, 1993) 7.00
Robotic Rocksteady (#5497, 1993) 6.00
  With trading card (#5497, 1994) 5.00
Gatekeeper Rocksteady + comic book
  "Warriors of the Forgotten Sewer"
  (#5268, 1994) 5.00
Kung Fu Rocksteady (#3026, 1994) 6.00
Sandstorm (#5491, 1993) 5.00
Scale Tail (#5284, 1992) 7.00
  On Pizza Back card (#5284, 1993) . . 4.50
Scratch (#5494, 1993) scarce 75.00
Scumbug (#5102, 1990) in type D1 pack . 10.00
  On Pizza Back card (#5399, 1993) . . 4.50
Sergeant Bananas (#5141, 1991) 7.50
  On Pizza Back card (#5141, 1993) . . 4.50
Shogun Shoate with card (#5163, 1994) . . 5.00
Shredder (#5007, 1988) in type A pack . . 25.00
  On Pizza Back card (#5389, 1993) . . 4.50
Slice 'n' Dice Shredder (Wacky Action) + joke
  book (#5617, 1990) in type W3 pack   18.00
Super Shredder (#5128, 1991) 10.00
  With trading card (#05128, 1994) 4.50
  With card and coin (#05128, 1995) . . 4.50
Movie Star Super Shredder on

Pizza Back card (#5128, 1993) 4.50
  With coin (#05128, 1995) 4.50
Mutatin' Shredder (#5236, 1993) 10.00
Road Ready Shredder (#5375, 1993) 7.50
Toon Shredder (#5411, 1993) 4.50
Cyber Samurai Shredder (#3008, 1994) . . . 6.00
Shogun Shredder with card (#5435, 1994) . 5.00
  With card and coin (#05435, 1995) . . 4.50
Metal Mutant Shredder with Tiger
  Spirit Armor (#3035, 1995) 6.00
Slash (#5105, 1990)
  Black Belt 15.00
  Purple Belt 30.00
Splinter (#5006, 1988) in type A pack . . . 25.00
  Reissue (#5006, 1990) 10.00
  On Pizza Back card (#5379, 1993) . . 4.50
  With trading card (#05379, 1994) 4.50
  With card and coin (#05379, 1995) . . 4.50
  With coin (#05379, 1995) 4.50
Creepy Crawlin' Splinter (Wacky
  Action) + joke book (#5616, 1990)
  in type W3 pack 18.00
Mutatin' Splinter (#5225, 1992) 10.00
Movie Star Splinter (#5295, 1992) 6.00
  On Pizza Back card (#5295, 1993) . . 4.50

Giant Movie III Samurai Raph and Samurai Leo (Playmates 1993)

Toon Cycle with Toon Raph (Playmates 1993)

On new card + card (#05295) 5.00	**Walkabout** (#5139, 1991) 7.50
Road Ready Splinter (#5374, 1993) 7.50	**Movie III Walker** (#5481, 1993) 4.50
Movie III Splinter (#5478, 1993) 4.50	**Movie III Warlord** (#5476, 1993) 4.50
Shogun Splinter with card (#5436, 1994) . . 5.00	**Wingnut and Screwloose** (#5103, 1990) in
Spellcaster Splinter + comic book "Warriors	type D1 pack 10.00
of the Forgotten Sewer" (#5269, 1994) 7.50	On Pizza Back card (#5383, 1993) . . 4.50
Shogun Splinter + coin (#5436, 1995) 5.00	**Wyrm** (#5134, 1991) 7.50
Tattoo (#5131, 1991) 5.00	**Zak, the Neutrino** (#5135, 1991) 5.00
Tokka (#5130, 1991)	**13" Giant Turtle Figures (Playmates)**
Dark Green Shell 10.00	Donatello (#5623, 1989) 30.00
Orange Shell 10.00	Leonardo (#5623, 1989) 30.00
On Pizza Back card (#5130, 1993) . . 4.50	Michaelangelo (#5623, 1989) 30.00
Mutatin' Tokka (#5239, 1993) 10.00	Raphael (#5623, 1989) 30.00
Toon Burne (#5403, 1993) 4.50	Bebop (#5521, 1991) 30.00
Toon Dask (#5401, 1993) 4.50	Krang's Android Body (#5526, 1991) 30.00
Toon Irma (#5408, 1993) 4.50	Rocksteady (#5522, 1991) 30.00
Toon Kala (#5402, 1993) 4.50	Giant Movie Star Raph (#5514, 1992) . . . 25.00
Toon Vernon (#5409, 1993) 4.50	Giant Movie Star Don (#5515, 1992) 25.00
Toon Zak (#5410, 1993) 4.50	Giant Movie Star Mike (#5516, 1992) 25.00
Triceraton (#5104, 1990) in type D2 pack 10.00	Giant Movie Star Leo (#5513, 1992) 25.00
Reissue in type F pack 5.00	Giant Movie III Samurai Raph
On Pizza Back card (#5397, 1993) . . 4.50	(#5508, 1993) 20.00
Shogun Triceraton with card (#5162) 7.00	Giant Movie III Samurai Don (#5507, 1993) 20.00
Usagi Yojimbo (#5054, 1989) in C pack . 12.00	Giant Movie III Samurai Mike
Reissue in type F pack 6.00	(#5509, 1993) 20.00
On Pizza Back card (#5380, 1993) . . 4.50	Giant Movie III Samurai Leo (#5506, 1993) 20.00
Space Usagi (#5137, 1991) 7.00	Giant Mutatin' Mike (#5564, 1993) 25.00
On Pizza Back card (#5137, 1993) . . 4.50	Giant Mutatin' Don (#5562, 1993) 25.00
Wacky Walking Mouser (Wacky Action) + joke	Giant Mutatin' Raph (#5563, 1993) 25.00
book (#5615, 1989) in type W1 pack 12.00	Giant Mutatin' Leo (#5561, 1993) 25.00

All prices listed are for *Near Mint* condition.

Figure/Vehicle Combinations

T he Cave Turtle figures are definitely Jurassariffic! Cave-Turtle Leo with Dingy Dino is the original figure in this line and appeared in late 1992. It was billed as the "First Collectible Turtle Combo" in the TMNT line. We don't normally recommend any of the four turtles for long-term collectibility because so many zillions are produced. However, these boxed, premium figures are a lot less common and the dinosaurs are attractive and wonderfully detailed. Many of the other special figure/vehicle combinations have good potential as well, particularly the ones involving April.

Cave-Beast Bebop with Bodacious
   Brontosaurus (#5359, 1994) 12.00
Cave-Turtle Don with Trippy
   Tyrannosaurus (#5362, 1993) 15.00
Cave-Turtle Mike with Silly Stegosaurus
   (#5361, 1993) 12.00
Cave-Turtle Raph with Tubular Pterodactyl
   (#5363, 1993) 12.00
(Original) Cave-Turtle Leo with Dingy Dino
   (#5301, 1993) i.e. late 1992 .... 15.00
Cave-Turtle Leo with Dingy Dino
   (#5364, 1993) 12.00
Cave-Woman April with Radical Raptor
   (#5358, 1994) 20.00
Channel 6 News Van with April figure
   (#5322, 1992) 60.00
Channel 6 News Van with April figure
   (#5346, 1993) 15.00
Cruisin' Leo with Classic Bike
   "Bodacious Biker" (#3402, 1994) ... 12.00
Farmer Don with Modern Mutant Tractor
   (#5326, 1994) 10.00
Farmer Mike and his Turtle Tractor
   (#5307, 1993) 10.00
Movie III Samurai Rebel War Horse with
   Rebel Soldier figure (#5305, 1993) .. 15.00
Movie III Samurai Evil War Horse
   with Castle Guard figure (#5304, 1993) 15.00
Movie III Turtlepult with Whit
   figure (#5306, 1993) 10.00
Road Racin' Mike with Kowabunga Bike
   "Bodacious Biker" (#3401, 1994) ... 12.00
Savage Leo with Sewer Warcat
   (#3477, 1994) 12.50
Scuba Divin' Raph with Psych Out Spin
   Out Scuba Tube (#3491, 1994) 12.50
Surfer Leo with Mondo Mutant Surfer
   Tube (#3492) 12.50
Toon Cycle with Toon Raph
   (#5347, 1993) 10.00

Cave-Beast Bebop with Bodacious Brontosaurus (Playmates 1994)

V ehicles and equipment for the TMNT figures may still be available in some toy stores. If so, they will probably be red tag specials by now. Most have not generated much collector interest yet. The vehicles with a special edition figure (see above) came in smaller boxes than these figures and are actually easier to find in toy stores, but they are more collectible. Look for the items below at flea markets from now until the next millennium.

Vehicles and Equipment

Bubble Bomber (Mutant Military)
   (#5312, 1992) 30.00
Cheapskate skateboard (#5017, 1988) 11.00
Cheapskate II Skateboard (#5017-2) 10.00
Don's Krazy Carnival Car (#5553, 1991) .. 15.00
Don's Pizza-Powered Parachute
   (#5314, 1992) 12.00
Don's Sewer Squirter (#5681, 1991) 10.00
Double Barreled Plunger Gun (#5662, 1990) 10.00
Flushomatic (#5661, 1990) 15.00
Foot Cruiser (#5625, 1989) 35.00
Footski (#5632, 1989) 11.00
Knucklehead (1988) 11.00
Leo's Jolly Turtle Tubboat (#5554, 1991) .. 15.00
Leo's Turtle Trike (#5698, 1991) 10.00
Lieutenant Leo's Bodacious Buggy
   (#5316, 1992) 20.00
Macho Mutant Module (#3412, 1994) 10.00
Mega Mutant Killer Bee (#5635, 1990) 10.00
Mega Mutant Needlenose (#5634, 1990) .. 20.00
Michaelangelo's Sidewalk Surfer
   (#5317, 1992) 15.00
Mike's Kowabunga Surf Buggy
   (#5556, 1991) 10.00
Muta-Party Wagon (#5325, 1993) 20.00
Mutant Module (#5624, 1990) 25.00
Mutant Sewer Cycle with Sidecar (1989) .. 15.00
Mutations Muta-Bike (#5331, 1992) 10.00
Mutations Muta-Carrier (#5324, 1992) 30.00
Mutations Muta-Raft (#5303, 1992) 10.00
Mutations Muta-Ski (#5332, 1992) 10.00
Ninja Grapplor, battery powered
   (#5318, 1993) 20.00
Ninja Newscycle (#5557, 1991) 10.00
Party Hearty Wacky Wagon (#3411, 1994) . 20.00
Pizza Powered Sewer Dragster
   (#5692, 1990) 15.00
Pizza Thrower (#5621, 1989) 35.00

Pizza Skimmin' Jetboat (#3496, 1994) 10.00
Pizza Powered Prop (#3498, 1994) 15.00
Psycho Cycle (#5691, 1990) 25.00
Raph's Sewer Speedboat (#5559, 1991) .. 10.00
Raph's Turtle Dragster (#5699, 1991) 10.00
Retrocatapault (#5663, 1990) 11.00
Retromutagen Rifle (#5643, 1992) 15.00
Rock N' Roll Muta-Bus (#5321, 1992) ... 30.00
Rocksteady's Pogocopter (#5558, 1991) . 10.00
Samurai Scooter (#5302, 1992) 8.00
Sewer Army Tube (#5651) 10.00
Sewer Dragster (#5692, 1990) 15.00
Sewer Party Tube (1990) 10.00
Sewer Playset (#5685, 1990) 50.00
Sewer Sandcruiser (#5313, 1992) 25.00
Sewer Seltzer Cannon (#5601, 1990) 15.00
Sewer Sub (#5572, 1991) 25.00
Sewer Subway Car (#3099, 1994) 20.00
Shell Top 4X4 (#5576, 1991) 25.00
Shreddermobile (#5555, 1991) 20.00
Slugemobile (Wacky Action) (#5551, 1991) 15.00
Supermutant Cyclone Cycle (#3019, 1994) . 11.00
Talkin' Turtle Communicator (#3495, 1994) 20.00
Technodrome 22" (#5684, 1988) 60.00
Techodrome Scout Vehicle (#5308, 1993) 18.00
Techodrome vehicle (#5684, 1993) 15.00
Toilet Taxi (#5552, 1990) 7.00
Turtle Blimp 30" vinyl (#5020, 1988) 30.00
Turtle Blimp II (#5050-2) 25.00
Turtle Communicator (#5682, 1993) 15.00
Turtle Party Wagon (#5622, 1989) 40.00
Turtle Popcan Racer (#5315, 1992) 20.00
Turtle Tank (#5571, 1991) 25.00
Turtle Trooper 22" parachute (#5019, 1988) 10.00
Turtlecopter (Mutant Military) (#5626, 1991) 25.00
Turtlemobile (#5323, 1992) 25.00

THE TICK

T hese action figures are based on the comic book characters created by Ben Edlund, now a hot animated TV show. The exploding Dyna-Mole looks a lot like my co-author Alex!

THE TICK
Bandai (1995)
6" action figures, Good Doers
Bounding Tick (#02601) 5.00
Fluttering Arthur (#02602) 5.00
Pose Striking Die Fledermaus (#02603?) not seen
Man Eating Cow (#02604?) .... not seen
Sewer Spray Sewer Urchin (#02605) 5.00

Exploding Dyna-Mole (Bandai 1995)

Projectile Human Bullet (#02606) 5.00
Evil Doers
Growing Dinosaur Neil (#02607) 5.00
Death Hug Dean (#02608) 5.00
Exploding Dyna-Mole (#02609) 5.00
Grasping El Seed (#02610) 5.00
Talking Tick, 16" (#02611) 20.00
Wacky Wind-Up Action
Hard Drivin Tick (#02614) 4.00
Wing Flutterin Arthur (#02615) 4.00
Submarine Sewer Urchin (#02616) 4.00
Cannon Human Bullet (#02617) 4.00
Crop Dustin' El Seed (#02618) 4.00
Time Bomb Dyna-Mole (#02619) 4.00
Series II, Good Doers (Fall 1995)
Twist and Chop American Maid (#02631) . . 5.00
Hurling Tick (#02633) 5.00
Color Changing Crusading
    Chameleon (#02635) 7.50
Evil Doers
Skippy the Propellerized Robot Dog (#02632) 5.00
Mucus Tick (#02634) 5.00
Evil Tongue Thrakkorzog (#02636) 5.00

ULTRAFORCE

T he UltraForce are "humans endow-
ed with awesome powers greater
than any known science can dupli-
cate." They first appeared in the Ultraverse line of comic books from Malibu in
1993 and now come in several monthly
titles and a TV series. Malibu is now
owned by Marvel and some of the Ultra-
Force have appeared with characters from
the Marvel universe, but the toys are
made by Galoob, which, unlike Toy Biz,
Marvel does not own.

The initial comic shop assortments
were guaranteed to include three Primes,
two each of Prototype, Night Man and
Hardcase and just one each of Ghoul,
Topaz and NM-E. Atalon appeared in toy
store assortments. Topaz, the only female
figure so far, is probably the best one to

Atalon Ultra Force figure (Galoob 1995)

collect. Various limited edition packaging mixes are scheduled for comic shops and different stores, with special UltraForce 5000 figures included in limited quantity. More of these will appear in 1996.

ULTRA FORCE
Galoob (1995)
5" Action Figures

0. Prime (deluxe edition) (#75640?)	15.00
1. Prime (#75597)	7.00
2. Prototype (#75598)	7.00
3. Hardcase (#75599)	7.00
4. Atalon (#75600)	8.00
6. Ghoul (in coffin) (#75603)	8.00
7. NM-E (#75604)	8.00
8. Topaz (#75605)	10.00
9. The Night Man (#57601)	7.00
10. NM-E (deluxe edition) (#75642)	12.50
15. Hardcase (deluxe edition) (#75643)	12.50
20. The Night Man (deluxe edition) (#75644)	12.50

Vehicles

Ultra Rage Rover vehicle (#76161)	10.00
Ultra Crasher Bike	not seen

Dozer (McFarlane 1995)

Wetworks toys are based on the Image comics characters created by Whilce Portacio. The figures appeared in the fall of 1995, except for Werewolf which is listed on the pack. It's too early for any significant price increases, although the female figure collectors have been buying Mother-One. No variations have been reported as yet, but the Spawn line by the same manufacturer had lots of them.

WETWORKS
McFarlane Toys (1995)
6" Action Figures

Dane (#12101)	8.00
Dozer (#12102)	8.00
Mother-One (#12103)	10.00
Vampire (#12104)	8.00
Werewolf (scarce, not seen)	17.00
Grail (#12106)	8.00

Great-looking new figures based on the Jim Lee comic book characters. Each figure comes with one of two different trading cards. Grifter and Daemonite were scarce at first, but appeared in quantity later. Five of the original characters were reissued in the summer in new outfits. Their packages say "New" so they are easy to identify. In October a third batch of three new figures appeared. These are somewhat scarce in toy stores as of December and the female figure collectors will probably drive the prices of Voodoo and Void up if this continues.

WILDC.A.T.S.
Playmates (1995)
6" action figures, with trading card

Spartan (#01801)	9.00
Zealot (#01802)	15.00
Grifter (#01803)	15.00
Maul (#01804)	10.00
Warblade (#01805)	9.00
Helspont (#01806)	15.00
Daemonite (#01807)	15.00

Zealot (Playmates 1995)

Second batch, all say "New"
Spartan in ECM Stealth Suit (#01816) 9.00
Zealot in Classic Coda Uniform (#01817) . . 12.00
WarBlade in Bio-Flexon Armor Suit (#01818) 9.00
Helspont in Daemonite Ceremonial
    Battle Gear (#01816) 10.00
Maul in Flexon All-Weather Combat
    Suit (#01820) 10.00
Third batch
Pike (#01810) 9.00
Voodoo (#01809) 11.00
Void (#01808) 10.00
Vehicle
Bullet Bike vehicle + card (#01851) 10.00
10" figures
Giant Spartan (#01831) 17.00
Giant Maul (#01832) 17.00
Giant Grifter (#01835) 17.00
Two-packs, limited editions with two trading cards
Spartan vs. Helspont (#01841) 16.00
The Grifter vs. Daemonite (#01842) 16.00

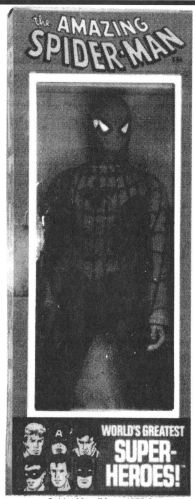

Spider-Man (Mego 1970s)

(OFFICIAL) WORLD'S GREATEST SUPER HEROES

W hile Captain Action was the closest thing to an actual super-hero action figure we had, the Mego company in 1972 gave us the real thing for the very first time.

The year 1972 saw the releases of the first 8" DC Comics character super offerings. These were boxed action figures of Batman, Robin, Aquaman, Superman, and

---

Shazam. Batman and Robin were also released that same year with a removable cowl for Batman and removable mask for Robin.

Catwoman, Batgirl, Green Arrow, Joker, Penguin, Mr. Mxyzptlk, Supergirl and The Riddler were made available the following year. All were still in boxes, but that was soon about to change. An interesting note here is that Superman's impish enemy, Mr. Mxyzptlk, was released that same year with two different styles. One depicted Mr. M. with his mouth open while the other had him with a smirk on his face. The smiling/smirking issue of the character is the rarer of the two and can be double the price of the other.

While the year 1974 saw no new DC Superheroes from Mego on the store shelves, there were three new additions to the line. Offered exclusively through Montgomery Ward were Alter Ego/Secret Identity figures that came in plain brown boxes through the mail. Clark Kent, Bruce Wayne and Dick Grayson were the three DC characters you could get through this offer. This same year, Mego was also to release the first in a series of accessories for the 8" line. The Supervator, Batcave and Batcycle found their way into the hands of wanting collectors as well as happy kids. Also available were the Batmobile, which came both boxed and carded, and the Batcopter, boxed and carded.

The Mobile Bat Lab and the Jokermobile were both offered in 1975. This year, however, saw no new 8" DC Superfolks releases.

Finally, in 1976, there was an action figure explosion from Mego. They introduced an 8" figure of the superfemale Isis, in both box and on card during the same year. The most important figures from this year were those made of the

Falcon and Green Goblin (Mego 1974)

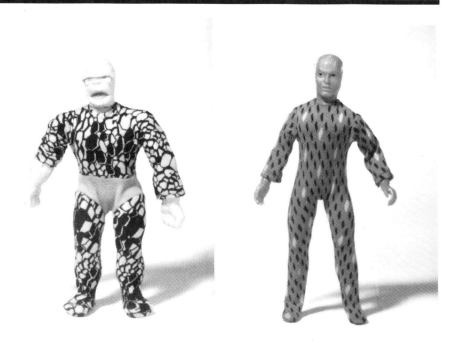

Thing and Human Torch (Mego 1970s)

Teen Titans. Each was a bit smaller than the standard 8" figures (they were roughly 6½" tall) and available only on cards. The set includes Wonder Girl, Speedy, Kid Flash and Aqualad. These four are some of the rarest action figures ever made, as they were only available during 1976. A new series of 8" figures called the Fist Fighters was also manufactured for sale this year. Batman, Robin, the Riddler and the Joker underwent cosmetic surgery and had devices installed on their backs that enabled them to wallop their chosen opponent. Mego added two more accessories that year with the Green Arrowcar and the Hall of Justice Playset.

All of the figures that were previously released in boxed packaging form were also available on blister cards. Batman, Robin, Superman, Aquaman, Penguin, Riddler, Shazam, Supergirl, Joker, Green Arrow, Batgirl, Catwoman and the open-mouthed version of Mr. Mxyzptlk were all repackaged thusly.

Actually, all of the figures had been available all along on blister cards, but only from S. S. Kresge stores (and a few others). These "Kresge Cards" can be identified by the §K logo on the back, at the bottom. Wonder Woman only appeared on a Kresge card and was not reissued in 1976. Figures on Kresge cards are worth as much, or more than boxed figures.

The last of the accessory pieces rolled out in 1977 and 1978. The very rare Wayne Foundation playset came first. Made of sturdy cardboard and vinyl plastic, it had four floors and was over 40" tall when assembled. The last of the accessories was the hard to find Aquaman and the Great White Shark.

In 1972, Captain America and Spider-Man (the same characters that had Captain Action outfits) were the first of the Mego/Marvel Super Hero 8" offerings.

For some unknown reason, there were no 8" Mego/Marvel action figures in 1973. However, Mego more than made up for this absence in the following year with five brand-new Marvel figure offerings for this series. Iron Man, The Hulk, The Falcon, The Green Goblin and The Lizard all rolled off the assembly line onto the shelves of toy stores and eventually into the awaiting hands of happy kids. The very rare and collectible Peter Parker figure, an exclusive 8" figure available only from Wards, could also be found during this time.

1975 was the last year of the Mego/Marvel 8" action figures. Six new characters made the scene, four of which comprised a team. Yes, I'm referring to the Fantastic Four. With the Fantastic Four, a minor milestone happened — for the first time in action figure history, a Marvel Comics SuperHeroine was made available. While there were a good amount of DC costumed females that made the action figure scene, Marvel's babes were more or less left out in the cold. However, the 8" figure of Sue Richards, The Invisible Girl, was not just the first Marvel SuperHeroine action figure, she was the last until the 1990s. Joining her were her fellow team members, husband Reed Richards, a.k.a. Mr. Fantastic, brother Johnny Storm, The Human Torch, and longtime friend and ace pilot, Benn Grimm, The Thing. The two remaining figures also available that year were Thor and Conan the Barbarian. Both of these are highly sought after by collectors.

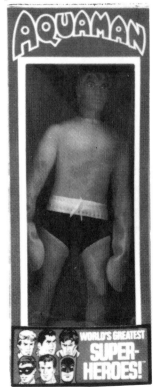  

Aquaman, Tarzan and Wonder Woman (Mego 1970s)

(OFFICIAL) WORLD'S GREATEST SUPER HEROES
Mego (1972–79)

Note: Figures on **Kresge** cards are from 1972–74 and are worth **as much or more** than the boxed figures from these years. Listed prices for carded figures are for the 1976–79 figure releases. Dates given below are for the first year of release.

8" Action Figures

Aqualad 6½" (carded) (1976) 300.00
Aquaman (solid box) (1972) 500.00
Aquaman (window box) 150.00
Aquaman (carded) (1976) 225.00
Batgirl (window box) (1973) 300.00
Batgirl (carded) (1976) 200.00
Batman (removable mask,
    solid box) (1972) 1,000.00
Batman (removable mask, window box) . . 375.00
Batman with out removable mask
    (window box) 150.00
Batman with out removable mask
    (carded) (1976) 80.00
Batman (Fist Fighting, window box) (1976) 400.00
Bruce Wayne (Mont. Ward's
    exclusive) (1974) 450.00
Captain America (window box) (1972) . . . 175.00
Captain America (carded) (1976) 125.00
Catwoman (window box) (1973) 300.00
Catwoman (carded) (1976) 200.00
Clark Kent (Mont. Ward's
    exclusive) (1974) 450.00
Conan (window box) (1975) 400.00
Conan (carded) (1976) 350.00
Dick Grayson (Mont. Ward's
    exclusive) (1974) 400.00
Falcon (window box) (1974) 120.00
Falcon (carded) (1976) 200.00
Green Arrow (window box) (1973) 175.00
Green Arrow (carded) (1976) 325.00
Green Goblin (window box) (1974) 250.00
Green Goblin (carded) (1976) 375.00
Human Torch (window box) (1975) 120.00
Human Torch (carded) (1976) 40.00
Incredible Hulk (window box) (1974) 75.00
Incredible Hulk (carded) (1976) 40.00
Invisible Girl (window box) (1975) 120.00
Invisible Girl (carded) (1976) 40.00
Iron Man (window box) (1974) 150.00
Iron Man (carded) (1976) 200.00
Isis (window box) (1976) 300.00
Isis (carded) (1976) 225.00

Joker (window box) (1973) 190.00
Joker (carded) (1976) 125.00
Joker (Fist Fighting, window box) (1976) . 300.00
Kid Flash 6½" (carded) (1976) 400.00
Lizard (window box) (1974) 200.00
Lizard (carded) (1976) 275.00
Mr. Fantastic (window box) (1975) 120.00
Mr. Fantastic (carded) (1976) 60.00
Mr. Mxyzptlk (window box,
    with smirk) (1973) 150.00
Mr. Mxyzptlk (window box, with
    mouth open) (1973) 90.00
Mr. Mxyzptlk (carded, with mouth open) . . 175.00
Penguin (window box) (1973) 125.00
Penguin (carded) (1976) 140.00
Peter Parker (Mont. Ward's
    exclusive) (1974) 450.00
Riddler (window box) (1973) 300.00
Riddler (carded) (1976) 400.00
Riddler (Fist Fighting, window box) (1976) 400.00
Robin (removable mask,
    solid box) (1972) 1,250.00
Robin (removable mask, window box) . . . 500.00
Robin (w/o removable mask; window box) 120.00
Robin (w/o removable mask; carded) (1976) 75.00
Robin (Fist Fighting) (1976) 400.00
Shazam (window box) (1972) 200.00
Shazam (carded) (1976) 200.00
Speedy 6½" (carded) (1976) 420.00
Spider-Man (window box) (1972) 120.00
Spider-Man (carded) (1976) 40.00
Supergirl (window box) (1973) 375.00
Supergirl (carded) (1976) 450.00
Superman (solid box) (1972) 250.00
Superman (window box) 140.00
Superman (carded) (1976) 100.00
Tarzan (window box) (1972) 75.00
Tarzan (carded) (1976) 150.00
The Thing (window box) (1975) 120.00
The Thing (carded) (1976) 40.00
Thor (window box) (1975) 375.00
Thor (carded) (1976) 425.00
Wonder Girl 6½" (carded) (1976) 400.00
Wonder Woman (window box) (1973) . . . 275.00
Wonder Woman (carded) (Kresge only) . . 400.00

Note: Batgirl, Catwoman, Supergirl and Wonder Woman packages say "World's Greatest Super Gals" and Isis package does not say "World's Greatest Super Heroes."

Vehicles and Playsets

The Amazing Spider Car (1976) 90.00
Aquaman vs. The Great White Shark 500.00

Batcopter (boxed) (1974) 120.00
Batcopter (carded) (1974) 100.00
Batcycle (1974) 160.00
Batmobile (boxed) (1974) 125.00
Batmobile (carded) (1974) 100.00
Captain Americar (1976) 300.00
Green Arrowcar (1976) 250.00
Jokermobile (1975) 225.00
Batcave playset (1974) 175.00
Batman's Wayne Foundation (1977) . . 1,200.00
Hall of Justice (1976) 200.00
Mobile Bat Lab (1975) 175.00
Supervator (1974) 125.00

Captain America Fly Away Action (Mego 1980)

LARGE FIGURES

T he 12½" Mego figures came out between 1976 and 1981. The Wonder Woman series of action figure dolls is based on the TV series with Lynda Carter. There were four figures in all. The second-issue box of Wonder Woman has no picture reference to the TV show. In 1979, Superman was reissued in a movie box, along with General

Zod, Jor-El and Lex Luthor. Five of the figures were reissued with "Fly Away Action" and Captain America had this feature in his only appearance.

Mego (1976–81)

12½" Action Figures

Batman (window box) 90.00
Batman "Fly Away Action" 140.00
Batman with magnetic power 125.00
Captain America "Fly Away Action" 125.00
Incredible Hulk 90.00
Incredible Hulk "Fly Away Action" 100.00
Lex Luthor 150.00
Robin (window box) 200.00
Robin "Fly Away Action" 140.00
Robin, with magnetic power 225.00
Spider-Man (window box) 90.00
Spider-Man with magnetic power 125.00
Spider-Man with spiderweb 70.00
Spider-Man "Fly Away Action" 125.00
Web-Spinning Spider-Man 150.00
Superman (window box) 100.00
Superman "Fly-Away Action" 150.00

Superman Movie figures in movie box (1979)

Superman 75.00
General Zod 40.00
Jor-El 40.00
Lex Luthor 40.00

Wonder Woman TV figures (1976)

Wonder Woman, Diana Prince outfit,
    Lynda Carter photo box 100.00
Wonder Woman, evening gown (2nd-issue box
    without Lynda Carter picture (1977) . . 40.00
Nubia 90.00
Queen Hippolite 90.00
Steve Trevor 75.00

DIE CAST METAL FIGURES

I n 1979 Mego produced "Limited Collector's Edition Die Cast Metal" superheroes from Mego. They are 5½" true action figures, with metal bodies, plastic heads and cloth capes (on Superman and Batman). They came in a combination window box and hanging card which is white with color lettering.

Mego (1979)

Batman (#91503) 110.00
Hulk (#91504) 75.00
Superman (#91505) 90.00
Spider-Man (#91506) 90.00

All prices listed are for *Near Mint* condition. **65**

X-FORCE

I n 1992 eleven new Marvel/X-Men/X-Force figures appeared all at the same time! Included were Warpath, Gideon and G.W. Bridge, the first of the X-Force figures. Cable and the rest of the figures appeared soon after. Deadpool has proved to be the most collectible so far, followed by Forearm.

X-FORCE
Toy Biz (1992)
5" Action Figures, with Impel X-Men (I) card
later shipments: SkyBox X-Men 2 card

Cable (I) (#4951)	9.00
Shatterstar (I) (#4952)	9.00
Kane (I) (#4953)	9.00
Warpath (#4954)	10.00
G.W. Bridge (#4955)	7.50
Stryfe (#4956)	12.50
Deadpool (#4957)	25.00
Forearm (#4958)	18.00
Gideon (#4959)	9.00

X-FORCE (1993)

T he only interesting development in the X-Force series in 1993 was the color variation in Cannonball's costume. The pink color is much scarcer that the purple color, and it has become a much-sought figure. It's not all that scarce because a number of dealers seem to have a copy. This probably means that collectors are still looking for one cheap.

X-FORCE (Cont.)
Toy Biz (1993)
5" Action Figures, with SkyBox X-Men 2 card

Cable 2nd (#4963)	6.00
Cable 3rd (#4964)	6.00
Kane (II) (#4965)	6.00
Cannonball (#4966)	
Pink, scarce	25.00
Purple	8.00
Grizzly (#4967)	6.00
Krule (#4968)	6.00

X-FORCE (1994)

E xcept for the switch to the Fleer Ultra X-Men trading card, none of the 1994 X-Force figures are remarkable. Any of these figures which have the older SkyBox X-Men 2 cards would be the earliest versions and worth a small premium.

X-FORCE (Cont.)
Toy Biz (1994)
5" Action Figures, with Fleer Ultra X-Men card

Cable 4th Edition (#49513)	5.00
Rictor (#49514)	5.00
Sunspot (#49515)	5.00

Cable 2nd, Cannonball, Kane II (Toy Biz 1993)

Quark (#49516) 5.00
Shatterstar 2nd Edition (#49518) 5.00
Pyro (#49519) 5.00
Mojo (#49528) (Toys "R" Us exclusive) . . . 4.00

Cable 4th Edition, X-Force (Toy Biz 1994)

Second 1994 batch, with Ultra X-Men card
X-Treme (#49520) 5.00
Black Tom (#49521) 5.00
Killspree (#49523) 7.50
Slayback (#49524) 5.00
Cable 5th Edition (#49525) 5.00
Commcast (#49526) 5.00
Warpath 2nd Edition (#49527) 5.00

X-FORCE (1995)

I n early 1995 the X-Force line got new, larger packaging along with the X-Men line. Black Tom was reissued in the new packaging.

X-FORCE (Cont.)
Toy Biz (1995)

First 1995 batch, with Fleer Ultra X-Men card
Mojo (#49528) 5.00
Black Tom (#49529) 5.00
Urban Assault Cable (#49530) 5.00
Avalanche (#49532) 5.00
Commando (#49533) 5.00
Exodus (#49534) 5.00
Second 1995 batch, with Flair Marvel Ann. card
Cable Cyborg (#49535) 6.00

The Blob (#49536) 6.00
Domino (#49537) 9.00
Caliban (#49538) 6.00
Nimrod (#49539) 6.00
Deadpool (#49540) 6.00
Tyler-Apocalypse III . . . . Not Yet Released
Genesis (#49543) 6.00
10" X-Force Figures
Cable (#49550, 1994) 11.00
Kane (#49551, 1994) 11.00
Shatterstar (#49552, 1994) 11.00
Cable, Venture exclusive (#49510, 1994) . . 15.00

(UNCANNY) X-MEN

C yclops, **Wolverine**, **Nightcrawler**, **Colossus** and **Magneto** made up the first wave of X-Men figures. Series two included **Archangel**, **Juggernaut**, **Apocalypse** and, hold onto your hats, **Storm**! Finally, another Marvel SuperHeroine made the action figure scene. She sat on the shelves for quite a while at first, as Toy Biz learned why

Storm, X-Men (Toy Biz 1991)

you should make the female figure the scarce figure: Boys will buy less female figures, but if the figure is scarcer than the others released at the same time,

---

collectors will hunt them all down! As all these early figures have been replaced by different issues, they have become collectible, and Storm has achieved the highest prices.

All the first nine X-Men figures came with Marvel Universe One trading cards which matched the toy. This requires a special card printing since only a few of the cards from that series were used. All later edition figures containing cards have used the entire card series, with cards included randomly. This simplifies the printing and toy production process, but it isn't as elegant. All the cards have a "Toy Biz" logo printed on the back, on top of the normal card back.

Iceman (1st), X-Men (Toy Biz 1992)

(UNCANNY) X-MEN
Toy Biz (1991)
5" Figures, with Impel Marvel Universe One card (which matches the figure)

Wolverine (#4901)	15.00
Archangel (white wings) (#4902)	15.00
Colossus (#4903)	15.00
Nightcrawler (#4904)	20.00
Storm (#4905)	25.00
Cyclops (#4906)	15.00
Apocalypse (#4907)	15.00
Magneto (#4908)	15.00
Juggernaut (#4909)	15.00

Vehicles and Accessories

Magneto Magnetron Vehicle (#4961, 1991)	11.00
Reissue, (#04961, 1994)	
Wolverine Mutant Cycle (#4962, 1991)	11.00
Reissue, (#04962, 1994)	10.00
Wolverine Combat Cave (#4971, 1991)	12.00
Cyclops Light Force Arena (#4973, 1991)	12.00

Super-Size 15" Super Heroes

Magneto (#4921, 1991)	20.00
Wolverine (#4922, 1991)	20.00

Accessory Playsets

Wolverine Dress Up Playset with mask and claw glove (#4981, 1991)	11.00
Magneto Dress Up Playset with Helmet and disk shooter glove (#4982, 1991)	11.00
Cyclops Laserlight Visor (#4983, 1991)	11.00

UNCANNY X-MEN (1992)

Toy Biz had very big plans for 1992 — 30 new Marvel, X-Men and X-Force figures — but they started slowly. The first four of the X-Men action figures, **Wolverine 2nd, Wolverine 3rd, Forge** and **Mr. Sinister**, appeared in early July. The figures come with an Impel trading card taken from the Uncanny X-Men (1) series which came out earlier that year, but the card has nothing to do with the particular action figure. The cards are identical to the regular trading card, except for an overprinted Toy Biz logo on the back. Eventually, near the end of the production of these figures, this became an X-Men 2 card.

Sabretooth came out next, followed by **Iceman** and several X-Force and Marvel figures, bringing the total released to 15.

Later 11 new Marvel/X-Men figures appeared from Toy Biz all at the same time! **Gambit** was the only one that disappointed us. His trademark raincoat looks like a cheap piece of thin brown plastic (which, of course, it is). Iceman was by far the most popular figure of the year with collectors. It was scarce in the toy stores, partly because of heavy buying by collectors and partly because it has been shipped in lesser quantity than the other figures. In the fall of 1992, Sears offered 4-pack sets of the Toy Biz figures in a box, with line drawings of the characters. The four figures were **loose, in a clear plastic bag**, with accessories in a separate bag. They cost $17.99 per set, plus shipping.

UNCANNY X-MEN (Cont.)
Toy Biz (1992)
5" Action Figures, with Impel X-Men (1) card
later shipments: SkyBox X-Men 2 or Fleer card
and 5 digit code on back, adding a "2"

Wolverine 2nd Edition (#4931)	10.00
Wolverine 3rd Edition (#4932)	18.00
Wolverine "Weapon X" green cords (#4933)	10.00
Iceman (#4934)	35.00
Forge (#4935), with yellow holster	8.00
Forge (#4935), with brown holster	20.00
Gambit (#4937)	8.00
later shipments: back (#49492)	8.00
Banshee (#4938)	6.00
Sabretooth (#4939)	15.00
Sauron (#4940)	6.00

Magneto (2) (#4941)	6.00
Mr. Sinister (#4942)	8.00

Sears X-Men sets, bagged, no card

Classic Heroes 4-Pack, with Spider-Man, Green Goblin, Venom and Punisher (#59501)	20.00
Classic Heroes 4-Pack, with Mr. Fantastic, Thing, Venom and Annihilus (#59506)	20.00
X-Force 4-Pack, with Cable, Stryfe, Forearm and Deadpool (#59505)	20.00
X-Men 4-Pack, with Mr. Sinister, Iceman, Sabretooth and Wolverine II (#59508)	20.00

UNCANNY X-MEN (1993)

There are also Canadian versions of these (and other X-Men toys) and some made their way to local Kay-Bee stores. They are from Charan Toy instead of Toy Biz, but otherwise, they are the same as the American versions of these toys and should sell for just a little bit less.

UNCANNY X-MEN (Cont.)
Toy Biz (1993)
5" reissue figures, Impel X-Men (1) card
later shipments: SkyBox X-Men 2 or Fleer card
and 5 digit code on back, adding a "6"

Juggernaut (#4943), reissue	6.00
Cyclops, blue and white (#4944), reissue	6.00

Wolverine, 2nd Edition (Toy Biz 1992)

Wolverine, 3rd Edition (Toy Biz 1992)

All prices listed are for *Near Mint* condition.

Cyclops, yellow-and-blue (#4944) 6.00
later shipments: back (#49491) 6.00
Magneto (#4945), reissue 6.00
Wolverine (I) (#4946), reissue 6.00
Archangel, white wings (#4947), reissue ... 6.00
Archangel, gray wings, back (#49495) 6.00
Apocalypse (#4948), reissue 6.00
Nightcrawler (#4950), reissue 10.00
Colossus (#4903), reissue, ... 6.00
later shipments: back (#49494) 6.00

X-MEN (Cont.)
Toy Biz (1994)
5" Action Figures, with SkyBox X-Men 2 card
later shipments: Fleer Ultra X-Men card
Cyclops (Light-Up Optic Blast) (#4917) 6.00
Professor X (#4918) 6.00
Longshot (#4923) 6.00
Sabretooth (Snarl & Swipe) (#4924) 6.00
Ahab (#4925) 6.00
Brood (#4926) 8.00

Omega Red, X-Men (Toy Biz 1993)

5" Action Figures, with Impel X-Men (1) card
or SkyBox X-Men 2 card
Wolverine 5th Edition (#4910) 10.00
Wolverine 5th Edition (Kay-Bee) (#4910) .. 7.50
Bishop (#4911) 10.00
Strong Guy (#4912) 6.00
Apocalypse (2nd) (#4913), resculpt 6.00
Tusk (#4914) 6.00
Omega Red (#4916) 7.00
Wolverine "Weapon X" red cords (#4933) .. 7.50

X-MEN (1994)

Brood from this series came out after Professor X, Ahab and Long-shot. Last to appear were the new Cyclops and a new Sabretooth. Note: Second batch 1994 display cards begin five-digit item numbers and no longer say "Uncanny" just "X-Men."

Brood, X-Men (Toy Biz 1994)

Second batch, with Fleer Ultra X-Men card
Beast (#49355) 10.00
Robot Wolverine (Albert) 6th (#49356) 6.00
Random (#49357) 6.00
Silver Samurai (#49358) 6.00
Trevor Fitzroy (#49360) 6.00
Morph (#49361) 6.00
Rogue (#49362) 7.00
Kylun (#49363) 6.00
Raza (#49364) 6.00
Ch'od (#49365) 6.00
Wolverine–Street Clothes 7th (#49366) ... 6.00
Bonebreaker (#49368) 6.00
Nightcrawler (#49369), reissue 10.00
Storm (#2) (#49370) 9.00
Magneto (Super Spark) (#49371) 6.00
Mr. Sinister, with goatee (#49372), reissue . 6.00
Wolverine "Weapon X" silver
cords (#49373), scarce 20.00
Sauron, black symbol on loincloth (#49374) 5.00

Iceman (#2): "Super Ice Slide" (#49375)
   Clear or blue 12.00
Senyaka (#49389) (Toys "R" Us exclusive) . 4.00

Phoenix (Toy Biz 1995)

X-MEN (1995)

T oy Biz redesigned the package for all of the X-Men figures and the new, larger, blue display cards appeared in the summer of 1995. The Phoenix Saga figures were the last ones released on the old, smaller, orange display cards. These figures were caught in the transition and quickly reappeared on the new cards. This makes the figures on the original display cards, especially Phoenix, highly collectible. In addition, the new package Gladiator and Wolverine figures have additional weapons and the new package Phoenix has a catapult (to go with light-up hair and eyes). Product codes are the same for both versions of each figure.

X-MEN (Cont.)
Toy Biz (1995)
5" Action Figures, with Fleer Ultra X-Men card
Phoenix Saga (Summer 1995)

Corsair (#49380) 6.00
   new larger package 5.00
Gladiator (#49381) 6.00
   new larger package 5.00
Space Wolverine, 8th Edition (#49383) 7.50
   new larger package 6.00
Warstar (#49384) 7.50
   new larger package 6.00
Phoenix (#49385) 15.00
   new larger package 8.00

5" Action Figures, with Fleer Ultra X-Men card
Mutant Genesis (August 1995)
Cameron Hodge Phalanx (#49386) 5.00
X-Cutioner (#49387) 5.00
Maverick (#49388) 5.00
Senyaka (#49389) 5.00
Wolverine Fang with Shi'ar Weapon (#49390) 5.00
Sunfire (#49399) 5.00

Invasion Series (October 1995)
Captive Sabretooth (#49392) 5.00
Battle Ravaged Wolverine (#49393) 5.00
Havok (#49394) 5.00
Iceman II (#49395) 5.00

Spiral (Toy Biz 1995)

All prices listed are for *Near Mint* condition.   **71**

Archangel II (#49396) 5.00
Spiral (#49397) 7.50
Eric The Red (#49398) 5.00

X-Men Vehicles and Accessories

X-Men Sentinel 14" (#49320, 1994) 25.00
X-Men Blackbird Jet (#49400, 1994) 25.00
X-Men Mini Blackbird Jet (#49690, 1995) . . 10.00
X-Men Wolverine Jeep (#49685, 1995) . . . 10.00
X-Men Headquarters Playset (#49810, 1995) 35.00

Maverick and Trevor Fitzroy
(KayBee exclusive) (Toy Biz 1994)

X-MEN MULTI–PACKS

T he X-Men Mutant Hall of Fame figure collection comes in a display box with name tags. The set includes the first version of Professor X available, together with the new yellow-and-blue Cyclops, Archangel with gray wings, Iceman and seven other figures. The only problem is that the figures can't be removed from the mounting platform and all the joints are glued.

The **X-Men Gift Set** is a four-figure set of some of your favorites (**Wolverine, Iceman, Mr. Sinister** and **Sabretooth**) in a display box. The key to collector interest in this item is **Iceman**. That figure is very hard to find alone, and this version includes the icebox which was missing in

the 10-figure Hall of Fame package which came out a few months earlier.

X-Men Mutant Hall of Fame, 10 figures
on collector display stand, numbered
(75,000 made) (#49800) 50.00
X-Men Gift Set (Wolverine, blue Iceman,
Mr. Sinister & Sabretooth) (#49100) . 20.00

WalMart 2-pack figures

Beast vs. Spiderman (Web Shooter) 10.00
Nightcrawler vs. Spider-Man (Web Racer) 10.00
Juggernaut vs. Spider-Man (Web Parachute) 10.00
Civilian Wolverine vs. Peter Parker 10.00

WalMart 2-packs with 4 cards

Wolverine vs. Sabretooth 10.00
Strong Guy vs. Tusk (#49602) 10.00
Professor X vs. Ahab (#49603) 10.00
Wolverine Spy vs. Omega Red 10.00
Bishop vs. Apocalypse 10.00
Cyclops vs. Mr. Sinister 10.00

F.A.O. Schwarz special

Trevor Fitzroy, Combat Cable, Forge
and Deadpool in mail-order box 45.00
Dark Phoenix Saga four pack: Phoenix, Corsair,
Ch'od, Wolverine Space (#49050) . . . 35.00

Kay-Bee Collector's Edition

Maverick and Trevor Fitzroy (with Steel Mutants
Wolverine) (Maverick sold exclusively
at Kay-Bee) (#49640, 1994) 13.00
Silver Samurai and Robot Wolverine (with Steel
Mutants Cyclops) (#49641, 1994) . . . 12.00

X-MEN DELUXE FIGURES

T he Deluxe Edition X-Men are a big 10" tall and come boxed rather than on blister cards. The first three figures were Sabretooth, Cyclops and Wolverine. They appear to be scaled-up versions of the smaller figures, but actually it's the other way around. This means that they are very attractive but somewhat disappointing since much more could have been done with this larger-size figure, such as electronic versions. They cost about twice as much as the smaller figures and come out in groups of three. Toy Biz also produced 10" figures for the Spider-Man, Fantastic Four, Iron Man, Ghost Rider and X-Force series.

10" X-Men Figures

Cyclops (#49755, 1993) 17.50
Wolverine (#49765, 1993) 17.50

Rogue, Deluxe X-Men (Toy Biz 1995)

Sabretooth (#49775, 1993) 20.00
Gambit (#49711, 1994) 8.00
Mr. Sinister (#49712, 1994) 8.00
Bishop (#49713, 1994) 8.00
Beast (#49721, 1994) 15.00
Weapon X (Wolverine) (#49722, 1994) 12.50
Apocalypse (#49723, 1994) 12.50
Beast (#49041, 1995) 10.00
Wolverine (#49042, 1995) 10.00
Magneto (#49043, 1995) 10.00
Wolverine (Battle Ravage) (#48409, 1995) . 10.00
Archangel II (#48410, 1995) 10.00
Wolverine Space (#48121, 1995) 10.00
Rogue (#48122, 1995) 15.00

X-MEN METALLIC MUTANTS

The first Deluxe Edition, 10" tall **Metallic Mutants** figures were metallic-painted versions of the same three large X-Men that first appeared in 1993 — Wolverine, Cyclops and Sabretooth. The paint jobs are nice, and each figure comes with a weapon and a sort of strip cartoon. Three more appeared in 1994, all KayBee store exclusives.

They have not been as popular with collectors as some of the other figures.

10" Metallic Mutant Figures
Wolverine (#49741, 1994) 9.00
Cyclops (#49742, 1994) 9.00
Sabretooth (#49743, 1994) 9.00
Spy Wolverine (#49621, 1994) 10.00
Omega Red (#49622, 1994) 10.00
Magneto (#49623, 1994) 10.00

X-MEN PROJECTORS

The new X-Men projectors are battery powered, 8" figures which contain film disks with action pictures from the X-Men animated series. You point the chest of the figure at the wall and project the pictures. They come with additional disks and originally sold for about $11.00, but were being discounted at the end of 1995 and haven't generated much collector interest yet. Three Spider-Man projectors and a batch of boxed projectors appeared in 1995.

X-MEN PROJECTORS
Toy Biz (1994–95)
8" Figure/Projectors with film disks, on cards
Wolverine (#49104) 9.00

Wolverine, X-Men Projector (Toy Biz 1994)

Cyclops (#49105) 9.00
Sabretooth (#49106) 9.00
Magneto (#49107) 9.00
Apocalypse (#49108) 9.00
Spider-Man (Spider-Man) (#47221, 1995) .. 9.00
Venom (Spider-Man) (#47222, 1995) 9.00
Hobgoblin (Spider-Man) (#47223, 1995) ... 9.00
8" Figure/Projectors, boxed (1995)
Civilian Wolverine (X-Men) (#48131) 10.00
Beast (X-Men) (#48132) 10.00
Iron Man (Iron Man) (#48133) 10.00
Lizard (Spider-Man) (#48134) 10.00
Thing (Fantastic Four) (#48135) 10.00
Mr. Sinister (X-Men) (#48211) 10.00
Cable (X-Men) (#48212) 10.00
Dr. Octopus (Spider-Man) (#48213) 10.00
Super Sense Spider-Man (#48214) 10.00
Bishop (X-Men) (#48215) 10.00

X-MEN CLASSICS

T he classic figures came out in mid 1995. They have their own packaging which features a special trading card which is not related to any other Marvel card series. Storm, in her white

costume, has received the most collector interest but she's not especially scarce.

X-MEN CLASSICS
Toy Biz (1995)
5" Action Figure, with special trading card
Wolverine (#43126) 6.00
Gambit (#43127) 6.00
Cyclops (#43128) 6.00
Storm (#43129) 9.00
Beast (#43130) 7.50
Magneto (#43131) 6.00

X-MEN 2099

T he first of the X-Men 2099 series appeared in quantity at local toy stores and comic shops in late November 1995. This is another one of Marvel's comic groups — like Iron Man, Fantastic Four and Ghost Rider — and it has its own unique packaging.

X-MEN 2099
Toy Biz (1995)
5" Action Figures, No trading card
Skullfire (#43106) 6.00

Storm (X-Men Classic) (Toy Biz 1995)

Bloodhawk (Toy Biz 1995)

Bloodhawk (#43107) 6.00
Meanstreak (#43108) 6.00
Metalhead (#43109) 6.00
Brimstone Love (#43110) 6.00

YOUNGBLOOD

Y oungblood figures are based on the
Image comic by Rob Liefeld. They
came out in the fall of 1995, except for Troll, who is listed on the package back but has not appeared. It's too
early to tell if any will be scarce. Watch
for variations in this line of toys as they
are manufactured by the same company
as Spawn figures. As of December 1995
they are all available in quantity. Chapel
in the Spawn series is actually a Youngblood character. More figures are planned
for 1996.

YOUNGBLOOD
McFarlane Toys (1995)
6" Action Figures
Troll (scarce, not seen) 17.00

Shaft (McFarlane Toys 1995)

Dutch (#13102) 8.00
Die Hard (#13103) 8.00
Shaft (#13104) 8.00
Crypt (#13105) 8.00
Sentinel (#13106) 8.00
Shaft & Mother-One boxed gift set (#92101) 9.00

Zen Intergalactic Ninja (Just Toys 1992)

ZEN INTERGALACTIC NINJA

T he Zen toys are based on a comic
book of the same name. Neither
the comic nor the toys caught on
with collectors. The figures hung around
in toy stores for a couple of years and
then disappeared without a trace. Toy
collector magazines hardly mention them
any more. Too bad, because they were
perfectly nice figures.

ZEN INTERGALACTIC NINJA
Just Toys (1992)
5" Action Figures
Zen (#14001) 7.00
Lord Contaminous (#14002) 7.00
Jeremy Baker, battery powered (#14003) .. 7.00
Garbage Man (#14004) 7.00
Can-It (#14005) 7.00
Lights Out, battery powered (#14012) 7.00

All prices listed are for *Near Mint* condition.

ACTION FIGURE—CHARACTERS

- These action figures are also listed in the Action Figure Series section.
- Marvel and DC characters are listed here, alphabetically for the most part.
- Some characters are listed under groups such as "Teen Titans."
- Alter-ego characters are listed under the superhero; for example, look for Clark Kent under "Superman."

Abbreviations:
MU1 — Marvel Universe One (card)
X1 — X-Men Series 1 (card)
X2 — X-Men Series 2 (card)
UX — Fleer Ultra X-Men (card)

If you can't find a figure here, it's probably not a DC or Marvel superhero or it's not an action figure. Try the previous section, or look under the Dolls or Models and Statues sections.

This section provides a detailed, alphabetical listing of the DC and Marvel characters included in the many series of action figures which have appeared over the last 30 years. These same figures appear in the previous section in this book, grouped by action figure series. Additional action figures, not part of any series, are also covered.

Why did we list DC and Marvel action figures two ways? Primarily because they are collected two different ways. Some collectors are interested in certain superhero characters. They can find all of the action figures of their favorite hero in this section, described in greater detail and listed together for comparison. Collectors who are interested in a series of figures will find a checklist of all the characters in the series, plus important comments about the series, in the previous section. Prices listed are the same in each section (unless we goofed).

BEFORE ACTION FIGURES

Before there were action figure series, there were toy figure series.

The Ideal Toy Company had a strangle-hold on the DC characters during the 1960s. They first produced a three-piece figure set called the Official Batman Figure Set. Also available during the same time were three other figure sets of this type, with four figures to a package and various playsets. See Justice League of America in the previous section.

Mechanical Marvel Super-Heroes: Captain America (Marx 1968)

The first actual Marvel figures were produced in 1967 by Marx Toys. They were made of a soft plastic and were also more of a statue nature than action figure. Thor, Captain America, Spider-Man, The Hulk, Iron Man and Daredevil were the characters picked to make up this set. These very same figures, by the way, were reissued in 1977, but with one difference, they were all hand-painted. The paint job was said by many to be very amateurish. Finding any of these figures today, with the paint job still intact, is something of a rarity, so it would be quite hard to put an actual price on these. Marx, also in 1968, manufactured a set of Mechanical Super-Heroes. These 5½" tall windup figures were made of tin, and there were four made altogether, including three Marvel Super Heroes — Thor, Captain America and Spider-Man.

Besides Mego, the Remco toy company also produced something akin to action figures in the 1970s. Their series of Energized Super Heroes came in two sizes, 9" and 12", in 1978. The figures were all battery operated and of a hard plastic. Captain America was the Marvel addition to the 9" line. Two other Marvel Super-Characters made the ranks of the 12" Energized gang, that being Spider-Man and The Green Goblin.

AHAB
Ahab with "Harpoon Shooting Gun," 5" + X2 or UX card "Uncanny X-Men" (Toy Biz #4925, 1994) 6.00

ALIEN SPIDER SLAYER
Alien Spider Slayer with "Twin Torso Spider Pincers," 5" "Spider-Man" (Toy Biz #47113, 1994) 5.00

ANNIHILUS
Annihilus with "Anti-Matter Wing Thrust," 5" "Marvel Superheroes" (Toy Biz #4840, 1992) 12.00
Annihilus with "Cosmic Control Rod Transforming Mutant," 5" "Fantastic Four" (Toy Biz #45123, 1995) 6.00

APOCALYPSE
Apocalypse with "Extending Body," 5" + MU1 card "Uncanny X-Men" (Toy Biz #4907, 1991) 15.00
Apocalypse with "Extending Body," 5" reissue + X1, X2 or UX card "Uncanny X-Men" (Toy Biz #4948, 1993) 6.00
Apocalypse 2nd Ed. with "Transforming Weapon Arms," 5" + card "Uncanny X-Men" (Toy Biz #4913, 1993) 6.00
Apocalypse Deluxe Figure, 10" "X-Men" (Toy Biz #49723, 1994) 12.50
·Tyler-Apocalypse III with "Removable Mask and Spine Figure," 5" + card "X-Force" (Toy Biz 1995) . . . . Not out yet

AQUAMAN
Aquaman 3" plastic figure "Justice League" (Ideal 1966–67) 90.00
Aquaman 8" "Official World's Greatest Super-Heroes" (Mego 1972) (solid box) . . . 500.00
Window box (1970s) 150.00
Carded (1970s) 300.00

Aquaman (Kenner 1984)

Aquaman 3¾" "Comic Action Hero" (Mego #62101-5, 1975–78) 75.00
Aquaman 3¾" "Pocket Super Hero" (Mego 1979) 50.00
Aquaman 5" + mini comic "DC Super Powers" (Kenner 1984) 35.00
Aquaman with "Fin Kick Action," 5" "DC Comics Super Heroes" (Toy Biz #4415, 1990) 25.00
Aquaman vs. The Great White Shark with 8" Aquaman figure, battery powered (Mego #51365, 1978) 500.00
Aqualad: See Teen Titans, below.
Mera: See Dolls section.

ARCHANGEL
Archangel with "Missile Shooting Wings," 5" (white wings) + MU1 Card, "Uncanny X-Men" (Toy Biz #4902, 1991) 15.00
Archangel with "Missile Shooting Wings," 5" reissue + X1 card "Uncanny X-Men" (Toy Biz #4947, 1993) with white wings 6.00
Later issue: gray wings, X2 card, (#49495 back, 1993–94) 6.00
Archangel II with "Wing-Flapping Action," 5" + card "X-Men: Invasion Series" (Toy Biz #49396, 1995) 5.00
Archangel II Deluxe Figure, 10" "X-Men" (Toy Biz #48410, 1995) 10.00

Archangel (Toy Biz 1991)

ARGENT SILVER DRAGON
Argent Silver Dragon Deluxe Figure, "Iron Man" (Toy Biz #46133, 1995) 10.00

ATTUMA
Attuma with "Sword Slashing Action," 5" "Fantastic Four" (Toy Biz #45125, 1995) 6.00

AUREUS GOLD DRAGON
Aureus Gold Dragon Deluxe Figure, "Iron Man" (Toy Biz #46132, 1995) 10.00

AVALANCHE
Avalanche with "Exploding Rock Platform," 5" + card "X-Force" (Toy Biz #49532, 1995) 5.00

BANE
Bane with "Body-Slam Arm Action" and "Venom Tube," 5½" "Batman: The Animated Series" (Kenner #64124, 1995) 25.00

BANSHEE
Banshee with "Sonic Scream," 5" + X1 or X2 card "Uncanny X-Men" (Toy Biz #4938, 1992) 6.00

BARON ZEMO
Baron Zemo 4¼" "Secret Wars" (Mattel #0139, 1984) 30.00

BATGIRL
Batgirl 8" "Official World's Greatest Super-Heroes" (Mego 1970s) (window box)

"Super Gals" 300.00
Carded 200.00
BATMAN
Batman Official Figures Set (with Robin and Joker) 3" figures on 9"x7" card (Ideal 1966) 125.00
Batman Figure 4 colors on 3½"x5" plastic pack display card (1966) 20.00
Batman Flying Batman (Ideal 1966) 175.00
Batman 3" plastic figure "Justice League" (Ideal 1966–67) 50.00
Batman 3" Painted Figure (Ideal 1967) 40.00
Batman 8" "Official World's Greatest Super-Heroes" (Mego 1970s)
   Removable mask (solid box) 1,000.00
   Removable mask (window box) 375.00
   Nonremovable mask (window box) .. 150.00
   Nonremovable mask (carded) 80.00
   "Fist Fighting" (window box) 400.00
Batman Bat Chute (Consolidated 1970s) .. 60.00
Batman Sky Diving Parachutist 4" plastic figure on 7"x11" color card (AHI 1973) 50.00
Batman 3¾" "Comic Action Hero" (Mego #62101-2, 1975–78) 75.00
Batman 12½" "Official World's Greatest Super-Heroes" (Mego 1970s) 90.00
Batman 12½" with Magnetic Power (Mego

Batman: Super Powers (Kenner 1984)

1970s) (window box) 125.00
Batman 12½" with fly-away action (Mego
1970s) 140.00
Batman 9" energized action figure
(Remco 1970s) 90.00
Batman Energized 12" plastic figure (Remco
1978) 120.00
Batman 3¾" "Pocket Super Hero" (Mego
1979) 40.00
Batman 5" + mini comic "DC Super Powers"
(Kenner 1984) 50.00
Small card (Kenner 1984) 30.00
Batman action figure, 8" movie version (Kid
Biz 1989) 65.00
Batman with "Bat Rope," 4¾" "Batman" (Toy
Biz #4401, 1989)
Keaton Face 10.00
Round Face 10.00
Square Jaw 12.00
Big Lip 10.00

Recent Batman Figures

Aero Strike Batman with "Ultrasonic Armor
and Flying Rocket," 4¾" "Batman
Returns" (Kenner #63649, 1993) 8.00
Air Attack Batman with "Camouflage Artillery
Gear," 4¾" "Batman Returns" (Kenner
#63610, 1992) 11.00
Air Assault Batman with "Transforming
Techno-Wing Backpack," 4¾" "Crime
Squad" (Kenner #64120, 1995) 6.00
Anti-Freeze Batman with "Firing Shield
Blaster," 4¾" "Batman: The Animated
Series" (Kenner #64018, 1994) 8.00
Arctic Batman with "Polar Armour and Ice
Blaster Weapon," 4¾" "Batman
Returns" (Kenner #63820, 1992) 11.00
Attack Wing Batman (Deluxe) with "Power
Flex Attack Cape," 4¾" "Batman
Forever" (Kenner #64161, 1995) 12.00
Batarang Batman with Spinning Batarang
and Radar System, 4¾" "Batman:
Forever" (Kenner #64166, 1995) 6.00
Batman Deluxe 15" figure "Batman Returns"
(Kenner #63990, 1992) 30.00
Batman with Blast Shield 4¾" "Dark Knight
Crime Master" boxed (Kenner #63460,
1991) 30.00
Batman with Claw Climber 4¾" "Dark Knight
Crime Master" boxed (Kenner #63540,
1991) 30.00
Batman with Night Glider 4¾" "Dark Knight
Crime Master" boxed (Kenner #63470,

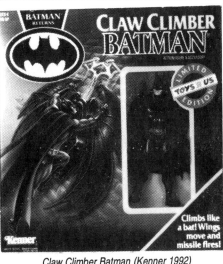

Claw Climber Batman (Kenner 1992)

1991) 40.00
Blast Cape Batman with "Assault Blades and
Launching Attack Cape," 4¾" "Batman
Forever" (Kenner #64149, 1995) 6.00
Bola Strike Batman "Batman Returns" (Toys
"R" Us Limited Edition) boxed (Kenner
#63102, 1992) 20.00
Claw Climber Batman "Batman Returns"
(Toys "R" Us Limited Edition) boxed
(Kenner #63104, 1992) 20.00
Combat Belt Batman with "Firing Grappling
Hook and Missile," 4¾" "Batman: The
Animated Series" (Kenner #64670,
1993) 10.00
Crime Attack Batman "Uses His Batarang
And Claw To Stop Dangerous
Criminals," 4¾" "Dark Knight" (Kenner
#63110, 1990) 18.00
Crime Attack Batman with "Firing Claw and
Batarang," 4¾" "Batman Returns"
(Kenner 1992) 20.00
Crusader Batman with "Powerful Punching
Action," 4¾" + card "Legends of
Batman" (Kenner #64026, 1994) 8.00
Special Warner Bros. Studio stores
edition (Kenner 1995) 10.00
Cyborg Batman with "Light-up Eye and
"Laser" Weapon," 4¾" + card "Legends
of Batman" (Kenner #64028, 1994) . . 8.00
Special Warner Bros. Studio stores
edition (Kenner #64781, 1995) 10.00
Cyber Gear Batman with "Hi-Tech Armor

All prices listed are for *Near Mint* condition.

and Power-Launch Weapon," 4¾"
"Batman: The Animated Series"
(Kenner #64119, 1995) 7.00

Dark Warrior Batman with "Slamming Mace
Attack," 4¾" + card "Legends of
Batman" (Kenner #64038, 1995) 6.00

Decoy Batman with "Crime-Fighting Decoy
Disguise," 4¾" "Mask of the Phantasm"
(Kenner #64017, 1994) 8.00

Deep Dive Batman (Kenner 1992)

Deep Dive Batman with "Torpedo Launching
Scuba Gear," 4¾" "Batman Returns"
(Kenner #63790, 1992) 10.00

Desert Knight Batman with "Whirling Metallic
Swords," deluxe figure + card "Legends
of Batman" (Kenner #64058, 1995) . . 12.00

Electronic Talking Batman, soft "Batman
Forever" (Kenner #29427, 1995) 20.00

Firebolt Batman Electronic Action Figure in
window box "Batman Returns" (Kenner
#63930, 1992) 40.00

Fireguard Batman with "Spinning Attack
Cape Action," 4¾" "Batman Forever"
(Kenner #64150, 1995) 6.00

Flightpak Batman with "Battle Metallic
Armor," deluxe figure + card "Legends
of Batman" (Kenner #64131, 1995) . . 12.00

Future Batman with "Pop-Up Aero Power
Wings," 4¾" + card "Legends of
Batman" (Kenner #64037, 1994) 8.00
Special Warner Bros. Studio stores
edition (Kenner 1995) 10.00

Ground Assault Batman "Deluxe Crime
Fighter Edition," 4¾" "Batman: The
Animated Series" (Kenner #63657,
1994) 10.00

High Wire Batman "Deluxe Crime Fighter
Edition," 4¾" "Batman: The Animated
Series" (Kenner #63998, 1994) 10.00

Hydro Charge Batman with "Water Blast
Missile," 4¾" "Batman Returns II"
(Kenner #64046, 1994) 7.00

Ice Blade Batman with Quick-Deploy Ski
Sled and Blade Runner, 4¾" "Batman
Forever" (Kenner #64164, 1995) 6.00

Infrared Batman with "Launching Bat-Signal
Disks," 4¾" "Batman: The Animated
Series" (Kenner #63997, 1994) 8.00

Iron Winch Batman with "BATARANG Winch
Reels Criminals In," 4¾" "Dark Knight"
(Kenner #63160, 1990) 18.00

Jungle Tracker Batman with "Shoulder
Mount Launcher," 4¾" "Batman
Returns II" (Kenner #64047, 1994) . . . 7.00

Knightquest Batman with "Battle Wings &
Blazing Missile," 4¾" + card "Legends
of Batman" (Kenner #64041, 1994) . . 8.00
Special Warner Bros. Studio stores
edition (Kenner #64785, 1995) 10.00

Knightsend Batman with "Aerial Torpedo
Launcher," 4¾" + card "Legends of
Batman" (Kenner #64127, 1995) 6.00

Knight Star Batman with "Star Blade Rocket
Launcher," 4¾" "Batman: The Animated
Series" (Kenner #64003, 1994) 8.00

Land Strike Batman with "Transforming
Techno-Claw Backpack," 4¾" "Crime
Squad" (Kenner #64121, 1995) 6.00

Laser Batman with "Missile Firing Radar
Dish," 4¾" "Batman Returns" (Kenner
#63810, 1992) 10.00

Lightning Strike Batman with "Transforming
Cape Glider," 4¾" "Batman: The
Animated Series" (Kenner #64002,
1994) 8.00

Long Bow Batman with "Arrow Slinging

Assault," 4¾" + card "Legends of
Batman" (Kenner #64043, 1995) 6.00
Manta Ray Batman with "Firing Sea Sled
and Pop-Out Breathing Gear," 4¾"
"Batman Forever" (Kenner #64153,
1995) 6.00

Flightpak Batman, deluxe (Kenner 1995)

Mech-Wing Batman "Deluxe Crime Fighter
Edition," 4¾" "Batman: The Animated
Series" (Kenner #63653, 1994) 10.00
Night Climber Batman with "Quick Climbing
Hook," 4¾" "Batman Returns II"
(Kenner #64048, 1994) 7.00
Night Hunter Batman with "Claw Glider Wing
and Night Vision Goggles," 4¾"
"Batman Forever" (Kenner #64154,
1995) 6.00
Piranha Blade Batman with "Transforming
Techno-Shield Backpack," 4¾" "Crime
Squad" (Kenner #64116, 1995) 6.00
Polar Blast Batman "Batman Returns" (Toys
"R" Us Limited Edition) boxed (Kenner
#63103, 1992) 20.00
Power Beacon Batman with Light Force Suit

and Flash Fire Weapon, 4¾" "Batman
Forever" (Kenner #64165?, 1995) ... 6.00
Power Guardian Batman with "Real Sword
Fighting Action," 4¾" + card "Legends
of Batman" (Kenner #64027, 1994) .. 8.00
Special Warner Bros. Studio stores
edition (Kenner 1995) 10.00
Power Vision Batman "Deluxe Crime Fighter
Edition," 4¾" "Batman: The Animated
Series" (Kenner #63656, 1994) 10.00
Powerwing Batman with "Fires missiles!
"Flying" wing lands upside down," 4¾"
"Dark Knight" (Kenner #63380, 1991) . 30.00
Powerwing Batman with "Flying Wing Can
Hang Upside Down," 4¾" "Batman
Returns" (Kenner #63880, 1992) 12.00
Radar Scope Batman with "Firing Turbo
Missiles and Sky-Scan Radar Gear,"
4¾" "Batman: The Animated Series"
(Kenner #64136, 1995) 7.00
Rapid Attack Batman with "Escape Hook and
Utility Belt," 4¾" "Mask of the
Phantasm" (Kenner #63965, 1994) .. 7.00
Reissue "Batman: The Animated
Series" (Kenner #63984, 1995) 6.00
Retro Batman with "Spinning Battle Spear,"
4¾" "Mask of the Phantasm" (Kenner
#63977, 1994) 7.00
Rocket Blast Batman Electronic Action
Figure in window box "Batman Returns"
(Kenner #63940, 1992) 40.00
Samurai Batman with "Slashing Sword &
Spiked Club," 4¾" + card "Legends of
Batman" (Kenner #64126, 1995) 6.00
Sea Claw Batman with "Transforming
Techno-Drive Backpack," 4¾" "Crime
Squad" (Kenner #64117, 1995) ... 6.00
Shadow-Wing Batman with "Cape Spreading
Pop-Up Arms and Handcuffs," 4¾"
"Dark Knight" (Kenner #63170, 1990) . 15.00
Shadow-Wing Batman with "Pop-Up Arms
and Capture Cuffs," 4¾" "Batman
Returns" (Kenner 1992) 20.00
Silver Knight Batman with "Battle Metallic
Armor," deluxe figure + card "Legends
of Batman" (#64132, 1995) 12.00
Sky Winch Batman with "Batarang Winch,"
4¾" "Batman Returns" (Kenner 1992) 25.00
Skydive Batman with "Working Mylar
Parachute," 4¾" "Batman: The
Animated Series" (Kenner 1993) 8.00
Sonar Sensor Batman with "Flying Disc

Blaster and Pop-Up Sonar Scope," 4¾"
"Batman Forever" (Kenner #64151,
1995) 6.00
Stealth Wing Batman with "Transforming
Techno-Flight Backpack," 4¾" "Crime
Squad" (Kenner #64118, 1995) 6.00
Tec-Shield Batman "Uses His Flight Pack
And Shield Suit To Escape From
Danger," 4¾" "Dark Knight" (Kenner
#63120, 1990) gold pull 15.00
   Black pull variation 25.00
Thunderwhip Batman with "Spinning Arm
Makes Weapons Whirl," 4¾" "Dark
Knight" (Kenner #63390, 1991) 30.00
Thunderwhip Batman with "Turbo Weapon
Spinning Arm," 4¾" "Batman Returns"
(Kenner #63890, 1992) 10.00
Tornado Batman with "Whirling Weapon,"
4¾" "Mask of the Phantasm" (Kenner
#63978, 1994) 7.00
   Reissue "Batman: The Animated
   Series" (Kenner #63982, 1995) 6.00
Torpedo Batman with "Transforming Techno-
Torpedo Backpack," 4¾" "Crime
Squad" (Kenner #64122, 1995) 6.00
Total Armor Batman with "Full Body Armor
and Shield," 4¾" "Mask of the
Phantasm" (Kenner #64001, 1994) . . 7.00
Turbojet Batman with "Firing Wrist Rocket &
Pivoting Engines," 4¾" "Batman: The
Animated Series" (Kenner #64660,
1993) 10.00
Ultimate Batman with "Light-Up Electric Eyes
and Bat Emblem" plus "Double-Barrel
Assault Weapon," 15" vinyl "Batman:
The Animated Series" (Kenner #64019,
1994) 25.00
Ultimate Batman 15" electronic figure
"Batman Forever" (Kenner #64177,
1995) 22.50
Viking Batman with "Swinging Battle Axe
Action," 4¾" + card "Legends of
Batman" (Kenner #64128, 1995 . . . . . 6.00
Wall Scaler Batman "Uses His Climbing
Action Pack To Scale Up and Down
Walls," 4¾" "Dark Knight" (Kenner
#63130, 1990) 15.00

BATMAN ALTEREGO: Bruce Wayne

Bruce Wayne 8" "Official World's Greatest
Super-Heroes" (Mego 1970s) (Mont.
Ward's exclusive) 450.00
Bruce Wayne with "Quick Change Suit

Changes Bruce Wayne Into BATMAN,"
4¾" "Dark Knight" (Kenner #63180,
1990) 15.00
Bruce Wayne with "Quick Change Batman
Armor," 4¾" "Batman Returns" (Kenner
#63970, 1992) 15.00
Bruce Wayne with "Snap-on Batman Armor,"
4¾" "Batman: The Animated Series"
(Kenner #64664, 1993) 10.00
Transforming Bruce Wayne with "Quick-
Change Bat Suit and Battle Blades,"
4¾" "Batman Forever" (Kenner #64152,
1995) 6.00

Bruce Wayne (Kenner 1993)

BATMAN and ROBIN

Ninja Power Pack Batman and Robin
"Batman: The Animated Series"
(Kenner #64110, 1994) 15.00
Guardians of Gotham City two-pack "Batman
Forever" (Kenner #64171, 1995) 12.00

BEAST

Beast with "Mutant Flipping Power," 5" + UX
card "X-Men" (Toy Biz #49355, 1994) . 10.00

Beast Deluxe Figure, 10" "X-Men" (Toy Biz #49721, 1994) 15.00
Beast with "Mutant Flipping Power," 5" + special card "X-Men Classic" (Toy Biz #43130, 1995) 7.50
Beast Deluxe Figure, 10" "X-Men" (Toy Biz #49041, 1995) 10.00

BISHOP
Bishop with "Quick-Draw Weapon Release," 5" "Uncanny X-Men" (Toy Biz #4911, 1993) 10.00
Bishop Deluxe Figure, 10" "X-Men" (Toy Biz #49713, 1994) 8.00

BLACK BOLT
Black Bolt with "Flight Ready Wings," 5" "Fantastic Four" (Toy Biz #45102, 1994) 7.00

BLACKLASH
Blacklash with Nunchak with "Whip Cracking Action," 5" "Iron Man" (Toy Biz #46016, 1995) 7.00

BLACKOUT
Blackout with "Vampire Attack Action," 5" + mini-comic "Ghost Rider" (Toy Biz #52306, 1995) 6.00

BLACK TOM
Black Tom with "Power Bio-Blast," 5" + UX card "X-Force" (Toy Biz #49521, 1994) 5.00
Black Tom with "Power Bio-Blast," 5" + UX card, new larger package "X-Force" (Toy Biz #49529, 1995) 5.00

BLASTAAR
Blastaar with "Power Blast Action," 5" "Fantastic Four" (Toy Biz #45117, 1995) 6.00

BLAZE
Blaze with "Mystical Flame Firing Action," 5" + mini-comic "Ghost Rider" (Toy Biz #52302, 1995) 6.00
Blaze Deluxe Figure, 10" "Ghost Rider" (Toy Biz #52402, 1995) 10.00

BLIZZARD
Blizzard with "Ice Fist punch," 5" "Iron Man" (Toy Biz #46116, 1995) 6.00

BLOB, THE
The Blob with "Rubber Blubber Belly," 5" + card "X-Force" (Toy Biz #49536, 1995) 6.00

BLOODHAWK
Bloodhawk with "Wing Flapping Action," 5" "X-Men 2099" (Toy Biz #43107, 1995) 6.00

BONEBREAKER
Bonebreaker with "Mutant Attack Tank," 5" +

UX card "X-Men" (Toy Biz #49368, 1994) 6.00

Brainiac (Kenner 1984)

BRAINIAC
Brainiac 5" + mini comic "DC Super Powers" (Kenner 1984) 30.00

BRAINSTORM
Brainstorm 3" plastic figure "Justice League" (Ideal 1966–67) 50.00

BRIMSTONE LOVE
Brimstone Love with "Back Slash Action," 5" "X-Men 2099" (Toy Biz #43110, 1995) 6.00

BROOD
Brood with "Wing Operated Snarl and Tail Whipping Action," 5" "Uncanny X-Men" (Toy Biz #4926, 1994) 8.00

CABLE
Cable with "Clobber Action," 5" + X1 card "X-Force" (Toy Biz #4951, 1992) 9.00
Cable 2nd Edition with "Deep Space Armor," 5" + card "X-Force" (Toy Biz #4963, 1993) 6.00
Cable 3rd Edition with "Rapid Rocket Firing Action," 5" + card, "X-Force" (Toy Biz #4964, 1993) 6.00
Cable 4th Edition with "Air Assault Action," 5" + card "X-Force" (Toy Biz #49513, 1994) 5.00
Cable 5th Edition with "Deep Sea Gear," 5"

Cable, 2nd Edition (Toy Biz 1993)

"X-Force" + UX card (Toy Biz #49525,
   1994) 5.00
Cable Deluxe Figure 10" "X-Force" (Toy Biz
   #49550, 1994) 11.00
Cable Cyborg with "Hidden Techno Bionics,"
   5" + UX card "X-Force" (Toy Biz
   #49535, 1995) 6.00
Urban Assault Cable Shoulder Cannon
   Blaster," 5" + card "X-Force" (Toy Biz
   #49530, 1995) 5.00

CALIBAN

Caliban with "Mutant Roaring Attack," 5" +
   card "X-Force" (Toy Biz #49538, 1995) 6.00

CAMERON HODGE

Cameron Hodge Phalanx with "Water
   Blasting Bio Weapon," 5" + card "X-
   Men: Mutant Genesis" (Toy Biz
   #49386, 1995) 5.00

CANNONBALL

Cannonball with "Catapult Launching Action," 5"
   + UX card "X-Force" (Toy Biz #4966, 1993)
   Pink outfit 25.00
   Purple outfit 8.00

CAPTAIN AMERICA

Captain America 6" plastic figure (Marx
   1966) 20.00

Captain America Mechanical Walking Figure
   (Marx 1967) 100.00
Captain America 8" "Official World's Greatest
   Super-Heroes" (Mego 1970s) (window
   box) 175.00
   Carded 125.00
Captain America 3¾" "Comic Action Hero"
   (Mego #62102-4, 1975–78) 90.00
Captain America 12" "Official World's
   Greatest Super-Heroes" (Mego 1976) . 90.00
Captain America with "Fly Away Action,"
   12½" (Mego 1979) 125.00
Captain America 3¾" "Pocket Super Hero"
   (Mego 1979) 90.00

Captain America (Mattel 1984)

Captain America 4¼" "Secret Wars" (Mattel
   #7205, 1984) 20.00
Captain America/Dr. Doom Set 40.00
Captain America flying figure (Transogram) 70.00
Captain America 9" energized action figure
   (Remco) 60.00
Captain America with "Shield Launcher," 5"
   "Marvel Superheroes" (Toy Biz #4801,
   1990) 15.00
   Reissue (Toy Biz #48001, 1993) 6.00

CAPTAIN MARVEL: See Shazam

CARNAGE

Carnage with "Weapon Arms," 5" "Maximum
Carnage" (Toy Biz #44100, 1994) . . . 10.00

Carnage with "Weapon Arms," 5" "Spider-
Man" (Toy Biz #47105, 1994) 5.00

Carnage Deluxe Figure, 10" "Maximum
Carnage" (Toy Biz 44200, 1994) 20.00

Carnage Deluxe Figure, 10" "Spider-Man"
(Toy Biz #47721, 1995) 10.00

CATWOMAN

Catwoman 8" "Official World's Greatest
Super-Heroes" (Mego 1970s) (window
box) "Super Gals" 300.00
Carded 200.00

Catwoman with "Whipping Arm Action and
Taser Gun," 4¾" "Batman Returns"
(Kenner #63870, 1992) 20.00

Catwoman with tail and cat-o'-nine-tails
(Distributor's prototype sample) 25.00

Catwoman with "Whipping Arm Action and

Catwoman (Kenner 1993)

Claw Hook," 4¾" "Batman: The
Animated Series" (Kenner #63652,
1993) 20.00

Catwoman with "Quick-Climb Claw and
Capture Net," 4¾" + card "Legends of
Batman" (Kenner #64033, 1994) 15.00

CENTURY

Century with "Cape and Battle Staff," 5" "Iron
Man" (Toy Biz #46124, 1995) 6.00

CHAMBER

Chamber with "Sparking Energy Portal," 5"
"Generation X" (Toy Biz #43117, 1995) 6.00

CHAMELEON

The Chameleon with "Transforming Identity,"
5" + pin "Spider-Man" (Toy Biz #47134,
1995) 5.00

CH'OD

Ch'od with "Double Arm Hurling Action," 5" +
UX card "X-Men" (Toy Biz #49365,
1994) 6.00

CLAYFACE

Clayface with "Launching Spiked Ball," 5"
"Batman: The Animated Series"
(Kenner #64005, 1994) 15.00

COLOSSUS

Colossus with "Power Lift Action," 5"
"Uncanny X-Men" + MU1 Card (Toy Biz
#4903, 1991) 15.00

Colossus with "Power Lift Action," 5" reissue
+ X1, X2 or UX card "Uncanny X-Men"
(Toy Biz #4903, 1993) 6.00
Later issue: X2 card (#49494 back) . . 6.00

COMMCAST

Commcast with "Mutant Hunting Hovercraft,"
5" + card "X-Force" (Toy Biz #49526,
1994) 5.00

COMMANDO

Commando with "Techno Sludge Liquid
Blaster," 5" + card "X-Force" (Toy Biz
#49533, 1995) 5.00

CONDUIT

Conduit with "Spinning Kryptonite Attack
Cables," ¾" + card "Man of Steel"
(Kenner #62906, 1995) 7.00

CONSTRICTOR

Constrictor 4¼" "Secret Wars" (Mattel #9631,
1984) 55.00

CORSAIR

Corsair "Swashbuckling Space Pirate," 5" +
card "X-Men Phoenix Saga" (Toy Biz
#49380, 1995) original package 6.00
New larger package 5.00

CYBORG
Cyborg 5" "DC Super Powers" (Kenner
1986) 175.00

CYCLOPS
Cyclops with "Laser Light Eyes," 5" + MU1
Card "Uncanny X-Men" (Toy Biz #4906,
1991) 15.00
Cyclops 5" "Marvel Electronic Talking
Superheroes" (Toy Biz #4896, 1991) . 12.00
Cyclops with "Laser Light Eyes," 5" reissue +
X1, X2 or UX card "Uncanny X-Men"
(Toy Biz (front) #4944, 1993):
Blue-and-white outfit (#49446 back) . . 6.00
Yellow-and-blue outfit (#49491 back) . 6.00
Cyclops Deluxe Figure 10" "X-Men" (Toy Biz
#49755, 1993) 17.50
Cyclops (3rd Edition) with "Light-Up Optic
Blast," 5" + X2 or UX card "Uncanny X-
Men" (Toy Biz #4917, 1994) 6.00
Cyclops Deluxe Figure "Metallic Mutant," 10"
"X-Men" (Toy Biz #49742, 1994) 9.00
Cyclops with "Light-Up Optic Blast," 5" +
special card "X-Men Classic" (Toy Biz
#43128, 1995) 6.00

CYCLOTRON
Cyclotron 5" "DC Super Powers" (Kenner
1986) 40.00

DAREDEVIL
Daredevil 6" plastic figure (Marx 1966) 20.00
Daredevil 4¼" "Secret Wars" (Mattel #914,
1984) 32.00
Daredevil with "Extending Billy Club," 5"
"Marvel Superheroes" (Toy Biz #4808,
1990) 50.00
Daredevil with "Exploding Grapple Hook," 5"
"Marvel Superheroes" (Toy Biz #48102,
1993) 7.00

DARKSEID
Darkseid 5¾" "DC Super Powers" (Kenner
#99960, 1985) 20.00

DEADPOOL
Deadpool with "Spring Out Dagger," 5" + X1
card "X-Force" (Toy Biz #4957, 1992) 25.00
Deadpool with "Mutagenic Hidden
Nightmare," 5" + card "X-Force" (Toy
Biz #49540, 1995) 6.00

DEATHLOK
Deathlok with "Hidden Cyber Strength," 5"
"Marvel Superheroes" (Toy Biz #4834,
1992) 12.00

DESAAD
Desaad 5" "DC Super Powers" (Kenner
1985) 18.00

Cyclops (Toy Biz 1991)

Darkseid (Kenner 1985)

DOCTOR DOOM

Doctor Doom 4¼" "Secret Wars" (Mattel
#7210, 1984) 15.00
Dr. Doom with "Power Driven Weapons," 5"
"Marvel Superheroes" (Toy Biz #4803,
1990) 15.00
Dr. Doom with "Power Driven Weapons," 5"
reissue "Marvel Superheroes" (Toy Biz
#48003, 1993) 6.00
Dr. Doom "Shooting Arm Action," 5"
"Fantastic Four" (Toy Biz #45106,
1995) 7.00
Dr. Doom Deluxe Figure 10" "Fantastic Four"
(Toy Biz 45503, 1995) 10.00

DOCTOR FATE

Dr. Fate 5" "DC Super Powers" (Kenner
1985) 35.00

Doctor Octopus (Mattel 1984)

DR. OCTOPUS

Doctor Octopus 4¼" "Secret Wars" (Mattel
#7213, 1984) 18.00
Dr. Octopus with "Suction Cup and Grasping
Tentacles," 5" "Marvel Superheroes"
(Toy Biz #4804, 1990) 15.00
Doctor Octopus with "Suction Cup and
Grasping Tentacles," 5" reissue "Marvel
Superheroes" (Toy Biz #48004, 1993)   6.00

Dr. Octopus Deluxe Figure 10" "Spider-
Man" (Toy Biz #47712, 1994) 10.00
Dr. Octopus with "Tentacle Whipping Action,"
5" "Spider-Man" (Toy Biz #47106,
1994) 5.00

DOMINO

Domino with "Twin Weapon Arsenal," 5" +
card "X-Force" (Toy Biz #49537, 1995)   9.00

DRAGON MAN

Dragon Man with ""Fire" Breathing Action,"
5" "Fantastic Four" (Toy Biz #45116,
1995) 6.00

DREADKNIGHT

Dreadknight with "Firing Lance Action," 5"
"Iron Man" (Toy Biz #46125, 1995) . . . 6.00

ELECTRO

Electro 4¼" "Secret Wars" (Mattel #9569,
1984) 65.00

EMPLATE

Emplate with "Arm Extending Action," 5"
"Generation X" (Toy Biz #43121, 1995) 6.00

ERIC THE RED

Eric The Red with "Super Metallic Armor," 5"
+ card "X-Men: Invasion Series" (Toy
Biz #49398, 1995) 5.00

EXODUS

Exodus with "Plasma Burst," 5" + card "X-
Force" (Toy Biz #49534, 1995) 5.00

FALCON

Falcon 8" "Official World's Greatest Super-
Heroes" (Mego 1970s) (window box) 120.00
Carded 200.00
Falcon 4¼" "Secret Wars" (Mattel #9141,
1984) 40.00

FIN FANG FOOM

Fin Fang Foom Deluxe Figure, "Iron Man"
(Toy Biz #46131, 1995) 10.00

FIRELORD

Firelord with "Cosmic Flame Launcher," 5"
"Fantastic Four" (Toy Biz #45114,
1995) 6.00

FIRESTORM

Firestorm 5" "DC Super Powers" (Kenner
1985) large card 30.00
Small card 20.00

FLASH

Flash 3" plastic figure "Justice League"
(Ideal 1967) 80.00
Flash 5" + mini comic "DC Super Powers"
(Kenner 1984) 13.00
The Flash with "Running Arm Movement," 5"
"DC Comics Super Heroes" (Toy Biz

#4414, 1990–91) Regular logo (1990)   7.00
Smaller logo (1991) 8.00
The Flash with "Turbo Platform," 5" "DC Comics
Super Heroes" (Toy Biz #4441, 1991)   15.00
Kid Flash: *See Teen Titans, below*

FOREARM
Forearm with "Four Arm Punching Action," 5"
+ X1 card "X-Force" (Toy Biz #4958,
1992) 18.00

FORGE
Forge with "Quick Draw Action," 5" + X1
card "Uncanny X-Men" (Toy Biz #4935,
1992) and yellow holster 8.00
Variation with brown holster and
see-through leg panel 20.00

GAMBIT
Gambit with "Power Kick Action," 5" + X1 card
"Uncanny X-Men" (Toy Biz #4937, 1992) 7.00
Later issue: X2 or UX card
(#49492 back, 1993–94) 6.00
Gambit Deluxe Figure 10" "X-Men" (Toy Biz
#49711, 1994) 8.00
Gambit with "Power Kick Action," 5" +
special card "X-Men Classic" (Toy Biz
#43127, 1995) 6.00

GENERAL ZOD
General Zod 12" (Mego 1978) 40.00
General Zod 3¾" "Pocket Super Hero"
(Mego 1979) 15.00

GENESIS
Genesis with "Spine Sidekick Feature," 5" +
card "X-Force" (Toy Biz #49543, 1995) 6.00

GHOST RIDER
Ghost Rider Deluxe Figure, 10" "Ghost
Rider" (Toy Biz #52401, 1995) 10.00
Ghost Rider with "Chain Whipping Action," 5"
+ mini-comic "Ghost Rider" (Toy Biz
#52301, 1995) 6.00
Ghost Rider II with "Transforming Action," 5"
+ mini-comic "Ghost Rider" (Toy Biz
#52307, 1995) 6.00

GIDEON
Gideon with "Sword Slashing Thrust," 5" + X1
card "X-Force" (Toy Biz #4959, 1992)   9.00
Later issue: X2 card (1993) 8.00

GLADIATOR
Gladiator with Super Strength Power Punch
5" + card "X-Men Phoenix Saga" (Toy
Biz #49381, 1995) original package . .   6.00
New larger package + new weapons .   5.00

GOLDEN PHAROAH
Golden Pharoah 5" "DC Super Powers"

(Kenner 1986) 75.00

GORGON
Gorgon with "Hoof Stompin' Action," 5"
"Fantastic Four" (Toy Biz #45113,
1995) 6.00

GREEN ARROW
Green Arrow 8" "Official World's Greatest
Super-Heroes" (Mego 1970s)
Window box 175.00
Carded 325.00
Green Arrow 5" "DC Super Powers" (Kenner
1985) 35.00
Green Arrowcar "featuring Green Arrow's
Flying Missiles" (Mego 1970s) 250.00

GREEN GOBLIN
Green Goblin 8" "Official World's Greatest
Super-Heroes" (Mego 1970s)
Window box 250.00
Carded 375.00
Green Goblin 12" energized action figure
(Remco) 90.00
Green Goblin 3¾" "Comic Action Hero"
(Mego #62102-3, 1975–78) 90.00
Green Goblin 3¾" "Pocket Super Hero"
(Mego 1979) 90.00
Green Goblin "Throws Pumpkin Bombs," 5"
with lever on back "Marvel
Superheroes" (Toy Biz #4815, 1991) . 35.00

Green Lantern (Kenner 1984)

Green Goblin "Throws Pumpkin Bombs," 5"
without lever (Toy Biz #4815, 1992) . . 15.00
*Note: The first Toy Biz figure was changed
because of safety regulations on stored
energy.*
Green Goblin with "Goblin Glider Attack," 5"
"Spider-Man" (Toy Biz #47125, 1995) . 5.00

GREEN LANTERN
Green Lantern, 5" + mini comic "Fan Club
Offer" (Kenner #99640, 1984) 50.00
Small card 25.00
Green Lantern with "Water Jet Ring," 4¾"
"DC Comics Super Heroes" (Toy Biz
#4413, 1990) 25.00

GREY GARGOYLE
Grey Gargoyle with "Stone Hurling Action,"
5" "Iron Man" (Toy Biz #46107, 1995)   7.00

GRIZZLEY
Grizzly with "Crushing Power Hammers," 5"
+ X2 card "X-Force" (Toy Biz #4967,
1993) 6.00

G.W. BRIDGE
G.W. Bridge with "Rapid-Fire Gun," 5" + X1
card "X-Force" (Toy Biz #4955, 1992)   7.50
Later issue: X2 card (1993) 7.00

HAVOK
Havok with "Projectile Throwing Action," 5" +
card "X-Men: Invasion Series" (Toy Biz

Hawkman (Kenner 1984)

#49394, 1995) 5.00

HAWKEYE
Hawkeye with "Bow and Arrow Arsenal," 5"
"Iron Man" (Toy Biz #46114, 1995) . . . 6.00

HAWKMAN
Hawkman 5" + mini comic "DC Super
Powers" (Kenner 1984) 50.00
Hawkman with "Flapping Wing Action," 5"
"DC Comics Super Heroes" (Toy Biz
#4421, 1990) 20.00

HOBGOBLIN
Hobgoblin with flying bat 4¼" "Secret Wars"
(Mattel #9138, 1984) 50.00
Hobgoblin with "Hurling Pumpkin Bomb," 5"
"Spider-Man" (Toy Biz #47107, 1994) . 5.00
Hobgoblin Deluxe Figure 10" "Spider-Man"
(Toy Biz #47703, 1994) 10.00

HUMAN TORCH
Human Torch 8" "Official World's Greatest
Super-Heroes" (Mego 1970s)
Window box 120.00
Carded 40.00
The Human Torch with "Fireball Flinging
Action," 5" "Marvel Superheroes" (Toy
Biz #4837, 1992) 15.00
Human Torch with "Glow-in-the-Dark Flames
with Catapult Launcher," 5" "Fantastic
Four" (Toy Biz #45109, 1995) 20.00
Human Torch with "Flame-On Sparking
Action," 5" "Fantastic Four" (Toy Biz
#45111, 1995) 6.00
Human Torch Deluxe Figure 10" "Fantastic
Four" (Toy Biz #45502, 1995) 10.00

ICEMAN
Iceman (European issue) "Marvel Secret
Wars" (Mattel #9561, 1984) 50.00
Iceman "Changes Color in Freezer," 5" +
card "Uncanny X-Men" (Toy Biz #4934,
1992) 35.00
Iceman (#2) "Super Ice Slide," 5" "X-Men"
(Toy Biz #49375, 1994) clear slide . . . 12.00
blue slide 12.00
Iceman II with "Extending Ice Limbs," 5" +
card "X-Men: Invasion Series" (Toy Biz
#49395, 1995) 5.00

THE INCREDIBLE HULK
Hulk 6" plastic figure (Marx 1966) 20.00
Incredible Hulk 8" "Official World's Greatest
Super-Heroes" (Mego 1970s)
Window box 75.00
Carded 40.00
Hulk 3¾" "Comic Action Hero" (Mego

Supersize Hulk (Toy Biz 1991)

#62102-1, 1975–78) 75.00
Incredible Hulk 12½" "Official World's
  Greatest Super-Heroes" (Mego 1978) . 90.00
Incredible Hulk "Fly-Away Action" (Mego
  1978) 100.00
Hulk 3¾" "Pocket Super Hero" (Mego 1979) 40.00
Hulk Rage Cage with Hulk figure (Toy Biz
  #4872, 1991) 15.00
Incredible Hulk with "Crushing Arm," 5"
  "Marvel Superheroes (Toy Biz #4809,
  1990) 15.00
Incredible Hulk with "Crushing Arm Action,"
  5" (small logo) "Marvel Superheroes"
  (Toy Biz #4809, 1991) 10.00
The Incredible Hulk 15" Supersize Super-
  hero (Toy Biz #4826, 1991) 18.00
Hulk 5" "Marvel Electronic Talking
  Superheroes" (Toy Biz #4893, 1991) . 10.00
Incredible Hulk with "Crushing Arm Action,"
  5" with small "Marvel Superheroes"
  logo reissue (Toy Biz #48007, 1993) . 6.00

INVISIBLE GIRL
Invisible Girl 8" "Official World's Greatest
  Super-Heroes" (Mego 1970s)
  Window box 120.00
  Carded 40.00

INVISIBLE WOMAN
Invisible Woman with "Vanishing Color
  Action," 5" "Marvel Superheroes" (Toy
  Biz #4836, 1992) 150.00
Invisible Woman (#2) with "Catapult Power
  Launcher," 5" "Marvel Superheroes"
  (Toy Biz #48101, 1994) 9.00
Invisible Woman (blue costume) with
  "Invisible Force Shield and Rolling
  Platform," 5" "Fantastic Four" (Toy Biz
  #45108, 1995) 25.00
Invisible Woman (clear) with "Invisible Force
  Shield and rolling Platform," 5"
  "Fantastic Four" (Toy Biz #45112,
  1995) 12.00

Iron Man (Mattel 1984)

IRON MAN
Iron Man 8" "Official World's Greatest Super-
  Heroes" (Mego 1970s) (window box) 150.00
  Carded 200.00
Iron Man Figure 6" (Marx 1976) 20.00
Iron Man 4¼" "Secret Wars" (Mattel #7206,
  1984) 20.00
Iron Man with "Quick Change Armor," 5"
  "Marvel Superheroes" (Toy Biz #4814,
  1991) large or small logo 20.00

Iron Man with "Plasma Cannon Missile
Launcher" 5" "Iron Man" (Toy #46101,
1995) 8.00
Iron Man Hydro-Armor with Deep Sea
Weapons (Toy Biz #46102, 1995) . . . 8.00
Iron Man Space Armor with "Power Lift
Space Pack," 5" "Iron Man" (Toy Biz
#46111, 1995) 6.00
Iron Man Stealth Armor with "Fight Action
Module," 5" "Iron Man" (Toy Biz
#46112, 1995 . . . . 6.00
Iron Man Hologram Armor with "Power
Missile Launcher," 5" "Iron Man" (Toy
Biz #46113, 1995) 6.00
Iron Man Arctic Armor with "Removable
Armor and Launching Claw Action," 5"
"Iron Man" (Toy Biz #46122, 1995) . . . 6.00
Hulk Buster Iron Man with "Power
Removable Armor," 5" "Iron Man" (Toy
Biz #46123, 1995) 6.00
Iron Man Deluxe Figure 10" "Iron Man" (Toy
Biz #46601, 1995) 10.00
Iron Man Space Armor Deluxe Figure 10"
"Iron Man" (Toy Biz #48126, 1995) . . . 11.00
IRON MAN ALTEREGO: Tony Stark
Tony Stark with "Armor Carrying Suitcase,"
5" "Iron Man" (Toy Biz #46121, 1995)   6.00
Tony Stark Techno-Suit Deluxe Figure 10"
"Iron Man" (Toy Biz #48407, 1995) . . . 11.00
ISIS
Isis 8" (Mego 1970s) (window box) 300.00
Carded 225.00
JOHNNY STORM
Johnny Storm Deluxe Figure, 10" "Fantastic
Four" (Toy Biz #48406, 1995) 10.00
JOKER
Joker 3" plastic figure "Justice League"
(Ideal 1966–67) 75.00
Joker Sky Diving Parachutist 4" plastic figure
on 7"x11" color card (AHI 1973) 50.00
Joker 3¾" "Comic Action Hero" (Mego
#62101-8, 1975–78) 75.00
Joker 8" "Official World's Greatest Super-
Heroes" (Mego 1970s) (window box) 190.00
Carded 125.00
"Fist Fighting," (window box) 300.00
Joker 3¾" "Pocket Super Hero" (Mego 1979) 40.00
Joker 5" + mini comic "DC Super Powers"
(Kenner 1984) 30.00
Joker with "Squirting Orchid," 4¾" "Batman"
(Toy Biz #4406, 1990)
Without curl 10.00

With curl 15.00
Sky Escape Joker "Uses Whirling Copter
Pack To Escape From Trouble," 4¾"
"Dark Knight" (Kenner #63140, 1990) . 25.00
Knock-Out Joker with "Bazooka and
"POW"erful Weapon," 4¾" "Dark

Joker (Kenner 1984)

Knight" (Kenner #63450, 1991) 50.00
The Joker with ""Laughing Gas" Spray Gun,"
4¾" "Batman: The Animated Series"
(Kenner 1993) 12.00
Jet Pack Joker with "Capture Nozzle," 4¾"
"Mask of the Phantasm" (Kenner
#64007, 1994) White face 15.00
Green face variation 20.00
The Joker with "Snapping Jaw," 4¾" + card
"Legends of Batman" (Kenner #64034,
1994) 12.00
Joker Companion
Bob, the Goon with "Power Kick," 4½"
"Batman" (Toy Biz #4407, 1990) 12.00
JOR-EL
Jor-El, 12" (Mego 1978) 40.00
Jor-El 3¾" "Pocket Super Hero" (Mego
1979) 15.00
JUBILEE
Jubilee with "Plasma Hurling Action," 5"
"Generation X" (Toy Biz #43120, 1995) 7.50

All prices listed are for *Near Mint* condition.

JUGGERNAUT
Juggernaut with "Power Punch Action," 5" +
MU1 Card "Uncanny X-Men" (Toy Biz
#4909, 1991) red boots 15.00
   Variation with orange boots 12.50
Juggernaut with "Power Punch Action," 5"
reissue + X1, X2 or UX card "Uncanny
X-Men" (Toy Biz #4943, 1993) 6.00

Kalibak (Kenner 1985)

KALIBAK
Kalibak 5" "DC Super Powers" (Kenner
#99950, 1985) 15.00

KANE
Kane with "Snap-Back Living Hand!," 5" + X2
card "X-Force" (Toy Biz #4953, 1992) 9.00
Kane (II) with "Double Fisted Weapons," 5" +
card "X-Force" (Toy Biz #4965, 1993) 6.00
Kane Deluxe Figure 10" "X-Force" (Toy Biz
#49551, 1994) 10.00

KANG
Kang 4¼" "Secret Wars" (Mattel #7212,
1984) 13.00
Dark Star flying wing with Kang figure
"Secret Wars" (Mattel #9692, 1984) . . 30.00

KEYMAN
Keyman 3" plastic figure "Justice League"
(Ideal 1966–67) 50.00

KILLER CROC
Killer Croc with "Power-Punch Arm and Pet
Crocodile," 5½" "Batman: The
Animated Series" (Kenner #64009,

1994) 15.00
KILLSPREE
Killspree with "Slashing Blade Arms," 5" +
card "X-Force" (Toy Biz #49523, 1994) 7.50
KINGPIN
KingPin with "Grab and Smash action," 5"
"Spider-Man" (Toy Biz #47114, 1994) . 5.00

Krule (Toy Biz 1993)

KOLTAR
Koltar 3" plastic figure "Justice League"
(Ideal 1966–67) 50.00
KRAVEN
Kraven with "Spear Throwing Action," 5"
"Spider-Man" (Toy Biz #47115, 1994) . 5.00
Kraven Deluxe Figure 10" "Spider-Man" (Toy
Biz #47722, 1995) 10.00
KRULE
Krule with "Shrunken Heads," 5" + card "X-
Force" (Toy Biz #4968, 1993) 6.00
KYLUN
Kylun with "Twin Striking Swords," 5" + UX
card "X-Men" (Toy Biz #49363, 1994) . 6.00
LEX LUTHOR
Lex Luthor 12½" (Mego 1976) 150.00
Lex Luthor 3¾" "Pocket Super Hero" (Mego
1979) 15.00
Lex Luthor, 5" + mini comic "DC Super
Powers" (Kenner #99670, 1984) 13.00

Lex Luthor, 4½" with "Power Punch," 5" "DC
    Comics Super Heroes" (Toy Biz #4408,
    1989) 8.00

LIZARD
Lizard 8" "Official World's Greatest Super-
    Heroes" (Mego 1970s) (window box) 200.00
    Carded 275.00

Lex Luthor (Kenner 1984)

The Lizard with "Lashing Tail action," 5"
    "Spider-Man" (Toy Biz #47116, 1994) . 5.00
The Lizard Deluxe Figure 10" "Spider-Man"
    (Toy Biz #47713, 1994) 10.00

LONGSHOT
Longshot "with Knife Throwing Action," 5" +
    UX card "Uncanny X-Men" (Toy Biz
    #4923, 1994; back: #49234) 6.00

MAGNETO
Magneto 4¼" "Secret Wars" (Mattel #7211,
    1984) 15.00
Magneto with "Magnetic Hands and Chest,"
    5" + MU1 Card "Uncanny X-Men" (Toy
    Biz #4908, 1991) 15.00
Magneto 5" "Marvel Electronic Talking
    Superheroes" (Toy Biz #4895, 1991) . 10.00
Magneto 15" Supersize Superhero with
    helmet & cape (Toy Biz #4921, 1991) 20.00
Magneto 2nd Edition with "Super Spark
    Action," 5" + X1 or X2 card "Uncanny
    X-Men" (Toy Biz #4941, 1992) 6.00

Later issue: UX card (#49371) 6.00
Magneto with "Magnetic Hands and Chest,"
    5" reissue + X1 card "Uncanny X-Men"
    (Toy Biz #4945, 1993) 6.00
Magneto Deluxe Figure "Metallic Mutant,"
    10" "X-Men" (Toy Biz #49623, 1994) . 10.00
Magneto with "Super Spark Action," 5" +
    special card "X-Men Classic" (Toy Biz
    #43131, 1995) 6.00
Magneto Deluxe Figure 10" "X-Men" (Toy
    Biz #49043, 1995) 10.00

MAN-BAT
Man-Bat with "Flapping Wings and Tow
    Cable," 5" "Batman: The Animated
    Series" (Kenner #64666, 1993) 10.00

MANDARIN
Mandarin with "Light Up Power Rings," 5"
    "Iron Man" (Toy Biz #46105, 1995) . . . 7.00
Mandarin Deluxe Figure 10" "Iron Man" (Toy
    Biz #46602, 1995) 10.00

MANTIS
Mantis 5" "DC Super Powers" (Kenner 1985) 30.00

MARTIAN MANHUNTER
Martian Manhunter 5" "DC Super Powers"
    (Kenner 1985) 30.00
    Small card 18.00

MAVERICK
Maverick with "Quick-Draw Weapon Action,"

Martian Manhunter (Kenner 1985)

All prices listed are for *Near Mint* condition.

5" + UX card "X-Men: Mutant Genesis"
(Toy Biz #49388, 1995) 5.00
MEANSTREAK
Meanstreak with "High Speed Action," 5" "X-
Men 2099" (Toy Biz #43108, 1995) . . 6.00
METALHEAD
Metalhead with "Heavy-Metal Punch," 5" "X-
Men 2099" (Toy Biz #43109, 1995) . . 6.00
MR. FANTASTIC
Mr. Fantastic 8" "Official World's Greatest
Super-Heroes" (Mego 1970s)
Window box 120.00
Carded 60.00
Mr. Fantastic with "5-Way Stretch," 5"
"Marvel Superheroes" (Toy Biz #4831,
1992) 18.00
Mr. Fantastic with "Super Stretch Arms," 5"
"Fantastic Four" (Toy Biz #45107,
1994) 7.00
MR. FREEZE
Mr. Freeze 5" "DC Super Powers" (Kenner
1986) 35.00
Mr. Freeze "Changes Color," 5" "DC Comics
Super Heroes" (Toy Biz #4412, 1989) 10.00

Mr. Freeze (Kenner 1994)

Mr. Freeze with "Firing "Ice" Blaster," ¾"
"Batman: The Animated Series"
(Kenner #64004, 1994) 12.00
MISTER MIRACLE
Mister Miracle 5" "DC Super Powers"
(Kenner 1986) 160.00
MR. MXYZPTLK
Mr. Mxyzptlk 8" "Official World's Greatest
Super-Heroes" (Mego 1970s)
Window box (with smirk) 140.00
Window box (with mouth open) 90.00
Carded (with mouth open) 175.00
MR. SINISTER
Mr. Sinister with "Power Light Eyes," 5" + X1
card "Uncanny X-Men" (Toy Biz #4942,
1992) 8.00
Mr. Sinister with "Power Light Blast," 5" + X2
or UX card "Uncanny X-Men" (Toy Biz
#49372, 1994) with goatee 6.00
Mr. Sinister Deluxe Figure 10" "X-Men" (Toy
Biz #49712, 1994) 8.00
MODOK
Modok with "Energy Brain Blasts," 5" "Iron
Man" (Toy Biz #46115, 1995) 6.00
MOJO
Mojo with "Wild Whipping Tail," 5" + UX card
(Toys "R" Us exclusive) "X-Force" (Toy
Biz #49528, 1994) 4.00
Mojo with "Wild Whipping Tail Action," 5" +
UX card in new, larger package "X-
Force" (Toy Biz #49528, 1995) 5.00
MOLE MAN
Mole Man with "Twirling Combat Staff," 5"
"Fantastic Four" (Toy Biz #45104,
1994) 7.00
MORBIUS
Morbius with "Missile Launching Jet Pack,"
5" + pin "Spider-Man" (Toy Biz #47144,
1995) 5.00
MORPH
Morph with "Mutant Shape Shifter," 5" + UX
card "X-Men" (Toy Biz #49361, 1994) . 6.00
MOUSERMAN
Mouserman 3" plastic figure "Justice
League" (Ideal 1966–67) 50.00
MYSTERIO
Mysterio with "Mist Squirting Action," 5" + pin
"Spider-Man" (Toy Biz #47133, 1995) . 5.00
Mysterio Deluxe Figure 10" "Spider-Man"
(Toy Biz #48124, 1995) 10.00
NAMOR
Namor Power Punch with "Undersea Trident

and Shield," 5" "Fantastic Four" (Toy
Biz #45122, 1995) 6.00
NICK FURY
Nick Fury with "Missile Launching Jet Pack,"
5" + pin "Spider-Man" (Toy Biz #47143,
1995) 5.00
NIGHTCRAWLER
Nightcrawler with "Super Suction," 5" + MU1
Card "Uncanny X-Men" (Toy Biz #4904,
1991) 20.00
Nightcrawler with "Super Suction," 5" reissue
+ X1 card "Uncanny X-Men" (Toy Biz
#4950, 1993) 10.00
Nightcrawler with "Super Suction," 5" reissue
+ UX card "X-Men" (Toy Biz #49369,
1994) 10.00
NIMROD
Nimrod with "Mutant Seeking Missiles," 5" + UX
card "X-Force" (Toy Biz #49539, 1995) 6.00
OMEGA RED
Omega Red with "Whipping Tendril
Weapons," 5" "Uncanny X-Men" (Toy
Biz #4916, 1993) 7.00
Omega Red Deluxe Figure "Metallic Mutant,"
10" "X-Men" (Toy Biz #49622, 1994) . 10.00
ORION
Orion 5" "DC Super Powers" (Kenner 1986) 30.00

Nightcrawler (Toy Biz 1991)

Orion (Kenner 1986)
PARADEMON
Parademon 5" "DC Super Powers" (Kenner
1985) 28.00
PENANCE
Penance with "Claw Slashing Action," 5"
"Generation X" (Toy Biz #43118, 1995) 7.50
PENGUIN
Penguin Sky Diving Parachutist 4" plastic
figure on 7"x11" color card (AHI 1973) 50.00
Penguin 8" "Official World's Greatest Super-
Heroes" (Mego 1970s) (window box) 125.00
Carded 140.00
Penguin 3¾" "Comic Action Hero" (Mego
#62101-7, 1975–78) 75.00
Penguin 3¾" "Pocket Super Hero" (Mego
1979) 40.00
Penguin 4" + mini comic "DC Super Powers"
(Kenner 1984) 38.00
The Penguin "Umbrella Fires Missiles," 4¼"
"DC Comics Super Heroes" (Toy Biz
#4409, 1989)
Small missile 35.00
Large missile 25.00
The Penguin "Missile Firing Umbrella," 4¼"
"DC Comics Super Heroes" (Toy Biz
#4409, 1989–90) 8.00
The Penguin with "Blast-Off Umbrella

Penguin (Toy Biz 1989)

Launcher," 4½" "Batman Returns"
(Kenner #63640, 1992) 25.00
The Penguin with "Hypno-Spin Umbrella and
Launcher," 4½" "Batman: The Animated
Series" (Kenner #64690, 1993) 25.00

Penguin Companions
Penguin Commandos with "Mind Control
Gear and Firing Missile" "Batman
Returns" (Kenner #63860, 1992) 15.00

PHALANX
Phalanx with "Live Captive Heads," 5"
"Generation X" (Toy Biz #43122, 1995) 6.00

PHANTASM
Phantasm with "Chopping Arm Action," 4¾"
"Batman: Mask of the Phantasm"
(Kenner #64006, 1994) 25.00

PHANTOM
The Phantom, 5½" "Defenders of the Earth"
(Galoob 1985) 15.00

PHOENIX
Phoenix with "Fiery Phoenix Power," 5" +
card "X-Men Phoenix Saga" (Toy Biz
#49385, 1995) original package 15.00
New larger package + catapult 8.00

PLASTIC MAN
Plastic Man, 5" "DC Super Powers" (Kenner
1986) 70.00

POISON IVY
Poison Ivy with "Snapping Venus Flytrap and
Dart Weapon," 4¾" "Batman: The
Animated Series" (Kenner 64012,

1994) 25.00
PROFESSOR X
Professor X with Secret Control Panels 5" +
X2 card "Uncanny X-Men" (Toy Biz
#4918, 1994) 6.00
PROWLER
The Prowler with "Extending Claws," 5" + pin
"Spider-Man" (Toy Biz #47135, 1995) . 5.00
PUNISHER
The Punisher with "Cap Firing Weapons," 5"
"Marvel Superheroes" (Toy Biz #4806,
1990) 15.00
Punisher with "Real Machine Gun Sounds,"
5" "Marvel Superheroes" (Toy Biz
#4813, 1991) 15.00
With "New Action" sticker (#4813) . . . 10.00
The Punisher 15" Supersize Superhero
(1991, mail-in, no box) 60.00
Punisher 5" "Marvel Electronic Talking
Superheroes" (Toy Biz #4892, 1991) . 10.00

Punisher (Toy Biz 1991)

Punisher with "Full Weapon Arsenal," 5" in
Trench Coat "Marvel Superheroes"
(Toy Biz #48104, 1994) 7.00
Punisher with "Immobilizing Arsenal," 5" +
pin "Spider-Man" (Toy Biz #47146,
1995) 5.00

Punisher Deluxe Figure 10" "Spider-Man"
(Toy Biz #48411, 1995) 10.00
PYRO
Pyro with "Flame Throwing Action," 5" + card
"X-Force" (Toy Biz #49519, 1994) . . . 5.00
QUARK
Quark with "2-Fisted Quick Draw," 5" + card
"X-Force" (Toy Biz #49516, 1994) . . . 5.00
RANDOM
Random with "Missile Blasting Arm," 5" + UX
card "X-Men" (Toy Biz #49357, 1994) . 6.00
RAZA
Raza with "Swashbuckling Sword Action," 5"
+ UX card "X-Men" (Toy Biz #49364,
1994) 6.00
RED TORNADO
Red Tornado 5" "DC Super Powers" (Kenner
1985) 32.00
Small card 20.00
RHINO
Rhino with "Head Ramming Action," 5"
"Spider-Man" (Toy Biz #47127, 1995) . 25.00
RICTOR
Rictor with "Seismic Shock Wave Action," 5"
+ card "X-Force" (Toy Biz #49514,
1994) 5.00
RIDDLER
Riddler 8" "Official World's Greatest Super-
Heroes" (Mego 1970s) (window box) 300.00
Carded 400.00

Riddler (Mego 1970s)

"Fist Fighting" (window box) 400.00
Riddler, 4½" with "Riddles & Clues" "DC
Comics Super Heroes" (Toy Biz #4411,
1989) 15.00
The Riddler with "Question Mark Launcher,"
4¾" "Batman: The Animated Series"
(Kenner #64700, 1993) 20.00
The Riddler with "Firing Question Mark
Launcher," 4¾" + card "Legends of
Batman" (Kenner #64130, 1995) 15.00
The Riddler with "Trapping Brain-Drain
Helmet," 4¾" "Batman Forever"
(Kenner #64148, 1995) 10.00

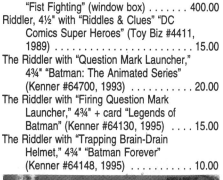

Robin (Kenner 1984)

ROBIN
Robin Figure, 5 colors on 3½"x5" plastic
pack display card (1966) 20.00
Robin 3" plastic figure "Justice League"
(Ideal 1966–67) 75.00
Robin 8" "Official World's Greatest Super-
Heroes" (Mego 1970s)
Removable mask (solid box) 1,250.00
Removable mask (window box) 500.00
Non-removable mask (window box) . 120.00
Non-removable mask (carded) 75.00
"Fist Fighting," window box) 400.00
Robin 3¾" "Comic Action Hero" (Mego
#62101-3, 1975–78) 75.00

Robin 12½" "Official World's Greatest Super-
  Heroes" (Mego 1970s) (window box) 200.00
Robin 12½" with fly-away action (Mego
  1976) 140.00
Robin 12½" with Magnetic Power (Mego
  1970s) (window box) 225.00
Robin 3¾" "Pocket Super Hero" (Mego
  1979) 40.00
Robin 4½" + mini comic "DC Super Powers"
  (Kenner 1984) 30.00
Robin 4½" with "Karate Chop" "DC Comics
  Super Heroes" (Toy Biz #4402, 1989)
  with grappling hook 10.00
  with gun 25.00
Robin with "Launching Grappling Hook," 4½"
  "Batman Returns" (Kenner #63630,
  1992) 20.00
Robin with "Turbo Glider and Drop Missiles,"
  4½" "Batman: The Animated Series"
  (Kenner #64680, 1993) 15.00

Ninja Robin (Kenner 1993)

Ninja Robin with "Chopping Arm Action and
  Ninja Weapons," 4½" "Batman: The
  Animated Series" (Kenner 1993) 10.00
Bola Trap Robin with "Whirling Battle

Blades," 4½" "Batman: The Animated
  Series" (Kenner #64134, 1995) 7.00
Glider Robin with "Winged Jet Pack and
  Firing Claw," 4½" "Batman: The
  Animated Series" (Kenner #64133,
  1995) 7.00
Ski Blast Robin with "Transforming Techno-
  Ski Backpack," 4½" "Batman: Crime
  Squad" (Kenner #64123, 1995) 6.00
Street Biker Robin with "Launching Grappling
  Hooks and Battle Staff," 4½" "Batman
  Forever" (Kenner #64144, 1995) 6.00
Hydroclaw Robin with "Aqua Attack
  Launcher and Diving Gear," 4½"
  "Batman Forever" (Kenner #64145,
  1995) 6.00
Martial Arts Robin with Ninja Kicking Action
  and Battle Weapons," 4½" Deluxe
  Figure "Batman Forever" (Kenner
  #64162, 1995) 10.00
Crusader Robin with "Firing Crossbow and
  Battle Shield," 4½" + card "Legends of
  Batman" (Kenner #64057, 1995) 6.00
Robin, 16" soft "Batman Forever" (Kenner
  #29417, 1995) 15.00

ROBIN ALTEREGO: Dick Grayson

Dick Grayson 8" "Official World's Greatest
  Super-Heroes" (Mego 1970s) (Mont.
  Ward's exclusive) 400.00
Dick Grayson/Robin "Transforms Into Robin
  with High-Tech Gear," 4½" "Batman:
  The Animated Series" (Kenner #64016,
  1994) 8.00
Transforming Dick Grayson with "Crime
  Fighting Suit and Sudden-Reveal
  Mask," 4½" "Batman Forever" (Kenner
  #64146, 1995) 6.00

Nightwing

Nightwing (Robin) with "Super-Strike Rocket
  Launcher," 4½" + card "Legends of
  Batman" (Kenner #64029, 1994) 8.00
  Special Warner Bros. Studio stores
  edition (Kenner 1995) 10.00

ROGUE

Rogue with "Power Uppercut Punch," 5" +
  UX card "X-Men" (Toy Biz #49362,
  1994) 7.00
Rogue Deluxe Figure 10" "X-Men" (Toy Biz
  #48122, 1995) 20.00

SABRETOOTH

Sabretooth with "Self-Healing Wounds," 5" +
  card "Uncanny X-Men" (Toy Biz #4939,

1992) 15.00
Sabretooth Deluxe Figure 10" "X-Men" (Toy
  Biz #49775, 1993) 20.00
Sabretooth (2nd) with "Snarl and Swipe
  Action," 5" + X2 card "X-Men" (Toy Biz
  #4924, 1994; back: #49244) 6.00
Sabretooth Deluxe Figure "Metallic Mutant,"
  10" "X-Men" (Toy Biz #49743, 1994) . 9.00
Captive Sabretooth with "Break-Away
  Action," 5" + card "X-Men: Invasion
  Series" (Toy Biz #49392, 1995) 5.00

SAMURAI
Samurai 5" "DC Super Powers" (Kenner
  1986) 60.00

SAURON
Sauron with "Savage Attack Wings," 5" + X1
  or X2 card "Uncanny X-Men" (Toy Biz
  #4940, 1992) 6.00
Sauron with "Savage Attack Wings," 5" +
  card, reissue with black symbol on
  loincloth (Toy Biz #49374, 1994) 5.00

SCARECROW
Scarecrow with "Thrashing Sickle," 4¾"
  "Batman: The Animated Series"

Scarecrow (Kenner 1993)

(Kenner 1993) 12.00
SCORPION
Scorpion with "Tail Striking Action," 5"
  "Spider-Man" (Toy Biz #47126, 1995) . 5.00
SENYAKA
Senyaka with "Whip Snapping Action," 5" +
  UX card (Toys "R" Us exclusive) "X-
  Men" (Toy Biz #49389, 1994) 5.00
Senyaka with "Whip Cracking Action," 5" +
  UX card "X-Men: Mutant Genesis" (Toy
  Biz #49389, 1995) 5.00
SHATTERSTAR
Shatterstar with "Dual Sword Action," 5" +
  X1 card "X-Force" (Toy Biz #4952,
  1992) 9.00
  Later issue: X2 card (1993) 8.00
Shatterstar 2nd Edition with "Dual Sword
  Slashing Action," 5" + UX card "X-
  Force" (Toy Biz #49518, 1994) 5.00
Shatterstar Deluxe Figure 10" "X-Force" (Toy
  Biz #49552, 1994) 10.00
SHAZAM
Shazam 3¾" "Comic Action Hero" (Mego
  #62101-4, 1975–78) 75.00
Captain Marvel 3¾" "Pocket Super Hero"
  (Mego 1979) 40.00
Shazam 8" "Official World's Greatest Super-
  Heroes" (Mego 1970s) (window box) 200.00
  Carded 200.00
Shazam (Captain Marvel) 5" "DC Super
  Powers" (Kenner 1986) 35.00
SHOCKER
Shocker with "Shooting Power Blasts," 5"
  "Spider-Man" (Toy Biz #47124, 1995) . 5.00
SILVER SAMURAI
Silver Samurai with "Metal Samurai Armor,"
  5" + UX card "X-Men" (Toy Biz #49358,
  1994) 6.00
SILVER SURFER
Silver Surfer with "Action Surfboard," 5"
  "Marvel Superheroes" (Toy Biz #4807,
  1990) silver matte 30.00
The Silver Surfer with "Speed Surfing," 5"
  "Marvel Superheroes" (Toy Biz #4835,
  1992) chrome 12.00
Silver Surfer "Space Surfing," 5" "Fantastic
  Four" (Toy Biz #45103, 1995) 8.00
Silver Surfer Deluxe Figure 10" "Fantastic
  Four" (Toy Biz #45501, 1995) 10.00
SKIN
Skin with "Growing Fingers," 5" "Generation
  X" (Toy Biz #43119, 1995) 6.00

All prices listed are for *Near Mint* condition.

SKINNER
Skinner with "Extending Rib Action," 5" +
mini-comic "Ghost Rider" (Toy Biz
#52305, 1995) 6.00
SKULLFIRE
Skullfire with "Glowing Energy Skeleton," 5"
"X-Men 2099" (Toy Biz #43106, 1995)   6.00
SLAYBACK
Slayback with "Extending Bio-Mechanical
Arms," 5" + UX card "X-Force" (Toy Biz
#49524, 1994) 5.00
SMYTHE
Smythe with "Punching Power," 5" "Spider-
Man" (Toy Biz #47103, 1994) 5.00

Spider-Man (Mattel 1984)

AMAZING SPIDER-MAN
Spider-Man 6" plastic figure (Marx 1966) . . 20.00
Spider-Man 12" energized action figure
(Remco) 90.00
Spider-Man 8" "Official World's Greatest
Super-Heroes" (Mego 1970s)
Window box) 120.00
Carded) 40.00
Peter Parker 8" "Official World's Greatest
Super-Heroes" (Mego 1970s) (Mont.

Ward's exclusive) 450.00
Spider-Man 3¾" "Comic Action Hero" (Mego
#62102-2, 1975–78) 75.00
Amazing Spider-Man 12½" with Spiderweb
(Mego #83001, 1977) (carded) 70.00
Amazing Spider-Man 12½" with Magnetic
Power (Mego 1970s) (window box) . 125.00
Amazing Spider-Man 12½" "Official World's
Greatest Super-Heroes" (Mego 1970s)
Window box) 90.00
Amazing Spider-Man 12½" "Fly-Away Action"
(Mego 1970s) 125.00
Web-Spinning Spider-Man 12½" (Mego) . . 150.00
Spider-Man 3¾" "Pocket Super Hero" (Mego
1979) 40.00
Spider-Man 4¼" "Secret Wars"
Black outfit (Mattel #9153, 1984) 48.00
Red outfit (Mattel #7207) 30.00
Spider-Man (black outfit) Captain America
and Daredevil gift set 4¼" "Secret
Wars" (Mattel #9482, 1984) 85.00
Spider-Man with "Web-Suction Hands," 5"
"Marvel Superheroes" (Toy Biz #4802,
1990) 20.00
Amazing Spider-Man with "Real Web-
Shooting Action," 5" "Marvel Super-
heroes" (Toy Biz #4811, 1991) 20.00
With "New Action" sticker (Toy Biz
#4811, 1991) 20.00
Amazing Spider-Man with "Real Web-
Climbing Action," 5" "Marvel
Superheroes" (Toy Biz #4812, 1991) . 25.00
(Toy Biz #4812, 1991) with "New
Action" sticker 25.00
Spider-Man 15" Supersize Superhero (Toy
Biz #4823, 1991) 20.00
Spider-Man 5" "Marvel Electronic Talking
Superheroes" (Toy Biz #4891, 1991) . 12.00
Spider-Man with "Multi Jointed Action
Poses," 5" "Marvel Superheroes" (Toy
Biz #4833, 1992) 10.00
Reissue (Toy Biz #48105, 1994) 7.00
Amazing Spider-Man with "Enemy Tracking
Tracer," 5" "Marvel Superheroes" (Toy
Biz #4838, 1992) 12.00
Spider-Man, 14" Electronic Talking (Toy Biz
#47361, 1994) 20.00
Spider-Man Deluxe Figure "Wall Hanging,"
10" black chest "Spider-Man" (Toy Biz
#47711, 1994) 10.00
Spider-Man Deluxe Figure "Web Hanging,"
10" (red chest) "Spider-Man" (Toy Biz

Spider-Man (Toy Biz 1992)

#47701, 1994) 10.00
Spider-Man "Web Racer," 5" "Spider-Man"
　(Toy Biz #47101, 1994) 5.00
Spider-Man "Web Shooter," 5" "Spider-Man"
　(Toy Biz #47102, 1994) 5.00
Spider-Man with "Web Parachute," 5"
　"Spider-Man" (Toy Biz #47111, 1994) . 5.00
Spider-Man with "Super Posable Action"
　(Multi-Jointed) 5" "Spider-Man" (Toy Biz
　#47121, 1995) 5.00
Spider-Man Spider Armor with "Super Web
　Shield," 5" "Spider-Man" (Toy Biz
　#47122, 1995) 5.00
Spider-Man Black Costume with "Web-
　Climbing Action," 5" + pin "Spider-Man"
　(Toy Biz #47131, 1995) 5.00
Spider-Man Web Glider with "Air Assault
　Action," 5" + pin "Spider-Man" (Toy Biz
　#47132, 1995) 5.00
Spider-Man Night Shadow with "Web
　Swinging Gear," 5" + pin "Spider-Man"
　(Toy Biz #47137, 1995) 5.00
Super Posable Spider-Man Deluxe Figure,
　10" "Spider-Man" (Toy Biz #48408,
　1995) 10.00
Six Arm Spider-Man with "Six Arm Arachnid
　Battle Attack," 5" + pin (Toy Biz
　#47141, 1995) 5.00
Battle Ravaged Spider-Man with "Secret

Storage Backpack," 5" + pin "Spider-
　Man" (Toy Biz #47142, 1995) 5.00
Super-Sense Spider-Man with "Wall Crawling
　Action," 5" + pin "Spider-Man" (Toy Biz
　47147, 1995) 5.00
Spider-Man Spider Armor Deluxe Figure 10"
　"Spider-Man" (Toy Biz 48123, 1995) . . 10.00
Spider-Man Web Trap 5" KayBee exclusive
　(Toy Biz #47046, 1995) 6.00
Spider-Man Web Lair 5" KayBee exclusive
　(Toy Biz #47047, 1995) 6.00
SPIDER-MAN ALTEREGO: Peter Parker
Peter Parker with "Camera Accessory," 5"
　"Spider-Man" (Toy Biz #47112, 1994) . 5.00
SPIDER-WOMAN
Spider-Woman with "Psionic Web Hurling
　Action," 5" "Iron Man" (Toy Biz #46104,
　1995) 10.00
SPIRAL
Spiral with "Arm-Spinning Action," 5" + card
　"X-Men: Invasion Series" (Toy Biz
　#49397, 1995) 7.50
STEEL
Steel (a.k.a. John Henry Irons) with
　"Pounding Hammer Blows," 4¾" + card
　"Man of Steel" (Kenner #62904, 1995) 7.00
STEPPENWOLF
Steppenwolf 5" "DC Super Powers" mail-in
　(Kenner 1984) 10.00
Steppenwolf 5" "DC Super Powers" (Kenner
　1985) 80.00
STORM
Storm with "Power Glow," 5" + MU1 Card
　"Uncanny X-Men" (Toy Biz #4905,
　1991) 25.00
Storm (#2) "Power Glow," 5" + UX card "X-
　Men" (Toy Biz #49370, 1994) 9.00
Storm with "Power Glow Action," 5" + special
　card "X-Men Classic" (Toy Biz #43129,
　1995), white costume 9.00
STRONG GUY
Strong Guy with "Power Punch," 5" + X2
　card "Uncanny X-Men" (Toy Biz #4912,
　1993) 6.00
STRYFE
Stryfe with "Flip-Up Helmet Reveals Identity,"
　5" + card "X-Force" (Toy Biz #4956,
　1992) 12.50
SUNFIRE
Sunfire with "Removable Solar Armor," 5" +
　card "X-Men: Mutant Genesis" (Toy Biz
　#49399, 1995) 5.00

All prices listed are for *Near Mint* condition.　　　**101**

Strong Guy (Toy Biz 1993)

SUNSPOT
Sunspot with "Explosive Power Punch," 5" + card "X-Force" (Toy Biz #49515, 1994) 5.00

SUPERBOY
Superboy with "Mammoth Claw and Taser Missiles," 4¾" + card "Man of Steel" (Kenner #62903, 1995) 7.00

SUPERGIRL
Supergirl 8" "Official World's Greatest Super-Heroes" (Mego 1970s) (window box) "Super Gals" 375.00
Carded 420.00

SUPERMAN
Superman 3" plastic figure "Justice League" (Ideal 1966–67) 75.00
Superman flying figure (Transogram) 60.00
Superman 12" energized action figure (Remco) 65.00
Superman 9" energized action figure (Remco) 50.00
Superman 8" "Official World's Greatest Super-Heroes" (Mego 1970s)
Solid box (1972) 250.00
Window box 140.00
Carded 100.00
Superman 3¾" "Comic Action Hero" (Mego #62101-1, 1975–78) 75.00

Superman 12½" "World's Greatest Super-Heroes" (Mego 1978) (window box) . 100.00
Superman 12½" with fly-away action (Mego 1970s) 150.00
Superman 3¾" "Pocket Super Hero" (Mego 1979) 40.00
Superman 5" + mini comic "DC Super Powers" (Kenner 1984) 25.00
Small display card 15.00
Superman 3¾" super hero (Mego) 50.00
Superman with "Kryptonite Ring," 5" "DC Comics Super Heroes" (Toy Biz #4403, 1989) 35.00
Laser Superman with "Super-charged "Laser" Cannon," 4¾" + card "Man of Steel" (Kenner #62902, 1995) 7.00
Power Flight Superman with "Take-off Force Arm Action," 4¾" + card "Man of Steel" (Kenner #62901, 1995) 7.00

SUPERMAN ALTEREGO: Clark Kent
Clark Kent 8" "Official World's Greatest Super-Heroes" (Montgomery Ward's exclusive) (Mego 1970s) 450.00
Clark Kent 5" "DC Super Powers" (mail-in offer or free with Superman figure from Sears) (Kenner 1986) 60.00

SUPER SKRULL
Super Skrull with "Super Extending Power Punch Action," 5" "Fantastic Four" (Toy Biz #45126, 1995) 6.00

TARZAN
Tarzan 8" "Official World's Greatest Super-Heroes" (Mego 1972) (window box) . . 75.00
Carded 150.00

TEEN TITANS
(Mego 1976–80s)
Aqualad 8" (#51316/1) (carded) 300.00
Kid Flash 8" (#51316/2) (carded) 400.00
Speedy 8" (#51316/4) (carded) 420.00
Wonder Girl 8" (#51316/3) (carded) 400.00
See (Official) World's Greatest Super-Heroes

TERRAX
Terrax with "Space Soaring Meteor," 5" "Fantastic Four" (Toy Biz #45105, 1994) 7.00

THANOS
Thanos with "Pulverizing Gauntlet Action," 5" "Fantastic Four" (Toy Biz #45115, 1995) 6.00

THING
Thing 8" "Official World's Greatest Super-Heroes" (Mego 1970s) (window box) 120.00

Carded 40.00
Thing with "Pulverizing Punch!," 5" "Marvel
Superheroes" (Toy Biz #4832, 1992) . 15.00
The Thing "Clobberin' Time Punch," 5"
"Fantastic Four" (Toy Biz #45101,
1995) 7.00
The Thing II with "Undercover Disguise," 5"
"Fantastic Four" (Toy Biz #45121,
1995) 6.00
The Thing Deluxe Figure 10" "Fantastic
Four" (Toy Biz #48125, 1995) 10.00

Thor (Toy Biz 1991)

THOR
Thor Mechanical Walking Figure
(Marx 1966) 100.00
Thor Figure 6" (Marx 1966) 15.00
Thor 8" "Official World's Greatest Super-
Heroes" (Mego 1970s) (window box) 375.00
Carded 425.00
Thor with "Smashing Hammer Action," 5"
with lever "Marvel Superheroes" (Toy
Biz #4817, 1991) 35.00
with short hammer 30.00
Thor with "Smashing Hammer Action," 5" no
lever "Marvel Superheroes" (Toy Biz
#4817, 1991) 20.00

THUNDERBOLT
Thunderbolt 3" plastic figure "Justice
League" (Ideal 1966–67) 50.00
TITANIUM MAN
Titanium Man with "Retractable Blade
Action," 5" "Iron Man" (Toy Biz #46127,
1995) 6.00
TREVOR FITZROY
Trevor Fitzroy with "Futuristic Crystal Battle
Armor," 5" + UX card "X-Men" (Toy Biz
#49360, 1994) 6.00
TRITON
Triton with "Smimming Action with Attack
Shark and Sea Trumpet," 5" "Fantastic
Four" (Toy Biz #45127, 1995) 6.00
TUSK
Tusk, "Surprise Attack Mutant," 5" "Uncanny
X-Men" (Toy Biz #4914, 1993) 6.00
TWO-FACE
Two-Face with "Coin Flipping Action," 4¾"
"DC Comics Super Heroes" (Toy Biz
#4427, 1989) 15.00
Two-Face with "Firing Roulette Wheel Gun,"
4¾" "Batman: The Animated Series"
(Kenner #64710, 1993) 18.00
Two Face with "Turbo-Change Cannon and
Good/Evil Coin," 4¾" "Batman Forever"
(Kenner #64147, 1995) 10.00
TYR
Tyr 5" "DC Super Powers" (Kenner 1986) . 45.00
U.S. AGENT
U.S. Agent with "Shield Launcher," 5"
"Marvel Superheroes" (Toy Biz #48103,
1994) 7.00
VENGEANCE
Vengeance with "Rib Clawing Action," 5" +
mini-comic "Ghost Rider" (Toy Biz
#52303, 1995) 6.00
Vengeance Deluxe Figure, 10" "Ghost Rider"
(Toy Biz #52403, 1995) 10.00
VENOM
Venom with "Living Skin Slime Pores," 5"
"Marvel Superheroes" (Toy Biz #4816,
1991) 20.00
Venom 15" Supersize Superhero (Toy Biz
#4825, 1991) 35.00
Venom 5" "Marvel Electronic Talking
Superheroes" (Toy Biz #4897, 1991) . 20.00
Venom with "Flicking Tongue," 5" "Marvel
Superheroes" (Toy Biz #4839, 1992) . 20.00
Venom "Squirts "Alien Liquid"," 5" "Marvel
Superheroes" (Toy Biz #48005, 1993) 8.00

Supersize Venom (Toy Biz 1991)

Venom Deluxe Figure 10" "Spider-Man" (Toy
  Biz #47702, 1994) 10.00
Venom, 14" Electronic Talking "Spider-Man"
  (Toy Biz #47362, 1994) 20.00
Venom with "Jaw Chomping Action," 5"
  "Spider-Man" (Toy Biz #47104, 1994) . 5.00
Venom II with "Removable Symbiotic Mask,"
  5" + pin "Spider-Man" (Toy Biz #47136,
  1995) . . . .

VULTURE
Vulture with "Spreading Wing Action," 5"
  "Spider-Man" (Toy Biz #47117, 1994) . 5.00
Vulture Deluxe Figure, 10" "Spider-Man"
  (Toy Biz #47723, 1995) 10.00

WAR MACHINE
War Machine with "Shoulder Mount
  Cannons," 5" "Iron Man" (Toy Biz
  #46103, 1995) 9.00
War Machine Deluxe Figure 10" "Iron Man"
  (Toy Biz #46603, 1995) 10.00

WARPATH
Warpath with "Thunder Punch Action," 5" +
  X1 card "X-Force" (Toy Biz #4954,
  1992) 10.00
Warpath 2nd Edition, with "Smashing Power
  Punch," 5" + UX card "X-Force" (Toy
  Biz #49527, 1994) 5.00

WARSTAR
Warstar Surprise Attack Team 5" + card "X-
  Men Phoenix Saga" (Toy Biz #49384,
  1995) original package 7.50
  New larger package 6.00

WHIRLWIND
Whirlwind with "Whirling Battle Action," 5"
  "Iron Man" (Toy Biz #46117, 1995) . . . 6.00

WOLVERINE
Wolverine 4¼" "Secret Wars" (Mattel #7208,
  1984) silver claws 60.00
  Black claws 90.00
Wolverine with "Snap-Out Claws," 5" + MU1
  card "Uncanny X-Men" (Toy Biz #4901,
  1991) 15.00
Wolverine with "Snap-Out Claws," 5" reissue
  + X1, X2 or UX card "Uncanny X-Men
  (Toy Biz #4946, 1993) 6.00
Wolverine 5" "Marvel Electronic Talking
  Superheroes" (Toy Biz #4894, 1991) . 15.00
Wolverine 15" Supersize Superhero with
  mask and sword (Toy Biz #4922, 1991) 20.00
Wolverine 2nd Edition with "Spring-Out
  Slashing Claws," 5" + card "Uncanny
  X-Men" (Toy Biz #4931, 1992) 10.00
Wolverine 3rd Edition with "Savage Strike
  Twist Action," 5" + card "Uncanny X-

Space Wolverine (Toy Biz 1995)

Men" (Toy Biz #4932, 1992) 18.00
Wolverine 4th Edition "Weapon X" with
   "High-Tech Training Helmet," 5" + X2
   card "Uncanny X-Men" (Toy Biz #4933,
   1992; back #49332), green cords 10.00
   Reissue (back #49600, 1993), red cords 7.50
   Reissue (#49373, 1994), silver cords . 20.00
Wolverine 5th Edition with "Thrusting Knife
   Action," 5" + card "Uncanny X-Men"
   (Toy Biz #4910, 1993) 10.00
   Kay-Bee special, dull green 7.50
Wolverine Deluxe Figure 10" "X-Men" (Toy
   Biz #49765, 1993) 17.50
Robot Wolverine VI (Albert) with "Robotic
   Arm Weapons," 5" + UX card "X-Men"
   (Toy Biz #49356, 1994) 6.00
Weapon X (Wolverine) Deluxe Figure 10" "X-
   Men" (Toy Biz #49722, 1994) 12.50
Wolverine–Street Clothes 7th Edition "Street
   Tough," 5" + UX card "X-Men" (Toy Biz
   #49366, 1994) 6.00
Wolverine Deluxe Figure "Metallic Mutant,"
   10" "X-Men" (Toy Biz #49741, 1994) . 9.00
Spy Wolverine Deluxe Figure "Metallic
   Mutant," 10" "X-Men" (Toy Biz #49621,
   1994) 10.00
Space Wolverine 8th Edition with "Slashing
   Space Armor," 5" + card "X-Men
   Phoenix Saga" (Toy Biz #49383, 1995)
   original package 7.50
   New larger package + new weapons . 5.00
Wolverine Fang with Shi'ar Weapon with
   "Super Slashing Claw Action," 5" +
   card "X-Men: Mutant Genesis" (Toy Biz
   #49390, 1995) 5.00
Wolverine with "Spring-out Slashing Claws,"
   5" + special card "X-Men Classic" (Toy
   Biz #43126, 1995) 6.00
Battle Raveged Wolverine with "Berserker
   Rage Action," 5" + card "X-Men:
   Invasion Series" (Toy Biz #49393,
   1995) 5.00
Wolverine Deluxe Figure, 10" "X-Men" (Toy
   Biz #49042, 1995) 10.00
Wolverine Space Deluxe Figure, 10" "X-Men"
   (Toy Biz #48121, 1995) 10.00
Wolverine (Battle Ravaged) Deluxe Figure,
   10" "X-Men" (Toy Biz #48409, 1995) . 10.00
WONDER WOMAN
Wonder Woman 3" plastic figure "Justice
   League" (Ideal 1966–67) 75.00
Wonder Woman 8" "Official World's Greatest

Wonder Woman (Kenner 1984)

Super-Heroes" (Mego 1970s)
   Window box "Super Gals" 275.00
   Carded 400.00
Wonder Woman 3¾" "Comic Action Hero"
   (Mego #62101-6, 1975–78) 75.00
Wonder Woman 12" with Diana Prince outfit,
   Lynda Carter photo box (Mego 1976) 100.00
Wonder Woman 12" with evening gown
   (2nd-issue box without Lynda Carter
   picture; Mego 1977) 40.00
Wonder Woman 3¾" "Pocket Super Hero"
   (Mego 1979) 40.00
Wonder Woman 4½" + mini comic "DC
   Super Powers" "Fan Club offer"
   (Kenner #99720, 1984) 20.00
   Small card version 10.00
   No comic, no offer (1985?) 10.00
Wonder Woman with "Power-Arm," 5" "DC
   Comics Super Heroes" (Toy Biz #4404,
   1989) 8.00
X-CUTIONER
X-Cutioner with "Battle Staff Spinning
   Action," 5" + card "X-Men: Mutant
   Genesis" (Toy Biz #49387, 1995) 5.00
X-TREME
X-Treme with "Axe Attack," 5" + UX card "X-
   Force" (Toy Biz #49520, 1994) 5.00

All prices listed are for *Near Mint* condition.

BENDABLE FIGURES

Mego also manufactured a set of bendy figures, roughly 4" tall, between 1972 and 1974. The set was largely made up of characters from DC Comics, though two of the 16 produced were from Marvel — Spider-Man and Captain America. Mego bendy figures are quite valuable, as are the other early figures from Deline and Lakeside.

Punisher Bend-Em (Just Toys 1991)

Most recent bendy figures are manufactured by Just Toys. They were called "Twistables" originally and are now called "Bend-Ems." They are available and fairly cheap, for now. Most come on display cards, but several of the X-Men were also originally sold loose.

AQUAMAN
Aquaman Superhero Bendable 5"
  (Mego 1970s) 75.00

ARCHIE
Archie (Jesco #1300, 1989) 4.00
Betty (Jesco #1320, 1989) 4.00
Jughead (Jesco #1310, 1989) 4.00
Reggie (Jesco #1340, 1989) 4.00

Veronica (Jesco #1330, 1989) 4.00

BADROCK
Badrock Youngblood Bend-em with comic
  book (Just Toys #12637, 1995) 5.00

BATGIRL
Batgirl Superhero Bendable 5"
  (Mego 1970s) 125.00

BATMAN
Batman bendie (Deline 1960s) 125.00
Batman Superhero Bendable 5"
  (Mego 1970s) 90.00
Batman Bendy Figure, 7" (Bully 1989) . . . 40.00

CAPTAIN AMERICA
Captain America Superhero Bendable
  (Mego 1970s) 90.00
Captain America bendie (Lakeside) 140.00
Captain America Marvel Super Heroes
  Twistable (Just Toys #12062, 1990) . . 7.50
  Bend-em (Just Toys #12062, 1991) . . 6.00

CATWOMAN
Catwoman 5" Superhero Bendables
  (Mego 1970s) 175.00

CHAPEL
Chapel Youngblood Bend-em with comic
  book (Just Toys #12639, 1995) 5.00

COLOSSUS
Colossus bendable, loose (Just Toys) 4.00
Colossus Uncanny X-Men Bend-em
  (Just Toys #12111, 1991) 6.00

CYCLOPS
Cyclops bendable, loose (Just Toys) 4.00
Cyclops Uncanny X-Men Bend-em
  (Just Toys #12110, 1991) 6.00

DAREDEVIL
Daredevil bendie (Just Toys) 6.00
Daredevil Marvel Super Heroes Bend-em
  (Just Toys #12061, 1991) 6.00

DICK TRACY
Dick Tracy Bendie (Lakeside) 80.00

DIEHARD
Diehard Youngblood Bend-em with comic
  book (Just Toys #12642, 1995) 5.00

GREEN HORNET
Green Hornet Bendie (Lakeside 1966) . . . 120.00

INCREDIBLE HULK
Hulk bendie (Just Toys) 6.00
Hulk Marvel Super Heroes
  Twistable (Just Toys #12058, 1990) . . 7.50
  Bend-em (Just Toys #12058, 1991) . . 6.00

JOKER
Joker 5" Superhero Bendables
  (Mego 1970s) 150.00

Juggernaut Bend-Em (Just Toys 1991)

JUGGERNAUT
Juggernaut bendable, loose (Just Toys) . . . 4.00
Juggernaut Uncanny X-Men Bend-em
    (Just Toys #12114, 1991) 6.00
MAGNETO
Magneto bendable, loose (Just Toys) 4.00
Magneto Uncanny X-Men Bend-em
    (Just Toys #12113, 1991) 7.00
MR. MXYZPTLK
Mr. Mxyzptlk Superhero Bendable
    (Mego 1972–74) 125.00
NIGHTCRAWLER
Nightcrawler bendable, loose (Just Toys) . . 4.00
Nightcrawler Uncanny X-Men Bend-em
    (Just Toys #12112, 1991) 7.00
OLIVE OYL
Olive Long Bendable Figure (Bronco 1978) 5.00
Olive Oyl Bendable Figure ("Popeye—Sixty Years"
    logo appears on package, Jesco 1988)
    Large 5.00
    Small 2.50
PENGUIN
Penguin Superhero Bendables
    (Mego 1970s) 150.00
PHANTOM
Phantom Bendie (Lakeside) 60.00
POPEYE

Popeye Long Bendable Figure (Bronco 1978) 8.00
Popeye Bendable Figure (with "Popeye—Sixty
    Years" logo on package, Jesco 1988)   4.00
Popeye BendiFace (Lakeside 1968) 15.00
PUNISHER
Punisher Marvel Super Heroes
    Twistable (Just Toys #12059, 1990) . . 7.50
    Bend-em (Just Toys #12059, 1991) . . 6.00
RIDDLER
Riddler Superhero Bendables 5"
    (Mego 1970s) 150.00
RIPTIDE
Riptide Youngblood Bend-em with comic
    book (Just Toys #12640, 1995) 5.00
ROBIN
Robin Superhero Bendable (Mego 1972–74) 75.00
Robin bendy figure (Diener) 75.00
SHAFT
Shaft Youngblood Bend-em with comic
    book (Just Toys #12641, 1995) 5.00
SHAZAM
Shazam Superhero Bendable
    5" (Mego 1972–74) 125.00
SILVER SURFER
Silver Surfer Marvel-Super Hero Twistable
    (Just Toys #12060, 1991) 6.00
AMAZING SPIDER-MAN
Spider-Man Superhero Bendable
    (Mego 1970s) 90.00
Spider-Man Marvel Super Heroes
    Twistable (Just Toys #12056, 1990) . . 7.50

Silver Surfer Twistable (Just Toys 1991)

All prices listed are for *Near Mint* condition.   **107**

Bend-ems (Just Toys #12056, 1991) . 6.00
SUPERGIRL
Supergirl Superhero Bendable
   (Mego 1972–74) 175.00
SUPERMAN
Superman Superhero Bendable 5"
   (Mego 1972–74) 75.00
TARZAN
Tarzan Superhero Bendable (Mego 1970s) 75.00
VOGUE
Vogue Bend-em 4¾" with comic book "Young-
blood" (Just Toys #12638, 1995) 5.00

Wolverine Twistable (Just Toys 1990)
WOLVERINE
Wolverine bendable, loose (Just Toys) 4.00
Wolverine Marvel Super-Hero
   Twistable (Just Toys #12057, 1990) . . 7.50
   Bend-Em (Just Toys #12057, 1991) . . 6.00
WONDER WOMAN
Wonder Woman Superhero Bendable
   (Mego 1970s) 100.00
UNCANNY X-MEN
X-Men gift set (Cyclops, Wolverine and
   Colossus) (Just Toys 1992) 15.00
ZEN INTERGALACTIC NINJA
Zen bendable figure with photon stick
   (Just Toys 1991–92) 6.00
Zen bendable prototype figure 30.00

DOLLS

This short section covers **Dolls**, which are distinguished from action figures in that they are not articulated, or are only slightly articulated, **Figures** and **Puppets**. **Models** and **Statues** are covered elsewhere. We live in an imperfect world and the distinctions between these categories are somewhat blurred, but they are real distinctions in the minds of collectors.

Ideal must have figured that Captain Action had to be pretty lonely being an action figure of 1,001 poses but just having only a youthful boy partner and villainous aliens around. They produced a female companion line in 1967 called the Super Queens Posing Dolls. These figures were all based on popular DC Comics character superheroines. Available were Aquaman's wife **Mera**, **Batgirl**, **Supergirl** and **Wonder Woman**. Collectors still go "gaga" over these superbabes, especially if they can be found in "mint in the box" (MIB) condition.

There were a good amount of superfemales from the Marvel line available at this time, such as Sif, Hela, The Wasp, The Invisible Girl and The Scarlet Witch. Unfortunately Ideal didn't produce any of them. Of course, the same can be said of many other manufacturers as well, I suppose.

BATGIRL
Batgirl 11½" "Super Queens Posin'
   Doll" (Ideal 1967) 2,200.00
Batgirl Action Figure (Extra Powers
   Custom-Made Figures 1991) 90.00
BATMAN
Batman Doll 24" cloth with vinyl face
   (Commonwealth 1966) 120.00
Batman plush doll 17" (1960s) 50.00
Batman Push-Up Puppet 3"
   plastic (Kohner 1966) 65.00
Batman face puppet head (Newfeld 1966) 75.00
Batman Handpuppet 10" vinyl
   (Ideal 1966) 80.00
Batman 12" Hand Puppet (Ideal) 60.00

Batman Marionette (Hazelle 1966)

Batman Marionette 15" cloth and plastic
  (Hazelle 1966) 250.00
Batman Stuffed Doll, 28" (Ace Novelty) . . 25.00
Batman 14" vinyl figure (Presents 1989) . . 25.00
Batman cloth figure, 8" (Applause 1989) . . 10.00
Batman 8" doll (Biken 1989) 35.00
Batman 14" vinyl figure (Presents, 1989) . 25.00
Batman Action Figure Doll, 12"
  (Takara 1989) 140.00
Batman Super Amigos Action Figure
  (Pacipa 1990) 25.00
Batman 5" Posable figure (Popi 1990) . . . 40.00
Batman Figure on stand, 15½" with vinyl
  and fabric 25.00
Batman 10" Vinyl Figure with fabric cape
  (Applause #45673, 1992) 15.00
Batman clear resin figure (Mexico 1990) . 16.00
Batman Plaster Figure Set,
  (Cowan de Groot 1989) 40.00
Batman Returns Fully posable 12" Action
  Figure w/Leatherette Outfit (Takara) . 15.00
Batman Returns 4" doll (Takara) 10.00
Batman Plush Doll 39" (A8145) 34.95
Batman Small Plush Doll 28" (A6145) . . . 19.95
Batman Very Small Plush Doll

13½" (A3145) 5.95

CAPTAIN AMERICA

Captain America 13" Vinyl
  figure (Hamilton #P7475) 27.50
Captain America Doll (#945027, 1991) . . . 34.95

CATWOMAN

The 10¾" Catwoman figure produced by Applause comes in a plastic bag with a wrist tag and rotates at the waist and shoulder only. As with most figures from this company, look for her at comic shops and specialty toy/collectible stores rather than at the large toy stores. It originally cost about $10.00. This slim figure is the biggest and best Catwoman on the market at the moment. However, we hope that other female figures are produced with the proportions of a human being rather than the overly skinny shape of a "Barbie" doll. It's not much of a problem with Catwoman because she was quite slim in the Batman Returns movie.

Catwoman Action Figure (Extra Powers
  Custom Made Figures 1991) 90.00
Catwoman 10" Vinyl Figure with fabric cape
  (Applause #45673, 1992) 15.00

DICK TRACY

Sparkle Plenty Doll (Ideal 1947) 125.00
Little Honeymoon Doll 150.00
Dick Tracy 15" "Special Collector's
  Edition" (Playmates #5797, 1990) . . 30.00
Breathless Mahoney 14" "Special Collector's
  Edition" (Playmates #5798, 1990) . . 35.00
Dick Tracy, 14" figure doll (Applause
  1990) 35.00
Breathless Mahoney, 14" figure
  doll (Applause 1990) 30.00
Breathless Mahoney 8" figure doll
  (Applause 1990) 12.00
Big Boy 8" figure doll (Applause 1990) . . . 10.00
Dick Tracy 8" figure doll (Applause 1990) . 10.00
Flattop 8" figure doll (Applause 1990) 12.00
Itchy 8" figure doll (Applause 1990) 10.00
Pruneface 8" figure doll (Applause 1990) . 12.00

DIRTY PAIR

Dirty Pair, Kei and Yuri 8" dolls, set 80.00

HULK

Incredible Hulk 16½" Vinyl
  figure (Hamilton #945064, 1991) . . . 45.00

All prices listed are for *Near Mint* condition.

Mary Jane Watson doll (Toy Biz 1995)

Breathless Mahoney (Playmates 1990)

JOKER

Joker 14" vinyl figure (Presents 1989)	25.00
Joker clear resin figure (Mexico 1990)	20.00
Joker musical ceramic figure	
(Price Imports)	60.00
Joker Plush Doll 40" (A8147)	34.95
Joker Small Plush Doll 29" (A6147)	19.95

LITTLE ORPHAN ANNIE

Little Orphan Annie Doll (ABC Toys 1940)	25.00
Little Orphan Annie Doll 7"	
(Well Toy Co. 1973)	30.00
Little Orphan Annie and Sandy Dolls 9¾"	
(Famous Artists Syndicate 1930)	90.00

MARY JANE (Spider-Man's wife)

Mary Jane Watson Special Collectors Edition	
12" figure with costumes (Toy Biz	
#48428, 1995)	35.00

MERA (Aquaman's wife)

Mera 11½" "Super Queens Posin'

Doll" (Ideal 1967) 1,500.00

PEANUTS

Charlie Brown (Hungerford Dolls 1958)	75.00
Linus (Hungerford Dolls 1958)	75.00
Lucy (Hungerford Dolls 1958)	75.00
Pigpen (Hungerford Dolls 1958)	90.00
Baby Sally (Hungerford Dolls 1958)	90.00
Schroeder with white rubber piano	
(Hungerford Dolls 1958)	200.00
Snoopy	75.00

PENGUIN

Penguin 8½" Vinyl Figure with fabric cape	
(Applause #45675, 1992)	15.00
Penguin clear resin figure (Mexico 1990)	18.00

POPEYE

Brutus Doll (medium size, Presents 1985)	18.00
Large size	30.00
Olive Oyl Doll (Uneeda 1980)	10.00
Olive Oyl Vinyl Doll (Dakin 1960s)	30.00
Olive Oyl Plastic Doll (Dakin late 1960s)	15.00
Olive Oyl Doll (Presents 1985)	30.00
Popeye Doll (16" tall; cotton-stuffed doll	
w/orange felt feet) (Columbia 1940s)	375.00
Popeye Cameo Doll (Ideal 1950s)	125.00
Popeye Doll (Dakin late 1960s)	20.00
Popeye Vinyl Doll (Uneeda 1979)	7.00
Popeye Doll large size (Presents 1985)	30.00
Popeye Doll medium size (Presents 1985)	15.00
Popeye Doll (Etone International 1983)	5.00
Sea Hag Doll (Presents 1985)	30.00

Swee'pea Doll (Presents, 1985) 15.00
Wimpy Doll large size (Presents 1985) 30.00
Wimpy Doll medium size (Presents 1985) . 15.00

ROBIN

Robin Figure, 5 colors on 3½"x5" plastic
   pack display card (1966) 20.00
Robin Handpuppet 10" vinyl (Ideal 1966) . 80.00
Robin Push-Up Puppet 3"
   plastic (Kohner 1966) 65.00
Robin Figure on stand, 12½" with vinyl
   and fabric 24.50
Robin 12" vinyl figure (Presents 1989) . . . 20.00
Robin clear resin figure (Mexico 1990) . . . 20.00

SPIDER-MAN

Spider-Man 12" Vinyl figure
   (Hamilton #P6800) 35.00
Spider-Man doll with stand 16" vinyl 30.00
Plush Spider-Man Doll (Toy Biz
   #42320, 1994) 30.00
Spider-Man Special Collectors Edition

Supergirl Posin' Doll (Ideal 1967)

12" figure with costumes (Toy Biz
   #48427, 1995) 25.00

SUPERGIRL

Supergirl 11½" "Super Queens Posin'
   Doll" (Ideal 1967) 1,500.00

SUPERMAN

Superman Carnival Chalk figure, 15"
   moulded plaster, painted (1940s) . . . 300.00
Superman jointed 13" wood figure
   (Ideal 1939) 1,500.00
Superman Syroco figure, brown with
   maroon details, black hair, 2½"x1½"
   base (1940s) 1,200.00
Superman plastic figure, 2½" on base
   ivory color, fine detail (Marx) 150.00
Push Button Puppets, boxed set of
   Superman & Supergirl (Koher 1968)   75.00
Superman 6" rubber figure (Fun Things) . . 25.00
Superman 15" plastic figure with cape
   (Warner Bros. Store 1988) 12.00
Superman Figure on stand 15" with vinyl
   and fabric (Hamilton) 24.50
Superman on base (Applause 1989) 5.00
Superman rubber figures (Chemtoy)
   3 different, each 15.00
Superman Doll #425, 11" (Japanese) 50.00
Superman Window Pop display toy
   (Horizon #WP001, 1990) 30.00

WOLVERINE

Wolverine Special Collectors Edition
   12" figure with costumes (Toy Biz
   #48426, 1995) 25.00

WONDER WOMAN

Wonder Woman 11½" "Super Queens
   Posin' Doll" (Ideal 1967) 1,200.00
Wonder Woman Figure on stand 14"
   with vinyl and fabric 24.50

Wonder Woman Companions

Nubia 12" (Mego 1976) 90.00
Queen Hippolite 12" (Mego 1976) 90.00
Steve Trevor 12" (Mego 1976) 75.00

MINI-FIGURES

A number of comics characters have been released as 2"–3" figures during the last two years. These mini-figures are die-cast metal, or plastic or both and some are articulated at the waist or arms. Their appearance from several manufacturers has blurred the distinction between die-cast and PVC figures and "mini-figures" has become the category name for all of these small figures.

We list those that come in two-packs and three-packs first, followed by die-cast and PVC figures.

MULTI-PACKS

CARNAGE

Maximum Carnage Die-cast
3-pack (Toy Biz #44500, 1994) 12.50

FANTASTIC FOUR
(2½" Die-Cast Figures—2 Per Pack)

Mr. Fantastic vs. Dr. Doom (Toy Biz #45211,
1994) 4.00
Human Torch vs. Dragon Man (Toy Biz
1994) 5.00
Silver Surfer vs. Terrax (Toy Biz 1994) 5.00
The Thing vs. Blastaar (Toy Biz #45214,
1994) 4.00

IRON MAN
(2½" Die-Cast Figures—2 Per Pack)

Iron Man vs. Mandarin (Toy Biz #46211,
1995) 4.00
War Machine vs. Modok (Toy Biz 1995) ... 5.00

Judge vs. Mutant (Mattel 1995)

JUDGE DREDD

These are small plastic figures and vehicles based on the popular comic book series and the unpopular Sylvester Stallone movie which opened in June 1995. Packs #5 and #6 are the most collectible because they have a large figure or vehicle (and one small figure) instead of three small figures.

1 Judge vs. Cons (Undercity Perp, Lawgiver
Dredd and Fergie) (Mattel #13927,
1995) 3.00
2 Judges vs. Mean Angel (Mean Machine
Angel, Chief Justice Fargo and Squad
Leader Judge Hunter) (Mattel #13928,
1995) 3.00
3 Judge vs. Uglies (Ugly Pugley, Block War
Dredd and Kink Angel) (Mattel #13929,
1995) 3.00
4 Judge vs. Anti-Judges (Rico, Street Judge
Hershey and Judge Death) (Mattel
#13930, 1995) 3.00
5 Judge vs. Mutant (Cursed Earth Mutant
and Judge Dredd Lawmaster Mark IV)
(Mattel #13931, 1995) 7.50
6 Judge vs. Machine (ABC Robot and Riot
Armor Dredd) (Mattel #13932, 1995) . 5.00

SPIDER-MAN: WEB OF STEEL
(2½" Die-Cast Figures—2 Per Pack)

Spider-Man vs. Smythe (Toy Biz #47316,
1995) 4.00
Spider-Man vs. Lizard (Toy Biz #47317,
1995) 4.00
Spider-Man vs. Kingpin (Toy Biz 1995) ... 5.00
Spider-Man vs. Vulture (Toy Biz 1995) 5.00
Spider-Man vs. Venom (Toy Biz #47211,
1994) 4.00
Spider-Man vs. Carnage (Toy Biz #47212,
1994) 4.00
Spider-Man vs. Hobgoblin (Toy Biz #47213,
1994) 4.00
Spider-Man vs. Dr. Octopus (Toy Biz
#47214, 1994) 4.00

X-MEN: STEEL MUTANTS
(2½" Die-Cast Figures—2 Per Pack)

Wolverine vs. Sabertooth (Toy Biz 1994) .. 5.00
Archangel vs. Apocalypse (Toy Biz #49206,
1994) 5.00
Juggernaut vs. Cyclops (Toy Biz #49207,
1994) 5.00
Spy Wolverine vs. Omega Red (Toy Biz
#49208, 1994) 5.00
Cable vs. Stryfe (Toy Biz #49221, 1994) .. 5.00

Professor X vs. Magneto (Toy Biz #49222,
   1994) 5.00
Gambit vs. Bishop (Toy Biz #49223, 1994) . 5.00
Cyclops vs. Mr. Sinister (Toy Biz #49224,
   1994) 5.00
Beast vs. Evil Morph (Toy Biz 1995) 4.00
Civilian Wolverine vs. Silver Samurai (Toy
   Biz #49232, 1995) 4.00
Rogue vs. Pyro (Toy Biz #49233, 1995) . . . 4.00
Longshot vs. Mojo (Toy Biz 1995) 4.00

Brahma and Riptide (Playco 1995)

YOUNGBLOOD
(2½" Articulated Figures—2 Per Pack)

Sentinel and Cougar (Playco #03810, 1995) 4.00
Brahma and Riptide (Playco #03810, 1995) 4.00
Photon and Shaft (Playco #03810, 1995) . . 4.00
Chapel and Vogue (Playco #03810, 1995) . 4.00
Die Hard and Link (Playco #03810, 1995) . 4.00
Combat and Psi-Fire (Playco #03810, 1995) 4.00
Badrock (Playco, #03810 1995) 5.00

DIE-CAST FIGURES

Ertl die-cast figures are mostly from the Batman movies and animated TV show. They include Batman characters (listed here) and Batman vehicles (listed in the Vehicles section). In 1990, they produced a series of DC characters. Recently Kenner has produced a series of "Action Master" die-cast figures which come with a trading card and include Batman and Catwoman (plus Aliens, Terminator and Star Wars) figures. Most die-cast figures are packaged singly and sold on display cards.

Practically all die-cast and PVC figures are 2" to 3" high and inexpensive enough to actually remove from their display card and put on a shelf or the top of a computer monitor. They are somewhat adicting — you can't seem to stop with one, or even just a few.

BATMAN
Batman standing figure, die-cast
   with collector card (Ertl #715, 1990) . . 5.00
Batman raised fist figure, die-cast
   with collector card (Ertl #723, 1990) . . 5.00
Batman die-cast, action pose "Batman
   Returns" (Ertl #2481, 1992) 3.00
Batman die-cast (standing) "Batman
   Returns" (Ertl #2485, 1992) 3.00
Batman: The Animated Series (standing
   erect) 2" die-cast (Ertl/AMT 1993) . . . 2.00
Batman: The Animated Series (bent knee
   stance) 2" die-cast (Ertl/AMT 1993) . . 2.00
Batman: Animated die-cast with card
   "Action Master" (Kenner 1994) 3.00
Legends Batman "Action Master" die-cast
   with card (Kenner #62622, 1994) 3.00
   See also: Vehicles section
CATWOMAN
Catwoman die-cast figure, light blue eyes
   (Ertl #2484, 1992) 3.00
Catwoman die-cast figure, dark blue eyes
   (Ertl #2484, 1992) 3.00
Catwoman 2" die-cast (Ertl/AMT 1993) 2.00
Catwoman "Action Master" die-cast figure
   with card (Kenner #62616, 1994) 3.00
GREEN LANTERN
Green Lantern die-cast with card
   (Ertl #727, 1990) 5.00

All prices listed are for *Near Mint* condition.

713AO Super Powers Assortment II

Super Powers II die-cast figures (Ertl 1990)

JOKER

The Joker figure, die-cast with collector
card (Ertl #728, 1990) 5.00
The Joker and Batman figures, die-cast
with collector card (Ertl #2490, 1990) . 5.00
The Joker 2" die-cast (Ertl/AMT 1993) 2.00

PENGUIN

The Penguin die-cast figure with collector
card (Ertl #718, 1990) 5.00
Penguin die-cast figure "Batman Returns"
(Ertl #2483, 1992) 2.00
Penguin Commando die-cast figure
"Batman Returns" (Ertl #2482, 1992) . 2.00
The Penguin 2" die-cast (Ertl/AMT 1993) .. 2.00

ROBIN

Robin figure, die-cast with collector
card (Ertl #726, 1990) 5.00
Robin 2" die-cast (Ertl/AMT 1993) 2.00

SHAZAM

Shazam die-cast with card
(Ertl #719, 1990) 5.00

SUPERGIRL

Supergirl die-cast with card
(Ertl #729, 1990) 5.00

SUPERMAN

Superman die-cast standing with card
(Ertl #716, 1990) 5.00
Superman die-cast raised fist with
card (Ertl #724, 1990) 5.00

THE TICK

Good Doers (Bandai 1995)
1. Crusading Chameleon 2.50
2. Human Bullet 2.50
3. The Tick 2.50
4. Arthur 2.50

5. American Maid 2.50
6. Sewer Urchin 2.50
Evil Doers (Bandai 1995)
1. Dyna Mole 2.50
2. Dinosaur Neil 2.50
3. Chairface Chippendale 2.50
4. Dean 2.50
5. El Seed 2.50

PVC FIGURES

In this section we list small PVC
figures (as opposed to statues and
figurines). They were issued as loose
figures and sold at comic shops or variety
stores. "PVC" means polyvinyl chloride,
a type of plastic also used in plumbing
pipes. Die-cast figures are stamped out of
metal. It can be hard to tell them apart
just by looking, but it's easy by touch as
the metal feels colder due to its greater
thermal conductivity.

The PVC figures listed here come from
just a few sources. The earliest DC
figures say "Presents" and are from 1988.
These include Batman and Robin, but the
best one is Superman. Batman, Robin and
villain figures were made by Applause in
1989 and 1992, which, of course, matches
the release dates of the two Batman
movies. All these figures were marketed
to variety stores at first and later through
the comic shop distributors as well. The
Dick Tracy and Popeye figures come

from this source, as do many movie, TV and other noncomic figures.

Most of the Marvel characters are from a series of almost 60 figures sold through comic shops, first by Marvel and later by Comic Images. The figures issued by Marvel say "© Marvel 1990 [or 1989 or 1991], Made in China." Currently, these figures say "© Marvel 1991 [or 1992 or 1994], China" and have a number. They are from Comic Images and are a continuation of the prior series because the first number is #34 (Wolverine). There are also three Marvel figures from Applause (Captain America, Hulk and Spider-Man) from 1992 and three massive 4" versions of these characters made by Hamilton Gifts in 1991 which stand on round bases. All of these figures were sold loose.

Superman PVC (Comics Spain 1988)

The most interesting PVCs are those made by "Comics Spain." They were imported into the USA and sold through comic shops in groups. They are more finely detailed and look more realistic than other PVC figures, except for the feet, which look like they belong on 7' basketball players. This does help them stand up for display. Comics Spain fig-

ures are mostly Marvel characters, but also include Superman, Batman, Flash Gordon, The Phantom and The Terminator, etc. They are from 1989 to 1992, but were sold to comic shops in mid-1992 in two groups of nine figures. (We have also seen some science fiction figures available, which included Flash Gordon.)

ARCHANGEL
Archangel 3½" PVC figure (Marvel 1991) . . 5.00

BATMAN
Batman 3½" PVC figure, on base, left hand
    extended (Presents #A2, 1988) 4.00
    Variation, with metal loop for hanging . 4.00
Batman 3½" PVC figure (Comics
    Spain 1989) 10.00
Batman 3½" PVC figure, hands on hips
    (Applause 1989) 5.00
Batman, caped, with rope and suction cup
    PVC figure (Applause 1992) 5.00
Batman 3½" PVC figure on base
    (Applause #5, 1992) 5.00
Batman 3" PVC figure on gargoyle base,
    throwing batarang (Applause 1992) . . 5.00
Batman Forever 3" PVC figure on base
    (Applause 1995) 4.00

BEAST
Beast 3" PVC figure #56, standing on head
    (Comic Images 1994) 4.00

BISHOP
Bishop 3½" PVC figure #52
    (Comic Images 1994) 5.00

CABLE
Cable 3½" PVC figure #36 (Comic Images
    1991) 5.00

CAPTAIN AMERICA
Captain America 3½" PVC figure
    (Marvel 1989) 5.00
Captain America 3½" PVC figure (Comics
    Spain 1990) 10.00
Captain America 3" PVC figure
    (Applause 1990) 4.00
Captain America 4" PVC figure
    on base (Hamilton Gifts 1991) 7.00

CAPTAIN BRITAIN
Captain Britain 3½" PVC figure
    (Marvel 1990) 5.00

CARNAGE
Carnage 3½" PVC figure #55
    (Comic Images 1994) 5.00

Captain America PVC (Hamilton Gifts 1991)

CATWOMAN
Catwoman with rope and suction
   cup 3½" PVC figure (Applause 1992) . 5.00
Catwoman on base 3½" PVC
   figure (Applause 1992) 5.00

CHARLIE BROWN
Charlie Brown PVC figure (Applause 1988) 4.00
Linus PVC figure (Applause 1988) 4.00
Lucy PVC figure (Applause 1988) 4.00
Snoopy PVC figure (Applause 1988) 4.50
Woodstock PVC figure (Applause 1988) ... 4.00

COLOSSUS
Colossus 4" PVC figure (Marvel 1990) 5.00

CYCLOPS
Cyclops 3½" PVC figure (Marvel 1990) ... 5.00
Cyclops 3½" PVC figure (Comics
   Spain 1990) 10.00
Cyclops 3½" PVC #50 (Comic Images 1994) 4.00

DAREDEVIL
Daredevil 3½" PVC (Marvel 1990) 5.00
Daredevil 3½" PVC figure (Comics
   Spain 1990) 10.00

DICK TRACY
Dick Tracy 3½" PVC, 2 different,
   (Applause 1991) 3.50
Breathless Mahoney 3½" PVC
   (Applause 1991) 6.00
Big Boy PVC figure (Applause 1991) 4.00
Flattop PVC figure (Applause 1991) 4.00
Itchy PVC figure (Applause 1991) 4.00
Pruneface PVC figure (Applause 1991) ... 4.00

DR. DOOM
Dr. Doom 3½" PVC figure (Marvel 1990) .. 5.00

Dr. Doom 3½" PVC figure (Comics
   Spain 1990) 10.00

DOCTOR OCTOPUS
Doctor Octopus 3½" PVC figure #41
   (Comic Images 1992) 5.00

DR. STRANGE
Dr. Strange 3½" PVC figure (Marvel 1991) . 5.00

FLASH GORDON
Flash Gordon PVC figure (Comics
   Spain 1990) 10.00

GAMBIT
Gambit 3½" PVC figure #37 with cloak
   (Comic Images 1991) 5.00

GHOST RIDER
Ghost Rider 3½" PVC figure (Marvel 1991) 5.00
Ghost Rider 3½" PVC figure #45
   (Comic Images 1992) 5.00

GREEN GOBLIN
Green Goblin 3½" PVC figure, detachable
   flying base (Marvel 1990) 5.00

HAVOC
Havoc 3½" PVC figure (Marvel 1991) 5.00

Joker PVC (Applause 1989)

HULK
Hulk, Grey 4" PVC figure (Marvel 1990) ... 5.00
Hulk, Green 3½" PVC figure
   (Comics Spain 1990) 10.00
Hulk, Green, small 3" PVC
   figure (Applause 1990) 5.00
Hulk, Green, Christmas 3½" PVC
   figure #39 (Comic Images 1991) 5.00
Hulk 4" PVC figure on base
   (Hamilton Gifts 1991) 7.00

ICEMAN
Iceman 3½" PVC figure #53 (Comic
   Images 1994) 4.00
IRON MAN
Iron Man 3½" PVC figure (Marvel 1990) . . . 5.00
Iron Man 3½" PVC figure (Comics
   Spain 1990) 10.00
JOKER
The Joker 2¾" PVC, hands on head
   (Applause 1989) 4.00
The Joker PVC hanging figure on
   suction cup (Applause 1989) 8.00
The Joker 3½" PVC figure #1 on base
   (Applause 1992) 5.00
LIZARD
Lizard 3½" PVC figure (Marvel 1991) 5.00
MAGNETO
Magneto 3½" PVC figure (Marvel 1991) . . . 5.00
Magneto 3½" PVC figure #49 (Comic
   Images 1994) 4.00
MARVEL GIRL
Marvel Girl 3½" PVC figure (Marvel 1990) . 5.00
Marvel Girl 3½" PVC figure #51 (Comic
   Images 1994) 4.00
MR. FANTASTIC
Mr. Fantastic 3½" PVC figure (Marvel 1990) 5.00
NIGHTCRAWLER
Nightcrawler 3½" PVC figure (Marvel 1990) 5.00
PENGUIN
Penguin 2" PVC figure, fencing with
   umbrella (Applause 1989) 5.00
Penguin, on base 3½" PVC figure
   (Applause #2, 1992) 5.00
Penguin, with rope and suction cup 3½"
   PVC figure (Applause 1992) 5.00
PHANTOM
Phantom 3½" PVC figure (Comics Spain
   1990) 2 different, each 10.00
POISON IVY
Poison Ivy 3½" PVC figure #2 on base
   (Applause 1992) 5.00
POPEYE
Presents (1989)
Brutus PVC figure (with bombs) 3.50
Olive PVC figure (holding heart) 3.50
Popeye PVC figure (with spinach can) 3.50
Swee'pea PVC figure (on alphabet block) . . 3.50
Wimpy PVC figure (with burgers) 3.50
PUNISHER
Punisher 3½" PVC figure (Comics
   Spain 1990) 10.00
Punisher 3½" PVC figure #44 (Comic

Punisher PVC (Comics Spain 1990)

   Images 1992) 5.00
RIDDLER
Riddler 3" PVC figure on base
   "Batman Forever" (Applause 1995) . . 4.00
ROBIN
Robin 3" PVC figure, A2 on base, right
   hand extended (Presents 1988) 4.00
Robin 3¼" PVC, arms folded
   (Applause 1989) 4.00
Robin PVC hanging figure on suction
   cup (Applause 1989) 8.00
Robin 3½" PVC figure on base
   (Applause 1992) 4.00
Robin 3" PVC figure on base
   "Batman Forever" (Applause 1995) . . 4.00
ROGUE
Rogue 3½" PVC figure (Marvel 1990) 5.00
Rogue 3½" PVC figure #54
   (Comic Images 1992) 5.00
SABRETOOTH
Sabretooth 3½" PVC figure #42
   (Comic Images 1992) 4.00
SCARLET WITCH
Scarlet Witch 3½" PVC figure (Marvel 1990) 5.00
SENTINEL
Sentinel 3½" PVC figure #57 (Comic
   Images 1994) 4.00
SHE-HULK
She-Hulk 3½" PVC figure (Comics
   Spain 1987) 10.00
She-Hulk 3½" PVC figure (Marvel 1990) . . . 5.00

All prices listed are for *Near Mint* condition.   **117**

SILVER SURFER
Silver Surfer 3½" PVC figure (Comics
Spain 1990) 10.00
Silver Surfer 3½" PVC figure #47
(Comic Images 1992) 5.00

SPIDER-MAN
Spider-Man 3½" PVC figure (Comics
Spain 1990) 10.00
Spider-Man 3" PVC figure (Applause 1990)   7.00
Spider-Man 4" PVC figure on base
(Hamilton Gifts 1991) 7.00
Spider-Man, Christmas 3½" PVC
figure #38 (Comic Images 1991) 5.00
Spider-Man 3½" PVC (Web Slinger pose)
figure #48 (Comic Images 1992) 5.00

Spider-Man PVC (Comic Images 1992)

SPIDER-WOMAN
Spider-Woman 3½" PVC figure
(Comics Spain 1987) 10.00

STORM
Storm 3½" PVC figure (Marvel 1990) 4.50
Storm 3½" PVC figure #35 (big cape)
(Comic Images 1991) 5.00

SUPERMAN
Superman 4" PVC figure, A1 on base
(Presents 1988) 7.00
Superman 3½" PVC figure (Comics
Spain 1988) 11.50
Superman on base PVC figure 3½"
(Applause 1991) 3.50

THANOS
Thanos 3½" PVC figure #40 (Comic
Images 1992) 5.00

Spider-Woman PVC (Comics Spain 1987)

THING
Thing 3½" PVC figure (Marvel 1990) 5.00

THOR
Thor 3½" PVC figure (Marvel 1990) 5.00
Thor 3½" PVC figure (Comics Spain 1990)   10.00

TWO-FACE
Two-Face 3½" PVC figure on base
(Applause 1992) 4.00
Two-Face 3" PVC figure on base
"Batman Forever" (Applause 1995) . . 4.00

VENOM
Venom 3½" PVC figure #43 (Comic
Images 1991) 5.00
Venom, flicking tongue 3½" PVC figure
#58 on base (Comic Images 1994) . . 5.00

VISION
Vision 3½" PVC figure (Marvel 1990) 5.00

WOLVERINE
Wolverine 3½" PVC figure (Marvel 1989) . . 5.00
Wolverine 3½" PVC figure (Marvel 1990) . . 5.00
Wolverine 3½" PVC figure #34 (Comic
Images 1991) 5.00
Wolverine 3½" PVC figure (Comics
Spain 1990) 10.00
Wolverine X-Mas 3½" PVC figure
(Comic Images #46, 1992) 5.00

WONDER WOMAN
Wonder Woman PVC (1990) 5.00

MODEL KITS & SCULPTURES

The Aurora Model Company got into the Super Hero figure kit biz with their highly prized Superman kit back in 1963. They decided to do Marvel Super Hero figure kits during the mid-1960s and picked three that would show up as mainstays with various other manufacturing companies: Spider-Man, The Incredible Hulk and Captain America. Toward the early to mid-1970s, these same three were part of a new kit series by the same company. The series was called "Comic Scenes," which came in a slightly smaller and differently illustrated box which contained a smaller-scaled kit

and a specially made comic book inside.

The first Superman figure by the Aurora Model Company was in 1963. This kit was produced two different times during the 1960s, each time with a different box style. The first issue of this kit had a painted box while the second, and rarer-variation was produced in 1965 and had a comic-styled illustration.

The Batman and Robin figure model kits from Aurora were spurred on by the success of the caped crusader's ABC-TV series, although the 1965 date would imply that the Batman kit was produced prior to the show's successful run. The dynamic duo's arsenal, the Batmobile, Batboat, Batcycle and Batplane, were

Classic Batman, Robin, Penguin and vehicle model kits (Aurora)

All prices listed are for *Near Mint* condition.

produced during the Bat craze, so that well-known TV series probably did have something to do with the production of those fantastically detailed and highly praised model kits.

And then there was the Penguin figure model kit produced in 1967. While it is, most certainly, quite unique to see a model kit of a major villain, and a foe of Batman's as well, why did the powers that be pick the Penguin, of all characters? Why did they not choose The Joker, who was, and still is, known to be *the* major archenemy of the Dark Knight detective? Why, indeed.

It's interesting to note that the Penguin was the only supervillain figure model kit ever produced up until the time that the Horizon company, in the late 1980s, began manufacturing their high-quality vinyl models. They've added supervillains to their line of Marvel-based model kits with characters such as Doctor Doom and Dark Phoenix. Hopefully, this already well-known model manufacturing outfit will do the same for DC villains.

Aside from the kits of Superman and the Batman-related series, the Aurora company produced fantastic action-oriented figures of Wonder Woman and Superboy. The Wonder Woman kit, released in 1964, depicted Princess Diana with magic lasso in hand, doing battle with, of all things, an octopus. What differentiates this model kit from the others produced by Aurora, or any others up to 1984, was the fact that it was the only female superhero model kit in existence up until that time. 1984 was the year that Tskuda of Japan released their jumbo kit of the Maid of Steel, Supergirl—the second model kit of a superheroine to be made.

The Boy of Steel, Superboy, was quite popular during the mid-1960s, and so Aurora produced a model kit featuring the lad. The model in question had the Superboy of Smallville, with his trusty super-

pet Krypto, encountering a dragonlike alien creature.

Aurora returned once more to the superhero model kit manufacturing spotlight in 1974. It was the year that they released their popular (to model kit builders, anyway—if it was popular to everyone, they'd still be in business) Comic Scenes series of kits. The once-large boxes were now smaller sized with new artwork on the lids. Also included inside the boxes were minicomics featuring the adventures of the kitted characters. The popular characters, Batman, Superman and Superboy, were the only DC characters that were featured in this series. Wonder Woman, considered a failed attempt in her first series, consequently proved to be too much of a risk to reproduce in this new line. As for Robin, it's hard to figure out why he was never reintroduced to the Comic Scenes line.

Sad to say, these were the last superhero kits offered by this great and grand company. The superhero figure kits were lost in "limbo land" only to be resurrected briefly by MPC in 1985 as part of the Super Powers series. Superman and Batman, retooled from the old Aurora molds, were the only two featured kits this time. You may find it interesting to know that Aurora had plans for three different Superman kits to follow after the first released one. Also, a kit of the Batcopter actually made it to the prototype stage but never into the hands of the kit-buying public.

As aforementioned, most figure model kits are produced by newer outfits such as Horizon, Tskuda and Billiken. These extremely well rendered kits aren't made of the same old styrene as the Aurora kits were but, rather, were made of vinyl. The box-office smash hit Batman film of 1989 helped bring the superhero back into demand, and model kits featuring the revamped DC Comics character and his

Superman model kit (Horizon 1994)

archenemy, The Joker, were the focus of these companies at that time.

Horizon's kit was the first to be fashioned after the movie and featured the Dark Knight standing with cape spread wide open. Billiken featured two versions of the Batman kit: the first depicted the caped crusader with open hands while the second portrayed him with grappling hook in hand. Billiken also produced a kit of The Joker which comes with two different heads. The Tskuda company also got on the Batman bandwagon with their figure kit as well.

Horizon also did what is called Window Pops. These are vinyl figures that are cut in half. The cut-off mark has an adhesive substance that allows each part to be attached to glass windows in order to give the illusion that the figure is actually walking through windows. Superman and Batman were both fashioned in this way during the late 1980s.

A great series of vinyl figure model kits based on the popular Marvel Super Heroes was begun in 1988 by the Horizon Model Company. To this day, they are still producing some high quality, top-notch kits.

MODEL KITS

Archie's Car, 1/25 scale,
    in 13"x4"x2" box (Aurora #582, 1969) 60.00
    in 8"x5"x4" box 50.00
Bane 1/8 scale solid model kit
    (Horizon 1995) 90.00
Batman, 1/8 scale, in 13"x7"x2" box
    (Aurora #467, 1964–68) 350.00
Batman Comic Scenes series, 1/8 scale, in
    7"x10½"x4" box w/ comic (Aurora #187,
    1974–75) 80.00
Batman Figure Model Kit (Super
    Powers) (MPC 1985) 30.00
Batman Figure Model Kit (Horizon 1989) . 35.00
Batman Figure Model Kit (Tskuda 1989) . 90.00
Batman Figure Model Kit
    (open hands) (Billikin 1989) 100.00
Batman Figure Model Kit (grappling
    hook) (Billikin 1989) 100.00
Batman vinyl model kit

    (Horizon #HC012, 1990) 30.00
Batman Window Pop display toy
    (Horizon #WP002, 1990) 30.00
Batman II Figure Model Kit (Batman
    Returns) (Horizon #HOR031, 1992) . 45.00
Batman, 1/6 scale, soft vinyl model
    (Tskuda 1992) 75.00
Batman 1/8 scale solid model kit
    (Horizon 1995) 90.00
Batman Forever Batman vinyl model
    kit (Revell 1995) 30.00
Batman Batboat Model Kit
    (motorized) (Imai [Japan] 1966) ... 600.00
Batboat, 1/32 scale, in 13"x5"x1½" box
    (Aurora #811, 1968) 600.00
Batman Forever Batboat plastic model
    kit (Revell 1995) 12.50
Batcycle, 1/24 scale, in 13"x5"x1½" box
    (Aurora #810, 1968) 800.00
Batman's Batmobile, 1/32 scale,
    in 13"x5"x1½" box with light blue
    background (Aurora #486, 1966) ... 450.00
    in variant box with purple background 500.00
Batplane, 1/60 scale, in 13"x5"x1½"
    box (Aurora #486, 1967–68) 300.00
Batman Forever Batplane plastic model
    kit (Revell 1995) 12.50
Batmobile Model w/removable Turbine
    Engine (Ertl/AMT #6650, 1992) 12.50
Batmobile, 1950s style solid model
    kit (Horizon 1995) 90.00
Batmobile, 1980s style solid model
    kit (Horizon 1995) 90.00
Batman Forever Batmobile plastic model
    kit (Revell 1995) 12.50
Batskiboat Snapkit Model (Ertl/AMT
    #6615, 1992) 11.00
Batmissile Snapfast Model
    (Ertl/AMT #6614, 1992) 11.00
Cable, 1/6 scale vinyl model kit
    (Horizon #HOR052, 1994) 45.00
Captain Action, 1/6 scale, in 13"x5"x2"
    box (Aurora #480, 1966–67) 200.00
Captain America (Tskuda 1984) 125.00
Captain America, 1/12 scale,
    in 13"x5"x2" box (Aurora #476, 1966) 325.00
Captain America Comic Scenes series,
    1/12 scale, in 7"x10½"x4" box
    w/ comic (Aurora #192, 1974–75) .. 75.00
Captain America 50th Anniversary 15" vinyl
    model kit (Horizon #HC014, 1990) .. 35.00
Carnage vinyl model kit

(Horizon #HOR051, 1994) 45.00
Catwoman Figure Model (Batman Returns)
(Horizon HOR032 1992) 40.00
Catwoman, 1/6 scale, soft vinyl model
(Tskuda 1992) 75.00
Catwoman 1/8 scale solid model kit
(Horizon 1995) 90.00
The Crow vinyl model, 12" (Inteleg 1994) . . 50.00
Cyclops vinyl model kit
(Horizon #HOR026, 1992) 45.00
Dark Phoenix vinyl model kit
(Horizon #HC016, 1991) 29.95
Doctor Doom vinyl model kit
(Horizon #HC017, 1991) 39.95

Dick Tracy, 1/16 scale, in 13"x5"x1½"
box (Aurora #818, 1968) 275.00
The Dick Tracy Space Coupe, 1/72 scale, in
13"x5"x1½" box (Aurora #819, 1968) 200.00
The Flash resin model kit
with base (Horizon 1995) 130.00
Flash Gordon and the Martian
(Revell 1965) 175.00
Flash Gordon (Screamin' 1993) 65.00
Ghost Rider vinyl model kit
(Horizon #HOR024, 1992?) 45.00
Gigantor solid model kit (Horizon 1995) . . . 80.00
Green Goblin, 1/6 scale, vinyl model kit
(Horizon #HOR055, 1994) 45.00

Silver Surfer and Iron Man model kits (Horizon 1990)

All prices listed are for *Near Mint* condition.

Green Hornet Black Beauty model kit
(Aurora 1966) 500.00
The Incredible Hulk, 1/12 scale,
in 13"x5"x2" box (Neal Adams art)
(Aurora #421, 1966–68) 250.00
The Incredible Hulk Comic Scenes series,
1/12 scale, in 7"x10½"x4" box w/
comic (Aurora #184, 1974–75) 75.00
Hulk model (MPC 1978) 40.00
Incredible Hulk 13" vinyl model kit
(Horizon #HC013, 1990) 35.00
Iron Man vinyl model kit
(Horizon #HC009, 1990) 30.00
Joker Figure Model Kit (Billiken 1989)
(with two different heads) 100.00
Joker vinyl model kit
(Horizon #HOR056, 1994) 45.00
Joker resin model kit
with diorama (Horizon 1995) 130.00
Judge Anderson vinyl model kit
(Halcyon/MRC #HT19, 1994) 30.00
Judge Dredd vinyl model kit
(Halcyon/MRC #HT16, 1994) 30.00
Judge Death vinyl model kit
(Halcyon/MRC #HT18, 1994) 30.00
Lobo, 1/6 scale vinyl model kit
(Horizon #HOR057, 1994) 50.00
Oh My Goodness Beldandy vinyl model,
10" (Inteleg #501-57, 1994) 90.00
The Penguin, 1/12 scale, in 13"x5"x2"
box (Carmine Infintino art)
(Aurora #416, 1967) 700.00
Penguin Figure Model (Batman Returns)
(Horizon #HOR033, 1992) 45.00
Penguin, 1/6 scale, soft vinyl model
(Tsukda 1992) 75.00
Phantom and the Voodoo Witch
Doctor model (Revell) 150.00
Punisher vinyl model kit (Horizon
#HC007, 1990) 30.00
Riddler 1/8 scale solid model kit
(Horizon 1995) 90.00
Robin the Boy Wonder, 1/12 scale,
in 13"x5"x2" box (Neal Adams art)
(Aurora #488, 1966–68) 120.00
Robin Comic Scenes series, 1/12 scale,
in 7"x10½"x4" box w/ comic (Aurora
#193, 1974–75) 50.00
Robin 1/8 scale solid model kit
(Horizon 1995) 90.00
Shadowhawk resin model, 1/6 scale,
with Gargoyle centerpiece base,

Spawn model kit (Interleg 1995)

by Jim Valentino, sculpted by
T. H. Bruckner (Geometric 1995) . . . 100.00
She Hulk vinyl model kit
(Horizon #HOR054, 1994) 45.00
Silver Surfer vinyl model kit
(Horizon #HC008, 1990) 30.00
Spawn vinyl model kit (Interleg 1995) 60.00
Speed Racer Mach 5 solid model
kit (Horizon 1995) 70.00
The Amazing Spider-Man, 1/12 scale,
in 13"x5"x2" box (Neal Adams art)
(Aurora #477, 1966–68) 325.00
Spider-Man Comic Scenes series, 1/12
scale, in 7"x10½"x4" box w/ comic
(Aurora #182, 1974–75) 90.00
Spider-Man model (MPC) 30.00
Spider-Man vinyl model kit
(Horizon #HC006, 1990) 30.00
Spider-Man vinyl model kit
(Horizon #HOR049, 1994) 45.00
Spider-Man resin model kit
with diorama (Horizon 1995) 130.00
Spider-Man 2099 vinyl model kit
(Horizon #HOR053, 1994) 45.00

Steel (John Henry Irons) vinyl model kit,
1/6 scale (Horizon HOR066, 1994) . . . 55.00
Steve Canyon model kit 1/8 scale
(Aurora 1958) 150.00
Superboy and his superdog Krypto,
1/8 scale, in 13"x5"x2" box
(Aurora #478, 1965–68) 275.00
Superboy Comic Scenes series, 1/8 scale,
in 7"x10½"x4" box w/ comic (Aurora
#186, 1974–75) 90.00
Supergirl model kit (Tskuda 1984) 175.00
Superman, 1/8 scale, in first issue
13"x5"x2" box with painted picture
(Aurora #462, 1963) 325.00
Superman 2nd issue box, comic style
art (Aurora #462, 1964–68) 400.00
Superman Comic Scenes series, 1/8 scale,
in 7"x10½"x4" box with comic
(Aurora #185, 1974–75) 75.00
Superman model kit (Monogram 1960s) . . 45.00
Superman Super Powers model kit (MPC) 25.00
Superman, 1/6 scale, vinyl model kit
(Horizon #HOR059, 1994) 45.00
Tarzan, 1/11 scale, in 13"x7"x2"
box (Aurora #820, 1967–68) 150.00
Tarzan Comic Scenes series, 1/10 scale,
in 10"x7"x4" box with comic
(Aurora #181, 1974–76) 75.00

The Thing vinyl model kit
(Horizon #HC018, 1991) 35.00
Thor vinyl model kit
(Horizon #HOR025, 1992) 45.00
Venom vinyl model kit
(Horizon #HOR023, 1992) 39.95
Venom resin model kit
with diorama (Horizon 1995) 130.00
Wolverine 11" scale vinyl model kit
(Horizon HC015, 1990) 35.00
Wolverine, new costume, vinyl model kit
(Horizon #HOR050, 1994) 45.00
Wolverine resin model kit
with diorama (Horizon 1995) 130.00
Wonder Woman, 1/12 scale, in 13"x5"x2"
box (Aurora #479, 1965–66) 400.00
Zen Intergalactic Ninja vinyl model, 1/6
scale, sculpted by Shawn Nagle
(Inteleg 1994) 40.00

SCULPTURES & STATUES

Badrock resin model kit, 9" x 18"
(Extreme Studios 1994) 100.00
Batman cold-cast resin statue on gargoyle,
sculpted by Randy Bowan, 5,000
copies (Graphitti Designs 1992) 750.00
The Beast Rider pewter figure +
serigraph by Jack Kirby 7"x7½" 250.00
Bone 4½" limited-edition cold-cast

Thing vs. Hulk Bisque figures (Dave Grussman Creations 1991)

All prices listed are for *Near Mint* condition.

figure (Dark Horse 1994) 125.00
Concrete cold-cast porcelain figure,
    sculpted by Randy Bowen (1991) . . 100.00
Death porcelain cold-cast statue,
    sculpted by Bowen Designs (1993) . 100.00
Dracula cold-cast figure kit, Thomas Kuntz
    sculptor, 11½" (Dark Horse 1994) . . 150.00
Faust Resin figure, signed by Tim Vigil
    (Michael Burnet Productions 1994) . . 110.00
Flash statue, sculpted by William Paquet
    (DC Comics 1995) 150.00
Gambit cold-cast figurine, hand-painted
    and numbered (Marvel 1994) 140.00
Judge Dredd Resin Statue #1 sculpted
    by Janine Bennett (1992) 50.00
Lady Death, sculpted by Clayburn Moore . 175.00
Lobo statue sculpted by Randy Bowen
    (Graphitti Designs 1992) 125.00
Madman cold-cast figurine 11" on base
    (Dark Horse 1994) 125.00
Mr. Natural porcelain statue (600 made)
    5" high, hand-painted 100.00
Omaha, The Cat Dancer cold-cast porcelain
    statue sculpted by Steve Kiwus (1993) 50.00
Pitt Sculpture sculpted by Dale Keown and
    Clayburn Moore (1994) 195.00
Ripclaw resin statue, 9"x9"x6" sculpted
    by Clayburn Moore (1994) 150.00
Robin Statue sculpted by Randy
    Bowen (DC Comics 1994) 200.00
Sandman cold-cast porcelain, sculpted
    by Randy Bowen, 10" (Graphitti
    Designs 1991) 600.00
Sandman (Arabian Nights) sculpted by
    Randy Bowen, 7,000 made (Graphitti
    Designs 1994) 150.00
Savage Dragon sculpture, 9" sculpted by
    Clayburn Moore (Image 1995) 150.00
Spider-Man versus Venom figural bookends
    (Marvel 1994) 175.00
Superman: Time for a Change sculpture on
    marble base (Ron Lee SP100, 1993) 280.00
Superman, sculpted by Randy Bowen . . . 250.00
Superman: Meteor Moment sculpture, on
    marble base (Ron Lee SP115, 1993) 315.00
Superman Quick Change Sculpture,
    pewter (Ron Lee SP120, 1994) 125.00
Superman to the Rescue Sculpture,
    pewter (Ron Lee SP125, 1994) 195.00
Superman Locomotive Sculpture, pewter
    (Ron Lee SP130, 1994) 420.00
Superman Good vs. Evil Sculpture,

pewter (Ron Lee SP135, 1994) 190.00
Thing versus Hulk bisque figures by Ron
    Frenz (Dave Grussman 1991) 100.00
Vampirella cold-cast porcelain model
    (Graphitti Designs 1994) 130.00
The Wolf Man cold-cast figure kit, John
    Rosengrant sculptor, 10" (Dark
    Horse 1994) 150.00
Wolverine cold-cast figurine, hand-painted
    and numbered (Marvel 1994) 140.00
The Yellow Kid, 13" with ring in secret
    compartment (Gemstone Publishing
    1995) bronze (100 made) 2,000.00
    gold (25 made) 3,500.00

Batboat and Trailer (Corgi 1966)

VEHICLES

W atch out! Here he comes tearing up the track. Is it Mario Andretti? Could it be Richard Petty? No, it's... Wolverine!?

The vehicle has been an integral aspect in the superhero's life, probably ever since Batman had his Batmobile. Perhaps even earlier than that were the modes of transportation Doc Savage and The Shadow utilized. Granted, there is a large majority of costumed characters that don't use conveyances, four-wheeled or otherwise, but some super folks just can't seem to live without them. Batman, for example, eventually graduated to accumulate the largest array of vehicles this side of the Thunderbirds. To even think of talking about them all would be a catastrophe! A number of them are covered below, but others are models and are covered in that section. The rest (those that are part of an action figure series) are covered in the Action Figures section. If you want to know all about Batman vehicles, you'll have to look all three places.

Though we have seen Captain America riding on a motorcycle, Spider-Man tooling around in a Spider-Car (not really his idea but more of a promotional endorsement) and The Punisher in his van, many toy companies take great liberties with these toys. What self-respecting superhero wants his name and logo emblazoned on anything? They certainly don't

want to attract attention when in pursuit of a criminal! Whatever happened to the element of surprise?

Now, let's go over, providing you're still reading this, which company has produced what for our costumed friends. **BUDDY L:** Metal and plastic vehicles were produced in conjunction with the **Marvel Super Heroes Secret Wars** license in 1984. Buddy L packaged these crafts two ways, in four-packs as well as seperately. Separate crafts known to exist are Captain America, Wolverine and Spider-Man on motorcycles. A Spider-Copter is also a separate vehicle. There are also two known four-packs: a Spider-Man set with Copter, Van, Car and Cycle, as well as a set with the Captain America Cycle (without figure), Wolver-

Kalibak Boulder Bomber Vehicle, DC Super Powers line (Kenner 1984)

ine Copter, Dr. Doom Race Car and Dr. Octopus Van.

Buddy L put out some remote-control superhero vehicles from this line as well, featuring Captain America (Rocket Racer), Doctor Doom (Dragster Racer), and Spider-Man (Spider-Racer).

MARX: Batman's Batcraft was a battery-operated little ditty from 1966 that reminded me of those trash can–type modes of transportation that Dick Tracy used in the 1960s. Two 4" Batmobiles were produced in 1966, in tin litho with either Batman or Robin as the driver.

MATTEL: In 1965, Mattel issued a Batman set for its **Switch 'n' Go** series. For those who already had a **Switch 'nN' Go** set, a Batmobile was available separately.

Hot Wheels cars for Marvel Super Heroes (The Human Torch, Spider-Man, Thor, The Hulk, The Thing and Captain America) were produced in 1979. There was also a track set called the Spider-Man's Web of Terror that was made available for this series of cars. You could blast your car out of the Cobweb Cave Tunnel, somersault through the Spidey Eye Loop and jump it through the Web of Terror.

From the impressive **Marvel Super Heroes Secret Wars** line, we were treated to vehicles and crafts such as The Freedom Fighter, The Doom Roller, The Turbo Cycle, The Turbo Copter, The Doom Chopper, The Dark Star (which came with a figure of Kang), The Star Dart (complete with a figure of Spider-Man in his black costume, which he, by the by, acquired during this series), Marvel Super Villains and Marvel Super Heroes Machine.

KENNER: Since Mattel was doing so well with their **Marvel Super Heroes Secret Wars** line, apparently DC Comics thought that a line of figures and vehicles based on characters from their comics line would do just as well. With the help of Kenner Toys, the DC Super Powers Collection was born and sold even better, and also lasted a year longer, than the Mattel series. The Batmobile, Batcopter, and Superman's Supermobile were modified vehicles that already appeared in comics. However, Kenner created some newer crafts just for the series, and thus the Justice Jogger (don't ask!), Kalibak's Boulder Bomber, Delta Probe One, Lex-Soar 7, and the Darkseid Destroyer were born.

Amazing Spider-Man four vehicle set (Buddy L 1985)

Batman: The Animated Series vehicles (Ertl 1993)

IDEAL: From the various Batman and JLA playsets produced by Ideal came miniature versions of the Batmobile and Batplane. Captain Action, that multi-persona super guy from Ideal (who would be a scream to get on a couch for analysis one day), had one of the greatest vehicles ever— The Silver Streak! As the Sears Wishbook for 1968 says, "The Silver Streak runs on land and floats on water to help Captain Action defend both the land and sea. The sleek twin-seater is custom-made for him and Action Boy. Spring-operated turbo rockets actually fire. Tri-wheel design. Removable deck, radar scanner. Plastic, 21 inches long. Stores in cardboard garage."

That cardboard garage that the catalogue alludes to was only available from Sears, and today is one of the most sought after Captain Action pieces. Sears packaged the Silver Streak in that garage and not in the original box. As a result, many were damaged and discarded instead of saved.

TOY BIZ: One of the most important licenses this young toy company ever acquired was for **Batman: The Movie**. They produced two versions of the Bat-mobile (one with/one without the cocoon that goes over the vehicle's cockpit), one Batwing, Batcycle, Joker Cycle and Joker Van. Oddly enough, although they were producing a line of DC super-heroes at the same time (or thereabouts), there were no vehicles issued to any of those characters. The only Batman figures produced at that time were for the movie license tie-in. The Robin figure from the comics series had to either go it solo or pal around with the movie incarnation of Batman in order to ride in the Batmobile.

When 1990 rolled along, Toy Biz also had the Marvel Super Heroes license. Currently, they just have a license to produce X-Men, X-Force and X-Factor–related figures and accessories. Once they acquired that Marvel license, though, we saw two incredibly "thought up" vehicles for our costumed pals that would, if they were actually real personas, truly embarrass them to no end: a Spider-Man Drag-ster and Captain America Turbo Coupe. The only vehicle the Biz produced that was "true to form" more or less for this line was the Punisher Van.

With the series of X-Men figures in 1991, Toy Biz just couldn't help them-

---

All prices listed are for *Near Mint* condition.   **129**

Marvel Super Heroes Spider-Man vans 2-pack (Corgi 1992)

selves, it seemed, by giving Wolverine a Wolverine Mutantcycle, which, just like Logan himself, had its own set of claws (popping out from the vehicle's front). Not one to be outdone, the Master of Magnetism, Magneto, had his four-wheeled Magneto Magnetron, which, according to its package, had a catapult that launched metallic disks. It seemed like the Mego days once again. One would expect a Hulk 4 x 4 to follow next in line.

ERTL: In conjunction with the **Batman: The Movie** license, this company issued die-cast versions, in different scales, of the Batmobile, Batwing and Joker Van. One micro set had all three vehicles featured, and there was also a Batman Wrist Racer set as well.

DUNCAN: Plastic versions of the Batmobile and Batboat were produced by this company in the 1970s.

FLEETWOOD: The elusive Ghost Rider Motorcycle (complete with figure) is this company's claim to superhero vehicle fame: a much sought after and extremely high-priced piece of plastic which came out in the late 1970s. I have seen this item go for anywhere from $150.00 to $300.00! Hard to believe it probably cost under a dollar originally.

CORGI: One of the leading die-cast car manufacturers produced some great superhero vehicles in the 1960s, with larger scale versions of the Batmobile, Batboat

(later packaged together) and The Black Beauty from The Green Hornet series. One of the best sets was the triple Batman vehicle pack Corgi produced in 1976. It contained the Batmobile, Batboat, and Batcopter in a nice-looking window box. However, toward the late 1970s to early 1980s, they got silly with a selection of vehicles from their line. Many of these were available in two different scales, the larger Corgi Scale Models and the Corgi Miniatures (or Corgi Juniors). The regular-sized crafts featured some truly memorable modes of transportation, such as the Batmobile, Batbike, Penguinmobile, Captain Marvel White Lightning, Daily Planet Copter, Metropolis Police Car, Spiderbuggy (complete with a capture net that contains a Green Goblin figure), Spidervan, Spiderbike, Spidercopter, Captain America Jetmobile, Hulkmobile (which came with a detachable cage and Hulk figure) and the Supermobile. The smaller series of these die-cast cars featured miniature versions of the majority listed above except for the Hulkmobile, Spiderbuggy, and Captain America Jetmobile. However, the miniature series included vehicles that did not show up in the regular-sized line, such as the Superman Van, Batmobile (available with Batboat), Batcopter, Jokermobile, Daily Planet Copter (with Truck) and Wonder Woman Car.

MEGO: Oh, brother! Do we have some

---

winners here! Corgi, Kenner, Toy Biz and Buddy L aside, this company was the leader in some of the most imaginary vehicles our heroes ever had to put up with.

*Spider-Man Electronic
Spider Copter (Buddy L 1980s)*

For their 8" figures, they gave us The Green Arrowcar (which shot three safe projectiles from under the hood as well as both sides of the vehicle); The Captain Americar (with Cap's shield as the weapon which served as more of a battering ram here); Spider-Car (no exciting features, but had a net made of webbing that could be sprung on unsuspecting criminal types); Jokermobile (the joke's on those who got too close to this Volkswagen-bus-turned-criminal vehicle—the Joker installed a squirting flower on the roof as well as a boxing glove on the van's rear); Batcopter (Batman got the boot with this one, literally, because that what this is shaped like); Batmobile (looks just like

the one on the TV series, more or less); Batcycle (came with a sidecar that was detachable but not powered on its own); and the Mobile Bat-Lab (the Volkswagen company must have sponsored the Joker as well as Batman), which was a VW bus-like vehicle with a bat trap on the top and a Bat wench on the rear.

One truly nice set was the Batmobile that came complete with figures of the dynamic duo. It was styled just like the TV series version.

BATBOAT
Batboat (Duncan 1970s) 100.00
Batboat and Trailer, w/Batman & Robin figures;
    black plastic boat on gold trailer; fits
    Batmobile (Corgi #107, 1966) 150.00
Batboat & Batmobile set (Corgi 1976) . . . 250.00
Batman Batboat (Eidai 1970s) 190.00
Batman Batcraft, 6½" Hovercraft
    (Marx 1966) 400.00
Batmobile and Batboat two-vehicle
    pack (Corgi Junior late 1970s) 60.00
Batboat "Batman: The Animated Series"
    (Ertl 1993) 3.00
Batboat "Batman Forever" die-cast
    (Kenner #28895, 1995) 5.00
BATCOPTER
Batman Flying Copter 12" plastic with
    guide-wire control (Remco 1966) . . . 100.00
Official Batman Batcopter, 7½"x11" card
    with Batman at controls (AHI 1973) . 50.00
Batcopter "Official World's Greatest Super-
    Heroes" (Mego 1975)
    Boxed 120.00
    Carded 100.00
Batcopter & Batboat & Batmobile triple-pack set
    17"x7" window box, with figures, 5"
    batmobile, 5" Batboat and 6" Batcopter
    (Corgi 1976) 300.00
Batcopter replica (Corgi 1976) 35.00
Batcopter (Corgi Junior late 1970s) 25.00
Batman Batcopter, Battery Operated
    (AHI 1977) 30.00
Batman Batcopter, 8" (LHT 1982) 35.00
Batcopter "DC Super Powers"
    (Kenner #67270, 1986) 90.00
Batcopter "Dark Knight" (Kenner
    #63220, 1990) 30.00
BATCYCLE
Batman Batcycle (with Batman and

All prices listed are for *Near Mint* condition.

Robin figures) (Taiwan 1970) 45.00
Batbike (Corgi late 1970s) 60.00
Batbike (Corgi Junior late 1970s) 30.00
Batcycle "Official World's Greatest Super-
Heroes" (Mego 1975) 160.00
Batcycle with Drop Down Wings
(Toy Biz #4436, 1990) 10.00
Batcycle "Dark Knight" (Kenner
#63190, 1990) 15.00
Batman Laser Blade Cycle with Disrupter
Device "Batman Returns" (Kenner
#63740, 1992) 10.00
Batcycle die-cast "Batman: The Animated
Series" (Ertl #2449, 1993) 3.00
Batcycle with "Motorized Turbo Power,
Turbo Sound and Wheelie Action" plus
Batman figure "Batman: The Animated
Series" (Kenner #63981, 1993) 12.00
Batcycle "Legends of Batman" (Kenner
#64981, 1994) 10.00
Batcycle, with Batman figure "Batman: Crime
Squad" (Kenner #64672, 1995) 9.00

BATMISSILE
Batmissile 3¾" die-cast vehicle "Batman

Returns" (Ertl #2478, 1992) 5.00
Batmissile Batmobile with Blastoff Sides "Batman
Returns" (Kenner #63910, 1992) . . . 40.00

BATMOBILE
Batmobile (Corgi 1966) 150.00
Batman Ride On Batmobile (Marx 1966) . 450.00
Batman (in Batmobile) Trinket
(Lawson Novelty 1966) 20.00
Batman Ceramic Batmobile (Lego 1966)
(Japanese) 200.00
Batmobile, 5" replica (Mattel 1966) 90.00
Batmobile, blue tin litho 12" battery-
powered bump 'n' go action,
metal/plastic figures (ASC 1966) . . . 250.00
Batmobile, 11" tin litho blue, one-seater
with Batman (ASC 1966) 175.00
Batmobile tin litho with Batman
driver, 4" (Marx 1966) 90.00
Batmobile tin litho with Robin
driver, 4" (Marx 1966) 90.00
Batmobile in red and blue with yellow-
and-black highlights, vinyl headed
figures (Taiwan 1970s) 60.00
Batmobile, blue metal, red outline, w/green-

Battery operated Batmobile & Batman (ASC 1966)

Batmobile, Batboat on Trailer and Batcopter three vehicle set (Corgi 1976)

tinted dome, battery powered, with
vinyl headed figures (AHI 1972) 150.00
Batmobile black die-cast car with blue-tint
cockpit dome and figures of Batman
& Robin in seats (Corgi #267, 1973)   80.00
Batmobile, blue plastic with green-tint
cockpit dome & vinyl figures(AHI 1974) 60.00
Batmobile 8" "Official World's Greatest
Super Heroes" (Mego 1970s)
   Boxed 125.00
   Carded 100.00
Batman Talking Batmobile
(Palitoy 1977) 150.00
Batman Batmobile, Radio Controlled,
Battery Operated (AHI 1977) 30.00
Batman Batmobile, Battery Operated,
Mystery Action (AHI 1978) 30.00
Batmobile (Corgi late 1970s) 60.00
Batmobile (Corgi Junior late 1970s) 30.00
Batmobile (Duncan 1970s) 100.00
Batmachine for 3¾" "Pocket Super Heroes"
figures (Mego 1979) 100.00
Batmobile with Batman & Robin 3¾" "Pocket
Super Hero" figures (Mego 1979) ... 200.00
Batmobile "DC Super Powers"
(Kenner #99780, 1984) 85.00
"Talking Batmobile" plastic, battery
powered vocals, manual-pushed car   125.00
Batmobile with Concealed Rocket Launcher
large, no figure (Toy Biz #4416, 1989) 30.00
   with Cocoon (Toy Biz 1989) 40.00
Batman Batmobile, R/C, 8",
(Matsushiro 1989) 80.00
Batmobile "Turbine Sound" (Toy Biz
#4432, 1989) 15.00
Batmobile, 1/43 scale, die-cast
(Ertl #2575, 1989) 5.00
Batmobile, 1/64 scale, and Joker Van set
die-cast (Ertl #2497, 1989) 7.50
Batmobile, 1/64 scale, die-cast, 3¾"

(Ertl #1064, 1989) 5.00
Batmobile, Batwing and Joker Van
micro set (Ertl #2498, 1989) 5.00
Radio control Batmobile (Toy Biz
#4429, 1990) 20.00
Remote-control Batmobile (Toy Biz
#4431, 1990) 9.00
Electronic Batmobile (Toy Biz
#4435, 1990) 11.00
Batmobile 13½" with "Launching Turbo
Missile" "Dark Knight" (Kenner
#63240, 1990) 60.00
Speed Sound Batmobile (Toy Biz 1990) ... 6.00
Batman Batmobile, Battery Operated,
Taiwan (New Thunder Pioneer 1991) 40.00
Batmobile and die-cast Batman figure "Batman
Returns" Set (Ertl #2477, 1992) 3.00
Batmobile 3¾" die-cast vehicle, glossy
finish (Ertl prototype) 5.00
Batmobile with Launching Pursuit Jet "Batman:
The Animated Series" (Kenner
#64730, 1993) 20.00
Batmobile with "Missile Detonator and Quick
Lift Canopy" "Legends of Batman"
(Kenner #64025, 1994) 20.00
Batmobile "Batman: The Animated Series"
(Ertl #2446, 1993) 3.00
Camo Attack Batmobile with Batman figure
"Batman Returns II" (Kenner #63919,
1994) 25.00
Batmobile "Batman Forever" die-cast
(Kenner #28893, 1995) 5.00
Electronic Batmobile with Light-Up Chassis
and Firing Long-Range Missile "Batman
Forever" (Kenner #64158, 1995) 30.00
            BATPLANE
Batplane friction, carded with
Batman figure in cockpit (AHI 1975) . 45.00
Batman Batplane, Battery-Operated
(AHI 1977) 30.00

All prices listed are for *Near Mint* condition.   **133**

Batman Batwing, Remote-Control Battery-
Operated (Blue Box #34031, 1989) . 90.00
Batwing with Villain Cruncher
(Toy Biz #4418, 1989) 35.00
With white back package 40.00
Batjet with Blast-Off Attack Missile "Dark
Knight" (Kenner #63210, 1990) 35.00
Turbojet Batwing "3 vehicles in 1" "Dark
Knight" (Kenner #63230, 1991) 40.00
Skyblade Vehicle with Ejecting Cockpit
"Batman Returns" (Kenner
#63400, 1992) 12.50
Bat Signal Jet mini vehicle "Batman: The
Animated Series" (Kenner 1993) 8.00
Batplane "Batman: The Animated Series"
(Kenner #64740, 1993) 20.00
Bat Plane die-cast "Batman: The Animated
Series" (Ertl #2447, 1993) 3.00
Aero Bat mini vehicle "Batman: The Animated
Series" (Kenner #64031, 1994) 8.00
Triple Attack Jet "Batman: Crime Squad"
(Kenner #64662, 1995) 15.00
Batwing "Batman Forever" die-cast
(Kenner #28894, 1995) 5.00
Batwing "Batman Forever "vehicle

(Kenner #64157, 1995) 25.00
BATSKIBOAT
Batskiboat 3¾" die-cast vehicle "Batman
Returns" (Ertl #2479, 1992) 3.00
All-Terrain Batskiboat with Torpedoes and
Skis "Batman Returns" (Kenner
#63920, 1992) 20.00
BRUCE WAYNE VEHICLES
Bruce Wayne Custom Coupe and Bruce
Wayne figure "Batman Returns"
(Kenner #63550, 1992) 20.00
With blue shirted figure 30.00
Bruce Wayne's Car die-cast "Batman: The
Animated Series" (Ertl #2458, 1993) . 3.00
Bruce Wayne Street Jet with Bruce Wayne
figure "Batman: The Animated Series"
(Kenner #63551, 1994) 20.00
OTHER VEHICLES
Batman Bola Bullet "Dark Knight" (Kenner
#63340, 1990) 12.50
Batman Strikewing "Dark Knight" (Kenner
#63350, 1990) 12.50
Four-Piece Vehicle Set: Batmobile; Bat
Missile; Duckmobile; Bat Ski Boat
"Batman Returns" (Ertl #2489, 1992)

Batmobile, Battery Operated, Mystery Action (AHI 1978)

All prices listed are for *Near Mint* condition.

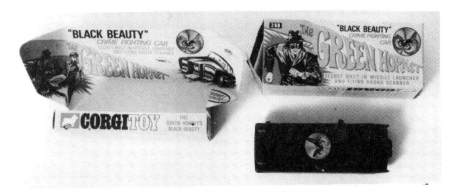

Green Hornet Black Beauty (Corgi 1960s)

and (Warner Bros. Catalog #9917) . . 12.50
Batman Sky Drop Airship with Hidden
    Compartment for Surprise Attack "Batman
    Returns" (Kenner #63680, 1992) . . . 20.00
B.A.T.V. mini vehicle "Batman: The Animated
    Series" (Kenner #63983, 1993) 8.00
Gotham City Police Helicopter "Batman:
    The Animated Series" (Ertl 1993) 3.50
Hoverbat mini vehicle "Batman: The
    Animated Series" (Kenner 1993) 8.00
Hydro Bat mini vehicle "Batman: The
    Animated Series" (Kenner #64032,
    1994) 8.00
Ice Hammer vehicle "Batman: The Animated
    Series" (Kenner #64039, 1994) 12.50
Electronic Crime Stalker "Batman: The
    Animated Series" (Kenner #64023,
    1994) 15.00
Dark Rider Batman "Legends of Batman"
    (on Stallion) (Kenner #64042, 1994) . 20.00
Batman Forever die-cast five-pack with
    Batmobile, Batwing, Batboat Two-Face
    Armored Car & Riddler Mobile (Kenner
    #28899, 1995) 15.00
Batman Forever Chasers, radio-controlled
    Batcopter and Riddler car (Tonka
    #27393, 1995) 20.00
BLAZE
Blaze's Dark Cycle, with figure "Ghost
    Rider" (Toy Biz #52437, 1995) 10.00
CADILLACS AND DINOSAURS
Jack Tenrec's Cadillac (Tyco 1994) 12.50
Jack Tenrec's Glider (Tyco 1994) 6.00
Hammer's Tribike (Tyco #13072, 1994) . . . 6.00
CAPTAIN AMERICA
Captain America's Jet Mobile (Corgi

late 1970s) 60.00
Captain Americar with Flip Out Deflector
    Shield "Official World's Greatest
    Superheroes" boxed (Mego 1970s) . 300.00
Captain America Super Heroes 4-vehicle
    set, boxed (Buddy L 1981) 40.00
Captain America Rocket Racer car Secret
    Wars remote-controlled battery-
    powered (Buddy L 1984) 40.00
Hot Wheels Captain America Racing
    Car (Mattel 1979) 15.00
Marvel Super Heroes Captain America limited
    edition van 2-pack (Corgi 1992) 40.00
Captain America Turbo Coupe for 5"
    figure (Toy Biz 1990) 25.00
CAPTAIN MARVEL
Captain Marvel White Lightning
    (Corgi late 1970s) 60.00
Captain Marvel White Lightning (Corgi
    Junior late 1970s) 30.00
DARKSEID
Darkseid Destroyer "Super Powers"
    (Kenner #67040, 1985) 25.00
DICK TRACY
Dick Tracy Police Squad Car, not distributed
    in United States (3rd Planet 1991) . . 95.00
Big Boy's Getaway Car, not distributed in
    United States (3rd Planet 1991) 95.00
DOCTOR DOOM
Doctor Doom Dragster Racer car Secret
    Wars remote controlled battery
    powered (Buddy L 1984) 40.00
Doom Chopper 16" "Secret Wars"
    (Mattel #9572, 1984) 45.00
Doom Cycle 8" "Secret Wars"
    (Mattel #7600, 1984) 15.00

All prices listed are for *Near Mint* condition.   **135**

Doom Roller Command Unit Vehicle
"Secret Wars" (Mattel #7474, 1984) . 20.00
FANTASTIC FOUR
Cosmic Modular Space Vehicle "Fantastic
Four" (Toy Biz #45320, 1995) 30.00
GARFIELD
Garfield in Volkswagen (Ertl) 4.00
Garfield in Lasagna Truck (Ertl) 4.00
Garfield on Ice Cream Cart (Ertl) 4.00
Garfield in Space Shuttle (Ertl) 4.00
Garfield on Rocking Horse (Ertl) 4.00
Odie on Doghouse (Ertl) 4.00
GHOST RIDER
Ghost Rider on motorcycle
(Fleetwood 1976) 250.00
Ghost Rider's Ghost Fire Cycle, with figure
"Ghost Rider" (Toy Biz #52436, 1995) 10.00
Green Arrowcar "Official World's Greatest
Superheroes" boxed (Mego 1970s) . 250.00
GREEN HORNET
Black Beauty 6" car (Corgi 1966) 600.00
Black Beauty 2½" slot car (Aurora 1966) . 250.00
Black Beauty H.O. scale race car
(Aurora 1966) 200.00

Black Beauty 12" battery car 600.00
HOBGOBLIN
Hobgoblin Pumkin Bomber "Spider-Man"
(Toy Biz #47457, 1995) 12.00
Hogoblin Wing Bomber "Spider-Man" (Toy
Biz #47410, 1995) 15.00
HULK
Incredible Hulk Super Heroes 4-vehicle
set, boxed (Buddy L 1981) 50.00
Hot Wheels Hulk Van (Mattel 1979) 15.00
Hulkmobile (Corgi late 1970s) 60.00
HUMAN TORCH
Hot Wheels Human Torch Racing
Car (Mattel 1979) 15.00
JOKER
Jokermobile (Corgi Junior late 1970s) ... 40.00
Jokermobile "Official World's Greatest Super-
Heroes" (Mego 1975) 225.00
Joker van, 1/43 scale, die-cast
(Ertl #2494, 1989) 5.00
Joker van, 1/64 scale, die-cast
(Ertl #1532, 1989) 3.00
Joker Cycle & Side Car (Toy Biz
#4437, 1989) 10.00

Jokermobile, Batman: The Animated Series (Kenner 1993)

Joker Van (Toy Biz #4438, 1990) 35.00
Joker Cycle "Dark Knight" (Kenner
   #63200, 1990) 15.00
Joker Mobile (Kenner 1990) 20.00
Jokermobile "Batman: The Animated Series"
   on card (Kenner #63530, 1993) 18.00

KALIBAK
Kalibak Boulder Bomber "Super Powers"
   (Kenner #67020, 1984) 20.00

LEX LUTHOR
Lex-Soar 7 "DC Super Powers" vehicle
   (Kenner 1984) 15.00

MAGNETO
Magneto Magnetron Vehicle "Uncanny X-Men"
   (Toy Biz #4961, 1991) 11.00
Reissue 10.00

MARVEL–SECRET WARS
Dark Star flying wing with Kang figure
   (Mattel #9692, 1984) 30.00
Turbo Copter (Mattel #9246, 1984) 40.00
   with Captain America figure 55.00
Turbo Cycle (Mattel #7473, 1984) 13.00
   with Figure 25.00

BUDDY L SECRET WARS VEHICLES
Buddy L (1984–85)
Four-piece set: Captain America Motorcycle,
   Wolverine Copter, Doctor Octopus Van
   and Doctor Doom Corvette (#1704J)   40.00
Constrictor Rocket Sled (#110KC) 15.00
Daredevil Jet Copter (#109KD) 15.00
Dr. Octopus Blaster Car (#108JA) 15.00
Dr. Doom Blaster Car (#108JB) 15.00
Electro Rocket Sled (#110KD) 15.00
Hobgoblin Rocket Sled (#110KA) 15.00
Iceman Jet Copter (#109KC) 15.00
Magneto Blaster Car 15.00
Spider-Man Spider Bike 10.00
Spider-Man Jet Copter (#109KA) 10.00
Wolverine Copter 15.00

PENGUIN
Penguinmobile (Corgi late 1970s) 60.00
Penguin mobile (Corgi Junior late
   1970s) 40.00
Penguin (Kenner #63640, 1992) 6.00
Penguin Commandos with Mind Control
   Gear and Firing Missile (Kenner
   #63860, 1992) 3.00
Penguin Umbrella Jet with "Spraying Knock-
   Out Gas and Umbrella Bombs" "Batman
   Returns" (Kenner #63690, 1992) 6.00
The Penguin's Duck Vehicle 2¼" die-
   cast vehicle "Batman Returns"

(Ertl #2480, 1992) 3.00
PHANTOM
Phantom Skull Copter vehicle
   (Galoob 1985) 45.00
POPEYE
Popeye Paddle Wagon, 5" metal red, yellow,
   white, blue wagon with moving
   figures of Olive, Popeye, Swee'Pea,
   Brutus and Wimpy (Corgi 1967) 150.00
Popeye Paddle Wagon on 5"x4" card; a
   "Corgi Junior Whizz Wheels Toy"
   die-cast vehicle with Olive steering,
   Swee'pea in rowboat and Popeye peering
   through telescope (Corgi 1970) 50.00
Popeye's Tugboat (Corgi 1980) 50.00
PUNISHER
Punisher Van (Toy Biz #4863, 1991) 30.00
ROBIN
Robin Jet Foil with Shooting Batarang
   "Batman Returns" on card
   (Kenner #63730, 1992) 10.00
Robin Dragster "Batman: The Animated
   Series" (Kenner #63995, 1993) 150.00
Robin Cycle with Ripcord Racing Power
   "Batman Forever" on card
   (Kenner #64156, 1995) 8.00
SMYTHE
Smythe Battle Chair "Spider-Man" (Toy
   Biz #47310, 1994) 17.00
SPAWN
Hot Wheels Spawn Mobile, promo
   (Mattel 1993) 40.00
Spawn Mobile "Spawn" (Todd Toys
   #10201, 1994) 20.00
Spawn Battle Horse "Spawn" (McFarlane
   Toys #10220, 1995) 20.00
Pilot Spawn Air Cycle "Spawn" (Todd Toys
   #10211, 1995) 25.00
   Reissue, with figure (McFarlane
   Toys #10211, 1995) 20.00
SPIDER-MAN
Amazing Spider-Car "Featuring Spidey's
   Web Trap" (Mego 1970s) 90.00
Spiderbuggy (Corgi late 1970s) 60.00
Spidervan (Corgi late 1970s) 60.00
Spiderbike (Corgi late 1970s) 60.00
Spidercopter (Corgi late 1970s) 60.00
Spidervan (Corgi Junior late 1970s) 25.00
Spiderbike (Corgi Junior late 1970s) 25.00
Spidercopter (Corgi Junior late 1970s) . . . 25.00
Spider-Man Helicopter (Empire 1970s) . . . 75.00
Spider-Car (with Spider-Man and

Hulk figures) "Pocket Super Hero"
(Mego 1979) 75.00
Spider-Car (with Spider-Man and Green Goblin
figures) "Pocket Super Hero"
(Mego 1979) 150.00
Spider-Machine "Pocket Super Hero"
(Mego 1979) 100.00
Hot Wheels Spider-Man Racing
Car (Mattel 1979) 15.00
Hot Wheels Spider-Man Web of Terror
(Mattel 1979) 75.00
Spider-Man Super Heroes 4-vehicle
set, boxed (Buddy L 1981) 50.00
Star Dart flying wing with black suited
Spider-Man figure "Secret Wars"
(Mattel #9693, 1984) 45.00
Spider-Racer car Secret Wars remote-
controlled battery-powered (Buddy L
1984) 40.00
Secret Wars 4-vehicle set: Spider-car,
Spider-cycle, Spider-copter and Spider-
van boxed set (Buddy L #1688P,
1985) 40.00
Spider-Man Electronic Spider Copter
(Buddy L #4665, 1980s) 15.00
Spider-Man Dragster (Toy Biz 1991) 20.00
Marvel Super Heroes Spider-Man limited
edition van 2-pack (Corgi 1992) 40.00
Tri-Spider Slayer "Spider-Man" (Toy
Biz #47330, 1994) 25.00

Spider-Man Wheelie Cycle, Motorized
"Spider-Man" (Toy Biz #47456, 1995) . 15.00
Spider-Man Mystery Bump and Go
motorcycle (#71400, 1995) 10.00
Spider-Man Radio Control Spider Cycle
"Spider-Man" (Toy Biz #47460, 1995) . 30.00

SUPERBOY
Superboy VOTL Cycle "Superman: Man of
Steel" (Kenner #62921, 1995) 11.00

SUPERMAN
Supermobile (Corgi late 1970s) 60.00
Supermobile (Corgi Junior late 1970s) . . . 30.00
Superman Van (Corgi Junior late 1970s) . 30.00
Daily Planet Copter (Corgi late 1970s) . . . 60.00
Metropolis Police Car (Corgi 1979) 75.00
Daily Planet Copter (Corgi Junior
late 1970s) 30.00
Metropolis Police Car (Corgi Junior
late 1970s) 30.00
Supermobile "DC Super Powers"
(Kenner 1984) 25.00

SWAMP THING
See series listing.

TARZAN
Tarzan car set (Corgi 1976) 75.00

TEENAGE MUTANT NINJA TURTLES
See series listing.

THING
Hot Wheels Thing Van (Mattel 1979) 15.00
Thing Sky Cycle "Fantastic Four"
(Toy Biz #45325, 1995) 10.00

Wolverine Mutantcycle (Toy Biz 1991)

All prices listed are for *Near Mint* condition.

X-Men van 2-pack (Corgi 1992)

THOR
Hot Wheels Thor Van (Mattel 1979) 15.00

TOM & JERRY
Tom's Go Cart (Corgi 1980) 50.00
Jerry's Banger (Corgi 1980) 50.00

TWO-FACE
Two-Face Armored Car "Batman Forever"
　die-cast (Kenner #28896, 1995) 6.00

VENGEANCE
Vengeance's Street Skeleton Cycle, with
　figure "Ghost Rider" (Toy Biz
　#52438, 1995) 10.00

VENOM
Venom Assault Racer "Spider-Man" (Toy
　Biz #47458, 1995) 12.00

VIOLATOR
Violator Monster Rig "Spawn" (Todd
　Toys #10202, 1994) 15.00
Violator Chopper "McFarlane Toys"
　(#10212, 1995) 25.00
　Reissue, with figure (McFarlane
　Toys #10212, 1995) 20.00

WILDC.A.T.S
WildC.A.T.s Bullet Bike "WildC.A.T.s"
　(Playmates #01851, 1995) 10.00

WOLVERINE
Wolverine Mutant Cycle "Uncanny X-Men"
　(Toy Biz #4962, 1991) 11.00
　Reissue 10.00

Wolverine Jeep "X-Men" (Toy Biz
　49685, 1995) 10.00
Wolverine Mystery Bump and Go
　motorcycle (#71400, 1995) 10.00

WONDER WOMAN
Wonder Woman Car (Corgi Junior
　late 1970s) 30.00
Invisible Jet "Pocket Super Hero"
　(Mego 1979) 125.00

X-MEN
Marvel Super Heroes X-Men limited edition
　van 2-pack (Corgi 1992) 40.00
X-Men Blackbird Jet "X-Men" (Toy
　Biz #49400, 1994) 25.00
X-Men Mini Blackbird Jet "X-Men"
　(Toy Biz #49690, 1995) 10.00

MICRO MACHINES

T here are three Marvel/X-Men
　Micro Machines packages, each
　containing three micro machines,
as listed below. All are vehicles, not
figures, in micro sizes. They first
appeared in the fall of 1993 and Galoob
finally produced them in quantity for
Christmas 1993.

X-Men (#65806) [X-Men Blackbird; Wolverine
　4X4 Tracker; Brotherhood of Evil Mutants
　Helecarrier] 5.00
Spider-Man #1 (#65804) [Spider-Man Hyper-
　Cycle; Spider-Man Sky Crawler; Carnage
　Road Killer] 5.00
Spider-Man #2 (#65805) [Spider-Man Turbo
　Car; Spider-Man Jet Cycle; Venom Flying
　All-Terrain Vehicle] 5.00

All prices listed are for *Near Mint* condition.　　　　**139**

COMIC STRIP TOYS

T his section covers toys based on comic strip characters and a few comic book characters who are not superheroes. Superhero toys are listed in the following section. A few additional figural items can be found in the Figures section, particularly in the Dolls, PVC and Model Kits subsections.

Comic strips preceded radio shows, comic books and television, and many of the most popular comic strips are from the early 1930s (Buck Rogers, Dick Tracy, Flash Gordon, Popeye, etc.). When the other mediums came into existence, they needed material, and so they quickly adapted comic strip characters. Radio show, and later TV show, sponsors adopted these same characters, and many of the best early comic strip collectibles are show or product premiums and give-aways.

Popularity was the major factor, but some comic strips just naturally yielded more toy possibilities than others. Buck Rogers and Flash Gordon used ray guns and flew around in spaceships while Dick Tracy had a wrist radio, a gun and a supply of detective equipment. All these props were made into popular toys many times over the years.

Of course, toy manufacturers also found that comic strip characters sold well enough as toy figures to justify the licens-

Walking Popeye (Marx 1930s)

ing fees. So instead of a walking farmer or a walking policeman, Marx marketed a walking Popeye carrying parrot cages.

Popular comic strips from the 1950s, such as Peanuts and Garfield, have a very different set of collectibles. They had no clubs to join and no props, just lovable characters. Most of the licensed toys show these lovable characters involved in everyday activities, but that has not reduced the number of possibilities; if anything, it has increased them!

It should go without saying that the original box is an essential part of any collectible. The values listed below assume the box is present.

Little Orphan Annie premiums: Decoder pin; Captain's Safety Guard Glowbird pin; Quaker Oats comic book

ARCHIES

Jughead Costume (Collegeville 1960)

Archie 5" pressed wood figure (1944)	75.00
Archie Costume (Collegeville 1960)	75.00
Jughead Costume (Collegeville 1960) . . .	65.00

McDonald's Happy Meal 1988
New Archies Figures in Cars (lim. dist.)

Archie in red car	6.00
Betty in blue car	6.00
Jughead in yellow car	6.00
Moose in pink car	5.00
Reggie in green car	5.00
Veronica in purple car	6.00

Burger King meal toys
Archies 1991 Vehicles

Archie in red car	4.00

Jughead in green car	4.00
Veronica in purple car	4.00
Betty in blue car	4.00
Set of Four	13.00

BC

BC Ice Age glasses, set of 6, Arby's premium (1981)	20.00

BEETLE BAILEY

Mort Walker's Beetle Bailey first appeared in 1950 as a daily comic strip and made it into the Sunday funnies in 1952. It's been there ever since. Unfortunately, we don't know of any collectible figures of Miss Buxley. She would be highly popular with the female action figure crowd.

Beetle Bailey telephone (1982)	85.00
Beetle Bailey 7" bobbin' head figure (1950s)	75.00
Sgt. Snorkel 7" bobbin' head figure (1950s)	75.00
Lt. Fuzz 7" bobbin' head figure (1950s) . .	75.00
Zero 7" bobbin' head figure (1950s)	75.00
Zero 11" hand puppet (Gund 1960)	35.00
Beetle Bailey Fold-A-Way Camp Swampy Playset (Multiple Products 1964) . . .	200.00
Beetle Bailey Halloween costume (1960s)	50.00
Sgt. Snorkle figure bank	40.00

BLONDIE and DAGWOOD

Alexander sirocco figure 3¾" (1930s)	65.00
Cookie sirocco figure 3¾" (1930s)	65.00

Arby's BC Ice Age Series glasses (1981)

Blondie Giant Puzzle (1966) 75.00
Blondie Jigsaw Puzzle (Jaymar 1960s) . . 50.00
Blondie and Dagwood Napkin Holder/
   ceramic 35.00
Dagwood Marionette Hazelle's 14" (1945) . 50.00
Blondie Costume (Collegeville 1960s) 80.00
Blondie lunch box (King Seeley 1969)
   Steel box 55.00
   Thermos (steel/glass) 24.00

BUCK ROGERS

Buck Rogers actually appeared first in a pulp magazine, but he became famous as a comic strip character in the early 1930s. Of course, he also appeared on the radio and in movie serials. Buck Rogers products were among the first to be mass-marketed, and there are many famous collectibles from the 1930s and 1940s.

Buck was the first of the great space heroes, and many of his accessories, such as his Rocket Gun and Space Helmet, have become part of the familiar background of all space adventures. Captain Kirk's phaser was a direct continuation of his type of weapon. The audience would have laughed out loud if he carried a mere "gun."

As a 1930s radio character, Buck had a club, the Solar Scouts, which you could join, and there were plenty of premiums for the young fan to acquire. These are all quite valuable today.

Buck was revived in the 1970s TV show starring Gil Gerard. TV show collectibles are typical of this era and include an action figure line, a utility belt, Starfighter vehicles, etc. As with most recent toy lines, look for the female figures, Wilma Deering and Ardella.

Comic Strip/Serial 1928–40s

Rocket Pistol XZ-31, 9½" (Daisy 1934) . . . 175.00
Holster, XZ-33 (Daisy 1934) 125.00
Combat Set, gun and holster, XZ-32
   (Daisy 1934) 700.00
Leather Helmet, XZ-34 (Daisy 1935) 750.00
Rocket Pistol XZ-35, 7¾" (Daisy 1935) . . . 225.00
Holster, leather, XZ-36 (Daisy 1935) 100.00
Combat Set, gun and holster, XZ-37
   (Daisy 1935) 300.00
Disintegrator pistol, XZ-38 (Daisy 1935) . . 225.00
Holster, XZ-39 (Daisy 1935) 150.00
Combat Set, gun and holster, XZ-40
   (Daisy 1935) 450.00
Cloth Helmet, XZ-42 (Daisy 1934) 425.00
Liquid Helium water pistol, XZ-44 (Daisy 1936)
   with red-and-yellow finish 400.00
   with copper finish 225.00
Daisy Equipment catalog of above
   equipment 350.00
Atomic Pistol, U-235 (Daisy 1945) 200.00
   Adventure book folder, b/w, for above 120.00
Atomic Pistol, U-238 (Daisy 1946) 225.00
   Leather holster 60.00
   Colored announcement flyer 40.00
Lite-Blaster flashlight (1936) 400.00
Pocket knife (Adolph Kastor 1934) 600.00
Pocket watch (E. Ingraham Co. 1935) . . . 100.00
Rocket roller skates (Louis Marx 1935)   3,000.00

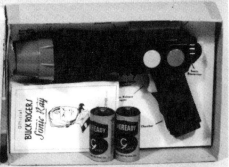

Buck Rogers Sonic Ray Gun (Norton-Honer 1952–55)

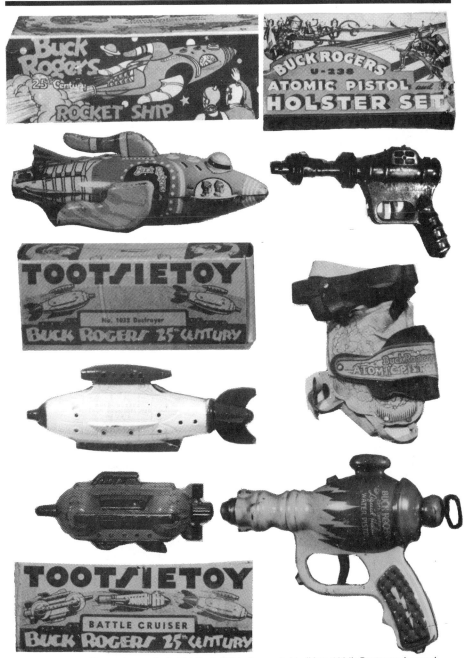

Buck Rogers ships and guns: (Left side) Rocket Ship, box and ship (Marx 1934); Destroyer, box and ship (Dowst. Mfg. 1937); Battle Cruiser, ship and box (Dowst. Mfg. 1937); (Right side) U238 Atomic Pistol and Holster Set, box, gun and holster (Daisy 1946); Liquid Helium water pistol (Daisy 1936)

Sneakers (U.S. Rubber Co. 1937) 150.00
"Sonic Ray" gun, yellow plastic, with code
    folder (Norton-Honer 1952–55) 75.00
Space Glasses (Norton-Honer 1955)   75.00
Super-Sonic Glasses (1953) 100.00

Buck Rogers Super-Scope (Norton-Honer 1952–55)

Super-Scope, 9" plastic telescope, in box
    (Norton-Honer 1955) 75.00
Super-Foto Camera (Norton-Honer 1955) . . 75.00
Walkie Talkies (Remco 1950s) 125.00
Toy Wrist Watch (GLJ Toys 1978) 20.00
Pocket watch (Huckleberry Time 1970s) . . 200.00
Pendant watch (Huckleberry Time 1970s) 250.00
Wrist watch (Huckleberry Time 1970s) . . . 140.00
Clock (Huckleberry Time 1970s) 50.00
Uniform (Sackman Bros. 1934) 2,000.00
Spaceships/Kits
Rocket Ship, 12" windup (Marx 1934) . . . 700.00
Rocket Ship motor kit 120.00
Interplanetary Space Fleet Construction
    Kits (1934):
       #1 Battle Cruiser 350.00
       #2 Martian Police Ship 350.00
       #3 Flash Blast Attack Ship 350.00
       #4 Superdreadnaught 350.00
       #5 Venus Fighting Destroyer 350.00
       #6 Pursuit Ship 350.00
       Fighting Fleet poster (backside of kit
       construction plan (17"x11") 125.00
Superdreadnaught model SD51X, 6½" balsa
    wood construction kit (1936) 600.00
Tootsietoy Rocket Ships with 2 grooved
    wheels to run on string (Dowst Mfg. 1937)
       Flash Blast Attack Ship 4½" 250.00
       Venus Duo-Destroyer 250.00
       Buck Rogers Battle Cruiser 300.00
Tootsietoy Cast figures for above 1¾" (1937)

Buck, gray 250.00
Wilma, gold 150.00
U.S.N. Los Angeles Dirigible 5" 225.00
Whistling rocket ship (Muffets 1939) 225.00
Police Patrol ship, windup (Marx 1939) . . 750.00
Puzzles and Paper Collectibles
Pop-up Buck Rogers (Random House) 10.00
Photo of Twiki, given at Detroit Autorama . . 7.00
Sticker set, 240 stickers (Panini) 25.00
Large Postcard (Quick Fox) 5.00
Big Thrill Chewing Gum Booklets, in color
    (Goudey 1934), set of 6 . . . . 400.00
    #1 *Thwarting Ancient Demons* 60.00
    #2 *A One-Man Army* 60.00
    #3 *An Aerial Derelict* 60.00
    #4 *The Fight Beneath the Sea* 60.00
    #5 *A Handful of Trouble* 60.00
    #6 *Collecting Human Specimens* 60.00
Planet Venus coloring map (1931) 200.00
Newspaper drawings, 8½"x11" of Buck
    or Wilma 200.00
Buck Rogers origin storybook,
    (Kellogg's 1933) 250.00
Solar System map (Cocomalt 1933) 750.00
Bucktoys cardboard figures (1933):
    #1 Buck Rogers 100.00
    #2 Wilma Deering 100.00
    #3 Killer Kane 100.00
    #4 Ardella 100.00
    #5 Gyrex-Bullet Space Racer 100.00
    #6 Doctor Huer 100.00
    Set 12 books 800.00
Colored face masks of Buck and Wilma
    (Einson-Freeman Co.), set 300.00
Paper plates, 2 sizes (Paper Art 1979) 6.00
Jigsaw puzzles (Milton Bradley), each 10.00
Strip cards, #425–#448, "Buck Rogers
    in the 25th-Century" (John F.
    Dille 1936), each 35.00
    Set of 24, in color 1,000.00
Dandy picture Buck Rogers, 8½"x5½"
    (1936) 175.00
Kite folder, #376 (PEP) 50.00
Bird folder, #331 (Corn Flakes) 50.00
Star Explorer chart, unmarked (1936) 75.00
Paper gun and helmet, Buck and Wilma
    versions (Einson-Freeman Co. 1933) 250.00
Photograph of Buck and Wilma in Grand
    Canyon (Cocomalt 1934) 125.00
Dixie ice cream cup lid, Matthew
    Crowley picture (1935) 60.00
Breyer's ice cream cup lid, Matthew

Crowley picture (1935) 60.00
Paperboard spaceship with suction cup
    (Morton Salt 1942) 90.00
Blotter with color scene (Chicago Herald
    American 1946) 50.00
Comic Traders series A-3 Color cards (1949)
    Buck Rogers 20.00
    Flame D'Amour 20.00
Flying saucer paper plates 75.00
Drawing of Buck, his friends and enemies
    (Yager 1950s) 50.00
Drawing of Buck, Wilma and Black Barney
    in space (Dworkins 1970s) 16.00
Greeting card (Bantam 1970s) 15.00
Buck Rogers Idea poster (S.D.
    Warren 1969) 40.00
    Paper Disintegrator noisemaker
    and postcard for above 75.00
Buck Rogers Magic Erasable Dot Pictures
    Set (Transogram 1950s) 90.00

Rocket Rangers Club
Rocket Rangers enlistment blank (1937) . . 75.00
Rocket Rangers *Flying Needle* rocket ship
    plan, red on white (1941) 60.00
Confidential Rocker Ranger bulletins 60.00
Rocket Rangers Membership cards 120.00
Rocket Rangers iron-on transfers,
    set of 3 . . . . 75.00
Rocket Rangers member oblong tab (L. J.
    Imber 1954) 90.00

Buck Rogers Solar Scouts

Buck Rogers Solar Scouts Radio Club
Solar Scouts Radio Club manual (1936) . . 200.00
Solar Scouts member badge, gold color
    (1935) 75.00
Spaceship Commander folder, with Chief
    Explorer application (1936) 100.00
Spaceship Commander banner (1936) . . . 200.00

Spaceship Commander stationery (1936) . 100.00
Spaceship Commander whistle
    badge (1936) 125.00
Wilma handkerchief (1936) 200.00
Chief Explorer badge (1936) 200.00
Chief Explorer folder (1936) 150.00

Buck Rogers Satellite Pioneers badge

Satellite Pioneers Club
Satellite Pioneers pinback, green or blue
    (Greenduck 1958) 40.00
Satellite Pioneers round tab
    (Greenduck 1958) 90.00
Satellite Pioneers membership
    card (1958) 50.00
Satellite Pioneers Cadet Commission
    with autographed postcard (1958) . . . 40.00
Satellite Pioneers Starfinder (1958) 40.00
Satellite Pioneers Secret Order #1 (1958) . 35.00
Satellite Pioneers Map of the Solar
    System (1958) 40.00
Confidential Satellite Pioneers Bulletins . . . 20.00

Buck Rogers Movie serials
Films, set of 6 (Irwin 1936) 250.00
    Movie projector for above, generic . . 125.00
Buck Rogers on Jupiter 16mm film (1936) . 40.00
Universal serial prints 16mm film,
    12 b/w chapters (Universal 1939) . . . 600.00
Lobby cards for serial (85 different),
    each 150.00
Posters for serial (1939) 1,200.00
Serial stills (original) (1939) 60.00
Serial press book, 3 versions: Universal Film-
    craft, Planet Outlaws (1939), each . . 250.00
Strange World Adventures Club pinback,
    2 colors (Philadelphia 1939) 300.00
Strange World Adventures Club
    membership card (1939) 125.00
Strat-O-Sphere Dispatch balloon with
    message (Thornecraft 1935) 135.00

All prices listed are for *Near Mint* condition.   **145**

Casting sets with midget, junior and electric
caster styles, manual and extra
3-figure mold 600.00
Eight extra molds (Rapaport Bros.
1934), each 150.00
Painted lead 2½" figures (Buck, Wilma
and Killer Kane) in cello bags
(Cocomalt 1934), set 160.00
Buck Rogers 1⅞" lead figure (1935–36) ... 75.00
25th-Century scientific laboratory,
with 3 manuals (Porter Chemical
Co. 1934) 1,500.00
Instruction envelope 125.00
Buck Rogers Chemistry set, with manual
(Grooper Co. 1937), simple set 500.00
Advanced set 700.00
Toyloons (Lee-Tex 1935) 125.00
Rubber balls (Lee-Tex 1935) 75.00
Paddle ball "Comet Socker"
(Lee-Tex 1935) 60.00
Pencil boxes (American Pencil 1934-38) . 160.00
Printing Set, boxed with cartoon sheets
(Stamperkraft 1930s) 500.00
School crayons ship box and pencils
(American Pencil 1935) 200.00

Rocket football, silver (Edward K.
Tryon 1935) 300.00
Space Ship that flies (Spotswood 1936) .. 400.00
School kit bag 120.00
Sweater emblem, 3 colors 700.00
Wilma pendant, brass color with chain ... 275.00
Repeller Ray ring (seal ring), brass
color with inset green stone 1,000.00
Britains lead figures — Buck, Wilma,
Kane, Ardella, Doctor Huer and Robot,
set of 6 .... 2,500.00
Doctor Huer's Invisible Ink Crystals
(1936) 170.00
Hearing Aid "Acousticon" Jr. (Dictograph
Products 1937), with large pinback . 475.00
Fireworks (National Fireworks Co. 1937)
Chase of Killer Kane 120.00
The Sun Gun of Saturn 70.00
The Battle of Mars 70.00
Battle Fleet of Rocket Ships 70.00
Fireless Rocket Ships 70.00
Catalog of above 125.00
Telescope (Popsicle premium) 100.00
Rubber band gun, 5"x10" punchout card
(Onward School Supplies 1940) 50.00

Buck Rogers Space Ranger Kit (Sylvania 1952)

         All prices listed are for *Near Mint* condition.

Popsicle Pete's Radio Gift News, 15"x10" . . 70.00
Punch-O-Bag, balloon with characters in
    color (Morton Salt 1942) 90.00
Ring of Saturn with red stone, glow-in-the-dark
    white plastic formed on crocodile
    base (Post Corn Toasties 1944) 300.00
    Instructions for above 75.00
Strato-kite (Aero-Kite Co. 1946) 40.00
Drawing of Pluton (Yager 1947) 50.00
Two-way Trans-Ceiver (DA Myco 1948) . . . 90.00
Space Ranger Kit, 6 punch-out sheets,
    11"x15" envelope (Sylvania 1952) . . . 60.00
Space Ranger HaloLight ring
    (Sylvania 1952) 100.00

Equipment/Guns/Costumes
Communications set (H-G Toys) 25.00
Space Communicators (Corgi) 25.00
Target set, 2 styles (Fleetwood) 30.00
Galaxy gun and holster set
    (Nichols-Kusan 1970s) 40.00
Utility belt, including play watch, decoders,
    eyeglasses, and disk-shooting
    gun (Remco 1970s) 30.00

Figures/Accessories/Vehicles
Captain Action Buck Rogers Outfit
    (Ideal 1967) 1,600.00

Glass/Mugs
Coca-Cola plastic tumblers, 16oz, each . . . 7.00
    Set, 8 tumblers 45.00
Coca-Cola plastic tumblers, 20oz, each . . . 8.00
    Set, 5 tumblers 40.00
Video game blue tumbler (Slurpee 1982) . . 7.00
Video game red tumbler (7-Eleven 1983) . . 7.00
Coca-Cola glass tumblers:
    Buck Rogers 30.00
    Wilma Deering 30.00
    Twiki 30.00
    Draco 30.00

Models/Molds/Lead Figures
Casting sets with midget, junior and
    electric caster styles, manual and
    extra 3-figure mold 600.00
Eight extra molds (Rapaport Bros. 1934),
    each 150.00
Painted lead 2½" figures (Buck, Wilma and
    Killer Kane) in cello bags
    (Cocomalt 1934), set 175.00
Buck Rogers 1⅞" lead figure (1935–36) . . . 50.00
Britain's lead figures (Buck, Wilma,
    Kane, Ardella, Doctor Huer and Robot),
    set of 6 . . . . 2,400.00
Starfighter Model Kit (Monogram 1979) . . . 20.00

Draconian Marauder Model Kit
    (Monogram 1979) 20.00
Lunch Boxes
Buck Rogers Lunch Box (Aladdin 1979)
    Steel box 45.00
    Thermos (plastic) 15.00

Buck Rogers Lunch Box (Aladdin 1979)

Watches/Clocks
Toy Wrist Watch (GLJ Toys 1978) 20.00
Pocket watch (Huckleberry Time 1970s) . . 200.00
Pendant watch (Huckleberry Time 1970s) 250.00
Wrist watch (Huckleberry Time 1970s) . . . 140.00
Clock (Huckleberry Time 1970s) 50.00
Miscellaneous
View-Master L-15 series, 3 stereo
    reels (Showtime) 15.00
Colorforms Adventure set, vinyl parts and
    scene board (1979) 20.00
Planet of Zoom video game (Sega) 15.00
Paint by Number set (Craft Master) 20.00
Pencil boxes (American Pencil 1934-38) . 160.00
School crayons ship box and pencils
    (American Pencil 1935) 200.00
25th-Century scientific laboratory, with
    3 manuals (Porter Chemical Co.
    1934) 1,500.00
    Instruction envelope 125.00
Strat-O-Sphere Dispatch balloon with
    message (Thornecraft 1935) 125.00
Buck Rogers Chemistry set, with manual
    (Grooper Co. 1937), simple set 500.00
    Advanced set 700.00
Toyloons (Lee-Tex 1935) 125.00
Rubber balls (Lee-Tex 1935) 75.00
Paddle ball "Comet Socker"
    (Lee-Tex 1935) 60.00

All prices listed are for *Near Mint* condition.   **147**

Rocket football, silver (Edward K.
Tryon 1935) 300.00
Wilma pendant, brass color with chain ... 275.00
Doctor Huer's Invisible Ink Crystals
(1936) 170.00
Hearing Aid "Acousticon" Jr. (Dictograph
Products 1937), with large pinback . 475.00
Telescope (Popsicle premium) 100.00
TV Characters, Action Figure (1979–81)
Ardella 3¾" (Mego 1979) 15.00
Buck Rogers 3¾" (Mego 1979) 30.00
Dr. Huer 3¾" (Mego 1979) 15.00
Draco 3¾" (Mego 1979) 15.00
Draconian Guard 3¾" (Mego 1979) 15.00
Killer Kane 3¾" (Mego 1979) 15.00
Tiger Man 3¾" (Mego 1979) 20.00
Twiki 3¾" (Mego 1979) 15.00
Wilma Deering 3¾" (Mego 1979) 25.00
Draconian Marauder (Mego 1979) 40.00
Landrover (Mego 1979) 40.00
Laser Scope Fighter (Mego 1979) 40.00
Star Fighter (Mego 1979) 40.00
Star Fighter Command Center (Mego 1979) 50.00
Spaceport playset (Mego 1979) 200.00
Buck Rogers 12½" (Mego 1979) 50.00
Dr. Huer 12½" (Mego 1979) 70.00
Draco 12½" (Mego 1979) 60.00
Killer Kane 12½" (Mego 1979) 60.00
Walking Twiki and Dr. Theo 7½"
(Mego 1979) 40.00
Wilma 12½" (Mego 1979) 50.00
Tiger Man 12½" (Mego 1979) 40.00
Draconian Guard 12½" (Mego 1979) 40.00
Radio-controlled Twiki, inflatable
(Daewoo 1979) 75.00
Die-cast Starfighter, 6" metal and plastic,

with Buck and Twiki (Corgi) 30.00
Galactic playset #892 (H-G Toys) 20.00
Gas-Powered Flying Starfighter (Cox) 50.00

CAPTAIN STERNN

Coffie Mug (Bernie Wrightson art) 7.95

CASPER

Casper 8" hand puppet, cloth,
plastic head 45.00
Casper Ceramic Figure Bank, holds a large
bag of money (1940s) 100.00
Casper tin windup toy (Linemar 1950s) .. 175.00
Casper Turnover Tank, tin litho, 4"
(Linemar 1950s) 250.00
Casper the Friendly Ghost musical pull toy,
5½"x9"x10¼" tall, wood with paper images
of him, on each side and music stand
in front of him, when toy moves he beats
drumsticks onto xylophone (1950s) . 300.00
Casper Figure Lamp 17" (Archlamp
Mfg. 1950) 50.00
Casper the Ghost push-button puppet 4¼"
depicting Casper rising from chimney of
house (late 1950s) 60.00
Casper's Ghost Train wooden pull toy,
20"-long (late 1950s) 70.00
Casper TV Promotional store display, 35"x26"
die-cut cardboard (Harvey 1960) ... 175.00
Casper Musical Stuffed Doll, 12" windup
musical doll (1960) 30.00
Casper Haunted House Balloon, 10x6"
display card with scary house and
Casper balloon (Van Dam 1960) ... 45.00
Casper the Ghost Cookie Jar, 13½" china
(American Bisque early 1960s) 750.00

Casper Delivery Truck (American Pre-School 1962); Casper Turnover Tank (Linemar 1950s)

All prices listed are for *Near Mint* condition.

Casper Pez dispenser (1960s) 70.00
Casper Hand Puppet, 12" (Gund 1960) . . 45.00
"I'm Casper the Talking Ghost!" 15" terrycloth
    doll, plastic head, pull-string voice box
    in box resembling Haunted House
    (Mattel 1961) 350.00
Casper Halloween Costume (Ben Cooper
    1961) 50.00
Casper Slide Tile Puzzle (Roalex 1961) . . 50.00
Casper View-Master pack (1961) 25.00
Casper Delivery Truck, wooden pull toy
    (American Pre-School–Harvey 1962) 60.00
Casper Party Set, 6 piece set incl. tablecloth
    cups, napkins, plates (Reed 1965) . . 32.00
Casper the Friendly Ghost vinyl lunch box,
    with steel/glass thermos (King
    Seeley 1966) 125.00
Casper the Ghost thermos, 6½" steel
    (King Seeley 1966) 55.00
Casper "Hi-C" Drink advertising poster,
    21x13" poster (Hi-C 1970) 30.00
Casper "Hi-C" large advertising poster,
    37x23" (Hi-C 1970) 40.00
Casper 4½" talking doll (Mattel 1971) 30.00
Casper Halloween Costume (Collegeville
    1971) 60.00
Casper the Friendly Ghost action figure
    (I. A. Sutton 1972) 40.00
Casper Night Light 6½" (Duncan 1975) . . 45.00
Casper Napkin Holders/set (Harvey
    Cartoons 1975) 20.00
Casper the Ghost miniature 1¼"
    plastic figure 5.00
Casper Stickon Figure (Tyco 1995) 6.00
Fatso Stickon Figure (Tyco 1995) 6.00
Stinkie Stickon Figure (Tyco 1995) 6.00
Stretch Stickon Figure (Tyco 1995) 6.00

Wendy the Good Little Witch

Wendy and Casper Kite (Saalfield 1960) . 25.00
Wendy the Witch hand puppet, 12" tall
    (Gund 1960) 42.00
Wendy the Witch tray puzzle (Built-Rite
    1960) 20.00
Wendy the Witch talking doll, 18" tall
    (Milton Bradley 1962) 85.00
Wendy the Witch Halloween Candy Bucket,
    bucket in the shape of Wendy's head
    (1973) 15.00

DENNIS THE MENACE
TV (1959–63)

Books and Puzzles

Dennis the Menace storybook, Hank
    Ketcham art (Random House 1960) . . 15.00
Dennis the Menace inlay jigsaw puzzle, TV
    photo (Whitman 1960) 12.00
Back-Yard Picnic setup kit. punch-out &
    cutout dolls, picnic items (Whitman
    1960) 25.00
Dennis the Menace Mischief Kit (1955) . . 35.00
Dennis the Menace squirty gun action
    figural toy, boxed 80.00
Dennis the Menace Little Golden
    Record #649 . . . . 15.00

DICK TRACY

Dick Tracy was successful for many reasons. It was the first action strip that reflected the headlines of the times. Crimes were aplenty in the 1930s so Chester Gould created a tough, no-nonsense detective who wouldn't take guff from any crook or mob leader. The

Dick Tracy Garage & Friction Car (Marx 1950s)

Top row: Dick Tracy Click Pistol, box and gun (Marx); Shoulder Holster Set (John Henry 1950s).
Middle row: Siren Squad Car (Marx 1950s); Flashlight, box and light (Bantam Lite 1950s).
Bottom row: "Premium" Junior Detective Kit (1944)

news-reading audience identified with this hero who fought the crime infestation in the city at the risk of his very life. He often suffered tortures from his enemies (being shot, gassed, etc.) but always endured to fight crime another day.

Heroes who were impatient with red tape, particularly nice guy vigilantes like Tracy, were extremely popular in the Depression years. By 1937, Dick Tracy was the syndicate's third most popular strip, topped only by The Gumps and Little Orphan Annie. In 1939, when Gould signed a new five-year contract, his strip was appearing in 160 newspapers. There was also a substantial income from comic book reprints, toys, a radio show and movie serials.

A lot of Dick Tracy's popularity was due to Gould's sinister cast of villains. They had ugly faces and unique characteristics. Since they were well crafted characters in their own right, they could be featured prominently in the strip and carry the story forward on their own. They were worthy adversaries for Tracy and thoroughly evil enough to deserve their violent deaths.

Dick Tracy's influence was eventually felt in the comic book world. As superheroes came and went, one of the few that survived was the Batman. Created in 1939 by Bob Kane, the early Batman was drawn in a very cartoony style. Whereas Dick Tracy's villains such as the Blank, Flattop, and Itchy, were evil in a caricatured albeit contemporary strip, Batman took this further. Not only were the villains grotesque but they were bizarrely costumed as well. The Joker, The Riddler and Two-Face wore outlandish outfits to emphasize their deformed appearances.

Dick Tracy also appeared in a long-running radio program, several serials and movies, as well as a 1950s TV series. One very famous "Tracy" incarnation was in Al Capp's parody of him as "Fearless Fosdick" in L'il Abner.

Never fear, Dick Tracy is here!
Dick Tracy Soaky container (Colgate-Palmolive 1963)

Tracy collectibles include the usual (and valuable) club premiums from the radio-show era and numerous other figures, guns, wrist radios and vehicles from

---

his 60+-year career. The 1990 Warren Beatty and Madonna movie produced some fine additions to the list, including the "Blank" figure which was sold only in Canada and is now worth over $150 in the United States.

Comic Strip from 1930s/Movie 1990 (Comic Strip Collectibles)

NBC Radio Script Plays
Vol 1. Dick Tracy and the Invisible Man (Gould 1939) 75.00
Vol 2. Dick Tracy and the Ghost Ship (Gould 1939) 75.00

Dick Tracy Target (Marx)

Video
Dick Tracy's Dilemma, VHS 1947 Movie .. 25.00
Dick Tracy 1939 serial, 15 chapters VHS .. 29.00
Dick Tracy rep. 1947, VHS (United American Video 1986) 7.00
Dick Tracy rep. 1946, VHS (United American Video 1990) 7.00
Dick Tracy unauthorized reproductions, various movies 15.00

Movie Posters
Dick Tracy (1937), starring Ralph Byrd ... 300.00
Dick Tracy Returns (1938) 250.00
Dick Tracy's G-Men (1939) 250.00
Dick Tracy versus Crime, Inc. (1941) 250.00
Dick Tracy, Detective (1945), rerelease of 1937 poster 200.00
Dick Tracy versus Cueball (1946), RKO picture 150.00
Dick Tracy's Dilemma (1947), RKO picture 150.00
Dick Tracy meets Gruesome, with Boris Karloff 175.00
Reprints, numbered, B&W (1990), each ... 25.00
Reprints, regular edition, Duo-Tone, each .. 20.00

Games and Puzzles
Target Game (Marx), G25 .... 50.00
Target Game (Marx), G34 .... 50.00
Rings
Dick Tracy Enameled Portrait Ring (Quaker 1937, premium) 50.00
Dick Tracy Air Detective Ring (1938) 60.00
Dick Tracy Secret Compartment Ring (1938) 75.00
Dick Tracy 4/c Metal Ring (Post Raisin Bran premium) 40.00
Cards
Tip Top Bread — Radio promotion on back, each 20.00
Dick Tracy Caramels, Johnson Candy Co. (1–120) (1930s), each 30.00
Dick Tracy Caramels (121–144), (1930s), each, reprints exist 10.00
Dick Tracy Caramels, Johnson Candy wrapper (1930s), each 20.00
Comic Booklets: Goudey Gum (1–6, 1934), each 50.00
Christmas Card with envelope (ca. 1950) .. 45.00
World War II propaganda card (ca. 1942) .. 40.00
Criss Cross Machines Card Display for 1-cent cards 125.00

Dick Tracy Crimestopper Play Set (1973)

Premiums/Giveaways
Dick Tracy Comics (Popped Wheat 1947) . 20.00
Secret Service Patrol Secret Code Book (Quaker 1938), 12p 60.00
Secret Detective Methods and Magic Tricks (Quaker 1939), 64p 60.00
Dick Tracy and Dick Tracy, Jr., Gould (Karmetz 1933), 48pp 75.00
Dick Tracy and Dick Tracy, Jr., Gould, 48pp (1933), with advertisement 60.00
Adventures of Dick Tracy (Karmetz 1933) . 75.00
Adventures of Dick Tracy (Karmetz 1933), with advertisement 60.00
Dick Tracy, Detective and Dick Tracy, Jr.

Gould (Perkins 1933) 75.00
Dick Tracy, Detective and Dick Tracy, Jr.
(1933), with advertisement 60.00
Dick Tracy Meets a New Gang, Gould,
Ice Cream (1934) 65.00
Dick Tracy's Secret Detective Methods
and Magic Tricks (1939) 60.00
Smashing the Famon Racket (Gould 1938),
Buddy Book Ice Cream 60.00
Buster Brown Shoes, 36pp (Gould 1938) . . 60.00
Buster Brown Shoes, 36pp (Gould 1939) . . 50.00
Hatful of Fun (Miller Bros./Gillmoe 1950-52) 50.00
Motorola, Harvey Comics Library (1953) . . . 45.00
Popped Wheat, Gould, Feuchtwanger
publ. (1940/47) 25.00
Family Fun Book (Tip Top Bread 1940) . . . 65.00
Family Fun Book (Tip Top Bread 1940),
Tracy on cover only 70.00
Harvey Info. Press (Esso Gasoline 1958) . . 35.00
Shoe Store Promo, 16pp (Gould 1939) . . . 70.00

Dick Tracy Oil Paint-By-Numbers (Hasbro)

Dick Tracy Sheds Light on the Mole
(Ray-o-Vac 1949) 50.00
Merry Christmas from Sears
Toyland (1939) 75.00
Super Book of Comics #1 (Pan Am and
Kelloggs 1943) 100.00
Super Book of Comics #1 (Omar
Bread 1944) 100.00
Super Book of Comics #1 (Hancock
Oil 1947) 80.00
Super Book of Comics #8 (Pan Am
and Kelloggs) 70.00
Super Book of Comics #13 (Omar
Bread 1945) 65.00
Super Book of Comics #13 (Hancock
Oil 1947) 60.00
Super Book of Comics #25 (Omar

Bread 1946) 60.00
Super Book of Comics no # (Hancock
Oil 1948) 60.00
Tastee-Freez Comics (Harvey
Comics #6 1957) 40.00
Secret Detective Scrapbook, 16 pgs. of
crime-solving tips (Amm-i-dent
Toothpaste 1950s) 45.00
Figures/Vehicles
B.O. Plenty and Sparkle Windup
Toy, 9" (Marx 1938) 200.00
Rocket Plane (1939) 125.00
Siren Plane (1938) 100.00
Copmobile, battery-powered 24" plastic
car with sirens (Ideal 1963) 200.00
Tin Squad Car, Friction power, 18" (Marx) 300.00

Dick Tracy Target Set (Larami 1969)

Squad Car with siren, 9" green plastic,
remote control (Marx) 250.00
Squad Car #1, windup/battery operated,
tin, 6½" 250.00
Hingee paper figures, set of six
(1940s) 35.00
Police Station with Authentic Siren
Car (Marx 1950s) 200.00
Garage and Friction Car (Marx 1950s) . . . 200.00
Riot Car, friction power, 7½" (ca. 1946) . . 175.00
Riot Car, friction power, 6" (ca. 1946) 150.00
Convertible Squad Car with flashing light,
friction power, 22" (Marx ca. 1948) . . 285.00
Windup Police Car (Marx 1949) 100.00
Dick Tracy plastic soap Soaky 10"

(Colgate-Palmolive 1963) 75.00
Hingers Cardboard figures, Tracy +
   7 others) (ca. 1944) 100.00
Lead figure, painted, 2¼" (ca. 1930) 75.00
Lead figure, Chief Brandon, painted, 2¼"
   (ca. 1930) 60.00
Hand Puppet 10½", fabric and vinyl (Ideal 1961)
   Dick Tracy 60.00
   Joe Jitsu 75.00
   Hemlock Holmes 75.00
Bonny Braids Stroll Toy (Charmore 1951) 125.00
Bonnie Braids Doll (Marx 1950s) 300.00
Movie Action Figures (Playmates 1990)
Dick Tracy (#5701) 5.00
Al "Big Boy" Caprice (#5705) 12.00
The Blank, not issued in United States ... 175.00
The Brow (#5703) 12.00
Flattop (#5706 .... 15.00
Influence (#5708) 12.00
Itchy (#5707) 12.00
Lips Manlis (#5713) 12.00

Mumbles (#5712) 12.00
Pruneface (#5709) 12.00
Rodent (#5714) 15.00
Sam Catchem (#5702) 12.00
Shoulders (#5704) 15.00
Steve the Tramp (#5711) (low dist.) 10.00
Vehicles
Police Squad Car, 13" 40.00
Big Boy's Getaway Car, 13" 40.00
Guns, Handcuffs and Whistles
Dick Tracy Automatic eagle design
   (Hubley) 75.00
Click Pistol, No. 36 (Marx) 75.00
G-Man windup gun 100.00
Siren Pistol (Marx late 1930s) 125.00
Siren Police Whistle, tin, No. 64 (Marx) ... 75.00
Sparkling Pop Pistol, tin, No. 96 (Marx) .. 125.00
Sub-Machine Gun, Raider (1946) 100.00
Dick Tracy Jr. Click Pistol, No. 78,
   Aluminum (Marx) 75.00
Dick Tracy's Handcuffs for Junior, John

Dick Tracy Riot Car (Marx 1940s)

Dick Tracy Crimestopper TV badge

Henry #700 (ca. 1946) 75.00
Water Pistol, plastic (1955) 35.00
Submachine Gun, 12", Tops, plastic 75.00
Kits
Crime Stoppers Set, John Henry
   (Handcuffs, Nightstick and Badge) . . 100.00
Junior Detective Kit (Certificate, Secret
   Code Dial, Wall Chart, Tape Measure,
   File Cards) (Sweets Company of
   Am. 1945) 150.00
Moviescope Viewer with two films
   (1940s) 100.00
Secret Detecto Kit (Secret Formula
   Q-11 and negatives) (1938) 125.00
Dick Tracy and Junior (Knife, Whistle,

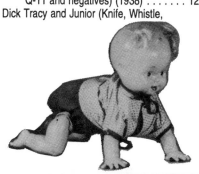

Bonny Braids Doll and box (Marx 1950s)

Clue Detector) 100.00
Detective Fingerprint Set (1933) 200.00
Deluxe Dick Tracy Set (Suspenders,
   Magnifying Glass, Badge, Whistle) . . 200.00
Suspenders and Badge on card
   (ca. 1940) 80.00
Chicago Tribune Suspender Set 75.00
Secret Detective Kit 75.00
Dick Tracy Crime Stopper Lab
   (Porter Chemical) 150.00
Black Light Magic Kit with U.V. bulb
   (Stroward 1952) 125.00
Target Playset (Dartgun, Handcuffs,
   8 Villains) (Placo 1982) 100.00

B.O. Plenty and Sparkle Wind-Up Toy (Marx 1938)

Pins/Badges/Buttons
Detective Club Badge: Crime Stoppers
   (Guild 1937) 75.00
Secret Service Patrol Member Button,
   Blue and Silver, litho, pinback,
   1¼" (1938) 35.00
Secret Service Patrol Badge—Sgt. (1938) . 85.00
Secret Service Patrol Badge—Lt. (1938) . 100.00
Secret Service Patrol Badge—Cpt. (1938) 125.00
Secret Service Patrol Badge—Inspector
   General (1938) 200.00
Secret Service Patrol Bar Pin—Leader,
   litho (1938) 25.00
Secret Service Patrol Badge — Girl's
   Division, litho (1938) 40.00

All prices listed are for *Near Mint* condition.

Dick Tracy Crime Stoppers lab (Porter Chemical)

Air Detective Badge, Winged,
   pin-back (1938) 35.00
Secret Service Patrol Badge—Member,
   Brass, star shape (1939) 25.00
Secret Service Patrol Badge—Member
   (1939) (2nd Yr. Chevron) 40.00
Detective Badge, with leather "secret"
   pouch (late 1930s) 60.00
Detective Club Pin, Yellow, tab
   Back (1942) 80.00
Detective Button, celluloid with portrait
   (Left, Right, or facing), each 40.00

Kellogg's Pep. Litho. pinback (1945) 20.00
Flattop Kellogg's Pep. Litho.
   pinback (1945) 20.00
Cleveland News Detective Badge,
   eagle design 55.00
Button with Dick Tracy and Little Orphan
   Annie, Genung promo 75.00

Miscellaneous

Dick Tracy's Electric Casting Outfit
   (Allied Mfg. 1930s) 150.00
Dick Tracy Halloween Costume
   (Ben Cooper 1967) 50.00
Detective Club Belt Buckle, with
   leather "secret" pouch (1937) 50.00
Tin Police Station (Marx 1948) 300.00
Secret Service Patrol Bracelet (1938) 50.00
Wing Bracelet (1938) 75.00
Air Detective Cap (1938) 75.00
Cereal Bowl 50.00
Secret Service Patrol Certificate 50.00
Detective Club Certificate (1945) 50.00
Secret Code Dial (1945) 35.00
Suspect Wall Chart (1945) 50.00
Tape Measure 35.00
File Cards 20.00
Moviescope (ex. Kit) 35.00
Flashlight, palm-sized metal
   (Bantam Lite 1940s) 40.00

Influence, Al "Big Boy" Caprice and Shoulders (Playmates 1990)

Dick Tracy's Electric Casting Outfit (Allied Mfg. 1930s)

Pocket Flashlight (1939) 100.00
Pocket Watch (Bradley 1959) 150.00
Private Telephones (1939) 125.00
Radio Watch (ca. 1940s) 125.00
Secret Detecto Kit "negatives" (1938) 100.00
Siren Code Pencil (1939) 100.00
Six-Shooter Wristwatch (1951) 150.00
Wristwatch, New Haven, Oblong
    face (1937) 250.00
Wristwatch, New Haven, Round
    face (1951) 150.00
Dick Tracy 2-Way Wrist Radio set,
    battery powered, plastic with powerpack
    (American Doll and Toy early 1960s) 100.00
Two Way Electronic wrist radios, 5",
    battery-powered set of two in box
    (Remco 1960s) 125.00
Pen-Lite (1940s) 75.00
Chicago Tribune Pocket Flashlight 75.00
Camera, Bakelite, (Seymour Prod. 1940) . 100.00
Pillowcase (ca. 1961) 25.00
Ceramic Plate, 9" 50.00
Green Decoder card (Post Cereals 1950s) . 50.00
Jr. Detective Secret Symbol Decoder,
    cardboard punch-out 65.00
Candy Bar Wrapper (1950s) 35.00
Play Case 200.00
    Bottle 75.00
    Thermos 75.00
Dick Tracy lunch box (Aladdin 1967)
    Steel box 350.00
    Thermos (Steel/glass) 60.00
Cartoon kit, vinyl pieces (Colorforms
    1962) 75.00
Target with Gould Art, 17" dia. (1930s) . . . 200.00

Wrist Watch — Magnetic Animated Musical
    Watch (Omni 1981) 250.00
Dick Tracy analog quartz watch
    (3rd Planet 1991) 50.00
Breathless Mahoney analog quartz watch
    (3rd Planet 1991) 50.00
Dick Tracy pop-open 2-way quartz watch
    (3rd Planet 1991) 50.00
Breathless Mahoney pop-open 2-way quartz
    watch (3rd Planet 1991) 50.00

Dick Tracy Wrist Radios (Remco 1960s)

Dick Tracy Movie Items (Applause 1990–91)
Breathless Mahoney Gift bag 6.00
Breathless Mahoney facial figural mug 15.00
Dick Tracy Cloisonné police badge 6.00
Dick Tracy facial figural mug 15.00
Dick Tracy Sticker book 4.00
Dick Tracy Pencil huggers 3.00
Dick Tracy with Kid Gift bag 6.00
Dick Tracy running Gift bag 6.00

All prices listed are for *Near Mint* condition.

Dick Tracy logo Gift bag 6.00
Dick Tracy police car Cloisonné keychain . . 4.00
Dick Tracy logo Cloisonné keychain 4.00
Dick Tracy Wheelie mug 15.00
Dick Tracy logo mug 10.00
Dick Tracy wrist radio figural handle mug . . 12.00
Dick Tracy gun figural handle mug, 2 diff. . . 15.00
Flattop Pencil huggers 2.00
Flattop facial figural mug 15.00

FLASH GORDON

Flash Gordon was created to compete with Buck Rogers. He first appeared in a comic strip in 1934 with some of the best comic art of all time. He had a fan club with many premiums and appeared in several action serials. Unlike most space heroes, Flash lived in the present, not the future. His spaceship, ray gun and heroism became necessary components of just about every subsequent science fiction series.

In many ways, Flash eclipsed Buck Rogers as the prototype space hero. For this young science fiction fan the reason was Ming the Merciless, as played to perfection by Charles Middleton in the movie serials (later made into TV episodes. (I was too young to be swayed by any differences in the sex appeal of Dale Arden versus Wilma Deering.) Anyway, you have to like a villain whose goal was to rule both Mongo and Earth (and everything else).

Cartoon/Serial 1934–1940s/TV 1953–54
Movie Figures/Figurines/Playsets
Flash Gordon, 9", with helmets, sword 75.00
Flash Gordon Large Box, set with 3
    figures, 2 ships (Tootsietoy) 50.00

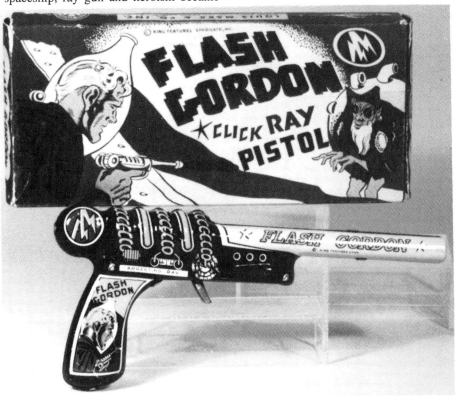

Flash Gordon Click Ray Pistol, box and gun (Marx 1950s)

Flash Gordon Water Pistol, box and gun (Marx early 1950s)

Dale Arden 9", with sword, gun (Mego 1976) 75.00
Dr. Zarkov 9", with sword, gun, helmets
    (Mego 1976). 60.00
Ming the Merciless 9", with various
    weapons (Mego 1976) 80.00
Flash Gordon playset (Mego 1977) 175.00
World of Mongo playset (Mego 1977) 150.00
Wood composition figure of Flash
    5" (1944) 250.00
Flash 4" (Mattel 1979) 20.00
Dr. Zarkov 4" (Mattel 1979) 20.00
Thun the Lion Man 4" (Mattel 1979) 20.00
Ming the Merciless 4" (Mattel 1979) 25.00
Beastman 4" (Mattel 1979) 20.00
Lizard Woman 4" (Mattel 1979) 30.00
Flash Gordon action figure (Defenders of
    the Earth) (Galoob) 18.00
Ming action figure (Defenders of the
    Earth) (Galoob) 20.00

Vehicles
Flash Gordon Starship (Tootsietoy) 20.00
Ming Starship (Tootsietoy) 20.00
Ming's Space Shuttle (Mattel 1979) 30.00
Inflatable Rocket Ship (Mattel 1979) 40.00

Weapons/Targets
Space Target 60.00
3-color Raygun (Nasta 1976) 30.00
Sparkling Raygun (Nasta 1976) 30.00
Flash Gordon Water Pistol 7½" plastic
    (Marx early 1950s) 150.00
Space Water Pistol (Nasta 1976) 30.00
MIP Soft Target set (King Features 1981) . 40.00
Click Ray Pistol (Marx 1950s) 300.00

Costumes/Clothing
Space-outfit including belt, goggles and wrist
    compass (Esquire Novelty 1951) . . . 175.00

Books and Puzzles
Three Puzzle boxed set (Milton
    Bradley 1951) 120.00
Tray puzzle (Milton Bradley 1951) 60.00
Ming punch-out (from Playboy magazine
    Jan. 1981) 3.00

Flash Gordon Space-Outfit (Esquire Novelty 1951)

Paper Collectibles
Paper plates (Unique Industries 1978) 6.00
Paper cups (Unique Industries 1978) 6.00
Table cover (Unique Industries 1978) 8.00
Loot bags 4.00
Candy box display 40.00
Candy boxes, 8 different, each 12.00
Film program (1979) 10.00
Lobby cards, each 3.00

All prices listed are for *Near Mint* condition.   **159**

King Feature Syndicate's Sparkling Rocket Fighter Ship

Buttons

Button, Flash and Ming	10.00
Flash Gordon Movie button (1980)	5.00
Ming Movie button (1980)	5.00
Vultan Movie button (1980)	5.00
Aura Movie button (1980)	5.00
Barin Movie button (1980)	5.00

Miscellaneous

Hand Puppet, rubber head (1950s)	30.00
Sun glasses (JA-RU 1981)	5.00
Wallet, with zipper (1949)	30.00
World Battle Fronts WWII map (1943)	60.00
Flash Gordon Pencil box (1951)	60.00
Space compass	50.00
Flash Gordon Kite	50.00
Gordon Bread wrappers	220.00
View-Master packet with 3 reels (1977)	15.00
Medals and insignia (Larami Corp. 1978)	6.00

GARFIELD

In 1978, when cartoonist Jim Davis's orange-and-black tabby burst onto the comic page of newspapers galore, he probably had no idea of how popular Garfield would be. The public did, though, and it certainly didn't take long before he garnered a considerable following for his lasagna-lovin' feline. Soon, Garfield was a household name like others of his kind, and his success grew to proportions as enormous as his stomach! Animated specials gave way for his own Saturday morning cartoon series, which, to this day, remains a stable of TV viewing for children nationwide. Naturally, all of this success also brought about a great deal of merchandise.

To this day, Garfield still remains a very strong license, be it coffee mugs, ornaments, PVC figures, notebooks, magnets, gift boxes, sleeping bags, Halloween costumes, bedspreads, cookie jars, drinking glasses, trading cards, lunch boxes, pencil toppers, activity toys, friction toys, games, Pez dispensers, and so on (you get the idea). The likenesses of Garfield, Odie, Nermal, Arlene and, of course, their ever-beleaguered master, Jon, appear as almost any kind of toy.

Figures/Figurines

Garfield Lying on Bed Blanket Over	25.00
Garfield Lying on Table	25.00
Garfield Lying on Top TV, Sitting	25.00

Garfield displays his sports prowess (or lack of same) (Enesco 1990s)

Garfield on Pink Chair with Coffee 25.00
Garfield Graduate Figurine (Enesco 1978) . 15.00
Garfield Easter Figurine (Enesco 1978) . . . 15.00
Garfield Six Different Figurines
   Saying on Base 60.00

Christmas

Garfield (Frosty the Snowman) ornament 3¼"
   artplas. (1990) 13.50
Garfield Christmas 1990 glazed porcelain items:
   Disk ornament 3¼" 7.50
   Miniplate with easel 4" 7.50
   Bell 4¾" 13.00
Garfield pocket watch ornament,
   1¼" artplas. 13.50
Garfield "Lighten Up" ornament, 2¾" 11.00
Garfield as Santa and Odie on seesaw ornament,
   2½" artplas. 15.00

Garfield Christmas ornaments, 2¼"–3" Artplas.
   Little Red Riding Cat. 13.50
   "Scrooge With the Spirit" 13.50
   "Ho-Ho Holiday Scrooge" 13.50
   "God Bless Us Everyone" 13.50

Miscellaneous

Garfield Swingin' in the Rain lighted
   action musical, key-wind and battery
   12" artplas. 60.00
Garfield switchplate, 6"x4" 7.95
Garfield Welcome door mat, 15"x25"
   rubberized vinyl 13.95
Garfield Halloween magnets, 1¼"–2" artplas.,
   set of 4 . . . . 12.00
Garfield Tramp Bank 7½" 25.00
Garfield Figural Music Box/Dancing 6¼"
   (Enesco 1981) 50.00

All prices listed are for *Near Mint* condition.

Garfield Figure Bank 4¾ (Enesco 1981) . . . 45.00
Garfield Chair Bank 6½" (Enesco 1981) . . . 55.00
Garfield Figural Sugar Containers 4½"
   (Enesco 1981) 80.00
Garfield Large Mug, Soup Mug
   and Snack Dish 25.00
Garfield Tree Bud Vase (Enesco 1978) . . . 20.00
Garfield Soap Dish with Toothbrush Holder
   (1978) 20.00
Garfield Among Flowers, Covered
   Jar (1978) 30.00
Garfield Sugar and Creamer Set
   (Enesco 1978) 50.00
Garfield Costume (Ben Cooper 1978) . . . 250.00
Garfield Pez Dispenser (1980s) 8.00
Garfield Watch (Armitron) 35.00
Garfield Plastic lunch pail
   and thermos 7.00
Garfield 1981 Ceramic Christmas
   Ornament 10.00
Odie Dunce Plush Figure (Dakin) 15.00
Odie Jester Plush Figure (Dakin) 15.00
Garfield Tennis Player Plush
   Figure (Dakin) 15.00
Garfield Devil Plush Figure (Dakin) 15.00
Garfield Red Riding Hood
   Plush Figure (Dakin) 15.00
Garfield Caped Avenger Plush
   Figure (Dakin) 15.00
Garfield and Arlene Salt and
   Pepper Shakers 85.00
Garfield Hawaiian Print Shirt Stuffed
   doll, Special Canadian ed. (Dakin) . . . 40.00
Garfield Gumball Machine,
   (Superior 1978) 45.00
Garfield 3-D Light Switch Plate
   (Presteigeline 1978) 14.00
Garfield McDonald's Premiums
   4 different (1988), each 4.00
Garfield Pin on Card 1.00
McDonald's Happy Meal
Garfield Glasses (1987):
Set of 4 . . . . 20.00
Poetry in Motion 5.00
Are We Having Fun Yet? 5.00
Home, James 5.00
Just Me and The Road 5.00
Mugs
Set of 4 . . . . 16.00
"I'm Easy to Get Along With
   When Things Go My Way" 4.00
"Use Your Friends Wisely" 4.00

"I'm Not One Who Rises to the
   Occasion" 4.00
"It's Not a Pretty Life but Someone
   Has To Live It" 4.00
Figures in Vehicles (1989):
Garfield on Roller Skates
   (under three) 6.00
Garfield with Pooky on Skateboard
   (under three) 6.00
Garfield with four-wheeler 5.00
Garfield with Skateboard 5.00
Garfield with Motorcycle (Odie in sidecar) . . 6.00
Garfield with Scooter 5.00

Herman windup (Linemar 1950s)

HERMAN AND KATNIP
Herman figure, windup 5"
   (Linemar 1950s) 100.00
Katnip doll, 9½" (1960s) 50.00

JOE PALOOKA
Daughter Joan Baby Doll 10" (National
   Puppetdoll 1950s) 75.00
Boxing Gloves (B&M Sports 1950s) 250.00

KATZENJAMMER KIDS
Pressed wood Sirocco figure, 3" (1940s)
   Fritz 75.00
   Hans 75.00
   The Captain (4½") 100.00

Li'l Abner and his Dogpatch Band (Unique Art 1945)

KING FEATURES

Pressed wood Sirocco figure, 5" (1944)

Tillie	150.00
Tim Tyler	100.00
Toots	150.00

LI'L ABNER

Li'l Abner and Dogpatch Band, tin litho,
windup (Unique Art 1945) 500.00
Li'l Abner and Daisy Mae Paper Dolls, Al Capp
art (Saalfield 1951) 150.00
Dog Patch Family vinyl dolls (Baby Barry 1957)
Li'l Abner 14" 200.00
Mammy Yokum 13" 150.00

Pappy Yokum 13" 150.00
Mammy Yokum figural Electric Lamp, cloth
and vinyl figure, nose light,
22" boxed (Barry Toys 1940s) 200.00
Dog Patch Li'l Abner Dish (1975) 40.00
Dog Patch Li'l Abner Tea Bag set (1975) . 40.00
Dog Patch Tray, brass trim (1972) 60.00
Li'l Abner Picto-Puzzle key chain 10.00
Daisy Mae Picto-Puzzle key chain 12.50
Ceramic Mugs (Pearce 1940s),
Li'l Abner, Daisy May,
Pappy or Mammy Yokum, each 35.00
Shmoo Bank, with display card
(Gould 1948) 60.00

Shmoo Bank (Gould 1948) and Shmoo Salt & Pepper Shakers (Japanese 1950s)

All prices listed are for *Near Mint* condition.

Li'l Abner Dogpatch Family Hand Puppets (1950s)

Shmoo Mystic Puzzle 10.00
Shmoo ceramic Salt and Pepper shakers
   4" (1950s) 35.00
Shmoo Air Deodorizer, ceramic (1940s) . . 25.00
Shmoos with Mystic Shmootomic Power,
   2 plastic Shmoos in 3"x2" box (1940s) 50.00
Li'l Abner Dog Patch Family Hand Puppets,
   3" puppet in window box (1950s),
   Mammy Yokum, Pappy Yokum,
   Wolf Gal or Moonbeam, each 25.00
Li'l Abner hand puppet, on card (Allied 1950s),
   Mammy Yokum, Pappy Yokum,
   Daisy Mae or Li'l Abner, each 40.00
Dog Patch Pappy Yokum Ashtray (USA
   Dish 1968) 40.00

LITTLE LULU

Books and Puzzles
Oh, Little Lulu! book by "Marge" 7"x8¼"
   hardcover, 60 pages with single-
   page cartoons (David McKay 1943) . . 35.00
Fun With Little Lulu book by "Marge" 7"x8¼"
   hardcover, 60 pages with single-
   page cartoons (David McKay 1944) . . 35.00
Little Lulu Plays Pirate 7½"x8¾" hardcover,
   42 pg + cartoons (McLoughlin

Little Orphan Annie Pastry set

Bros. 1946) 35.00
Paper Collectibles
Little Lulu Kleenex Store Display sign,
   9"x9" (1949) 35.00

Little Lulu, Tubby & Dog cutouts (1950s)

Little Lulu, Tubby and dog die-cut cardboard
   color figures (1950s) 25.00
Little Lulu Kleenex display sign with
   free cutout doll (1952) 30.00
Miscellaneous
Little Lulu Bank, 8" vinyl figure (Play
   Pal Plastics 1970s) 25.00
Little Lulu Clothes Line and Pin set
   (Arandell 1940s) 50.00
Little Lulu Doll Maker Kit
   (Happycraft) 50.00

LITTLE ORPHAN ANNIE

Miscellaneous
Annie Pez Dispenser (1970s) 20.00
Little Orphan Annie Head Pipe Scrimshaw
   (Edmonton Pipe Co. 1970) 40.00
Little Orphan Annie Ovaltine Cup

Little Orphan Annie Wrist Watch (New Haven Watch Co. 1930s)

(Harold Gray 1930) 60.00
Little Orphan Annie Figural Music Box
  (N. Y. News Co. 1970) 50.00
Litle Orphan Annie Soaky bottle 30.00
Little Orphan Annie Pastry set 40.00
Little Orphan Annie Knitting Outfit
  (Pressman 1930s) 75.00
Little Orphan Annie Hankie Holder
  (Famous Artists Syndicate 1930s) . . 75.00
Little Orphan Annie and Sandy Tea Set,
  complete service for 4 with cups,
  saucers, dishes, serving dish, creamer,
  and pitcher, glazed china
  (Famous Artists Syndicate 1930s) . . 200.00
Little Orphan Annie Embroidery Set
  (Pressman 1930s) 75.00
Little Orphan Annie Wrist Watch

(New Haven Watch Co. 1930s) 250.00
Little Orphan Annie Shadowettes (1938) . 150.00
Little Orphan Annie Halloween Costume with
  Famous Artist Syndicate marking, in
  colorful box (1930s) 350.00

MADMAN
Madman Glow-in-the-dark Flippy Flyer 6.00

MR. NATURAL
Mr. Natural puppet pulltoys 16.00
Mr. Natural vinyl figure, 4" high 20.00
Mr. Natural metal advertising sign 15.00
Angel Food McSpace puppet pulltoys . . . 16.00

MOON MULLINS
Tin Litho railroad handcar (Marx 1930s) . . 500.00

PEANUTS
T he Peanuts comic strip, by Charles
Schulz, was introduced in 1950 and
quickly became the most popular
strip in the world, appearing in over
2,000 newspapers and in 26 different
languages. If you don't already know
Charlie Brown, Lucy and Snoopy, you
must have been born on another planet.
There have been four feature-length films,
numerous TV specials and a Broadway
play and the Peanuts gang regularly appears in Metropolitan Life Insurance
commercials.

Tons of Peanuts merchandise are sold
every year, and we can list only a small
sampling. The large quantities available
tend to keep prices more or less reasonable.

Little Orphan Annie Knitting Outfit

Snoopy Skediddler

(Applause late 1980s)

Baby Snoopy plush toys, 3", 7"
    or 8" .... CRP
Baby Snoopy, 8", and Belle with
    pacifier plush .... CRP
Baby Snoopy musical plush toy .... CRP
Belle plush figures, 10" or 13" .... CRP
Belle with Snoopy—beach beagle 10" plush CRP
Belle (bride) 10" figure .... CRP
Snoopy (groom) 11" figure .... CRP
Snoopy (in tux) figure, 6", 11" or 18" ..... CRP
Snoopy plush figures, 5", 11", 15" or 18" .. CRP
Snoopy 6" miniplush puppet .... CRP
Pencils, Charlie Brown, Snoopy
    Woodstock or Lucy .... CRP
Chirping Woodstock 7" .... CRP
Snoopy and Belle, wheel shoes, 2 diff. ..... CRP
Snoopy (Joe Cool) 11" plush figure ...... CRP
Snoopy 10" sleeve puppet .... CRP
Snoopy hugging Woodstock, 11" plush figure CRP
Snoopy 7" bank .... CRP
Snoopy (Racing) 11" plush figure .... CRP
Snoopy (Flying Ace) 11" plush figure ..... CRP
Snoopy 13" body puppet .... CRP
Snoopy 4" plush minifigure, 6 diff. .... CRP
Woodstock 5" miniplush puppet .... CRP
Woodstock 6" bank .... CRP
Woodstock (standing) 9" plush figure ..... CRP
Woodstock 9" body puppet .... CRP

(Anri)

Snoopy and the Peanuts Gang Music Boxes,
    set of 6 (1968) 325.00
(Aviva mid 1970s)
#1776 All-American Mechanical Windup
    Wood Train Express 80.00
Snoopy Die-Cast Metal Toy Vehicles (1977)
#710 Orange Car, Charlie Brown as
    driver; Snoopy, Lucy and Woodstock . 35.00
#700 Yellow and Red Roadster, Snoopy as
    driver and Woodstock as passenger . 15.00
(Aviva late 1970s)
Balance Toys, Series #555
    Charlie Brown and Woodstock on skis 20.00
    Snoopy and Woodstock on skis 20.00
    Snoopy Biplane 20.00
Snoopy Action Toys, Series #200
    Charlie Brown playing baseball 25.00
    Snoopy playing football 20.00
    Snoopy playing hockey 20.00
Snoopy Balance Bar, Series #155
    Charlie Brown, Woodstock and Snoopy 20.00
    Snoopy, Charlie Brown and Lucy 20.00
    Snoopy Family Car, battery
    operated (1978) 50.00
    Snoopy Mechanical Windup Wood
    Train Express (1977) 70.00
Snoopy Motorized Toys, Series #966
    Charlie Brown's Mound Buggy 35.00
    Linus's Blanket Mobile 30.00

Lucy's Doctor Booth 25.00
Schroeder's Piano Mobile 35.00
Snoopy's Desk Mobile 30.00
Snoopy Push 'N' Pull Toys, Series #855
Charlie Brown's Ice Cream Van 15.00
Lucy's Car 15.00
Snoopy's Helicopter 20.00
Snoopy's Rescue Squad 15.00
Snoopy Skis windup action toys, Series #711
Charlie Brown and Woodstock 20.00
Lucy and Woodstock 20.00
Snoopy and Woodstock 25.00
Windup Snoopy "Joe Cool" Walker, 4"
    (Mid 1970s) 15.00
Woodstock Formula-1 Racing car (1978) . . 75.00
(Avon)
Charlie Brown plastic figural container
    with nontear shampoo (1960) 20.00
Lucy Shampoo Mug (1969) 15.00
Schroeder Bubble Bath (1970) 20.00
Woodstock brush and comb set (1975) . . . 15.00
(Chein late 1960s)
Peanuts Drum 80.00
Peanuts Parade Drum 100.00
Peanuts Tea Set 110.00
(Child Guidance mid to late 1970s)
Charlie Brown's All-Stars Dugout 30.00
Charlie Brown's Backyard 25.00
Snoopy's Beagle Bugle 75.00
Snoopy's Good Grief Glider 45.00

(Colorforms 1970s)
Carry On, Nurse Lucy! 20.00
Hit the Ball, Charlie Brown! 20.00
Let's Go to the Beach, Snoopy! 30.00
Hold That Line, Charlie Brown! 25.00
Yankee Doodle Snoopy 25.00
What's Cooking, Snoopy? 15.00
Happy Birthday, Snoopy!; pop-up 40.00
Snoopy, You're a Star!
    Colorforms Theater 40.00
Snoopy's Beagle Scouts, 3-Dimensional . . . 35.00
#2397 Tell Us a Riddle, Snoopy! 45.00
(Determined 1973)
Baseball Bank Series
Charlie Brown, Linus or Lucy, each 30.00
Peppermint Patty, Schroeder or Snoopy . . . 35.00
Ceramic "Snoopy, Come Home" planter/vase;
    Snoopy wears green supper dish on top
    of his head, carries suitcase in one
    hand, Woodstock sits on his nose. No box
    7½" 30.00
    4½" 20.00
Ceramic Planter; Snoopy and Woodstock
    asleep in haystack. No box (mid 1970s),
    4¼" 20.00
Ceramic Planter; Snoopy holding green flag
    with heart, Woodstocks surround him.
    No box (mid 1970s) 4¾" 20.00
Ceramic Snoopy "Happy" Banks; Snoopy is
    sitting down, wearing a red collar.
    No box, 5" (mid 1970s) 8.00

Peanuts figures and collectibles

Snoopy Lunch Box

5½" 10.00
11" 80.00
16" 95.00
(Figurescenes early 1970s)
Charlie Brown and Snoopy, "Happiness is
    Having Someone to Lean On" 15.00
Linus and Sally, "Love Is Walking
    Hand in Hand" 10.00
Lucy, "Bleah" 15.00
#354 Snoopy Doghouse Radio 55.00
(Hallmark)
Peanuts Yo-Yo, Charlie Brown (mid 1960s) 20.00
Snoopy Hummingbird Yo-Yo; Snoopy tangled
    up in string (late 1960s) 15.00
(Ideal)
Peanuts Push Puppets 1977
Lucy Nurse 25.00
Snoopy as Joe Cool 20.00
Snoopy as World War I Flying Ace 25.00
Snoopy in Formal Attire, including top hat . 25.00
Snoopy Sheriff 25.00
Peanuts Rag Dolls 1978
Charlie Brown, Linus, Lucy
    or Peppermint Patty 35.00
Snoopy 40.00
Peanuts "Show Time" finger puppets 25.00

(King Seeley)
Lunch Boxes
Peanuts (1966–67), Snoopy sitting on piano
    Steel box 55.00
    Thermos (steel/glass) 20.00
Peanuts (1967–68), red box, gang flying kite
    Vinyl box 60.00
    Thermos (steel/glass) 30.00
Peanuts (1969–70), red box, playing baseball
    Vinyl box 60.00
    Thermos (steel/glass) 30.00
Peanuts (1973–75), Charlie leaning against tree
    Steel box 45.00
    Thermos (plastic) 20.00
Peanuts (1976–79), red, Charlie pitching
    Steel box 40.00
    Thermos (plastic) 15.00
Peanuts (1980), yellow, Charlie pitching
    Steel box 30.00
    Thermos (plastic) 10.00
Snoopy's Doghouse (1969–72)
    Steel box 45.00
    Thermos 15.00
Snoopy Munchies Bag (1977)
    Vinyl bag 55.00
    Thermos (plastic) 15.00

(Lego)

Bobbers 1958

Charlie Brown 60.00
Linus 50.00
Pigpen or Schroeder, each 45.00
Snoopy or Lucy, each 55.00

(Mattel)

Skediddlers

Linus, Lucy or Snoopy, each 40.00
Charlie Brown 45.00
Snoopy and his Sopwith Camel 100.00
Plush Point Craft Kit of
  Snoopy "Rats" (1972) 20.00
Snoopy pop-up figure in 5" steel
  music box (1966) 40.00

(Monogram)

Snap Tite Kits, battery operated:

Snoopy and his Bugatti (1970) 55.00
Snoopy and his Motorcycle (1971) 50.00
Snoopy and his Sopwith Camel (1970) 60.00
Snoopy is Joe Cool (1973) 60.00

(Schmidt)

Peanuts Music Box (1980) 40.00
Peanuts Gang 5 Figural Music Boxes,
  set (1970) 100.00

(Synergistics late 1970s)

Peanuts Magic-Catch Puppets, Series SP

Charlie Brown, Lucy, Snoopy
  or Woodstock, each 15.00

(United Features)

Peanuts Gang 5 Figural Banks set (1970)   125.00
Snoopy Figural Bank 7" (1968) 40.00
Snoopy and Peanuts Gang Figurines set . . 75.00

JAPANESE PRODUCTS

"A Beagle Tale" Tape Cassette Caddy; metal
  with plastic handle (late 1980s) 15.00
Ceramic Bank; Snoopy dressed in Japanese
  attire (late 1980s) 5" 25.00
  6" 35.00
Ceramic Teapot with bamboo handle
  (mid 1980s) 40.00
#J-861 Snoopy 154-piece puzzle, assembled
  size 37.5x26cm (late 1980s) 10.00
Wooden Snoopy figural bank from France
  (Villac 1990) 50.00
Ceramic plate from England; Snoopy lying
  on top of the roof of his house; "I
  Love My Home," 7" diameter (Carriaga-
  line Pottery late 1960s) 40.00
8" Glass Lamp from Hong Kong; shade
  and lamp are one piece 40.00
Bobbing Head 5½" Figures 1960s

Charlie Brown, Snoopy or Lucy 50.00
Vinyl Character Figures
Set, 7 figures, 9" (1958) 400.00
Each figure 50.00

Peanuts wall clock

Christmas

Peanuts Gang Baseball ornaments 2" porcelain
  bisque, set of 6 . . . .   45.00
  Charlie Brown, Snoopy, Linus
  Peppermint Patty or Schroeder 8.00
Peanuts Christmas pageant ornaments, porcelain
  Snoopy 1¾" 10.00
  Charlie Brown 2¼" 10.00
Peanuts Christmas pageant 1"–2½" figurines,
  Set of 7 . . . .   60.00
Snoopy, Linus, Lucy, Charlie Brown,
  Baby Jesus, Sally or Schroeder, each   9.00
  With musical crèche, key windup,
  wood 30.00
Snoopy musical snow globe, Christmas tree
  inside, 5½" 27.50
Snoopy Santa musical, windup, 5¼" 50.00
Snoopy Christmas figural bell, 5" 17.50
Snoopy Christmas Musical, windup, 7¾" .   35.00
Snoopy figurine ornament, 3¼" ceramic . .   12.50
Snoopy Christmas collectors 2¾" dia.
  disc ornament 11.00
Snoopy Christmas collectors 7½" dia.
  plate ornament 22.50
1990 annual Snoopy Christmas snowfall musical,
  windup, 5½" 40.00
Snoopy/Lucy 2" porcelain sports ornaments,
  set of 6 . . . .   49.50
  Lucy Football, Snoopy Hockey, Snoopy
  Basketball, Snoopy Tennis, Snoopy Golf,
  or Snoopy Soccer, each 8.50

All prices listed are for *Near Mint* condition.

Peanuts table-top appointments, ceramic:
Linus creamer, 5" 12.50
Snoopy Sugar Bowl 4½" 12.50
Charlie and Lucy (sitting on sofa), salt
and pepper, 5", pair 30.00
Snoopy "Baby's First Christmas" ornament
3" porcelain 10.00

40th Anniversary Items

Peanuts characters cake musical 100.00
Snoopy Musical snowfall, key
windup, 5½" 40.00
Peanuts 40th Anniv. figurines 2" PVC,
set of 6 . . . . 19.00
Linus, Lucy, Snoopy, Charlie Brown,
Woodstock and Snoopy M.C., each . . 3.50
Snoopy 40th Anniv. figurines, 1½"–2" PVC,
set of 4 (Applause) 14.50
Peanuts 40th Anniv. Musical, key windup,
Charlie Brown, Snoopy and Woodstock,
on sofa, 4½" 50.00
Peanuts 40th Anniv. bell, Snoopy handle,
5" ceramic 17.50
Peanuts 40th Anniv. plate, 7½" porcelain . 22.50
Peanuts 40th Anniv. disk ornament, 2¾"
porcelain 10.00
Peanuts 40th Anniv. minifigurines, 2"–2¾"
glazed porcelain, all in party hats,
Set of 8 . . . . 69.50
Snoopy, Charlie Brown, Sally, Peppermint
Patty, Schroeder, Lucy, Marcie or Linus . . . 9.00
Snoopy 40th Anniv. 2¼" figurines, PVC,
set of 12 . . . . 36.00

Miscellaneous

Snoopy musical figurines, key windup, porcelain:
Snoopy decorated doghouse 7" 30.00
Snoopy sledding, 6" 30.00
Charlie Brown "Go Fly A Kite" musical figurine,
windup glazed ceramic 7"h, 5"dia. . . 50.00

Snoopy Joe Surfer figurine musical, windup
7½" porcelain 45.00
Peanuts Gang Happiness Ride Musical, windup,
9"long, porcelain 70.00
Lucy with football musical figurine, "Trust Me,"
7" ceramic, key windup 45.00
Snoopy and Woodstock on surfboard musical
figurine, "Super Snoopy" 7" ceramic,
key windup 50.00
Snoopy and Woodstock musical, glazed ceramic,
key windup, 5½" "Holiday Hug" 30.00
Snoopy and Woodstock musical, glazed
ceramic, key windup, 5½" "Trimming
the Tree" 30.00
Snoopy musical, glazed ceramic, key windup,
5½" "Snoopy Plays Snowman" 30.00

McDonald's Happy Meal 1983

Peanuts Camp Snoopy Glasses: Set of 5 . 16.00
Charlie Brown, Snoopy #1, Snoopy #2,
Lucy, or Linus, each 4.00
Charlie Brown Glass Promoting Series:
"Good Grief! McDonald's 'Camp
Snoopy' Glasses Are Coming" 85.00
Happy Meal 1989, Figures pushing carts:
Snoopy/Woodstock, Charlie Brown,
Lucy, or Linus/Cat, each 5.00
Snoopy or Charlie Brown (under 3) . . 5.50

POPEYE

"**W**ell Blow Me Down!" Popeye the Sailorman entered the hearts of America in 1929 and is still swabbing the decks of cartoon history after more than sixty years.

The feisty one-eyed spinach eater evolved from Elzie Segar's 1919 strip entitled "Thimble Theatre" which focused

Brutus Chase Car (1950s)

　　　　All prices listed are for *Near Mint* condition.

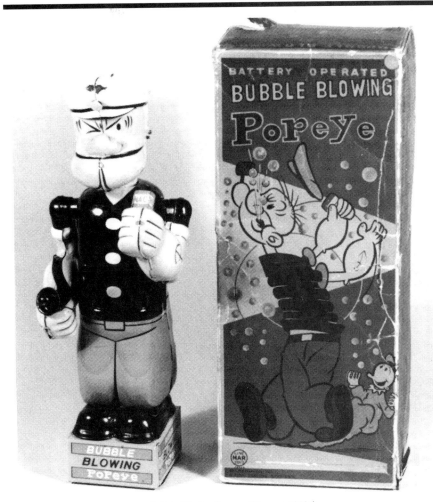

Bubble Blowing Popeye (Linemar 1950s)

on the adventures of the Oyl family: Castor Oyl, his sister Olive, and Olive's then boyfriend, Ham Gravy. In one of Segar's early episodes, Castor roamed the docks in search of a sailor who could transport his family to Dice Island, an offshore resort for gambling. He came upon a peppery, fat forearmed sailor and asked him, "Hey there, are you a sailor?"

"Ja think I'm a cowboy?" replied the scowling old salt, and with this famous one-liner, Popeye the Sailorman was born.

Intended as a temporary addition to the cast (he was only slated for this one adventure), Popeye was dropped from the strip on that fateful day, January 17, 1929. Segar, however, was flanked with letters from fans who immediately fell in love with this wisecracking hired hand and demanded he be added to the "Thimble Theatre" cast. And so, Ham Gravy was cast overboard and Popeye the Sailorman took over at the helm.

He's been there ever since. Segar died in 1938, and during the next twenty years Popeye declined somewhat until Bud Sagendorf took over the illustration, followed by George Wildman in 1969.

There are a lot of Popeye collectibles from the past 65+ years, but they do not follow the typical pattern of a 1930s hero because Popeye did not have the typical radio show/TV show incarnations with a fan club.

Comic Strip from 1929–/
TV Cartoon 1960–61; 1978–83/Movie
Barnacle Bill

Figures

Barnacle Bill Tin Windup Toy Bill
   resembles Popeye (Chein 1930s) .. 300.00
Barnacle Bill in A Barrel Tin Windup
   Toy, 7" high (Chein 1932) 400.00

Brutus

Figures/Vehicles

Brutus "Fun On Wheels" (Empire 1950s) .. 25.00
Brutus Chase Car Scene, 15"-long wooden
   Brutus push toy with Brutus behind wheel
   of racing car and Olive screaming in
   backseat; scarce (1950s) 200.00
Brutus Jump-Up Toy (Imperial Toy
   Co. 1979) 5.00
Brutus Steamroller vehicle (Matchbox 1980) 10.00
Brutus Pewter Figure, 3" tall
   (Spoontiques 1980) 20.00
Frosted Crystal Figurine (Italy 1980s) 35.00
Brutus Ceramic Figure, Brutus holds two
   bombs (Presents 1989) 3.00

Glass/Mugs

Brutus Coca-Cola Glass (Coca-Cola
   Co. 1975) 5.00
Brutus Drinking Glass (Popeye's Chicken)
   1978–79 .... 25.00
   1982 .... 8.00
Brutus Ceramic Mug (Presents 1990) 17.00
Brutus Ceramic Mug (Vandor 1990) 15.00

Miscellaneous

Brutus Marionette, about 12" long
   (late 1950s) 60.00
Brutus Soaky, soap container depicting
   Brutus in striped shirt and Captain's
   hat (Colgate Pamolive 1960s) 20.00
Brutus "Popeye and Pal Bookmark" (Durham
   Industries 1980) 5.00
Brutus Ceramic Ornament (1987) 10.00

Brutus TV-style Magnet 5.00
Brutus (Bluto) Comic strip–style Magnet ... 5.00

Jeep

Figures/Vehicles

Jeep Wood Jointed figure, 4½" (1930s) .. 100.00
Jeep Wood/Composition Jointed figure,
   8" tall (1930s) 150.00
Jeep Wood/Composition Jointed figure,
   12" tall (1930s) 400.00
Jeep Pewter figure (Spoontiques 1980) ... 20.00

*Olive Oyl Halloween Costume
(Collegeville 1950s)*

Olive Oyl

Figures

Olive Oyl Figural Toy 8" (King
   Features 1940) 75.00
Olive Oyl 8" figure (Dakin 1974) 50.00
Olive Oyl 7" figure, "TV Cartoon
   Theater" (Dakin 1976) 50.00
Olive Ramp Walking Figure from the "Thimble
   Theatre Figures" series, 5" tall; hollow
   figure; black/red and creme coloring
   (1929) 100.00
Olive Lead Figure (1940s) 30.00
Olive Oyl Rubber Squeeze Toy, 8" tall;
   Olive is in running position
   (Rempel 1950s) 80.00
Olive Oyl Squeeze Toy, 8" tall; Olive
   holds flower (Bayshore 1950s) 75.00
Olive Plastic Figure (Marx 1950s) 25.00
Friction "Olive Oyl Ballet Dancer," 5½" tall;
   Olive dances on her toes; her nose is
   made of rubber (Linemar 1950s) ... 400.00
Olive The Sportscar Driver, 1.5" long; Olive

---

in plastic Astin Martin convertible
(Empire 1950s) 20.00
Olive "Fun On Wheels," 1"x1.5" tall; Olive
on four-wheeler holding Swee'Pea on her
lap (Empire 1950s) 20.00
Olive Movable Figure (Kohner
Bros. 1960s) 15.00
Olive Bike Bobber (1960s) 18.00
Olive Oyl Rubber Figure (Ben
Cooper 1974) 20.00
Olive Pewter Figure (Spoontiques 1980) .. 20.00

Olive Oyl Ballet Dancer (Linemar 1950s)

Olive Oyl Little Figure (Iti Hawaii
Inc. 1980s) 5.00
Olive Frosted Crystal Figure
(Italy 1980s) 35.00
Vehicles/Playsets
Olive Oyl Friction Convertible, yellow tin
MG car with Olive behind the wheel with
flowing black hair (Linemar 1950s) .. 600.00
Olive Oyl TV Cartoon Theater (1976) 40.00
Olive Oyl Car, Olive in sportscar
(Matchbox 1980) 10.00
Glass/Mugs
Olive Ceramic Container/Mug (Presents
1990) 17.00
Olive Oyl Drinking Mug (Deka 1971) 5.00
Olive Oyl Drinking Glass (Popeye's
Chicken 1978) 25.00
Olive Oyl Drinking Glass (Popeye's
Chicken 1979) 25.00
Olive figural head ceramic mug
(Vandor 1980) 20.00
Olive Oyl Drinking Glass (Popeye's

Chicken 1982) 8.00
Miscellaneous
Olive Oyl TV-style Magnet 5.00
Olive Oyl Comic strip–style Magnet 5.00
Olive Oyl Pez Dispenser (1960s) 125.00
Olive Oyl Hand puppet (Gund 1938) 20.00
Olive Oyl String and Wood Puppet,
5" tall (Jaymar 1940s) 55.00
Olive Oyl Hand puppet, plastic head
with King Features TV, cloth body
(Gund 1960s) 30.00
Olive Oyl Halloween Costume, 9"x11"
box (Collegeville 1950s) 55.00
Olive "Popeye and Pal Bookmark" (Durham
Industries 1980) 5.00
Olive Musical Jewelry Box, Olive as a
dancer (1980) 25.00
Olive Phone Rest (Comvu
Corporation 1980s) 8.00
Olive Hand puppet (Presents 1985) 10.00
Olive Oyl Pen (N.J. Croce 1985) 5.00
Olive Ceramic Christmas Ornament
(Presents 1987) 10.00
Popeye
Figures/Mechanical Toys
Popeye spinach pop-up toy, 4½" steel
spinach can with plastic popeye
(Mattel 1957) 90.00
Popeye 8" figure with spinach can (Dakin 1974)
Can in left hand 60.00
Can in right hand 60.00
Popeye 7" figure, "TV Cartoon Theater"
(Dakin 1976) 50.00
Popeye Figural Toy 9½" 50.00
Popeye Figural Toy 4¼" (Kohner) 25.00
Popeye Figure 8" (Duncan Mold 1970) 35.00
Popeye and Friends Figurines (1980) 80.00
Popeye and Swee'pea Wooden Pull Toy,
7½"x10" tall; wood wheels with red
base and Popeye hitting drum while
Swee'pea is on his lap (Fisher
Price 1929) 150.00
Popeye Ramp Walking Figure from
"Thimble Theatre Figure" collection,
6" tall, hollow figure (1929) 200.00
Popeye Celluloid Figure, 5½" tall (1929) .. 160.00
Popeye on Tricycle (Line Mar no date) . 1,200.00
Popeye "Shadow Boxer" Tin and Celluloid
Toy, 7" tall; wears orange boxing
gloves with black trim; has movable
head (Chein 1930) 900.00
Popeye Jigger On Rooftop, 7" tall;

Popeye dances atop 5"x3"x2" tall
illus. roof (Marx 1930s) 750.00
Popeye Wood Jointed Figure, 5½" tall
(1930s) 65.00
Mechanical Popeye Floor Puncher,
4"x2" base with 7" tall figure of
Popeye standing atop green base
wearing boxing gloves and standing

Popeye & Olive Slinky Handcar
(Linemar 1950s)

before punching bag (Chein 1930s) 2,000.00
Popeye Toy Walking Figure (Chein 1932)
MIB 500.00
Popeye Figure, 11" tall; wood and
composition (Chein 1932) 900.00
Popeye Joint Composition figure, 10"
tall (Chein 1932) 400.00
Mechanical "Walking Popeye" Tin Windup,
7¾" tall, depicts Popeye carrying
parrots in cages (Marx 1935) 250.00
Popeye In Rowboat Toy (Hoge 1935)   11,000.00
Popeye Express Windup Toy a/k/a "Popeye
and Baggage," 8½"x8½" box; Popeye is
pushing box with parrot on top and
"Popeye Express" written along side
(Marx 1935) 650.00
Large Popeye Composition Figure With Felt
Collar, wooden figure with compo.
head; has unusual orange sailor's
collar with yellow trim (1935) 750.00
Mechanical "Popeye and Olive Oyl Jiggers,"
4"x3"x2" tall base; tin litho toy depicting
Popeye dancing as Olive plays an

accordian (Marx 1936) 1,400.00
Popeye Miniature Lead Figure (1940s) 20.00
Musical Popeye the Sailorman, 16" tall;
wooden, cloth and vinyl Popeye at
ship's wheel; turns head and plays "I'm
Popeye The Sailorman" (Woolnough) 175.00
Popeye Stuffed Figure with Rubber Arms and
Head, 20" tall (Gund 1958) 22.00
"Popeye and Olive Oyl Playing Ball," 18"-
long base with 1½" width; Popeye and
Olive stand at opposite ends of base;
each fig. is 4½" tall and when both are
wound, the red/yellow ball in center
swings from Popeye to Olive (Linemar
1950s) 1,200.00
Wooden Popeye, 4" tall; Popeye with very
round head that bobs on a spring;
wears blue/black hat, blue pants, and
black shirt with yellow buttons and red
collar (Linemar 1950s) 600.00
Smoking Popeye, 9" tall; Popeye sits atop a
spinach can waving his right arm while
holding a pipe with light-up bulb in
other hand; has "smoking action"
(Linemar 1950s) 1,500.00
Bubble Blowing Popeye, battery powered
(Linemar 1950s) 1,000.00
Mechanical Popeye, 5" tall; tin litho Popeye
with white/yellow tin pipe that moves,
body rocks and head nods (Linemar
1950s) 1,000.00
Popeye "Fun On Wheels," 1"x1.5" tall; plastic
toy featuring Popeye on four wheeler
with telescope (Empire 1950s) 20.00
Popeye The Sportscar Driver, 2.1" long;
Popeye drives a green race car with
gray wheels (Empire 1950s) 20.00
Mechanical Popeye Basketball Player,
features Popeye standing below basket
with ball in hands; backboard depicts
Olive and Wimpy (Linemar 1950s) 1,600.00
Popeye Movable Figure (Kohner Brothers
1960s) 20.00
Popeye Rubber Figure (Combex 1960s) ... 20.00
Popeye Bike Bobber (1960s) 20.00
Popeye and Wimpy Walk-A-Way Toy, 5" tall;
plastic toy of Popeye and Wimpy with
nodding heads and when string pulled
it causes "walking action" (Marx 1964) 35.00
Popeye Rubber Doll, 12" tall
(Lakeside 1968) 20.00
Popeye rubber figure (Ben Cooper 1974) .. 20.00

Popeye Soda Ad Sign (1929)

Popeye Little Figure (Iti Hawaii
Inc. 1980s) 5.00
Mechanical Popeye Celluloid Walker, 8½"
tall; in black captain's uniform; moves
with vibrating motion and his head
goes in and out of neck at different
angles; backside marked "foreign"
(Japan 1929) 900.00
Mechanical "Popeye Flyer," 9.5" diam. base
marked "Popeye Express"; two 4"-long
planes attached to 8"-tall "Popeye
Flyer" tower; planes circle the tower in
up and down motions (Marx 1930s) . 700.00
Popeye "Eccentric Airplane," 6¼"x8"; "Popeye
The Pilot" airplane performs crazy stunts
and twirls (Marx 1940) 900.00
Popeye Ramp Walker, 5½" tall; red/blue/
fleshtone plastic walker that waddles
forward (Irwin 1949) 45.00
Popeye and Olive Slinky Handcar, 6½" tall;
red tin base with figures on slinky coil
springs; figures move in seesaw action
(Linemar 1950s) 1,500.00
Friction Popeye Convertible, red tin MG
car with Popeye behind wheel
(Linemar 1950s) 750.00
Popeye Plastic Walkie, Popeye pushes
wheelbarrow (Marx 1950s) 10.00
Popeye Tricky Walker (Jaymar Inc.
mid 1960s) 20.00

Popeye's Paddle Wagon 5" (Corgi 1967) . 150.00
Popeye's Paddle Wagon (Corgi 1969) . . . 50.00
Popeye Patch, Popeye in his sailor's uniform
from the King Features TV cartoon series
(1970s) 7.00
Popeye Santa Ornament Figure (Presents
1987) 10.00
Books/Puzzles
Popeye complete activity book #2831
(Lowe 1960) 35.00
Popeye (and Krazy Kat) 2-1 activity book
#3097 (Lowe 1963) 30.00
Popeye The Juggler Bead Game, 3½"x5"
box (1929) 30.00
Popeye Bingo Game, 5"x3½" metal bingo
sheet; depicts Popeye punching Oxheart
(Bar Zim 1929) 30.00
Popeye Intelligence Test-Dexterity Game,
5"x4" metal frame with glass cover;
game has die-cut figures of Popeye, Olive,
and Wimpy which can be shaken in order
to put in proper slots (no date) 30.00
Popeye Ring Toss Game, 16"x12" box; full
color cardboard figures of Olive/Popeye in
base with rings for tossing (Rosebud Art
1933) 75.00
Popeye Shipwreck Game (Einsen-Freeman
1933) 40.00
Popeye Playing Card Game
(Whitman 1934) 40.00
Popeye Cartoon Book, 13"x8" book; cover
depicts Popeye fighting Oxheart; 36 color
pages of Segar illustrations
(Saalfield 1934) 45.00
Popeye Pipe Toss Game (Rosebud Art
Co. 1935) 35.00
Popeye Roly Poly Target Game, 6"-long
plastic cork gun with ammo, five 4"-tall
character targets which when hit "rock
and roll" (Knickerbocker 1958) 40.00
Popeye Plastic Puzzle, slide tile puzzle
(Roalex Co. 1950s until 1970s) 20.00
Popeye Card Game (Ed-U-Cards 1960s) . . 20.00
Popeye Cards (Primrose Sweets,
early 1960s), complete set 30.00
Popeye Ring Toss (Happy-Mates 1980) . . . 3.00
Paper and Utensil-Related Collectibles
Popeye Magic Slate (Lowe 1963) 20.00
Popeye trading cards (Ad-Trix 1950s), each 2.50
Set: 66 Cards 175.00
Popeye Pencil Sharpener, 3"x3"; metal desk
sharpener with crank handle; front/back with

Popeye Pirate Pistol (Marx 1935); Popeye Modeling Clay (1936);
Popeye TV Eras-O-Board (Hassenfeld 1950s); and Popeye Friction Car (Linemar 1950s)

color illus. of Popeye with balloon captions
(Irwin 1929) 60.00
Popeye's 12 Pieces Colored Chalk, 2½"x7"
tall box containing 12 pcs. of colored
chalk (American Crayon 1929) 15.00
Popeye School Writing Tablet, 7"x9" tablet;
illus. of Popeye on front and multiplication
tables on back (1929) 20.00
Popeye Soda Advertising Sign, 11"x12" sign
in yellow/black/red/white/blue depicting
Popeye holding a bottle of Popeye soda;
logo reads "I yam what I yam and I yam
tops" (1929) 85.00
Popeye Embossed Napkins, 7"x7"; thirty
napkins with illus. in red/blue (Tuttle
Press 1930s) 45.00

Popeye Paints, American Crayon Co. 1933) 20.00
Popeye Pencil Case, 9"x5"x1"; illus.
in blue, silver and brown on every side
(Eagle 1933) 35.00
Popeye Pencil Case With Popeye Ruler,
10½"x6"x1" case and 10" ruler;
green cardboard with illus. in black
and red (Eagle 1933) 40.00
Popeye Pencil Case, 8"x4"x1" tall; green,
silver and brown cardboard case
(Eagle 1933) 30.00
Popeye White Chalk, 4"x7" box (American
Crayon Co. 1936) 30.00
Popeye Paint and Crayon Set, 15½"x9½"
box (Whitman 1938) 55.00
Popeye Hingee Paper Figures, No. 102 (Reed

Mechanical Juggling Popeye and Oliveoyl (Linemar)

& Associates 1940s), each cutout ... 6.00
Popeye "Pop-Ons", 8"x11" card contains full
   sheet of 12 circular decals to be placed
   "on your muscles like Popeye" (Weldon
   1940s–50s) 40.00

Popeye TV Eras-O-Board Set, 19"x9"x1" cover,
   color plastic coated pictures with wipe-
   off crayons (Hassenfeld 1950s) 40.00
Popeye Numbered Pencil Coloring Set,
   13"x10"x1" box (Hasbro 1950s) 25.00

Popeye Cartoon Kit, 17"x13"x1" cover
(Colorforms 1957) 40.00
Popeye Numbered Pencil and Coloring Set
(Hassenfeld Bros. 1957) 45.00
Popeye the Weatherman
(Colorforms 1959) 320.00
Popeye Paint and Crayon Set
(Hasbro 1960s) 20.00
Popeye Sticker Fun-Pre-School Activity
(Lowe 1960s) 20.00
Popeye Peg Pals (Colorforms 1960s) 35.00
Popeye Magic Slate (Lowe 1960) 20.00
Popeye Presto Paints (Kenner 1961) 25.00
Popeye Vending Machine Sticker (also on
sticker is "The Little King" and
"Felix the Cat") 18.00
Popeye Wrap-A-Round Playmates (Payton
Products 1961) 20.00
Popeye Birthday Party Colorforms
(Colorforms 1960s) 30.00
Popeye Sun Cards, labeled "Sun-eze"
(Tillman's 1962) 12.00
Popeye Paints—14 Brilliant Colors
(American Crayon Co. 1965) 25.00
Popeye's TV Cartoon Kit
(Colorforms 1966) 25.00
Popeye Sparkle Paints (Kenner 1966) 20.00
Popeye Paint and Crayon Set (Hasbro
1970s) 15.00
Popeye Cartoon Set (Colorforms 1970s) .. 25.00

Popeye and Pal Bookmarks. (Durham
Industries 1980) 5.00
Popeye Stickers (Fasson 1981) .... .69
Popeye Pencil Top Erasers (Diener
Industries 1981) 4.00
Popeye Puffy Sticker Set (Diamond
Toymakers 1983) 3.00
Popeye Valentine Day Cards (1983),
Boxed Set 3.00
Popeye Pen (N.J. Croce Co. 1985) 2.00
"Popeye and Son" Wood Slate
(Ja-Ru 1987) 3.00
Music Boxes/Banks/Puppets
Popeye Figural Puppet 4" (Kohner 1960) .. 20.00
Popeye in the Music Box, metal, crank
wound with plastic pop-up Popeye
in spinach can (Mattel 1957) 120.00
Popeye 4 Music Boxes (King
Features 1979) 120.00
Popeye and Olive Oly Figural Music
Box 8¼" (Schmid) 100.00
Popeye Dime Register Bank, 2½"x
2½" (1929) 75.00
Popeye String Puppet, 5" tall
(Jaymar 1940s) 50.00
Popeye Daily Quarter Bank,
4"x4"x5" tall (Kalon 1950s) 150.00
Popeye and Olive Oyl Push Button Puppets,
4" tall plastic figures; both figures
have buttons underneath bases that

Popeye Shadow Boxer, Popeye "In the Barrel" and Popeye Floor Puncher (Chein 1930s)

when pushed, cause them to perform
crazy maneuvers (Kohner 1956), each   18.00
Popeye Daily Dime Register Bank, 2"
    square tin Bank (Kalon 1956) 50.00
Popeye Puppetforms (1960s) 35.00
Popeye Hand puppet (Gund 1960s)
    Puppet has device in cloth body
    which squeaks 25.00
    Popeye head on cloth body
    decorated with ships 30.00
    Plastic head on a Popeye comic
    strip costume body 20.00
Popeye Talking Hand puppet (Mattel 1968)   40.00
Popeye Head Bank (Play-Pal
    Plastics 1972) 25.00
Popeye Plastic Bank (Renz Corp. 1976) ... 10.00
Popeye Music Box, when drawer is opened
    "I'm Popeye the Sailor Man" music
    plays (1980) 25.00
Popeye Money Bank (BBI Toys
    International 1986) 5.00
Popeye Money Bank Figure (Spardose-
    Tirelire 1988) 5.00
Popeye Brand Yellow Popcorn Bank, 6½"
    tall can with coin slot on top
    (Purity Mills 1949) 50.00
Kitchen and Bathroom Collectibles
Popeye Cookie Jar/head (Vandor 1979) ... 30.00
Popeye Figural Spoon Rest 6¾"
    (Vandor 1980) 35.00
Popeye Figural Toothbrush Holder 5"
    (Vandor) 15.00
Popeye 50th Birthday Plate 8½" (1979) ... 35.00
Popeye and Friends 4 Ceramic Mugs 3½"
    (Vandor 1980) 30.00
Popeye and Olive Figural Salt and Pepper
    Shakers 7½" (Vandor 1980) 60.00
Popeye and Sweet Pea Salt and Pepper
    Shakers 3" (Vandor) 30.00
Popeye and Olive Oyl Glass, 4½" tall; depicts
    Olive with hands clasped and Popeye in
    boxing shorts and gloves (1929) 50.00
Popeye and Oscar Glass, 4½" tall; illus.
    in blue/fleshtone (1929) 50.00
Popeye and Wimpy Glass, 4½" tall; illus.
    in blue/black (1929) 50.00
Popeye Brush, 4½" long (1929) 50.00
Popeye Boxed Soap Set, includes Popeye,
    Olive and Wimpy (Kerk Guild Soap
    1930s) 275.00
Popeye and Olive Salt and Pepper Shakers,
    3" tall; bisque shakers of Popeye in

black sailor uniform and Olive in apron
    (Japan) 75.00
Popeye and Jeep Glass, 4½" tall; illus.
    illus. in red/yellow (1936) 50.00
Popeye Brand Yellow Popcorn Tin, 3"x2"x5"
    tall; tin litho can in red, white, blue
    and yellow (Purity Mills 1949) 50.00
Popeye Ceramic Cookie Jar, Popeye's
    head (1950s) 400.00
Popeye Tattoo Bubble Gum (Topps
    Chewing Gum 1950s/1960s) 20.00

Popeye Dynamite Music Machine (Emerson)

Popeye Soaky, 10" tall (Colgate
    Palmolive 1960s) 20.00
Popeye Ceramic Cookie Jar
    (McCoy 1960s) 75.00
Popeye Soap Container (Woolfoam Corp./
    Placon 1960s) 20.00
Popeye Children,s Dish set, 5.5" diam. Popeye
    bowl, 4" tall b/w tumbler and 7" diam. dish
    depicting color illus. of Olive/Popeye/Wimpy/
    Swee'pea (Boontonware 1964) 55.00
Popeye Cast Drinking Mug (Deka 1971) ... 5.00
Popeye Cereal Bowl (Deka 1971) 5.00
Popeye Drinking Glass (Deka 1971) 5.00
Popeye Coca Cola Glass (1975) 7.00
Popeye Candy and Prize Boxes, 5"x2½"
    (Phoenix Candy Co. 1979), each ... 5.00
Popeye Shaving Kit (Larami 1979) 3.00
Popeye Toothbrush Set (Nasta 1980s) 12.00
Popeye Cake Pan (Wilton 1980) 8.00
"Popeye & Son" Pop Maker (Ja-Ru 1987) . 2.00
Popeye Pop-Up Wash Cloth, 13"x13"
    (Magical Mystery Products 1987) 5.00

All prices listed are for *Near Mint* condition.

Popeye Sparkler (Chein 1959)

Miscellaneous

Popeye Alarm Clock (New Haven 1932) . . 800.00
Official Popeye pipe "It Lites, It Toots" 5"
    stem, 2" bowl, battery powered (1958)100.00
Popeye figure Lantern, metal, battery
    powered (Linemar 1960s) 250.00
Popeye Snow Dome, 5" plastic figure
    holding 2½" plastic sphere 60.00
Popeye Figural Head Pipe (Edmonton
    Pipe Co. 1970) 35.00
Popeye Figural Box 1¾" (Vandor 1980) . . . 20.00
Popeye Figural Box 3½" (Vandor) 25.00
Popeye Figural Doorstop 14" (1930) 30.00
Popeye Wristwatch (Bradley 1979) 35.00
Popeye and Friends Figural Book Ends
    (Vandor 1980) 50.00
Popeye TV–style Magnet (1974) 5.00
Popeye Comic strip–style Magnet (1974) . . 5.00
Popeye Cheers Christmas Lights, 9"x5"x2"
    box, lid features Popeye holding
    Swee'pea; eight colored plastic bulbs
    with decals of Popeye and friends
    (Clemco/General Electric 1929) 225.00
Popeye "Blow Me Down Handkerchiefs,"
    8¼"x8¼" box (1929) 50.00
Popeye and Olive Oyl Sand Toy, red tin
    base and funnel with black tin 9" tall
    poles; as sand is poured into funnel,
    lever shifts sand into one side of
    jointed swing (1930s) 750.00
Popeye Lightbulb, 4" tall bulb; clear glass
    bulb with gray metal 2" tall figure of
    Popeye holding torch inside (1930s) 150.00
Popeye Christmas Tree Set With Mazda Lamps
    (8 tree bulb lights each with bulb cover
    depicting illus. scenes (1930s) 500.00

Popeye Tin litho "In The Barrel" Key Windup
    Toy, 7" tall; Popeye in black/yellow barrel
    with orange feet sticking out of bottom
    (Chein 1932) 400.00
Popeye Yazoo Pipe (Northwestern
    Productions 1934) 150.00
Popeye Peg Board "Hammer Peg", 20"x11"
    set; peg board, pegs instructions
    and hammer (Bar Zim Toys 1934) . . . 50.00
Popeye Pocket Watch, 2" diam. (New
    Haven 1934) 400.00
Popeye Pocket Watch (New Haven 1935) 350.00
Popeye Wrist Watch (New Haven 1935) . . 450.00
Popeye Halloween Costume, 4 pc. outfit
    with blue sailor hat, blue pants and
    blue or b/w shirt (Halco 1935) 200.00
Popeye Pirate Pistol, 10" long; lithoed
    pistol with illustration of Popeye dressed
    as Pirate and four other characters
    along barrel (Marx 1935) 200.00
Popeye Bubble Set with two pipes, 5"x
    7½" box (Transogram 1936) 150.00
Popeye "Song Folio", 12"x9" cover with 24
    original songs incl. "I'm Popeye The Sailor
    Man" (Popular Melodies 1936) 35.00
Popeye Tin Litho listed as both "The Big Fight"
    and "Popeye the Champ", 7" square boxing
    ring; 3½" tall figures of Popeye and Brutus
    fighting inside ring (Marx 1936) . . 2,500.00
Popeye Jack Knife, celluloid (1930s–40s) . 100.00
Popeye The Sailor Child's Hat, 8" diam.
    (1940) 100.00
Popeye's Pow-Er Strength Test Toy, like
    carnival toy test of strength; when
    hit base with mallet, spinach can is
    sent up into Popeye's mouth to ring bell
    (Harett-Gilmar-Wood 1950s) 65.00
Popeye Rollover Tank (no date) 400.00
Popeye Lantern, 7.5" tall; Popeye with clear
    glass chest to hold bulb; has jointed
    arms and black rubber pipe
    (Linemar 1950s) 300.00
Popeye Costume and Mask, 9"x11" box
    (Collegeville Costumes 1950s) 75.00
Popeye Rubber Squeeze Toy, 8" tall,
    Rempel 1950s) 80.00
Popeye Pick-Up Sticks (Lido 1950s) 25.00
Popeye Boxing Gloves, 10"x13" package
    (Everlast 1950s) 125.00
Popeye Sand Set (Peer Productions 1950s) 20.00
Official Popeye Wallet, vinyl wallet with picture
    of Popeye that illus. him swallowing a can

---

of spinach when tilted; color illus. of
Popeye and Olive yelling "Lookee!"
(Chase Creations 1950s) 65.00
Popeye Strength Tester–Muscle Builder,
7"x7"; color illus. toy depicting Popeye
pulling on metal handles and strength
scale; depicts 4 Popeye characters using
the tester (Welded Plastics 1950s) . . 100.00
Popeye Magic Playaround, 15"x10" cover;
punch-out town and figures to be assembled
on 15"x10"x4" base (Amsco 1950s) . . 40.00
Popeye Getar (Mattel 1951/1953) 85.00
Popeye Jack-In-The-Box Spinach Can,
6" tall (Mattel 1957) 60.00

Popeye Halloween Costume (Halco 1935)

Popeye Metal Tapping Set, six 4½"x4½"
wooden boards with metal sheets of diff.
characters, tools and instructions
(Handicraft 1957) 40.00
Popeye Nightlight, vinyl figure (Alan
Jay 1959) 50.00
Popeye head Silly Puddy containers
(1950s/1960s) 7.00
Popeye "Dynamite Music Machine," 12x9x4"
tall; record player depicting Popeye in
captain's uniform and illus. of stick of
dynamite (Emerson) 35.00
Popeye Pez dispenser, original Popeye
wearing his Captain's hat (Pez 1950s
–early 1960s) 35.00
S.S. Popeye wallet (1960s) 20.00
Popeye Sparkler, 3½" diam.; toys shoots
sparks from Popeye's open mouth
(Chein 1959) 125.00
Popeye Holster Set, two 5"-long guns marked
"Pal" with illustration of Popeye
(Halco 1961) 35.00
Popeye Lunchbox (Universal 1962) 100.00
Popeye Jack-In-The-Box (Mattel 1963) 50.00
Give-A-Show Projector (Kenner 1964) 35.00
Popeye Lunch Box (King Seeley
Thermos 1964) 50.00
Popeye Gumball Machine (Hasbro 1968) . 100.00
Popeye Alarm Clock (Smiths 1968) 100.00
Popeye Blow Bubble Pipe (1969) 25.00
Popeye Pez dispenser, Popeye in sailor's
hat (Pez mid 1960s–1970s) 50.00
Popeye Mask and Costume, based on King
Features TV series (Collegeville
Costumes 1960s–1970s) 60.00
Popeye Bubble Liquid (M. Shimmel Sons
Inc. 1970s) 20.00
Popeye Hauling and Construction Set
(Toys For All Seasons 1970s) 50.00
Popeye Transistor Radio (Philgee 1970s) . . 50.00
Popeye Wrist Watch (Sheffield 1971) 125.00
Popeye Wallet (Larami 1978) 20.00
Popeye Lite-Brite (Hasbro 1978),
refill only 10.00
Popeye Carrying Holder, Halloween Bucket
(Renz Corp. 1979) 10.00
Popeye "The First Fifty Years" Trash Can
(1979) 15.00
Popeye Watch (Bradley 1979) 75.00
Popeye Jump-Up (Imperial Toy Co. 1979) . 5.00
Popeye Phone Rest (Comvu Corp. 1980s) . 10.00
Popeye Big Band Combo (Larami 1980s) . . 5.00

Popeye Harmonica (Larami 1980s) 15.00
Popeye Crazy Color Foam (American Aerosol
   Corporation 1980) 10.00
Popeye Lunch Box (Aladdin 1980)
   Steel box 25.00
   Thermos (plastic) 15.00
Popeye Lunch Box (King Seeley 1964)
   Steel box 90.00
   Thermos (steel/glass) 35.00
Popeye's Spinach Truck (Matchbox 1980) . 15.00
Popeye's Pipe (Continental Plastics/
   Harmony Toys 1980) 5.00
Popeye and Swee'Pea Mirror (Creative
   Accessories late 1980s) 48.00
Popeye Mask and Costume (Collegeville
   Costumes late 1980s) 4.00
Popeye Doodle Ball (Ja-Ru 1981) 2.00
Popeye Telephone, 10" tall; plastic phone featur-
   ing Popeye holding spinach can receiver in
   his hand (Comvu Corporation 1982) . . 60.00
Popeye Telephone, small one-piece
   telephone (Comvu 1982) 40.00
Popeye View-Master Showbeam Cartridge
   (View-Master 1982) 3.69
Official Popeye Gumball Dispenser
   (Superior Toy 1983) 5.00
Popeye Wood Slate (Ja-Ru 1983) 2.00
Popeye Duck Shoot (Ja-Ru 1983) 3.00
Popeye Tube-A-Loonies (Larami 1981) . . . 3.00
Popeye Glo-Whistle (Helm Toys 1984) 4.00
Popeye Pool Table (Larami 1984) 4.00
Popeye Magnets (Larami 1984) 1.09
Popeye Boat Bubble Blower (Larami 1984) 4.00
"Popeye & Son" Plastic Lunchbox (Thermo-
   Serv 1987) 6.00
"Popeye & Son" Grabber (Ja-Ru 1987) . . . 2.00

Sea Hag

Magnets
The Sea Hag TV–style Magnet 5.00
The Sea Hag Comic strip–style Magnet . . . 5.00
Sea Hag Puffy Vinyl Magnets, part of set
   (1974) 2.00
Miscellaneous
Sea Hag Hand puppet (Presents 1985) . . . 10.00
Sea Hag Rubber Stamp, says "No Seahags"
   (L.A. Stampworks) 4.00
Sea Hag Rubber Stamp, Sea Hag on broom
   (L.A. Stampworks) 4.00

Swee'Pea

Figures/Playsets
Swee'Pea Plastic Figure (Marx 1950s) 12.00
Swee'Pea Pewter Figure

   (Spoontiques 1980) 20.00
Swee'Pea Frosted Crystal Figurine
   (Italy 1980s) 35.00
Paper Collectibles
Swee'Pea Hingees No. 102 Paper Punchouts
   (Reed & Associates 1944) 5.00
Glass/Mugs/etc .
Swee'Pea Drinking Glass (Popeye's
   Chicken 1978) 25.00
Swee'Pea Drinking Glass (Popeye's
   Chicken 1979) 25.00
Swee'Pea Ceramic Egg Cup (Vandor 1980) 20.00
Swee'Pea Drinking Glass (Popeye's
   Chicken 1982) 10.00
Swee'Pea Ceramic Container/Mug
   (Presents 1990) 17.00
Swee'Pea Figural Cup 3½" (Vandor 1981) . 15.00
Miscellaneous
Swee'Pea Hand puppet, plastic head on lamb-
   printed cloth body (Gund 1960s) 30.00
Swee'Pea and Jeep Musical Jewelry
   Box (1980) 25.00
Swee'Pea Ceramic Nightlight
   (Presents 1980) 25.00
Swee'Pea Ceramic Christmas Ornament
   (Presents 1985) 10.00
Swee'Pea Pen (N.J. Croce Co. 1985) 5.00
Swee'Pea Figural Bank 6½" (Vandor 1980) 25.00

Wimpy

Figures
Wimpy Ramp Walking Toy from "Thimble

Mechanical Celluloid Wimpy (1930s)

Theatre Figures" collection, 6" tall; hollow figure; wears black/brown and red tie (1929) 200.00
Mechanical Celluloid Wimpy, 7" tall; Wimpy wears black jacket, red tie, tan shirt, black shoes, hat and coat and black-striped pants 850.00
Wimpy Chalk Figure (1930s) 50.00
Wimpy Character Mini-Lead Figure (1940s) 35.00
Wimpy Vinyl Squeeze Toy (Rempel 1950s) 65.00
Wimpy 7" figure, "TV Cartoon Theater" (Dakin 1976) 50.00
Wimpy Pewter Figure (Spoontiques 1980) . 20.00
Wimpy Ceramic Figure, Wimpy holds hamburgers (Presents 1989) 3.00

Glass/Mugs
Wimpy Ceramic Container/Mug (Presents 1980) 17.00
Wimpy Ceramic Kitchen Utensil Holder (Vandor 1980s) 8.00
Wimpy Ceramic Mug (Vandor 1990) 15.00

Miscellaneous
Wimpy Pen (N.J. Croce Co. 1985) 8.00
Wimpy Hand puppet, plastic head on checkered cloth body (Gund 1960s) . . 20.00
Wimpy Ceramic Christmas Ornament (Presents 1980) 10.00
Wimpy TV–style Magnet 5.00
Wimpy Comic strip–style Magnet 5.00
Wimpy Figural Music Box 6" (King Features 1980) 40.00

PRINCE VALIANT
Prince Valiant syrocco figure (1940s) 100.00

STEVE CANYON
Comic Strip; TV (1958–59)
Paper Collectibles
Meet Steve Canyon – NBC-TV ad poster (Chesterfield 1950s) 50.00
Air Rangers Membership Card (1959) ... 10.00
Costumes/Clothing
Jet Helmet, boxed (Ideal 1959) 75.00
Steve Canyon mask and costume (Halco 1959) 75.00
Steve Canyon outfit for Captain Action figure
See Captain Action in Action Figure Series
Steve Canyon lunch box (Aladdin 1959)
Steel box 120.00
Thermos (Steel/glass) 55.00

Tom Hand puppet (Mattel 1965)

TOM and JERRY
(TV 1965–72)
Tom and Jerry Ceramic Set (1940) 150.00
Tom and Jerry "Lars" doll 12" Tom stuffed felt and flannel plus 4½" hat, Tom holds aluminum sauce pan containing Jerry (Lars 1950s) 250.00
Tom the Cat Halloween Costume (Halco 1952) 40.00
Tom and Jerry Locomotive, tin litho and plastic, 10" (MT Japan 1960s) 300.00
Tom and Jerry English Cup, 3¼" tall, depicting Tom and Jerry with bomb ("Made In England" mid 1960s) 35.00
Tom and Jerry Fire Engine, mechanical, 7" long, 7 colors, plastic (MT Japan 1960s) . . 400.00
Tom Handcar, battery powered, 8"x9" plastic and vinyl (MT Japan 1960s) . 150.00
Jerry Handcar, battery powered, 8"x9"

Jerry Handcar (MT Japan 1960s)

plastic and vinyl (MT Japan 1960s) . 150.00
Tom and Jerry Talking Hand Puppets, plastic and
cloth 7"x12"x4" box (Mattel 1965) . . 70.00
Tom and Jerry Crayon by Number coloring set in
10"x16" box (Transogram) 20.00
Tom the Cat Halloween Costume
(Kusan 1968) 30.00
Tom and Jerry white china mug (Staffordshire
1970) 20.00
Tom and Jerry on a scooter, plastic, friction
drive (Marx 1971) 65.00
Tom and Jerry Go Kart, friction drive,
plastic 3½"x5½"x4" (Marx 1973) . . . 65.00
Tom and Jerry Scooter, friction drive,
plastic (Marx 1973) 50.00
Tom 6" figure, boxed (Marx 1973) 35.00
Jerry 4" figure, boxed (Marx 1973) 30.00

Tom and Jerry porcelain china figures, 3¾" Tom,
2" Jerry in case (George Wade 1973) 45.00
Tom and Jerry and Droopy Walking Figures
(MGM 1975), set 40.00
Tom and Jerry Figural Bank 6"
(Gorham 1980) 40.00
Tom and Jerry Figural Bookends 8"
(Gorham 1980) 40.00
Tom and Jerry Figural Bank 5" (Gorham
1980) 40.00
Tom and Jerry Mugs (Gorham 1980) 40.00
Tom and Jerry vehicles on cards (Corgi)
Tom's Go-Cart (#38) 15.00
Jerry's vehicle (#58) 15.00
Tom Pez dispenser (1980s) 10.00
Jerry Pez dispenser (1980s) 10.00
Spike Pez dispenser (1980s) 10.00
Droopy Dog Pez dispenser (1980s) 10.00
Tyke Pez dispenser (1980s) 10.00
Tom and Jerry Music Box, 3"x5½"x 6½",
both on skateboard, box plays "King of
the Road" (Gorham 1981) 25.00
Tom figure (Multi-Toys 1990) 5.00
Jerry figure (Multi-Toys 1990) 5.00
Spike figure (Multi-Toys 1990) 5.00
Tyke figure (Multi-Toys 1990) 5.00
Droopy figure (Multi-Toys 1990) 5.00
Quackers figure (Multi-Toys 1990) 5.00
Tom and Jerry large posable figures, boxed
(Multi-Toys 1990) 15.00
Spike and Tyke large posable figures, boxed
(Multi-Toys 1990) 15.00

WIZARD OF ID

Wizard of Id glasses, set of 6, Arby's
Premium (1983) 20.00

Wizard of Id glasses (Arby's 1983)

SUPERHERO TOYS

M any superhero items are listed in the Action Figures, Dolls and Vehicles sections. The rest are listed below. Batman and Superman have a long history and consequently they have many items listed. Recently, very few Superman toys have been produced but there have been tons of Batman toys. Many Spider-Man and the X-Men items appeared in the 1980s and 1990s and some other Marvel characters have toys, but the largest number of entries after Batman and Superman are for the Teenage Mutant Ninja Turtles.

For the future, look for a continuing number of toys based on Marvel Comics characters, now that Marvel owns Toy Biz, and the emergence of toys and collectibles based on comics characters from Image comics and Todd McFarlane (Spawn). Batman is still going strong with the 1995 **Batman Forever** movie and Superman may return to the toy lines based on the popularity of the "Lois and Clark" TV series. The Mighty Morphin Power Ranges have pretty much replaced the Teenage Mutant Ninja Turtles as the kings of the licensed characters, but they won't last forever either.

ANGEL
Angel Marvel Flyer (Topps 1966) 45.00

AQUAMAN
Aquaman Halloween costume, boxed
    (Ben Cooper 1967) 225.00
Aquaman superhero moon glass
    (Pepsi 1976) 35.00

ARCHANGEL
Archangel Flying Marvel Superheroes
    Glider, on card (Toy Biz #4990,
    1992) 10.00

BATGIRL
Batgirl Pez dispenser, soft head (1970s) . 40.00
Batgirl Drinking Glass (Pepsi 1976) 25.00
Batgirl Haloween Costume (1977) 25.00

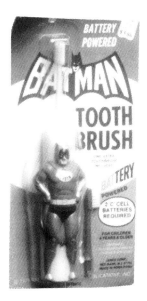

Batman Toothbrushes (battery powered and hand powered)

Batman sneakers (Randy)

BATMAN
(Comics 1939–Present)
(TV 1966–68; Movies 1989–95)

Batman collectibles can be divided into eras. The first period runs from 1939 to 1965 and includes the toys based on the early comic books, comic strips and Saturday morning serials. As you may notice, there aren't very many, particularly compared to Superman or Captain Marvel. Batman licensing didn't really take off until 1966, when the campy Batman TV series began. Indeed, most Batman collectibles made before 1989 come from this era, and so collectors are stuck with the image of Batman as a somewhat comedic figure. This did not change until the Tim Burton–directed Batman movie appeared in 1989. Licensing companies started to take notice and many toys and other products were created. If you are in doubt about the vintage of a particular toy, look at Batman's costume. Most older items have Batman

in a blue-and-gray outfit and most newer items depict Batman in his basic black outfit. The newest toys are of Batman from the animated series, and the artwork is distinctive and easily recognized.

Many Batman collectibles are also listed in the Action Figure Series, Vehicles and other sections of this book. Thousands of Batman toys have appeared in the 1990s, but hardly any Superman items. Someday somebody will write a thesis explaining the cosmic meaning behind this and then we will all understand how it makes sense! (Don't hold your breath.)

1940s and 1950s

Batman club card, serial premium (1940s)	50.00
Batman Pep Pin (1940s)	50.00
Batman Mask, movie serial premium (1940s)	75.00
Batman Premium Mask, 5"x8½" cardboard, with comic strip illustration on reverse (Philadelphia Record newspaper, early 1940s)	200.00

Batman Decal set (1944)

Batman decal set, 21 color decals
with booklet (1944) 50.00
Batman press release pamphlet, 10 pages,
11"x16" (Columbia Pictures 1954) . . 75.00
1960s and 1970s
Artistic
Batman 4" Cake Decoration Figures (1966) 30.00
Batman Paint Box (Whitman 1966) 20.00
Batman Colorforms Set (Colorforms 1966) 50.00
Batman Print Putty (Colorforms 1966) . . . 55.00
Batman Star Dust Paint Set "Touch
of Velvet" (Hasbro 1966) 125.00
Batman Color Pencil Set (Hasbro 1966) . . 80.00
Batman Oil Painting Set (Hasbro 1965) . . 100.00
Batman Stamp Set (Kellogg's 1966) 50.00
Batman Cartoon Kit (Colorforms 1966) . . . 45.00
Batman Paint By Numbers Book
(Whitman 1966) 45.00
Batman Oil Painting Set (Hasbro 1973) . . 40.00
Batman–Tru Dimension 3-D action picture
kit, boxed (Colorforms 1976) 30.00
Batman Colorforms Set (Colorforms 1976) 35.00
Banks
Batman Figural Bank (Transogram 1966) . 150.00

Batman Bank (Transogram 1966) 135.00
Batman Ceramic Bank 7" glazed china on
2"x3" base (1966) 60.00
Buttons, Badges and Club Items
Batman code card (1966) 5.00
Batman Coins, set of 25, plastic, on 9"x12"
card (Transogram 1966) 35.00
Batman print set, in envelope 35.00
Batman Membership Button
(Button World 1966) 20.00
Batman Bat Ring (Samsons 1966) 25.00
Batman Flasher Rings, silver
or gold (VariVue 1966) 16.00
Batman Flicker Rings blue
plastic (VariVue 1966) 10.00
Batman Brass Badge, 2½" metal clasp . . . 20.00
See also: "Rings" section, page 261.
Clothing, Costumes and Masks
Batman Raincoat yellow (Sears 1975) . . . 60.00
Batman and Robin child's sweatshirt (1966) 30.00
Batman Playset with cape and mask
(Ben Cooper 1965) 160.00
Batman outfit, mask, 4-piece costume
(Berwick 1966) 140.00

All prices listed are for *Near Mint* condition.

Batman Deluxe roller skates
(Laramie 1970s) 50.00
Batman gloves 12" black vinyl, with
Batman emblem (Wells Lamont 1966) 135.00
Batman Play Costume (Ideal 1966) 75.00
Batman Felt Hat (Arlington 1966) 80.00
Batman-Robin face mask, 8"x11", cardboard,
color (General Electric TV 1966) . . . 20.00
Batman belt (Morris Belt 1966) 25.00
Batman sneakers (Randy 1960s) 75.00
Batman outfit (Lindsay #579, 1960s) 75.00
Batman helmet and cape in 11"x9" color box
plastic and vinyl (Ideal 1966) 125.00
Batman Utility Belt with rope and hook,
Grenades, Batarang, handcuffs, flashlight
Bat-pistol and radio belt-buckle
(Ideal 1966) 1,250.00
Official Batman Utility Belt in 8"x14" Window
box containing Bat Belt Grappler,
Cuffs, Clicker Gun and Walkie Talkie
(Remco 1976) 120.00

Food and Candy

Batman Pez Candy Dispenser (1966)
hard head with cape 90.00
Batman Pez Candy Dispenser (1970s)
Soft head 40.00
Hard head 5.00
Batman Crusader Fudge Bar
Wrapper (M.U. 1966) 25.00
Batman Slam Bang Ice Cream Box (1966) 20.00
Batman Ice Cream Carton (1966) 50.00
Batman orange drink container (1966) . . . . .
Batman Punch-o Drink Mix (1966) 50.00
Batman breadloaf bag featuring Batman, Robin
Bat Plane, Batmobile and enemies
(New Century Bread 1966) 35.00
Batman Candy Premium sign 17"x22"
(Holloway Candies 1966) 50.00

Glass and Tableware

Batman drinking glass (Pepsi 1976) 25.00
Batman Drinking Cup Holder
(Burger King 1984) 15.00

Batman's Closet: Outfit (Berwick); Raincoat (Sears); Kid's Sweatshirt

Batman stainless steel silverware (Imperial 1966)
 Fork and spoon, on card 125.00
 Fork or spoon, each 50.00
Batman and Robin Coffee Mugs (1966), pair 30.00

Batman Helmet & Cape (Ideal 1966)

Household Items
Batman Talking Alarm Clock (Janex 1975)　85.00
Batman Felt Pennent, 18" (M.U. 1966) ... 40.00
The Penguin Versus Batman 16"x27", color
 cloth hanging on wooden rod (1966) 75.00
The Joker Versus Batman 16"x27", color cloth
 hanging on wooden rod (1966) 75.00
Batman Napkins (M.U. 1966) 30.00
Batman and Robin party centerpiece
 (Hallmark 1966) 120.00
Batman "Hotline" Talking Batphone, 8"
 red plastic (Marx 1966) 225.00
Batman Executive Set (Batsharpener, Batcalen-
 dar and Joker Stapler) (Janex 1977)　45.00
Batman Waste Paper Basket (1966) 40.00
Batman Pillow (1966) 45.00

Batman Light Up Battery
 Tester (Nasta 1975) 15.00
Batman and Robin lunch box (Aladdin 1966)
 Steel box 120.00
 Thermos 50.00

Miscellaneous.
Batman theme record (RCA 1966) 65.00
Batman Pix-a-Go Go Double Feature Show
 featuring The Catwoman (Embree/
 NPPI 1966) 50.00
Batman *"The Catwoman's Revenge"*
 33⅓ RPM record (Peter Pan 1975) . 15.00
Batman 45 RPM record *"The Battiest Car
 Around"* (Synthetic Plastic 1966) ... 45.00
Batman 45 RPM record *"The Penguin and A
 Penguin Caper"* (Synthetic
 Plastic 1966) 35.00
Batman and Robin 33⅓ RPM stereo record
 "Batman Theme" (Tifton 1966) 40.00

Shaker Maker (Ideal 1974)

Batman Shaker Maker Playset, 11"x9"
 box with ingredients to mold Batman,
 Robin and Joker (Ideal 1974) 65.00
Batman Sneak Previews Movie Cassette, with
 collector's card (Galoob 1984) 15.00
Batman View-Master Reel set (GAF 1966) 60.00

Batman Pix-a-Go Go (Embree/NPPI 1966); "The Catwoman's Revenge" record (Peter Pan 1975)

Batman View-Master Reels (1976) 15.00
Batman picture pistol, 15" plastic
    projector, with 4 films (Marx 1966) . . 300.00
Batman Talking View-Master Cartridges
    (View-Master Intl. 1983) 15.00
Batman and Joker Story Sticker Book
    10"x12" (German 1960s) 35.00
Batman and Penguin Story Sticker Book
    10"x12" (German 1960s) 35.00
Batman Valentine Cards
    (Hallmark 1966), pack. 15.00
Batman Postcards (8) (Dexter 1966) 30.00
Super Friends Pencil Sharpener (1980) . . 12.50
Batman Crazy Foam container 8" tall
    (American Aerosol 1974) 30.00
Batman Futuristic Racer tin litho, 9"
    friction powered, spring antenna
    (Alps 1960s) 80.00
Batman Batmobile License Plate, 4" long
    (Marx 1966) 35.00

Batman Robot (Japanese 1960s)

Batman Kite (Ski-Hi 1979) 15.00
Batman Talking Command Console
    (Mego 1977) 120.00
Batman HO Freight Car (Tyco 1977) 20.00
Batman and Robin Rolykins
    (Marx 1966) (pair) 450.00
Batman Robot battery powered with vinyl
    head and cloth cape (Japanese) . . . 500.00
Batman Robot (Marx) 650.00
Batman Yo-Yo (Duncan 1978) 15.00

Playsets

Batman Magic Magnetic Gotham City Playset
    with 6 figures, cardboard city & vehicles
    in 36"x20" box (Remco 1966) . . . 1,000.00
Batman 6-piece Playset in plain box
    (Ideal/Sears 1966) 150.00

Bat Plane ad sign (Durham 1960s)

Batman advertising sign for Bat Plane
    cardboard (Durham) 25.00
Batplane 43" wingspan Styrofoam (Durham) 75.00
Batman Electronic Question and Answer
    Quiz Machine in box with 11"x9"
    cartoon sheets (Lisbeth 1966) 40.00
Official Batman Bicycle ornament on card
    8" plastic Batman (Empire 1966) . . . 35.00
Batman Bike Reflector (Charhill 1978) . . . 15.00
Batman Wingo (Irwin 1966) 120.00
Batman and Robin figural walkie
    talkies (M.U. 1974) 80.00
Batmobile "spin out" cars (AHI 1970) 35.00

Batmobile Bubble Bath (Avon 1978)

Batman Playset (6 piece) (Ideal 1966) . 1,700.00
Batman Playset (23 pieces, with Batcave
    carrying case) (Ideal/Sears 1966) . 1,500.00
Batman 23-piece Playset in plain box
    (Ideal/Sears 1966) 500.00
Batman Playset Batcave Carrying Case
    for 3" figures (Ideal/Sears 1966) . . . 300.00
Batman 11-piece Playset with Robin, Wonder
    Woman, Superman, Robot and other
    villains, Bat Car, Bat Plane, Sonar
    Ray Weapon (Ideal #3305, 1966)   1,100.00
Batman 11-piece Playset in plain box
    (Ideal/Sears 1966) 350.00
Mobile Bat-lab (Mego 1975) 300.00
Batcave 15" cardboard and vinyl
    playset (Mego 1970s) 250.00
Batcave for 3¾ Pocket Super Heroes
    figures (Mego 1979) 300.00
Wayne Foundation 40" playset
    (Mego 1975) 1,200.00
Batcave 15" "Official World's Greatest
    Super Heroes" cardboard and vinyl playset
    (Mego 1979) 175.00
Batman Playset (Ideal 1970s) 120.00

Puzzles
Batman Sliding Puzzle (APC 1977) 10.00
Batman and Robin Rub-Down Transfer
    Game (American Pub. 1979) 5.00

Road Race Sets
Batman Road Racing set, inc. Batmobile
    and Jokermobile and track
    (Azrak-Hamway 1976) 100.00
Batman Road Race Set (AHI 1976) 225.00
"Switch 'N' Go" Batmobile road race set,
    battery power, with track, etc.
    (Mattel 1966) 300.00

Soap and Soaky
Batman Soaky Bottle (Colgate-
    Palmolive 1966) 65.00
Batmobile blue plastic with screw-off
    trunk nozzle for Bubble bath soap
    (Avon 1978) 65.00
Vehicles: See "Vehicles" section, page 131–35.

Weapons and Devices
Batman-Robin tin rifle, 18" (Japanese) . . . 150.00
Batman Periscope, 14" (Kellogg's 1966) . . 45.00
Batman Official Directional Finder on card
    7" card with compass (1966) 25.00
Batman Escape Gun, plastic (Lincoln
    International 1966) 75.00
Batman Bullhorn, carded 10½" black plastic
    (Bayshore Ind. 1966) 75.00

Batman Bullhorn (Bayshore Ind. 1966)

Batman Bat Chute (Poynter 1966) 65.00
Batman Grenade (Lincoln
    International 1966) 125.00
Batman Super Heroes Code Flasher
    (Gordy Intl. 1978) 6.00
Batman Bat-Ray, plastic (Remco 1977) . . 80.00

BATMAN
The First Movie (1989–91)
Artistic
Batman figural crayons set (M.U. 1989) . . 10.00
Batman Adventure Set (Colorform
    #727, 1991) 7.50
Batman Deluxe Playset (Colorform
    #2382, 1991) 10.00
Batman Easy Painting (#38650) 5.00

Banks
Batman Vinyl Bank (from cereal)
    (Ralston-Purina 1989) 15.00
Batman Bank (Australia,
    manufacturer unknown, 1989) 15.00
Batman gumball bank (#09401) 15.00

Food
Batman Batmobile premium (from cereal),
    (Ralston-Purina 1990) 10.00

Puzzles
Batman Sliding Puzzle (Jotastar 1989) . . . 25.00
Batman Puzzle (Schmidt
    [Germany] 1989) 50.00

Household
Batman mug (Applause late 1980s) 10.00
Batman 14oz. Logo mug (1990) 2.50
Batman 33.8oz. Super Logo Mug (1990) . . 3.00
Batman 10oz. logo travel mug (1990) 3.00
Batman bat towel (1990) 16.00
Batman bag (1990) 20.00
Black Visor with logo (1990) 3.00

Supersqueeze Sports Bottle (1990) 3.50
Batman logo Frisbee (1990) 3.00
Batman superfoam can cooler (1990) 2.50
Batman Foam Can Cooler (Betras 1989) .. 4.00
Bat Wall Clock 8", battery
   powered (1990) 20.00
Batman Magnets (1990) 4.00
Batman Wall Mask plaque, 6½" ceramic . 16.50
Batman AM Radio (Jotastar 1989) 45.00
Batman Telephone Intercoms
   (Bandai 1989) 50.00

Miscellaneous

Batman Water Fun Ball,
   English (M.U. 1989) 35.00
Batman Water Fun Ball (Kidworks 1989) . 25.00
Batman LCD watch (1990) 10.00
Batman Quartz Watch (1990) 30.00
Batman Flying Disk (Betras 1989) 6.00
Batwing Verti-Bird (Blue Box 1989) 10.00
Batman Tin Windup, 7" (Billiken 1990) ... 120.00
Batman Nite Writer ballpoint pen (1990) ... 7.00
Batman Key Chains (1990), each 5.00
Bat Earrings (1990), pair 9.00
Batman Christmas ornament 3¾" P.V.C. .. 9.00
Batman Wrist Racers (#0702) 8.00
Batman YoYo (Pikit 1989) 30.00
Batman YoYo (Spectra Star 1989) 5.00
Batcave playset (Toy Biz #4417, 1989) .. 40.00

Batman Bat-Ray (Remco 1977)

Batman soaky-type bottle, Japan
   (M.U. 1989) 4.00
Batwing Water Blaster (Blue Box
   Toys #34029) 10.00
Batman Hand Cuffs (Gordy Intl. 1989) 4.00
Batman Batsignal Gun (Gordy Intl. 1989) .. 4.00
Batman Binoculars/Scope
   (Gordy Intl. 1989) 4.00
Bat Flashgun, battery powered (1990) 3.00
Bat Gun, spark shooting (1990) 3.00
Batman Pistol, with vinyl bullets (1990) ... 3.50
Batman Water Gun (Pikitoys 1989) 25.00
Batman Binoculars (Pikitoys 1989) 25.00
Batman Batwing Water Blaster
   (Blue Box 1989) 10.00
Batman Armor Set (mask, cape, armor
   chest, armor glove) (Kenner
   #63290, 1990) 25.00
Batman Crime Control Set (binoculars,
   Walkie Talkie, microphone & freeze-ray
   weapon (Kenner #63270, 1990) 20.00
Crossbow assault weapon
   (Kenner #63320, 1990) 15.00
Batarang "Dark Knight" blaster
   (Kenner #63250, 1990) 15.00
Sonic Neutralizer Dark Knight
   weapon (Kenner #63280, 1990) 15.00
Batman Armor Set "Batman: The Animated
   Series" (Kenner #63651, 1993) 25.00
Batman Accessory Set (Toy Biz
   #4419, 1990) 13.00
Batman Projector Gun (Toy Biz
   #4429, 1990) 8.00

Batman & Robin Soaky Bottles

All prices listed are for *Near Mint* condition.

BATMAN RETURNS
The Second Movie (1992–93)

The number of Batman collectibles spawned by the second Batman movie is truly legion. More than 500 are listed below, and many others are contained in other sections of this book. Few of the ones below have attracted enough collector interest to rise in value from their original retail price, and there are so many available that future prices are speculative at best. The undeterred collector should look for Penguin and particularly Catwoman items (listed later, under those characters). There are less of them around, and there are very few Catwoman items that date from before 1992.

Many of the Batman licensees continue to make essentially the same products today with graphics from *Batman: The Animated Series, The Adventures of Batman and Robin*, or *Batman Forever.*

Artistic
Batman Returns Play Doh playset with 4
    character molds (#23005) 12.00
Batman Chalk (Noteworthy #BMCH33B)
    Full figure 3.00
    Bust, purple background 2.00
    Bust, city and red background 2.50
Batman Returns 2-color stamp Pad (Note-
    worthy #BMSP38) 2.50
Batman Plastic Half Figure Rubber Stamper,
    on card (Noteworthy #BMCS31B)
    Black Costume, 2 different 3.00
    Blue and Gray Costume 3.50
Batman Wooden Rubber Stampers, 5 different,
    (Noteworthy #BMR37), each 3.00
Batman Returns Colorforms sets:
    Adventure Set (#749) 6.00
    Deluxe Adventure Set (#2399) 9.00
Batman Returns Restickables sheet with 15
    stickers, playmat (Colorforms #83007) 3.00
Batman Returns Action Stamper
    (Colorforms #5404) 7.50
Batman Returns Adventure Playset with
    Playmat (Colorforms) 12.50
Batman Returns Glo-Doodler (Colorforms
    #7100) 15.00
Batman Returns Sparkle Art (Colorforms
    #879) 7.50

Batman Returns color by numbers with
    markers (Colorforms) 5.00
Batman Returns crayon by Numbers
    (Colorforms) 5.00
Batman Returns deluxe comic kit with comic
    book–type pieces and playset
    (Colorforms #2382) 15.00
Batman Returns Goof-Proof Easy Color Two
    11"x16" posters with 4 markers
    (Colorforms) 5.00
Batman Crayon by Number set (Craft
    House #50821, 1991) 6.00
Batman Easy Painting Brush with 6 paints
    (Craft House), 3 diff., each 5.00
Batman 5 oz. Pocket Figural Gumball
    Dispenser (#09301) 5.00
Batman Poster Pen set (Craft House
    #63076) 4.00
Batman trace plates, 6 two-sided plates,
    tray and Pencils (Hasbro #2546) 10.00
Action clay playset with 3 characters,
    molds and clay (Tonka) 10.00
Batman Returns Crayon Case (Kids
    Katchalls) 4.00

Batman Lip Balm (Kid Care 1992)

Batman Returns Toothbrush (Janex 1992)

Bath and Health Care

Batman Talking Electric Toothbrush (Janex)
With stand (#43200) 25.00
Boxed, with 2 brushes 20.00
Carded, with 2 brushes (#43210) 17.50
Batman Soap on a Rope (Cosrich SP 236,
1989) 4.50
Batman Tissues 3 pack, 3 diff. wrappers (Kid
Care #00044) 1.00
Batman Anti-Chap Lip Protector, on
blister card (Kid Care) 1.00
Batman Lip Balm, Cherry Flavored on
blister card (Kid Care #00041) 1.00
Batman Bubble Bath container (Kid Care),
16 oz. with Batman picture (#00040) . 1.00
Standing Batman 10 in. figural
plastic 10 oz. (#00023) 5.00
Crouching Figure, top for 7 oz.
"Crime Fighter Slime" (#00021) 4.00
Batman Foam Soap 5.5 oz. container with
Batman pictured (Kid Care #00042) . . 2.00
Batman Floating Soap Dish (Kid Care
#00024) 1.00
Batman Liquid Soap, torso figural plastic
10 oz. container (Kid Care #00022) . . 3.25
Batman Crime Fighter Survival Kit
(Kid Care #00028) 3.00
Batman Locker Bag (Toothbrush and case,
Soap and case, comb, brush, cup and

tissues) (Kid Care #00029) 5.00
Batman Play Shaving Kit (Kid Care #00027) 4.00
Batman Sculpted Hair Brush (Kid
Care #00026) 3.00
Batman Returns 30 Bandages (Kid Care) . . 1.00

Bikes

Batmobile, battery-operated Kid Ride (Power
Drivers) . . . . CRP
Batman 16" Cycle (Power Cycle #50543) . . CRP
Batman 16" Mountain Bike (Rand) . . . . CRP
Batman 12" Boys Bike (Rand) . . . . CRP
Batman Low Rider with Guard (Rand) . . . . CRP
Batman Toddler Bike (Rand) . . . . CRP
Batman 8¾ Kids Bike Helmet (Rand #957) . 25.00
Batman Six-Piece Bicycle Accessory
Value Pack (Rand #936) 20.00
Pedal Batmobile, 55"x23"x18" (Sears
#86019K) 100.00

Clothing, Costumes and Masks

Batman Costume, One-piece flame-retardant

Batman Sculpted Hair Brush (Kid Care 1992)

polyester suit (Hood, cape, boots,
belt in two sizes: ages 4–6 (Sears #3634)
or ages 8–10 (Sears #3635), each . . . 30.00
Batman child's Vacu-form Mask
(Ben Cooper) 10.00
Batman costume with Mask, Chest and
Cape (Ben Cooper #1537), child or
adult 15.00
Batman Cowl, 3 different (Ben Cooper) . . . 10.00
Batman Armour Set with Cowl, Chest, Boot
tops, Gloves, Belt, Leotard (Ben
Cooper) 15.00
Batman adult Mask (Collegeville
#12467-HD) 20.00
Batman Costume classics (S-M-L)
(Collegeville #5747) 50.00
Batman Adult costume with Cowl, Belt,
Cape, Wrists and Spats (Collegeville
#8587) 75.00
Batman Costume (Costume Classics #5747) 60.00
Batman Rubber Mask on hang tag (Morris) 30.00
Deluxe Batman attire (New Dimension Comics)
Costume (#BM100) 255.00
Cape (#BM112) 60.00
Body Suit (#BM113) 43.00
Belt (#BM111) 23.00
Gloves (#BM110) 24.00
Spats (#BM110) 30.00
Mask (#BM115) 42.00
Mask without face (#BM114) 40.00

Food and Candy

Batman Returns Cereal (Ralston Purina)
with Glo Window Slick, 4 diff., each . . 5.00
With Puzzle, 3 different, each 6.00
With To & Fro Book Marker, 3 diff. . . . 5.00
Hanging promo with logo 5.00
1 oz. Batman Tortilla Chips (Street Kids) . . 1.00
Box of nine 1-oz.Tortilla chips with or without
order form (Street Kids) 5.00
With Batman Bank (Street Kids) 10.00
Big Bag of Tortilla Chips (Street Kids) 1.50
Batlogo Nightlight (mail-in) (Street Kids) . . . 3.00
Batlogo Keychain (mail-in) (Street Kids) . . . 3.00
Batlogo coin purse (mail-in) (Street Kids) . . 4.00
Batman figural Bank, from 9-pack box
(Street Kids) 5.00
Batman Returns Head candy container, old
(Topps #502, 1989) 1.50
Batman Squeeze Tube Gum (Topps
#00651, 1991) 1.50
Batman Medallion candy container (Topps
#587), 12 different, each 1.50

Special Edition "R" Treat Box with 2 masks
(Toys "Я" Us) 5.00

Batman head candy container

McDonald's Fast-Food Promotions

Batmobile/Batman Happy Meal Vehicle . . . 2.50
Batmissile Happy Meal Vehicle 2.50
Penguin Happy Meal Vehicle, umbrella spins 2.50
Catwoman Happy Meal Vehicle, tail wags . 2.50
Batman Cup with Batdisk Lid 2.50
Batmobile Cup with Batdisk Lid 2.50
Catwoman Cup with Batdisk Lid 2.50
Penguin for Mayor Cup with Batdisk Lid . . . 2.50
Penguin on Duck Cup with Batdisk Lid 2.50
Selina and Bruce Wayne Cup with
Batdisk Lid 2.50
*Note: cup variations: copyright symbol either right
of logo or left of logo, also White Band or no
White Band.*
Batman Returns McDonald's Cup Display
72" standing figure, holds 6 cups 75.00
Batman Returns McDonald's Cup Counter
Display, holds 1 cup 50.00
Batman Returns McDonald's Happy Meal
Display, holds 4 vehicles 50.00
Batman Returns McDonald's Happy
Meal/Cups Plastic Menu Display,
3 ft. sq. 25.00
Batman Returns McDonald's Outdoors
Hanging Banner (gold, black print) . . . 25.00
Gotham City and Batsignal 25.00
Batman 25.00
Batman and Batmobile 35.00

All prices listed are for *Near Mint* condition.

Large Fries carton, Batman, Catwoman or
Penguin (#13172) 1.00
Happy Meal Bag with Activities (#26172) . . 1.00
6-Item bag w/3 coupons, pictures (#11729) 1.00
Batman Head Enamel Pin (#56119) 3.00
White Logo Enamel Pin 3.00
Batman Returns Baseball Hat (#56114) . . . 10.00
Welcome to Gotham City Button (#56110) . 1.00
Batman Returns Sunglasses (#56123) 3.50
Batman Returns Lapel Pin (#56120) 3.00
Batman Returns Flip Top Watch (#56122) . 5.00
Batman Watch (#56121) 10.00
Batman Returns Trayliner with Batman's
Hand Up or Batman Standing 1.00
Batman Returns Happy Meal Crew Poster . 5.00
Batman Returns Plastic Cup Crew Poster . 5.00

Glasses and Tableware

Batman sipper straw (Applause #45672) . . 2.00
Batman figural mug (Applause #45669) . . . 15.00
Diving Batman cup with lid and straw, small
(Betras Plastics) 2.00
Diving Batman cup with lid and straw, large
(Betras Plastics) 2.50
Batman superhero 12-oz. mug, limited
edition of 5,000, hero on handle
(Warner #8299, 1992) 12.00
Batarang cup with lid and straw (Betras
Plastics), small or large 2.50
Batman Returns Snack and Play T.V. Tray
(Marsh Allen) 7.50
Gothamesque Lunch Box with Thermos . . . 10.00
Blue Lunch Box with comic Batman on roof
(Thermos) 10.00
Soft insulated lunch cooler (Thermos) 5.00
Batman Returns Tableware (Zak Designs)
Spoon/Fork Set (#BT112) 5.95
Plate (#BT117) 4.95
Bowl (#4BT118) 4.95
Cup (#BT119) 4.95
Plate, Dish and Cup set 12.50
12oz. Tumbler 5.00
Tumbler Cup 5.00
7oz. double wall tumbler (#BT137) 5.95
8oz. single wall tumbler (#BT137) . . . 2.95
14oz. face tumbler (#BT220) 3.95
14oz. logo tumbler (#BT223) 3.95
12oz. double bottom tumbler (#BT230) 6.95
20oz. jumbo tumbler (#BT234) 3.95
12oz. double wall tumbler (#BT225) . . 5.95
Catwoman/Penguin/Batman
Place Mat (#BT111) 2.95
Batman with Batmobile 12oz. Tumbler 5.00

Household Items

Batman, 3-piece twin bed sheets and
pillowcase (Bibb) 25.00
Batman, 3-piece full bed sheets and pillow-
case (rep. samples only, not produced)
(Bibb) 50.00
Batman Comforter (Bibb) 20.00
Batman Pillowcases, 2-pack (Bibb) 10.00
Batman Flat Sheets, twin (Bibb) 15.00
Batman Elastic Edged Sheets, Twin (Bibb) . 15.00
Batman Curtains (Bibb) 15.00
Batman Shower Curtains (Bibb) 15.00
Batman Comforter/Slumber Bag 30"x57"
(Ero #71564) 20.00
Batman Slumber Mate Carry Case
(Ero #12864) 10.00
Batman Fabric Luggage (Ero #95625) 15.00
Batman Returns Slumber Playtent 30"x57"
(Ero #11964) 25.00
Batman Duffle Bat (Ero) 10.00
Batman Vehicle Playtent 57"x28"x32"
(Ero #11614) 25.00
Batman Bean Bag Chair 80" (Lewco #6290) 33.00
Batman Pillow (Nickry) 12.00
Batman Returns Inflatable TV Chair
(Playtime #1541) 20.00
Batman beanbag kids chair, PVC
(Sears #11045) 20.00
Batman Comforter
Twin (Sears #97780) 30.00
Full size (Sears #97781) 40.00
Batman Bed coordinates
Bed ruffle, twin size (Sears #97788) . . 20.00
Bed ruffle, full size (Sears #97789) . . 25.00
Pillow (Sears #97782) 13.00
Sheets, twin size (Sears #97786) 27.00
Sheets, full size (Sears #97787) 30.00
Batman Window Fashions
Panels, 82"x63", with tiebacks
(Sears #97783), pair 25.00
Valance 84"x11" (Sears #97785), each 15.00
Batman Beach Towel 30"x60" 18.00
Batman Slumber Tent, 45"x33"x33"
(Sears #77538) 24.99
Batmobile playhouse, vinyl with PVC
frames, 57"x32"x28" (Sears #77537) . 30.00
Batman slumberbag, 30"x57" (Sears
#70270) 25.00
Batman Nap Mat 22"x45" (Spectra Star
#8815) 10.00
Batman Silkscreened Mirror (Zanart) 15.00
Catwoman Silkscreened Mirror (Zanart) . . . 20.00

Bat Logo Silkscreened Mirror (Zanart) 12.50
Batman Soft-Glow Nightlight 5.00

Batman logo keychain
Jewelry, Key Rings, Buttons
Batman Torso Key Buddy Key Holder
  (#BMKB36B) 3.50
Batman Keychains (Applause), 7 different
  configurations, on ring or carded 4.00
Batman Enamel Hat Pin on hang card (Gift
  Creation), 4 diff. styles, each 4.00
Enamel Hat Pins on hang card (Gift Creations)
  Gotham Public Works Gear 5.00
  Gotham Public Works with Statue ... 5.00
  Batski Boat 5.00
  Batmobile 5.00
  Silver Batlogo 4.00
  White Batlogo 4.00
Batman Enamel on metal Keychain (Gift
  Creations), 5 diff. styles, each 5.00
Waterdisk Pendant (Rosecraft) 3.00
White Logo Stamped Metal Pendant
  (Rosecraft) 3.00
Removable Tatoos–Sheet A or B (Rosecraft) 3.00
White Logo Stamped Metal Pin (Rosecraft) 3.00
White Logo stamped metal earrings
  (Rosecraft) 6.00
Plastic Logo earrings (Rosecraft) 2.50
Glitter Plastic Logo Earrings (Rosecraft) ... 3.00
Plastic Logo Ring (Rosecraft) 2.00
Stamped Metal Logo Ring (Rosecraft) 4.00
Glitter Plastic Logo Ring (Rosecraft) 3.00
Plastic Logo Pin (Rosecraft) 2.50
Glitter Plastic Logo Pin (Rosecraft) 3.00
Glitter Enamel Logo Pin (Rosecraft) 3.00
Gold-tone Enamel Logo Pin (Rosecraft) ... 3.00
Plastic Black Logo Pendant with plastic
  chain (Rosecraft) 3.50
Metal Pendant with Metal Chain (Rosecraft) 5.00
Batman hologram rectangle button
  (Comic Images) 2.00
The Bat, The Cat and the Penguin promo
  button (Warner Bros.) 5.00

Miscellaneous
Batman Figural Coin Bank (Noteworthy
  #BMK34B) 15.00
Batman Sewing Pattern 10.00
Batman 1 oz. silver coin, plastic case
  (Chicagoland Processing) 10.00
Set of Batman, Catwoman and Penguin 1
  oz. silver coins with decals, hand folder
  plus certificate (Chicagoland
  Processing) 25.00
Batman Jr. Executive Play and Carry Case
  (Creative Plastics) 10.00
Batman Kid's Katchalls Plastic Storage case
  (Creative Plastics) 7.50
Batman small Pencil Box Carry Case
  (Creative Plastics) 5.00
12-figure collector case (Tara Toys #20560) 9.00
Batman Figure handle kid's umbrella 5.00
Batsignal with buildings vacuform clock with
  store name (Dealers only) (DC) 20.00
Batlogo cutout Acrylic Clock with white
  hands (DC) 15.00
Medallion Flashlight with Bat Logo (Garrity
  Ind. Intl.) 5.00
Batman Flashlight (Playtime #8009) 5.00
Batman Returns Talking Gumball Bank
  (Janex #43215) 25.00
Batman Super Button Value 6-pack, comic
  version, carded (O.S.P.) 10.00
Batlogo Plastic Book Marker (O.S.P. #26-
  262) 1.00
Batman Face Book Marker (O.S.P. #26-263) 1.50
Batman Shadow with Bats Plastic Book
  Marker (O.S.P. #26-265) 1.00
Batman Novelty Plastic License,
  4 styles (O.S.P. #6-2038) 2.50
Party Items
Batman Head Quick and Easy Self-Sealing
  Balloon, small or large (Anagram Intl.) 5.00
  Large 3-D scene with all 3 characters 7.50
Batman party items (Unique)
  Party Set (#14010) 10.00
  Napkins (16) (#14001) 2.00
  Tablecloth (#14003) 4.00
  Paper plates 7" (#14004) 2.00
  Paper plates 9" (#14005) 2.00
  Cups, 7 oz. (#14006) 2.00
  Party Pack (#14007) 10.00
  8 paper Party Hats (#14011) 3.50
  8 Blowouts paperhorns (#14012) 3.50
  8 Loot Bags (#14013) 2.50
  8 Party Invitations (#14014) 3.00

All prices listed are for *Near Mint* condition.

8 Party Balloons (#14015) 2.00
8 oz. Ice Cream Cups (#14022) 2.00
Party Horns (#14023) 3.50
12-foot Party Flag Banner (#14024) . . 5.00
Cake Decorator (#14025) 5.00
Batman Party Game (#14026) 5.00
Batman party rings, 8 (#1739) 5.00
Gift Wrap Set (#14017) 6.00
Ball Puzzle Party Favors (#14018) . . . 5.00
80 Dollar Bills, including Catwoman
  and Penguin (#14020) 7.50

Batman Party Favors Sliding Puzzles (Unique 1992)

Batman Sliding Puzzles, including Catwoman
  and Penguin (Unique #14021) 7.50
Batman Piñata (Unique) 13.00
Play Toys and Games
Batmobile 3" vinyl rollalong (Applause) 4.00
Duckmobile 3" vinyl rollalong (Applause) . . 4.00
Batman Returns Stikball (Colorforms)
  With 3 Velcro balls and hook (#3704) . 7.95
  With Target (#3702) 5.95
  With 2 catch mitts (#3705) 7.95
Batman Returns First Games for young kids

(Colorforms #7961) 9.95
Power Punch Batman versus Penguin
  Boxing Ring toy (KayBee special)
  (Kenner #00938) 30.00
Batman Returns Fast Flipper pinball
  (Playtime #4868) 14.95
Batman Returns Electronic Pinball Game
  (Playtime #4864) 29.95
Batman Returns Electronic Hyper Action
  Pinball Game (Playtime #4869) 39.95
Batman Batdisk (Spectra Star #8302) 5.95
Batdisk Jr. Outdoor Fun Pack with YoYo,
  Kite and String (Spectra Star #3319) . 8.00
Batman Streamer Kite 78" (Spectra Star
  #06210) 4.00
Batman Returns Radical YoYo (Spectra Star
  #01529) 2.95
The New Batman Movie View-Master (Tyco) 9.95
View-Master 3-D reel 3-pack, 21 pictures
  (Tyco #4137) 10.00
View-Master gift set, 3-D viewer, in box
  (Tyco #2436) 15.00
Gotham City Chase B/O racing set (Tyco
  #8203) 25.00
Batman Playing Cards, on card (U.S. Playing
  Card Co. #00296) 2.00
Batman Playing Cards, wrapped with hang
  tag (U.S. Playing Card Co. #00296) . . 2.00
Batman Projector Gun (#4428) 3.00
Prints, Stickers
Batman Returns Calendar (Landmark) 7.50
Batman blue-and-black promo sheet (DC) . 3.00
Batman blue-and-black promo sticker (DC) . 1.00
Batman Bat yellow-and-black promo sticker
  (DC) 1.00
Batman Shiny Sticker (Mello Smello) 1.00
Batman Paper Sticker (Mello Smello) 1.00
Batman Returns Giant Big Sticker (2 diff.)
  (Mello Smello) 2.00
Batman Cutout Stand-Up, medium or large
  (Starmakers) 4.00
Batman/Gotham City Lithoprint (Warner
  Bros. #9923) 20.00
Batman/Batmissile Lithoprint (Warner Bros.
  #9924) 20.00
Batmobile (Profile view) blueprint, 15"x19½"
  framed in silver metal (Warner Bros.
  #9940) 50.00
Batmobile (Overhead view) blueprint, 15"
  x19½" framed in silver metal (Warner
  Bros. #9939) 50.00
Set of 2 Batmobile blueprints (Warner Bros.

#9941) 90.00
Batman Returns Movie Cards 11"x14" set of
8 (Warner Bros. Catalog #9921) 10.00
The Art of Batman Returns Print Portfolio
11"x14" cards (Warner Bros. #9922) . 10.00
Batman Returns 2-layer cardboard
movie stand-up (Warner Bros.) 15.00
Batman Returns 3-layer cardboard movie
stand-up with spinning umbrella
(Warner Bros.) 20.00
Batman small cardboard counter stand-up
(Warner Bros.) 7.50
Three-heads small cardboard counter stand-
up (Warner Bros.) 5.00
Poster giveaway with AMC popcorn, soda
purchase (Warner Bros.) 5.00
Flyer advertising Dolby Surround Sound
theaters (Warner Bros.) 3.00
Press Release folder with 8"x10" photos and
articles (Warner Bros.) 15.00
2-layer movie promo stand-up (Video and LP
version) (Warner Bros.) 7.50
Batman Movie Cards, 8 items, 11"x14"
prints, Special Collectors Ed. (Zanart)   9.95
Art of *Batman Returns* print portfolio, 8
items, 11"x14" prints (Zanart) 9.95
Framed lithographs 11"x14" (Zanart)
Batman 19.95
Bat Logo 19.95
Batman in Flight 19.95
Gotham City 19.95
Batmobile 19.95
Serigraph, 24"x36" signed and numbered by
John T. Dismukes (Zanart) 50.00
16"x20" series of 4 views of Batmobile
Unframed (Zanart) 14.95
Framed (Zanart) 19.95
24"x30" series of 4 views of Batmobile
Unframed (Zanart) 19.95
Framed (Zanart) 29.95
Batman Silkscreened Mirror (Zanart) 20.00
Bat Logo Silkscreened Mirror (Zanart) 15.00
School Supplies
Batman Action Pencil (Applause #45668) . . 1.00
Batman figural bookmarker (Applause
#2748) 2.00
Minipad pocket folders (Impact Intl.),
Batman, standing; Batmissile or
Batmobile (#4930) 1.00
Spiral Notebooks 8½"x11" (Impact Intl.
#4936), Batman, Batmissile or
Batmobile 2.00

Study Kits (Impact Intl. #4940)
Batman and Batmobile 5.00
Batman and Gotham City 5.00
Batman 3-ring binder, with flap (Impact Intl.
#4945) 6.00
Batman Folders (Impact Intl. #4953),
Batman, Batmissile or Batmobile 2.00
Batman Pencil Box (Impact Intl. #4957)
Head, blue 2.00
Figure, black 2.00
Batman 3-Pack of Pencils (Noteworthy
#BM3PAK) 2.00
Batman Pencil with Bust top (Noteworthy
#BMCT30B), carded or loose 2.50
Batman mini notepad and pencil topper
(Noteworthy #BMMS35B) 2.99

Batman wallet (Roseart 1992)

School Equipment
Backpacks (Ero)
Batman Glow (#96025) 13.00
Batman Silver Screen (#99031) 12.00
Batman Big Impressions large 15.00
Batmobile Big Impressions large 15.00
Batman 3-D Face Locker Back Pack, Blue,
Purple or Red (Ero #98025) 20.00
Black, sample only (Ero #98025) 30.00

All prices listed are for *Near Mint* condition.   **199**

Batman Belt Bag (Ero #97525) 2.50
Penquin Belt Bag (Ero #97525) 3.00
Sports Items
Batman child's snorkle set with snorkle,
   mask and flippers (Coral Diving) 20.00
Batman 42" PVC Blaster Float Ring
   with Water Gun (Coral Diving) 25.00
Batman Returns Wallet (Ero #97038) 7.50
Batman Returns Wallet (Sears) 7.50
Batman Sunglasses, 4-piece set
   (Eye Spy #41671) 8.00
Batman Returns Sunglasses, 4-piece
   set (Eye Spy #41673) 8.00
Gotham Public Works cap (Warner Bros.
   #9929) 12.00
Cap with Batlogo, Baseball style, 3 diff.
   colors; Multicolor Batman Returns
   Leather Cap (Warner Bros. #9928) . . 24.00
Video, Audio and Electronic
Batman Returns Video Cartridge (Atari
   #PA2101) 10.00
Batman Returns in Mail-Away box (free with
   purchase) (Atari #PA2101) 10.00
Batman Returns mail-in coupon (Atari) 5.00
Batman Returns store display (fits
   around Game Unit) (Atari) 10.00
Limited Edition Water Proof White AM/FM
   Player (Mail-In-Offer) (Memorex) 15.00
Mail-In Form for AM/FM Cassette Player with
   Phones (Memorex) 3.00
Batman Returns Super Nintendo Game

Cartridge (NES/Kanami) 20.00
Batman Returns video game
   cartridge (Sega) 20.00
Batman Returns LCD Video Game (Tiger
   #78-507) 20.00
Batman Returns LCD Watch Game (Tiger) . 12.50
Watches
Bat Logo Watch, Men's or Women's (Consort)
   Black on Silver 35.00
   Silver on Black 35.00
   On Granite Face 30.00
Batman LCD watch (Quintel)
   Glo-logo 10.00
   Gotham 10.00
   Batsymbol 10.00
Batman Returns Batlogo Watch, leather
   band (Warner Bros. Catalog #9907) . . 30.00

BATMAN:
THE ANIMATED SERIES
The 1993–94 Animated TV Show

Many of the Batman licensees from the **Batman Returns** movie have continued to make essentially the same products with "Batman: The Animated Series" logo and artwork. Life is too short to research all of them again. None of these products have attained much collector interest yet, which means that they can all be obtained for retail price or even at discount. However, the animated series is highly regarded by fans and the artwork is quite good, so when the products finally disappear, collectors will wake up. Just keep checking for those "Red Tag" specials for interesting toys and collectibles. Look for anything with Phantasm, Poison Ivy or any of the other villains. Of course, there is always active collector interest in action figures and other special toy categories.

Batman: The Animated Series LCD Game (Tiger 1994)

Batman: Animated neon framed picture
(Neonetics 1994) 225.00
Batman Wall Light 45.00
Batman Animated Bat-Beam Talking Alarm Clock
battery powered (#TB1071, 1994) . . 40.00
Classic Batman Watch with lapel pin
and box (Fossil Features 1994) 70.00
Batman: The Animated Series 11"x14" lithocels
(Zanart 1993), framed, four different
featuring The Penguin, Two Face, Poison
Ivy, or Catwoman 19.95
Batman Animated hand-held game #72505 19.95
Batman: The Animated Series framed TV Card,
11"x14" from production cels (Zanart 1993)
Eight different, each 9.95
Batman: The Animated Series Slumber Play-
tent 45"x33"x33" (Ero #11030, 1993) . 27.00
Adventures of Batman and Robin Playhouse
(Ero #11656, 1995) 22.00

BATMAN FOREVER
The Third Movie (1995)
Batman Forever Power Armor Suit (Kenner
#64174, 1995) 20.00
Batman Forever Snack Maker Snack Playset
(Toy Max #8902, 1995) 10.00
Batman Forever Creator Pak Set (Toy Max
#9986, 1995) 25.00
Batman Forever Colorforms kit (Colorform
#00792, 1995) 5.00
Batman Forever Magic Rocks (Craft House
#50835, 1995) 9.00
Batman Forever Bean Bag Chair 30.00
Batman Forever face mugs: Batman, Robin,
Riddler, Two-Face (Warner Bros.
1995), each 12.00
Batman Forever PlayDoh 2-pack with Batman
and Riddler (PlayDoh #22101, 1995) . 15.00
Batman Forever metal wastebasket (Warner
Bros. 1995) 15.00
Batman Forever audio casset + trading
cards (TW Kids #266-4, 1995) 8.00
Batman Forever Snackmaker (Toymax
#8988, 1995) 25.00

CADILLACS & DINOSAURS
Cadillacs & Dinosaurs candy and box . . . 30.00

CAPTAIN ACTION
Accessory Sets
20-Piece Survival Kit (#3450) 350.00

10-Piece Weapons Arsenal (#3451) 300.00
Inter-Galactic Jet Mortar (#3452) 300.00
Four-Ft. Working Parachute (#3453) 300.00
Inter-Spacial Directional Communicator
(#3454) 400.00
Anti-Gravitational Power Pack (#3455) . . . 300.00
Captain Action Halloween costume
(Ben Cooper 1960s) 150.00

CAPTAIN AMERICA
Captain America Sentinel of Liberty Club
Badge (Timely Comics, early 1940s) 275.00
Membership card (early 1940s) 40.00
Captain America costume, boxed
(Ben Cooper 1966) 150.00

Captain America Strapper Snapper (Hope 1990)

Captain America Kite (Pressman 1966) . . . 50.00
Captain America T-shirt Transfer (1960s)   20.00
Captain America View-Master Pack (1974)   15.00
Captain America Drinking glass (7-11 1977) 10.00
Captain America Pez Dispenser (1970s) . 10.00
Captain America Flashlight (Gordy
    International 1980) 10.00
Captain America mug (Applause late 1980s)   3.00
Captain America tumbler 3.00
Captain America 20oz. bowl 5.00
Captain America placemat 3.00
Captain America Secret Wars watch (1984) 20.00
Captain America Secret Wars pocket gumball
    dispenser (Superior 1985) 15.00
Captain America costume Accessory
    playset (Toy Biz 1991) 15.00
Captain America Button Biter 4.95
Captain America Strapper Snapper
    (Hope #31904, 1990) 5.00

CAPTAIN MARVEL
(Fawcett Comics 1940s)

T he toys listed below are based on the **original** Captain Marvel comic books from the 1940s. He and his family were incredibly popular back then and gave Superman a run for his money. However, Superman eventually won out in a complicated copyright infringement case in the 1950s. The Captain Marvel who appeared in Marvel comics in the late 1960s is not the same character. DC Comics ended up owning the character and renamed him Shazam!

Captain Marvel Balloon Whistle (1944) . . . 45.00
Captain Marvel Club Membership
    code card (1941) 30.00
Captain Marvel Beanie, Fawcett
    premium (1940s) 200.00
Captain Marvel color photo (1941) 90.00
Captain Marvel club letters
    B&W stationery (1941) 35.00
    4-Color stationery (1941) 40.00
Captain Marvel club offers forms (1941) . . 45.00
Captain Marvel felt emblem (1941) 90.00
Captain Marvel X-mas card (1941) 60.00
War Bond Stamp Book Envelope (1941) . 70.00
Captain Marvel necktie (1941) 50.00
Capt. Marvel E. Z. Code Finder (1943) . . . 300.00
Captain Marvel Secret Message
    postcard (1943) 60.00
Captain Marvel Adventures in Paint, set of
    6 unpainted plaster figures, boxed
    (S.A. Resco 1946) 750.00
Captain Marvel "Toss Bags" (1943)
    Capt. Marvel flying 50.00
    Capt. Marvel standing at attention . . 50.00
    Mary Marvel flying, 5" 50.00
    Mary Marvel standing alert 50.00
    Hoppy 50.00
Captain Marvel Statuette, scarce (1944) 1,000.00
Captain Marvel Tie Clip (1946) 65.00
Captain Marvel Flying Glider (1944) 25.00
Captain Marvel Stationery,
    8½"x10½" (1940s) 20.00
Captain Marvel felt pennant, blue
    (1944–46) 100.00
Captain Marvel cloth emblems (1944–46)
    Captain Marvel 50.00

Captain Marvel felt pennant (1941)

Mary Marvel 50.00
Capt. Marvel, Jr. 50.00
Captain Marvel Overseas cap (1944–46) . 90.00
Captain Marvel Magic Folder (1944–46) . . 80.00
Captain Marvel Felt Hat (1944–46) 140.00
Captain Marvel Pencil Clip (1944–46) . . . 40.00
Captain Marvel Skull Cap (1944–46) 90.00
Captain Marvel 4" tin windup cars
   (Automatic Toy 1947), set of 4 . . . . . 150.00
Mary Marvel fiberboard pin (1944–46) . . . 80.00
Shazam Membership/Code card 40.00
Captain Marvel Magic Flute 30.00
Captain Marvel Balloon Flute 30.00
Flying Captain Marvel Felt Pennant 120.00
Marvel Glow Pictures (1944–46) set of 4 . 500.00
   Captain Marvel, Mary Marvel,
   Captain Marvel, Jr. or Hoppy the
   Marvel Bunny 125.00

Mary Marvel Wrist Watch (Fawcett 1948)

Marvel plastic statues (1946):
   Captain Marvel 6", Mary Marvel 6",
   Capt. Marvel Jr. 6", Marvel Bunny,
   set of 4 . . . . 500.00
Captain Marvel paper punch-outs
   (Reed 1944–45):
   "3 Famous Flying Marvels" 25.00
   "Flying Captain Marvel" 25.00
   Captain Marvel's "Magic Picture" . . . 25.00
   Captain Marvel's "Rocket Raider" . . . 25.00
   "Captain Marvel Jr. Ski Jump" 25.00
   Captain Marvel "Picture Puzzle" . . . 25.00
   Captain Marvel "Buzz Bomb" 25.00
   Captain Marvel "Magic Lightning Box" 50.00
Captain Marvel Wrist Watch with Vinylite
   Band, in box (Fawcett 1948) 200.00

Captain Marvel Deluxe Wrist Watch
   (smaller) with Vinylite Band, in box
   (Fawcett 1948) 275.00
Mary Marvel Wrist Watch
   In box (Fawcett 1948) 250.00
   In plastic box (Fawcett 1948) 225.00
CAPTAIN MARVEL: see also SHAZAM

CARNAGE
Maximum Carnage Watch (Marvel 1994) . 50.00

CATWOMAN
Batman Returns (1992–93)
Catwoman Chalk (Noteworthy #BMCH33B)
   Crouching or standing sideways 3.50
Catwoman Wooden Rubber Stampers
   (Noteworthy #BMR37), two styles:
   Catwoman alone or with cats, each . . 3.00
Batman Returns Easy Painting with 6 paints,
   Brush (Catwoman) (Craft House
   #38654) 15.00
Catwoman 16" Girl's Bike (Rand) 150.00
Catwoman child's Vacu-form Mask
   (Ben Cooper) 25.00
Catwoman Adult Mask (Collegeville
   #12444-HD) 35.00

Catwoman Keychain

Catwoman Studio classics (S-M-L)
   (Collegeville #8590) 25.00
Catwoman costume classics (S-M-L)
   (Collegeville #5749) 45.00
Catwoman Rubber Mask on hang tag
   (Morris) 30.00
Deluxe Catwoman Mask (New Dimension
   Comics BM2002) 45.00
Deluxe Catwoman Mask no face (New
   Dimension Comics BM2003) 40.00
Catwoman Mask cloth (New Dimension

Comics BM310) 20.00
Deluxe Catwoman Costume (New
    Dimension Comics BM300) 140.00
Catwoman Happy Meal Vehicle, tail wags . 2.50
Catwoman Cup with Batdisk Lid 2.50
Catwoman Large Fries carton (#13172) ... 1.00
Catwoman sipper straw (Applause #45672) 2.00
Catwoman figural mug (Applause #45671) . 15.00

Catwoman jewelry (Rosecraft)

Catwoman Tableware (Zak Designs)
    12oz. Tumbler, with cats (#BT251) ... 3.50
    12oz. Tumbler, circular 3.50
    Tumbler Cup 3.50
    14oz. tumbler (#BT221) 3.95
    12oz. double bottom tumbler (#BT231) 5.95
Catwoman Comforter/Slumber Bag 30"x57"
    (Ero #71578) 25.00
Catwoman Pillow (face) (Nickry) 12.00
Catwoman Pillow (figure, from side) (Nickry) 12.00
Catwoman Returns Inflatable TV Chair
    (Playtime #1542) 35.00
Catwoman slumberbag, 30"x57" (Sears
    #70047) 25.00
Catwoman Silkscreened Mirror (Zanart) ... 35.00
Catwoman Head Keychain on ring with
    product sticker (Applause #45666) ... 4.00
Catwoman keychain on card (Applause
    40439) 4.00
Catwoman keychain with ring sticker
    (Applause #40705) 3.50
Catwoman Enamel Hat Pin on hang card
    (Gift Creations), 2 different, each 5.00
Catwoman Head Enamel Hat Pin on hang
    card (Gift Creations) 5.00
Catwoman Enamel on metal Keychain (Gift
    Creations), 2 different, each 5.00
Catwoman Sewing Pattern 12.50
Catwoman 1 oz. silver coin, plastic case

(Chicagoland Processing) 10.00
Catwoman Flashlight (Playtime #8006) 5.00
Catwoman Face Book Marker (O.S.P. #26-
    264) 1.50
Catwoman Novelty Plastic License
    (O.S.P. #6-2038) 5.00
Catwoman Head Quick & Easy Self-Sealing
    Balloon (Anagram Intl.), 2 diff., each . 7.50
Catwoman party items (Unique)
    Napkins (16) (#13972) 3.00
    Paper Tablecover (#13973) 5.00
    Paper plates 7" (#13974) 3.00
    Paper plates 9" (#13975) 3.00
    Cups, 7 oz. (#13976) 2.50
    Party Pak for 8 (#13977) 12.50
    Party Pack (#13980) 10.00
    Party Hats (#13981) 3.50
    Blow Outs (#13982) 4.00
    Loot Bags (#13983) 3.00
    Invitations (#13984) 4.00
    Balloons (#13985) 3.00
    Gift Wrap (#13986) 2.50

Catwoman Party Favors Ball Puzzles (Unique 1992)

Gift Wrap Set (#13987) 10.00
Ball Puzzle Party Favors (#13988) . . . 5.00
Party Rings (#13989) 7.50
Ice Cream Cups (#13990) 3.00
Catwomanmobile 3" vinyl rollalong
    (Applause) 4.00
Catwoman magenta and black promo
    sheet or sticker (DC), each 1.50
Catwoman Shiny Sticker (Mello Smello) . . . 1.00
Catwoman Paper Sticker (Mello Smello) . . . 1.00
Catwoman Cutout Stand-Up, medium or
    large (Starmakers) 25.00
Catwoman Lithoprint (Warner Bros. #9925) 20.00
Catwoman and Penguin 11"x14" framed
    lithograph (Zanart) 19.95

#45668) 1.00
Catwoman minipad pocket folder
    (Impact Intl. #4930) 1.00
Catwoman Spiral Notebook 8½"x11"
    (Impact Intl. #4936) 3.00
Catwoman Study Kit (Impact #4940) 5.00
Catwoman 3-ring binder, with flap
    (Impact Intl. #4945) 6.00
Catwoman folder (Impact Intl. #4953) 2.50
Catwoman Pencil Box, red (Impact Intl.
    #4957) 3.00
Pencil with Catwoman Bust top, on card
    (Noteworthy #BMCT30B) 3.00
Pencil with Catwoman Bust top, loose
    (Noteworthy #BMCT30B) 3.00

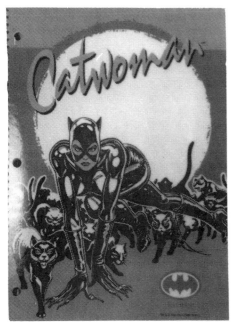

Catwoman Spiral Notebook (Impact Intl. 1992)

Catwoman/The Penguin Lithoprint (Warner
    Bros. #9926) 20.00
Catwoman small cardboard counter
    stand-up (Warner Bros.) 15.00
Wall-sized Catwoman Clawing pose
    on foam core (Warner Bros.) 25.00
Catwoman 11"x14" framed lithographs (Zanart)
    Catwoman 19.95
    Catwoman with cats 19.95
Catwoman Silkscreened Mirror (Zanart) . . . 25.00
Catwoman Action Pencil (Applause

Catwoman Study Kit (Impact Intl. 1992)

Catwoman minipad and pencil topper
    (Noteworthy #BMMS35C) 3.00
Catwoman Glitter Lips Backpack
    (Ero #96051) 12.00
Catwoman Big Impressions large
    Backpack (Ero #) 17.50

All prices listed are for *Near Mint* condition.

Catwoman 3-D Face Locker Back Pack
Red (Ero #98051) 25.00
Purple (Ero #98051) 25.00
Blue, sample only (Ero #98051) 30.00
Black, sample only (Ero #98051) 30.00
Catwoman Sunglasses, 4-piece set
(Eye Spy #41675) 10.00
Catwoman, Men's Watch (Consort) 30.00
Catwoman, Ladies' Watch (Consort) 30.00
Catwoman Glo LCD watch (Quintel) 15.00
Catwoman Watch, leather band (Warner
Bros. Catalog #9908) 30.00

CYBERFORCE

Cyberforce Stryker Complete
Skateboard (1994) 129.95

CYCLOPS

Cyclops Laserlight Visor (Toy Biz
#4983, 1991) 11.00
Light Force Arena (Toy Biz #4973)
"The Uncanny X-Men" (1991) 20.00
"X-Men" (1993) 10.00

DAREDEVIL

Daredevil Drinking Glass (7-11 1977) 10.00
Daredevil TV Script (1989) 40.00
Daredevil Halloween Costume (Ben
Cooper 1966) 150.00

DARK HORSE

Dark Horse logo men's watch (1992) 40.00
Dark Horse logo ladies' watch (1992) 40.00

DC SUPERHEROES

Super Heroes Drinking Glass 4½" (1960s) 50.00
Superadventure Colorforms set
(Colorforms 1974) 20.00
DC Superheroes plastic cups
(7-11 1974), each 10.00
DC Super Friends Lunch Box, with thermos
(Aladdin 1976) 50.00
Super-Friends Napkins (1976) 5.00
Mr. Bubble and the Super Friends
Bubble Bath (1984) 20.00
Super Hero Cup Holders (Burger King 1984)
Superman 7.50
Batman 6.00
Robin 6.00
Wonder Woman 7.00
DC figural handle mugs (5,000 made, numbered)
#1 Batman in Gotham City (1991) . . 15.00
#2 Superman Around the World (1991) 15.00
#3 Glow of the Green Lantern (1992) 15.00
See also: Super Powers

DOCTOR DOOM

Doctor Doom Secret Wars watch (1984) . 20.00
Doctor Doom Halloween Costume, boxed

Cyclops Light Force Arena (Toy Biz 1993)

(Ben Cooper 1965) 75.00
Tower of Doom 15" (Mattel #7472, 1984) . 30.00
Doctor Doom Secret Wars pocket gumball
   dispenser (Superior 1985) 15.00

DOCTOR OCTOPUS
Doctor Octopus Secret Wars pocket gumball
   dispenser (Superior 1985) 15.00

EXTREME STUDIOS
Prophet Skateboard, Dan Panosian art . . 150.00
Youngblood Faces Skateboard, Rob
   Liefeld art 150.00
Troll Skateboard, Jeff Matsuda art 150.00
Badrock Skateboard, Rob Liefeld art 150.00
Glory Skateboard, Rob Liefeld art 150.00
Extreme Back to School set, 20 folders,
   30 pencils, 5 erasers 25.00

FALCON
Falcon (Mattel #9141, 1984) 40.00

FANTASTIC FOUR
Fantastic Four Halloween Costume, boxed
   "Mr. Fantastic" (Ben Cooper 1965) . . 125.00
Fantastic Four Drinking glass (7-11 1977) 10.00
Fantastic Four Viewmaster Reel Set
   (GAF 1979) 20.00
Fantastic Four mug (Applause late 1980s) 10.00

FLASH
Flash costume, boxed (Ben Cooper 1967) 100.00

Flash Color-a-Deck card game (Russell)

Flash Two Way Flasher Ring 20.00
Flash mug (Applause late 1980s) 10.00
Flash Color-a-Deck cards (Russell) 15.00
Flash Superhero moon glass (Pepsi 1976) 35.00

GHOST RIDER
Ghost Rider figure, on motorcycle with
   interchangeable Johnny Blaze head
   (Fleetwood 19970s) 250.00

GREEN ARROW
Green Arrow mug (Applause late 1980s) . 10.00
Green Arrow Superhero moon glass
   (Pepsi 1976) 37.50

GREEN HORNET
T he Green Hornet actually started in 1936 on the radio. By the early 1940s there were comic books and movie serials. The most valuable collectibles date from this era. The Green Hornet, Kato and his sleek Black Beauty car next appeared in 1966 as a TV show. It was very popular, but it is most famous as the initial appearance of the legendary Bruce Lee (as Kato). Most Green Hornet collectibles date from this era, which also gave us the Superman and Batman TV shows. Most of the companies that produced licensed Batman products also produced Green Hornet items but in much smaller quantities. Currently, the Green Hornet appears in Now Comics.

Green Hornet Soundtrack record, with logo
   on back (20th Century Fox
   Records 1966) 100.00
The Green Hornet record, same cover as
   Gold Key #1 comic book (20th
   Century Fox Records 1966) 75.00
Horn Meets the Hornet record, Al Hirt
   (RCA Victor 1966) 75.00
Theme Album, Green Mask on cover
   (Crown Records 1966) 35.00
Adventures of the Green Hornet serials
   from 1940s (1966) 45.00
Radio Reruns, serials from the 1940s
   (Golden Age Records 1977) 20.00
Green Hornet Playing cards (Ed-U-
   Cards 1966) 75.00
Barris Custom Car (single stickers) 6.00

Saturday Serials Cards, inc. 3 Green
Hornet cards (1988) 15.00
Black Beauty Balloon Toy (Oak
Rubber 1966) 275.00
Green Hornet Pez dispenser variation #1
(Hat has a wider hat brim and taller
hat band), generally darker in
color (1966) 175.00
Variation #2 . . . . 150.00
Variation #3, brown hat 250.00
Variation #4, black hat 325.00
Pez counter display box (empty) 1,500.00
Green Hornet Walkie-Talkies
(Remco 1966) 250.00
Green Hornet Wrist Radios (Remco 1966) 375.00

Green Hornet Print Putty (Colorforms 1966) 95.00
Green Hornet View-Master Reels
(Sawyers 1966) 95.00
Green Hornet Movie Viewer (Active 1966) 95.00
Green Hornet Stardust Paint Set
"Touch of Velvet" (Hasbro 1966) . . . 250.00
Green Hornet Paint-by-Number Set
(Hasbro 1966) 600.00
Green Hornet Wallet, with card 75.00
Green Hornet Halloween Costume, boxed
(Ben Cooper 1966) 350.00
Green Hornet Colorforms set (1966) 275.00
Green Hornet Fork and Spoon set
(Imperial Knife Co. 1966) 125.00
Green Hornet Kite (Roalex 1966) 150.00

Green Arrow and Green Lantern superhero glasses (Pepsi 1976)

Green Hornet Lunch Box and Thermos

Green Hornet Vernors Trick or Treat bag
   (premium) (1966) 250.00
Green Hornet Felt Hat, with mask
   (Arlington Hat Co. 1966) 150.00
Green Hornet Punch Balloon (Oak
   Rubber 1966) 295.00
Green Hornet Flashlight Whistle
   (Bantam Light) 125.00
Green Hornet Signal Ray Flashlight
   (Colorforms 1966) 50.00
Green Hornet Hand puppet (Ideal 1966) . . 200.00
Green Hornet Frame Tray Puzzles, box
   of four (Whitman 1966) 175.00
Green Hornet Magic Rub-off Set
   (Whitman 1966) 175.00
Green Hornet Bike Badge with Varivue
   Flasher (Burry Premium 1966) 350.00
Green Hornet Lunch Box (Thermos 1966) 250.00
   Thermos for above 125.00
Green Hornet Masks (Hornet and Kato
   on single card) 175.00
Green Hornet Electric Drawing Set
   (Lakeside 1966) 250.00
Green Hornet Pennants (Blue or Orange)
   (RMS 1966) 75.00
Green Hornet Charm Braclet 75.00

Green Hornet Medallion (Toys for Boys) . . 200.00
Golden Jersey Milk Glasses (1940)
   Green Hornet 150.00
   Green Hornet with call letters 175.00
   Kato/Black Beauty 150.00
   Kato/Black Beauty with call letters . . 200.00
   Miss Case 140.00
   Mike Axford 140.00
   Membership Card 125.00
Federal Glass Company (1966)
   Green Hornet 125.00
   Kato 100.00
   Milk Mug 65.00
Green Hornet Chateau Lime Vodka drink
   glass (1966) 65.00
Green Hornet Pencils, 5 on card
   (Empire Pencil 1966) 175.00
Green Hornet Pencil Case
   (Hasbro 1966) 125.00
Green Hornet Notebook
   (U.S. Envelope 1966) 75.00
Green Hornet Folders
   (U.S. Envelope 1966) 75.00
Green Hornet Writing Pads
   (U.S. Envelope 1966) 75.00
Green Hornet Flasher Ruler

All prices listed are for *Near Mint* condition.   **209**

Green Hornet Eating Set (Imperial Knife 1966)

(Varivue 1966) 95.00
Green Hornet T-Shirt (Norwich
   Mills 1966) 30.00
Green Hornet Sweatshirt "Green Hornet
   Strikes Again" (Movie Tees 1989) .. 20.00
   Patch (Movie Tees 1989) 10.00
Green Hornet Iron-On Transfer
   (Funny Fronts 1966) 65.00
Green Hornet Ski Mask (Captron
   Headwear 1966) 175.00
Green Hornet Movie Serial lobby
   card (1940s) 200.00
Green Hornet Movie Serial press kit
   (1940s) 50.00
Green Hornet Strikes Again Movie Serial
   press kit (1940s) 50.00
Green Hornet TV Show press kit (1966) .. 75.00
Photos from Green Hornet 1940 Serials
   (many different), each 10.00

Photos from Green Hornet 1966 TV
   Show (many different), each 10.00
Photo from TV show autographed by
   Bruce Lee (Kato) 1,000.00

GREEN LANTERN
Green Lantern costume, boxed (Dessart
   Bros. 1961) 200.00
Green Lantern costume, boxed (Ben Cooper
   1967) 100.00
Green Lantern Superhero moon glass
   (Pepsi 1976) 37.50

HOWARD THE DUCK
Howard the Duck Drinking glass
   (7-11 1977) 10.00

THE INCREDIBLE HULK
Incredible Hulk Halloween Costume
   (Ben Cooper 1966) 100.00
Hulk costume (Ben Cooper 1978) 15.00
Incredible Hulk Carry-All Bag (Accessories
   Corner 1979) 10.00
Incredible Hulk 15" green-molded
   plastic bank (AJ Renz 1978) 25.00
Incredible Hulk Key Case (Nasta 1978) .. 10.00
Incredible Hulk Pez Dispenser (1970s) 5.00
Hulk View-Master Pack (1974) 10.00
Hulk mug (Applause late 1980s) 10.00
Hulk comic scene (Aurora) 60.00
Hulk Drinking glass (7-11 1977) 10.00
Hulk 3-D Kazoo (1979) 10.00
Hulk Keychain 4.95
Hulk Bean Bag Chair (Lewco #6261, 1992) 26.95
Hulk 20oz. bowl 5.00
Hulk placemat 3.00
Hulk Wall Mounted Mask (1979) 10.00
Incredible Hulk lunch box (Aladdin 1979–80)
   Steel box 45.00
   Thermos (plastic) 19.00

IMAGE
Image Chromium Watch (Image 1994) ... 50.00

IRON MAN
Iron Man Marvel Flyer (Topps 1966) 45.00
Iron Man Halloween Costume (Ben
   Cooper 1966) 100.00
Iron Man View-Master Pack (1974) 10.00
Iron Man mug (Applause late 1980s) 10.00

JOKER

Joker Pez Candy Dispenser, soft
    head (1970s) 65.00
Joker Drinking Glass (Pepsi 1976) 25.00
Joker Super Friends puzzle (APC 1974) .. 30.00
Joker Hand–Puppet 12" (Ideal 1966) 100.00
Joker Hand puppet 10" vinyl (Ideal 1966) . 80.00
Joker Water Fun Ball, English
    (M.U. 1989) 35.00
Joker Water Fun Ball (Kidworks 1989) ... 25.00
Joker Laughing Ball (Hyman
    Products 1989) 25.00
Joker Super Amigos Action Figure
    (Pacipa 1990) 15.00
Joker mug (Applause late 1980s) 5.00
Joker YoYo (Spectra Star 1989) 5.00
Joker LCD Watch (1990) 10.00
Joker Watch (Fossil Co. 1989) 125.00
Joker Hologram rectangle button
    (Comic Images) 5.00
The Joker (Batman Animated) Framed
    TV Card, 11"x14" from production cel
    (Zanart 1993) 9.95
Joker Sunglasses (Pan Oceanic 1993) 2.50

JUSTICE LEAGUE OF AMERICA

Justice League of America mug
    (Applause late 1980s) 10.00
Justice League Plate 40.00
Justice League of America paint-by-number
    set, boxed (Hasbro 1967) 50.00

KANG

Dark Star flying wing with Kang figure
    (Mattel #9692, 1984) 30.00

MAGNETO

Magneto Dress Up Playset with
    Helmet and disk-shooter glove
    (Toy Biz #4982, 1991) 11.00
Magneto Flying Marvel Superheroes
    Glider, on card (Toy Biz #4990, 1992) 7.50

MALIBU

Bravura logo Watch (Malibu 1994) 50.00
Malibu Comics logo Watch (Malibu 1994) . 50.00

MARVEL SUPERHEROES

Marvel World Adventure Playset
    (Amsco 1975) 200.00
Marvel lunch box (Aladdin 1976–80),

Steel box 45.00
Thermos 16.00
Marvel Superheroes Colorforms Set
    (Colorform 1983) 15.00
Marvel Super Heroes Training
    Center for 5" figure (Toy Biz 1990) .. 40.00
Marvel Super Heroes bop bag (#1773) 5.95
Marvel Super Heroes toys (Henry Gordy 1991):
    Ball Blaster (#814) 2.00
    Binocular Set with compass (#823) .. 2.50
    Vinyl Stickers (#863) 1.00
    Handcuffs (#925) 2.00
    Flash Gun (#930) 2.00
    Sunglasses (#931) 1.50
    Watergun (#933) 2.00
    Action Set, inc. sun glasses,
    handcuffs and badge (#934) 2.50
    Disk Shooter (#935) 2.00
    Bubble Blaster (#939) 3.00
    Crimefighter kit, handcuffs, walkie talkie,
    watch and case (#940) 2.50
    Soft Darts Target Set (#941) 2.50
    TV View 'N' Color (#942) 2.50
    Glider Launcher with 2 gliders (#943) . 2.00

Marvel Super Heroes Handcuffs
(Henry Gordy 1991)

Party Items
Marvel Super-Heroes party items
    Beverage Napkins (16) (R-1161-BN) . 2.00
    Luncheon Napkins (16) (R-1161-LN) . 2.00
    Tablecloth (R-1161-TC) 4.00
    7" Dessert Plates (8) (R-1161-P7) . . . 2.00
    9" Dinner Plates (8) (R-1161-P9) 2.00
    7oz. Cups (8) (R-1161-C7) 2.00
    Invitations (8) (R-1161-V) 3.00
    Party Blowouts (8) (R-1161-FB) 3.50
    Party Hats (8) (R-1161-FH) 3.50
    Party Horns (8) (R-1161-FN) 3.50
    Party Bags (8) (R-1161-FP) 2.50

MEGO ACCESSORIES
Super Action Flyby Supervator
    (Mego mid 1970s) 100.00
The Mangler vehicle for 3¾"
    superhero (Mego) 125.00
Hall of Justice acc. for 3¾ figures
    (Mego) 300.00
Hall of Justice playset for 8" figures
    (Mego mid 1970s) 350.00

PENGUIN
Penguin Pez Candy Dispenser (1970s),
    soft head 65.00
Penguin Drinking Glass (Pepsi 1976) 25.00
Penguin Bike Reflector (Charhill 1978) . . . 15.00
Penguin Super Amigos Action Figure

Penguin record

(Pacipa 1990) 25.00
Batman Returns Items
Penguin Chalk (Noteworthy #BMCH33B) . . 2.00
Penguin Plastic Half Figure Rubber Stamper,
    on card (Noteworthy #BMCS31B) . . . 2.00

Penguin Wooden Rubber Stampers
    (Noteworthy #BMR37) 2.00
Batman Returns Easy Painting with 6 paints,
    Brush (Penguin) (Craft House #38653) 12.50
Penguin child's Vacu-form Mask (Ben
    Cooper) 15.00
Penguin Adult Mask with separate jaw
    (Collegeville #12443-HD) 20.00
Penguin Costume classics (S-M-L)
    (Collegeville #5748) 35.00
Penguin Commando costume with Hood,
    Helmet, Inflatable backpack
    (Collegeville #7597) 35.00
Penguin Make-Up kit (Collegeville #13248-
    CL) 15.00
Penguin Make-Up kit with two-piece mask
    (Collegeville #) 25.00
Penguin Costume (Costume Classics #5748)40.00
Penguin Rubber Mask on hang tag, with
    separate jaw (Morris) 35.00
Masks and costumes (New Dimension Comics)
    Penguin Mask (BM2004) 40.00
    Penguin Costume (dressy) (BM600) . 150.00
    Penguin Costume (sewer) (BM20087) 140.00
    Penguin Hat (BM612) 65.00
    Penguin Wig (BM616) 26.00
    Penguin Cigarette Holder (BM617) . . . 17.00
    Penguin Umbrella (BM614) 20.00
    Penguin Gloves (BM613) 25.00
    Penguin Nose (BM619) 6.00
    Make-Up Kit (BM2005) 15.00
Penguin Happy Meal Vehicle, umbrella spins 2.50
Penguin for Mayor Cup with Batdisk Lid . . . 2.50
Penguin on Duck Cup with Batdisk Lid 2.50
Penguin Large Fries carton (#13172) 1.00
Penguin sipper straw (Applause #45672) . . 2.00
Penguin figural mug (Applause #45670) . . . 15.00
Penguin tableware (Zak Designs)
    Tumbler Cup 4.00
    14oz. face tumbler (#BT222) 4.00
    12oz. double bottom tumbler (#BT232) 6.00
Penguin Pillow (face) (Nickry) 12.00
Penguin Returns Inflatable TV Chair
    (Playtime #1543) 20.00
Penguin Head Keychain on ring with
    product sticker (Applause #45666) . . . 4.00
Penguin keychain on card, scarce
    (Applause #40439) 5.00
Penguin keychain with ring sticker
    (Applause #40705) 4.00
Penguin Enamel Hat Pin on hang card (Gift
    Creations) 4.00

Flashy Flickers Magic Picture Gun (Marx 1960s)

Penguin Commandos Enamel Hat Pin on
   hang card (Gift Creations) 4.00
Penguin Enamel on metal Keychain (Gift
   Creations) 4.00
Penguin Sewing Pattern 10.00
Penguin 1 oz. silver coin, plastic case
   (Chicagoland Processing) 10.00
Penguin Flashlight (Playtime #8007) 5.00
Penguin Novelty Plastic License
   (O.S.P. #6-2038) 2.50
Small Penguin Head Quick & Easy Self-
   Sealing Balloon (Anagram Intl.) 5.00
Large Penguin Head Quick & Easy
   Self-Sealing Balloon (Anagram Intl.) . . 6.00
Penguin green-and-black promo sheet (DC) 2.50
Penguin green-and-black promo sticker (DC) 2.50
Penguin Shiny Sticker (Mello Smello) 1.00
Penguin small cardboard counter stand-up
   (Warner Bros.) 5.00
Wall-sized Penguin pose on foam core
   (Warner Bros.) 15.00
Penguin Action Pencil (Applause #45668) . 1.00
Pencil with Penguin Bust top (Noteworthy
   #BMCT30B), carded or loose 2.00
Penguin minipad and pencil topper
   (Noteworthy #BMMS35P) 3.00
Penguin Silver Ink Backpack (Ero #99031) . 12.00
Penguin Big Impressions large
   Backpack (Ero #) 15.00

PHANTOM

The Phantom started out as a newspaper comic strip in 1936 and shortly after appeared in comic books. There was a movie serial in 1943, and he appeared in various comic books in the 1950s and 1960s. DC Comics acquired the rights to the character in 1988, and he appeared in his own DC comic book for a while. The number one Phantom collectible is the Captain Action costume, with ring, which is listed in the Action Figure section. For a 1930s and 1940s hero, there are less Phantom collectibles than you might think but more than appear here. Look for them in the sections on Bendies, Books, PVC figures, Model Kits, Games, etc.

Phantom Oil Painting Set, 12"x10"
   (Hasbro 1965) 100.00
Phantom Rub On Magic Transfer Set
   (Hasbro 1965) 50.00
Flashy Flickers Magic Picture Gun with
   films of The Phantom, Prince
   Valiant, Blondie, and Hi and Lois
   (Marx 1960s) . . . .
Phantom Jungle Playset (Larami 1976) . . 75.00
Phantom sirocco wooden statue (1940s) . 150.00
Phantom (in red costume) on horse

Phantom Jungle Play Set (Larami 1976)

(K.F.S. Inc. [Spain] 1960s) 50.00
Phantom costume (Ben Cooper 1963) . . . 90.00
Phantom costume (Collegeville 1956) . . . 250.00

PITT

Pitt Attack Skateboard 150.00
Pitt Punch Skateboard 150.00

PUNISHER

Punisher wrist watch LCD (MVW629) 24.99

RIDDLER

Riddler Drinking Glass (Pepsi 1976) 25.00
Riddler Nightlight (Price Imports 1978) . . . 75.00
Riddler Super Amigo Action Figure
(Pacipa 1989) 50.00

ROBIN

Robin Ceramic Bank (M.U. 1966) 65.00
Robin Composition Bank, 7" figure on
2"x3" base (1966) 60.00
Robin Boots (Parco 1966) 175.00
Robin Drinking Glass (Pepsi 1976) 25.00
Robin Memo Pad (Alco 1980) 9.00
Robin Super Friends Pencil
Sharpener (1980) 12.50
Robin Soaky Bottle (Colgate/
Palmolive 1966) 65.00
Robin Marionette 15" cloth and plastic
(Hazelle 1966) 200.00

Robin hand puppet (Ideal) 30.00
"There goes Robin" 45 RPM record with
figure sleeve 60.00
Robin Rolykins, 1" ball-bearing
base (Marx 1966) 80.00
Robin Christmas ornament 3½"
P.V.C. (1989) 9.00
Robin cup holder (Burger King 1984) 6.00

ROGUE

Rogue ministand-up 4.00

Shazam Pepsi glass (1976)

SANDMAN
Death watch (1991) 30.00

SHAZAM
Shazam Superhero moon glass
(Pepsi 1976) 35.00
Shazam Super Hero playing
card game (Russell 1977) 6.00

SHE-CAT
She-Cat 10" ministand-up 3.95

SILVER SURFER
Silver Surfer Flying Marvel Superheroes
Glider, on card (Toy Biz #4990, 1992) 6.00
Silver Surfer ministand-up 4.00

SPAWN
Spawn autographed baseball, with Spawn
logo in collector's case 35.00
Spawn Hand Watch 41.00
Spawn card game "Power Cardz" (1995) .. 10.00

AMAZING SPIDER-MAN
Spider-Man Pez Candy Dispenser (1960s)
Hard head, with Cape 75.00

Pez dispenser (1970s) 5.00
Spider-Man costume (Ben Cooper 1972) . 35.00
Amazing Spider-Man adventure set
(Colorforms 1974) 15.00
Spider-Man Bed Cover (1977) 15.00
Spider-Man Nite Lites (1977) 10.00
Amazing Spider-Man Super-Hero
watch, 1¼" dia. (Dabs 1977) 125.00
Spider-Man Drinking glass (7-11 1977) .. 10.00
Spider-Man Promotional Packet
(Marvel 1977) 40.00
Spider-Man Presto Majix set (1978) 15.00
Spider-Man Sting Ray Gun (Remco 1978) 125.00
Spider-Man Sharp Shooter (Larami 1978) . 20.00
Amazing Spider-Man 11" plastic
figure bank (Renzi 1979) 25.00
Spider-Man 3-D Kazoo (1979) 10.00
Spider-Man mug (Applause late 1980s) .. 10.00
Spider-Man Walkie Talkies (Nasta 1984) .. 75.00
Spider-Man Secret Wars pocket gumball
dispenser (Superior 1985) 15.00
Spider-Man Secret Wars AM radio (1986) 40.00
Spider-Man figural Flashlight (1991) 5.95
Spider-Man Flying Marvel Superheroes
Glider, on card (Toy Biz #4990, 1992) 6.00
Spider-Man Attack Tower for 5"
figure (Toy Biz #4874, 1991) 25.00

Spider-Man Camera (1994)

Spider-Man costume Accessory
playset (Toy Biz 1991) 15.00
Spider-Man Play Putty (#3001) 3.95
Spider-Man Action Phone (SST-200, 1994) 45.00
Spider-Man Camera (#47340, 1994) 20.00
Spider-Man 2099 ministand-up (Comic
Images 1994) 3.95
Classic Spider-Man Watch with lapel pin
and box (Fossil Features 1994) 75.00
Spider-Man Bean Bag chair
(Lewco #6262 1992) 26.95
Spider-Man bop bag (#1770) 5.95
Spider-Man button biter 4.95
Spider-Man hand-held game (#7853) 19.95
Spider-Man Party Items
Beverage Napkins (16) (R-1151-BN) . 2.00
Luncheon Napkins (16) (R-1151-LN) . 2.00
Table Cloth (R-1151-TC) 4.00
7" Dessert Plates (8) (R-1151-P7) . . . 2.00
9" Dinner Plates (8) (R-1151-P9) 2.00
7oz. Cups (8) (R-1151-C7) 2.00
Invitations (8) (R-1151-V) 3.00
Party Blowouts (8) (R-1151-FB) 3.50
Party Hats (8) (R-1151-FH) 3.50
Party Horns (8) (R-1151-FN) 3.50
Party Bags (8) (R-1151-FP) 2.50
Spider-Man Happy Meal (McDonald's 1995)
Characters
Spider-Man, Venom, Dr. Octopus, Peter
Parker or Mary Jane Watson, each . . 1.00
Vehicles
Hobgoblin, Venom, Scorpion or
Spider-Man Transports, each 1.00
Spider-Man Dress-Up Set (Toy Biz #47351,
1995) 25.00
Spider-Man Mini Fun Fan, battery operated
(Janex #44450, 1995) 8.00

SPIDER-WOMAN
Spider-Woman Halloween Costume (Ben
Cooper 1970s) 200.00

SUPERGIRL
Supergirl costume (Ben Cooper 1973) . . . 20.00
Supergirl (Comic Heroines/Super Queens)
(Ideal 1967) 1,800.00
Supergirl superhero moon glass
(Pepsi 1976) 37.50

Superman Sirocco figure (1940s)

SUPERMAN
(Comics 1939–present)
(Radio 1940–51; TV 1951–57)
(Movies 1979–80s)

Jerry Siegel and Joe Shuster understood the marketing possibilities of their comic *strip* character in the mid 1930s. While they were strong on seeing the future, they were weak on seeing tomorrow because Superman had to wait several years and be recycled as a comic *book* character in 1938 before anybody would print the stories. It didn't take long from there. Within a couple of years of the first comic book, Superman was also a comic strip, a radio show and a series of cartoons. The first toys appeared in 1939, and there were tons produced in the 1940s. The Superman TV show created more and so did the movies.

In the 1990s, Superman is still going strong with four different comic books

---

*Superman & Supergirl puppets (Kohner 1960s); Superman wrist watch (New Haven Clock Co. 1939)
Superman figural nutcracker (1979); Superman Paint by Numbers (Transogram/NCP 1954)
Superman Turnover Tank box (Louis Marx 1940); Superman Lunchpail (Universal 1950s)*

each month, the "Lois and Clark" TV show and the publicity bonanzas of the death of Superman (in. 1992) and the death of Clark Kent (in early 1995). And so naturally, the 1990s have produced hardly any Superman toys. By contrast, Batman started in 1940 but didn't produce many toys until the 1966 TV show came along. Today there are so many Batman toys that you can't possibly count them all. You figure it out — we can't.

The earliest Superman toys are probably the most collectible superhero items in existence. In some cases from the 1940s, there are only a couple of examples of the toy known to exist. That makes the prices on such items somewhat speculative. The only thing you can be sure of is that Superman collector extraordinaire Danny Fuchs has one (or, more likely, two). He lives at 209-80 18th Avenue, Bayside, NY 11360. Write him. Maybe you can convince him to sell you the one you want.

1938–48

Superman Sirocco figure, brown with
    maroon details, black hair, 2½"x1½"
    base (1940s) 2,000.00
Superman Wrist Watch, in box

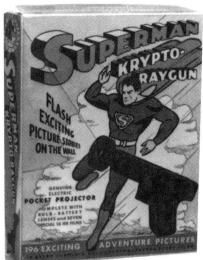

Superman Krypto-Raygun (Daisy 1940)

(New Haven Clock Co. 1939) . . . 1,500.00
(New Haven Clock Co. 1948) 750.00
Superman Mechanical Turnover Tank, silver
    tin litho tank and turret, with tin Superman
    on underside who turns over tank in
    motion, in 4" litho box, windup
    (Marx 1940) 1,000.00
Secret Code Wheel 4" dia. (Junior Justice
    Society of America premium 1940s) . 300.00
Superman cutouts, 10"x14½" book with 4

Superman Mechanical Turnover Tank (Marx 1940)

color cutouts of figures and objects
(Saafield #1502 1940) 1,000.00
Superman Dime Register Bank, 2½"x2½ tin
litho (DC 1940s) 250.00
Superman Premium Comic Book, 8 pages, 5"x7"
(Py-Co-Pay Tooth Powder 1940s) . . 300.00
Official Superman Costume, 40" long suit
with belt, mask and cape, illustrated
box (Ben Cooper 1940s) 500.00
Superman Record and Story Book, 7½"x8"
with two-sided record "The Flying Train"
and 10 story pages (Musette 1947) . 125.00
Superman Krypto-Raygun, black metal
with Superman embossed on stock
(Daisy 1940) 1,500.00
Superman Krypto-Raygun advertisement
on back of Children's Activities Magazine
dated December 1941 . . . . 50.00
Superman Cinematic Picture Pistol, with
Feature Film (Daisy #96, 1940) 600.00
Superman Boxes Set of 5 Films, in 6"x2½"
box (Acme/FAS 1946) 75.00
Superman Magic Ring record set
in story jacket (Musette 1947) 125.00
Superman Hair Brush, 4¼" wood (Superman,
Inc. 1940), various versions, each . . 75.00
Superman Sweater Patch 12"x13" wool
(Irvin Foster 1940s) 200.00
Superman Paint Set with illus. and dried
paint tablets & mixing dish (American
Toy Works #32, 1941) 150.00
Superman Pencil Box, 8"x4"x1" cardboard
box with raised illus. Superman
(American Pencil Co. 1940s) 75.00

Supermen of America emblem award

Pencil Case, cardboard-simulated
leather, Blue (Hassenfeld Bros.) 150.00
Superman Billfold (Hidecraft 1947) 300.00
COMICS and RADIO PREMIUMS
1938–42
Supermen of America Member Ring . 40,000.00
Supermen of America Membership
Certificate (Action Comics) 200.00
Supermen of America cello button 75.00
Supermen of America Code Card 75.00
Supermen of America Cloth Patch
(only two known to exist) 5,000.00
Action Comics Button (large picture) 150.00
Action Comics Button (small picture) 150.00
Secret Compartment Initial Ring
with paper picture inside 10,500.00
Secret Compartment Initial Ring
with Superman stamped in metal 10,000.00
Crusaders Ring 250.00
Junior Defense League Pin 300.00
Superman Defense America Pin 400.00
Superman Defense Club of America
Member Card (Roberts) 400.00
Superman Badge (Gum, Inc.) 2,000.00
Superman's Christmas Adventure
Comic (Macy's) 950.00
1942–50
Superman Parachute Rocket (H-O Oats) . 900.00
Superman Bread Promotional Card,
24 different, each 200.00
Superman Buckle and Belt
(Kellogg's Premium) 400.00
Kellogg's Corn Flakes cereal box with Norman
Rockwell picture on front & advertisement
for Buckle and Belt on back 50.00
Press Card for Stamps 100.00
Pennant 350.00
1950–59
Flying Superman (Kellogg's) 700.00
Kellogg's Corn Flakes cereal box with ad
for Flying Superman on back 40.00
Superman T Shirt (Kellogg's) 200.00
Krypton Rocket (red) and Launcher 300.00
Extra Rockets, blue and green, set 150.00
Superman Quoit Set (1950s) 75.00
Kellogg's Corn Flakes cereal box with ad
for Krypton Hydrojet Rocket 40.00
Superman Space Satellite
Launcher Set (gun and propellers) . . 500.00
Superman Dangle Dandy paper
cutout (Kellogg's) 150.00

All prices listed are for *Near Mint* condition.

SUPERMAN-TIM
Clothing Store and Radio Premiums
(1942–50)

Superman-Tim Club Pin ¾" litho
with secret code on back (1940s) . . . 75.00
Membership Button, profile 75.00
Membership Button, Tim's head
insert in circle 75.00
Membership card 200.00
Superman-Tim Ring 5,000.00
Superman-Tim store Monthly Membership
Pamphlet with stories, games and puzzles
1942, 16 pages, each 100.00
1943, 16 pages, each 100.00
1944, 16 pages, each 100.00
1945, 16 pages, each 100.00
1946, 14–16 pages, 5"x8", each . . . 100.00
1947, 14–16 pages, 5"x8", each . . . 100.00
1948, 14–16 pages, 5"x8", each . . . 100.00
1949, 14–16 pages, 5"x8", each . . . 100.00
1950, 14–16 pages, 5"x8", each . . . 100.00
Superman-Tim Club for Boys
Birthday Postcard 200.00
Puzzle Card 200.00
Superman Puzzle, 300 pieces, small
blue box (1940) 85.00
Superman-Tim Club Patch,
6 different (1944–45), each 600.00
Superman Action Target Set, boxed
(American Toy Works 1942) 750.00
Christmas Play Book (1944) 400.00
Superman-Tim's Press card, reverse has 12
squares to paste in Superman-Tim
stamps (1940s) 200.00
Superman-Tim Stamp Album (1946) 150.00
Stamps (1946), each 75.00
Stamps (1947–50) 75.00
Superman-Tim Red Backs certificate
redeemable for merchandise (1944) . 20.00
Supermen of America Button (1950) 75.00

1950s (Television Era)

George Reeves photo card 5"x7" postcard,
with comics pictured on back (1950s) 150.00
Kellogg's cereal cutout 3-D picture
(mid 1950s) 150.00
Superman Krypton Rocket premium, in
mailing box, red plastic with water
pump launcher (Kellogg's 1956) 500.00
Superman Belt, brown leather (1940s) . . . 150.00
Belt, red plastic with aluminum buckle
(Kellogg's premium (early 1950s) . . . 300.00
Superman Tank, Battery Operated

Superman Official Costume (Ben Cooper 1950s)

(Linemar 1958) 2,000.00
Superman Official Costume, red fabric
pants & cape, blue shirt, logo + belt
(Ben Cooper 1950s) 300.00
"Superman Space Satellite Launcher set"
plastic gun with satellite wheel
(Kellogg's premium 1950s) 700.00
Superman Pocket Watch, boxed
(Bradley 1959) 800.00
Superman Senior Swim Goggles
in box (Super Swim mid 1950s) 100.00
Superman Junior Swim Goggles
in box (Super Swim mid 1950s) 100.00
Superman Snorkle in box (Super
Swim mid 1950s) 250.00
Official Superman Swim Fins, blue rubber
in 7"x12" box with color illus. and
Safety Swim Club membership card
(Super Swim 1950s) 150.00
Official Superman Kiddie Paddlers,
blue rubber in 5"x8" box with color
illus. & Safety Swim Club membership
card (Super Swim mid 1950s) 300.00
Superman Leather zipper wallet 150.00
Superman Golden Muscle Building set
with 1½" "Superman Muscle Building
Club" pinback, 18"x11"x3" box, with
cartoon story inside, 2 handgrippers,
chest expander, chart & certificate
(Peter Puppet/Natl. Comics 1954) . . 800.00
Superman Lunchpail with robot picture and

---

bottle (Universal #4083SM, 1950s) . . 600.00
Superman Paint By Number Water Color set,
    4 pictures, paints (Transogram 1954) 100.00
Superman Lighter (Dunhill 1950s) 1,500.00

1960s

Superman M. Polaner and Son Jam Glasses
    labeled – "Polaners TV Treat Pure
    Concord Grape Jam" (5¾"or 4¼") (1964)
    Superman uses X-ray vision 75.00
    Superman in action 75.00
    Superman with Spaceship 75.00
    Superman versus Dragon 75.00
    Clark Kent changing into Superman . 75.00
    Superman to the rescue 75.00
Superman Stardust Art Set
    "Touch of Velvet" (Hasbro 1966) . . . 40.00
Paint by number book (Whitman 1966) . . 60.00
Superman club membership kit, record,
    card, patch and Button 150.00
"Superman Superwatch" plastic, movable hands
    on store card (Toy House 1967) . . . 75.00
Superman and Supergirl Push button
    puppets, 7"x5½"x2" window box with

Superman Swim Fins (Super Swim 1950s)

3½" plastic figures on bases (Kohner
    Bros. 191U, 1968) 200.00
Movie Viewer, plastic hand viewer, with
    two boxes of film (1965) 50.00
Cloth picture, color, rod through top
    edge for hanging, 16"x25" (1966) . . . 150.00

Vinyl wallpaper roll 20½" wide (1966) 100.00
Superman Colorforms 12"x8" box
    (Colorforms #260, 1964) 35.00
Boontonware Children's set, plate, bowl
    and cup (Boontonware 1966) 75.00
White glass mug, with picture (1966) 20.00
Superman Paper Plate and Cup Set (1966) 50.00
Superman Pillow Case (1966) 25.00
Superman Lunch Box, steel
    (King-Seeley 1967) 300.00
    Thermos for lunch box 6½" metal . . 40.00
Superman Metropolis Playset, with Krypton
    Kid, enemies, Superman Car and Solar
    Ray Weapon (Ideal #3323) . . . . . Unknown
Superman Musical Stories Record Album
    12" sq. (Tifton 1966) 40.00
Superman Body Building Set on 14"x24"
    card, red plastic barbell, blue plastic
    dumbbells, can be filled with water
    or sand (Irwin 1967) 200.00
Superman Water Gun (Multiple
    Toymaker 1967) 75.00
Superman Wallpaper roll, with full color illus.
    of Superman, Clark Kent, etc., 20" wide
    (United Wallpaper 1966) 100.00
Superman Ball on 7"x4" card (Natl.
    Latex 1966) 50.00
Superman Hand Puppet, cloth with vinyl head,
    full costume, 10", plastic with
    header card (Ideal 1965) 125.00
Flying Superman, 10" blue plastic, with
    cape, shoots in air with rubber band,
    on 10"x14" "Daily Planet" card
    (Hassenfeld 1965) 25.00
Superman Vinyl Wallet, brown (Standard
    Plastic Products 1966) 50.00
Superman Sparkle Paints set with
    5 pictures, on 8"x11" card (Kenner
    1960s) 50.00
Superman Outfit on 11"x15" cardboard
    illus. hanger (Lindsay #573, 1960s) . 75.00
Superman Rub-Ons magic picture transfers,
    12"x10"x1" cartoon illus. box with two
    8½"x11" pictures (Hasbro 1964) 85.00
Superman movie viewer, on 5"x7½"
    color card, with 2 boxed films
    (Chemtoy 1965) 50.00

1970s

Superman Wristwatch (Timex 1976)
    Large, boxed 60.00
    Small, boxed 50.00
Avon bottle 9½" vinyl bubble bath figure

All prices listed are for *Near Mint* condition.

bottle (Avon 1978) 10.00
Superman Ceramic Planter (1978) 15.00
Superman Drink Carton (1972) 15.00
Superman Star Dust paint set 45.00
Superman Soaky bottle 60.00
Superman color and paint book (Whitman) 25.00
Superman sparkle paints (Kenner) 45.00
Superman fork and spoon set (Imperial) .. 50.00
Superman Christmas ornament 3½" PVC .. 9.00
Superman Motorcycle, 11" yellow plastic
   cycle with decals and working headlight
   plus 6" full Superman figure (Taiwan
   late 1970s) 55.00
Kryptonite Rock, glows in dark, in box
   (1977) 25.00
Superman 11" figural nutcracker (1979) .. 25.00
Phonograph with carrying case (1978) ... 100.00
Superman Figural Telephone (ATE) 200.00
Superman Superhero moon glass
   (Pepsi 1976) 35.00
1980s and 1990s
Superman the Movie glasses
   Child to Man of Steel 10.00
   Kal-El Comes to Earth 10.00
   Lois Is Saved 10.00
   Superman Saves the Day 10.00
   Caped Wonder to the Rescue 10.00
   The Characters 10.00
Superman photo frame, 10"x8" holds 4"x6"
   photo (Warner Bros. #9515) 12.00
Superman watch, quartz, gold rim
   (Warner Bros. #9302) 30.00
Superman superhero 12-oz. mug, limited
   edition of 5,000, hero on handle
   (Warner Bros. #8300) 12.00
Superman: Better than Ever neon framed
   picture (Neonetics 1994) 225.00
Superman Red Beam Hologram, 8"x10"
   (Lightrix Studios 1994) 25.00
Superman: The First Anniversary of
   his Death watch 70.00

[DC] SUPER POWERS
(Kenner)
Color poster of the 12 first year
   characters, 18"x24" (Kenner) 10.00
Collector's Case 11" (Kenner) 20.00
Play Doh playset (Kenner 1985) 30.00
Birthday party plates (1986) 5.00
Super Powers signature stamp set (1985) 10.00
Birthday party centerpiece (1986) 5.00
Super Powers flashlights (1985) 10.00

Super Powers Lunch Box (Aladdin 1984–85)

Burger King cups (1987–88), set 45.00
   Batman, Darkseid, Superman,
   Wonder Woman, each 10.00
Sunglasses (1984)
   Superman (#14995) 5.00
   Batman (#14995) 5.00
   Wonder Woman (#14995) 5.00
Super Powers lunch box (Aladdin 1984–85)
   Steel box 30.00
   Thermos (plastic) 12.00
Super Powers (Burger King 1987)
   Superman Birthday Coin 5.00
   Batman Toothbrush Holder 5.00
   Aquaman Tub Toy 5.00
   Super Powers Stick-On Door Shield .. 5.00

SWAMP THING
Swamp Thing pencil toppers, 3 diff., each . 4.00
Swamp Thing stampers (1991) 3.00

TEENAGE MUTANT NINJA TURTLES
(Comics 1984–91; Movies 1990–91)

Playmates is the primary licensee of TMNT products. See the huge list of their action figures and vehicles in the Action Figures Series section. The much shorter list below consists of the other toy items from Playmates. Right after that is the huge list of TMNT toys by other manufacturers!

Playmates
Gags, Jokes and Crazy Weapons packs (1988):
   Set #1 Turtle ring squeeze bulb; joke
   book #1, weapons and shields 5.00

All prices listed are for *Near Mint* condition.

Set #2 Invisible Ink powder; Retromutagen squirter; joke book #2, weapons and shields 5.00

Set #3 Turtle Call razzer; Mutant turtle eggs; joke book #3; weapons & shields 5.00

Retromutagen Ooze, per 4oz. bucket (Playmates #5531, 1989) 3.00

Oozey (#5602, 1990) 5.00

Leonardo Sewer Force Sword (#5683, 1990) 10.00

Raphael Sewer Spy Goggles (#5642, 1990) 5.00

Michaelangelo Sewer Exploration Belt (#5641, 1990) 5.00

TMNT Battle Fun Set (#5026, 1989) 15.00

Turtle Bubble Sword (#5345, 1992) 13.00

Don's Sewer Squirter water gun (#5681, 1991) 5.00

Sewer Sports Football (#5199, 1991) 5.00

Sewer Sports Soccer Ball (#5198, 1992) . . 5.00

Sewer Sports (Baseball) Ball (#5190, 1991), four different turtles, each 4.00

Don's Telephone Line Rider Backpack (#5574, 1991) 10.00

Mike's Pizza Chopper Backpack (#5575, 1991) 10.00

Turtle Communicator (#5682, 1991) 10.00

Mutant Cartoon Maker Crazy Character kit (#5695, 1990) 15.00

Movie III Mike Samurai Fun Set (#5343, 1993) 10.00

Movie III Samurai Sword (#5344, 1993) . . . 5.00

Movie III Raph Samurai Fun Set (#5342, 1993) 10.00

Movie III Samurai Fun Set (#5340) 10.00

Talkin' TMNT Quick Strips, three different types (#5185) 4.00

Raphael, Your Ninja Practice Pal, large soft body (#5353, 1992) 20.00

My First Teenage Mutant Ninja Turtle, bath time toy (#5511, 1992) . . 5.00

TMNT Battle Fun Set (Playmates #5026, 1989) 10.00

TURTLE FORCE PRODUCTS
Fan Club

4" color turtle stickers 2.00

Pizza Point Premiums

Volume I

Poster of All 4 Turtles 5.00

Bookcover 3.00

Volume II

Keychain (#10740) 5.00

Sticker Set (#10520) 3.00

TMNT Memo Pad (#05400) 2.00

Leonardo full color lim. ed. poster (#05500)   3.00

Post-it Note Pad (#10700) 2.00

TMNT Pen Set of 4 (#10580) 3.00

TMNT Pencil Set of 4 (#05800) 3.00

Book Bag (#10620) 5.00

Cloth Lunchbag (#10625) 5.00

Beverage Bag (#10670) 5.00

3-piece Dinnerware Set (#10650) 10.00

TMNT Silverware (#10652) 10.00

Tumbler, 7 oz. (#10661) 2.50

Tumbler, 16 oz. (#10660) 3.50

Placemat (#10651) 3.00

Totally Tubular Tabulator calculator (#10710) 5.00

Mike Head Patch (#10565) 3.00

Don Head Patch (#10566) 3.00

Leo Head Patch (#10568) 3.00

Raph Head Patch (#10567) 3.00

TMNT logo patch 2.50

Mike Turtle Patch (#05600) 3.00

Don Turtle Patch (#05601) 3.00

Leo Turtle Patch (#05603) 3.00

Raph Turtle Patch (#05602) 3.00

Door Knob Hanger "Turtle Turf" (#05700) . . 2.00

Door Knob Hanger "Enter With Pizza" (#05701) 2.00

Door Knob Hanger "Fresh From the Sewer" (#10570) 2.00

Sun Visor (#10850) 2.00

OTHER TMNT PRODUCTS

T he pizza-powered four have generated a quantity of other licensed items that is truly staggering. Somebody will be collecting them all, someday . . . but so far very few, if any, have appreciated over their original retail price. This list is certainly not complete, but it is huge. It's designed to remind you that there are plenty of items to go around, so don't pay a premium price for any of these items and expect to get rich. Look for them at surplus stores and other secondary outlets where you can get them cheap! Look for items based on the characters **other than** the four turtles. There are a lot less of them.

Artistic

TMNT Light Art Board (Rose Art #1390) . . . CRP

TMNT Drawing Desk (Rose Art #8674) . . . CRP

TMNT Colorforms Set (Colorforms

#725, 1989) 7.00
Colorforms Adventure Set (Colorforms 1990) 9.00
World's Largest Colorforms Set
   (Colorforms #4801 1990) 12.95
TMNT Busy Builders (Colorforms
   #6014, 1991) 17.95
TMNT deluxe playset Colorforms
   #2384, 1991) 8.95
Character chalk (Janex), four different
   turtles, each 2.50
TMNT Design and Wear Magic
   Paint Set (Rose Art #1725) 10.00
TMNT Poster Pen set (Rose Art #1313) ... 5.00
TMNT Paint by Number (Rose Art #1999) . 10.00
TMNT Crayon by Number (Rose Art #1290) 7.50

Shredder Bubble Bath (Kid Care 1990)

Bath, Health and Grooming
Talking Turtles electric toothbrush
   (Janex 1988) 25.00
TMNT Adhesive Bandages (Ducair) 1.00
TMNT Bubble Bath (Ducair 1988) 2.50

TMNT printed tissues (Kid Care) 1.00
TMNT printed adhesive bandages (Kid Care) 1.00
TMNT full-figure bubble bath (Kid Care),
   Don, Mike, Raph or Leo, each 4.00
Figural soap (Kid Care), Donatello, Leonardo,
   Michaelangelo or Raphael, each 3.00
TMNT Foam Soap (Kid Care) 2.50
TMNT Mug, Brush, Comb and Toothbrush
   Set (Kid Care) 4.00
Shredder Ooze Bubble Bath (Kid Care) ... 3.00
Michaelangelo Ooze Bubble Bath (Kid Care) 3.00
TMNT Play Shaving Kit (Kid Care) 2.50
TMNT Locker Bag (Kid Care) 4.00
Bath Scribbler (Sears Page 293, 1992) ... 3.00
Soapdish (Sears Page 293, 1992) 3.00
TMNT Toothbrushes (U.K. only)
   (Search 1990) 5.00
Talking Raphael Toothbrush
   (J.C. Penney Page 434, 1990) 15.00
Buttons, Pins and Jewelry
TMNT movie Button collection of
   6 buttons (Button-Up #443902) 5.00
Big Buttons (Button-Up)
   TMNT The Movie, with all 4 turtles ... 2.00
   TMNT The Movie, with Leonardo
   and Raphael 2.00
   Cartoon Donatello 2.00
   Cartoon Leonardo 2.00
Buttons, 1" (Button-Up)
   TMNT Logo on blue background 1.00
   TMNT 4 turtles on white background . 1.00
   TMNT The Movie, Donatello in a truck 1.00
   TMNT The Movie, Raphael & Leonardo 1.00
   Splinter on red background 1.50
   Leonardo on yellow background 1.00
   Raphael on blue background 1.00
   Donatello on orange background 1.00
   Michaelangelo, background unknown . 1.00
Movie Limited-edition silver medallion
   (Chicagoland Processing 1990) 10.00
Necklace (Stephan Adrian 1990) 15.00
Earrings (Stephan Adrian 1990) 5.00
Pin (Stephan Adrian 1990) 5.00
Teenage Mutant Hero Turtles original
   buttons (Jeff Rudolph 1984) (U.K.) ... 10.00
Clothing, Costumes and Masks
Beach Slippers (Angel-etts of CA 1989),
   four different turtles, each 5.00
Sneakers (Angel-etts of CA 1989),
   four different turtles, each 10.00
Sneaker Strappers (Hope Industries
   #60834, 1990) 5.00

Belt Biter (Hope Industries
  #60934, 1990) 2.50
TMNT Belt Buckle (Lee Belt Co. 1989) 10.00
TMNT Battle Costumes (Sears Page 538, 1991),
  four different turtles, each .... CRP
TMNT Child's life jacket (Stearns
  #21318) 20.00

Fast-Food Toys
Turtel Head Mugs, four different turtles,
  in different colors, each 1.00
TMNT Badges (Burger King 1990):
  Raphael 5.00
  Leonardo 5.00
  Michaelangelo 5.00
  Donatello 5.00
  Shredder 5.00
  Heroes In A Halfshell 5.00
Turtle Translight 7.00
Turtles Horn 7.00
Spike Sliders (Burger King), four different
  turtles, each 5.00
TMNT Mini-Squeeze Bottle 3.00
TMNT License Plate 2.00
TMNT Bike Bag 4.00
TMNT Static Window Stick-on 1.00
Plastic Cup, Dig This (Playing Volleyball) .. 1.50
Plastic Cup, April 2.50
TMNT Translight for Kid's Meal 2.00
Shredder premium (Chef Boy Ardee) 2.50
Soda Cup and Lid (Pizza Hut), four different
  turtles, each 2.00

Food
TMNT in tomato and cheese sauce (Chef
  Boy Ardee) 2.50
TMNT sauce (with Shredder) (Chef
  Boy Ardee) 3.00
TMNT in tomato and cheese sauce
  with meatballs (Chef Boy Ardee) 2.50
TMNT sauce and meatballs (with Shredder)
  (Chef Boy Ardee) 2.50
TMNT Super Van (Party Wagon shaped) Box
  of Apple Cinnamon Grahams (Delicious
  Cookies 1988) 4.00
TMNT Cookie bank (Delicious Cookies 1989) 5.00
TMNT Pizza Cracker box (Delicious
  Cookies 1990) 3.00
TMNT Cookie box (Delicious Cookies 1988) 3.00
Ooze Gelatin (Nabisco), 2 diff., each 2.00
TMNT Pasta Dinner box (Primera 1990) ... 1.00
TMNT Pasta Dinner can (Primera 1990) ... 1.00
TMNT tube Candy Container with figural heads
  (1990), four different turtles, each ... 2.00

Shredder 3.00
Bebop 3.00
Splinter 3.00
Rocksteady 3.00
TMNT Cereal Box (Ralston Purina 1988) .. 1.00
TMNT Cereal comic book (Ralston Purina)
  Baxter Stockman cover 2.00
  Ray Fillet cover 2.00
  Wingnut cover 2.00

TMNT Cereal with free comic book

TMNT Wall Clock (Ralston Purina 1989) .. 10.00
TMNT Fruit Snacks (Farley) 3.00
Bag of Candy Gummi Turtles
  (small candies) (Alma [Leo]) 3.00
Large Gummi Candy Figures (Alma [Leo]),
  Four different turtles, each 2.00
  Shredder 3.00
  Splinter 3.00
Suckers (Amurol Products 1990), boxed ... 3.00
Donatello half figure, from candy
  container (Holiday Deliter) 5.00

Games and Puzzles
TMNT Shooting Gallery (Helm) 20.00
TMNT Pinball game (Helm) 25.00
TMNT City Sewer Turtle Chain Game
  (Helm #65) 15.00

All prices listed are for *Near Mint* condition.

TMNT Action Game (International
   Games 1990) 15.00
TMNT Tower of Doom action race and rescue
   game (International Games #7610) .. 25.00
TMNT Handheld electronic video
   game (Konami) 20.00
TMNT Talking Handheld Video
   Game (Konami 1990) 30.00
TMNT II: Splinter Speaks handheld
   video game (Konami 1990) 25.00
TMNT III Shredder's Last Stand handheld
   video game (Konami) 25.00
TMNT Sewer Ball game (Milton Bradley
   #4150) 20.00
TMNT Shooting Gallery pinball game
   (Playtime #62) 30.00
TMNT Pinball game (J.C. Penney
   Christmas catalog page 463, 1992) .. 30.00
TMNT Totally Awesome Dueling Dudes in
   boxing ring, Shredder versus Mike
   (Remco #18545) 30.00
TMNT Miniature Golf Course
   (Remco #18519) 13.00
TMNT Subterranean Sewer Hockey game
   39½"x24½" (Remco #18501, 1990) . 85.00
TMNT Pizza Toss Game (Remco #18544) . 15.00
TMNT Cowabunga Catch ball and paddle . 15.00
   Glove (Remco #18553, 1991) 10.00
TMNT Poppin Pins Bowling game
   (Remco #18524) 20.00
TMNT Fun Dough Pizza Maker
   (Rose Art #8670) 15.00
TMNT My Turtle Maker Fun-Dough
   Playset (Rose Art #8677) 15.00
TMNT II Arcade Game (Ultra Games) 25.00
TMNT III (Ultra Games) 25.00
TMNT Computer Game (Ultra Games) 25.00
TMNT Playing cards (U.S. Playing Card)
   purple or yellow box 5.00
Raphael Ball Bearing Game 10.00
TMNT Adventure Set (Paul Lamond
   Games [U.K.] 1990) 10.00

Glasses and Tableware

TMNT Mug (Peter Pan) 5.00
TMNT Cup (Peter Pan) 5.00
TMNT Plate (Peter Pan) 7.00
TMNT Cereal Bowl (Ralston Purina 1990),
   four different turtles, each 7.00

Holiday

Christmas Stocking (International Silver),
   four different turtles, each 3.00
TMNT Christmas Stockings (Wallace

International 1990) 3.00
TMNT Christmas ornaments (Wallace
   International 1990) 2.00
TMNT Easter Basket (Wallace
   International 1990) 3.00

Michaelangelo Bubble Bath (Kid Kare)

Household

TMNT Door Knob Hanger (all 4 turtles)
   (Antioch Publishing) 2.00
TMNT Door Knob Hanger (Welcome to
   the Sewer) (Antioch Publishing) 2.00
TMNT Slumber Bag/Comforter
   (Ero #71554) 20.00
TMNT Inflatable TV Chair (Helm 1989) ... 25.00
Christmas 1990 (J.C. Penney Catalog)
   Slumber Tent (Page 287) 30.00
   Overnight Bag (Page 287) 15.00
   Slumber Bag (Page 287) 20.00

Donatello Plush Chair (Page 491) . . . 20.00
Leonardo Plush Chair (Page 491) . . . 20.00
Michaelangelo Plush Chair (Page 491) 20.00
Raphael Plush Chair (Page 491) 20.00
Christmas 1991 (Sears Catalog)
  Slumber Tent (Page 436) 30.00
  Slumber Mates (Page 436) 12.50
  Slumber Bags (Page 436) 20.00
  Fun Hut (Page 436) 25.00
Christmas 1992 (J.C. Penney Catalog)
  Playhouse (Page 272) 30.00
  Slumber Tent (Page 272) 30.00
  Locker Bag (Page 272) 15.00
  Overnight Tote (Page 272) 10.00
  Comforter (Page 292) 15.00
  Pillow Sham (Page 292) 5.00
  Ruffled Bed Skirt (Page 292) 5.00
  Drapes (Page 292) 15.00
  Valance (Page 292) 5.00
  Tiers (Page 292) 5.00
  Blanket (Page 292) 12.00
  Sheets (Page 292) 10.00
Christmas 1992 (Sears Catalog)
  Sleeping Bag (Page 435) 20.00
  Slumber Mat (Page 435) 10.00
  Slumber Tent (Page 435) 25.00
TMNT Pillow (Springs Performance 1990) . 5.00
Raphael Night Lite (Street Kids) 2.50
Donatello Cookie Cutter 2.00
Leonardo Cookie Cutter 2.00
Michaelangelo Cookie Cutter 2.00
Raphael Cookie Cutter 2.00
TMNT Cake Pan 2.00
TMNT Beach Towel (Jay Franco 1988) . . . 3.00
Miscellaneous stuff
TMNT Plastic Squeeze bottles (Betras Plastic),
  four different colors, each 1.00
Flashlights (Happiness Enterprises 1990),
  four different turtles, each 1.00
TMNT Real Magnets (Hope Industries)
  Don and Mike (#60215) 1.00
  Leo and Raph 1.00
TMNT Wallet (Imaginings 3 1989) 3.00
Talking Turtle bubblegum bank (Janex
  1988) 10.00
Talking Gumball Bank (Janex #83215) 15.00
TMNT Supersipper Juice Box
  Holders, 4 diff. (Little Kids) 1.00
Soft Flying Disk sewer saucer (MB),
  four different turtles, each 2.00
TMNT Punch Ball (National Latex 1988) . . . 1.00
TMNT Aquarium (Nature's Toyland #NT-1C) 20.00

Leonardo Streamers (Rand) 3.00
TMNT 3-ft. Chain and Lock (Randor #472) . 5.00
TMNT Wrist Pocket (Randor #336) 2.00
TMNT 110 pocket camera (Remco 1990) . . 10.00
TMNT 35mm camera (Remco 1990) 15.00
TMNT Movie Music Kazoo (SBK 1990) . . . 2.00
TMNT Foot Lockers (Seward) 10.00
Sneaker zipper pulls (Stephan
  Adrian 1990) 1.00
Collector's Case (Tara Toy #20400, 1988) . 7.50
Collector's Case (Tara Toy #20400, 1991) . 5.00
Collector's Deluxe action figure Case
  (Tara Toy #20420, 1993) 10.00
TMNT View-Master 3-D three reel
  pack (Tyco #4210) 9.00
TMNT Movie II View-Master 3-D three
  reel pack (Tyco #4213) 9.00
TMNT Movie II View-Master reels
  (Tyco #4114) 4.00
TMNT View-Master Set (Tyco #2393) 4.00
TMNT Cartoon View-Master reels
  (Tyco #1073) 3.00
X-O Graph Button, Heroes in a Halfshell . . 2.00
TMNT Hotwater Bottle (Golden Bear
  Products [U.K.] 1990) 3.00
Party Items
TMNT Napkins, 16-pak (Unique #1181) . . . 2.00
TMNT Luncheon Napkins (Unique #1182) . 2.00
TMNT Tablecloth, paper (Unique #1183) . . 4.00
TMNT Plates, 7" diameter (Unique #1184) . 2.00
TMNT Plates, 9" diameter (Unique #1185) . 2.50
TMNT 7 oz. Party Cups (Unique #1186) . . . 2.00
TMNT Party Pak for 8 (Unique #1187) 5.00
TMNT Accessory Pak for 4 (Unique #1188) 4.00
TMNT Gift Wrap roll (Unique #1189) 1.50
TMNT Gift Wrap Set (Unique #1190, 1989) 2.25
TMNT Party Hats (Unique #1191, 1989) . . . 1.75
TMNT Blowouts, 8-pak (Unique #1192) . . . 2.00
TMNT Loot Bags (Unique #1193) 1.25
TMNT Invitations, 8-pak (Unique #1194) . . 3.00
TMNT Thank Yous (Unique #1195) 3.00
TMNT Christmas Wrapping Paper
  (Unique #1199) 2.50
TMNT Candles (Unique) 2.50
TMNT Instant Gift Wrap (Unique #11989) . . 2.75
TMNT Party Banner (Unique #11994, 1990) 1.25
TMNT 65-piece Party Set for 8
  (Unique #11985) 10.00
TMNT Candles, set of 4 . . . . 2.50
TMNT Erasers, set of 4 . . . . 1.00
TMNT Balloons, pack of five 14"
  balloons (National Latex) 3.00

All prices listed are for *Near Mint* condition.

Play Toys

TMNT Bow and Arrow Set (Daco)	15.00
TMNT Skateboard (Dynacraft)	15.00
Swim Mask and Snorkle (Ero #54490)	10.00
Beach Ball (Ero #F93220)	4.00
Swim Aids (Ero #F93217)	3.00
Swim Ring (Ero #F93214)	4.00
TMNT Fishing Kit (Woodstream 1990)	10.00
TMNT Cycle helmet (#8900)	15.00
TMNT Snowboard (SLM 1990)	10.00
Inflatable Pool (SLM #1661)	15.00
TMNT 42" kite (Spectra Star #6128)	5.00
TMNT skis (K2 1990)	25.00
TMNT Baseball Glove (Remco 1990)	15.00
TMNT Wacky Poppin' Pool (Remco)	15.00
TMNT Skates (Sears Page 554, 1991)	35.00
TMNT Ice Skates (Sears Page 562, 1991) .	35.00
TMNT Sno-Kart (Sears Page 565, 1991) . .	20.00
TMNT Flying Disks, with picture of Turtle	
(Spectra Star), 4 diff. turtles, each . . .	3.00
TMNT Wacky Winder (Spectra Star)	2.50
TMNT Poly Diamond Kite (Spectra	
Star #9905)	7.00
TMNT Marbles (Spectra Star)	1.00
Leonardo Yo-Yo (Spectra Star)	1.00
TMNT Green Water Pistol (TK #6821)	2.50
Skateboard (J.C. Penney Page 515, 1990) .	15.00
Pedal Driver (J.C. Penney Page 519, 1990)	CRP

Plush Figures

Plush figures, small or large (Ace Toy Company),	
four different turtles, each	10.00

School Supplies

TMNT Calculator (AJM Market	
Enterprises 1990)	4.00
PVC Bookmarks (Button-Up), four different	
turtles, each	1.00
TMNT Pencil Case (Henry Gordy)	2.00
TMNT Calculators (Hope Industries), four	
different turtles, each	3.00
TMNT School Kit (Imaginings 3 1989)	4.00
TMNT Belt Bag (Imaginings 3 #5260-1) . . .	5.00
Spiral notebooks (Imaginings 3)	
4 TMNT from waist up (#923)	1.50
Comic book illustrations (#283)	1.50
Cartoonish drawings (#923)	1.50
Movie, coming out of sewer (#923) . .	1.50
Don and Mike on purple (#923)	1.50
TMNT attacking Rocksteady (#923) . .	1.50
Folders (Imaginings 3)	
Don and Mike on purple (#924)	1.00
TMNT attacking Rocksteady (#924) . .	1.00
Movie II "Recycle Dude" (#924)	1.00

4 TMNT on school bus (#924)	1.00
Movie II Secret of the Ooze (#924) . .	1.00

TMNT Flying Props (Henry Gordy 1989)

Movie II Splinter (#924)	1.00
TMNT lime green pencil case	
(Kid's Katchalls)	2.00
Pencil, with Water Globe (Noteworthy),	
four different turtles, each	2.50
Water Globe Stamp (Noteworthy), four	
different turtles, each	3.00
Stamps (Noteworthy), four different	
turtles, each	1.50
Mininotepad (Noteworthy), four different	
turtles, each	1.00
TMNT Pencil Box (Tin Box Co. 1990)	2.00
TMNT Backpack, purple	5.00
TMNT Lunch Box, red, with	
Shredder in background (Thermos) . .	5.00

Stickers

TMNT Sticker Book (Diamond)	1.00
TMNT Sticker Pack (Diamond)	.50
TMNT Sticker Packs, Bag of 5 (Diamond) .	2.50
VHS video tapes, Bad Guys Stickers	
in every box (number unknown)	
(Family Home Entertainment)	1.00
TMNT Shiny Stickers (Mello Smello)	.50

TMNT Scratch and Sniff stickers
(Mello Smello) 1.00
TMNT Glow in the Dark stickers
(Mello Smello) 1.00
Miscellaneous toys
Sewer Scope Periscope (Tamfort
#173, 1989) 4.00

TMNT Action Set (Henry Gordy 1989)

TMNT toys, on card (Henry Gordy 1989)
Flying Props (propellers) set (#853) .. 3.00
Action Set, handcuffs and
glasses (#854) 4.00
Stamp and Color Set (#982) 3.00
Karate Punch Target Game (#869) .. 4.00
Sun Glasses 3.00
Binocular Set (#875) 3.00
Giant Puffy Sticker (#957) 2.00
Small Puffy Stickers 2.00
Pop-Pistol Target Game (#855) 3.50
Bubble Blaster (#847) 3.00
TMNT toys (Henry Gordy 1992)
Flying Props (propellers) set (#853) .. 2.00
Action Set, handcuffs & glasses (#854) 3.00
Marksman Target Set (#204) 2.50
Whirlwind Pinball Game (#206) 2.00

Karate Punch Target Game (#869) .. 2.50
Wall Art
Animation Cels (sold thru Toys "Я" Us) (MWS)
Four different turtles, each 5.00
Turtle in sailor suit 5.00
April 5.00
Bebop 5.00
Gengis Frog 5.00
Irma 5.00
Krang 5.00
Krang's Android Body 5.00
Rat King 5.00
Rocksteady 5.00
Shredder 5.00
Splinter 5.00
Wall Paper Wall Boarders (Plaid
Enterprises #27367) 5.00
Watches
TMNT watches, LCD digital, plastic strap, flip
up figure to see time (Hope Industries 1991)
Donatello (#60011, 1991) 9.00
Leonardo (#60021, 1991) 9.00
Michaelangelo (#60031, 1991) 9.00
Raphael (#60041, 1991) 9.00
April (1991) 9.00
TMNT watch, can be customized
to any turtle (Sears, 1991) 5.00
TMNT Talking Watches (Hope Industries)
Donatello (#60201) 7.00
Leonardo (#60202) 7.00
Michaelangelo (#60203) 7.00
Raphael (#60204) 7.00
TMNT Gold watch (Hope Industries 1989) . 10.00
Gift Set (Watch and 3 other items,
various assortments (Hope Industries
1990), each 15.00

TEKNO COMIX

Tekno Comix wristwatch (Tekno
Comix 1994) 60.00

THING

Thing ministand-up (Comic Images 1994) .. 4.00

THINGMAKER ACCESSORY KITS

Batman 20–55.00
Superman 20–55.00
Green Hornet 40–85.00

THOR

Thor Pennant (1966) 15.00

Thor Halloween Mask (Ben Cooper 1967) . 75.00
Thor Drinking glass (7-11 1977) 10.00
Thor mug (Applause late 1980s) 10.00
Thor Pez Candy Dispenser (1970s) 60.00

TWO-FACE
Two-Face divided head bookends 9"
(Warner Bros. 1995) 35.00

VENOM
Venom Dress-up Set (Toy Biz
#47352, 1995) 25.00
Venom ministand-up (Comic Images 1994) 4.00

WOLVERINE
Wolverine Combat Cave Danger
Room (Toy Biz #4971, 1991) 15.00
Wolverine Flying Marvel Superheroes
Glider, on card (Toy Biz #4990, 1992) 6.00
Wolverine ministand-up (Comic Images 1994) 4.00
Wolverine Action Phone (XWT-100, 1994) 45.00
Wolverine Wall Light 45.00
Wolverine Watch (Marvel 1994) 50.00
Wolverine PVC Bank (#1827, 1994) 8.50
Wolverine full body 7" flashlight (#1797) . . . 7.00
Wolverine 5" flashlight (#1796) 5.00
Wolverine nite lite (#1790) 4.00
Wolverine switchplate (#1795) 2.75
Wolverine Dress-Up Playset with mask and
claw glove (Toy Biz #4981, 1991) . . 11.00
Wolverine Motorized Mystery Bump & Go
Motorcycle, with figure (#71700, 1995) 7.00

WONDER WOMAN
(Comics 1941–present) (TV 1974, 1976–79)
Wonder Woman 7" plastic train car
(Tyco 1977) 15.00
Wonder Woman Pez Candy Dispenser (1970s)
Soft head 35.00
Hard head 5.00
Wonder Woman Dabs Super
Hero Watch 125.00
Wonder Woman Super Hero playing
card game (Russell's 1977) 7.50
Wonder Woman Ceramic Planter (1978) . 15.00
Wonder Woman mug (Applause late 1980s) 10.00
Wonder Woman clock (1970s) 65.00
Wonder Woman cake pan set
(Wilton 1970s) 25.00
Wonder Woman Colorforms set 15.00
Wonder Woman 12" hand puppet, plastic head,

Wonder Woman card game (Russell's 1977)

boxed (Ideal 1966) 25.00
Wonder Woman costume (Ben
Cooper 1976) 20.00
Wonder Woman Collapsible Tower playset
with Invisible Plane and Wonder
Woman 3¾" figures (Mego 1974) . . . 150.00
Wonder Woman Invisible Jet Pocket
Super Heros (Mego 1979) 125.00
Wonder Woman superhero moon glass
(Pepsi 1976) 35.00
Wonder Woman lunch box (Aladdin 1977)
Vinyl box 50.00
Thermos (plastic) 23.00

X-MEN
X-Men Collectors Case (Targa
#20570, 1991) 8.95
X-Men bean bagchair (Lewco
#6265, 1992) 26.95
X-Men bop bag (#1777) 5.95
X-Men fast flipper pinball
(Playtime #4819, 1992) 14.95
X-Men electronic pinball
(Playtime #4818, 1992) 29.95
X-Men Electronic hyperaction pinball with
digital sound (Playtime #4893, 1992) 39.95

All prices listed are for *Near Mint* condition.

Wolverine Combat Cave (Toy Biz 1991)

X-Men Clip Board (#17009) 1.95
X-Men Die-cut Erasers (#17004) 1.95
X-Men Magnetic wipe-off board (#17015) . . 2.95
X-Men Plastic storage box (#17008) 2.95
X-Men puzzle pen (#17003) 2.45
X-Men Stencil Kit (#17006) 5.95
X-Men Study Kit (#17007) 1.95
X-Men 3-D Sharpener (#17005) 2.45
X-Men 3-D stamper (#17011) 1.95
X-Men 3-D pencil toppers (#17002) 2.45
X-Men 3-pack pencils (#17001) 1.50
X-Men wipe-off board (#17010) 1.95
X-Men Value pack, 11 pieces
    (Impact #3885, 1994) 7.95
X-Men Handheld game (#7854, 1992) . . . 19.95
X-Men: Project X Handheld game
    (#78504, 1992) 19.95
X-Men LCD Watch (CD176) 9.95
X-Men Playtent 45"x33"x33" (Ero
    #11005, 1994) 27.00
X-Men Play Putty (#3003, 1994) 3.95
X-Men Analog Watch (Innovative
    Time 1994) 20.00
Xavier's Institute Analog Watch
    (Innovative Time 1994) 20.00
X-Men 2099 ministand-up (Comic Images
    1994) 3.95
Uncanny X-Men carded toys (Henry Gordy 1991)
    Surveillance Kit (#155) 2.00
    Bubble Blaster (#156) 3.00
    Watergun (#159) 2.00

Sunglasses (#160) 2.00
Glider Launcher with 2 gliders (#161) . 2.00
Soft Darts Target Set (#162) 2.50
"Flying Props" Propeller Gun with
    two propellers (#164) 2.00
Karate Punch Target Set (#165) 2.50
Cap Bomb Set (#166) 1.50
Vinyl Stickers (#167) 1.00
Color Changing Flash Gun B/O (#168) 2.00
Sparkle Gun (#169) 2.00
Signal Flash Gun B/O (#177) 2.50
Handcuffs (#196) 2.00
X-Men playing cards (U.S. Playing Card) . . 3.00
X-Man Candy Tube Figures, 3" with movable
    arms, Hulk or Spider-Man 2.50
X-Men Pocket Comics with trading card, tiny
    figures, accessories (Toy Biz 1994–95)
    Danger Room (#49201, 1994) 5.00
    Asteroid 'M' (#49202, 1994) 5.00
    Spy Mission (#49203, 1994) 5.00
    Jet Hangar (#49204, 1994) 5.00
    Weapon X Lab (#49301, 1995) 5.00
    Master Mold (#49302, 1995) 5.00
    Cerebro Room (#49303, 1995) 5.00
    War Room (#49304, 1995) 5.00

GAMES

G ame collecting, a hobby which has seen enormous growth in the last ten years, has become a new and widely accepted pastime. There are several rules of thumb novice game collectors should familiarize themselves with before encountering the chutes and ladders of the business.

One of the important concerns for game enthusiasts is the buying or trading of unseen games from auction, fixed-price lists or through correspondence via mail or phone. Grading is then very important to the buyer. The grading of games is, at best, subject to one's own individual opinions. So many factors come into play that a single grade can never truly tell the story.

Guidelines, however, have been set down by dealers and collectors alike. The standard grades for games break down as follows: Mint, Near Mint, Excellent, Very Good, Good, Fair, and Poor. The outside box, the colors, the inside box, completeness and the condition of the pieces are all factors which determine the grading of games. Paper and cardboard are the main ingredients in games, but the occasional metal spinner, tokens and wooden tokens must also be judged where grading is concerned.

Games deteriorate much quicker than most collectibles, such as plastic toys, metal toys, cards, stamps and coins. Boxes eventually flatten, parts inevitably get lost, and mildew, water and light soon take their harsh toll. The result is that games just don't hold up to their environment.

A game played only five or six times will usually show decisive wear; even careful storage of games can result in warped boxes or sagged centers. In addition, misplaced game pieces, die and instructions present continual roadblocks

in game collecting. The popular and pricey game of Milton Bradley's **Dark Shadows** was issued with white plastic fangs to be worn by players. These fangs are rarely found with the game today.

Snip Snap Newspaper Premium Game (1905–7)

On the positive side of collecting games is the fact that families rarely threw out their games; they were kept and stored in attics or basements. The result is that interesting and rare games are always surfacing for sale. This aspect is what allows the hobby to remain ever exciting and fresh. Primarily, it is a hobby still in its infancy, and it is not uncommon to find a game which no expert ever knew to exist. In another sense, game playing is a pastime as old as this country, with several American card games published in the late 1700s.

The outside box is the collector's first and prime concern in terms of grading. The points on the corners of the box should be the primary focal point since it is here that the game usually shows the first signs of wear. From this point, the other areas of the outside box should be examined, including the state of the box top graphics. If the box is totally damaged and defaced, it is hardly collectible, and a game without a box top is good for playing only.

The inside, or components of the game,

is also an important attribute. A great box without a board is of very limited value since the board is the foremost collectible item in the game. Even early boards (pre-1940), in and of themselves, have a collectible value. Minor parts missing from the inside does lessen the value, but major parts missing can devastate the value of a game to a collector. For example, missing items which are unique to a game, such as the scales or special spinner found in the **Game of Justice** by Lowell, can decrease the value of a game significantly.

Lack of special metal tokens or punched cardboard graphic images can also lessen the value. Instructions are important in the higher grades, but often Xerox copies are acceptable in the lesser conditions. Remember that you *cannot* play a game without the instructions.

Now that you have some idea of the aspects that are integral to game collecting, investing in reference guides and newsletters will help you go to the head of the class. Numerous quality books on games have been printed including *Spin Again* by Rick Polizzi and Fred Schaefer and *Warman's Antique American Games 1840–1940* by Lee Dennis. Polizzi and Schaefer's book is devoted to the board games of the fifties and sixties while the Dennis book, in its second issue, includes revised market values and several hundred photos. *Games: American Boxed Games and Their Makers 1822–1992 with Values* by Bruce Whitehill is an excellent overview of games in general.

Publications such as these, along with various toy catalogues which feature games, continue to create new collectors. The formation of groups devoted to the game cause, such as the American Game Collectors Association, has also helped nurture new enthusiasts. The AGCA publishes two scholarly newsletters, including *Game Times* and *Game Researcher's Notes.*

Good research and exposure to game conventions will ensure that the road to collecting will not be a trivial pursuit. Who knows, perhaps you'll even be able to monopolize the games market without passing go!

COMIC AND CARTOON GAMES

Comic game history dates back to a late-19th century game series called the Brownies Related Games. In 1883, Palmer Cox created the first illustrated story of **The Brownies Ride**; this creation of new, funny, illustrated characters with ongoing stories was the inspiration for numerous comic games.

The first comic-related board game was called **The New Game of Social Brownies** by C. L. Sirenne (1894). This rare game was sold at auction for $1,000 (including the buyer's fee). Two years after Sirenne's Brownies, R. F. Outcault's **The Yellow Kid** debuted in a Sunday comic strip. This character was later immortalized in a wooden ladder game.

Shortly thereafter, **KatzenJammer Kids** by Dirks and **Happy Hooligan** by Opper were having their own adventures in the game world. Other popular comic strips such as **Little Nemo** and **Buster Brown** were also made into board games.

Selchow and Righter, an early game manufacturer, made comic character games from the early 1900s to the early 1920s. **Foxy Grandpa's Card Game**, **Foxy Grandpa's Christmas Tree Game** and **Reg'lar Fellers Bowling Game** are among some of their titles.

On December 2, 1906, the *New York Sunday American and Journal* produced a Christmas game supplement called **The Game of Maud**, or **Hee Haw**. This card game, which had to be cut from the paper to be played, featured various popular comic characters of the time. These cards featured characters such as Alfonse, Buster Brown, Yellow Kid, Maud, Katzen-Jammer Kids, Foxy Grandpa, Tiger and Happy Hooligan.

A small game company in Chicago, the Hendriksen Manufacturing Company, made comic character games in the 1920s with wonderful covers: **Oh Min!**, **Funny Fellers** and **Mama's Darlings with the KatzenJammer Kids**.

Milton Bradley decided to capitalize on its success in comic character games and continued to expand its line in the 1930s, adding **Harold Teen, The Nebs, Smith Game, Walt and Skeezix, Gasoline Alley Game** and **Chester Gump Game** in deluxe editions. They even added a budget line of comic games with the bottom of the box serving as the board! These games also included a specific theme, as in the following games: **Moon Mullins Automobile Race, Winnie Winkle Glider Race Game, The Gumps at the Seashore, Skeezix and the Air Mail, Skeezix Visits Nina** and **Moon Mullins Gets the Run-A-Round**.

The Gumps at the Seashore (Milton Bradley 1935)

All Fair Game Company produced one spectacular comic game in 1928, called **Highway Henry**, with a very ornate comic cover featuring Henry traveling down a long, winding road, meeting various cartoon characters. All Fair also produced a fine card game titled **Buck Rogers in the 25th Century**, with a multitude of highly colorful characters from the strip.

One of the most sought after games from the 1930s is the Lutz and Steinkman

game of **Buck Rogers** (1934). This game has three very colorful boards which take Buck on three different adventures. Buck Rogers was both an adventure hero and a science fiction figure. He certainly was an inspiration for many of the superheroes that followed!

Whitman entered comic strip game manufacturing in the mid 1930s after gaining licenses for some very popular characters. They produced card and board games of **Popeye, Dick Tracy, Skippy, Oh Blondie, Little Orphan Annie** and **Terry and the Pirates.** Several versions of different adventures were produced by Whitman featuring these characters.

EARLY COMIC CHARACTERS

Adventure of the Nebbs Deluxe Board Game
(Milton Bradley 1925) 250.00
All Star Comics Card Game (Whitman
Publishing 1934) 100.00
Alley Oop Jungle Game (Whitman
Publishing 1930s) 150.00
Alley Oop Can Edition (Royal Toy) 50.00
Alley Oop Boxed Set (Slesinger 1937) . . . 75.00
Andy Gump; His Game (Milton
Bradley 1927) 125.00
Andy in the White House (Milton
Bradley 1935) 125.00
Barney Google and Spark Plug Game
(Milton Bradley 1926) 200.00
Bringing Up Father Game
(Embee Dist. Co. 1920s) 125.00
Brownie Horseshoe Game
(M.H. Miller Co. 1920s) 100.00
Brownie Kick-in Top (M.H.
Miller Co. 1920s) 100.00
Brownie Ring Toss (M.H.
Miller Co. 1920s) 100.00
Brownie Ladder (Bliss 1900) 700.00
Brownies Auto Race (1920s) 150.00
Brownies and other Queer Folk
(Parker Bros. 1894) 350.00
Brownies Ten Pin set
(McLaoghlin 1900) 1,100.00
(Buck Rogers) Game of the
25th Century (1934) 350.00
(Buck Rogers) Interplanetary Games, set
of 3 boards in illustrated box (1934) . 550.00

Cocomalt version, plain red box 500.00
All-Fair card game, "Buck Rogers in the 25th
  Century," 36 cards (E. E. Fairchild 1936),
  in box 425.00
(Buck Rogers) Combat game, interlocking
  panels with stand-up figures
  (Warren 1937) 375.00
Buster Brown at Coney Island
  (Ottman 1910) 200.00
Buster Brown Bean Bag Toss, Double
  Tier (Bliss 1900) 800.00
Buster Brown and His Dog Tige,
  cards (1920s) 150.00
Buster Brown Neck Tie Party,
  cloth game 200.00
Buster Brown Bean Bag Toss
  (Bliss 1900) 450.00
Chester Gump Hops Over the Pole
  (Milton Bradley 1935) 100.00
Chester Gump Game with treasure cover
  (Milton Bradley 1938) 300.00
Chester Gump In the City of Gold Game
  (Milton Bradley 1930s) 225.00
Climbing Brownie; Litho paper on wood
  climbing figures 350.00
Detective Game, Famous Artist Syn.
  board (1937) 75.00
Dick Tracy Whitman Card Game (1934) . . 75.00
Dick Tracy Whitman Card Game (1937) . . 60.00
Dick Tracy Playing Card Game;
  2 diff. boxes (Whitman Pub. 1934) . . 75.00
Dick Tracy Detective Game
  (Whitman 1937) 150.00
Dick Tracy Super Detective Mystery
  Card Game (Whitman Pub. 1933) . . 80.00
Dick Tracy Detective Game
  (Einson Freeman 1933) 250.00
Foxy Grandpa World's Fair
  (Ottman 1904) 300.00
Foxy Grandpa Hat Party
  (Selchow & Righter) 150.00
Foxy Grandpa World's Fair
  (Ottman 1904) 300.00
Foxy Grandpa Card Game
  (Ottman 1900s) 125.00
Foxy Grandpa, An Up To Date Game
  (Selchow & Righter 1910s) 100.00
Foxy Grandpa Christmas Tree
  (Baker and Bannnot 1905–15) 300.00
Funny Fellers (Hendkson 1920) 300.00
Game of Maud, Buster Brown, Foxy Grandpa,
  Yellow Kid, Alphonse, KatzenJammer Kids,

N.Y. American Sunday supplement
  card game 200.00
Game of Skippy (Milton Bradley 1932) . . . 225.00
The Gumps at the Seashore (Milton
  Bradley 1935) 100.00
H-Bar-Q, Radio premium
  (H-Bar-Q Ranch 1930s) 75.00
Happy Hooligan Popgun Target
  Game (Milton Bradley 1925) 300.00
Happy Hoppers and Game Solitaire;
  Brownies on cover (Parker
  Bros. 1899) 250.00
Harold Teen, A Game; deluxe
  (Milton Bradley 1920s) 250.00
Harold Teen, A Game (Milton
  Bradley 1920s) 150.00
Harold Teen Game, Up The Ladder
  (Milton Bradley 1936) 125.00
Henry Rings the Bell (Parker
  Bros. 1930s) 400.00
Hi Way Henry (All Fair 1928) 2,200.00
Little Nemo—A Game (small box)
  (Milton Bradley 1905–10) 1,000.00
Little Nemo—A Game (Milton
  Bradley 1905–10) 500.00
Little Orphan Annie to the Rescue
  (Milton Bradley 1935) 150.00
Little Orphan Annie Rummy
  (Whitman Pub. 1930) 60.00
Little Orphan Annie Treasure Isle of Health
  and Happiness (Ovardne Premium) . 150.00

Little Orphan Annie Game (Milton Bradley 1927)

Little Orphan Annie Game, Deluxe
  Edition (Milton Bradley 1927) 250.00
Little Orphan Annie Game
  (Milton Bradley 1935) 125.00
Little Orphan Annie Travel Game
  (Milton Bradley 1935) 125.00
Moon Mullins Gets the Run-A-Round
  (Milton Bradley 1935) 100.00
Moon Mullins Automobile Race
  (Milton Bradley 1935) 150.00

All prices listed are for *Near Mint* condition.

Moon Mullins Game Deluxe
(Milton Bradley 1927) 225.00
Moon Mullins Game (Milton
Bradley 1930s) 225.00
Moon Mullins Game, yellow deluxe cover
(Milton Bradley 1938) 250.00
Nebbs Card Game, Deluxe Large
Edition (Milton Bradley 1925) 100.00
Nebbs Card Game (Milton Bradley 1925) . 75.00
New Game of Social Brownies
(C. L. Sirenne 1894) 1,000.00
Og, Son of Fire (Whitman Pub. 1930s) . . . 150.00
Oh Min! (Henricksen 1920s) 200.00
Our Comic Ladder (Bliss 1900) 450.00
Popeye Card Game; red box;
(Whitman Pub. 1937) 50.00
Popeye Party Game (Whihan Pub. 1937) . 75.00
Popeye the Sailor Shipwreck Game
(Einson-Freeman 1933) 250.00
Popeye Card Game; 3 dfff. boxes;
(Whitman Pub. 1934) 50.00
Popeye Pipe Toss (Rosebud Art 1935) . . 50.00

Popeye Ring Toss Game (Rosebud Art 1937)

Popeye Ring Toss (Rosebud Art 1937) . . 75.00
Popeye's Game: Tiddly Winks type
(Parker Bros.) 225.00
Poppin' Popeye Target Game (1930s) . . . 250.00
Red Ryder Target Game
(Whitman Pub.) 125.00
Reg'lar Fellers Bowling Game
(Milton Bradley 1926) 125.00
Reg'lar Fellers (Selchow &
Righter 1920s) 600.00
Skeezix Game (w/police car)
(Milton Bradley 1930s) 300.00
Skeezix Card Game (Milton
Bradley 1930s) 100.00
Skeezix Visits Nina (Milton
Bradley 1937) 100.00

Skeezix and the Air Mail
(Milton Bradley) 80.00
Skippy Card Game (All Fair 1930s) 75.00
Smitty Game (Milton Bradley 1930s) 300.00
Smitty Speed Boat Race Game
(Milton Bradley 1935) 125.00
Snip Snap Newspaper Premium Game, with
Alphonse, Foxy Grandpa, Leander,
KatzenJammer Kids, Gaston, Uncle
Heine, Happy Hooligan, Tiger, Noah
(1905–7) 200.00
Terry and the Pirates Game
(Whitman Pub. 1937) 250.00
The Game Of Keeping Up With the
Joneses (Philips 1920s) 125.00
The Nebbs on the Air,
radio game (Milton Bradley 1930) . . 100.00
The Alphabet Game; Brownies on Cover
(Parker Bros. 1893) 100.00
Toonerville Trolley Game
Deluxe (Milton Bradley 1927) 300.00
Walt and Skeezix (Milton
Bradley 1920s) 275.00
Winnie Winkle Glider Race Game
(Milton Bradley 1920s) 125.00
Winnie Winkle Game (Milton
Bradley 1930s) 300.00
Yellow Kid Comic Ladder (Bliss 1900) . . . 500.00

COMIC CHARACTER GAMES
1940s–90s

After World War II, when many game companies went under, Bradley introduced a new line of six cartoon games, including **Gordo and Pedito, The Game of Li'l Abner, Ella Cinders, The KatzenJammer Kids, Blondie and Dagwood's Race for the Office Game** and **The Game of Abbie An' Slats**. Milton Bradley continues to license comic character games today, including the popular animated movie **Who Framed Roger Rabbit?**

Transogram introduced several comic characters that worked well in fun comic games. **Prince Valiant: A Game of Valor** and various Terry Toon games, including the **Hide 'N' Seek Game**, were produced by Transogram.

By the 1950s, new companies started

producing games. Lowell Toy Company made **Steve Canyon**. In this exciting Air Force game, you're a real jet pilot. Players must fly through storms, and make emergency landings; instrument flying and an actual fuel gauge were among this game's features. They also made a **Joe Palooka Boxing Game**.

The young toy manufacturer Hassenfeld Brothers, now Hasbro, made a 1965 3-D game group known as **The Thimble Theatre Game**. These were titled **Popeye: The Strongest Man in the World**; **Olive Oil: I'll Catch My Popeye**, and **Wimpy: Where Are My Hamburgers?**

During this period, television was producing new comic cartoon characters, and these largely supplanted comic strip characters as the source for games. Of course, this didn't stop comic strip characters from making their way onto game boards. It just meant that they had to make their way into a TV show first!

Alfred's Other Game (Selchow &
   Righter 1985) 15.00
Adventures of Popeye
   (Transogram 1957) 75.00
The Archie Game (Whitman 1969) 35.00
Beetle Bailey (Jaymar) 80.00
Blondie Playing Card Game
   (Whitman 1941) 50.00
Blondie Game (Parker Brothers) 35.00
Blondie Sunday Funnies Board Game
   (Ideal 1972) 50.00
Blondie Goes to Leisureland
   (Westinghouse Premium 1940) 55.00
Blondie Playing Card Game
   (Whitman Pub. 1941) 45.00
Blondie, The Hurry Scurry Game
   (Transogram 1966) 50.00
Blondie and Dagwood's Race for the
   Office (Jaymar 1950) 50.00
Buck Rogers Adventures in the 25th
   Century Game (Transogram 1970s) . . 65.00
Buck Rogers 25th Century
   (Transogram 1965) 45.00
Buck Rogers: Battle for 25th Century
   (TSR 1988) 24.00
Buck Rogers Martian War (TSR) 25.00

Captain And The Kids (Milton
   Bradley 1946) 75.00
Cartoon Capers Game (Warren-Built
   Rite 1970s) 50.00
Casper the Friendly Ghost (Milton
   Bradley 1959) 65.00
Casper the Ghost, Glow in the Dark
   (Schaper 1974) 35.00
Comic Card Game (Milton Bradley 1972) . . 35.00
The Curious George Game (Parker
   Brothers 1977) 20.00
Dick Tracy, A Sunday Funnies Game
   (Ideal 1972) 175.00
Dick Tracy (Selchow & Righter 1961) 65.00
Dick Tracy Crime Stopper (Ideal 1963) . . . 125.00
Dick Tracy Mystery Card Game
   (Whitman 1941) 60.00
The Dick Tracy Game (University
   Games 1990) 20.00
Dondi Finders Keepers (Hasbro 1959) 60.00
Dondi Potato Race (Hasbro 1960) 50.00
Ella Cinders (Milton Bradley 1944) 100.00
Elsie And Her Family (Selchow &
   Righter 1941) 50.00
Elsie and Her Family, Jr. Edition
   (Selchow & Righter 1941) 60.00
Felix The Cat (Milton Bradley 1968) 50.00
Felix The Cat Game (Milton
   Bradley 1960) 50.00
Flash Gordon (Game Gems 1965) 40.00
Game of Abbie And Slats (Milton
   Bradley 1946) 100.00
The Game of Abby 'N' Slatts
   (Milton Bradley 1944) 125.00
Game of Li'l Abner (Milton Bradley 1944) . . 85.00
Gay Puree Board Game (UPA Cartoon
   Show 1962) 50.00
Garfield (Parker Brothers 1981) 15.00
Garfield Card Game (Bicycle
   Games 1978) 10.00
Gordo And Pepito (Milton Bradley 1947) . . 95.00
Good Ol' Charlie Brown Game (Milton
   Bradley 1971) 25.00
Hashimoto Sam (Transogram 1960) 65.00
Heathcliff, Munch Out (Warren 1982) 15.00
Heckle And Jeckle's Ski Trail Game
   (Whitman 1971) 25.00
Hide 'N' Seek Game (Transogram) 50.00
High Spirits With Calvin, Game Of
   (Milton Bradley 1962) 125.00
Jim Prentice Electric Comin' Round The
   Mountain (Electric Game Co. 1950s) 100.00

All prices listed are for _Near Mint_ condition.   **237**

Joe Palooka Boxing Game (Lowel
Toy Co.) 200.00
KatzenJammer Kids Hockey
(Jaymar 1940s) 125.00
King Leonardo and his Subjects
(Milton Bradley 1960) 75.00

Li'l Abner, His Game (Milton Bradley)

The Li'l Abner Game (Parker
Brothers 1969) 65.00
Li'l Abner Game (Milton Bradley 1944) . . . 125.00
Li'l Abner Spoof Game (Milton
Bradley 1960) 50.00
Little Orphan Annie (Selchow
& Righter 1978) 25.00
Little Lulu Adventure Game (Milton
Bradley 1946) 150.00
Lucy's Tea Party Game (Milton
Bradley 1971) 45.00
Mad's Spy Vs. Spy (Milton Bradley 1956) . . 35.00
Mad Magazine Game (Parker
Brothers 1979) 35.00
Mad Magazine Card Game (Parker
Brothers 1980) 22.00
MAD's Spy Vs. Spy (Milton Bradley 1986) . 15.00
The Master Detective Game (Dick Tracy)
Sechow & Rightez (1962) 75.00
Nancy & Sluggo Game (Milton
Bradley 1944) 125.00
Nickelodeon, The Ren & Stimpy Show,
Target Toss (Cereal give-away) (1994) 5.00
Oh Blondie (Whitman 1940) 75.00
Peanuts (Selchow & Righter 1959) 75.00
Peter Potamus (Ideal 1964) 150.00
Popeye's 3 Game Set (Built-Rite 1956) . . . 70.00
Popeye's Sliding Boards and Ladders Game
(Warren 1958) 65.00
Popeye's Old Maid (Jaymar 1970s) 25.00
Popeye Card Game (Ed-U-Cards 1960s) . . 20.00
Popeye Games (Built-Rite 1958) 70.00
Popeye's Game, tiddly winks–type game
(Parker Brothers 1948) 135.00
Popeye Card Game, Based on the Arcade

Game (Parker Brothers 1983) 15.00
Popeye Board Game, based on Popeye 1980
film (Milton Bradley 1980) 5.00
Popeye Party Game (Unique Ind. 1980) . . . 2.00
Popeye Board Game (Parker Bros. 1983) . 5.00

Prince Valiant Crossbow Pistol Game (Parva 1948)

Prince Valiant Crossbow Pistol Game
(Parva Products Co. 1948) 150.00
Prince Valiant: A Game of Valor
(Transogram 1950s) 65.00
Rex Morgan Sunday Funnies Board Game
(Ideal 1972) 55.00
Richie Rich Big Money Game
(Pressman 1977) 20.00
Ruff and Ready Game
(Transogram 1962) 50.00
Ruff and Ready Spelling Game (Exclusive
Planning Card 1960s) 25.00
"Screwball" The Mad Mad Game
(Transogram 1958) 60.00
"Screwball" The Mad Mad Game
with Microphone (Transogram 1960) . 45.00
Sigmund and the Sea Monsters Game
(Milton Bradley 1974) 35.00
Silly Sidney (Transogram 1963) 65.00
Snoopy (Selchow & Righter 1960) 65.00
Snoopy Come Home Game (Milton
Bradley 1966) 50.00
Snoopy Card Game (Milton Bradley 1965) . 25.00
Snoopy Versus the Red Baron (Milton
Bradley 1970) 35.00
Snoopy Snack Attack Pop-O-Matic
Game (Gabriel #70345, 1980) 30.00
Snagglepuss Picnic Game
(Transogram 1962) 50.00

Snuffy Smith's Hoot 'N' Holler Bug Derby
(Jaymar 1940s) 75.00
Space Mouse Card Game
(Fairchild 1964) 35.00
Spooky, Marble Maze Game
(Warren 1971) 20.00
Steve Canyon (Lowel Toy 1959) 75.00
Super Detective Mystery Card Game
(Whitman 1941) 50.00
T. Simpsons Mystery Of Life
(Cardinal 1990) 15.00
Thimble Theatre Game, Olive Oyl: I'll
Catch My Popeye (Hasbro 1965) 75.00
Thimble Theatre Game, Wimpy: Where Are
My Hamburgers? (Hasbro 1965) 75.00
Thimble Theatre Game, Popeye: The Strongest
Man In The World (Hasbro 1965) 75.00
The Tom & Jerry Game (Selchow &
Righter 1962) 80.00
Tom and Jerry Game (Milton
Bradley 1968) 55.00
Top Cat (Whitman 1962) 75.00
TMNT Pizza Powers Game (Random
House 1987) 15.00
Turtles (Entex 1982) 10.00
Underdog Game (Milton Bradley 1964) . . . 50.00
Woody Woodpecker Up The Game
(Whitman 1969) 75.00
Yertle, Game Of (Revell 1960) 100.00

SUPERHEROES GAMES

Superhero games are a quickly growing part of the game market. In 1941, Milton Bradley announced the first superhero games, based on the comics superhero Superman. Bradley's press release said "from the greatest cartoon sensation of the year — Superman — eagerly followed by millions of children, in cartoon papers (comics) and in the movies — now incorporated into three popular Milton Bradley Games."

The finest (and rarest) is **The Adventures of Superman**. In this game, the players represent reporters who set out to reach the center "Editorial Sanctum" with their stories. The play is governed by the influence of Superman, and a Superman cloak fits over the playing pieces. This game originally sold new for $1.00; it

now brings $300 to $400. Issued along with this game was the **Superman Speed Game** and the **Superman Target Game**.

DC's superheroes were made into games by Hasbro in two periods: 1965 and 1978. The scarce but popular 1965 series of five games is titled **Super Boy Game: Can Superboy Escape the Deadly Green Kryptonite?**; **The Batman Game: The Adventures of the Caped Crusader**; **The Superman Game: Search for Superman's Deadliest Enemy**; **The Batman and Robin Game: Help Batman and Robin Capture the Joker**; and **The Wonder Woman Game**.

One year later, Transogram released the **Mighty Comics Superheroes Game**. This scarce game involved ten superheroes named The Shield, The Hood, Captain Flagg, Mr. Fox, The Web, Mr. Justice, Mr. Jag and Mr. Steel, Fly Man and Girl. This game sells for $200.00 now!

The Incredible Hulk Smash-Up Action Game
(Ideal 1970s)

Marvel Comics' first game was issued in 1967 by Milton Bradley and was called **The Amazing Spider-Man Game**, with "Marvel Superheroes" depicted fighting two villains with fists flying. Wok! and K-RAK! and Thor, Sub-Mariner, Hulk and Iron Man are in fast pursuit. The object of this game is to capture villains as a superhero while racing along on the spiderweb.

Milton Bradley also produced **The Captain America Game, The Amazing Spiderman Game**, with the Fantastic Four, and **The Incredible Hulk Game**. Ideal produced a motorized Hulk in **The Incredible Hulk Smash-Up Action Game**.

More recently, Pressman has issued **The Uncanny X-Men Alert! Adventure Game**, featuring the most popular superhero team of the 1980s and 1990s. Included inside the game are 18 collectible X-Men figures. In the last two years, over two dozen role-playing superhero games and related products have been released. This is probably just the beginning, as the superhero gains new speed in the game world.

The Amazing Spider-Man Web Spinning Action Game (Ideal 1979)

The Adventures of Superman (Milton
Bradley 1941) 250.00
Deluxe edition 350.00
The Amazing Spider-Man Game (Milton
Bradley 1977) 30.00
The Amazing Spider-Man Web-Spinning
Action Game (Ideal 1979) 45.00
The Amazing Spider-Man Game (Milton
Bradley 1967) 40.00
Batman (Hasbro 1965) 50.00

Batman game 20"x9" color box, 18"x15"
board, 4 figural playing pieces,
etc. (Milton Bradley 1966) 35.00
Batman MiniBoard Card Game (Milton
Bradley 1964) 30.00
Batman Pinball Game (Marx 1966) 175.00
Batman Card Game (Ideal 1966) 45.00
Batman Card Game (Koide
[Japan] 1966) 250.00
Batman Card Game (Milton
Bradley 1972) 20.00
Batman Game (Hasbro 1973) 35.00
Batman Game (Hasbro 1978) 35.00
Batman Electronic Pinball Game,
Jotastat (B.O. 1989) 85.00
Batman Card Game (Schmidt
[Germany] 1989) 50.00
The Batman Game (University
Games 1989) 25.00
Batman Road Race Game (Gordy
Intl. 1989) 4.00
Batman 50th Anniversary
board game (1990) 15.00

Batman and Robin Game (Hasbro 1965)

Batman & Robin Game, 16"x8" color cover
picturing Batman, Robin & Joker;
16" sq. board (Hasbro 1965) 85.00
Batman & Robin Marble Maze Game,
12" sq. box pinball type (Hasbro 1965) 50.00
Batman & Robin Bagatelle Game 10"x21" with
illustrations of Catwoman, Commissioner,
Penguin, Riddler (Marx 1966) 120.00
Batman Swoops Down game 11" sq. color
cover with Batman & Robin figures and
9 enemies litho panels (Sears 1966) 175.00
Batman Animated Game (Parker
Bros. 1992) 30.00
Batman Returns, 3-D Board Game (1992) . 30.00
Batman Returns card game (Parker
Bros. 1992) 6.00
Batman Forever, Battle at the Big Top game
(Parker Bros. #40350, 1995) 13.00

The Green Hornet Quick Switch Game (Milton Bradley 1966)

Calling Superman – A Game of News
  Reporting with plastic pieces
  (Transogram 1954) 150.00
Captain America Game (Milton
  Bradley 1966) 40.00
Captain America Game (Milton
  Bradley 1977) 25.00
Electra Woman and Dyna Girl
  (Ideal 1977) 50.00
Fantastic Four, Featuring Herbie The Robot
  (Milton Bradley 1978) 45.00
The Flash (Russell Mfg. 1977) 10.00
The Green Hornet Quick Switch Game
  (Milton Bradley 1966) 150.00
The Incredible Hulk Smash-Up Action
  Game (Ideal 1970s) 50.00
Incredible Hulk/Fantastic Four
  (Milton Bradley 1978) 25.00
Judge Dredd (Games Workshop 1983) . . . 16.00
Justice League of America and:
  Aquaman (Hasbro 1967) 100.00
  The Flash (Hasbro 1967) 125.00
  Wonder Woman (Hasbro 1967) 100.00

Marvel Comics Super-Hero card game
  (Milton Bradley 1978) 35.00
Marvel Super Heroes (TSR 1986) 15.00
Marvel Superheroes with 30 trading cards
  (Pressman 1993) 11.00
Mandrake The Magician Game
  (Transogram 1966) 75.00
Mighty Comics Super Heroes Game
  (Transogram 1966) 100.00
The Phantom Game (Transogram 1966) . 165.00
Robin card game (Russell) 10.00
Shazam (Reed & Assoc. 1940s) 50.00
Spawn, The Game (Pressman 1995) 18.00

The Phantom Game (Transogram 1966)

Super Hero, Batman (Russell 1977) 10.00
Super Hero, Robin (Russell 1977) 10.00
Super Hero, Shazam (Russell 1977) 10.00
Super Hero, Superman (Russell 1977) 10.00
Super Hero, Wonder Woman
  (Russell 1977) 10.00
Super Heroes Bingo Game
  (Hasbro 1976) 75.00
Super Heroes Strategy Game (Milton
  Bradley 1980) 32.00

Mighty Comics Super Heroes Game
(Transogram 1966)

All prices listed are for *Near Mint* condition.

Super Powers (Parker Brothers 1984) 20.00
Super Powers skyscraper caper game
    (Parker Bros. 1986) 20.00
Superboy (Hasbro 1965) 100.00
Superfriends Magnetic Pa'cheesie Game
    (Nasta 1980) 20.00
Superman Official 8-Piece Junior Quoit set
    game in box + membership card ... 250.00
Superman Card Game (Ideal 1966) 45.00
Superman Comic Game (Mattel 1971) 65.00
Superman Electronic Question & Answer
    Quizz Machine Game 14"x9"
    (Lisbeth Whiting 1966) 150.00

Superman Game (Hasbro 1965)

Superman Game (Hasbro 1965) 60.00
Superman Game (Hasbro 1973) 50.00
Superman Game (Hasbro 1978) 40.00
Superman/Fantastic Four (Milton
    Bradley 1977) 30.00
Super Hero, Superman Card game
    (Russell 1977) 15.00
Superman Flying Bingo (Whitman 1966) .. 65.00
Superman Game, "Search For Superman's
    Deadliest Enemy" (Hasbro 1965) ... 150.00
Superman Match II (Ideal 1979) 35.00
Superman II Game (Milton Bradley 1980) .. 15.00
Superman III game (Parker Bros. 1983) ... 10.00
Superman Spin Game (Pressman 1967) . 100.00

Superman Speed Game (Milton Bradley 1941)

Superman Speed Game (Milton
    Bradley 1941) 150.00
Superman and Superboy game (Milton

Bradley 1967) 100.00
TMNT Heroes in a Halfshell card game
    (International Games #3610, 1990) .. 6.00
TMNT Ready For Battle board game
    (Rose Art #03017) 15.00
TMNT Pizza Power board game
    (Rose Art #03018) 15.00
The Tick Versus Doer of Evil Game
    (Pressman 1995) 15.00
Uncanny X-Men Game (Pressman 1992) .. 30.00
Wonder Woman Game (Hasbro 1978) 30.00
X-Men X-Mansion Under Siege, with 18
    figures (Pressman #4444, 1994) 28.00
X-Men Crisis in the Danger Room with four
    figures (Pressman #4443, 1994) 15.00
X-Men Alert Adventure (Pressman
    #4440, 1994) 27.00

SUPERHERO ROLE-PLAYING GAMES

Allies (ICE) 13.00
Avengers Archives (TSR 1993) 15.00
Champions (Hero Games 1982) 8.00
Champions Presents Adventures
    (ICE 1993) 20.00
Daredevils (Fantasy Games Unlimited) 10.00
DC Heroes 1st, 2nd 25.00
DC Heroes 3rd (Mayfair) 20.00
DC Technical Manual (Mayfair 1993) 20.00
Enemies (Hero Games) 6.00
Enemies II (Hero Games) 6.00
Games Handbook of the Marvel Universe
    1993 Update (TSR) 15.95
Ghost Rider & Midnight Sons Boxed
    Set (TSR) 15.00
Hero Systems Rulebook (ICE) 20.00
Horror Hero (ICE 1993) 20.00
Infinity Watch Boxed Set (TSR) 20.00
Marvel Super Heroes Basic Set
    1st and 2nd (TSR 1993) 20.00
Marvel Super Heroes Advanced Set
    1st and 2nd (TSR 1993) 20.00
Marvel 2099 Boxed Set (TSR 1993) 15.00
Official Superhero Game (Mayfar
    Games 1982) 12.00
Super Squadron (Adv. Simulations 1983) .. 12.00
Supervillains (Task Force Games 1982) ... 10.00
Underworld Enemies (ICE) 13.00
Villains and Vigilantes (Fantasy
    Games Unlimited) 10.00
Viper Sourcebook (ICE) 20.00
Webs: Spider-Man Dossier (TSR 1993) ... 15.00

Who's Who #3 (Mayfair 1993) 24.95
X-Men Boxed Set (TSR) 15.00

JIGSAW PUZZLES

Aquaman Jigsaw Puzzle 14"x18"
(Whitman 1968) 30.00
Batman Jigsaw Puzzle 150 pieces
(Whitman #4608, 1966) 35.00

Batman Jigsaw Puzzle Game (Milton Bradley 1966)

Batman Jigsaw Puzzle Game
(Milton Bradley 1966) 35.00
Batman 200-piece Jigsaw Puzzle, in
can (Amer. Publ. Corp. 1973) 15.00
Batman Magic Slate (Golden #4113, 1992) 5.00
Batman Frame Tray Puzzle (Golden
#4127, 1992) 5.00
Batman minipuzzle (Golden #5606B,
1992) 5.00
Batman 300-piece Jigsaw Puzzle (Golden
#5158, 1992) 10.00
Batman 200-piece Jigsaw Puzzle (Golden
#5247A, 1992) 7.50
Batman 200-piece Jigsaw Puzzle (Golden
#5247B, 1992) 7.50
Batman 3-heads movie poster 500-piece 24"x36"
puzzle (Milton Bradley #4273, 1992) . 10.00
Buck Rogers and His Atomic Bomber, boxed
set of 3 inlaid jigsaw puzzles
(Puzzle Craft 1945) 250.00
Inlaid jigsaw puzzle, space station scene,
14"x10" in paperboard picture sleeve
(Milton Bradley 1952) 20.00
Captain America frame tray puzzle 11"x14"
(Whitman 1966) 30.00
Captain Marvel Jigsaw Puzzle (1940s) . . . 100.00
Catwoman minipuzzle (Golden #5606C,
1992) 6.00
Catwoman and Batman minipuzzle (Golden
#5606D, 1992) 6.00
Catwoman 200-piece Jigsaw Puzzle (Golden

#5247C, 1992) 10.00
Conan the Barbarian Jigsaw Puzzle
(Marvel 1971) 40.00
Conan the Barbarian Puzzle (movie poster
art (Jaymar 1982) 50.00
Dick Tracy 10"x14" jigsaw puzzle
(Jaymar 1960s) 20.00
Dr. Strange Jigsaw Puzzle 500 piece
15"x22" (Third Eye 1971) 50.00
Fantastic Four jigsaw puzzle
(Whitman 1969) 10.00
Fantastic Four Jigsaw Puzzle 500 piece
15"x22" (Third Eye 1971) 50.00
Fantastic Four jigsaw frame tray puzzle
(Whitman 1977) 10.00
Fantastic Four Big Little Book jigsaw
puzzle, 99 piece (Whitman 1968) 15.00
Fantastic Four Junior Jigsaw Puzzle, 100 piece
(Milton Bradley 1967) 40.00
Felix Tray Puzzle (Built-Rite 1960) 20.00
Green Hornet Frame Tray Puzzle 9"x12"
(Whitman 1966) 75.00
The Hulk Jigsaw Puzzle 500 piece
15"x22" (Third Eye 1971) 50.00
Incredible Hulk Jigsaw Puzzle, 100 piece
(Whitman 1978) 10.00
Marvel Superheroes Jigsaw Puzzle, 100 piece
(Milton Bradley 1966) 65.00
Marvel Superheroes Jigsaw Puzzle, 100 piece
(Milton Bradley 1967) 50.00
Penguin minipuzzle (Golden
#5606A, 1992) 6.00
Penguin 200-piece Jigsaw Puzzle (Golden
#5247D, 1992) 10.00
Popeye Picture Puzzle Set (10 x 8" box
with 4 jigsaw puzzles inside)
(Saafield 1932) 75.00
Popeye Jigsaw Puzzle (22" by 13½"
puzzle) (Jaymar 1945) 30.00
Popeye Inlaid Puzzle (Popeye battles a
tiger) (Jaymar 1950s–60s) 10.00
Popeye Interlocking Puzzle (entitled
"Three's a Crowd") (Jaymar 1950s–60s) 15.00
Popeye 28-Piece Kiddie Puzzle
(Jaymar 1980s) 3.00
"Popeye & Son" Puzzle (Popeye's son in
skateboard contest) (Milton
Bradley 1988) 3.00
"Popeye & Son" Puzzle (Popeye, son and
Olive on ship) (Milton Bradley 1988) . . 3.00
Silver Surfer Jigsaw Puzzle 500 piece
15"x22" (Third Eye 1971) 50.00

Spider-Man Giant Floor Puzzle, 30"x18"
(Waddington 1977) 25.00
Spider-Man with Thor Jigsaw Puzzle, 75 piece
12" diameter (4-G TOys 1977) 25.00
Superman picture puzzle, 300 pieces,
12"x16" titled "Superman and the
Submarine" (Saafield 1940) 500.00
Superman picture puzzle, 500 pieces,
16"x20" titled "Superman Saves a
Life" (Saafield #1516, 1940) 500.00
Superman Jigsaw Puzzle 8½"x11" box
100-piece 14"x18" puzzle
(Whitman 1965) 15.00
Superman Jigsaw Puzzle 9"x11" box
150-piece 14"x18" puzzle
(Whitman 1965) 25.00
Superman frame tray puzzles
(Whitman 1966), each 20.00
TMNT Giant Floor Puzzle (Paul
Lamond Games 1990) (U.K.) 25.00
TMNT Jigsaw puzzles (Rose Art)
Ninja Pizza (#08018) 5.00
Samurai Leonardo (#08018) 5.00
Surfing Michelangelo (#08018) 5.00
Turtles in sewer (#08018) 5.00
Turtles party wagon (#08018) 5.00
Slash (#08018) 5.00
TMNT Movie Poster II Jigsaw puzzle
(Rose Art #08021) 5.00

The Flash 10.00
Flash Gordon 12.50
Gasoline Alley 5.00
Green Arrow 10.00
Green Lantern 10.00
Junior and Honey Moon 5.00
Killer 5.00
Lex Luthor 10.00
Little Orphan Annie 10.00
Lois Lane 10.00
Olive Oyl and Swee'pea 7.50
Penguin 10.00
The Phantom 12.50
Plastic Man 10.00
Popeye 10.00
Robin 7.50
Shazam 10.00
Supergirl 10.00
Superman (Birthday) 7.50
Superman 10.00
Veronica 5.00
Wimpy 5.00
Wonder Woman 10.00

MEDALLIONS

BATMAN SERIES
(1970s)
Batman, Robin & Catwoman medallion .. 25.00
Catwoman and Robin medallion 20.00
Penguin medallion 20.00
Riddler medallion 20.00

CARTOON CELEBRITIES SERIES
American Medallion Corporation (1987)
1½" Bronze medallion on card
Archie 5.00
Aquaman 10.00
Batman 10.00
Beetle Bailey and Sarge 7.50
Betty Boop 10.00
Blondie and Dagwood 7.50
Brenda Starr 10.00
Brutus 5.00
Dick Tracy 7.50
Mr. and Mrs. Dithers 5.00

Phantom Medallion
(American Medallion Corporation 1987)

PINS

Planet Studios has been producing pins of Marvel characters for the last eight years. In the last few years they have added other comic characters. The list below includes selected popular pins, but is not complete. The product numbers used are catalog numbers and do not appear on the pins. Over the years, they have produced many different pins of the most popular Marvel characters. Most comics shops have a few of these pins for sale, but they do not seem to be collected heavily.

Other companies have issued pins from time to time with the same result. We think that these pins may become collectible in the future, but it is too early to tell which will be the most sought after items. The best bets would be the female characters and pins by better known artists.

MARVEL PINS
Planet Studios (1987–95)
#1 Spidey cutout pin	10.00
#3 Punisher Panel #1	10.00
#4 Wolverine profile cutout	10.00
#5 Wolverine panel	10.00
#6 Wolverine cutout	10.00
#7 Black Spider-Man cutout	10.00
#10 Silver Surfer panel	10.00
#14 Daredevil cutout	8.00
#15 Small Punisher Skull	8.00
#16 Fantastic Four Symbol	8.00
#19 Iron-Man	8.00
#21 X-Men logo	6.95
#22 Spider-Man head	6.95
#28 Dr. Doom	6.95

Xavier's School and Punisher pins

Ghost Rider & Spider-Man 30th Anniversary pins

#39 Punisher logo cloisonné	6.95
#40 Captain America shield	6.95
#41 Thing Head	6.95
#48 U.S. Agent	6.95
#51 Galactus panel	6.95
#52 Wolverine "I'm the best..."	6.95
#54 Spider (McFarlane art)	6.95
#58 Punisher Skull	6.95
#59 Punisher figure	6.95
#63 Silver Surfer Panel	6.95
#78 Captain America	6.95
#83 Spidey Tracer	6.95
#86 Spider-Man cutout	6.95
#87 Punisher Big Gun	6.95
#88 Lockheed	6.95
#92 Mr. Fantastic	6.95
#97 Wolverine	6.95
#105 Wolverine (Orig. Costume) cutout	6.95
#111 Thor	6.95
#121 Punisher panel	6.95
#123 Iron Man	6.95
#126 Ghost Rider Logo	6.95
#127 Captain America 50th	6.95
#130 Spidey cutout (McFarlane art)	6.95
#147 Elektra panel #4	6.95
#150 Ghost Rider cutout	6.95
#151 I "Punisher logo" NY	6.95
#153 Weapon X logo	6.95
#155 Wolverine slashing	6.95
#156 Spider #2 (McFarlane art)	6.95
#159 Xavier's School pin	6.95
#160 Ghost Rider figure	6.95
#161 Ghost Rider Skull	6.95
#164 Ghost Rider skull	6.95
#171 Captain America figure	6.95
#177 Green Hulk cutout	6.95
#180 Black Spider-Man panel	6.95
#182 Silver Surfer cutout	6.95
#184 Elektra panel	6.95
#185 Storm Panel	6.95

#187 Wolverine cutout 6.95	#265 Wolverine head 6.95
#191 Gambit cutout 6.95	#269 Punisher 2099 . . . . 6.95
#192 Archangel panel 6.95	#270 Avengers 30th year 6.95
#193 Beast cutout 6.95	#272 Spidey/Venom 6.95
#195 Jubilee cutout 6.95	#275 Spider-Man clinging, cutout 6.95
#196 Rogue cutout 6.95	#276 Rogue, cutout 6.95
#197 Wolverine panel 6.95	#280 X-Men 30th Anniv. 6.95
#198 Iron Man cutout 6.95	#282 Wolverine cutout 6.95
#202 Spider-Man Christmas 6.95	#284 Flaming Fist (Ghost Rider) 6.95
#203 Punisher Skull Christmas 6.95	#293 Magneto 6.95
#208 Ghost Rider/Bike 6.95	#294 Sentinal 6.95
#209 Punisher War Zone logo 6.95	#295 Hulk 2099 . . . . 6.95
#211 "DD" (Daredevil) 6.95	#296 Carnage Claw 6.95
#213 Spider-Man panel 6.95	#298 Carnage cutout 6.95
#216 Venom skull 6.95	#304 Wolverine figure 6.95
#219 Silver Surfer 6.95	#305 Nightcrawler figure 6.95
#220 Spider-Man's 30th Year 6.95	#307 Vision cutout figure 6.95
#225 Wolverine 6.95	#308 Jubilee cutout figure 6.95
#229 Rogue 6.95	#310 Spider-Man face 6.95
#232 Punisher panel (Jim Lee art) 6.95	#312 Captain America Head 6.95
#236 Carnage Head 6.95	#313 Punisher 2099 Skull 6.95
#238 Spider-Man 2099 Figure 6.95	#314 Spider-Man 2099 . . . . 6.95
#239 Ghost Rider head 6.95	#315 Ghost Rider Symbol 6.95
#240 Silver Spider 6.95	#316 Storm cutout 6.95
#242 Wolverine Holiday 6.95	#317 Hulk Holiday 6.95
#246 Spider-Man w/moon Panel 6.95	#320 Daredevil Panel 6.95
#247 Ravage 2099 . . . . 6.95	#326 Jean Grey cut out 6.95
#248 Venom leaping figure 6.95	#328 Mutatis (Xavier's School) 6.95
#249 Bishop's Medallion 6.95	#329 Sabretooth 6.95
#250 Silver Surfer 6.95	
#251 Spider-Man 2099 head 6.95	
#252 Wolverine w/moon 6.95	
#255 Punisher 2099 skull cutout 6.95	
#256 Spider-Man 2099 figure cutout 6.95	
#257 Psylocke cutout 6.95	
#258 Cable cutout 6.95	
#259 Venom cutout 6.95	

Rogue & Cable Head pins

1994

#332 Ghost Rider 2099 Skull 6.95
#334 Beast 6.95
#335 Spider-Man 6.95
#338 Iron Man 2020 . . . . 6.95
#341 Hulk corner box 5.95
#346 Psylocke 6.95
#347 Wolverine 6.95
#350 Cyclops 6.95
#351 Nightcrawler 6.95
#352 Silver Surfer 6.95

X-Men pin

1993

#260 Punisher 2099 . . . . 6.95
#261 Doom 2099 . . . . 6.95
#262 Venom Head 6.95
#264 Spidey's Spider pin 6.95

#353 Elektra 6.95
#355 Hobgoblin & Pumpkin Bomb pin pair . 7.95
#357 Rogue 6.95
#361 Venom Holiday 6.95
#362 Wolverine 6.95
#363 Jubilee 6.95
#366 Penance 6.95
#372 Rogue 6.95
#374 Emplate 6.95
#376 Rogue swimsuit 6.95
#378 Jubilee cutout 6.95

ALIENS
Aliens pin set #1, 5 pins by John
    Bolton (Dark Horse) 50.00

ARCHIE
AR-1 Archie Head (1991) 5.95
AR-2 Betty Heart (1992) 5.95
ARP-1 Veronica pin (1994) 3.99
ARP-2 Jughead pin (1994) 3.99
ARP-3 Betty pin (1994) 3.99
ARP-4 Archie pin (1994) 3.99
ARP-5 Reggie pin (1994) 3.99

ARZACH
Planet Studios (1993)
ARZ-1 Arzach skull, 2" black 12.95
ARZ-2 Arzach skull, 2" blue 12.95

BONE
Planet Studios (1992–94)
BN-1 Bone Logo cloisonné pin 6.95
BN-2 Fone Bone cloisonné pin 6.95
BN-3 Ted the Bug cloisonné pin 6.95
BN-4 Rat Creatures cloisonné pin 6.95
BN-5 Fone Bone in Love pin 6.95
BN-6 Red Dragon pin 6.95
BN-7 Phoney Bone cloisonné pin 6.95
BN-8 Smiley Bone cloisonné pin 6.95
BN-9 Grandma Ben cloisonné pin 6.95

CADILLACS AND DINOSAURS
Planet Studios
CD01 Cadillacs and Dinosaurs logo
    cloisonné pin 6.95
CD02 Poacher's logo cloisonné pin 6.95
CD03 Wassoon logo cloisonné pin 6.95
CD-1 Cadillacs & Dinosaurd panel #1 .... 10.00

CEREBUS
Graphitti Designs (1994)
Cerebus the Barbarian cloisonné pin #1 ... 6.95
Cerebus the Candidate cloisonné pin #2 ... 6.95
Cerebus the Prime Minister cloisonné #3 ... 6.95
Cerebus the Most Holy cloisonné pin #4 .. 6.95
Young Cerebus cloisonné pin #5 .... 6.95
Hellboy Ceramic Pin (Media Arts 1994) ... 5.95

Monkeyman and O'Brien brass pin
    (Media Arts 1994) 5.95

CONAN
(S/Q Productions 1992)
Conan pin by Jim Lee 12.00
Conan Cover pin #2 (Jim Lee) 12.00
Conan Cover pin #3 (Barry Windsor-Smith) 12.00

CONCRETE
Dark Horse (1991)
Set of 5 Concrete cloisonné pins 35.00

CROW
Crow cloisonné pin, B&W 6.95
Crow cloisonné pin #2 .... 7.95

CYBERNARY
Planet Studios (1993)
CN-1 Cybernary pin 6.95

DC COMICS
Robin cloisonné pin (Graphitti
    Designs 1991) 5.95

DEATHBLOW
Planet Studios (1993)
DB-1 Deathblow logo 6.95
DB-2 Deathblow figure 6.95
DB-3 Deathblow figure cloisonné pin 6.95

ELFQUEST
Elfquest autographed, boxed pin collection
    (Planet Studios EQ-BX1, 1995) 19.95

FANTASTIC FOUR
Planet Studios (1994)
Four pins in acrylic collector's case 17.95

FEM FORCE
Planet Studios (1993)
AC-1 Ms. Victory 6.95
AC-2 Synn 6.95

GROO
Graphitti Pins (1991)
#1 Groo 5.95
#2 Rufferto 5.95
#3 Taranto 5.95
#4 Sage 5.95
#5 Minstrel 5.95
#6 Chakaal 5.95

HUNTSMAN
The Huntsman cloisonné Pin (Planet Studios
    HM-1, 1994) 6.95

IMAGE
Planet Studios
J-1 Fuji 6.95
J-2 Diva 6.95
J-3 Winter 6.95
J-4 Grifter II 6.95
J-5 Zealot II 6.95

All prices listed are for *Near Mint* condition.

J-6 Warblade 6.95
Gen #6 Freefall 6.95
Gen #7 Burnout 6.95
Gen #8 Fairchild 6.95
Gen #9 Grunge 6.95
Gen 13 boxed pin set #1 . . . . 14.95
Image Team 7 logo pin (Planet
 Studios IM03) 3.95

JACK KIRBY PIN COLLECTION
Planet Studios (1992)
6-pin collection, die-cut cloisonné pins of X-
Men, Thor, Hulk, Captain America and
Silver Surfer in acrylic case with Kirby
bio-booklet & numbered foil stamped
Silver Surfer Plate, orig. 1992 at $70
(reissued 1994) 100.00

JUDGE DREDD
Dredd Head, soft enamel pin, 1"
 (Fleetway 1991) 6.95

KINDRED
Kindred Logo 24K gold pin IM01 . . . . 3.95

KITCHEN SINK
Kitchen Sink Press square logo pin (1991)
 Yellow and gold 5.95
 Silver and white 5.95

MADMAN
Tundra (1993)
Madman #1 color cloisonné pin
 by Mike Allred 6.95
Madman #2 head shot color cloisonné
 pin by Mike Allred 6.95

MALIBU
Bravura logo cloisonné pin (Malibu) 5.95
Malibu Comics logo cloisonné pin (Malibu) . 5.95
Ultraforce logo cloisonné pin (Malibu) 4.95

MARVEL COVER PINS
Cover Pins, 1"x2", boxed, plated in 24k gold
 (2,500 made) (1991–92)
Wolverine Cover #1 (Frank Miller) 10.00
Platinum Spider-Man #1 . . . . 10.00
X-Men #1 cover version A to D, each 10.00
X-Men #1 version E (Jim Lee) 10.00
X-Men #2 cover (Jim Lee) 10.00
X-Men #3 cover (Jim Lee) 10.00
X-Men #4 cover (Jim Lee) 10.00
X-Force #1 cover 10.00
X-Force #2 cover pin (Rob Liefeld) 10.00
X-Force #3 cover pin (Rob Liefeld) 10.00
X-Force #4 cover pin (Rob Liefeld) 10.00
X-Force #5 cover pin (Rob Liefeld) 10.00
Uncanny X-Men #1 (Jack Kirby) 12.00
Spider-Man #2 cover pin 10.00

MARVEL HEAVY METAL PINS
Planet Studios (1994)
1001 X-Men Symbol 3.95
1006 Spider-Man Panel 3.95
1007 Gambit Panel 3.95
1008 Fantastic Four 3.95
1009 Spider-Man tracer 3.95
1010 X-Men logo 3.99
1011 Generation X logo, gold plated 3.95
1012 Spider-Man head, gold plated 3.95
1013 Venom head, gold plated 3.95
1014 Generation X Icon 3.95

MARVEL "MUTANT GEAR" PINS
Planet Studios
Pins on blister cards
M1-1 Wolverine badge 3.99
M1-2 Cyclops badge 3.99
M1-3 Storm badge 3.99
M1-4 Rogue badge 3.99
M1-5 Gambit badge 3.99
M1-6 Wolverine badge (no name) 3.99
M1-7 Gambit badge (no name) 3.99
M1-9 Cyclops panel 3.99
M1-10 Cable panel 3.99
M1-11 Spider-Man panel 3.99
M1-12 Venom Panel 3.99
M1-13 Iron Man 3.99
M1-14 Spider-Man 3.99
M1-15 Venom 3.99
M1-16 Wolverine 3.99
M1-17 Gambit 3.99
M1-18 The Thing 3.99
M1-19 Human Torch 3.99
M1-20 Spider-Man 3.99
M1-21 Hobgoblin 3.99
M1-22 Wolverine profile cutout 3.99

Nancy pin in box (Kitchen Sink 1991)

M1-23 Storm cutout 3.99
M1-24 Cyclops cutout 3.99
M1-25 Jubilee cutout 3.99
M1-26 Rogue cutout 3.99
MRV-1 X-Men symbol . . . . ˙3.99
MRV-2 Spider-Man head 3.99
MRV-3 Xavier's School pin 3.99
MRV-4 Captain America Shield 3.99

MARVEL BIG PINS
Planet Studios (1991)
BP-2 Big Punisher Skull 2" 9.95
BP-3 Captain America Shield 9.95
BP-4 Ghost Rider Skull 9.95
BP-5 Cutout Punisher Skull 9.95
BP-6 Spidey Head 9.95
BP-7 Triple Skull 9.95
BP-8 Silver Spider 11.95
BP-9 Jumbo Carnage Pin 9.95
BP-10 Silver Surfer (1993) 9.95
BP-11 Ghost Rider (1993) 9.95
BP-12 Venom cutout 9.95
BP-19 Generation X logo pin (2 pin backs) . 8.95

MARVEL SCULPTED PINS
SP-1 Adam Warlock Skull Sculped big pin . 14.95
SP-3 Punisher Skull Sculpted big
      pin, sterling silver, boxed 19.95
Big Venom Head 11.95

MAXIMUM FORCE
Planet Studios (1993)
MF-1 Maximum Force 6.95

MAXIMUM CARNAGE
Planet Studios (1994)
MC-P1 Spider-Man & Carnage + logo pins . 14.95

MR. NATURAL
Kitchen Sink (1993)
#1 Mr. Natural, color, boxed (R. Crumb art) 8.00
#2 Mr. Snoid, color, boxed (R. Crumb art) . 8.00
#3 Smelly Old Cat, color, boxed
   (R. Crumb art) 8.00

NANCY
Kitchen Sink (1991)
Nancy cloisonné pin (Ernie Bushmiller art)
   Boxed, yellow or red ribbon 7.95
   Blue ribbon (rare) 25.00
Sluggo tie tack (Ernie Bushmiller art),
   boxed, red or yellow hat 5.95

PUNISHER MEETS ARCHIE
Planet Studios (1994)
PAR-1 Punisher meets Archie 4.95

SHMOO
Kitchen Sink (1992)
Shmoo cloisonné pin (Al Capp art) 7.95

Shmoo cloisonné pin, gold border, rare . . . 25.00

SHADOW
Graphitti Designs (1991)
#1 Shadow Pin (profile) 5.95
#2 Shadow Pin 5.95
#3 Shadow Pin (head, 2 guns) 5.95
#4 Shadow Pin (gun, "The Weed of Crime") 5.95

SPIDER-MAN
Planet Studios (1993–94)
VSC-1 Spider-Man, Venom, Carnage boxed
   set of cloisonné pins (1993) 14.95
Spider-Man pin/pendant and chain
   Silver 50.00
   Gold (150 made) 100.00
Boxed pin set 9.95
SM-P1 Spider-Man versus Punisher, boxed 14.95
Spider-Man's 30th Anniversary Pins
   Set I (by John Romita, Sr.) (1992) . . . 30.00
   Set II (signed by Stan Lee) (1992) . . . 30.00
Vote-1 Spider-Man Campaign (1992) 6.95

The Tick pin

STORMWATCH
Planet Studios (1993)
SW 1 Stormwatch logo pin 6.95
SW 2 Backlash figure pin 6.95
SW 3 Battalion 6.95

THE TICK
Comic Images (1994–95)
The Tick logo cloisonné pin 6.95
The Tick Face cloisonné pin 6.95
Tick cloisonné pin 6.95
Arthur cloisonné pin 6.95
Dr. Stupid cloisonné pin 6.95

All prices listed are for *Near Mint* condition.   **249**

ULTRAVERSE
Mantra cloisonné pin, designed by
   Adam Hughes 3.95
Mantra cloisonné pin, designed by
   Norm Breyfogle 3.95
Rune cloisonné pin, designed by Barry
   Windsor-Smith 3.95

UNION
Planet Studios (1993)
UN-1 Union logo 6.95
UN-2 Union #1 (Jim Lee) 6.95
UN-3 Union #2 (Mark Texeira) 6.95

VALIANT PINS
Planet Studios (1993)
#V-1 X-O Manowar figure 6.95
#V-2 X-O Manowar Icon 6.95
#V-3 Solar Icon 6.95
#V-4 Shadowman Icon 6.95
#V-5 Master Darque figure 6.95
#V-6 Turok figure 6.95
#V-7 Bionosaurus figure 6.95
#V-8 Valiant logo 6.95
#V-9 Eternal Warrior Icon 6.95
#V-10 Bloodshot figure 6.95
#V-11 Ninjak 6.95
#V-12 Dr. Mirage 6.95
#V-13 Harbinger Icon 6.95
#V-14 Solar the Destroyer 6.95
#V-15 Armorine 6.95

VAMPIRELLA
Vampirella logo cloisonné pin
   (Graphitti Designs 1995) 6.95

WETWORKS
Wetworks logo 24K gold pin IM02 . . . . 3.95

WILDC.A.T.S
Planet Studios (1993–94)
WC-4 Warblade figure 6.95
WC-5 WildC.A.T.S. logo 6.95
WC-6 Voodoo 6.95
WC-7 Spartan 6.95
WC-8 Void 6.95
WC-9 Emp 6.95
WC-10 Maul 6.95
WC-12 Spartan 6.95
WC-13 Voodoo 6.95

Planet Studios (1994)
WS-1 Grifter 3.99
WS-2 Voodoo 3.99
WS-3 Spartan 3.99
WS-4 Maul 3.99
WS-5 Warblade 3.99
WS-6 Emp 3.99

BUTTONS

BATMAN
Batman – pin back, B&W, 1¾" (1966) 20.00
Batman pin back, 3" Ron Riley's Batman
   Club (WBKB-TV 1966) 25.00

Batman: Mask of the Phantasm button

Batman: Mask of the Phantasm movie promo
   button, 2⅛"x3⅛" (DC/Warner 1993) . . 2.50

CAPTAIN AMERICA
Captain America – ⅞" litho pin
   back (1976) 15.00
• Pin back badge, Sentinels of
   Liberty (1940s) 100.00
• Deluxe Sentinels of Liberty 125.00
• Marvel, 3-D (1966) 15.00

CAPTAIN MARVEL
Captain Marvel – Club buttons:
   "Shazam" tin litho (1941) 25.00
   "Shazam" cello button (1943) 25.00
   "Shazam" button (1944) 20.00
   "Shazam" button (1946) 25.00
   Button (1947) 50.00
Captain Marvel – Comic Buttons
   Set of 10 . . . . 450.00
   Captain Marvel 50.00
   Billy Batson 50.00
   Mary Marvel 50.00

Captain Marvel Club pin

Captain Marvel Jr.	50.00
Hoppy the Marvel Bunny	50.00
Ibis	50.00
Bulletman	50.00
Radar	50.00
Nyoka	50.00
Golden Arrow	50.00

Cerebus & Captain Marvel pins

CEREBUS
Cerebus – 1½" enamel 5.00

DC BUTTONS
DC Hero Buttons (OS 1991)
400 Superman Flying "Many Lives, Many Worlds"	1.25
401 Superman logo "Many Lives, Many Worlds"	1.25
402 Superman Bursting Through: "The Man of Steel"	1.25
403 Superman Flying: "The Man of Steel"	1.25
404 "This Is a Job for Superman"	1.25
405 Batman on yellow	1.25
406 Batman and Robin	1.25
407 Batman and Robin on Skyline	1.25
408 Batman Bursting Through	1.25
409 Wonder Woman	1.25

410 Shazam on Red	1.25
411 Shazam on Blue	1.25
412 Flash	1.25
413 Justice League of America Member	1.25
430 Yellow Bat Symbol	1.25
431 Batman Head	1.25
432 Batman Standing	1.25
433 Riddler	1.25
434 Batman Poised for Action	1.25
435 Batman Looking Proud	1.25
436 Joker Laughing	1.25
437 Batman: Beware the Power of the Bat	1.25
438 Batman Head and Spotlight	1.25
439 Batman Fists Flying	1.25
440 Joker Face	1.25
441 Joker with Flower	1.25

DC COMICS
DC Comics Hologram Buttons set,
   10 die-cast buttons from Robin II:
   Joker's Wild 20.00

Carl Barks pin (Kitchen Sink 1975)

FAMOUS CARTOONIST SERIES
Kitchen Sink (1975)
1 Sergio Aragones	10.00
2 Robert Armstrong	10.00
3 Carl Barks	30.00
4 C. C. Beck	20.00
5 Joel Beck	10.00
6 Fershid Bharucha	10.00
7 Tim Boxell	10.00
8 Sol Brodsky	10.00
9 Leslie Cabarga	10.00
10 Al Capp	25.00
11 Dan Clyne	10.00
12 Richard Corben	25.00
13 Robert Crumb	35.00
14 Howard Curse	10.00

All prices listed are for *Near Mint* condition.   **251**

15 Kim Deitch	10.00
16 Will Eisner	25.00
17 Will Elder	10.00
18 Vince Fago	10.00
19 Kelly Freas	20.00
20 Evert Geradts	10.00
21 Justin Green	10.00
22 Bill Griffith	10.00
23 Hugh Hefner	25.00
24 Fred Julsing	10.00
25 Jay Kinney	10.00
26 Denis Kitchen	15.00
27 Aline Kominsky	10.00
28 Harvey Kurtzman	10.00
29 Peter Loft	10.00
30 Jay Lynch	10.00
31 Jim Mitchell	10.00
32 Will Murphy	10.00
33 Grim Natwick	10.00
34 Peter Poplaski	10.00
35 John Pound	10.00
36 Ted Richards	10.00
37 Trina Robbins	10.00
38 Spain Rodriguez	10.00
39 Sharon Rudahl	10.00
40 Bill Sanders	10.00
41 Ronald Searle	10.00
42 John Severin	10.00

Gilbert Shelton pin (Kitchen Sink 1975)

43 Gilbert Shelton	20.00
44 Barry Smith	25.00
45 Art Spiegelman	10.00
46 John Stanley	10.00
47 Steve Stiles	10.00
48 Bil Stout	20.00
49 Mort Walker	10.00
50 Skip Williamson	10.00

51 Gahan Wilson	25.00
52 Basil Wolverton	10.00
53 Neal Adams	15.00
54 Rick Meyerowitz	10.00

MARVEL

Marvel Mania Fan club, set of 8 buttons
1" - 3" (Marvel 1969) 100.00

MEGATON MAN
Kitchen Sink (1985)

Megaton Man buttons, six diff., each 5.00

MISS VICTORY
Pin back buttons, 2¼" metal

New Ms. Victory	1.25
Rad	1.25
Original Ms. Victory	1.25
Golden Age Miss Victory	1.25

TEENAGE MUTANT NINJA TURTLES
(1991)

6088 Michelangelo	1.25
6089 Donatello	1.25
6090 Raphael	1.25
6091 Donatello with stick	1.25
6092 Leonardo Running	1.25
6093 Leonardo	1.25
6094 Raphael holding logo	1.25
6095 Michelangelo with chucks & logo	1.25
6096 Four Breaking Wall	1.25
6097 Four Breaking Screen	1.25
6098 Four squares	1.25
6099 Group	1.25
6488 Shredder	1.25
6489 Four Standing	1.25
6490 Splinter	1.25
6491 Four from Movie with logo	1.25
6492 Four sitting in Director's chair	1.25
6493 Four looking at light	1.25

Big Buttons

6584 Four breaking screen	4.00
6585 Group	4.00
6586 Leonardo	4.00
6587 Raphael	4.00
6588 Donatello	4.00
6589 Michelangelo	4.00
6590 Four looking at light	4.00

SUPER HERO CLUB
Button World (1966)

Bagged, with header card:

Hawkman 3"	40.00
Captain America 3"	40.00
Daredevil 3"	40.00

*"Official Member Superman Club" button
in cello pack (Button World 1966)*

Incredible Hulk 3"	40.00
Iron Man 3"	40.00
The Amazing Spider-Man 3"	40.00
The Mighty Thor 3"	40.00
Green Hornet 3"	40.00
Superman 3½"	40.00
Any of above, loose	20.00

SUPERMAN
Superman
- pin back button, 7-Up, 1¾" 20.00
- litho tab, Brookdale Ford (1972) 20.00
- pin back, ⅞" Breaking Chains
  Action Comics (1939) 75.00
- pin back, ⅞" Superman-Tim Club
  with boy 45.00
- pin back, 2" (1976) 12.00
- litho pin back, National Comics 1⅜"
  Muscle Building Club 120.00

- litho pin back (Kellogg's Pep 1945) . 25.00

Supermen of America Club, 1½" pin back:
- 1940—Action 75.00
- 1961 .... 35.00
- no date 30.00

TICK
Ben Edlund art
Tick #1: The Red Eye	1.25
Tick #2: Spoon	1.25
Tick #3: Arthur, The Moth	1.25
Tick #4: Chainsaw Vigilante	1.25
Tick #5: Classic Tick	1.25

*Supermen of America and
Superman-Tim Club pins*

WONDER WOMAN
Wonder Woman – pin back 1½" Sensation
  Comics, rare 70.00
YOUNGBLOOD
Youngblood Home Team button (1992) ... 8.95
Youngblood Away Team button (1992) 8.95

COMIC STRIP BUTTONS

Abie – 1¼" Cel, newspaper premium 25.00
Abner's Ma – 1³⁄₁₆" Litho (Saturday
  Daily News) 25.00
Abretha Breeze – Tin Litho, pin back
  (Kellogg's Pep 1945) 20.00
Aesop's Fables – ⅞" Litho (Western
  Theatre premium):
  Al 35.00
  Countess 35.00
  Don 35.00
  Judge 35.00
  Mike 35.00
  Puffie 35.00
  Waffles 35.00
Alley Oop – Pin Back (Newspaper
  Enterprises) 25.00
Andy Gump – ⅞" Litho (Western
  Theatre premium) 25.00

All prices listed are for *Near Mint* condition.

- 1⅜", Pin Back Teeple Shoes 40.00
- ⅞" Pin Back, B&W, For President . . . 35.00
- ⅞" Pin Back, B&W, For Congress
  Evening Sun 30.00
- Tin Litho, Pin Back (Kellogg's
  Pep 1945) 25.00

Apple Mary – ¹³⁄₁₆" Litho (Saturday
Daily News) 25.00

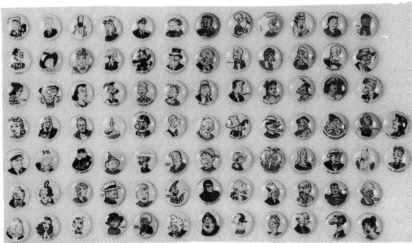

Archie Club pin

Archie – Litho pin back, Reggie ⅞"
Archie Power 25.00
- Litho pin back, ⅞" Archie Fan 25.00
- Litho pin back, ⅞" Archie Jingle
  Jangle Fan 25.00
- 1¼" cel, newspaper premium 45.00

Auntie Blossom – tin litho, pin back
(Kellogg's Pep 1945) 25.00

Barney Google – ⅞" litho (Western Theatre
premium) 40.00

- Tin Litho, pin back (Kellogg's
  Pep) 25.00
- 1¼" cel, newspaper premium 35.00

B.C. – pin back, 3" Arby's signed
Mart (1981) 15.00

Beezie – Litho pin back (Kellogg's
Pep 1945) 25.00

Benny – 1¼" cell, newspaper premium 30.00

Ben Webster – 1¼" Cel, newspaper
premium 30.00

Betty Boop – ⅞" litho (Western Theatre
premium 35.00
- Cello, pin back, color, 2" 65.00
- Pin back, B&W (King Features 1979) . 15.00
- Enameled pin back (1979) 15.00
- Clothing button, sew on, various 15.00

Bimbo – ⅞" Litho (Western Theatre
premium) 35.00
- Cello pin back, B&W, Betty
  Boop's dog 40.00

Blackie – ⅞" litho (Western Theatre
premium 35.00

Blondie – Litho, ⅞" litho pin back,
(Kellogg's Pep 1946) 30.00

Boob McNutt – 1¼" cel, newspaper
premium 30.00

Boots and Her Buddies – 1¼" cel
(Sweater Co.) 30.00

B.O. Plenty – ⅞" litho, pin back,
(Kellogg's Pep 1945) 25.00

Bosko – ⅞" litho (Western Theatre
premium 35.00

Complete set of Kellogg's Pep pins (1940s)

Bosko's Dog Bruno – ⅞" litho (Western
Theatre premium 35.00
Bound to Win – 1¼" cel, newspaper
premium 30.00
Brenda Starr – ⅞" litho pin back
(Kellogg's Pep 1945) 25.00
Bringing Up Father – 1¼" cel, newspaper
premium 35.00
Buck Rogers – Litho pin back badge (Solar
Scout) (Cream of Wheat 1934) 120.00
• (Space Commander) (1934) 140.00
• (Chief Explorer) (1934) 165.00
• Litho pin back (Chicago
American 1934) 125.00
• (Pittsburgh Post Gazette 1934) 125.00
• and Dr. Huer, pin back (1936) 125.00
• Club Member, pin back (1937) 140.00
• 25th Century, pin back (1935) 125.00

Buck Rogers Solar Scouts pin

• Rocket Ranger, pin back (1936) 140.00
• Satellite Pioneer, pin back 125.00
• I Saw Buck Rogers–pin back, Chicago
World's Fair (1934) 140.00
• Rocket Rangers Member, pin
back (1946) 125.00
• 1" litho (Saturday Chicago American) . 50.00
• Rocket Ranger, pin back (1936) 100.00
Buttercup – 1¼" cel, newspaper premium . 35.00
"Cap" Stubbs – 1¼" cell, newspaper
premium 35.00
The Captain – pin back (Kellogg's Pep) .. 25.00
Captain Zilog – 3½" pin back 20.00
Casper – ⅞" litho (Western Theatre
premium 35.00
• pin back, cash prizes (L.A.
Herald Express) 35.00

• litho pin back (Kellogg's Pep 1945) . 25.00
Castor Oyl – 1¼" cel, newspaper premium . 35.00
Chester Gump – litho pin back (Kellogg's
Pep 1945) 25.00
Chester – ⅞" litho (Western Theatre
premium) 35.00
Chief Brandon – litho pin back,
(Kellogg's Pep 1945) 20.00
Chief Wahoo – 1⅛" litho (Journal
Transcript Funnies Club) 35.00
Cindy – litho pin back (Kellogg's
Pep 1945) 20.00
Corky – litho pin back (Kellogg's
Pep 1945) 20.00
The Comic – pin back buttons (L.A.
Evening Herald & Express)
– Orphan Annie 40.00
– Casper 35.00
Conan the Conqueror – pin back
(Caldwell 1974) 15.00
Dagwood – litho pin back (Kellogg's
Pep 1945) 25.00
Dagwood and Blondie – 1" litho 15.00
Daisy – litho pin back (Kellogg's
Pep 1945) 25.00
Dale Arden – ¹³⁄₁₆" litho
(King Features Syndicate) 30.00
Danny Dunn – ¹³⁄₁₆" litho (Saturday
Daily News) 25.00
Dan Gunn – Tin Badge, pin back (1930s) . 55.00
Dennie – ¹³⁄₁₆" litho (Saturday
Daily News) 25.00
Denny – litho pin back (Kellogg's
Pep 1945) 25.00
Der Captain – 1¼" cel, newspaper
premium 35.00
Der Professor – 1¼" cel, newspaper
premium 35.00
Dick Tracy – litho pin back (Kellogg's
Pep 1945) 25.00
Dick Tracy litho pinback Secret
Service Badges (1938)
• Patrol Member 35.00
• Patrol Sergeants 80.00
• Patrol Lieutenants 100.00
• Patrol Captains 125.00
• Patrol Inspector General 175.00
• Patrol Leader, bar pin 25.00
• Patrol Girl's Division 40.00
• Patrol Member (1939) 30.00
Dick Tracy – pin back Air Detective
badge (1938) 35.00

All prices listed are for *Near Mint* condition.

Dick Tracy Secret Service Patrol Badge (1938)

- pin with tab–Detective Club (1942) . . 75.00
- Detective Button, celluloid pin back
  three types, each 50.00
- Badge, Eagle Top (Cleveland News) . 60.00
- pin back, Orphan Annie (Genung's
  premium) 80.00
Don Winslow – Badge, Ensign (1939) . . . 60.00
- Badge, Lt. Commander 75.00
- litho pin back (Kellogg's Pep 1945) . 25.00
Dora – 1¼" cel, newspaper premium 35.00
Ella – ⅞" litho (Western Theatre
  premium) 35.00
Ella Cinders – 1¼" cel, newspaper
  premium 35.00
Etta Kett – 1¼" cel, newspaper
  premium 35.00
Emmy – litho pin back (Kellogg's
  Pep 1945) 25.00
Fatso – 1" litho (Saturday Chicago
  American) 30.00
Fat Stuff – litho pin back (Kellogg's
  Pep 1945) 25.00
Felix the Cat – cloth button 30.00
- pin enameled 75.00
- litho pin back (Kellogg's Pep 1945) . 25.00
The Fire Chief – litho pin back (Kellogg's
  Pep 1945) 25.00
Flash – pin back button, 1⅜" "Fastest
  Man Alive" 15.00
Flash Gordon – 1¼" cel, newspaper
  premium 35.00
- ¹³⁄₁₆" litho (King Features Syndicate) . 55.00
- Pin back button, Raymond,
  Dueling Ming 3" 30.00
- litho pin back (Kellogg's Pep 1945) . 25.00

Flattop – litho pin back (Kellogg's
  Pep 1945) 25.00
Foxy Grandpa – Button, color 1¼" (New
  York Journal) 30.00
- Button, Color, 1⅜" 30.00
- pin back, color, 2nd year 30.00
- Button Color, six months in N.Y. . . . 25.00
Fritz – litho pin back (Kellogg's
  Pep 1945) 25.00
- Litho, 30 comics (Herald & Examiner) 35.00
Garfield – Enameled Pins, set of 9
  United Features Syndicate (1978) . . 40.00
- pin back, 2¼", set of 6
  (United Features 1978) 20.00
Goofy – litho pin back (Kellogg's
  Pep 1945) 25.00
Goopy – ⅞" (Western Theatre
  premium) 35.00
Gordo – B&W litho pin back, (Phoenix
  Gazette) 30.00
Gravel Gertie – litho pin back (Kellogg's
  Pep 1945) 25.00
Gus and Gussie – 1¼" cel, newspaper
  premium 35.00
Hans – litho pin back (Kellogg's
  Pep 1945) 25.00
Happy Hooligan – die-cast pin,
  pink and green 50.00
- 1¼" cel, newspaper premium 35.00
Harold – ⅞" (Western Theatre premium) . 35.00
Harold Teen – litho pin back (Kellogg's
  Pep 1945) 25.00

Just Kids pins

Henry – litho pin back (Kellogg's
  Pep 1945) 25.00
Herby – litho pin back (Kellogg's
  Pep 1945) 25.00
Honey – ⅞" (Western Theatre premium) . 35.00
Ignatz Mouse – 1¼" cel, newspaper
  premium 35.00
Inspector – litho pin back (Kellogg's
  Pep 1945) 25.00
Jeff – Enamel pin, B&W/Tan 30.00

- Metal Stick pin 30.00
- ¹³⁄₁₆" litho (Saturday Daily News) . . . 25.00

Jiggs – ⅞" (Western Theatre premium) . . 35.00
- cello pin back (Detroit Times) 45.00
- R, W & B pin, 1½" (N.Y. Evening Journal 35.00
- litho pin back (Kellogg's Pep 1945) . 25.00
- litho, 30 comics (Herald & Examiner) 30.00

Jimmie – ⅞" (Western Theatre premium) . 35.00
Joe – ⅞" (Western Theatre premium) . . . 35.00
Joe Jinks – 1¼" cel, newspaper premium . 35.00
Joe Palooka – cello pin back, 1¼" (Tangle Comics) 35.00
Judy – litho pin back (Kellogg's Pep 1945) 25.00
Junior Tracy – litho pin back (Kellogg's Pep 1945) 25.00
Just Kids Safety Club pins, 1¼" (Montreal Herald 1930s)
     Mush 20.00
     Peanut 20.00
     Nicodemus 20.00
     Marjory 20.00
     Fatso 20.00
Just Kids – cello pin back (Mom-Plainfield Courier News) 25.00
- pin back, Safety Club buttons (1920s) 40.00
- 1¼" cel (Sweater Co.) 35.00

KatzenJammer Kids – 1¼" cel, newspaper premium 35.00
- ⅞" (Western Theatre premium) 35.00

Kayo Club pin

Kayo – cello pin back, Chocolate, Kayo Club member 40.00
- litho pin back (Kellogg's Pep 1945) . 25.00

Kit 'N' Katz – pin back button, 1½" B&W . 15.00
Kitty Kat – ⅞" (Western Theatre premium) 35.00
Ko-Ko – ⅞" (Western Theatre premium) . . 35.00
Krazy Kat – ⅞" (Western Theatre premium) 35.00
- 1¼" cel, newspaper premium 35.00

Li'l Abner – cello pin back 1¼" (Tangle Comics) 35.00
- Plastic pin back, badge 25.00
- brass figure pin, 2½" 55.00
- 1⅛" litho (Journal-Transcript Funnies Club) 45.00
- ¹³⁄₁₆" litho, Saturday Daily News 35.00

Lillums – litho pin back (Kellogg's Pep 1945) 25.00
Little Annie Roonie – ¹³⁄₁₆" litho (King Features Syndicate) 35.00
- 1¼" cel, newspaper premium 35.00

Little Joe – litho pin back (Kellogg's Pep 1945) 25.00
Little King – litho pin back (Kellogg's Pep 1945) 25.00
Little Moose – litho pin back (Kellogg's Pep 1945) 25.00
Little Wilbur – ⅞" (Western Theatre premium) 35.00

Little Orphan Annie Decoder Pin and Secret Guard Captain's Glow in the Dark badge

Little Orphan Annie – Secret Compartment Pin (1939) 75.00
- Decoder pins, 1936–39, each 75.00
- Mysto Snapper Membership Badge Clicker (1940) 60.00
- Radio, Captain's Secret Guard pin (1942) 60.00
- Radio Star pin (1934) 35.00
- School Pin (1937) 30.00
- School Pin #2 (1939) 30.00
- Secret Society Membership Pin (1934) 40.00
- Safety Guard Whistle Badge (Quaker 1942) 45.00
- Joe Corntassel Button (1931) 30.00
- Pin (Kellogg's Pep 1945) 30.00
- Button (1931) 35.00
- pin back, (Red Cross Macaroni) 50.00

All prices listed are for *Near Mint* condition.

- pin back, (New York Sunday American)40.00
- color, 1¼" Some Swell Sweater
  2 portraits (c. 1930s) 50.00
- Funny Frosty's Club Member
  1½" (1930) 50.00
- Genung's Portrait with Dick Tracy . . 75.00
Lord Plushbottom – litho pin back (Kellogg's
  Pep 1945) 25.00
Lum & Abner – Weather Prophet Badge,
  Litmus Type Counter (1936) 75.00
- Celluloid, pin back, 1¾" 35.00
Mac – ⅞" (Western Theatre premium) . . . 35.00
Mac – litho pin back (Kellogg's
  Pep 1945) 25.00
Maggie – ⅞" (Western Theatre premium) . 35.00
Maggie – litho pin back (Kellogg's
  Pep 1945) 25.00
- 1¼" cel, newspaper premium 35.00
Maggie and Jiggs, 1" litho 20.00
Mama Des Stross – litho pin back,
  (Kellogg's Pep 1945) 25.00
Mama KatzenJammer – litho pin back,
  (Kellogg's Pep 1945) 25.00
Mamie – litho pin back (Kellogg's
  Pep 1945) 25.00
Mandrake The Magician – pin back, Club
  Membership, die-cut (Taystee) 50.00
Margy – 1¼" cel, newspaper premium . . . 35.00
Marty Monk Cartoons – ⅞" (Western
  Theatre premium) 35.00
Marvel Comics – cello pin back, Spider-Man,
  Thor, Human Torch, 3-D Marching
  Society 35.00
Maud – 1¼" cel, newspaper premium . . . 35.00
Min Gump – litho pin back (Kellogg's
  Pep 1945) 25.00
Minute Movie – 1¼" cel, newspaper
  premium 35.00
Moon Mullins – litho pin back (Kellogg's
  Pep 1945) 25.00
Mr. Bailey – litho pin back (Kellogg's
  Pep 1945) 25.00
Mr. Bibs – litho pin back (Kellogg's
  Pep 1945) 25.00
Mr. Bungle – pin back, 1" (Newark
  Star Eagle) 30.00
- 1¼" cel, newspaper premium 35.00
Mr. Winkle – litho pin back (Kellogg's
  Pep 1945) 25.00
Muggs – 1¼" cel, newspaper premium . . . 35.00
- pin back, 1" (Newark Star-Eagle) . . . 30.00
Mush – 1¼" cel, newspaper premium 35.00

Mutt – Metal stick pin 30.00
- ¹³⁄₁₆" litho (Saturday Daily News) . . . 25.00
Mutt & Jeff – litho pin back, B&W, ⅞", various
  types (American Tobacco 1910) 45.00
- Litho pin back, B&W 1⅜"
  (Evening Telegraph) 40.00
Nancy – 1⅛" litho (Journal-Transcript
  Funnies Club) 45.00
- 1½" litho (Museum of
  Cartoon Art c.1990) 5.00
Nebs – 1¼" cel, newspaper premium 35.00
Nina – litho pin back (Kellogg's
  Pep 1945) 25.00
Old Doc – ⅞" (Western Theatre premium) 35.00
Olive Oyl – litho pin back (Kellogg's
  Pep 1945) 25.00

Nancy pin (1991)

- ¹³⁄₁₆" litho (King Features) 40.00
Oswald The Lucky Rabbit – ⅞" (Western
  Theatre premium) 35.00
Oswald's Kitty – ⅞" (Western Theatre
  premium) 35.00
Pa – ⅞" (Western Theatre premium) 35.00
Pam – 1¼" cel, newspaper premium 35.00
Pa Perkins – 1¼" cel, newspaper
  premium 35.00
Pat Patten – litho pin back (Kellogg's
  Pep 1945) 25.00
Peanuts – 1¾" cel (c. 1960s) Simon Simple
  cartoon:
- "Batting Average .001" 25.00
- "Big Man" 25.00
- "Curse You, Rad Baron" 25.00
- "Dogs Accept..." 25.00
- "Good Grief" 25.00
- "Here's Beav.." 25.00
- "I Believe In..." 25.00
- "I Don't Care If..." 25.00
- "I Wonder If..." 25.00
- "You're a Good Man Charlie Brown" . 25.00
- 1¼" cel (c. 1960s) Saying Buttons . . 15.00
Perry – ⅞" (Western Theatre premium) . . 35.00

Perry Winkle – litho pin back (Kellogg's
Pep 1945) 25.00
Petting Patty – 1¼" cel, newspaper
premium 35.00
The Phantom – litho pin back (Kellogg's
Pep 1945) 30.00
Pogo – "Pogo for President" 12" 25.00
• "I Go Pogo," pin back (1952) 20.00
Popeye – pin back button, 1¼" (N.Y.
Evening Journal) 55.00
• Set 6 pin back buttons, King
Features (c. 1980) 15.00
• litho pin back (Kellogg's Pep 1945) . 25.00
• pin back, Sailorman, ¾" Marion Theatre
Popeye Club (1935) 65.00
• pin back, Popeye the Sailor, ⅞"

I Go Pogo pin (1956)

Marion Theatre Popeye Club 65.00
• litho, 1¼" "I Yam Strong
for King Comics" 75.00
• pin back, Popeye the Sailor, ⅞"
red and white 60.00
• pin back, B&W, ⅞" (Penney's) 65.00
• pin back, newspaper, 1" litho beige . 50.00
• pin back, litho, ⅞" various color types
King Features Syndicate (1956) 50.00
• ¹³⁄₁₆" litho, King Features Syndicate . 50.00
• pin back, Sailorman, 3" full figure ... 60.00
• pin back, Douglas Popeye Club
Blue and White ¾" 60.00
Enamel, ½" 75.00
Pop Jenkins – litho pin back (Kellogg's
Pep 1945) 25.00
Punjab pin (Kellogg's Pep 1945) 30.00

Rainbow Duffy – 1¼" cel, newspaper
premium 35.00
Rip Winkle – litho pin back (Kellogg's
Pep 1945) 25.00
Rod – 1¼" cel, newspaper premium 35.00
Rosie – 1¼" cel, newspaper premium ... 35.00
Sandy Pin (Annie's Dog) (Kellogg's
Pep 1945) 25.00
Scrappy – ⅞" (Western Theatre premium) 35.00
Shadow – litho pin back (Kellogg's
Pep 1945) 25.00
• Club Stud Bottom magazine
premium 100.00
Shield – G-Man, litho celluloid, Pep Comics
premium 1¾" (1942) 75.00
• G-Man, litho celluloid, Pep Comics
premium, 3" 100.00
Shmoo – Pin in Gold Color 40.00
• Tin litho tab (Sealtest Ice Cream) ... 30.00
Skeezix – ⅞" (Western Theatre premium) 35.00
• litho pin back (Kellogg's Pep 1945) . 25.00
• Cello pin back, 1¼" (Red Cross
Macaroni 1930s) 50.00
• color pin back, 1⅝" 45.00
• 1¼" cel, Sweater Company 35.00
• 1¼" cel, newspaper premium 35.00
Skippy – 1" litho (Saturday Chicago
American) 40.00
• 1¼" cel, newspaper premium 35.00
• Cello, Efenbee, "I Am Skippy
Real American Boy" 50.00
S'Matter Pop – 1¼" cel, newspaper
premium 35.00
Smilin' Jack – pin back, in plane,
(Kellogg's Pep) 30.00
• pin back, Cindy (Kellogg's Pep) 25.00
• pin back, Fat Stuff (Kellogg's Pep) .. 25.00
• litho pin back (Kellogg's Pep 1945) . 30.00
Smitty – pin back, cello, Genung's 1⅝" .. 35.00
• pin back, Advertising Smitty
sweaters, 1¼" 50.00
• pin back cell, Ad for Caps (1945) ... 45.00
Smokey Stover – litho pin back (Kellogg's
Pep 1945) 25.00
Snoopy – Enamel Pins, various, city types 15.00
• pin back, sayings, 2¾" United
Features (1955) 25.00
• tab litho, B&W, Snoopy for President
HDQTRS-Ivar Theater 25.00
• pin back, Snoopy for President,
Webers's For Lunch (c. 1968) 15.00
• pin backs, holidays, set of four 20.00

All prices listed are for *Near Mint* condition.

- pin back buttons, promotional,
  Knotts Berry Farm, 7½" 20.00
Snuggle Pup – 1⅛" litho, newspaper,
  Savings (1923) 25.00
Snuffy Smith – litho pin back (Kellogg's
  Pep 1945) 25.00
Sunny Jim – Jim Running-Bran Daniels . . 40.00
Tailspin Tommy – 1¼" cel, newspaper
  premium 35.00
Tarzan – pin back button—Giant 5⅞"
  (c. 1974) 15.00
- pin back button, set of four 35.00
- pin back, ⅞" Safety Club 30.00
- pin back Celluloid, Signal Club 40.00
- pin back, Radio Club 50.00
- pin back, Radio Club,
  (Bursley Coffee) 65.00
Terry And The Pirates – tin litho, pin back
  various members, each 20.00
Tess Truehart – litho pin back (Kellogg's
  Pep 1945) 25.00
Tilda – litho pin back (Kellogg's
  Pep 1945) 25.00
Tillie – ⅞" (Western Theatre premium) . . . 35.00
Tillie the Toiler – litho pin back (Kellogg's
  Pep 1945) 25.00
- 1¼" cel, newspaper premium 35.00
Tiny Tim – litho pin back (Kellogg's
  Pep 1945) 25.00
Toots – litho pin back (Kellogg's
  Pep 1945) 25.00
- 1¼" cel, newspaper premium 35.00
Uncle Avery – litho pin back (Kellogg's
  Pep 1945) 20.00
Uncle Bim – litho pin back (Kellogg's
  Pep 1945) 20.00
Uncle Walt – litho pin back (Kellogg's
  Pep 1945) 20.00
- 1¼" cel, newspaper premium 35.00
Uncle Willie – litho pin back (Kellogg's
  Pep 1945) 20.00
The Villain – 1¼" cel, newspaper premium 35.00
Vitamin Flintheart – litho pin back,
  (Kellogg's Pep 1945) 20.00
Vontzy – ⅞" litho (Western Theatre
  premium) 35.00
Walt – ⅞" litho (Western Theatre premium) 35.00
Warbucks – (Kellogg's Pep 1945) 25.00
- Cel pin back, $1 Daddy Warbucks . . 60.00
Wilmer – litho pin back (Kellogg's
  Pep 1945) 20.00
Wimpy – litho pin back (Kellogg's

Pep 1945) 20.00
- pinback, enameled, 1¼" (1930s) . . . 50.00
- ¹³⁄₁₆" litho (King Features Syndicate) . 45.00
- 1" litho (Saturday Chicago American) 35.00
Winnie Winkle – litho pin back (Kellogg's
  Pep 1945) 20.00
- 1¼" cell newspaper premium 35.00
Yellow Kid – Metal Stick Pin (1890s) 75.00
- Metal Pin Cello, Occupations
  Sports, each 50.00
- Cello, various types, numbered, each 50.00
- White Metal Stick Pin—Painted 50.00
- pin back ⅞" Bubble Chewing Gum . . 40.00
Yippy – ⅞" litho (Western Theatre
  premium) 35.00
Ziggy – pin back buttons, 4" (1972)
  two types, each 15.00
- pin back buttons, set of four,
  T. Wilson 1¾" (1979) 15.00

JEWELRY

Cadillacs & Dinosaurs Bolo Tie (Planet
  Studios #CD-1B, 1991) 17.95
Crow Keychain 8.95
Generation X Stud Earring (Planet Studios
  #359A, 1994) 3.95
Generation X logo bolo tie (Planet Studios
  #359B, 1995) 14.95
Ghost Rider Skull Stud Earring (#161A) . . . 3.95
Ghost Rider Skull earrings (#161-A) 4.95
Ghost Rider Skull Bolo Tie (Planet Studios
  #161-B, 1991) 17.95
Judge Dredd heavy metal keyring (1992) . . 7.95
Punisher Skull earrings (#015-A) 4.95
Punisher Skull Stud Earring (#015A 3.95
Punisher Skull earrings (#139-D) 12.95
Punisher Skull Stud Earring (Planet Studios
  #015A, 1994) 3.95
Punisher Skull Belt Buckle (Planet Studios
  #BB-P, 1994) 19.95
Silver Surfer keychain (#182-K) 7.95
Silver Surfer Sterling silver pin/pendant
  (Planet Studios #PD-2S, 1994) 37.50
Spider Dangle Earrings (#267D) 12.00
Spider Stud Earring (#267A) 3.95
Spidey Head Earrings (#022-D) 12.95
Spider-Man Symbol Belt Buckle (Planet
  Studios BB-S) 19.95
Storm Earrings (Planet Studios 1993) 12.95
Venom Head Stud Earring (Planet Studios
  #262A, 1994) 3.95
X-Men Belt Buckle (#BB-X) 24.95

X-Men bolo tie (#190-B) 19.95
X-Men Symbol earrings (#190-D) 12.95
X-Men Tie-Tack (Planet Studios
     #190-T, 1992) 6.95

RINGS

R ings were among the most popular of the early radio premiums. They have been a symbol of power, both real and magical, since at least the Middle Ages and appear constantly in the movies and literature. Consequently, there is more collector interest in rings than in pins and buttons.

This listing is just a sampling of the many types of collectible rings. A complete listing would take an entire book in itself. In addition, identification of rings can be quite complicated without detailed photos, and many collectible rings were worn by the original owner and are now in less than mint condition, making grading (and pricing) difficult. For instance, The Supermen of America Membership prize ring is worth about $25,000 in good condition and would probably be worth $125,000 in mint condition, but none of the ten known examples of this ring are in this condition. Most of them are in very good condition and are worth about $40,000 (and are the most valuable comics collectibles in existence).

If you can find a ring at a flea market cheap, you can probably buy it and turn a profit. If you want to start collecting rings seriously, you'll need more than this book, not to mention a lot of money.

Archie sterling silver ring (Stabur 1993)
     Silver ring (495? made) 99.95
     Gold ring (100? made) 395.00
Batman Bat Signal (Diamond Comics
     Distribution 1992), 14k gold
     with diamond chips (25 made) . . 2,500.00
     Silver (550 made) 225.00
Batman Flicker rings, 12 different,
     silver base, (1960s), each 16.00
Batman Flicker Rings, blue plastic base,
     (VariVue 1966), 12 different, each . . . 10.00
Batman Bat Ring (Samsons 1966) 25.00

Batman Plastic Logo Ring (Rosecraft 1992)   5.00
Batman Stamped Metal Logo Ring
     (Rosecraft 1992) 10.00
Batman Glitter Plastic Logo Ring
     (Rosecraft 1992) 5.00
Batman Plastic Logo Pin (Rosecraft 1992) .   5.00
Buck Rogers Repeller Ray ring (seal
     ring), brass color with inset
     green stone 900.00
Buck Rogers Ring of Saturn with red
     stone (Post Corn Toasties 1944) . . . 300.00
Buck Rogers Space Ranger HaloLight
     ring (Sylvania 1952) 100.00
Captain America ring (1980s), metal 60.00
Captain Marvel compass ring (1940s),
     metal, rare 2,000.00
Cat Woman metal cloisonné ring
     (Rosecraft 1991) 10.00
Crow Silver Ring "Real love is forever—
     The Crow" (1994) 30.00

Green Lantern Water Jet Ring

Dick Tracy Enameled Portrait Ring (ca.
     1937, Quaker prem.) 50.00
Dick Tracy Air Detective Ring (1938) 60.00
Dick Tracy Secret Compartment Ring
     (1938) 75.00
Dick Tracy 4/c Metal Ring (Post Raisin
     Bran premium) 40.00
FemForce rings (1994), metal with
     enamal detail, 5 diff., each 12.50
Flash Two Way Flasher Ring 20.00
Garfield flicker rings (1970s),
     3 different, each 5.00
Green Hornet flicker rings (1960s),
     12 different, each 10.00
Green Lantern Water Jet Ring (Toy
     Biz 1989), came with action figure . . 10.00
Hägar the Horrible sterling silver
     ring (Stabur 1993)
     Silver ring (495 made) 100.00
     Gold ring (100 made) 395.00

All prices listed are for *Near Mint* condition.

Incredible Hulk ring (1980s), metal 60.00
King Comics Strip figural rings (1953)
   Blondie 10.00
   Felix the cat 10.00
   Flash Gordon 20.00
   Henry 10.00
   Little Lulu 10.00
   Olive Oyl 10.00
   Swee'Pea 10.00
   Other comic strip characters 10.00
Little Orphan Annie metal cloisonné
   rings (1980s) 3 different, each 10.00
Marvel Flicker rings (1970s),
   12 different, each 10.00
Marvel Super-Hero rings (1980s), 2 rings
   on card, 3 different, each 50.00
Ninjak Bronze Ring, in box (Planet Studios
   #Har-Br, 1994) 25.00
Phantom Silver Crossbones Ring (Planet
   Studios #SPR-2, 1994) 52.00
Phantom Silver Skull Ring (Planet
   Studios #SPR-1, 1994) 52.00
Popeye metal cloisonné ring (1980s) 10.00

Shadow Carey Salt ring

Post Cereal tin premium rings (1940s)
   Andy Gump 10.00
   Dagwood 10.00
   Dick Tracy 15.00
   Felix the Cat 10.00
   Flash Gordon 20.00
   Henry 10.00
   Little Orphan Annie 10.00
   Olive Oyl 10.00
   Phantom 15.00
   Popeye 15.00
   Smilin' Jack 10.00
   Swee'Pea 10.00
   Wimpy 10.00
Shadow Carey Salt glow-in-the-dark
   ring (1947) 350.00
Spawn (Image 1993)
   Gold, with diamond 1,000.00
   Silver 250.00
Spider-Man (Marvel 1994)

   (1,200 made max.) 75.00
Spider-Man (Marvel 1993)
   Gold (12 made max.) 3,000.00
   Silver (50 made max.) 600.00
   Bronze (50 made max.) 400.00
Supermen of America Member Ring . 40,000.00
Superman Secret Compartment Initial Ring
   with paper picture inside 10,500.00
Superman Secret Compartment Initial Ring
   w/Superman stamped in metal . 10,000.00
Superman Crusaders Ring 250.00
Superman-Tim Club Ring 5,000.00
Superman Ring (S/logo) (Nestle 1978) . . . 100.00

Superman Kryptonite Ring

Superman Kryptonite ring (Toy Biz
   1989), came with action figure 20.00
Teenage Mutant Ninja Turtles plastic
   rings (1990s), 8 different, each 20.00
Tekno•Comix Ring (Tekno Comix 1994) . . . 5.95
Wonder Woman metal logo rings (1980s) . . 50.00
Xavier Institute graduation ring (1994)
   10k gold (250 made max.) 400.00
   Sterling Silver (2500 made) 75.00
   Bronze-plated pewter 20.00
X-Men Ring (Diamond Comics Dist. 1993)
   Gold, with diamond chip (25 made) . 850.00
   Silver 150.00
X-O Valiant comics (1993) 50.00
   Note: In 1967, Videomatic (flicker) rings were
included with various Captain Action figures, such
as Aquaman, Batman, Buck Rogers, Captain
America, etc. See the Action Figure Series section
for more information.

S unday comics pages have long been a collectible in the comics sphere. Only recently has the full potential of their value been realized. Age is a prime factor, together with the title and the artist, when evaluating Sunday comics. The values represented below indicate Sunday comics in attractive, readable condition. Trimmed down, stained, torn or pages in generally poorer condition will bring a lower value. Superb quality pages will demand a higher value. The most sought after titles are the strips executed by the creator, the original artist thereof.

Tabloid pages will tend to bring a slightly lower value overall. A collector can expect to find pages in various formats, such as one-third pages, half pages and full pages. These varieties also appear in the tabloids mentioned above. Most comics from the first year of production have a 30% value premium over the second and later years.

ABBIE AN' SLATS
Raeburn Van Buren

per 10/ per year/

1937-39	12.00	75.00
1940-49	10.00	60.00
1950-59	5.00	15.00
1960-69	1.00	5.00
1970	1.00	5.00

BEN CASEY
Neal Adams

1962-66	2.00	10.00

ALLEY OOP
Vincent T. Hamlin

1933-39	50.00	250.00
1940-49	30.00	150.00
1950-59	8.00	45.00
1960-69	3.00	15.00
1970-71	4.00	20.00

Dave Grave

1971-79	6.00	25.00
1980-89	4.00	20.00
1990-present	1.00	5.00

ANDY CAPP
Reginald Smith

1957-59	3.00	15.00
1960-69	1.50	7.50
1970-79	.50	4.00
1980-89	.50	4.00
1990-present	.50	4.00

AMAZING SPIDER-MAN
Stan Lee

1977-79	5.00	25.00
1980-89	4.00	20.00
1990-present	.50	4.00

APARTMENT 3-G
Alex Kotsky

1961-69	10.00	55.00
1970-79	1.50	17.00
1980-89	1.00	8.00
1990-present	.50	4.00

ARCHIE

1960-69	1.50	7.50
1970-79	.50	4.00
1980-89	.50	4.00
1990-present	.50	3.00

ACCORDING TO HOYLE

1930-39	20.00	100.00

BARNEY GOOGLE
Billy DeBeck

1916-19	60.00	350.00
1920-29	30.00	150.00
1930-39	20.00	100.00
1940-42	10.00	55.00

and SNUFFY SMITH
Fred Lasswell

1942-49	10.00	55.00
1950-59	3.00	15.00
1960-69	1.50	7.50
1970-79	1.00	6.00
1980-89	.50	3.00

BATMAN

1944-46	100.00	500.00

B.C.
Johnny Hart

1958-59	6.00	32.00
1960-69	2.75	14.00
1970-79	2.00	10.00
1980-89	1.50	8.00
1990-present	.50	2.50

BEETLE BAILEY
Mort Walker

1950-59	5.00	25.00
1960-69	3.00	15.00
1970-79	3.00	15.00
1980-89	3.00	15.00
1990-present	.50	2.50

BIG BEN BOLT
John Cullen Murphy

1950-59	6.00	30.00

BLONDIE
Chic Young

1930-39	20.00	160.00
1940-49	10.00	55.00
1950-59	6.00	30.00
1960-69	3.00	15.00
1970-73	2.50	12.50

Jim Raymond

1973-79	2.50	12.50
1980-84	1.25	6.00

Stan Drake

1984-89	1.25	6.00
1990-present	.50	2.50

BOOTS & HER BUDDIES

1930-39	10.00	55.00
1940-49	3.00	15.00
1950-59	3.00	15.00
1960-69	2.00	10.00

BLOOM COUNTY
Berke Brethed

1970s	4.00	20.00
1980s	3.00	15.00
1990-present	.50	2.50

BOBBY THATCHER
George Storm

1927–29	20.00	100.00
1930–38	15.00	75.00

Sheldon Mayer

1938	12.00	60.00

BONER'S ARK
Mort Walker

1968–69	2.50	13.00
1970–71	1.75	9.00

Frank Johnson

1971–79	1.70	9.00
1980	1.25	6.00

BRENDA STARR
Dale Messick, Ramona Fradon

1945–49	20.00	100.00
1950–59	5.00	25.00
1960–69	2.50	12.50
1970–79	2.00	11.00
1980–89	1.80	8.00
1990–present	.50	2.50

BRINGING UP FATHER
George McManus

1918–19	80.00	425.00
1920–29	40.00	240.00
1930–39	25.00	130.00
1940–49	15.00	75.00
1950–59	5.00	25.00
1960–69	2.50	13.00
1970 on	1.20	6.00

BROOM HILDA
Russell Myers

1970–79	1.50	7.50
1980–89	1.00	5.00
1990–present	1.00	5.00

BUCK ROGERS
Dick Calkins

1929	300.00	1500.00
1930	220.00	1100.00
1931	200.00	1000.00
1932	150.00	750.00
1933	125.00	600.00
1934–36	100.00	550.00
1937–39	90.00	500.00
1940–47	50.00	250.00

Leon Dworkins

1949–51	30.00	150.00
1952–58	20.00	100.00

Murphy Anderson

1958–59	22.00	110.00

George Tuska

1959–64	20.00	100.00
1965–67	10.00	50.00

Gray Morrow

1979–89	5.00	25.00

1990–present	5.00	25.00

BUGS BUNNY

1945–49	10.00	55.00
1950–59	10.00	55.00
1960–69	6.00	35.00
1970–79	5.00	25.00
1980 on	1.50	7.50

BUNGLE FAMILY
Clarence Grey

1932–39	50.00	250.00
1940–49	25.00	125.00
1950–57	18.00	80.00

Paul Norris

1957–59	10.00	50.00
1960–69	2.00	10.00
1970–79	1.50	7.50
1980–89	1.00	5.00
1990–present	.50	2.50

BUSTER BROWN
Outcault, Richard

1905–9	100.00	500.00
1910 on	60.00	300.00

BUZ SAWYER

1943–49	10.00	50.00
1950–55	5.00	25.00
1956–on	2.00	10.00

CAPTAIN MIDNIGHT
Rudolph Dirks

1914–19	30.00	150.00

CAPTAIN MIDNIGHT

1940–49	30.00	150.00
1951–59	10.00	50.00

CAPTAIN AND THE KIDS
Rudolph Dirks

1914–19	80.00	400.00
1920–29	40.00	165.00
1930–39	20.00	100.00
1940–49	10.00	55.00
1950–59	6.00	30.00
1960–68	3.00	15.00

John Dirks

1968–69	2.00	10.00
1970–79	1.50	7.50
1980–89	1.00	5.00
1990–present	1.00	5.00

CHARLIE CHAN
Alfred Andriola

1938–39	25.00	125.00
1940–42	15.00	75.00

CONAN

1978–79	5.00	25.00

CONNIE
Frank Godwin

1927–29	80.00	400.00
1930–39	60.00	300.00
1940–44	20.00	100.00

DATELINE: DANGER
Al McWilliams

1968–74	4.00	20.00

DENNIS THE MENACE
Hank Ketcham

1951–59	10.00	55.00
1960–69	5.00	25.00
1970–79	2.50	12.00
1980–89	1.00	5.00
1990–present	1.00	5.00

DESPERATE DESMOND
Harry Hirshfield

1910–19	50.00	250.00
1920–29	30.00	150.00
1930–34	20.00	100.00

DICKIE DARE
Milton Caniff

1933–34	60.00	300.00

Coulton Eaugh

1934–44	25.00	125.00

Mabel Adin Burvick

1944–49	12.00	60.00
1950–55	8.00	40.00

DICK'S ADVENTURES IN DREAMLAND
Neil O'Keefe

1947–49	15.00	75.00
1950–56	8.00	40.00

DICK TRACY
Chester Gould

1931–39	150.00	750.00
1940–49	40.00	200.00
1950–59	30.00	150.00
1960–69	20.00	100.00
1970–77	15.00	75.00

Rick Fletcher

1977–83	7.50	35.00

Dick Locher

1983–89	5.00	25.00
1990–present	.50	2.50

DIXIE DUGAN
John Striebel

1929–39	60.00	300.00
1940–49	20.00	100.00
1950–59	11.00	55.00
1960–69	6.00	30.00
1970–79	2.00	10.00
1980–89	2.00	10.00
1990–present	.50	2.50

DR. KILDARE
Ken Bald

1964–69	5.00	25.00
1970 on	1.00	5.00

DONDI
Gus Edson

1954–59	8.00	40.00
1960–66	4.00	20.00

Irwin Hasen

1966–69	2.00	10.00
1970 on	1.00	5.00

DON DIXON AND THE HIDDEN EMPIRE
Carl Pfeufer

1935–39	30.00	150.00
1940–41	20.00	50.00

DON WINSLOW
Leon Beroth

1936–39	25.00	125.00
1940–45	20.00	100.00

DOONESBURY
Gary Trudeau

1970–79	6.00	30.00
1980–89	4.00	20.00
1990–present	.50	2.50

DRAGO
Burne Hogarth

1945–46	55.00	275.00

DREAMS OF THE RAREBIT FIEND
(Silas) Winsor McCay

1904–7	75.00	375.00

DUMB DORA
Chic Young

1925–30	25.00	125.00

Paul Fung

1930–32	20.00	100.00

Bil Dwyer

1932–33	20.00	100.00

ELLA CINDERS
Charlie Plumb

1927–29	20.00	100.00
1930–39	12.50	62.00
1940–49	10.00	50.00
1950–55	7.50	35.00

FAMOUS FICTION
Chad Gropkopf and others

1938–39	20.00	100.00
1940–45	15.00	75.00

FEARLESS FOSDICK
Al Capp

1942–49	20.00	100.00
1950–59	15.00	75.00
1960–69	10.00	50.00
1970 on	7.50	37.50

FEIFFER
Jules Feiffer

1956–59	5.00	25.00
1960–69	3.00	15.00
1970–79	1.50	7.50

FELIX THE CAT
Pat Sullivan

1923–29	50.00	250.00
1930–34	40.00	200.00

Mesmer

1935–43	30.00	150.00
1944–49	15.00	75.00

FAR SIDE
Gary Larson

1984–present	3.00	15.00

FLAMINGO
Matt Baker

1952–53	13.00	65.00

FLASH GORDON
Alex Raymond

1934	250.00	1500.00
1935	200.00	1100.00
1936–39	100.00	550.00
1940–44	60.00	300.00

Austin Briggs

1944–48	20.00	100.00

Mac Raboy

1948–49	30.00	150.00
1950–59	15.00	75.00
1960–67	13.00	65.00

Dan Barry

1967–69	10.00	50.00
1970–79	7.50	37.50
1980–89	5.00	25.00

1990–present	1.00	5.00

FLINTSTONES
Joe Barbara/Bill Hanna

1961–69	7.50	37.50
1970–79	5.00	25.00
1980–85	4.00	20.00

FRIDAY FOSTER
Jorge Langorian

1970–74	7.50	37.50

Gray Morrow

1974	5.00	25.00

GASOLINE ALLEY
Frank King

1918–19	35.00	175.00
1920–29	25.00	125.00
1930–39	20.00	100.00
1940–49	15.00	75.00
1950–51	7.50	37.50

Bill Perry

1951–59	7.50	37.50
1960–69	6.00	30.00

Dick Morres

1970–79	5.00	25.00
1980–89	3.00	15.00
1990–present	.50	2.50

GARFIELD
Jim Davis

1978–79	3.00	15.00
1980–89	1.00	5.00
1990–present	.50	2.50

GENE AUTRY
Till Goodan

1940–45	35.00	175.00

Bob Stevens

1953	7.50	37.50

GORDO
Gus Arriola

1941–43	15.00	75.00
1946–49	12.00	60.00
1950–59	10.00	50.00
1960–69	7.50	37.50
1970–79	5.00	25.00
1980–89	3.00	15.00
1990–present	.50	2.50

GUMPS
Sidney Smith

1919–29	20.00	100.00
1930–35	15.00	75.00

Gus Edson

1935–39	12.00	60.00

All prices listed are for *Near Mint* condition.

1940–49	10.00	50.00
1950–59	7.50	37.50

HÄGAR
Dik Browne

1973–79	3.00	15.00
1980–89	2.00	10.00
1990–present	.50	2.50

HAIRBREADTH HARRY
C. W. Kahles

1906–9	50.00	250.00
1910–19	35.00	175.00
1920–29	25.00	150.00
1930–31	20.00	100.00

F. O. Alexander

1931–39	17.00	87.00

HALF HITCH
Hank Ketcham

1970–75	2.00	10.00

HEATHCLIFF
George Gately

1970–79	2.50	10.00
1980–89	1.00	5.00
1990–present	.50	2.50

HERMAN
G. Forton, C. Weber

1980–present	1.00	5.00

HAPPY HOOLIGAN
Fred Opper

1900–9	75.00	375.00
1910–19	50.00	250.00
1920–29	30.00	150.00
1930–32	25.00	125.00

HAROLD TEEN
Carl Ed

1919–29	15.00	750.00
1930–39	10.00	50.00
1940–49	5.00	25.00
1950–59	1.00	5.00

HEART OF
JULIET JONES
Stan Drake

1953–59	12.00	60.00
1960–69	10.00	50.00
1970–79	6.00	30.00
1980–89	3.00	15.00
1990–present	.50	2.50

HENRY

1936–39	15.00	75.00

1940–49	7.50	37.50
1950–59	6.00	30.00
1960–69	5.00	25.00
1970–79	3.00	15.00
1980–89	1.00	5.00
1990–present	.50	2.50

HI AND LOIS
Dik Browne

1954–59	5.00	25.00
1960–69	3.00	15.00
1970–79	1.20	6.00
1980–89	1.00	5.00
1990–present	.50	2.50

HOWARD THE DUCK

1978	1.00	5.00

INVISIBLE SCARLET
Russel Stamm

1941–49	30.00	150.00
1950–54	20.00	100.00

INCREDIBLE HULK

1978–79	20.00	75.00
1980–82	7.50	37.50

JANE ARDEN
F. Ellis, B. Schoenke, R. Ross

1928–29	15.00	75.00
1930–39	10.00	55.00
1940–49	8.00	40.00

Hargis, Jim Seed

1950s	5.00	25.00

JOE PALOOKA
Ham Fisher

1928–29	30.00	150.00
1930–39	20.00	100.00
1940–49	10.00	50.00
1950–55	7.50	37.50

Tony DiPreta

1955–59	7.50	37.50
1960–69	6.00	30.00
1970–79	3.00	15.00
1980–89	3.00	15.00
1990–present	.50	2.50

JOHNNY HAZARD
Frank Robbins

1944–49	12.50	60.00
1950–59	10.00	50.00
1960–69	10.00	50.00
1970–79	6.00	30.00

JUDGE PARKER
Dan Heilman

1952–59	4.00	20.00
1960–65	3.00	15.00

Harold LeDoux

1965–69	3.00	15.00
1970–79	2.00	10.00
1980–89	1.00	5.00
1990–present	.50	2.50

JUNGLE JIM
Alex Raymond

1934	150.00	750.00
1935	100.00	500.00
1936–39	60.00	300.00
1940–44	40.00	200.00

Austin Briggs

1944–48	12.00	60.00

Paul Norris

1948–49	12.00	60.00
1950–54	10.00	50.00

KERRY DRAKE
Alfred Andriola

1943–49	15.00	75.00
1950–59	12.00	60.00
1960–69	7.50	37.50
1970–79	3.00	15.00
1980–89	2.00	10.00
1990–present	.50	2.50

KING OF
THE ROYAL MOUNTED
A. Dean, C. Flanders, J. Gary

1935–39	30.00	150.00
1940–49	20.00	100.00
1950–59	10.00	50.00

KRAZY KAT
George Herriman

1916–19	75.00	375.00
1920–29	60.00	300.00
1930–39	50.00	250.00
1940–44	40.00	200.00

LANCE
Warren Tufts

1955–57	30.00	150.00

LI'L ABNER
Al Capp

1935–39	20.00	100.00
1940–49	10.00	55.00
1950–59	10.00	55.00
1960–69	6.00	30.00
1970–77	5.00	25.00

Buck Rogers Sunday page (detail)

Darrell McClure

LITTLE ANNIE ROONIE				LITTLE IODINE	
Ed Verdier				Jimmy Hatlo	
1929	30.00	150.00	1930–39 .... 10.00 . 55.00	1943–49 .... 8.00 . 40.00
Ben Batsford			1940–49 .... 7.50 . 37.50	1950–59 .... 3.00 . 15.00
1929–30 .... 20.00	100.00		1950–59 .... 5.00 . 25.00	1960–63 .... 2.00 . 10.00
			1960–66 .... 3.00 . 15.00	

All prices listed are for *Near Mint* condition.

Bob Dunn
1963–67 . . . . 2.00 . 10.00
Hy Eisman
1967–69 . . . . 2.00 . 10.00
1970–79 . . . . 2.00 . 10.00
1980–89 . . . . 1.00 . 5.00
1990–present . . . . . . .50 . 2.50

LITTLE JOE
Ed Leffingwell
1934–39 . . . . 10.00 . 55.00
1940–49 . . . . 7.00 . 35.00
1950–56 . . . . 5.00 . 10.00

THE LITTLE KING
Otto Soglow
1934–39 . . . . 20.00 . 100.00
1940–49 . . . . 15.00 . 75.00
1950–59 . . . . 10.00 . 50.00
1960–69 . . . . 7.50 . 37.50
1970–79 . . . . 6.00 . 30.00
1980–89 . . . . 3.00 . 15.00
1990–present . . . . . . .50 . . 2.50

LITTLE NEMO
IN SLUMBERLAND
Winsor McCay
1905–9 . . . . 120.00 . 600.00
1910–14 . . . . 80.00 . 400.00
1924–26 . . . . 120.00 . 600.00

LITTLE ORPHAN ANNIE
Harold Grey
1924–29 . . . . 35.00 . 175.00
1930–39 . . . . 30.00 . 150.00
1940–49 . . . . 15.00 . 75.00
1950–59 . . . . 10.00 . 50.00
1960–69 . . . . 5.00 . 25.00
Leonard Starr
1970–79 . . . . 3.00 . 15.00
1980–89 . . . . 2.50 . 12.00
1990–present . . . . . . .50 . . 2.50

LONE RANGER
Ed Kressy
1938–39 . . . . 25.00 . 125.00
Charles Flanders
1939–49 . . . . 20.00 . 100.00
1950–59 . . . . 15.00 . 75.00
1960–69 . . . . 7.50 . 37.50
Russ Heath
1970–71 . . . . 7.50 . 37.50

MANDRAKE
THE MAGICIAN
Phil Davis
1935–39 . . . . 50.00 250.00

1940–49 . . . . 35.00 175.00
1950–59 . . . . 20.00 100.00
1960–64 . . . . 10.00 . 50.00
Fred Fredericks
1964–69 . . . . 10.00 . 50.00
1970–79 . . . . 4.00 . 20.00
1980–89 . . . . 2.50 . 12.00
1990–present . . . . . . .50 . . 2.50

MAIAH MOOVIE
H. Cornel Greening
1910–19 . . . . 60.00 300.00

MARMADUKE
Brad Anderson
1970s . . . . 4.00 . 20.00
1980–89 . . . . 2.00 . 10.00
1990–present . . . . . . .50 . . 2.50

MARK TRAIL
Ed Dodd
1946–49 . . . . 10.00 . 50.00
1950–59 . . . . 5.00 . 25.00
1960–69 . . . . 3.00 . 15.00
1970–79 . . . . 2.00 . 10.00
1980–89 . . . . 1.00 . 5.00
1990–present . . . . . . .50 . 2.50

MARY WORTH
Mary Orr
1932–40 . . . . 25.00 . 125.00
Dale Conner
1940–42 . . . . 15.00 . 75.00
Ken Ernst
1942–49 . . . . 10.00 . 50.00
1950–59 . . . . 5.00 . 25.00
1960–69 . . . . 3.00 . 15.00
1970–79 . . . . 2.00 . 10.00
1980–89 . . . . 1.00 . . 5.00
1990–present . . . . . . .50 . 2.50

MEDAL OF HONOR
1945–49 . . . . 20.00 100.00

MEDIEVAL CASTLE
Hal Foster
1944–45 . . . . 25.00 125.00

MICKY FINN
Lank Leonard
1936–39 . . . . 10.00 . 50.00
1940–49 . . . . 7.50 . 37.50
1950–59 . . . . 5.00 . 25.00
1960–70 . . . . 4.00 . 20.00
Morris Weiss
1970–75 . . . . 3.00 . 15.00

MICKEY MOUSE
Floyd Gottfredson
1932–39 . . . . 30.00 150.00
1940–49 . . . . 20.00 100.00
1950–59 . . . . 15.00 . 75.00
1960–69 . . . . 15.00 . 75.00
1970–79 . . . . 12.00 . 60.00
1980–89 . . . . 5.00 . 25.00
1990–present . . . . . 3.00 . 15.00

MR. BREGER
Dave Breger
1942–44 . . . . 10.00 . 50.00
1945–49 . . . . 10.00 . 50.00
1950–59 . . . . 5.00 . 25.00
1960–70 . . . . 3.00 . 15.00

MR. ABERNATHY
Bud Jones
1957–59 . . . . 5.00 . 25.00
1960–69 . . . . 5.00 . 25.00
1970–79 . . . . 3.00 . 15.00
1980–89 . . . . 1.00 . . 5.00
1990–present . . . . . . .50 . . 2.50

MR. & MRS.
1923–29 . . . . 15.00 . 75.00
1930–39 . . . . 10.00 . 50.00
1940–49 . . . . 7.50 . 37.50
1950 on . . . . 5.00 . 25.00

MOON MULLINS
Frank Willard
1923–29 . . . . 30.00 150.00
1930–39 . . . . 20.00 100.00
1940–49 . . . . 15.00 . 75.00
1950–58 . . . . 10.00 . 50.00
Fred Johnson
1958–59 . . . . 7.50 . 37.50
1960–69 . . . . 5.00 . 25.00
1970–79 . . . . 3.00 . 15.00
1980–89 . . . . 1.00 . . 5.00
1990–present . . . . . . .50 . . 2.50

MUTT AND JEFF
Ham Fisher
1907–9 . . . . 50.00 250.00
1910–19 . . . . 40.00 200.00
1920–29 . . . . 30.00 150.00
1930–39 . . . . 15.00 . 75.00
1940–49 . . . . 12.50 . 63.00
1950–59 . . . . 10.00 . 50.00
1960–69 . . . . 5.00 . 25.00
1970–79 . . . . 4.00 . 20.00
1980–89 . . . . 1.00 . . 5.00
1990–present . . . . . . .50 . . 2.50

Flash Gordon Sunday page (detail)

NANCY
Ernie Bushmiller

1938–39	20.00	100.00

Jerry Scott

1940–49	10.00	50.00
1950–59	7.50	37.50
1960–69	5.00	25.00
1970–79	3.00	15.00
1980–89	2.00	10.00
1990–present	.50	2.50

NAPOLEON

1930–39	15.00	75.00
1940–49	10.00	50.00
1950–59	7.50	37.50

THE NEBBS

1933–39	10.00	50.00
1940 on	7.50	37.50

OAKY DOAKS
Ralph Briggs Fuller

1945–49	10.00	50.00
1950–59	7.50	37.50
1960–61	5.00	25.00

ON STAGE
Leonard Starr

1950–59	10.00	50.00
1960–69	7.50	37.50
1970–79	5.00	25.00

OUR BOARDING HOUSE
Gene Ahern

1923–29	20.00	100.00
1930–36	15.00	75.00

Bill Freyse

1936–39	15.00	75.00
1940–49	10.00	50.00
1950–59	7.50	37.50
1960–61	5.00	25.00
1973–77	2.50	12.50

PEANUTS
Charles Schultz

1952–59	12.00	60.00
1960–69	10.00	50.00
1970–79	5.00	25.00
1980–89	3.00	15.00
1990–present	3.00	15.00

PHANTOM
Ray Moore

1936–39	50.00	250.00
1940–47	25.00	125.00

Wilson McCoy

1947–49	20.00	100.00
1950–59	15.00	75.00
1960–61	7.00	35.00

Bill Lignante

1961–62	7.00	35.00

Sy Barry

1962–69	7.00	35.00
1970–79	5.00	25.00
1980–89	3.00	15.00
1990–present	1.00	5.00

POGO
Walt Kelly

1949	18.50	95.00
1950–59	15.00	75.00
1960–69	12.00	60.00
1970–73	10.00	50.00

Selby and Stephen Kelley

1973–75	5.00	25.00

All prices listed are for *Near Mint* condition.

POLLY
Cliff Scerrett
1914–19	50.00	250.00
1920–29	40.00	200.00
1930–33	25.00	125.00

PRINCE VALIANT
Hal Foster
1937–39	75.00	375.00
1940–49	65.00	325.00
1950–59	35.00	175.00
1960–69	15.00	75.00
1970–71	10.00	50.00

John Cullen Murphy
1971–79	7.50	37.50
1980–89	4.00	20.00
1990–present	.50	2.50

RED BARRY
Will Gould
1934–40	40.00	200.00

REDEYE
Gordon Bess
1967–69	7.50	37.50
1970–79	5.00	25.00
1980–89	3.00	15.00
1990–present	.50	2.50

RED RYDER
Fred Harmon
1938–39	50.00	250.00
1940–49	20.00	100.00
1950–60	15.00	75.00

REX MORGAN
Frank Edgington and Marvin Bradley
1948–49	10.00	50.00
1950–59	7.50	37.50
1960–69	5.00	25.00
1970–79	3.00	15.00
1980–89	2.00	10.00
1990–present	.50	2.50

RICK O'SHAY
Stan Lynde
1958–59	7.50	37.50
1960–69	5.00	25.00
1970–74	3.00	15.00

RIGHT AROUND HOME
1940–49	5.00	25.00
1950–54	3.00	15.00

ROOM AND BOARD
1936–39	12.00	60.00
1940–49	10.00	50.00
1950–51	7.50	37.50

ROY ROGERS
Al McKimson
1950–59	20.00	100.00

SAD SACK
George Baker
1948–49	10.00	50.00
1950–59	5.00	25.00

SCORCHY SMITH
Ed Good
1944–46	30.00	150.00

Rodlow Willard
1946–49	30.00	150.00
1950–59	20.00	100.00
1960–61	10.00	50.00

THE SHADOW
Vernon Greene
1938–42	40.00	200.00

SHOE
Jeff MacNelly
1977–79	5.00	25.00
1980–89	2.00	10.00
1990–present	.50	2.50

SMILIN' JACK
Zack Mosely
1933–35	50.00	250.00
1936–39	30.00	150.00
1940–49	20.00	100.00
1950–59	15.00	75.00
1960–69	10.00	50.00
1970–73	7.50	37.50

SMITTY
Walter Berndt
1928–29	20.00	100.00
1930–39	15.00	75.00
1940–49	12.00	60.00
1950–59	10.00	50.00
1960–69	7.50	37.50

SMOKEY STOVER
Bill Holman
1935–39	25.00	125.00
1940–49	15.00	75.00
1950–59	10.00	50.00
1960–69	7.50	37.50

SNUFFY SMITH
1957–59	6.00	30.00
1960–69	5.00	25.00

1970–79	4.00	20.00
1980–83	3.00	15.00

SPIRIT
Will Eisner
1940–49	120.00	600.00
1950	120.00	600.00

Wally Wood
1950–52	120.00	600.00

STAR TREK
1979–81	7.50	37.50

STAR WARS
1979–83	5.00	25.00

STEVE CANYON
Milt Caniff
1947–49	20.00	100.00
1950–59	15.00	75.00
1960–69	12.00	60.00
1970–79	10.00	50.00
1980–89	5.00	25.00
1990–present	.50	2.50

STEVE ROPER
Bill Overgard
1948–49	10.00	50.00
1953–59	7.50	37.50
1960–69	5.00	25.00
1970–79	3.00	15.00
1980–89	1.00	5.00
1990–present	.50	2.50

SUPERMAN
Joe Shuster
1939	100.00	1000.00
1940–45	40.00	200.00
1946–49	30.00	150.00

Wayne Boring
1950–59	15.00	75.00
1960–67	10.00	50.00
1979–79	5.00	25.00
1980 on	.50	2.50

TAILSPIN TOMMY
Hal Forest
1928–29	30.00	150.00
1930–40	20.00	100.00

TARZAN
Hal Foster
1931–32	100.00	500.00
1933–37	60.00	300.00

Burne Hogarth
1937–46	40.00	200.00
1947–48	20.00	100.00

John Lehti
1949 . . . . 20.00 100.00
Paul Reinman
1949–50 . . . . 20.00 100.00
Nick Cardy
1950 . . . . 15.00 . 75.00
Bob Lubbers
1950–53 . . . . 15.00 . 75.00
John Celardo
1953–59 . . . . 15.00 . 75.00
1960–67 . . . . 15.00 . 75.00
Russ Manning
Late 1960s 20.00 100.00
Mike Grell
1970s . . . . 15.00 . 75.00
Gray Morrow
1980s . . . . 10.00 . 50.00

TEENIE WEENIES
1915–19 . . . . 50.00 250.00
1920–29 . . . . 20.00 100.00
1930–39 . . . . 10.00 . 50.00
1940–49 . . . . 5.00 . 25.00
1950s . . . . 2.00 . 10.00

TERRY AND THE PIRATES
Milt Caniff
1934–39 . . . . 40.00 200.00
1940–46 . . . . 25.00 125.00
George Wunder
1946–49 . . . . 15.00 . 75.00
1950–59 . . . . 10.00 . 50.00
1960–69 . . . . 7.50 . 37.50
1970–73 . . . . 5.00 . 25.00

THIMBLE THEATER
With Popeye, after 1929
Bud Segar (Elzie C. Segar)
1919–29 . . . . 75.00 375.00
1930–38 . . . . 50.00 250.00
Bud Sagendorf
1938–39 . . . . 30.00 150.00
1940–49 . . . . 20.00 100.00
1950–59 . . . . 15.00 . 75.00
1960–69 . . . . 12.00 . 60.00
1970–79 . . . . 10.00 . 50.00
1980–89 . . . . 5.00 . 25.00
1990–present . . . . . . .50 . . 2.50

TIGER
Bud Blake
1965–69 . . . . 7.50 . 37.50
1970–79 . . . . 5.00 . 25.00
1980–89 . . . . 3.00 . 15.00
1990–present . . . . . . .50 . . 2.50

TILLIE THE TOILER
Russ Westover
1921–29 . . . . 35.00 175.00
1930–39 . . . . 20.00 100.00
1940–49 . . . . 15.00 . 75.00
Bob Gustafson
1950–59 . . . . 10.00 . 50.00

TIMID SOUL
1936–39 . . . . 15.00 . 75.00
1940–49 . . . . 7.50 . 37.50

TIM TYLER'S LUCK
Lyman Young
1931–39 . . . . 40.00 200.00
1940–49 . . . . 20.00 100.00
1950–52 . . . . 15.00 . 75.00
Tom Massey
1952–59 . . . . 10.00 . 50.00
1960–69 . . . . 7.50 . 37.50
1970–72 . . . . 5.00 . 25.00

TINY TIM
1933–39 . . . . 12.00 . 60.00
1940–49 . . . . 10.00 . 50.00
1950–58 . . . . 7.50 . 37.50

TOONERVILLE FOLKS
Fontaine Fox
1920–29 . . . . 30.00 150.00
1930–39 . . . . 15.00 . 75.00
1940–49 . . . . 10.00 . 50.00
1950–55 . . . . 7.50 . 37.50

TUMBLEWEEDS
Tom K. Ryan
1965–69 . . . . 10.00 . 50.00
1970–79 . . . . 5.00 . 25.00
1980–89 . . . . 3.00 . 15.00
1990–present . . . . . . .50 . . 2.50

WASH TUBBS
Roy Crane
1930–39 . . . . 30.00 150.00
1940–43 . . . . 40.00 200.00
Leslie Turner
1943–49 . . . . 20.00 100.00
1950–59 . . . . 15.00 . 75.00
1960–69 . . . . 10.00 . 50.00
1970–79 . . . . 7.50 . 37.50
1980–89 . . . . 5.00 . 25.00
1990–present . . . . . . .50 . . 2.50

WALT DISNEY
1936–39 . . . . 20.00 100.00
1950–59 . . . . 10.00 . 50.00
1960–69 . . . . 5.00 . 25.00

1970–79 . . . . 3.00 . 15.00
1980–89 . . . . 1.00 . . 5.00
1990–present . . . . . . .50 . . 2.50

WEE PALS
Morrie Turner
1965–69 . . . . 4.00 . 20.00
1970–79 . . . . 2.00 . 10.00
1980–89 . . . . 1.00 . . 5.00
1990–present . . . . . . .50 . . 2.50

WINNIE WINKLE
Martin Branner
1920–29 . . . . 25.00 125.00
1930–39 . . . . 15.00 . 75.00
1940–49 . . . . 10.00 . 50.00
1950–59 . . . . 7.50 . 37.50
1960–62 . . . . 5.00 . 25.00
Max Van Bibber
1960s . . . . 5.00 . 25.00
Joe Kubert School
1970s . . . . 3.00 . 15.00
Frank Bolle
1980s . . . . 3.00 . 15.00

WINTHROP
1966–69 . . . . 3.00 . 15.00
1970–77 . . . . 2.00 . 10.00

WIZARD OF ID
Brant Parker
1964–69 . . . . 5.00 . 25.00
1970–79 . . . . 3.00 . 15.00
1980–89 . . . . 1.00 . . 5.00
1990–present . . . . . . .50 . . 2.50

YELLOW KID
Richard Outcault
1895 *per page* 200.00
1896 *per page* 150.00
George Luks
1897 *per page* 100.00
1898 *per page* 100.00
Richard Outcault
1898 *per page* 100.00

ZIGGY
Tom Wilson
1970s . . . . 3.00 . 15.00
1980s . . . . 2.00 . 10.00

All prices listed are for *Near Mint* condition.

O riginal comics art collecting has sprung up as a hobby in just the last ten years. Much original art from prior years has been lost or destroyed, but now the originals are returned to the artists and often offered for sale, by the artists and by dealers, at comics conventions.

Sotheby's comic book and art auction in December 1991 is generally credited with giving mainstream acceptance to this type of art collecting.

This listing of original art prices serves as a guideline for retail art prices. These are average prices, with a high and low end to help you in the purchasing process.

Under each artist we have listed a few titles (obviously, we can't list all titles for all artists) so those unfamiliar with an artist may have a reference point. Those wanting to know specific titles an artist worked on should refer to *Comic Book Artists* edited by Alex G. Malloy, published in 1993 by Wallace-Homestead division of Chilton Book Company (ISBN: 0-87069-707-2).

Interior pages are priced in different classes, depending on the content:

Class—Interior Pages
A: Main character, general views
B: Main character, main foe
C: Main character, action
D: Support characters, main foe
E: Special importance
F: None of the above

ART ADAMS
Covers	800.00–1,000.00
Splash page	300.00–500.00

Action Comics, Armageddon, Batman, X-Men, Cloak and Dagger, Longshot, Uncanny X-Men
Class A	250.00
Class B	175.00
Class C	150.00
Class D	125.00
Class E	100.00
Class F	75.00
Sketches	75.00
Autographed	plus 25%
Misc. pages	75.00

NEAL ADAMS
Covers	1,000.00–2,500.00
Splash page	800.00–1,000.00

Avengers, Batman, Conan, JLA, Savage Sword, Teen Titans, World's Finest, X-Men
Class A	250.00–500.00
Class B	250.00–400.00
Class C	200.00–300.00
Class D	150.00–175.00
Class E	100.00–150.00
Class F	75.00–100.00
Sketches	50.00–100.00
Autographed	plus 50%
Misc. pages	75.00–100.00

MURPHY ANDERSON
Covers	150.00–300.00

Splash page	100.00–150.00

Action, Adventure, Brave and the Bold, JLA, Robotech, Superman (Pal), Thunder Agents
Class A	75.00–100.00
Class B	50.00–75.00
Class C	50.00–75.00
Class D	25.00–50.00
Class E	25.00–50.00
Class F	25.00
Sketches	20.00
Autographed	same
Misc. pages	25.00

ROSS ANDRU
Covers	200.00–250.00
Splash page	100.00–125.00

Amazing Spider-Man, Fantastic Four, Superman, World's Finest, Zen Intergalactic Ninja
Class A	75.00–100.00
Class B	50.00–75.00
Class C	25.00–50.00
Class D	25.00
Class E	10.00
Class F	10.00
Sketches	20.00
Autographed	plus 10%
Misc. pages	10.00

JIM APARO
Covers	200.00–300.00
Splash page	150.00–200.00

Aquaman, Batman, Detective, Jonah Hex, JLA, Phantom Stranger,

Teen Titans
Class A	75.00–100.00+
Class B	75.00–100.00+
Class C	75.00–100.00+
Class D	50.00–75.00
Class E	25.00–50.00
Class F	10.00–25.00
Sketches	20.00+
Autographed	plus 25%
Misc. pages	10.00–25.00

SERGIO ARAGONES
Covers	200.00–500.00+
Splash page	150.00–200.00+

Destroyer Duck, Groo, House of Mystery, Jonah Hex, Mad, Starslayer, Wonder Woman
Class A	100.00–150.00+
Class B	75.00–100.00+
Class C	50.00–75.00+
Class D	50.00–75.00+
Class E	25.00–50.00+
Class F	25.00–50.00+
Sketches	20.00+
Autographed	plus 25%
Misc. pages	25.00–50.00

DICK AYERS
Covers	300.00–400.00
Splash page	200.00–400.00

Avengers, Daredevil, Fantastic Four, Hulk, Outlaw/Rawhide Kid(s), Sgt. Fury, X-Men
Class A	150.00–175.00
Class B	100.00–150.00

Class C 75.00–100.00
Class D 50.00
Class E 50.00
Class F 25.00
Sketches 100.00
Autographed . . . . same
Misc. pages 25.00

CHRIS BACHALO
Covers . . . . 200.00–700.00+
Splash page . . . . 500.00+
*Death: The High Cost of Living,
Death, Ghost Rider 2099, X-Men
Unlimited*
Class A . . . . 150.00+
Class B . . . . 100.00+
Class C . . . . 75.00+

Class D . . . . 60.00+
Class E . . . . 50.00+
Class F 25.00–50.00
Sketches . . . . 50.00+
Autographed . . . . plus 25%
Misc. pages . . . . 25.00+

MARK BADGER
Covers 150.00–300.00
Splash page 75.00–100.00
Shadow, Excalibur, American Flagg
Class A . . . . 50.00–75.00+
Class B . . . . 65.00–75.00+
Class C . . . . 40.00–50.00+
Class D 25.00–30.00
Class E 25.00–30.00
Class F 15.00–20.00

Sketches 20.00
Autographed . . . . plus 10%
Misc. pages 10.00

MARK BAGLEY
Covers . . . . 200.00–300.00+
Splash page . . . . 150.00–250.00+
*Amazing Spider-Man, Avengers,
Captain America, New Mutants,
Uncanny X-Men*
Class A 100.00–175.00
Class B 75.00–100.00
Class C 75.00–100.00
Class D . . . . 50.00–75.00+
Class E . . . . 50.00–75.00+
Class F 25.00–40.00
Sketches . . . . 20.00+

Mike Mignola X-Force panels. ® & © Marvel Entertainment Group

Autographed . . . . plus 25%
Misc. pages . . . . 15.00+

CARL BARKS
Covers . . . . 5,000.00+
Splash page . . . . 3,000.00+
Dell Giant, Donald Duck (all titles), New Funnies, Uncle Scrooge, Walt Disney
Class A . . . . 500.00+
Class B . . . . 500.00+
Class C . . . . 500.00+
Class D . . . . 500.00+
Class E . . . . 300.00+
Class F . . . . 200.00+
Sketches . . . . 100.00+
Autographed . . . . plus 50%
Misc. pages . . . . 100.00+

C. C. BECK
Covers 1,000.00
Splash page 800.00
Shazam, Special Edition Comics, Tom Mix Western, Whiz, Wild Western, Wow
Class A 200.00
Class B 200.00
Class C 200.00
Class D 150.00
Class E 100.00
Class F 100.00
Sketches 100.00
Autographed . . . . plus 75%
Misc. pages 100.00

SIMON BISLEY
Covers . . . . . . 1,500.00–3,000.00+
Splash page . . 1,000.00–1,500.00+
A1, A.B.C. Warriors, Batman, Doom Patrol, Dredd Rules, Lobo, Slaine, 2000 A.D.
Class A . . . . . . 400.00–500.00+
Class B . . . . . . 400.00–500.00+
Class C 300.00–400.00
Class D 200.00
Class E 200.00
Class F 200.00
Sketches . . . . 75.00–100.00+
Autographed . . . . plus 50%
Misc. pages 75.00–100.00

STEVE BISSETTE
Covers . . . . 200.00–300.00+
Splash page . . . . . 150.00–200.00+
A1, Amazing High Adventure, Critters, Dark Horse Presents, Saga of the Swamp Thing
Class A . . . . . . 100.00–150.00+
Class B . . . . 75.00–100.00+

Class C . . . . 50.00–75.00+
Class D . . . . 40.00–50.00+
Class E . . . . 40.00–50.00+
Class F 25.00–50.00
Sketches . . . . 25.00+
Autographed . . . . plus 10%
Misc. pages . . . . 25.00+

JON BOGDANOVE
Covers 250.00–300.00
Splash page 175.00–200.00
Action Weekly, Adventures of Superman, Alpha Flight, X-Factor, X-Terminators
Class A 125.00–150.00
Class B 125.00–150.00
Class C 100.00–125.00
Class D 100.00–125.00
Class E . . . . 75.00+
Class F 25.00–50.00
Sketches . . . . 25.00+
Autographed . . . . plus 50%
Misc. pages . . . . 25.00+

BRIAN BOLLAND
Covers . . . . . 1,500.00–3,000.00+
Splash page . . . . 500.00+
Action, Adventure, Batman, Camelot 3000, Doom Patrol, Outsiders, Robin, 2000 A.D.
Class A . . . . 200.00+
Class B . . . . 150.00+
Class C . . . . 150.00+
Class D 100.00
Class E 75.00
Class F 50.00
Sketches . . . . 50.00+
Autographed . . . . plus 10%
Misc. pages . . . . 50.00+

JOHN BOLTON
Covers . . . . 500.00+
Splash page . . . . 200.00+
Aliens, Classic X-Men, Clive Barker's Freak Show, Halls of Horror, Wonder Woman
Class A . . . . 200.00+
Class B . . . . 200.00+
Class C . . . . 150.00+
Class D 100.00
Class E 100.00
Class F 75.00
Sketches 50.00–75.00
Autographed . . . . plus 10%
Misc. pages 75.00

WAYNE BORING
Covers . . . . 200.00–300.00+
Splash page . . . . 200.00+
Action, Adventure, All Star

Squadron, Superboy, Superman, Superman's Pal
Class A 150.00–200.00
Class B 150.00–200.00
Class C 100.00–150.00
Class D 75.00–100.00
Class E 50.00–75.00
Class F 50.00
Sketches . . . . 30.00+
Autographed . . . . plus 20%
Misc. pages . . . . 30.00+

NORM BREYFOGLE
Covers . . . . 200.00–300.00+
Splash page . . . . . 150.00–200.00+
Batman, Batman: Shadow of the Bat, Detective Comics, Hardware, Prime
Class A . . . . 125.00–150.00+
Class B 100.00–125.00
Class C 75.00–100.00
Class D 50.00–75.00
Class E 50.00
Class F 25.00
Sketches . . . . 25.00+
Autographed . . . . plus 15%
Misc. pages 25.00

FRANK BRUNNER
Covers . . . . 150.00–200.00+
Splash page . . . . . 100.00–125.00+
Doctor Strange, Howard the Duck, Seven Samurai
Class A . . . . 75.00–100.00+
Class B . . . . 75.00–100.00+
Class C 50.00–75.00
Class D . . . . 50.00+
Class E . . . . 40.00+
Class F 25.00
Sketches . . . . . . 25.00–50.00+
Autographed . . . . plus 20%
Misc. pages . . . . 25.00+

RICH BUCKLER
Covers 75.00–150.00
Splash page 50.00–75.00
Avengers, Astonishing Tales, Thor, Starhunters, World's Finest, Super Villains
Class A 50.00
Class B 40.00
Class C 25.00–40.00
Class D 15.00–25.00
Class E 15.00–25.00
Class F . . . . 10.00+
Sketches . . . . 15.00+
Autographed . . . . same
Misc. pages 10.00

---

274   **All prices listed are for *Near Mint* condition.**

Mark Badger & Mike Mignola collaboration ® & © Marvel Entertainment Group

JOHN BUSCEMA

Covers . . . . 150.00–300.00+
Splash page . . . . . 100.00–150.00+
Avengers, Captain America,
Daredevil, Fantastic Four, Kull, She-
Hulk, X-Men
Class A . . . . 75.00–100.00+
Class B 50.00–75.00
Class C 25.00–50.00
Class D . . . . 25.00+
Class E . . . . 25.00+
Class F 15.00
Sketches 20.00
Autographed . . . . plus 20%
Misc. pages . . . . 15.00+

SAL BUSCEMA

Covers . . . . 150.00–200.00+
Splash page 75.00–125.00
Amazing Spider-Man, Conan,
Daredevil, Dull, Master of Kung Fu,
Power Man and Iron Fist
Class A 50.00–175.00
Class B 50.00–75.00
Class C 30.00–50.00
Class D 25.00
Class E 15.00
Class F 15.00
Sketches . . . . 20.00+
Autographed . . . . same
Misc. pages 15.00

JOHN BYRNE

Covers . . . . 250.00–500.00+
Splash page . . . . . 175.00–200.00+
Avengers, Batman, Doomsday+1,
Green Lantern, Next Men, She-Hulk,
Superman
Class A 150.00–175.00
Class B 100.00–250.00
Class C 75.00–100.00
Class D . . . . 75.00+
Class E 50.00
Class F . . . . 25.00+
Sketches . . . . 25.00+
Autographed . . . . plus 20%
Misc. pages . . . . . . 15.00–25.00+

PAUL CHADWICK

Covers . . . . 250.00–300.00+
Splash page . . . . . 200.00–250.00+
Cobalt Blue, Concrete, Dazzler,
Mighty Mouse, New Titans,
Underdog
Class A 150.00–200.00
Class B 125.00–150.00
Class C . . . . 100.00+
Class D . . . . 50.00–75.00+
Class E . . . . 50.00+
Class F . . . . 25.00+

Sketches . . . . 20.00+
Autographed . . . . plus 20%
Misc. pages . . . . 20.00+

HOWARD CHAYKIN

Covers 200.00–600.00
Splash page 150.00–300.00
Big Black Kiss, Conan, Detective,
Kull, Star Wars, Vampire Tales,
Weird War Tales
Class A 150.00–275.00
Class B 100.00–150.00
Class C 75.00–100.00
Class D 75.00
Class E 50.00–75.00
Class F . . . . 25.00+
Sketches 30.00–50.00
Autographed . . . . plus 10%
Misc. pages 25.00

DAVE COCKRUM

Covers 100.00–250.00
Splash page 150.00–175.00
Avengers, Batman, Captain
America, Detective, Iron Man,
Swamp Thing, World's Finest, X-
Men.
Class A 100.00
Class B 75.00
Class C 50.00
Class D 25.00
Class E 25.00
Class F 15.00
Sketches . . . . 20.00+
Autographed . . . . plus 20%
Misc. pages 15.00

GENE COLAN

Covers 200.00–500.00
Splash page 175.00–200.00
Astonishing Tales, Batman,
Daredevil, Red Sonja, New Teen
Titans, Wolverine, What If?
Class A 150.00–175.00
Class B . . . . 100.00+
Class C . . . . 60.00+
Class D . . . . 50.00+
Class E . . . . 40.00+
Class F . . . . 40.00+
Sketches 20.00
Autographed . . . . plus 20%
Misc. pages . . . . 15.00+

DENYS COWAN

Covers 300.00–500.00
Splash page 200.00–275.00
Deathlok, Detective, Lobo, Prince,
Question, Sable, Superman, Teen
Titans Spotlight

Class A . . . . 150.00+
Class B . . . . 125.00–150.00+
Class C 75.00
Class D 60.00–75.00
Class E . . . . 50.00+
Class F . . . . 25.00+
Sketches . . . . 25.00+
Autographed . . . . plus 25%
Misc. pages 15.00

REED CRANDALL

Covers . . . . 3,000.00+
Splash page . . . . 3,000.00+
The Ray, Dollman, Firebrand,
Blackhawk, Eerie, Creepy
Class A . . . . 2,500.00+
Class B . . . . 2,000.00+
Class C . . . . 1,000.00+
Class D . . . . 1,000.00+
Class E . . . . 1,000.00+
Class F . . . . 1,000.00+
Sketches . . . . 1,000.00+
Autographed . . . . . . plus 35%–40%
Misc. pages . . . 250.00–1,000.00+

ROBERT CRUMB

Covers . . . . . . 3,000.00–4,000.00+
Splash page . . 1,500.00–2,000.00+
Arcade, Despair, Fritz the Cat, Mr.
Natural, Snarf, Weirdo, Young Lust,
Yum Yum, Zap
Class A . . . . 1,000.00+
Class B . . . . 800.00+
Class C . . . . 500.00+
Class D . . . . 500.00+
Class E . . . . 500.00+
Class F . . . . 500.00+
Sketches . . . . 150.00–300.00+
Autographed . . . . plus 75%
Misc. pages 200.00–500.00

ALAN DAVIS

Covers . . . . 200.00–300.00+
Splash page 150.00–200.00
Action Weekly, Batman, Captain
Britain, New Mutants, 2000 A.D.,
Uncanny X-Men, Wolverine
Class A 100.00–125.00
Class B . . . . 75.00+
Class C . . . . 75.00+
Class D . . . . 50.00+
Class E 30.00
Class F 25.00
Sketches . . . . 20.00+
Autographed . . . . plus 10%
Misc. pages . . . . 20.00+

STEVE DITKO

Covers . . . . 400.00–6,000.00+
Splash page . . . 250.00–4,500.00+

*Action Weekly, Amazing Spider-
Man, Captain Atom, Daredevil,
World's Finest, X-O Manowar*
Class A .... 150.00–2,500.00+
Class B .... 125.00–2,500.00+
Class C .... 100.00–1,800.00+
Class D ...... 75.00–1,000.00+
Class E .... 60.00–800.00+
Class F .... 60.00–400.00+
Sketches .... 50.00–100.00+
Autographed .... plus 75%
Misc. pages 50.00–100.00
**High prices for *Amazing Spider-
Man***

COLLEEN DORAN
Covers .... 150.00–200.00+
Splash page ...... 75.00–100.00+
*A Distant Soil, Amazing Spider-
Man, Elfquest, Sandman, Warp,
Wonder Woman, X-Factor*
Class A 75.00
Class B .... 60.00+
Class C .... 50.00+
Class D .... 25.00+
Class E 25.00
Class F 20.00
Sketches .... 15.00+
Autographed .... plus 10%
Misc. pages 15.00

STAN DRAKE
Covers 150.00–200.00
Splash page 75.00–100.00
*Armor, Captain Marvel, Conan,
Megalith, Pitt, She-Hulk, Solar: Man
of the Atom, Solo Avengers*
Class A .... 60.00+
Class B .... 50.00+
Class C .... 40.00–50.00+
Class D .... 30.00+
Class E 25.00
Class F .... 25.00+
Sketches .... 15.00+
Autographed .... plus 10%
Misc. pages 15.00

KEVIN EASTMAN
Covers .... 500.00–700.00+
Splash page .... 350.00+
*Teenage Mutant Ninja Turtles,
Grimjack, Plastron Cafe, Zombie
Wars*
Class A ...... 175.00–200.00+
Class B 100.00–150.00
Class C 100.00
Class D 75.00
Class E 75.00
Class F 60.00
Sketches 40.00

Autographed .... plus 30%
Misc. pages 40.00

FRANK FRAZETTA
Covers 5,000.00–75,000.00
Splash page ... 4,000.00–7,000.00
*Fantasy and Science Fiction novel
covers, Conan, Many E.C. books*
Class A .... 2,000.00–3,500.00+
Class B .... 2,000.00–3,500.00+
Class C .... 2,000.00–3,500.00+
Class D .... 2,000.00–3,500.00+
Class E .... 2,000.00–3,500.00+
Class F .... 2,000.00–3,500.00+
Sketches .... 500.00–1,500.00+
Autographed .... plus 75%
Misc. pages ... 500.00–1,500.00+

RON FRENZ
Covers 150.00–275.00
Splash page 75.00–100.00
*Action Weekly, Amazing Spider-
Man, Brave and the Bold, Green
Lantern, She-Hulk*
Class A .... 75.00+
Class B .... 60.00+
Class C .... 50.00+
Class D .... 40.00+
Class E .... 25.00+
Class F .... 20.00+
Sketches 20.00
Autographed .... plus 10%
Misc. pages .... 15.00+

DAVE GIBBONS
Covers ..... 1,500.00–2,000.00+
Splash page ... 700.00–800.00+
*Flash, Give Me Liberty, Green
Lantern, Mr. Monster, 1963, 2000
A.D., Watchmen*
Class A .... 500.00+
Class B .... 300.00+
Class C .... 200.00+
Class D .... 200.00+
Class E .... 175.00+
Class F 75.00–100.00
Sketches 40.00
Autographed .... plus 30%
Misc. pages .... 50.00+

KEITH GIFFEN
Covers .... 200.00–350.00+
Splash page 175.00–200.00
*Action, Ambush Bug, Defenders,
Heckler, Legion, Trencher, Video
Jack, Wonder Woman*
Class A .... 100.00+
Class B 75.00–100.00
Class C 50.00–75.00
Class D 50.00

Class E 25.00–30.00
Class F 25.00
Sketches 20.00
Autographed .... plus 15%
Misc. pages 150

DICK GIORDANO
Covers ...... 200.00–2,500.00+
Splash page ... 100.00–1,500.00+
*Action, Archie, Batman, Hawk &
Dove, JLA, Kull, Shazam,
Superman, Wonder Woman*
Class A 75.00–100.00
Class B .... 75.00+
Class C .... 75.00+
Class D 60.00–70.00
Class E 40.00–50.00
Class F 15.00–30.00
Sketches 15.00–30.00
Autographed .... plus 25%
Misc. pages 15.00–30.00

JACKSON GUICE
Covers 250.00–1,000.00
Splash page 125.00–175.00
*Action, Aliens, Creepy, Daredevil,
Flash, Squadron Supreme, X-
Factor, X-Men*
Class A 75.00–100.00
Class B 60.00–80.00
Class C .... 50.00+
Class D 30.00–40.00
Class E 25.00
Class F 20.00
Sketches 20.00
Autographed .... plus 10%
Misc. pages 20.00

DON HECK
Covers 250.00–400.00
Splash page 250.00–300.00
*Avengers, Champions, Defenders,
Ghost Rider, Iron Man, Teen Titans,
Wonder Woman*
Class A 175.00–200.00
Class B 100.00–125.00
Class C 75.00–80.00
Class D 50.00–60.00
Class E .... 40.00+
Class F 25.00
Sketches .... 30.00+
Autographed .... plus 25%
Misc. pages 25.00

CARMINE INFANTINO
Covers 150.00–250.00
Splash page 100.00–125.00
*Adventure, Airboy, Captain
America, JLA, Secret Origins,
Savage Sword, Supergirl, What If?*

Rich Buckler/Dick Giordano collaboration ® & © DC Comics

Class A . . . . 75.00–100.00+	
Class B 50.00–80.00	
Class C 40.00–60.00	
Class D . . . . 30.00+	
Class E 25.00	
Class F 15.00	
Sketches . . . . 20.00+	
Autographed . . . . plus 20%	
Misc. pages 10.00	

KLAUS JANSON (Miller pages only)

Covers 250.00–6,000.00
Splash page 200.00–4,000.00
　Class A 150.00–2,000.00
　Class B 125.00–1,500.00
　Class C 100.00–1,000.00
　Class D 100.00–750.00
　Class E 75.00–475.00
　Class F 50.00–400.00
Sketches 20.00
Autographed . . . . plus 40%
Misc. pages 20.00

DAN JURGENS

Covers . . . . . . 500.00–1,000.00+
Splash page . . . 800.00–1,000.00+
Action, Detective, JLA, Outsiders, Superman, Tales of the Legion, Warlord
　Class A . . . . 200.00+
　Class B 100.00–150.00
　Class C 75.00–100.00
　Class D 75.00
　Class E 60.00
　Class F 25.00–50.00
Sketches . . . . 25.00+
Autographed . . . . plus 50%
Misc. pages . . . . 20.00+

JACK KIRBY

Covers 500.00–10,000.00
Splash page 300.00–6,000.00
Avengers, Fantastic Four, Kamandi: The Last Boy on Earth, X-Men, and just about everything else
　Class A 150.00–4,000.00
　Class B 150.00–3,000.00
　Class C 150.00–2,000.00
　Class D 100.00–175.00
　Class E 75.00–300.00
　Class F . . . . 50.00+
Sketches 25.00–50.00
Autographed . . . . plus 50%
Misc. pages 50.00

ADAM KUBERT

Covers 150.00–200.00
Splash page 100.00–175.00
Wolverine, X-Men, Sgt. Rock,

Ghost Rider and Blaze: Spirits of Vengeance
　Class A 100.00–125.00
　Class B 100.00–125.00
　Class C . . . . 100.00+
　Class D . . . . 70.00+
　Class E . . . . 50.00+
　Class F . . . . 35.00+
Sketches . . . . 25.00+
Autographed . . . . plus 10%
Misc. pages . . . . 35.00+

ANDY KUBERT

Covers . . . . 200.00–300.00+
Splash page . . . . 100.00–175.00+
Adam Strange, Batman versus Predator, Ghost Rider, Warlord, Uncanny X-Men, X-Men
　Class A . . . . . . 100.00–150.00+
　Class B . . . . 100.00+
　Class C . . . . 75.00+
　Class D . . . . 65.00+
　Class E . . . . 50.00+
　Class F . . . . 40.00+
Sketches . . . . 30.00+
Autographed . . . . plus 10%
Misc. pages . . . . 40.00+

JOE KUBERT

Covers 500.00–6,000.00
Splash page . . . 300.00–5,000.00
All American Men of War, Brave and The Bold, Flash, G.I. Combat, Our Army at War
　Class A 300.00–2,000.00
　Class B 200.00–1,500.00
　Class C . . . . . . 150.00–750.00+
　Class D 150.00–250.00
　Class E 75.00–150.00
　Class F . . . . 100.00+
Sketches . . . . 75.00+
Autographed . . . . plus 50%
Misc. pages . . . . 75.00+

HARVEY KURTZMAN

Covers 500.00–8,000.00
Splash page 500.00–6,000.00
Frontline Comics, Hey Look!, Little Annie Fanny, Two-Fisted Tales, Mad, Weird Science
　Class A 175.00–3,000.00
　Class B 150.00–2,500.00
　Class C 150.00–1,500.00
　Class D 125.00–700.00
　Class E 125.00–500.00
　Class F . . . . 100.00+
Sketches 200.00–300.00
Autographed . . . . plus 50%
Misc. pages 75.00–100.00

ERIK LARSEN

Covers . . . . . . 500.00–1,500.00+
Splash page . . . . 300.00–750.00+
Amazing Spider-Man, Doom Patrol, Marvel Comics Presents, Punisher, Savage Dragon
　Class A . . . . 200.00+
　Class B . . . . 175.00+
　Class C . . . . 125.00+
　Class D . . . . 100.00+
　Class E . . . . 75.00+
　Class F . . . . 50.00+
Sketches . . . . 25.00+
Autographed . . . . same
Misc. pages 25.00

BOB LAYTON

Covers . . . . 300.00+
Splash page . . . . 150.00+
Hercules Unbound, Iron Man, Magnus: Robot Fighter, Solar Man of the Atom, What If?
　Class A . . . . 100.00+
　Class B 100.00
　Class C 75.00
　Class D 60.00
　Class E 35.00
　Class F 25.00
Sketches 25.00
Autographed . . . . same
Misc. pages 25.00

JAE LEE

Covers 600.00–2,000.00
Splash page 500.00–1,200.00
Marvel Comics Presents, Hellshock, Youngblood Strikefile, WildC.A.T.S. Trilogy
　Class A 300.00–500.00
　Class B 150.00–400.00
　Class C 125.00–200.00
　Class D . . . . 100.00+
　Class E . . . . 90.00+
　Class F . . . . 75.00+
Sketches 50.00
Autographed . . . . same
Misc. pages 75.00

JIM LEE

Covers . . . . 300.00–3,000.00+
Splash page . . . 300.00–1,500.00+
Alpha Flight, Punisher War Journal, Stormwatch, Uncanny X-Men, WildC.A.T.S.
　Class A . . . . 300.00+
　Class B 200.00–300.00
　Class C 175.00
　Class D 175.00
　Class E . . . . 75.00+
　Class F . . . . 60.00+

All prices listed are for *Near Mint* condition.　　　　　**279**

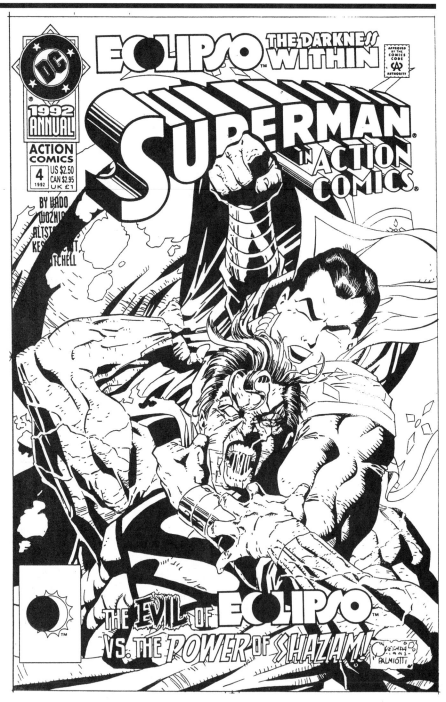

Joe Quesada/Jim Palmiotti Superman collaboration. ® & © DC Comics

Sketches . . . . 75.00+
Autographed . . . . same
Misc. pages . . . . 60.00+

RICK LEONARDI

Covers . . . . 500.00+
Splash page . . . . 300.00+
Amazing Spider-Man, Cloak and Dagger, Spider-Man 2099, Vision and Scarlet Witch
Class A . . . . 150.00+
Class B . . . . 100.00+
Class C . . . . 75.00+
Class D . . . . 50.00+
Class E . . . . 40.00+
Class F . . . . 20.00+
Sketches . . . . 25.00+
Autographed . . . . plus 10%
Misc. pages . . . . 10.00+

ROB LIEFELD

Covers 300.00–1,000.00
Splash page 200.00–750.00
Brigade, Deathmate, Darker Image, Marvel Comics Presents, X-Force, Youngblood
Class A 200.00
Class B 175.00
Class C 150.00
Class D 100.00
Class E 75.00
Class F 50.00
Sketches 25.00
Autographed . . . . plus 10%
Misc. pages 50.00

RON LIM

Covers . . . . 200.00+
Splash page . . . . 150.00+
Avengers, Badger, Captain America, Infinity Crusade, Infinity Gauntlet, Infinity War, Silver Surfer, Venom
Class A . . . . 100.00+
Class B . . . . 75.00+
Class C 75.00
Class D . . . . 50.00+
Class E 50.00
Class F 35.00
Sketches 25.00
Autographed . . . . plus 10%
Misc. pages 30.00

MIKE MANLEY

Covers 150.00–200.00
Splash page 100.00–125.00
Alpha Flight, Batman, Darkhawk, Deathlok, Quasar, Sleepwalker, X-O Manowar
Class A . . . . 100.00+

Class B . . . . 75.00+
Class C 75.00
Class D 60.00
Class E 50.00
Class F 25.00
Sketches 25.00
Autographed . . . . plus 10%
Misc. pages 25.00

DAVID MAZZUCHELLI

Covers 175.00–225.00
Splash page 100.00
Batman, Daredevil, Rubber Blanket, Marvel Fanfare, World's Finest, X-Factors
Class A . . . . 75.00+
Class B 75.00
Class C 60.00
Class D 50.00
Class E . . . . 40.00+
Class F 25.00
Sketches . . . . 50.00+
Autographed . . . . plus 25%
Misc. pages 25.00

TODD McFARLANE

Covers . . . . . . 300.00–6,000.00+
Splash page . . . 300.00–6,000.00+
Amazing Spider-Man, Incredible Hulk, Marvel Tales, Spawn, Spectacular Spider-Man
Class A 300.00–1,250.00
Class B 200.00–750.00
Class C 150.00–300.00
Class D 100.00–300.00
Class E 75.00–100.00
Class F 60.00–75.00
Sketches . . . . 75.00+
Autographed . . . . plus 40%
Misc. pages 50.00

MIKE MIGNOLA

Covers . . . . 200.00–800.00+
Splash page . . . . 350.00+
Alpha Flight, Aliens, Dracula, Phantom Stranger, World of Krypton, X-Force
Class A . . . . 175.00+
Class B . . . . 150.00+
Class C . . . . 125.00+
Class D . . . . 100.00+
Class E 75.00
Class F 60.00
Sketches . . . . 75.00+
Autographed . . . . plus 10%
Misc. pages 60.00

FRANK MILLER

Covers 200.00–6,000.00
Splash page 200.00–3,000.00

Batman/Dark Knight Returns, Daredevil, Dark Horse Presents, Give Me Liberty, Ronin
Class A 150.00–2,000.00
Class B 150.00–1,500.00
Class C 150.00–1,000.00
Class D 150.00–750.00
Class E 100.00–500.00
Class F 100.00–450.00
Sketches . . . . 100.00+
Autographed . . . . plus 50%
Misc. pages . . . . 100.00+

MOEBIUS (JEAN GIRAUD)

Covers 2,000.00–4,000.00
Splash page . . . . 2,000.00+
Batman, Batman: Shadow of the Bat, Detective Comics, Hardware, Prime
Class A . . . . 500.00–1,000.00+
Class B . . . . 500.00–1,000.00+
Class C 500.00–750.00
Class D 300.00–500.00
Class E 200.00–300.00
Class F . . . . 100.00+
Sketches . . . . 150.00+
Autographed . . . . plus 40%
Misc. pages . . . . 100.00+

KEVIN NOWLAN

Covers . . . . 600.00+
Splash page 250.00–400.00
Batman: Sword of Azrael, Outsiders, Grimwoods Daughter, New Mutants
Class A 175.00–200.00
Class B 150.00–175.00
Class C 100.00–125.00
Class D 75.00–100.00
Class E . . . . 75.00+
Class F . . . . 50.00+
Sketches . . . . 75.00+
Autographed . . . . plus 25%
Misc. pages 50.00

JERRY ORDWAY

Covers 200.00–1,000.00
Splash page 100.00–750.00
All Star Squadron, Crisis on Infinite Earths, Infinity Inc., Superman, Wildstar
Class A . . . . 100.00–250.00+
Class B . . . . 100.00–200.00+
Class C 100.00–150.00
Class D 75.00–100.00
Class E 15.00–25.00
Class F . . . . 50.00+
Sketches . . . . 25.00+
Autographed . . . . plus 50%
Misc. pages 25.00

All prices listed are for *Near Mint* condition.   **281**

GEORGE PEREZ

Covers 200.00–2,000.00
Splash page 200.00–1,500.00
Action, Astonishing Tales,
Avengers, Flash, JLA, New Teen
Titans, Sachs and Violence
Class A 175.00–300.00
Class B 150.00–200.00
Class C .... 100.00+
Class D .... 50.00+
Class E .... 40.00+
Class F .... 35.00+
Sketches .... 75.00+
Autographed .... plus 25%
Misc. pages .... 35.00+

MIKE PLOOG

Covers .... 200.00–600.00+
Splash page .... 200.00–300.00+
Dracula Lives, Frankenstein, Man-
Thing, Terror of the Planet of the
Apes
Class A 150.00–175.00
Class B .... 150.00+
Class C .... 125.00+
Class D .... 75.00+
Class E .... 60.00+
Class F .... 40.00+
Sketches .... 30.00+
Autographed .... plus 25%
Misc. pages 35.00

WHILCE PORTACIO

Covers .... 250.00–500.00+
Splash page .... 175.00–200.00+
Avengers, Batman, Doomsday+1,
Green Lantern, Next Men, She-Hulk,
Superman
Class A 150.00–175.00
Class B 100.00–250.00
Class C 75.00–100.00
Class D .... 75.00+
Class E 50.00
Class F .... 25.00+
Sketches .... 25.00+
Autographed .... plus 20%
Misc. pages ..... 15.00–25.00+

JOE QUESADA

Covers 150.00–450.00
Splash page 100.00–200.00
Batman: Sword of Azrael, Solar:
Man of the Atom, The Ray, X-
Factor, X-O Manowar
Class A .... 100.00+
Class B 100.00
Class C .... 75.00+
Class D 75.00
Class E .... 60.00+
Class F .... 50.00+

Sketches .... 25.00+
Autographed .... plus 50%
Misc. pages .... 50.00+

JOHN ROMITA

Covers 500.00–3,000.00
Splash page 500.00–2,000.00
Big Black Kiss, Conan, Detective,
Kull, Star Wars, Vampire Tales,
Weird War Tales
Class A ...... 300.00–750.00+
Class B 200.00–500.00
Class C 100.00–250.00
Class D .... 75.00–175.00+
Class E .... 75.00–150.00+
Class F .... 100.00+
Sketches .... 100.00+
Autographed .... plus 50%
Misc. pages .... 75.00+

JOHN ROMITA, JR.

Covers 200.00–2,000.00
Splash page ..... 75.00–200.00+
Avengers, Batman, Captain
America, Detective, Iron Man,
Swamp Thing, World's Finest
Class A 150.00–200.00
Class B 100.00–150.00
Class C 125.00
Class D .... 75.00+
Class E .... 60.00+
Class F .... 50.00+
Sketches .... 25.00+
Autographed .... plus 10%
Misc. pages 50.00

STEVE RUDE

Covers .... NA–Rare
Splash page 150.00–600.00
Nexus/Next/Legend/Origin
Class A 150.00–300.00
Class B .... 150.00+
Class C .... 125.00+
Class D .... 100.00+
Class E .... 75.00+
Class F .... 50.00+
Sketches .... 75.00+
Autographed .... plus 25%
Misc. pages 50.00

P. CRAIG RUSSELL

Covers ...... 300.00–3,000.00+
Splash page .... 150.00–300.00+
Amazing Adventures, Cloak and
Dagger, Elric, Justice League
International, Sandman, Uncanny X-
Men
Class A .... 200.00+
Class B ...... 125.00–150.00+

Class C .... 100.00+
Class D ...... 75.00–100.00+
Class E 75.00–100.00
Class F .... 50.00+
Sketches 50.00–75.00
Autographed .... same
Misc. pages 50.00

PAUL RYAN

Covers 150.00–200.00
Splash page .... 100.00+
Avengers West Coast, Fantastic
Four, Iron Man, Ravage 2099,
Squadron Supreme
Class A 75.00–100.00
Class B 75.00
Class C 65.00
Class D 50.00
Class E 35.00
Class F 25.00
Sketches 20.00–30.00
Autographed .... plus 10%
Misc. pages 15.00–20.00

BART SEARS

Covers 350.00–1,000.00
Splash page 200.00–750.00
JLA, Invasion, Turok: Dinosaur
Hunter
Class A 150.00–200.00
Class B 100.00–150.00
Class C .... 75.00+
Class D 50.00
Class E .... 45.00+
Class F 35.00
Sketches 25.00–30.00
Autographed .... plus 15%
Misc. pages .... 25.00+

BILL SIENKIEWICZ

Covers 300.00–3,000.00
Splash page .... 500.00+
Dazzler, Elektra: Assassin,
Fantastic Four, Moonknight, New
Mutants, Stray Toasters
Class A ...... 200.00–300.00+
Class B .... 175.00+
Class C .... 150.00+
Class D .... 125.00+
Class E .... 75.00+
Class F 75.00
Sketches ...... 50.00–100.00+
Autographed .... plus 20%
Misc. pages .... 35.00+

MARK SILVESTRI

Covers .... 500.00+
Splash page .... 200.00+
Conan the King, Uncanny X-Man,
Web of Spider-Man, Wolverine, X-

John Romita, Jr. Daredevil page ® & © Marvel Entertainment Group

Factor
Class A	150.00+
Class B	100.00+
Class C	75.00+
Class D	65.00+
Class E	50.00+
Class F	35.00+
Sketches	20.00–30.00
Autographed	plus 15%
Misc. pages	20.00–30.00

WALT SIMONSON
Covers	150.00–300.00+
Splash page	100.00–200.00+

Cyberforce, Detective, Fantastic Four, Metal Men, Star Wars, Thor, X-Factor
Class A	100.00+
Class B	75.00+
Class C	65.00+
Class D	50.00+
Class E	50.00
Class F	40.00
Sketches	25.00–50.00+
Autographed	plus 15%
Misc. pages	35.00+

PAUL SMITH
Covers	150.00–300.00
Splash page	75.00–150.00

American Flagg, Dr. Strange, Marvel Fanfare, Nexus, Uncanny X-Men, X-Factor
Class A	100.00–125.00
Class B	75.00–100.00
Class C	50.00–75.00
Class D	50.00
Class E	35.00+
Class F	30.00
Sketches	15.00–20.00+
Autographed	plus 10%
Misc. pages	25.00+

Barry Smith, see Barry Windsor-Smith

CHRIS SPROUSE
Covers	150.00–300.00+
Splash page	100.00–200.00

Shadow of the Bat
Class A	75.00–100.00
Class B	50.00–75.00
Class C	50.00+
Class D	45.00+
Class E	40.00+
Class F	30.00+
Sketches	25.00–30.00+
Autographed	plus 15%
Misc. pages	25.00+

JIM STARLIN
Covers	300.00–1,000.00+
Splash page	150.00–500.00+

Amazing Adventures, Amazing Spider-Man, Silver Surfer, Warlock
Class A	100.00–300.00+
Class B	75.00–150.00+
Class C	75.00+
Class D	50.00+
Class E	50.00
Class F	45.00
Sketches	50.00–150.00+
Autographed	plus 20%
Misc. pages	40.00+

JOE STATON
Covers	200.00+
Splash page	150.00+

Adventure, Avengers, Deadly Hands of Kung Fu, E-Man, Green Lantern(s), Wonder Woman
Class A	100.00+
Class B	75.00+
Class C	50.00+
Class D	50.00
Class E	40.00
Class F	25.00
Sketches	20.00+
Autographed	plus 10%
Misc. pages	15.00–20.00

BRIAN STELFREZE
Covers	250.00–1,500.00+
Splash page	150.00–200.00+

Batman: Shadow of the Bat, Zorro
Class A	100.00+
Class B	75.00+
Class C	75.00
Class D	50.00+
Class E	50.00
Class F	40.00
Sketches	25.00–30.00+
Autographed	plus 15%
Misc. pages	25.00+

JIM STERANKO
Covers	1,000.00–5,000.00+
Splash page	500.00–2,500.00+

Captain America, Doc Savage, Fantastic Four, Nick Fury, Strange Tales
Class A	500.00–1,000.00+
Class B	400.00–750.00+
Class C	300.00–500.00+
Class D	200.00–300.00
Class E	150.00–175.00
Class F	100.00–150.00
Sketches	100.00–250.00+
Autographed	plus 25%
Misc. pages	100.00+

LARRY STROMAN
Covers	200.00–300.00
Splash page	150.00+

Strykes Strikefile, X-Factor, Wolverine, Tribe
Class A	75.00–150.00
Class B	50.00–100.00
Class C	50.00–75.00
Class D	40.00–60.00
Class E	35.00–40.00
Class F	25.00+
Sketches	20.00–30.00+
Autographed	plus 10%
Misc. pages	20.00+

CURT SWAN
Covers	200.00–400.00+
Splash page	150.00–300.00+

Action, Adventure, DC Comics Presents, Long runs on most Superman Titles
Class A	100.00+
Class B	75.00+
Class C	75.00
Class D	50.00+
Class E	50.00
Class F	35.00
Sketches	15.00–30.00+
Autographed	plus 20%
Misc. pages	15.00+

MARK TEXIERA
Covers	250.00–350.00+
Splash page	175.00–200.00+

Ghost Rider, Punisher, Punisher War Journal, Sabretooth, Wolverine, X-Men
Class A	175.00+
Class B	150.00+
Class C	75.00+
Class D	50.00
Class E	40.00
Class F	35.00
Sketches	25.00–50.00+
Autographed	plus 10%
Misc. pages	25.00+

HERB TRIMPE
Covers	200.00–400.00
Splash page	100.00–200.00

Defenders, F.F. Unlimited, G.I. Joe, Incredible Hulk, Iron Man Unlimited
Class A	100.00+
Class B	75.00
Class C	50.00
Class D	45.00
Class E	30.00
Class F	25.00
Sketches	15.00–25.00
Autographed	plus 10%

Joe Staton work for Batman ® & © *DC Comics*

Misc. pages 20.00

DWAYNE TURNER
Covers 200.00–300.00
Splash page .... 150.00+
Cable, Cage, Excalibur Specials,
2099 Unlimited, Wolverine
Class A 75.00–125.00
Class B .... 75.00+
Class C .... 65.00+
Class D .... 50.00+
Class E .... 45.00+
Class F .... 35.00+
Sketches .... 15.00+
Autographed .... plus 10%
Misc. pages ..... 25.00–30.00+

GEORGE TUSKA
Covers .... 200.00–500.00+
Splash page .... 150.00–200.00+
Avengers, Crime Does Not Pay,
Iron Man, Jungle Comics, JLA,
World's Finest
Class A .... 100.00+
Class B .... 75.00+
Class C 50.00–75.00
Class D .... 50.00+
Class E 45.00
Class F 40.00
Sketches .... 25.00+
Autographed .... plus 10%
Misc. pages .... 25.00+

JIM VALENTINO
Covers .... 150.00–200.00+
Splash page ..... 100.00–150.00+
Avengers Spotlight, Dr. Strange,
Guardians of the Galaxy,
Shadowhawk, What If?
Class A .... 100.00+
Class B 75.00–100.00
Class C .... 65.00+
Class D .... 50.00+
Class E 50.00
Class F 45.00
Sketches 15.00–25.00
Autographed .... plus 10%
Misc. pages .... 25.00+

BORIS VALLEJO
Covers .... 2,000.00+
Splash page .... 2,000.00+
Card Sets, Conan and sword and
sorcery book covers, Movie posters
Class A .... NA
Class B .... NA
Class C .... NA
Class D .... NA
Class E .... NA
Class F .... NA

Sketches ...... 200.00–500.00+
Autographed .... plus 25%
Misc. pages .... NA

RICK VEITCH
Covers .... 200.00–300.00+
Splash page ..... 150.00–200.00+
Brat Pack, From Hell, The One,
Saga of Swamp Thing
Class A .... 150.00+
Class B .... 125.00+
Class C .... 100.00+
Class D .... 75.00+
Class E 50.00
Class F 25.00
Sketches .... 25.00–50.00+
Autographed .... same
Misc. pages .... 25.00+

CHARLES VESS
Covers ...... 500.00–2,000.00+
Splash page .... 250.00–500.00+
Dark Horse, Spider-Man Graphic
Novel, Sandman, Marvel Fanfare,
Raven Banner
Class A .... 200.00+
Class B .... 175.00+
Class C .... 150.00+
Class D .... 100.00+
Class E 75.00
Class F .... 50.00+
Sketches .... 50.00+
Autographed .... plus 20%
Misc. pages .... 50.00+

TIM VIGIL
Covers .... 500.00+
Splash page ..... 250.00–300.00+
Badger, Faust, Faust Specials, J.N.
Williamson's Masque, Weird Tales
Illustrated
Class A .... 200.00+
Class B .... 175.00+
Class C .... 150.00+
Class D .... 125.00+
Class E .... 100.00+
Class F .... 50.00+
Sketches .... 25.00+
Autographed .... plus 20%
Misc. pages .... 35.00+

TREVOR VON EDEN
Covers .... 200.00+
Splash page .... 125.00+
Batman: Shadow of the Bat, Black
Lightning, Green Arrow, World's
Finest
Class A .... 75.00–100.00+
Class B .... 60.00–75.00+

Class C .... 50.00+
Class D 40.00
Class E 40.00
Class F .... 25.00+
Sketches .... 25.00+
Autographed .... same
Misc. pages .... 25.00+

MIKE VOSBURGH
Covers .... 175.00–200.00+
Splash page .... 100.00+
Archer & Armstrong, American
Flagg, Secret Society of Super
Villains, Wonder Woman
Class A .... 75.00+
Class B .... 60.00+
Class C .... 50.00+
Class D .... 40.00+
Class E .... 35.00+
Class F .... 25.00+
Sketches .... 15.00–20.00+
Autographed .... same
Misc. pages .... 15.00+

MATT WAGNER
Covers 500.00–2,000.00
Splash page 100.00–200.00
Grendel, Legends of the Dark
Knight, Mage, Sandman Mystery
Theater
Class A ...... 175.00–200.00+
Class B ...... 150.00–175.00+
Class C ...... 125.00–150.00+
Class D 75.00–125.00
Class E 50.00–75.00
Class F .... 40.00+
Sketches .... 50.00+
Autographed .... same
Misc. pages .... 40.00+

CHRIS WARNER
Covers 200.00–300.00
Splash page .... 150.00+
Batman, Comics Greatest World,
Dr. Strange, Moon Knight,
Terminator
Class A 75.00–125.00
Class B .... 75.00+
Class C .... 65.00+
Class D .... 50.00+
Class E .... 45.00+
Class F .... 35.00+
Sketches .... 15.00+
Autographed .... plus 10%
Misc. pages ...... 25.00–30.00+

BOB WIACEK
Covers .... 200.00+
Splash page .... 175.00+
Avengers West Coast, Legion of

Dwayne Turner work for Excalibur Special ® & © Marvel Entertainment Group

Super Heroes, Deathmate, She-Hulk
Class A . . . . 100.00–125.00+
Class B . . . . 75.00–100.00+
Class C . . . . 75.00+
Class D . . . . 65.00+
Class E . . . . 50.00+
Class F . . . . 25.00+
Sketches . . . . 10.00–15.00+
Autographed . . . . plus 10%
Misc. pages 25.00

KENT WILLIAMS
Covers 1,000.00–2,000.00
Splash page . . . . 1,000.00+
Epic Magazine, Havok and
Wolverine, Prince, X-Men
Class A . . . . 300.00+
Class B . . . . 750.00+
Class C . . . . 750.00+
Class D . . . . 500.00+
Class E . . . . 275.00+
Class F . . . . 250.00+
Sketches . . . . 30.00+
Autographed . . . . same
Misc. pages . . . . . . 50.00+–200.00

SCOTT WILLIAMS
Covers . . . . 500.00+
Splash page . . . . 300.00+
Strikeforce: Moritori, Uncanny X-
Men, WildC.A.T.S., X-Men
Class A . . . . 200.00+
Class B . . . . 175.00+
Class C . . . . 100.00+
Class D . . . . 50.00+
Class E . . . . 35.00+
Class F . . . . 25.00+
Sketches . . . . 20.00–30.00+
Autographed . . . . plus 10%
Misc. pages . . . . 25.00+

AL WILLIAMSON
Covers . . . . . . 1,000.00–2,000.00+
Splash page . . 1,000.00–1,500.00+
Daredevil, Flash Gordon, Star
Wars, Superman, Tales From the
Crypt
Class A . . . . . 800.00–1,000.00+
Class B . . . . 500.00–800.00+
Class C . . . . 250.00–400.00+
Class D . . . . 200.00–250.00+
Class E . . . . 200.00+
Class F . . . . 175.00–200.00+
Sketches 100.00–150.00
Autographed . . . . plus 50%
Misc. pages . . . . 75.00+

BILL WILLINGHAM
Covers . . . . 200.00+
Splash page . . . . 175.00+

Batman, Green Lantern Corps,
Elementals, Justice League
International
Class A . . . . 80.00–100.00+
Class B . . . . 75.00+
Class C . . . . 60.00+
Class D . . . . 40.00+
Class E 30.00–40.00
Class F 25.00
Sketches . . . . 10.00–15.00+
Autographed . . . . NA
Misc. pages . . . . 15.00+

BARRY WINDSOR-SMITH
Covers . . . . . . 500.00–5,000.00+
Splash page . . . 300.00–2,000.00+
Archer & Armstrong, Avengers,
Conan, Eternal Warrior, Daredevil,
Rune, X-Men
Class A . . . . . . 275.00–400.00+
Class B . . . . . . 200.00–300.00+
Class C . . . . . . 150.00–200.00+
Class D . . . . 150.00+
Class E . . . . 125.00+
Class F . . . . 75.00–100.00+
Sketches . . . . 75.00–100.00+
Autographed . . . . plus 20%
Misc. pages . . . . 50.00+

CHUCK WOLTKIEWICZ
Covers 150.00–200.00
Splash page . . . . 100.00+
Adventures of Superman Annual,
Marvel Comics Presents
Class A 80.00–100.00
Class B 75.00
Class C 50.00
Class D 40.00
Class E 30.00
Class F 25.00
Sketches . . . . 15.00–20.00+
Autographed . . . . plus 10%
Misc. pages 15.00

WALLY WOOD
Covers . . . . . . 500.00–1,000.00+
Splash page . . . . 500.00–700.00+
All Star Comics, Captain Action,
T.H.U.N.D.E.R. Agents, Weird
Science
Class A . . . . 400.00+
Class B . . . . 300.00+
Class C . . . . 100.00+
Class D . . . . 75.00–100.00+
Class E . . . . 75.00+
Class F . . . . 60.00+
Sketches . . . . 100.00+
Autographed . . . . plus 50%
Misc. pages . . . . 50.00+

CHRIS WOZNIAK
Covers . . . . 150.00+
Splash page 100.00
Adventures of Superman Annual,
Comics Greatest World
Class A 85.00–100.00
Class B 75.00
Class C 50.00
Class D 40.00
Class E . . . . 30.00+
Class F . . . . 25.00+
Sketches . . . . 15.00–20.00+
Autographed . . . . plus 10%
Misc. pages . . . . 25.00+

BERNIE WRIGHTSON
Covers . . . . . 1,000.00–3,000.00+
Splash page . . . . 1,000.00+
Creepy, House of Mystery, House
of Secrets, The Weird, Swamp
Thing
Class A . . . . 200.00+
Class B . . . . 500.00+
Class C . . . . 200.00+
Class D . . . . . . 150.00–175.00+
Class E . . . . . . 125.00–150.00+
Class F . . . . 75.00–100.00+
Sketches . . . . 75.00–150.00+
Autographed . . . . plus 50%
Misc. pages . . . . 50.00+

MIKE ZECK
Covers . . . . 200.00–600.00+
Splash page . . . . . 175.00–400.00+
Captain America, Punisher,
Amazing Spider-Man, Spectacular
Spider-Man
Class A . . . . 200.00+
Class B . . . . 175.00+
Class C . . . . 150.00+
Class D . . . . 125.00+
Class E . . . . 100.00+
Class F 50.00
Sketches . . . . 25.00–50.00+
Autographed . . . . plus 10%
Misc. pages . . . . 20.00+

DC POSTERS

T he secondary poster market is somewhat limited. A few popular titles (by important artists) will command a premium price but not many, unless they are signed by the artist. Special giveaway posters are hard to find but usually do not command higher values.

Both DC and Marvel have published posters regularly for several years. The growth of the other comic book publishers has resulted in a good supply of their posters in recent years.

Wonder Woman through the Ages 22"x28"
    color poster by George Perez (1992) . 5.95
Superman at War 22"x34" color poster
    by Jerry Ordway (1991) 5.95
Death 22"x34" color poster (1993) 4.95
Doom Patrol 22"x34" color poster by Richard
    Case and Stan Woch (1993) 4.95
Robin 22"x34" color poster Tom Lyle
    and Scott Hanna (1993) 4.95

Catwoman by Jim Balent (DC 1994)

Women of the DC Universe 22"x34" color
    poster by Adam Hughes (1993) 4.95
Aquaman 22"x34" color poster,
    by Craig Hamilton (1994) 4.95
Batman Rogues Gallery 22"x34" color
    poster by Joe Quesada and Kevin
    Nowlan (1994) 4.95
Black Orchid 22"x34" color poster
    by Jill Thompson (1994) 4.95
Catwoman 22"x34" color poster
    by Jim Balent (1994) 4.95
Countdown to Zero Hour 22"x34" color
    poster by Dan Jurgens and Jerry
    Ordway (1994) 4.95

Shazam by Jerry Ordway (DC 1994)

DC Universe 22"x34" color poster
    by Alex Ross (1994) 4.95
Death I 22"x34" color poster
    by Mike Dringenberg (1994) 4.95
Death II 22"x34" color poster
    by Chris Bachalo (1994) 4.95
Doom Patrol 22"x34" color poster
    by Richard Case and Stan Woch (1994) 4.95
Flash 22"x34" color poster
    by Brian Stelfreeze (1994) 4.95

All prices listed are for *Near Mint* condition.   **289**

Superboy by Grummett & Hazlewood; Steel by Bogdanove & Janke (DC 1994)

Hardward 22"x34" color poster by
  Denys Cowan and Kent Williams (1994) 4.95
Hellblazer 22"x34" color poster
  by Glen Fabry (1994) 4.95
Superman/Doomsday: Hunter/Prey 22"x34"
  color poster by Dan Jurgens
  and Brett Breeding (1994) 4.95
Icon 22"x34" color poster
  by Moebius (1994) 4.95
Knights End: Batman 22"x34" color
  poster by Joe Quesada and Joseph
  Rubenstein (1994) 4.95
The Last Green Lantern 22"x34" color poster by
  Darryl Banks & Romeo Tanghal (1994) 4.95
Legion of Super-Heroes 22"x34" color poster by
  Stuart Immonen and Ron Boyd (1994) 4.95
Lobo: Smokin'! 22"x34" color poster
  by Joe DeVito (1994) 4.95
Lois and Clark TV 24"x36" color photo poster
  (Collector's Warehouse 1994) 10.00
New Batman (Azrael-era) 22"x34" color
  poster by Kelley Jones (1994) 4.95
New Titans 22"x34" color poster
  by Tom Grummett and Al Vey (1994) . 4.95

The Ray: In a Blaze of Power 22"x34"
  color poster by Joe Quesada
  and Brian Stelfreeze (1994) 4.95
Robin 22"x34" color poster
  by Tom Lyle and Scott Hanna (1994) . 4.95
Sandman: Brief Lives 22"x34" color poster by
  Jill Thompson and Vincent Locke (1994) 4.95
Shazam! 22"x34" color poster
  by Jerry Ordway (1994) 4.95
Spectre: City of Lost Souls 22"x34" glow-in-the-
  dark poster by Tom Mandrake (1994) . 4.95
Steel 22"x34" color poster by Jon Bogdanove
  and Dennis Janke (1994) 4.95
Superboy 22"x34" color poster by Tom
  Grummett and Doug Hazlewood (1994) 4.95
Superman: Faster Than A Speeding Bullet
  22"x34" color poster by Joe
  DeVito (1994) 4.95
Swamp Thing 22"x34" color poster
  by Michael Zulli (1994) 4.95
Women of the DC Universe 22"x34" color
  poster by Adam Hughes (1994) 4.95
Wonder Woman 22"x34" color poster
  by Brian Bolland (1994) 4.95

Xombi 22"x34" color poster
by Moebius (1994) 4.95

BATMAN RETURNS POSTERS
One Stop Posters (1992)
Bat, Cat and Penguin (#2083) 5.95
Batman and Costumes (#2076) 5.95
Batman Throwing Batarang (#2049) 5.95
June 19th Movie (#2074) 5.95
Catwoman (#2077) 5.95
Catwoman and Cats line art (#2053) 5.95
Catwoman's Head "Meow" (#2075) 5.95
Batman leaping (#2054) 5.95
Batman on Gargoyle Glow 5.95
Bat Logo Glow 5.95
Batman Fist-Up line art (#2025) 5.95
Batman Diving line art 5.95
Batmobile Plans 5.95
Splashed Logo 5.95
Closeup of Silver Logo w/June 19th 5.95
Batmissile 5.95
Batski Boat and Duckmobile 5.95
BATMAN: THE ANIMATED SERIES
Batman Animated (#2164, 1994) 5.95

MILESTONE
Milestone poster (1994) 3.00
SANDMAN
Sandman cards poster (1993) 2.00
DC/MARVEL
Crossover posters—fit together
DC Comics Heroes and Villains 22"x34" color
poster by John Byrne & Terry
Austin (1991) 5.95
Marvel Super Heroes 22"x34" color poster
by John Byrne and Terry Austin (1991) 5.95

MARVEL POSTERS

She-Hulk (John Byrne) 5.00
Punisher I 5.00
Punisher II 5.00
Cloak and Dagger II (Rick Leonardi) 5.00
Magik (Mike Kaluta) 5.00
Captain America (Mike Zeck
and Phil Zimmelman) 5.00
Scarlet Witch (P. Craig Russell) 5.00
Punisher III 5.00
Spider-Man 5.00
Marvel Universe 15.00

Marvel and DC Crossover poster(s) by John Byrne and Terry Austin (DC 1991 and Marvel 1991)

All prices listed are for *Near Mint* condition.

Excalibur by Davis & Farmer (Marvel #124, 1992)

Wolverine	5.00	Fantastic Four (Mike Mignola		
Groo (Sergio Aragones)	5.00	and Mark Chiarello)		5.00
Power Pack (June Brigman and		Captain America 50th Anniv. (Mike		
P. Craig Russell)	5.00	Zeck and Phil Zimmelman)		5.00
Wolverine	5.00	Punisher IX		5.00
Silver Surfer (Moebius)	5.00	Elektra III (Moebius)		5.00
X-Factor	5.00	Dracula (Jon Jay Muth)		5.00
Rogue (Cindy Martin)	5.00	Hellraiser (John Bolton)		5.00
Punisher IV	5.00	Storm II		5.00
Wolverine	5.00	Wolverine		5.00
Hulk II	5.00	X-Men Triptych I		5.00
Elektra II (Frank Miller)	5.00	Black Widow (Joe Chiodo)		5.00
Punisher VI	5.00	Marvel Universe II		6.00
Mutants	5.00	Spiderman IX		5.00
Spider-Man V	5.00	Deathlok I		5.00
Marshal Law (Kevin O'Neill)	5.00	Wolverine VI		5.00
Avengers II (Paul Ryan)	5.00	Silver Surfer		5.00
Wolverine/Nick Fury	5.00	Thing I		5.00
Iron Man (Moebius)	5.00	Mary Jane 30"x59" (Joe Jusko)		13.00
Spider-Man VI	5.00	X-Men III (Jim Lee and Scott Williams)		6.00
Sub-Mariner (Scott Hampton)	5.00	Hulk versus Thing (Matt Wagner)		6.00
Punisher VII	5.00	Captain America (Joe Jusko)		6.00
Daredevil III (Moebius)	5.00	Punisher (Moe)		6.00
Wolverine V	5.00	Wolverine VII (Sam Kieth)		6.00
She-Hulk III (Joe Chiodo)	5.00	Wolverine, Ghost Rider and Punisher		6.00
Spider-Man VII	5.00	Spiderman X (Leonardi and Williamson)		6.00
Major Grubert (Moebius)	5.00	Daredevil and Elektra (Kent Williams)		6.00

Spider-Man and Mary Jane (Marvel #145, 1993)

(1992)

Ironman (Bob Layton)	5.00
Ghost Rider (1st solo) (Mark Texeira)	5.00
Dr. Strange	5.00
X-Men (Jim Lee, Scott Williams and Chiado)	7.00
Thor Corps	5.00
Infinity (Ron Lim and Terry Austin)	5.00
Spider-Man and Mary Jane (Ken Steacy)	5.00
Wolverine and Cable	5.00
X-Men Villains Gallery (Jim Lee and Scott Williams)	7.00
Original X-Men (Jim Lee and Scott Williams)	7.00
X-Men, Things To Come (Jim Lee and Scott Williams)	7.00
X-Men Time Off (Jim Lee and Scott Williams)	7.00
Ghost Rider (Bill Sienkiewicz)	5.00
Guardians of the Galaxy (Rob Liefeld and Jim Valentino)	7.50
Punisher (Joe Jusko)	5.00
Wolverine (Ken Steacy)	5.00
X-Men Door Poster 30"x59" (Jim Lee and Scott Williams)	15.00
Ghost Rider: Rise of Midnight Sons (Adam and Joe Kubert)	5.00
X-Men Door Poster II 30"x59" (Jim Lee/Scott Williams and Joe Chido)	7.00
Excalibur (Alan Davis and Mark Farmer)	5.00

Spiderman 2099 (Leonardi and Williamson)	5.00
Hulk (Bob Larkin)	5.00
Psylocke (Jim Lee)	8.00
Marvel Universe III Trading Card I 25"x35"	5.00
Marvel Universe III Trading Card II 25"x35"	5.00
X-Men Triptych Door Poster III 30"x59" (Jim Lee and Scott Williams)	15.00
X-Men (Whilce Portacio and Scott Williams)	5.00
Spider-Man versus Venom (Joe Chiodo)	5.00
Ghost Rider (Brett Blevins)	5.00
Deaths Head II (Liam Sharp)	5.00
(1993)	
Silver Sable (Joe Chiodo)	5.00
Punisher (Mick Zeck and Phil Zimmelman)	5.00
Cable (Art Thibert)	5.00
Wolverine (Quesada and Palmiotti)	5.00
Ghost Rider IV (Mark Texeira)	5.00
Wolverine versus Sabretooth (Joe Chiodo)	5.00
Carnage/Spider-Man/Venom (Mark Bagley and Randy Emberlin)	5.00
Hulk and Friends swimsuit (Dale Keown and Mark Farmer)	5.00
Dead Pool (Joe Adureira and Mark Farmer)	5.00
Magneto I (Jim Lee and Alex Toth)	7.00

Magento (Marvel #144, 1993)

All prices listed are for *Near Mint* condition.

The Infinity Crusade (Marvel #146, 1993)

Spider-Man and Mary Jane (Jan Duursema)	5.00
The Infinity Crusade (Jim Starlin)	5.00
Wolverine (Mark Beachum)	5.00
Avengers 30th Anniversary (George Perez)	6.00
Storm swimsuit (Mark Silvestri)	5.00
New Warriors	5.00
Sabretooth (Mark Texeira)	5.00
Daredevil (Frank Miller)	7.00
Venom (Ken Steacy)	5.00
Midnight Sons II (Garney and Ivy)	5.00

(1994)

X-Mas Promo Poster	3.00
Punisher poster	3.00
Punisher Door Signs	3.00
Dr. Strange Door Signs	3.00
X-Men Poster	3.00
Avenger Poster	3.00
Infinity Crusade Poster	3.00
Cable poster	3.00
Heavy Hitters promo poster	3.00
Spidey poster	3.00
Marvel UK posters	3.00
Infinity Crusade promo poster	3.00
Thunderstrike promo poster	3.00

OTHER COMICS POSTERS

ALL WINNERS
All Winners golden-age poster by Alex
Schomburg (1990) 6.00
BATMAN
Batman 41"x 27" movie serial poster
(Columbia Pictures 1954) 140.00
Batman Pin-Up Posters (DC Comics 1966) 30.00
BONE
Bone 1995 poster calendar 24"x36"
(Comic Images 1994) 8.00
CAPTAIN AMERICA
Captain America golden-age poster by Alex
Schomburg (1990) 6.00
CHAOS
Lady Death #1 poster 24"x36"
by Steve Hughes and Jason Jenson . 5.95
Lady Death all chromium poster 19"x27"
by Steve Hughes and Jason Jenson 29.95
COLD BLOODED
Cold Blooded Poster, signed (Kyle Holtz)
and numbered poster, 24"x36" color
(Comico 1993) 9.95
Cold Blooded Poster (Kyle Holtz art)
poster, 24"x36" color (Comico 1993) . 6.95
CONAN
Barry Smith Conan Blacklight Poster (same
as puzzle art) (Marvel 1971) 60.00
CONCRETE
Concrete wall poster, 26"x72" by Paul
Chadwick (Dark Horse 1994) 24.95
CROW
Kitchen Sink (1994)
Crow movie poster 10.00
Crow door-sized poster 26"x72" 16.95
Crow sitting poster 24"x30" 6.95
Crow with gun poster by James O'Barr ... 6.95
CYBERFORCE
Cyberforce Poster #1 (Marc Silvestri/
Joe Chiodo art) 22"x34" (Image
Comics 1993) 4.95
DARK, THE
The Dark Poster, George Perez pencils,
Tom Vincent painted 22"x14"
color (Continum 1993) 3.95
DEATHBLOW
Deathblow Poster (Jim Lee art),
24"x36" (Homage Studios 1993) 7.50
EXTREME
Black Flag poster 24"x36" by Dan Fraga .. 4.95
Black-and-White poster, 24"x36"

by Art Thibert 4.95
Chapel poster 24"x36" by Jae Lee 4.95
Die Hard poster 24"x36" by Joe
   Madureira 4.95
Dutch poster 24"x36" 4.95
Extreme poster 24"x36" 4.95
Youngblood poster 24"x36" by George
   Perez 5.95
Doom's IV poster by Mark Pacella 4.95
Prophet poster by Stephen Platt 4.95
Shaft poster, Richard art, Rob
   Liefeld design (1992) 4.95

GEN 13
Gen 13 poster G6 . . . . 5.95

GEN-X
Gen-X Poster color 26"x20" (Homage
   Studios 1993) 5.95

HELLBOY
Hellboy poster, Mike Mignola 4.95

HOMAGE STUDIOS
Kindred poster 26"x20" 5.95
Killer Instinct poster 26"x20" by Jim Lee
   and Marc Silvestri 7.50
WildC.A.T.S. poster 26"x20" (Jim Lee) 7.50
Deathblow poster 26"x20" (Jim Lee) 7.50
Stormwatch poster 26"x20" (Scott Clark
   and Trevor Scott) 5.95

HUMAN TORCH
Human Torch golden-age poster by Alex
   Schomburg (1990) 6.00

IMAGE
Image Universe Jam poster 26"x20" color . 6.50
Ballistic/Cyberforce #6 dover poster,
   22"x34" by Joe Chiodo 4.95
Black Anvil 22"x34" 4.95
Ripclaw Special cover poster 22"x34" 4.95
The Pack poster 22"x34" 4.95

JUDGE DREDD
Judge Dredd No Smoking Sign, 8½"x11"
   color (Fleetway 1993) 2.00

LETHARGIC COMICS
Poster Pack, 6 posters of Lethargic
   Comics characters, 11"x17"
   (Lethargic 1992) 25.00

LORELEI
Lorelei #0 poster 15"x22" by Louis
   Small, Jr. (Starwarp 1994) 10.00

MADMAN
Madman Door Poster 26"x72", Mike
   Allred art (Dark Horse 1994) 24.95
Madman Adventures Timewarp poster,
   M. Dalton Allred and friends art,

(Tundra 1992) 8.95

MALIBU
Dreadstar (1994) 2.00
Starslammers (1994) 2.00
Rune (1993) 2.00
Ultraverse (1994) 2.00
Bravura (1994) 2.00
Freex and Ultraverse (1993) 2.00
Edge (1994) 2.00
Dinosaurs For Hire (1992) 2.00
Breed (1993) 2.00
Firearm (1993) 2.00
Solitaire (1993) 2.00
Intro-Ultraverse (1993) 3.00

MELTING POT
Melting Pot metal poster, 12"x18",
   Simon Bisley art 20.00
Melting Pot poster Simon Bisley art
   (Tundra 1992) 6.95

MONKEYMAN AND O'BRIEN
Monkeyman and O'Brien, Art Adams 4.95

NEXTMEN
Nextmen poster (Dark Horse 1994) 2.00

NORTHSTAR COMICS
Klownshock poster #1, Tommy Pons
   art, 24"x36" (Northstar 1992) 9.95
Skull Rocker poster #1, James O'Barr
   art (Northstar 1992) 8.95
Skull-Rocker Poster #1, Jim O'Barr,
   2nd printing (Northstar 1993) 8.95
Skull Rocker poster #2, James O'Barr
   art, 24"x36" (Northstar 1992) 9.95
Cold Blooded Poster #2 (Kelley Jones
   art) 24"x36" (Comico 1993) 8.95

PLASM
Plasm poster (The River Group 1993) 1.00

SHADOWHAWK
Shadowhawk The Secret Revealed
   poster 22"x34" by Bill Sienkiewicz . . . 4.95
Shadowhawk poster #1, color, 22"x34"
   (Jim Valentino and Chance Wolf)
   (Image Comics 1993) 4.95
Shadowhawk/Savage Dragon poster #1,
   color, 22"x34" (Jim Valentino
   and Erik Larson) (Image Comics 1993) 4.95

SLAINE
SQ Productions (1991)
Slain, 17"x24" (Simon Bisley) 6.95

SPAWN
Spawn poster 22"x34" 5.95

STORMWATCH
Stormwatch poster (Scott Clark, Jim

All prices listed are for *Near Mint* condition.

Spawn (Todd McFarlane 1994)

Lee and Dale Keown art) color
(Homage Studios 1993) 5.95
SUPERMAN
Superman the Movie Poster (Warner
Bros. #0437, 1980) 50.00
Superman two-sided poster (Mark's
Memorabilia 1993) 15.00
Superman Bursting Out of His Shirt,
#2210, 33"x23", color (One-Stop 1993) 4.95
Superman's Funeral, #2197, 23"x33",
color (One-Stop 1993) 4.95
Superman's Grave Stone, #2186,
23"x33", color (One-Stop 1993) 4.95
TEENAGE MUTANT NINJA TURTLES
TMNT poster series, volume 1 (A. C.
Farley art) (Mirage 1992) 5.95
TMNT/Savage Dragon Poster series #3,
color (Eric Larsen and Michael Dooney
art) (Mirage 1993) 5.95
Don (Star Makers #2904) . . . . CRP
Leo (Star Makers #2901) . . . . CRP
Mike (Star Makers #2902) . . . . CRP
Raph (Star Makers #2903) . . . . CRP
TMNT The Movie II (New Line Cinema) . . . CRP
TMNT The Movie III (New Line Cinema) . . CRP

TEKNO COMIX
Tekno Comix poster 24"x36" color 3.95
TICK
Tick: Omnibus bus poster 4.95
Tick: Nightmare Buildings poster 4.95
Tick: A Typical day on the lower East Side . 4.95
Tick triple poster, 24"x18" (New
England 1992) 7.49
Tick versus Multiple Santa full-color poster,
Ben Edlund art (New England 1993) . 4.95
Tick versus Multiple Santa full-color poster,
Ben Edlund art, signed (New England
1993) 8.95
VALIANT
X-O Manowar poster, Joe Quesada
art (Valiant 1993) 4.95
VAMPIRELLA
Vampirella poster 16"x24"(Harris 1972) . . 10.00
VOYAGER COMMUNICATIONS
Alpha-Omega-Solarman poster (1994) 3.00
WETWORKS
Wetworks Poster (Whilce Portacio art),
24"x36" (Homage Studios 1993) 5.95
WILDC.A.T.S.
WildC.A.T.S. poster 26"x20" Jim Lee art
(Image Comics 1992) 7.50
WildC.A.T.S. Trilogy Collector's poster,
(Jae Lee art) 26"x20" (Homage
Studios 1993) 5.95
WildC.A.T.S. 1995 Calendar poster,
Jim Lee art 7.50
WildC.A.T.S. poster, WC16 . . . . 5.95
WildC.A.T.S. poster, WC17 . . . . 5.95
WILDSTORM
WUP01 Wildstorm Universe poster,
Whilce Portacio art 6.95
Wetworks poster, WW#3 . . . . 5.95
X-MEN
X-Men 1995 poster calendar 24"x36"
(Comic Images 1994) 8.00
YOUNGBLOOD
Youngblood poster 24"x36", George Perez
art (Extreme Studios 1994) 4.95
Youngblood poster, Rob Liefeld art
(Image Comics 1992) 7.50

BOOKS

T his section includes information on several different types of collectible books that are based on or derived from comic books or comic strips. The first listing covers paperback books which reprint comic book or comic strip stories. There are numerous large paperback and hardcover reprints of comic books, but the ones listed below are standard size (small) paperbacks. This isn't really a very good size or format for comic book stories and so not very many such books were published, which may be the reason book collectors and some comics collectors are interested in these books as collectibles.

COMIC PAPERBACKS

Batman, by Bob Kane, Signet D2939, 1966 15.00
Batman vs. Three Villains of Doom, by Winston Lyon, Signet D2940, 1966 . . . . . . 15.00
Batman vs. The Joker, Signet D2969, 1966 12.50
Batman vs. The Penguin, Signet D2970, 1966 . . . . 12.50
Batman vs. The Fearsome Foursome, by Winston Lyon, Signet D2995, 1966 . . 12.50
Blackmark, by Gil Kane, Bantam N5871, Jan. 1971, $0.95, cover by Gil Kane 12.50
Conan the Barbarian, Vol. 1, by Roy Thomas, Ace 11692-2, 1979, $1.95, illustrated and cover by Barry Smith 11.00
Conan the Barbarian, Vol. 2, by Roy Thomas, Ace 11693-0, 1979, $1.95, illustrated and cover by Barry Smith 10.00
Conan the Barbarian, Vol. 3, by Roy Thomas, Ace 11694-9, 1979, $1.95, illustrated and cover by Barry Smith 10.00
Conan the Barbarian, Vol. 4, by Roy Thomas, Ace 11695-7, 1979, $1.95, illustrated and cover by Barry Smith 10.00
Conan the Barbarian, Vol. 5, by Roy Thomas, Ace 11696-5, 1979, $1.95, illustrated and cover by Barry Smith 10.00
Conan the Barbarian, Vol. 6, by Roy Thomas, Ace 11697-3, 1979, $2.25, illustrated and cover by Barry Smith 10.00
Here Comes Daredevil, Lancer 72-170, 1967, $.50, ... 20.00

The Fantastic Four Collector's Album, by Stan Lee, Lancer 72-111, 1966, $0.50, Jack Kirby art 15.00
The Fantastic Four Return, by Stan Lee, Lancer 72-169, 1967, $0.50, Jack Kirby art . . 10.00

Flash Gordon, Vol. 6 (Tempo 1980)

The Amazing Adventures of Flash Gordon, Vol. 1, Ace-Tempo 17349, 1980 . . . . 5.00
The Amazing Adventures of Flash Gordon, Vol. 2, Ace-Tempo 17348, 1980 . . . . 5.00
The Amazing Adventures of Flash Gordon, Vol. 3, Ace-Tempo 17347, 1980 . . . . 5.00
The Amazing Adventures of Flash Gordon, Vol. 4, Ace-Tempo 17154, 1980, cover by Boris Vallejo 7.50
The Amazing Adventures of Flash Gordon, Vol. 5, Ace-Tempo 17208, 1980, cover by Davis Meltzer? 6.00
The Amazing Adventures of Flash Gordon, Vol. 6, Ace-Tempo 17245, 1980, cover by Davis Meltzer 6.00
Green Lantern and Green Arrow #1, by Denny O'Neill, Paperback Library #64-729, 1972, $0.75 . . . . 10.00

All prices listed are for *Near Mint* condition.

Green Lantern and Green Arrow #2, by
Denny O'Neill, Paperback Library #64-
755, 1972, $0.75 . . . . 10.00
The Incredible Hulk Collector's Album, Stan
Lee script, Lancer 72-124, 1966, $0.50,
Steve Ditko and Jack Kirby art 10.00

The Amazing Spider-Man Collector's Album
(Lancer 1966)

The Amazing Spider-Man Collector's Album,
Stan Lee script, Lancer 72-112, 1966,
$0.50, Steve Ditko art 12.50
2nd printing 7.00
Star Hawks, by Gil Kane and Ron Goulart,
Ace #78150, 1979, Gil Kane cover . . . 10.00
Star Hawks, by Gil Kane and Ron Goulart,
Tempo 17311, 1981, $1.75, Gil Kane
cover 7.50
Star Hawks II, by Gil Kane and Ron Goulart,
Tempo 17272, July 1981, $1.75, Gil
Kane cover 7.50
Superman, (author and artists not credited),
Tempo #14532-4, 1978, $1.25, 5
classic stories 10.00

Superman (Tempo 1978)

Swamp Thing, written by Len Wein, Tor 49-
012, April 1982, $1.95, Berni Wrightson
art 6.00
The Mighty Thor Collector's Album, Stan Lee
script, Lancer 72-125, 1966, $0.50,
Jack Kirby art 10.00
Thunder Agents reps., Larry Ivie; Wally Wood art:
Dynamo, Tower 42-660, 1966 . . . . . . 10.00
Noman, Tower 42-672, 1966 . . . . 10.00
Menthor, Tower 42-674, 1966 . . . . . . 15.00
The Terrific Trio, Tower 42-687, 1966 15.00
Tales From the Crypt, Ballantine Books
#U2106, Dec. 1964, $0.50, Frank
Frazetta cover 25.00
The Vault of Horror, Ballantine Books
#U2107, Aug. 1965, $0.50 . . . . 20.00
Tales of the Incredible, Ballantine Books
#U2140, Mar. 1965, $0.50, Frank
Frazetta cover 25.00
The Best of Creepy, Tempo Books #05368, Feb.
1971, $0.75, Frank Frazetta cover . . . 25.00

COMIC NOVELIZATIONS

T he first comic novelization was **The Adventures of Superman** by George Lowther in 1942. It contained illustrations by Joe Shuster, which is what makes it so incredibly valuable. Amazingly enough, there have been very few other attempts to turn comic books into fiction. Byron Preiss published a series of books in 1976 and Marvel tried a series two years later and the Superman movies were novelized, but that's about it until the 1990s. Recently, quite a few comic characters have made their way into novels. The Batman movies had a lot to do with this, as director Tim Burton's Batman is a much more adult character than the 1960s TV show Batman was. Given the success of the novelizations of

the several Star Trek series, many of which made the *New York Times* bestseller lists, it is not surprising that book publishers are giving superheroes another try.

The Avengers Battle The Earth-Wrecker,
  Otto Binder, Bantam 3569, 1967 .... 7.50
The Further Adventures of Batman, edited
  by Martin H. Greenberg, Bantam
  28270, July 1989, $3.95, 14 stories,
  Kyle Baker cover 5.00
The Further Adventures of the Joker, edited
  by Martin H. Greenberg, Bantam
  #28531, Feb. 1990, $4.50, Kyle Baker
  cover 5.00
The Further Adventures of Batman II: Fea-
  turing the Penguin, edited by Martin H.
  Greenberg, Bantam Spectra #56012,
  1992, 425p, $4.99, Joe DeVito cover,
  11 stories 5.00
The Further Adventures of Batman III: Fea-
  turing Catwoman, edited by Martin H.
  Greenberg, Bantam Spectra #56069,
  Mar. 1993, 468p, $5.50, 13 stories ... 6.00
Batman: Knightfall, by Dennis O'Neil, Ban-
  tam #09673, 1994 HC, $19.95 ..... 20.00
Batman: Knightfall and Beyond, by Alan
  Grant, Bantam #48187, 1994, PB, Joe
  DeVito cover 4.00
Batman Returns, movie book, Bantam,
  Hard cover 15.00
  Trade paperback 5.00
Batman Returns, 92-page adaption by
  Helfer, Little Brown #17782 .... 7.50
Batman Returns, by Craig Shaw Gardner,
  Warner PB, July 1992 .... 7.50
Catwoman, by Lynn Abbey and Robert
  Asprin, Warner #36043, Sept. 1992,

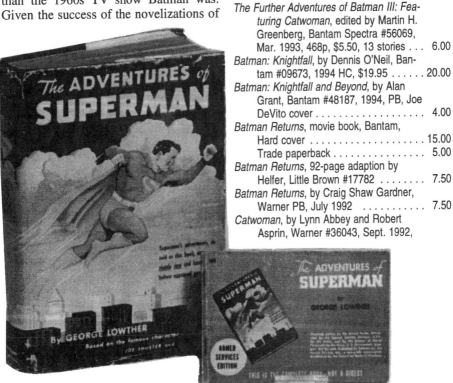

The Adventures of Superman
(Random House 1942)

The Adventures of Superman
(Armed Services Edition 1945)

---

paperback 7.50
SFBC #03870, Apr. 1994, 7.98, 196p,
Dave Dorman cover 7.50
The Batman Murders, by Craig Shaw
Gardner, Warner #36040, Oct. 1990,
$4.95, Dave Dorman cover 6.00
Batman: To Stalk a Specter, by Simon
Hawke, Warner #36041, Feb. 1991,
$4.95, 249p, Dave Dorman cover . . . 5.00

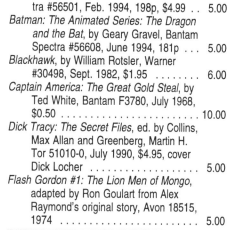

tra #56501, Feb. 1994, 198p, $4.99 . . 5.00
*Batman: The Animated Series: The Dragon
and the Bat*, by Geary Gravel, Bantam
Spectra #56608, June 1994, 181p . . . 5.00
Blackhawk, by William Rotsler, Warner
#30498, Sept. 1982, $1.95 . . . . 6.00
Captain America: The Great Gold Steal, by
Ted White, Bantam F3780, July 1968,
$0.50 . . . . 10.00
Dick Tracy: The Secret Files, ed. by Collins,
Max Allan and Greenberg, Martin H.
Tor 51010-0, July 1990, $4.95, cover
Dick Locher 5.00
Flash Gordon #1: The Lion Men of Mongo,
adapted by Ron Goulart from Alex
Raymond's original story, Avon 18515,
1974 . . . . 5.00

Flash Gordon (Avon 1975)

Batman Captured by the Engines, by Joe R.
Lansdale, Warner #36042, July 1991,
$4.99, 241p, Dave Dorman cover . . . 5.00
*Batman: Mask of the Phantasm: The
Animated Movie*, by Geary Gravel,
Bantam Spectra #56581, Jan. 1994,
232p, $4.99 . . . . 5.00
*Batman: The Animated Series: Shadows of
the Past*, by Geary Gravel, Bantam
Spectra #56365, Nov. 1993, 180p,
$4.99 . . . . 5.00
*Batman: The Animated Series: Duel to the
Death*, by Geary Gravel, Bantam Spec-

Howard the Duck (Berkley 1980s)

Flash Gordon #2: The Plague of Sound,
adapted by Ron Goulart from Alex
Raymond's original story, Avon 19166,
1974 . . . . 5.00
Flash Gordon #3: The Space Circus,

adapted by Ron Goulart from Alex Raymond's original story, Avon 19695, 1974 .... 5.00

Flash Gordon #4: The Time Trap of Ming XIII, adapted by Carson Bingham from Alex Raymond's original story, Avon 20446, 1974 .... 5.00

Flash Gordon #5: The Witch Queen of Mongo, adapted by Carson Bingham from Alex Raymond's original story, Avon 21378, 1974 .... 5.00

Flash Gordon #6: The War of the Cybernauts, adapted by Carson Bingham from Alex Raymond's original story, Avon 22335, 1975 .... 5.00

Howard the Duck, by Ellis Weiner, Berkley 09275, 1980s, from screenplay by Willard Huyck and Gloria Katz 5.00

The Ultimate Spider-Man, edited by Stan Lee, Berkley 14610-3, 12 stories, TPB   6.00

Spider-Man, The Venom Factor, by Diane Duane, Putnam #14002-6, illustrated by Ron Lim, 348p, Nov. 1994, HC, Bruce Jenson cover, with trading card 20.00

Supergirl, by Norma Fox Mazer, Warner #32367, Nov. 1984 .... 5.00

The Adventures of Superman, by George Lowther, Random House, 1942, illustrated by Shuster
in dust jacket 1,500.00
without dust jacket 700.00

The Adventures of Superman, by George Lowther, Armed Services Edition #656, May 1945 .... 400.00

The Adventures of Superman, by George Lowther, Applewood facsimile edition, 228pgs, HC, 1995 .... 17.95

Superman: Last Son of Krypton, by Elliot S. Maggin, Science Fiction Book Club edition, Spring 1979, $3.98 (movie tie-in) 15.00

Superman: Last Son of Krypton, by Elliot S. Maggin, Warner #82319, Sept. 1980, $2.25 .... 7.00

Superman: Miracle Monday, by Elliot S. Maggin, Warner #91196, June 1981, $2.50, photo cover and 8 pages of photos from Superman II movie 7.00

Superman III, by William Kotzwinkle, Warner #30699, June 1984, $2.95 (movie tie-in) 5.00

Superman IV, by B. B. Hiller, Scholastic

Point #41195, July 1987, $2.75 (movie tie-in) 3.50

The Death and Life of Superman, by Roger Stern, novelization, Bantam Spectra #09582, Sept. 1993, 416p, $19.95 ... 25.00
Science Fiction Book Club #02262, Dec. 1993, 416p, $9.98 .... 10.00
Paperback: Bantam Spectra #56930-9, Nov. 1994, 528p, $5.99 .... 6.00

The Further Adventures of Superman, edited by Martin H. Greenberg, Bantam Spectra #28568, Nov. 1993, 360p, $5.99 (10 stories) 6.00

Vampirella #1: Bloodstalk, by Ron Goulart, Warner 76-928, 1975, $1.25 .... 7.50

Vampirella #2: On Alien Wings, by Ron Goulart, Warner 76-929, 1975, 138p, $1.25 .... 5.00

Vampirella #3: Deadwalk, by Ron Goulart, Warner 76-930, 1976, 144p, $1.25 ... 5.00

Vampirella #4: Blood Wedding, by Ron Goulart, Warner 86-088, 1976, 140p,

Vampirella (Warner 1976)

All prices listed are for *Near Mint* condition.

$1.25 . . . . 5.00

Vampirella #5: Deathgame, by Ron Goulart, Warner 86-089, 1976, 138p, $1.25 . . . 5.00

Vampirella #6: Snakegod, by Ron Goulart, Warner 86-090, 1976, 139p, $1.25 . . . 5.00

The Further Adventures of Wonder Woman, edited by Martin H. Greenberg, Bantam Spectra #28624, Sept. 1993, 337p, $5.99 (8 stories) 6.00

[Tales From] The House of Mystery #1, by Jack Oleck, Warner #75-226, Apr. 1973, $0.95, Berni Wrightson cover and illustrations 6.00

[Tales From] The House of Mystery #2, by Jack Oleck, Warner #75-256, Aug. 1973, $0.95, Berni Wrightson cover and illustrations 6.00

MARVEL NOVEL SERIES

#1 The Amazing Spider-Man in Mayhem in Manhattan, by Len Wein and Marv Wolfman, Pocket #82044, Apr. 1978,

The Amazing Spider-Man in Crime Campaign (Pocket 1979)

$1.50, Bob Larkin cover 10.00

#2 The Incredible Hulk in Stalker From the Stars, by Len Wein, Marv Wolfman and Joseph Silva, Pocket #82084, Nov. 1978, $1.75 . . . . 9.00

#3 The Hulk in Cry of the Beast, by Richard S. Meyers, Pocket #82085, Apr. 1979, $1.75 . . . . 9.00

#4 Captain America in Holocaust for Hire, by Stan Lee, Pocket #82086, May 1979, $1.95 . . . . 9.00

#5 Fantastic Four in Doomsday, by Stan Lee, Pocket #82087, 1979, $1.95 . . . 9.00

#6 Iron Man in Call My Killer...Modok!, by William Rotsler, Pocket #82089, June 1979, $1.95 . . . . 9.00

#7 Doctor Strange in Nightmare, by William Rotsler, Pocket #82088, July 1979, $1.95, Bob Larkin cover 9.00

#8 The Amazing Spider-Man in Crime Campaign, by Paul Kupperberg, Pocket #82090, August 1979, $1.95, Bob Larkin cover 9.00

#9 The Avengers in The Man Who Stole Tomorrow, by Stan Lee, Pocket #89093, Oct. 1979, $1.95 . . . . 9.00

WEIRD HEROES SERIES

#1 Weird Heroes: Vol. 1, edited by Byron Preiss, Pyramid A3746, Oct. 1975, $1.50 . . . . 8.00

#2 Weird Heroes: Vol. 2, edited by Byron Preiss, Pyramid A4044, Dec. 1975, $1.50, James Steranko cover 7.50

#3 Quest of the Gypsy, by Ron Goulart, edited by Byron Preiss, Pyramid A4034, Sept. 1976, $1.50, Alex Nino cover and illustrations 10.00

#4 Nightshade, by Tappan King and Beth Meacham, Pyramid A4035, Oct. 1976, $1.50, Ralph Reese cover 7.00

#5 Doc Phoenix—The Oz Encounter, by Ted White and Marv Wolfman, Pyramid A4036, Jan. 1977, $1.50, Jeff Jones cover 7.00

#6 Weird Heroes: Vol. 6, edited by Byron Preiss, Pyramid M4037, Apr. 1977, $1.75 . . . . 6.00

#7 Eye of the Vulture, A Quest of the Gypsy Novel, by Ron Goulart, edited by Byron Preiss, Jove A4293, Oct. 1977, $1.50, Alex Nino cover and illustrations 6.00

Weird Heroes, Vol. 5: The Oz Encounter (Pyramid 1977); Supergirl: The Girl of Steel (Archway 1984)

#8 *Weird Heroes: Vol. 8*, edited by Byron
Preiss, Jove M4257, Nov. 1977, $1.75,
Stephen Hickman cover 6.00
  Which Way "Super Powers"
#1 *Superman: The Man of Steel*, by Andrew
Helfer, Archway 64332, 1984 . . . .   3.50
#2 *Supergirl: The Girl of Steel*, by Andrew
Helfer, Archway 47566, 1984 . . . .   3.50
#3 *Justice League of America*, by Richard
Wenk, Archway, 1984 . . . .   3.50
#4 *Batman: The Doomsday Prophecy*, by
Richard Wenk, Archway 62454, 1985 .   3.50

BIG LITTLE BOOKS

Big Little Books, which were written
for children and were about half
pictures anyway, were a natural
place for comic book and comic strip
characters to appear in stories. There are
many collectors of Big Little Books and

few copies around in good condition, so
prices are high. However, the books were
generally printed on relatively cheap
paper, so they won't last forever, and the
collectors are getting old, too, so prices
will probably stay high until either the
collectors or the books die or both.

Betty Boop in Snow White (1934) 48.00
Betty Boop in Miss Gulliver's Travels 42.00
Blondie 48.00
Blondie and Baby Dumpling (1939) 31.00
Blondie and Baby Dumpling (1937) 25.00
Blondie and Bouncing Baby Dumpling 25.00
*Blondie and Dagwood — Everybody's
  Happy* 25.00
Blondie and Dagwood in Hot Water 25.00
Blondie and Dagwood — Some Fun! 26.00
Blondie — Baby Dumpling and All! 26.00
*Blondie — Cookie and Daisy's Pups,
  (1943), 432p* 25.00
*Blondie — Cookie and Daisy's Pups,
  2nd ed.* 32.00

All prices listed are for *Near Mint* condition.

Blondie — Count Cookie in Too! 25.00
Blondie — Fun For All! 21.00
Blondie — No Dull Moments 21.00
Blondie, or Life Among the Bumsteads 25.00
Blondie — Papa Knows Beast 25.00
Blondie — The Bumsteads Carry On 25.00
Blondie — Who's Boss? 25.00
Buck Rogers and the Planetoid
    Plot (1936) 54.00
Buck Rogers and the Super Dwarf of Space 42.00
Buck Rogers and the Overturned World ... 42.00
Buck Rogers and the Doom
    Comet (1935) 42.00
Buck Rogers and the Depth Men
    of Jupiter (1935) 66.00
Buck Rogers and the City Below
    the Sea (1934) 90.00
Adventures of Buck Rogers 50.00
Buck Rogers in the 25th Century
    A.D. (1938) 48.00
Buck Rogers in the 25th Century
    A.D. (1933) 58.00
Buck Rogers in the 25th Century
    A.D. vs. the Fiend of Space 42.00
Buck Rogers in War with the
    Planet Venus 54.00
Buck Rogers on the Moon of
    Saturn (1934) 72.00
Chester Gump and His Friends 43.00
Chester Gump at Silver Creek Ranch 16.00
Chester Gump Finds the Hidden
    Treasuer 25.00
Chester Gump in the City of Gold 32.00
Chester Gump in the Pole-to-Pole Fight ... 21.00
Dick Tracy and Chains of Crime 36.00
Dick Tracy and Dick Tracy Junior 43.00
Dick Tracy and His G-Men 36.00
Dick Tracy and Phantom Ship 32.00
Dick Tracy and the Racketeer Gang 36.00
Dick Tracy and the Mad Killer 29.00
Dick Tracy and the Man with No Face,
    #1491 (1938) 36.00
Dick Tracy and the Spider Gang 40.00
Dick Tracy and the Maroon Mask Gang ... 36.00
Dick Tracy and the Mystery of
    the Purple Cross 36.00
Dick Tracy and the Hotel Murders 36.00
Dick Tracy and the Blackmailers 44.00
Dick Tracy and the Boris Arson Gang 50.00
Dick Tracy and the Bicycle Gang 47.00
Dick Tracy and the Wreath Kidnapping Case 32.00
Dick Tracy and the Stolen Bonds 36.00

Dick Tracy and the Frozen Bullet Murders . 36.00
Dick Tracy and the Chain of Command ... 36.00
Adventures of Dick Tracy (1932) 125.00
Dick Tracy and the Yogee Yama 29.00
Dick Tracy, Detective 14.00
Dick Tracy, Detective and Federal Agent .. 38.00
Dick Tracy from Colorado to Nova Scotia .. 36.00
Dick Tracy Gets His Man 39.00
Dick Tracy Meets a New Gang 36.00
Dick Tracy on the High Seas 36.00
Dick Tracy on the Trail of Larceny Lu 36.00
Dick Tracy on Voodoo Island 40.00
Dick Tracy Out West, #723 (1933) 43.00
Dick Tracy Returns 50.00
Dick Tracy Solves the Penfield Mystery ... 48.00
Dick Tracy, Special FBI Operative 32.00
Dick Tracy, Super Detective 36.00
Dick Tracy, the Tiger Lilly Gang 29.00
Dick Tracy vs. Crooks in Disguise 36.00
Felix the Cat (1935) 48.00
Felix the Cat (1943) 38.00
Felix the Cat (1945) 28.00
Flash Gordon and the Emperor of
    Mongo (1936) 108.00
Flash Gordon and the Fiery Desert of
    Mongo (1948) 40.00
Flash Gordon and the Tournaments of
    Mongo (1935) 50.00
Flash Gordon and the Ape Men of Mor ... 78.00

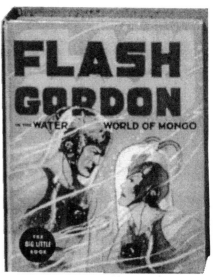

Flash Gordon on the Water World of Mongo
Big Little Book (Whitman 1937)

Flash Gordon and the Tyrant of Mongo ... 30.00
Flash Gordon and the Monsters
   of Mongo (1935) 132.00
Flash Gordon and the Red Sword
   Invaders (1945) 108.00
Flash Gordon and the Witch Queen of
   Mongo (1936) 132.00
Flash Gordon and the Power Men
   of Mongo 108.00
Flash Gordon in the Ice World of
   Mongo (1942) 132.00
Flash Gordon in the Forest Kingdom of
   Mongo 40.00
Flash Gordon in the Jungles of Mongo 35.00
Flash Gordon in the Water World
   of Mongo (1937) 54.00
Flash Gordon on the Planet Mongo (1934) 180.00
Kayo and Moon Mullins 30.00
Li'l Abner in Sadie Hawkins Day 75.00
Little Lulu, Alvin and Tubby 60.00
Little Orphan Annie 100.00
Little Orphan Annie and the Haunted Man-
   sion 50.00
Little Orphan Annie and Her Dog Sandy ... 75.00
Little Orphan Annie and Daddy Warbucks . 50.00
Little Orphan Annie and Chizzler 50.00
Little Orphan Annie in Rags to Riches 60.00
Little Orphan Annie in the Movies 50.00
Little Orphan Annie with the Circus 50.00
Nancy and Sluggo 20.00
Popeye and Castor Oyl the Detective 50.00
Popeye and the Jeep 45.00
Popeye in Chose Your Weppins 75.00
Popeye the Superfighter 30.00
Terry and the Pirates and the Giant's
   Revenge 30.00

Superheroes

Aquaman in Scourge of the Sea (#2017) .. 10.00
Batman and Robin in the Cheetah Caper
   (#2031) 15.00
The Fantastic Four in The Case of the Many
   Missing Things (#2014) 10.00
The Fantastic Four in The House of Horrors
   (#2019) 10.00

LITTLE GOLDEN BOOKS

Buck Rogers and the Children of Hopetown,
   by Raven Dwight, ill by Kurt
   Schaffenberger (1971) 7.50
Dennis the Menace, by Carl Memling, ill. by

Fantastic Four in The House of Horrors
(Whitman 1968)

Hawley Pratt and Lee Holley (1959) .. 8.00
Dennis the Menace and Ruff, by Carl
   Memling and Lee Holley, ill. by Hawley
   Pratt (1959) 8.00
Dennis the Menace, A Quiet Afternoon, by
   Carl Memling, ill. by and Lee Holley
   (1960) 8.00
Little Lulu and Her Magic Tricks, ill. by
   Marjorie H. Buell (1954) 15.00
Steve Canyon, written and ill. by Milton
   Caniff (1959) 12.00
Tom and Jerry, ill. by Harvey Eisenberg
   and Don MacLaughlin (1951) 10.00
Tom and Jerry Meet Little Quack, ill. by
   Harvey Eisenberg and Don
   MacLaughlin (1953) 6.00
Tom and Jerry Photo Finish, by Jean Lewis,
   ill. by Al Anderson (1974) 4.00
Tom and Jerry's Merry Christmas, by Peter
   Archer, ill. by Harvey Eisenberg (1954) 8.00
Tom and Jerry's Party, by Steffie Fletcher, ill.
   by Harvey Eisenberg, Marjorie Hartwell
   and Samuel Armstrong (1955) 5.00

All prices listed are for *Near Mint* condition.

COLORING BOOKS

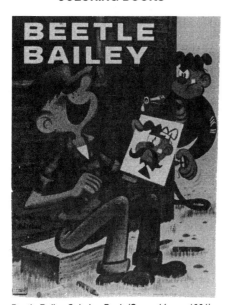

Beetle Bailey Coloring Book (Samuel Lowe 1961)

Andy Panda Paint Book (Whitman #681, 1946) 15.00

Archies Coloring Book (Western #1045, 1970) 10.00

Baby Huey Coloring Book (Saalfield #4536, 1959) 10.00

Batman Meets Blockbuster (Whitman 1966) 20.00

Batman Coloring Book #1140 (Whitman, 1967) 3 different, each 20.00

Batman Coloring Book (Whitman 1970) . . . 10.00

Batman Follow the Color/Magic Rub-Off 8 pictures, and crayons, in box (Whitman 1966) 35.00

Batman With Robin the Boy Wonder sticker fun book (Whitman) 30.00

3-D Batman Adventures 8½"x11" comic book with 3-D glasses 35.00

Batman Magic Slate 8½"x14" (Whitman 1966), with wood stylus 35.00

Beetle Bailey Coloring Book (Samuel Lowe #2860, 1961) 10.00

Blondie Paint Book (Whitman 1945) 20.00

Blondie Coloring Book (Saalfield #9961, 1968) 10.00

Blondie Coloring Book (Saalfield #4541, 1968) 10.00

Boots and Her Buddies Coloring Book (Saalfield #331, 1942) 20.00

Boots and Her Buddies Coloring Book (Saalfield #1182, 1952) 10.00

Brenda Starr Coloring Book (Saalfield #9675, 1964) 15.00

Bringing Up Father Paint Book (Whitman #663, 1942) 20.00

Buck Rogers Paint Book (Whitman 1935)

Buck Rogers Paint Book #679 (Whitman 1935) 200.00

Buster Brown's Paint Book (1916) 75.00

Captain America Coloring Book (Whitman 1966) 25.00

Captain Marvel Paint Book (Lowe 1943) . . 100.00

Dick Tracy Coloring Book (Whitman #399, 1935) 60.00

Dick Tracy Paint Book (Whitman #665, 1935) 60.00

Dick Tracy Coloring Book (Saalfield #2536, 1946) 30.00

Felix the Cat Coloring Book (Saalfield #4655, 1959) 15.00

Flash Gordon Mission of Peril (Rand McNally #06538, 1979) 15.00

Henry Paint Book (Whitman #696, 1951) . . 20.00

Hulk in 3 Incredible Tales 10.00

Hulk in Wisdom of the Watcher 10.00

Incredible Hulk at the Circus (Western #1040, 1977) 10.00

Jughead Coloring Book (Western #1045, 1972) 10.00

Li'l Abner Coloring Book (Saalfield #121, 1941) 50.00

The Incredible Hulk Coloring Book (Western 1977)

Li'l Abner and Daisy Mae Coloring Book
  (Saalfield #2391, 1942) 50.00
Little Annie Rooney Paint Book (Whitman
  #666, 1935) 50.00
Little Audry Coloring Book (Saalfield #9535,
  1959) 15.00
Little Lulu Coloring Book (Whitman #1186,
  1950) 25.00
Little Orphan Annie Crayon & Coloring Book
  10"x13" (McLoughlin Bros. 1933) . . . 100.00
The Great Big Little Orphan Annie Paint &
  Crayon Book (McLoughlin #2017,
  1935) 100.00
Little Orphan Annie's Coloring Book Junior
  Commandos (Saalfield #300, 1945) . . 45.00
Little Orphan Annie Coloring Book (Saalfield
  #4689, 1974) 15.00
Mandrake the Magician (Ottenheimer #2942-
  4, 1940s) 25.00
Nancy and Sluggo (Western #1053, 1972) . 15.00
Peanuts Box of 5 coloring books
  (Saalfield #6546) 35.00
Peanuts (Saalfield #5331, 1960) 15.00
Popeye Coloring Book (Bonnie Books
  #2925, 1958) 30.00
Popeye Coloring Book (Bonnie Books
  #2945, 1958) 30.00
Popeye Coloring Book (Lowe #2834, 1959) 30.00

Popeye Coloring Book (Lowe #2834, 1961) 25.00
Popeye Coloring Book (Lowe #4924, 1961) 30.00
Popeye Secret Picture #3097
  (Lowe, 1962) 30.00
Popeye TV Coloring Book #2834 (Lowe,
  1964) 30.00
Popeye #1062-54 (Golden, 1978) 8.00
Popeye Funtime Fiesta #1045-52 (Golden,
  1979) 8.00
Popeye Outer-Space Zoo (Golden, 1980) . . 10.00
Popeye #1833-44 (Golden, 1981) 6.00
Popeye Sailor and the Spinach Stalk #1045-
  51 (Golden, 1982) 6.00
Popeye Color and Re-Color Book,
  cardboard, with washable crayons
  (Jack Built, 1957) 30.00
Popeye Dot-to-Dot #1062-65
  (Golden 1978) 8.00
Popeye Paint with Water #1822-1
  (Golden 1981) 6.00
Popeye Coloring Book #939 (Lowe 1963) . . 25.00
Popeye color by numbers #2959E (Lowe
  1963) 30.00
Prince Valiant Coloring Book
  (Saalfield 1954) 20.00
Smilin' Jack Coloring Book (Saalfield #397,
  1946) 40.00
Steve Canyon Coloring Book (Saalfield
  #123410, 1952) 30.00

Steve Canyon Coloring Book (1952)

All prices listed are for *Near Mint* condition.

Superman Coloring Book (Whitman 1965)

Superman Coloring Book, 32 pages
    11"x15"(Saafield #196, 1940) 250.00
Superman Coloring Book, 48 pages
    11"x15"(Saafield #196, 1940) 350.00
Superman Coloring Book (Saalfield 1958) . 35.00
Superman Coloring Book, 60 pages
    8"x11" "The Missile Base Mystery"
    (Whitman #1031, 1965) 15.00
Superman Coloring Book, 96 pages
    8"x11" (Whitman 1965) 15.00
Tarzan Coloring Book (Whitman #1157,
    1968) 15.00
Terry and the Pirates Coloring Book
    (Saalfield #398, 1946) 45.00
Tubby (Little Lulu) coloring book, 8"x11"
    32p (Whitman 1963) 35.00
Wonder Woman "The Menace of the Mole
    Men" (Western #1653, 1975) 10.00

POP-UP/PUNCH-OUT BOOKS

Buck Rogers Pop-Up "A Dangerous Mission"
    book (Blue Ribbon Press 1934) 200.00
Captain Marvel Comic Hero Punch-Out
    book (Fawcett 1940s) 30-50.00
Dick Tracy Pop-Up book (Pleasure
    Books 1935) 90.00
Dick Tracy Junior Detective Kit
    (Golden Press 1962) 40-100.00
Superman (Whitman 1966) 60-100.00
Batman (Whitman 1966) 65-130.00
Steve Canyon's Interceptor Station
    (Golden Press 1959) 60-95.00
Superman: The Movie (Warner Books

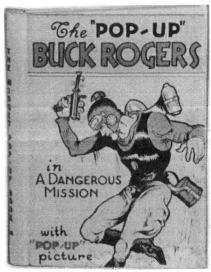

*Buck Rogers Pop-Up book
(Blue Ribbon Press 1934)*

1977) 45-70.00
Supergirl (Grosset and Dunlap
    1984) 25-35.00
Batman Activity Box (Whitman
    1966) 60-200.00
Little Orphan Annie "Pop-Up" book, 8"x9"
    three circus pictures (Blue
    Ribbon Press 1935) 150.00
Marvel World Activity Box
    (Amsco 1975) 60-150.00
Popeye punch-out/sticker fun #2631
    (Lowe 1962) 35.00

Captain Marvel Punch-Out book (Fawcett 1940s)

Three Flying Marvels punch-out (Fawcett 1945)

Popeye sticker book #2631 (Lowe 1961) . . 35.00
Popeye sticker fun #2631 (Lowe 1963) . . . 35.00
The Three Flying Marvels (Fawcett
Publishers 1945) 30-45.00
X-Men Mask Book (Random House
#986143, 1994) 7.00
X-Men Pop-Up Book (Random House
#986390, 1994), 7"x10", 10p 12.00
X-Men Poster Book (Random House TPB,
1994), 8 posters 9.00
*X-Men X-Tra Large Coloring and Activity
Book* (Random House #986864, 1994) 4.00

COVER REPRINTS

If you liked comic books in your
youth but don't want to collect them
now, you can get some cheap
nostalgia from looking at the covers. The
early Batman and Superman covers in the
Abbeville Press volumes are lots of fun,
but if you are old enough for some
serious nostalgia, look for the Gerber
volumes. They are simply incredible. The
two more expensive ones reprint every
Golden Age comic book cover known to
exist. Assembling all these covers was a
task worthy of Hercules. The two books
of Marvel covers are equally impressive.

We have seen copies of these books for
sale at comics shows at reasonable prices
recently. Check them out.
Batman in Detective Comics, Abbeville Press
1993, 4"x4" TPB reprinting early covers 11.00
Batman in Detective Comics II, Abbeville
Press 1994, 4"x4" TPB reprinting early
covers 11.00
Superman in Action Comics, Abbeville Press
1993, 4"x4" TPB reprinting early
covers 11.00
Superman in Action Comics II, Abbeville
Press 1994, 4"x4" TPB reprinting early
covers 11.00
The Golden Age of Batman, Abbeville Press
1994, 9"x12" HC reprinting early
covers 19.00
The Golden Age of Superman, Abbeville
Press 1994, 9"x12" HC reprinting early
covers 19.00
*Photo Journal Guide to Comics: Volume 1:
A–J*, by Ernst and Mary Gerber, 425
pages (Gerber 1991) 75.00
*Photo Journal Guide to Comics: Volume 1:
K–Z*, by Ernst and Mary Gerber, 425
pages (Gerber 1991) 75.00
*Photo Journal Guide to Marvel Comics:
Volume A–J*, by Ernst and Mary Gerber
(Gerber 1991) 30.00
*Photo Journal Guide to Marvel Comics:
Volume K–Z*, by Ernst and Mary
Gerber (Gerber 1991) 30.00

COMIC STRIP REPRINTS

Kitchen Sink press has been doing a
great job of reprinting classic
newspaper comic strips for the last
several years. If you liked these comic
strips when you were young, you will
simply love having them assembled this
way and reprinted on quality paper. Most
of these volumes can be obtained for
cover price or less and many are still "in
print" at Kitchen Sink. We have listed as
many of the ISBN numbers as we could
track down in the hope that this will help
you order them through your bookstore or
comic shop. The prices listed are cover
price or current catalogue price.

Alley Oop Vol. 3 (Kitchen Sink 1995)

ALLEY OOP

Alley Oop, Vol. 1: 1946–47, by V. T. Hamlin,
   reprinting daily strips, B&W, 156pgs
   TPB (Kitchen Sink 1990) 13.95
   HC (1990) 35.00
Alley Oop, Vol. 2: 1947–48, by V. T. Hamlin,
   reprinting daily strips, B&W, 156pgs
   TPB (Kitchen Sink 1991) 13.95
   HC (1990) 35.00
Alley Oop, Vol. 3: First Trip to the Moon, by
   V. T. Hamlin, reprinting daily strips, B&W,
   244pgs, TPB (Kitchen Sink 1995) . . . 19.95
   HC (1995) 35.00
   Signed HC (1995) (250 made) 45.00

BATMAN

Batman: The Dailies reprinting the comic
   strip, B&W, TPB, DC/Kitchen Sink
   1990–91. Pete Poplaski covers.
   Vol. 1, from 1943–44, 176pgs 15.00
   Vol. 2, from 1944–45, 192pgs 12.95
   Vol. 3, from 1945–46, 176pgs 12.95
Batman: The Dailies, 1943–1946, all three
   volumes in one book, 550pgs, HC
   DC/Kitchen Sink (1992) 60.00
   Deluxe HC, signed and numbered . . 150.00
Batman: The Sunday Classics 1943–1946,
   reprinting Sunday strips, color,
   DC/Kitchen Sink 1991, 208pgs. 30.00
   Reissued, 1993:
   Softcover (0-87816-149-X) 19.95
   HC, lim. ed. (0-87816-163-5) 75.00
   Deluxe HC, signed and numbered . . 150.00

BUCK ROGERS

*The Collected Works of Buck Rogers in the
   25th Century*, ed. by Robert C. Dille,
   Dick Culkins art, written by Nowlan and

others, stories from 1929 to 1943, HC
370p (Chelsea House 1969) 75.00

*Batman: The Sunday Classics 1943–46
(Kitchen Sink 1991)*

CALVIN AND HOBBES

Calvin and Hobbes, by Bill Watterson,
   foreward by Garry Trudeau, B&W,
   TPB, Andrews & McMeel (1991) 7.95

FEARLESS FOSDICK

Fearless Fosdick, by Al Capp (from Li'l
   Abner comic strip) B&W, TPB, 128pgs,
   Kitchen Sink 1990 (0-87816-108-2) . . 11.95
Fearless Fosdick: The Hole Story, by Al
   Capp (from Li'l Abner comic strip) black
   and white, 128pgs, Kitchen Sink 1992,
   softcover (0-87816-164-3) 11.95

FLASH GORDON

Flash Gordon, reprints of the original Alex
Raymond Sunday color comic strips:
   Volume 1: *"Mongo, The Planet of Doom,"*
   from 1934–35, Kitchen Sink 1990
   Hardcover (0-87816-114-7) 34.95
   Softcover 19.95
   Volume 2: *"Three Against Ming,"* from
   1935–37, Kitchen Sink 1991
   Hardcover (0-87816-120-1) 34.95
   Softcover (0-87816-139-2) 19.95
   Volume 3: *"The Tides of Battle,"* from
   1937–39, Kitchen Sink 1992
   Hardcover (0-87816-161-9) 34.95

Flash Gordon #1 (Kitchen Sink 1990)

Softcover (0-87816-162-7) 21.95
Volume 4: *"The Fall of Ming,"* from
1939–41, Kitchen Sink 1993
Hardcover (0-87816-167-8) 34.95
Softcover (0-87816-168-6) 21.95
Volume 5: *"Between Worlds at War,"*
from 1941–43, Kitchen Sink 1993
Hardcover (0-87816-176-7) 34.95
Softcover (0-87816-177-5) 21.95
Volume 6: *"Triumph in Tropica"* from
1943–44, Kitchen Sink 1994, 96pgs.
Hardcover (0-87816-198-8) 34.95
Softcover (0-87816-199-6) 21.95
Flash Gordon, reprints of the original Austin
Briggs daily black-and-white comic strips:
The Dailies, Volume 1, strips from
1940–42, Kitchen Sink 1993, 96pgs.
Softcover (0-87816-172-4) 10.95
The Dailies, Volume 2, strips from
1941, Kitchen Sink 1993, 108pgs.
Softcover (0-87816-187-2) 10.95
Flash Gordon, The Daily Strip, 1951,
reprinting the original strips from
1951–53 by Dan Barry, Harvey

Kurtzman and Frank Frazetta, black
and white, 136pgs, Kitchen Sink 1988
Hardcover, signed 25.00
Also Trade Paperback (1988) 12.00
Reprint 1991 (0-87816-134-5) 10.00
                    KRAZY KAT
Komplete Kolor Krazy Kat, reprinting Sunday
color comic strips from 1935–36 by
George Herriman, 94pgs., HC, Kitchen
Sink 1991 (0-924359-06-4) 34.95
Komplete Kolor Krazy Kat, Vol. 2, reprinting
Sunday color comic strips from
1936–37 by George Herriman, 94pgs.
HC, Kitchen Sink 1991 . . . . 34.95
Krazy & Ignatz: The Komplete Kat Comics,
reprinting George Herriman's Sunday
comic strips, TPB, 64pg (Eclipse 1990?)
Vol. 1 1916 . . . . 9.95
Vol. 2 1917 . . . . 9.95
Vol. 3 1918 . . . . 9.95
Vol. 4 1919 . . . . 9.95
Vol. 5 1920 . . . . 9.95
Vol. 6 1921 . . . . 9.95

All prices listed are for *Near Mint* condition.   **311**

Li'l Abner, Vol. 21 (Kitchen Sink 1995)

LI'L ABNER

Li'l Abner reprints the classic comic strips by
Al Capp, Kitchen Sink 1988–93.

Vol. 1. 1934–35 HC (0-87816-036-1) 27.95
Vol. 1. 1934–35 Softcover (0-87816-037-X) 16.95
Vol. 2. 1936 HC (0-87816-040-0) 27.95
Vol. 2. 1936 Softcover (0-87816-041-8) . . . 16.95
Vol. 3. 1937 HC (0-87816-042-6) 27.95
Vol. 3. 1937 Softcover (0-87816-043-4) . . . 16.95
Vol. 4. 1938 HC (0-87816-051-5) 27.95
Vol. 4. 1938 Softcover (0-87816-052-3) . . . 16.95
Vol. 5. 1939 HC (0-87816-056-6) 27.95
Vol. 5. 1939 Softcover (0-87816-057-4) . . . 16.95
Vol. 6. 1940 HC (0-87816-058-2) 27.95
Vol. 6. 1940 Softcover (0-87816-059-0) . . . 16.95
Vol. 7. 1941 HC (0-87816-064-7) 27.95
Vol. 7. 1941 Softcover (0-87816-065-5) . . . 16.95
Vol. 8. 1942 HC (0-87816-068-X) 29.95
Vol. 8. 1942 Softcover (0-87816-069-8) . . . 16.95
Vol. 9. 1943 HC (0-87816-073-6) 29.95
Vol. 9. 1943 Softcover (0-87816-074-4) . . . 16.95
Vol. 10. 1944 HC (0-87816-078-7) 29.95
Vol. 10. 1944 Softcover (0-87816-079-5) . . 18.95
Vol. 11. 1945 HC (0-87816-082-5) 29.95
Vol. 11. 1945 Softcover (0-87816-083-3) . . 18.95
Vol. 12. 1946 HC (0-87816-091-4) 29.95
Vol. 12. 1946 Softcover (0-87816-092-2) . . 18.95
Vol. 13. 1947 HC (0-87816-098-1) 29.95
Vol. 13. 1947 Softcover (0-87816-099-X) . . 18.95
Vol. 14. 1948 HC (0-87816-115-5) 29.95
Vol. 14. 1948 Softcover (0-87816-116-3) . . 18.95
Vol. 15. 1949 HC (0-87816-126-0) 34.95
Vol. 15. 1949 Softcover (0-87816-127-9) . . 18.95
Vol. 16. 1950 HC (0-87816-143-0) 34.95
Vol. 16. 1950 Softcover (0-87816-144-9) . . 18.95
Vol. 17. 1951 HC (0-87816-209-7) 34.95
Vol. 17. 1951 Softcover (0-87816-210-0) . . 18.95

Vol. 18. 1952 HC 34.95
Vol. 18. 1952 Softcover 18.95
Vol. 19. 1953 HC 34.95
Vol. 19. 1953 Softcover 18.95
Vol. 20. 1954 HC (with Frank Frazetta) . . . 34.95
Vol. 20. 1954 Softcover 18.95
Vol. 21. 1955 HC (with Frank Frazetta) . . . 34.95
Vol. 21. 1955 Softcover (0-87816-262-3) . . 18.95

LIFE IN HELL

Binky's Guide to Love, Harper Collins
#095078, 1994, Matt Groening art,
B&W 11"x11", 128p 16.00

ERNIE BUSHMILLER'S NANCY

Nancy Eats Food

Nancy Eats Food (Kitchen Sink 1991)

NANCY

Nancy Eats Food, reprints Ernie Bushmiller's
strips, Kitchen Sink 1991, B&W, 96pgs. 7.95
Nancy's Dreams and Schemes, reprints
Ernie Bushmiller's strips, Kitchen Sink
1991, B&W, 98pgs. 7.95
*Nancy: Bums, Beatniks & Hippies/Artists &
Con Artists*, reprints Ernie Bushmiller's
strips, Kitchen Sink 1991, B&W, 96pgs. 9.95

POPEYE

The Complete Segar Popeye, reprinting 2 year's
worth of E. C. Segar's Thimble Theater
strips, TPB, B&W (Fantagraphics 1988?)
Vol. 1 thru Vol. 11, each 14.95

PRINCE VALIANT

Prince Valiant, Volume 1, Fantagraphics
Books 1990, 48p, reprints Hal Foster
comic strips from 1937 . . . . 14.95

Prince Valiant: The Singing Sword, Volume
2, Fantagraphics Books 1991, 48p,
reprints Hal Foster comic strips from
1938 . . . . 14.95
Prince Valiant: Knights of the Round Table,
Volume 3, Fantagraphics Books 1991,
48p, reprints Hal Foster Sunday comic
strips from 1938–39 . . . . 14.95
Prince Valiant: Menace of the Hun, Volume
4, Fantagraphics Books 1991, 48p,
reprints Hal Foster comic strips from
1940–41 . . . . 14.95
Prince Valiant: The Sea King, Volume 5,
Fantagraphics Books 1991, 48p,
reprints Hal Foster comic strips from
1941–42? 14.95
Prince Valiant: Journey to Africa, Volume 6,
Fantagraphics Books 1991, 48p,
reprints Hal Foster comic strips from
1941–42 . . . . 14.95
Prince Valiant: The Roman Wall, Volume 7,
Fantagraphics Books 1991, 48p,
reprints Hal Foster sunday color comic
strips from 1942–43? 14.95
Prince Valiant: Prince of Thule, Volume 8,
Fantagraphics Books 1991, 48p,
reprints Hal Foster comic strips from
1943–44 . . . . 14.95
Prince Valiant: Journey to the Misty Isles,
Volume 9, Fantagraphics Books 1991,
48p, reprints Hal Foster comic strips
from 1944 . . . . 14.95
Prince Valiant: Aleta, Volume 10,
Fantagraphics Books 1991, 48p,
reprints Hal Foster color comic strips
from 1945? 14.95
Prince Valiant: Intrigues at Camelot, Volume
11, Fantagraphics Books 1991, 48p,
reprints Hal Foster comic strips from
1946 . . . . 14.95
Prince Valiant: Volume 12, Fantagraphics
Books 1991, 48p, reprints Hal Foster
comic strips from 1947? 14.95
Prince Valiant: Volume 13, Fantagraphics
Books 1992?, 48p, reprints Hal Foster
comic strips from 1948? 14.95
Prince Valiant: Volume 14, Fantagraphics
Books 1992?, 48p, reprints Hal Foster
comic strips from 1949? 14.95
Prince Valiant: Volume 15, Fantagraphics
Books 1993?, 48p, reprints Hal Foster
comic strips from 1950? 14.95

Prince Valiant: Love and War, Volume 16,
Fantagraphics Books 1994, 48p,
reprints Hal Foster comic strips from
1950–51 . . . . 16.95
Prince Valiant: Return from Rome, Volume
17, Fantagraphics Books 1994, 48p,
reprints Hal Foster comic strips from
1951 . . . . 16.95
Prince Valiant: Prisoner of the Khan, Volume
21, Fantagraphics Books 1994, 48p,
reprints Hal Foster comic strips to June
1955 . . . . 16.95
Prince Valiant: Homeward Bound, Volume
22, Fantagraphics Books 1994, 48p,
reprints Hal Foster comic strips from
June 1955 to May 1956 . . . . 16.95

Secret Agent X-9 (Kitchen Sink 1990)

SECRET AGENT X–9
Secret Agent X–9, by Dashiell Hammett and
Alex Raymond, Kitchen Sink 1990,
reprints strips from the 1930s, TPB . . 20.00

TARZAN
*Obviously there are earlier volumes in this
series, but unfortunately we don't have any
information on them.*
Tarzan, Vol. 6 (1936–37), NBM 1994, 64p,
reprints Hal Foster/Burne Hogarth art
from comic strips 35.00
Tarzan, Vol. 8 (1938–39), NBM 1994, 64p,
reprints Burne Hogarth art from comic
strips 35.00
Also: Lim. Ed. (300 made) 60.00
Tarzan, Vol. 9 (1939–40), NBM 1994, 64p,
reprints Burne Hogarth art from comic
strips 35.00
Also: Lim. Ed. (300 made) 60.00

TERRY AND THE PIRATES
The Complete Color Terry and The Pirates,
Vol. 1, reprints the daily and Sunday

strips by Milton Caniff from 1934–35,
96pgs., Kitchen Sink 1990 (0-924359-
19-6) HC 34.95
The Complete Color Terry and The Pirates,
Vol. 2, reprints the daily and Sunday
strips by Milton Caniff from 1935–36,
96pgs., Kitchen Sink 1991, HC 34.95

REFERENCE BOOKS

*Comics Values Annual, 1995 Edition
(Wallace-Homestead Books 1994)*

Adventures of Superman Collecting, HC,
Russ Cochran (1991) 200.00
Archie: His First Fifty Years, by Charles
Phillips, Abbeville Press 55859-206-7
(1992) 30.00
Collector's Guide to Comic Books, by John
Hegenberger, Wallace-Homestead
Books (1990) 15.00
Comic Book Artists, edited by Alex G. Malloy
with Brian Kelly & Kevin Ohlandt, TPB,
Wallace-Homestead Books (1993) ... 15.00
Comic Book Heroes, Carol (1994), trivia

questions, TPB, 256p 10.00
*The Comic Book in America: An Illustrated
History*, by Mike Benton, hardcover,
Taylor (1989) 30.00
Comics Values Annual, by Alex G. Malloy,
edited by John Laub, TPB, Wallace-
Homestead Books (1992) 20.00
Comics Values Annual 1993–94, by Alex G.
Malloy, edited by John Laub, TPB,
Wallace-Homestead Books (1993) ... 15.00
Comics Values Annual 1995 Edition, by Alex
G. Malloy, edited by John Laub, TPB,
Wallace-Homestead Books (1994) ... 13.00
Comics—Anatomy of a Mass Medium, by
Reitburger-Fuchs (1971) 35.00
The Encyclopedia of American Comics, by
Ron Goulart, Facts on File (1990) ... 35.00
The Encyclopedia of Super-Heroes, by Jeff
Rovin, 464 pgs, Facts on File 1990) . 19.95
The Encyclopedia of Super-Villains, by Jeff
Rovin, 416 pgs, Facts on File 1990) .. 19.95
50 Years of American Comic Books, by Ron
Goulart, Mallard Press (1991) 25.00
*From Aargh! to Zap!, Harvey Kurtzman's
Visual History of the Comics*, Kitchen
Sink (1991) 25.00
The Great Comic Book Artists, by Ron
Goulart, St. Martins Press (1986) 25.00
The Great Comic Book Heroes, by Feiffer
(1965) 50.00
Illustrated History of Horror Comics, by Mike
Benton, Taylor Publishing (1991) 25.00
*Marvel: Five Fabulous Decades of the
World's Greatest Comics*, by Les
Daniels, HC, 8109-3821-9, color
Abrams (1991) 45.00
*Masters of Imagination: The Comic Book
Artists Hall of Fame*, by Mike Benton,
Taylor (1994) 250 color illus., 184p .. 29.95
*Men of Steel: The Adventures of Superman
on Film*, TPB Cinemaker Press (1994) 15.00
*The Overstreet Comic Book Price Guide,
25th Edition*, by Robert Overstreet
Avon Books (1995) 10.00
Original Comic Art, by Jerry Weist, Avon
Books (1992) 20.00
The Superhero Women, by Stan Lee,
Marvel (1977) 15.00
The World Encyclopedia of Comics, by
Maurice Horn, Chelsea House (1976) . 25.00

MAGAZINES

AMAZING HEROES

1 Fantastic Four, Dial H for Hero 10.00
2 Teen Titans 5.00
3 Justice Society 4.00
4 Daredevil 3.00
5 Ka-Zar, Steve Ditko's Spidey 3.00
6 Doom Patrol 3.00
7 Gil Kane on Micronauts 2.00
8 Thunder Agents 2.00
9 Capt. Carrot 2.00
10 Metal Men, Swamp Thing 2.00
11 Horror Issue, Night Force 3.00
12 X-Men, Paul Smith 5.00
13 Star Wars (reissued 1992) 5.00
14 Camelot 3000 . . . . 2.00
15 Keith Giffen 2.00
16 New Mutants 3.00
17 Supergirl, Wolverine 2.00
18 Nexus 2.00
19 E-Man 2.00
20 Hembeck, Amethyst 2.00
21 Coyote 3.00
22 Alpha Flight 3.00
23 Crystar 2.00
24 DNAgents, Daredevil 2.00
25 Ronin, Frank Miller cover 2.00
26 Gray Morrow, Ron Goulart 2.00
27 Batman, Mike Barr 3.00
28 Gil Kane, Sword of the Atom 2.00
29 American Flagg 2.00
30 Thriller, J'onn J'onzz 2.00
31 Tom Sutton 2.00
32 Somerset Holmes 2.00
33 Mars 2.00
34 Redeemer 2.00
35 Dan Jurgens 2.00
36 DC 3.00
37 Nova, Dave Stevens 3.00
38 Wendy Pini 3.00
39 1984 Preview 2.00
40 Ironman, Sun-Runners 2.00
41 . . . . 2.00
42 Josh Quagmire 2.00
43 Warlock 2.00
44 Alien Legion 2.00
45 Hannigan 2.00
46 Legend of Super Heroes 2.00
47 Kirby's New Gods 2.00
48 Mr. X 2.00

49 Dalgoda 2.00
50 George Perez, Marv Wolfman 2.00
51 Golden 2.00
52 Judge Dredd 3.00
53 Elementals 2.00
54 X-Men 4.00
55 B. Sienkiewicz 2.00
56 Super-heroines, Kevin Nowlan 2.00
57 Starstruck 2.00
58 Badger, Nexus 2.00
59 Secret Wars, Mike Zeck 2.00
60 Mantlo 2.00
61 Groo 2.00
62 1985 Preview 2.00
63 Masked Man 2.00
64 Moon Knight 2.00
65 Black Dragon 2.00
66 Perez, Crisis on Infinite Earths 2.00
67 Jim Shooter, Secret Wars II 2.00
68 Ambush Bug 2.00
69 Elektra, Dark Knight 2.00
70 Squadron Supreme 2.00
71 . . . . 2.00
72 Vision, Scarlet Witch 2.00
73 Eternals 2.00
74 Futurians 2.00
75 Chris Claremont 2.00
76 Hulk/Alpha Flight 3.00
77 Mr. Monster 2.00
78 New Outsiders, Denis Kitchen 2.00
79 DC Challenge 3.00
80 Blood of Innocents 2.00
81 Scout 2.00
82 Mutants, SunRunners 2.00
83 X-Factor 3.00
84 Batman history 3.00
85 Miracleman 2.00
86 Hawkmoon 2.00
87 Electric Warrior 2.00
88 Shadow 2.00
89 Threat 2.00
90 Bruce Jones 2.00
91 Post Crisis issue 2.00
92 Normal Man 2.00
93 Demon 2.00
94 Unicorn Isle 2.00
95 Johnny Quest 2.00
96 . . . . 2.00
97 Invaders 2.00
98 Jim Starlin 2.00
99 Elektra 2.00
100 Jack Kirby tribute 2.00

All prices listed are for *Near Mint* condition.   **315**

101 New Universe 2.00
102 .... 2.00
103 William Messner-Loebs 2.00
104 Dynamo Joe 2.00
105 Evanier 2.00
106 Wonder Woman 2.00
107 Teenage Mutant Ninja Turtles 2.00
108 The Atom 2.00
109 Zot!, Scott McCloud 2.00
110 Fallen Angels 2.00
111 Ty Templeton 2.00
112 Concrete 2.00
113 Justice Machine 2.00
114 Punisher 2.00
115 Swim Suit 3.00
116 Justice League International 2.00
117 Dark Horse, Captain Eo 3.00
118 Manga 2.00
119 Superman, Max Collins 2.00
120 Green Arrow 2.00
121 Metamorpho, Alien Fire 2.00
122 X-Men's Rogue 3.00
123 Joker, Frank Thorne 3.00
124 Blackthorne 2.00
125 Cirocco 2.00
126 Millennium, Charles Vess 2.00
127 Starblaze 2.00
128 Mike Baron 2.00
129 Funny Animals 2.00
130 Shadow Line 2.00
131 Comico's 5th Anniversary 2.00
132 American Flagg, Blackhawk 2.00
133 Concrete 5.00
134 Excalibur 3.00
135 Superman 2.00
136 Superman 3.00
137 Flash Gordon 2.00
138 Swimsuit Issue, Neal Adams 3.00
139 Aliens 2.00
140 Wolverine, Marvel Universe 3.00
141 Women Creators 2.00
142 Eclipse 10th Anniversary 2.00
143 Gays in comics, pt.I 2.00
144 Gays in comics, pt.II 2.00
145 D. Stevens 2.00
146 Captain America 2.00
147 Megaton Man 2.00
148 Suburban Nightmare 2.00
149 GrimJack 2.00
150 Elfquest 10th Anniversary 2.00
151 Stray Toasters 2.00
152 Black Orchid 2.00

Amazing Heroes #174
(Fantagraphics Books 1989)

153 Now Comics 2.00
154 Maze Agency 2.00
155 Klaus Janson 2.00
156 George Perez 2.00
157 1989 Preview, giant size 4.00
158 3-D Issue 2.00
159 Paul Gulacy 2.00
160 International issue 2.00
161 Hero Hotline 2.00
162 Roachmill, Power of the Atom 2.00
163 The Question 2.00
164 1989 Swimsuit issue 2.00
165 Japanese Comics 2.00
166 S.H.I.E.L.D. 2.00
167 Batman, Bob Kane 3.00
168 Jim Lee 2.00
169 Xenozoic Tales 2.00
170 Summer '89 .... 2.00
171 Teenage Mutant Ninja Turtles 2.00
172 Legion 2.00
173 Dave Gibbons 2.00
174 Clive Barker 2.00
175 Peter David 2.00
176 Grant Morrison 2.00

177 Gil Kane 3.00
178 Batman & Wolverine 3.00
179 Todd McFarlane 3.00
180 Hawkworld 3.00
181 Star Trek 4.00
182 Marshal Law 3.00
183 King Kong 3.00
184 Avengers 3.00
185 Sandman, Neil Gaiman 4.00
186 Deathlok 4.00
187 Stan Sakai, Usagi Yojimbo 4.00
188 Barry Windsor-Smith 4.00
189 Indiana Jones 4.00
190 Doom Patrol, Adam Hughes 4.00
191 10th Anniversary 5.00
192 X-Men 5.00
193 Excalibur, Alan Davis 4.00
194 Tundra comics 4.00
195 Ghost Rider 4.00
196 Batman versus Predator 4.00
197 Wonder Woman 4.00
198 The Incredible Hulk 4.00
199 Valiant comics 4.00
200 All Comics issue 4.00
201 Dave Sim, Cerebus 4.00
202 New Company, Wraparound cover . . . 4.00
203/204 Batman/Green Lantern/Lobo
    flip cover: Concrete, P. Chadwick,
    final issue (1992) 6.00

BEST OF AMAZING HEROES
1 . . . . 4.00

SWIMSUIT SPECIALS
Swimsuit '90 . . . . 12.00
Swimsuit '91 . . . . 11.00
Swimsuit Special '92, Red Sonja cover . . 10.00
Swimsuit #4, with 2 cards (1993) 7.50
Summer Swimsuit #5 with cards (1994) . . . 5.00
Summer Swimsuit #6 (1995) 5.00

AMAZING HEROES 1993
1 Siege of Darkness 5.00
2 Intergalactic War 5.00

AMAZING HEROES INTERVIEWS
Friendly Comics (1993)
1 Walter Koenig interview and card 5.00
2 Scavengers cover and card 5.00
3 Chromium Man cover and card 5.00
4 DeForest Kelley interview and card 5.00
5 thru 8 48 pages, weekly, each 3.00
9 96 pages, monthly 5.00
10 still monthly 3.00

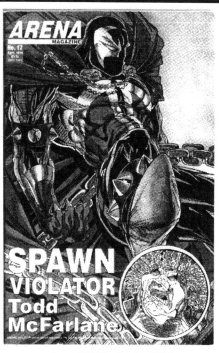

Arena #17 (Sky Comics 1994)

[COMICS] ARENA
1 Punisher, George Perez poster 4.00
2 Superman/Justice League,
    Continuity poster 3.00
3 Hulk and Superman, Sky Comics Poster . 3.00

ARENA
Sky Comics (1992)
4 Eclipso/Batman 3.00
5 Tribe 3.00
6 Val Semeiks 3.00
7 Lurene Haines 3.00
8 Wildstar (Wildstar card, Image postcard) . 3.00
9 Wolverine (Tribe #1 card) 3.00
10 Aliens (Dave Dorman) (Tribe #2 card) . . 3.00
11 Next Men, flip cover: Solution (Next
    Men card) 3.00
12 Shaft and Bloodshot (Trencher card) . . 3.00
13 Spider-Man and Venom (Evil Ernie card) 3.00
14 . . . . 3.00
15 Freak Force (Parts Unknown card) 3.00
16 Frank Miller (Rune card) 3.00
17 Spawn 3.00
18 Art Thibert's Black and White
    (Deathgrip card) 3.50
Arena Yearbook '92, Wolverine + card 5.00

Combo #1 (1995)

Comic Book Collector #19 (Century 1994)

COMBO

1 Todd McFarlane (with 2 cards)	3.50
2 thru 5, each	3.00

COMIC BOOK COLLECTOR
Century Publishing Company

1 January 1993	3.00
2 Spawn	3.00
3 Valiant	2.00
4 Golden Age Collecting	2.00
5 Jim Shooter Interview	2.00
6	2.00
7	2.00
8 Freex (Nightman card)	2.00
9	2.00
10 Zen	2.00
11	2.00
12 (A.R.Comics card)	2.00
13 (Zen Intergalactic Ninja card)	2.00
14	2.00
15 (Press Pass's Nelson card)	2.00
16 John Byrne interview	2.00
17 Dan Jurgens interview	2.00
18 Image	2.00
19 Rob Liefeld	2.00
20	2.00
21 Dark Horse	2.00
22 S. Platt	2.00
23	2.00
24 Last Issue, B. Sears	2.00

THE BUYER'S GUIDE
FOR COMIC FANDOM

1 (Founded by Allen Light in 1971)	50.00
2 through 10, each	25.00
11 through 100, each	10.00
101 through 482 (Last Light issue)	5.00

Becomes

COMIC BUYER'S GUIDE
Krause Publications

484 through 499, each	2.00
500	3.00
501 through 599, each	1.50
600	2.00
601 through 699, each	1.00
700	2.00
701 through 749, each	1.00
750 (new cover price $1.95, 4-1-88)	2.00
751 through 799, each	1.00
800	3.00
801 through 899, each (cover price $2.25)	1.00
900	3.00
901 through 999, each	1.00
1000 Jim Lee cover	5.00

Comics Buyer's Guide (Krause)

Comics Collector #10 (Krause 1986)

1001 through 1099, each (cover price $2.50) 1.00
1100 .... 2.00
1101 and subsequent 1.00

COMIC CULTURE
1 thru 12 Newspaper format (1994), each . 1.00
Vol. 2-1 to 2-3 Magazine format, each 2.00

COMIC FANDOM FORUM
1 thru 10, each .... .50

COMIC NEWS
1 and 2, each 1.00

COMICS COLLECTOR
Krause Publications
1 Superman 10.00
2 X-Men 5.00
3 Teen Titans 5.00
4 Thor 5.00
5 .... 5.00
6 New Teen Titans 5.00
7 .... 5.00
8 .... 5.00
9 .... 5.00
10 X-Factor 5.00

COMICS FEATURE
1 Legion of Superheroes (1980) 5.00
2 Iron Man 3.00
3 Micronauts 3.00
4 X-Men 3.00
5 Fantom Zone 3.00
6 Terry and the Pirates 3.00
7 Dazzler 3.00
8 .... 3.00
9 Annie 3.00
10 to 14, each 3.00
15 Legion 2.00
16 Powerman and Iron Fist 2.00
17 Fantastic Four 2.00
18 Year Review 2.00
19 Wally Wood 2.00
20 thru 39, each 2.00
40 Spider-Man 2.00

COMICS INTERVIEW
1 Omega Men 5.00
2 Ronin 5.00
3 New Teen Titans 5.00
4 Warlock 5.00
5 Elfquest 5.00
6 Justice League America 5.00
7 D'Arc Tangent 4.00
8 Nexus 5.00

All prices listed are for *Near Mint* condition.

9 Walt Simonson 5.00
10 Star Wars 5.00
11 X-Men 7.00
12 Teen Titans 5.00
13 Conan 5.00
14 Secret Wars 5.00
15 Grimjack 5.00
16 Legion of Superheroes 5.00
17 Elementals 5.00
18 Captain Marvel 5.00
19 Judge Dredd 5.00
20 Ambush Bug 4.00
21 Shatter 5.00
22 Fred Hembeck 5.00
23 Robotech 5.00
24 Sal Buscema 5.00
25 John Byrne 5.00
26 Crisis 5.00
27 Teenage Mutant Ninja Turtles 5.00
28 X-Factor 5.00
29 Elric 5.00
30 Spider-Man 5.00
31 Dark Knight 5.00
32 Swamp Thing 5.00
33 Alan Weiss 4.00
34 Elektra 5.00
35 Southern Knights 5.00
36 New Universe 4.00
37 G.I. Joe 5.00
38 Howard the Duck 4.00
39 X-Factor 5.00
40 Flaming Carrot 5.00
41 Jack Kirby 5.00
42 Frazetta 5.00
43 Sex and Violence 5.00
44 Party 4.00
45 Moebius 5.00
46 X-Men 5.00
47 Peanuts 5.00
48 Watchmen 5.00
49 Micra 4.00
50 Perez 5.00
51 Grendel 5.00
52 Lone Wolf 5.00
53 The 'Nam 5.00
54 New Universe 4.00
55 Southern Knights 5.00
56 Excalibur 5.00
57 Airboy 5.00
58 X-Men 5.00
59 "Omaha" 5.00
60 Elfquest 5.00

Comics Interview #139 (1994)

61 Concrete 5.00
62 Wolverine 5.00
63 Punisher 5.00
64 Silver Surfer 5.00
65 Watchman 5.00
66 Justice League 5.00
67 Conan 5.00
68 Aliens 5.00
69 007 .... 5.00
70 Batman 5.00
71 John Byrne 5.00
72 Punisher 5.00
73 Beauty and the Beast 5.00
74 Joker 5.00
75 Flagg 5.00
76 New X-Men 5.00
77 Batman 5.00
78 Nexus 5.00
79 Teenage Mutant Ninja Turtles 5.00
80 Dark Knight 5.00
81 Spider-Man 5.00
82 Robocop 5.00
83 Grendel 5.00
84 Aliens and Wolverine 5.00
85 Spider-Man 5.00
86 John Byrne 5.00

All prices listed are for *Near Mint* condition.

Comics Interview #140 (1994)

87 Aliens versus Predator	....	5.00
88 Flash	....	5.00
89 Rocketeer	....	5.00
90 Love and Money	....	5.00
91 Neal Adams	....	5.00
92 Ghost Rider	....	5.00
93 Robin	....	5.00
94 Infinity Gauntlet	....	5.00
95 Teenage Mutant Ninja Turtles	....	5.00
96 X-Force	....	5.00
97 Rocketeer	....	5.00
98 X-Men	....	5.00
99 Lobo	....	5.00
100 100 most powerful people in comics	..	5.00
101 Batman versus Dredd	....	5.00
102 John Byrne	....	5.00
103 Sandman	....	5.00
104 Wolverine	....	5.00
105 X-Factor	....	5.00
106 Aliens	....	5.00
107 Cerebus	....	5.00
108 Maus	....	4.00
109 Tarzan	....	4.00
110 Star Trek	....	5.00
111 Robocop versus Terminator	....	5.00
112 X-Men on TV	....	5.00

113 Frank Miller	....	5.00
114 Shadow of the Bat (Stelfreeze)	......	5.00
115 Topps: Dracula	....	4.00
116 Death	....	5.00
117 Batman versus Lobo	....	5.00
118 Deep Space Nine	....	5.00
119 Image	....	5.00
120 Death of Superman	....	5.00
121 Jack Kirby	....	5.00
122 Ren and Stimpy	....	5.00
123 X-Men 2099	....	5.00
124 Deathmate	....	5.00
125 Batman	....	5.00
126 Star Trek	....	5.00
127 Clive Barker	....	5.00
128 Judge Dredd	....	5.00
129 Bat versus Spawn	....	5.00
130 Star Wars	....	5.00
131 Ren and Stimpy	....	5.00
132 Lois and Clark	....	5.00
133 to 140, each	....	5.00
Superman Super Special: The Many Lives		
of Superman (1993)	....	7.50
X-Men X-Tra Super Special (1993)	......	6.00
Cerebus special	....	6.00
Sandman Super Special	....	6.00

THE COMICS JOURNAL

1	....	4.00
2 thru 36, each	....	3.00
37	....	3.00
38 Gil Kane	....	3.00
39 Joe Staton	....	3.00
40 Jim Shooter	....	3.00
41 to 44, each	....	3.00
45 E-Man	....	3.00
46 Will Eisner	....	3.00
47 Will Eisner	....	3.00
48 Len Wein	....	3.00
49 Heavy Metal	....	3.00
50	....	3.00
51 Frank Brunner	....	3.00
52 Plasticman	....	3.00
53 Harlan Ellison	....	3.00
54 to 57, each	....	3.00
58 Writing Comics	....	3.00
59 Heavy Metal	....	3.00
60 Jim Shooter	....	3.00
61 Roy Thomas	....	3.00
62 D. Giordano	....	3.00
63	....	3.00
64 Gil Kane	....	3.00

All prices listed are for *Near Mint* condition.

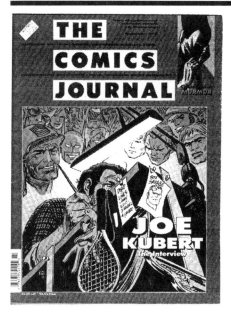

The Comics Journal #173 (1994)

65 Jack Kirby		3.00
66 D. O'Neil		3.00
67		3.00
68 F. Miller		3.00
69		3.00
70		3.00
71 Popeye versus Hulk		3.00
72 Neal Adams		3.00
73 Carl Barks		3.00
74 X-Men		3.50
75 J. Strand		3.00
76		3.00
77 Gil Kane		3.00
78 Censorship		3.00
79		3.00
80 Marv Wolfman		3.00
81		3.00
82 D. Sim		3.00
83 D. Sim		3.00
84 Harlan Ellison		3.00
85		3.00
86 Love and Rockets		3.00
87 D. Rosa		3.00
88 Jim Shooter		3.00
89 Will Eisner		3.00
90 A. Williamson		3.50
91 Convention		4.00
92		3.50
93		3.50

94 International		3.50
95 C. C. Beck		3.50
96 H. Nostrand		3.50
97 H. Pekar		3.50
98 A. Toth		3.50
99 X-Men		4.00
100 Giant size		6.00
101 Frank Miller		4.00
102 H. Foster		5.00
103 Mike Kaluta		3.50
104 Savage Tales		3.50
105 Jack Kirby		4.00
106 Wierdo		5.00
107 Bill Sienkiewicz		5.00
108 M. Caniff		3.50
109 Howard Chaykin		3.50
110 Jack Kirby		3.50
111 D. Day		3.50
112		3.50
113 R. Crumb		4.00
114 D. Knight		4.00
115 Harlan Ellison		4.00
116 Watchman		4.00
117		4.00
118 Moebius		4.00
119 Political Cartoonists		5.00
120 F. Gottfredson		5.00
121 R. Crumb		5.00
122 British Comics		5.00
123 K. Deitch		4.00
124 Jules Feiffer		4.00
125 Will Eisner		4.00
126 B. Breathod		4.00
127 B. Watterson		4.00
128 Sergio Aragones		4.00
129 Christin-Bilal		5.00
130 Cerebus		4.00
131 G. Groth		4.00
132 P. Chadwick		5.00
133 Nude cover		6.00
134 Violence		4.00
135 Mummy Fur		4.00
136 Vietnam		4.00
137 S. McCloud		4.00
138 Serjio Aragones		4.00
139 Alan Moore		4.00
140 Walt Kelly		4.00
141 Matt Groening		4.00
142 A. Roth		4.00
143		4.50
144 J. Jackson		4.50
145 Eddie Campbell		4.50
146 Will Eisner		4.50

147 P. Craig Russell 4.50
148 Charles Burns 4.50
149 Dan Clowes 4.50
150 Xenozoic Tales 4.50
151 Carl Barks 4.50
152 Todd McFarlane 4.50
153 Harvey Kurtzman 4.50
    2nd printing 2.50
154 Dan Clowes 4.50
155 Neil Gaiman and Dave McKean 4.50
156 Gahan Wilson 4.50
157 Underground Comics (H. Kurtzman) . . 4.50
158 R. Crumb 4.50
159 . . . . 4.50
160 Black comics artists 4.50
161 Robert Williams 4.50
162 Autobiographical Comics Artists 4.50
163 Vertigo 4.50
164 Jim Woodring 4.50
165 Matt Wagner 4.50
166 Burne Hogarth 4.50
167 Paul Mavrides 4.50
168 Elfquest 4.50
169 Neil Gaiman 4.50
170 . . . . 4.50
171 . . . . 4.50
172 J. Kubert 4.50
173 Joe Kubert Interview 4.00

COMICS SCENE
Starlog (1981-83)
1 Stan Lee, Jim Shooter 7.50
2 Jack Kirby 5.00
3 Byrne Hogarth 4.00
4 thru 11, each 3.00
One shot (1988) 4.00

COMICS SCENE
Starlog (1988–95)
1 Chaykin, Claremont 10.00
2 Chaykin, Claremont 4.00
3 Simonson 4.00
4 Alan Moore 4.00
5 John Byrne 4.00
6 Frank Miller, Mike Grell 5.00
7 Bernie Wrightson 10.00
8 Wendy Pini 15.00
9 Michael Keaton 3.00
10 Arnold Schwarzenegger 3.00
11 B. Sienkiewicz 3.00
12 Sienkiewicz, Byrne 3.00

Comics Scene #33 (Starlog 1993)

13 Mike Barr 3.00
14 Gray Morrow 3.00
15 Dave Gibbons 3.00
16 Harvey Kurtzman 3.00
17 Frank Miller 3.00
18 Dave Stevens 3.00
19 Jim Starlin 4.00
20 Jim Shooter 4.00
21 Jim Lee 4.00
22 Wilce Portacio 3.00
23 Addams Family 3.00
24 Bob Layton 5.00
25 Youngblood 3.00
26 Justice League 3.00
27 Todd McFarlane 3.00
28 Batman Returns 3.00
29 Batman: The Animated Series 5.00
30 Jim Lee 3.00
31 Wildstar 5.00
32 John Romita 3.00
33 Magnus Robot Fighter 3.00
34 Superman 3.00
35 X-Men 3.00
36 Clive Barker 3.00
37 Chris Claremont 3.00
38 X-Men 2099 . . . . 3.00
39 Lois and Clark 3.00

All prices listed are for *Near Mint* condition.   **323**

40 Batman: Mask of the Phantasm 3.00
41 .... 3.00
42 The Critic 3.00
43 .... 3.00
44 Flash Gordon comics 3.00
45 Mask 3.00
46 .... 3.00
47 Generation X 3.00
48 Spider-Man 3.00
49 Marvel movies 3.00
50 Tank Girl 3.00
Yearbook #1 Batman Returns (1992) 5.00
Yearbook #2 Doc Savage (1993) 5.00
Yearbook #3 Batman/Punisher/Archie (1994) 4.00

Comics Spectacular #5 (Starlog 1991)

COMICS SPECTACULAR
1 Batman 4.00
2 Simpsons 3.00
3 Teenage Mutant Ninja Turtles 3.00
4 Flash 3.00
5 Judge Dredd 4.00
6 Stan Lee 3.00

COMICS SCOREBOARD
1 .... 2.00
2 to 9, each 1.75
10 to 75, each 1.50

COMICS SOURCE
American Collectors Exchange (1993)
1 Published by former Overstreet editor ... 5.00
2 thru 17, each 1.50

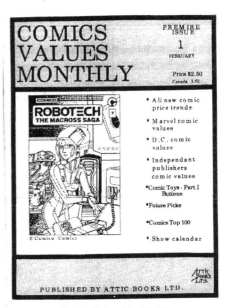

Comics Values Monthly #1
(Attic Books 1986)

COMICS VALUES MONTHLY
1 Robotech 10.00
2 Thundercats 5.00
3 Fish Police 3.00
4 G.I. Joe 3.00
5 Albedo 3.00
6 Man of Steel 3.00
7 Red Fox 3.00
8 Star Brand 3.00
9 Boris the Bear 3.00
10 Dragonring 3.00
11 Star Trek 5.00
12 Gobbledygook 3.00
13 The 'Nam 3.00
14 The Survivors 3.00
15 Justice League 3.00
16 Concrete 3.00
17 Captain America 3.00
18 Justice League 3.00
19 Groo 3.00
20 Donald Duck 3.00
21 Lone Wolf and Cub 3.00

22 Green Lantern	3.00
23 Honeymooners	3.00
24 Joker	4.00

Comics Values Monthly
Superman Memorial Issue

25 Excalibur	3.00
26 Wolverine	3.00
27 Green Lantern/Green Arrow	3.00
28 Alf (beige picture)	4.00
28a Alf (black picture)	3.00
29 Aliens	3.00
30 The Cult	3.00
31 The Prisoner	3.00
32 Teenage Mutant Ninja Turtles	3.00
33 Batman	3.00
34 X-Men	4.00
35 Catwomen	3.00
36 She-Hulk	3.00
37 Detective	3.00
38 Joker	3.00
39 Punisher	3.00
40 Predator	3.00
41 Wolverine	3.00
42 Fantastic Four	3.00
43 Green Hornet	3.00
44 Judge Dredd	3.00
45 Emerald Dawn	3.00
46 Teenage Mutant Ninja Turtles	3.00

47 Ghost Rider	3.00
48 Roger Rabbit	3.00
49 Dick Tracy	3.00
50 Spider-Man	3.00
51 World's Finest	3.00
52 Terminator	3.00
53 Lobo	3.00
54 Fantastic Four	3.00
55 Superman (1st color cover)	4.00
56 Mummy	4.00
57 The New Mutants	4.00
58 Robin	4.00
59 Magnus Robot Fighter	4.00
60 Amazing Spider-Man (1st slick cover)	4.00
61 War of the Gods	4.00
62 Terminator	4.00
63 X-Men X-Travaganza (1st with comic cards listing, 1991)	5.00
64 Batman versus Judge Dredd	5.00
65 Ghost Rider	5.00
65a Dracula	4.00
66 X-Force	4.00
66a Star Trek cover	5.00
67 Lobo	4.00
68 1992 Picks	4.00
69 Justice League of America	4.00
70 Incredible Hulk	4.00
71 Batman Returns	4.00
72 Spider-Man 30th Anniversary	4.00
73 Battles	4.00
74 Marvel 2099	4.00
75 British Invasion	4.00
76 Dracula	4.00
77 Tribe	4.00
78 1993 Preview	4.00
79 Rai and the Future Force	4.00
80 Youngblood (Poster)	6.00
81 Death's Head (Poster)	5.00
82 Superman (Poster)	5.00
83 Three New Universes (Dark Horse Poster)	5.00
84 Deathmate (Poster)	5.00
85 X-Men/Avengers (Poster)	5.00
86 New Batman (Poster)	6.00
87 Ninjak (Poster)	5.00
88 Marvel (Poster)	5.00
89 Batman: Animated (Poster)	5.00
90 Ultraverse (Poster)	5.00
91 Spawn/Batman (Poster)	6.00
92 Vertigo (Poster)	5.00
93 Extreme (Prophet Poster)	5.00

All prices listed are for *Near Mint* condition.

94 Axis (Poster) 5.00
95 Zero Hour (Poster) 4.00
96 Youngblood (Poster) 4.00
Becomes: **CVM**
97 Star Trek (internal color) 4.00
98 never issued
99 never issued
Special Issues
Dick Tracy special 10.00
Superman Memorial Issue + poster 8.00

CVM #100 (Sunrise 1994)

CVM
Sunrise Publications (1994–95)
100 Fantastic Four 3.00
101 Stormquest 3.00
102 DC's Black Lightning 3.00

COMIC TIMES
1 Spider-Man 4.00
2 . . . . 3.00
3 . . . . 2.00
4 Charles Vess cover 2.00
5 . . . . 2.00
6 Popeye 3.00

FANDOM DIRECTORY
1 1979 issue 10.00
2 1980 issue 8.00

3 to 12, 1981 to 1990 issues, each 6.00
13 1991 issue 9.00
14 1992–93 issue 16.00

FANDOM FEATURE
1 . . . . 2.00
2 Bill Sienkiewicz 1.00

FOOM MAGAZINE
1 . . . . 10.00
2 . . . . 5.00
3 to 10, each 3.00
11 to 20, each 2.00

Hero Illustrated #15
(Warrior Publications 1994)

HERO ILLUSTRATED
Warrior Publications (1993–95)
1 Dr. Mirage with two ashcans 4.00
2 Aliens versus Predator with two ashcans . 3.00
3 Cyber Force with two ashcans 3.00
4 Bane with 2099 ashcan and 3 cards 3.00
5 Vampirella with Shadowhawk ashcan . . . 3.00
6 Spider-Man with Solitaire Joker card 3.00
7 WildC.A.T.S. with Wetworks ashcan 3.00
8 Shadowman with Extreme ashcan and card 3.00
9 Pitt with Bravura ashcan 3.00

---

10 Spawn with ashcan and card 3.00
11 Black Ball Jam cover with 2 cards
    With Bongo ashcan 2.50
    With Dreadstar ashcan 2.50
12 Doomsday/Superman with card 2.50
13 Chang and Ordway cover with ashcan . 2.50
14 . . . . 2.50
15 Jimmy the Idiot Boy with ashcan 2.50
16 Bone with Superman scratch-off card . . 2.50
17 . . . . 2.50
18 Sin CIty 2.50
19 with Prototype ashcan 2.50
20 Ripclaw 2.50
21 Spawn Unleashed cover 2.50
22 Mask (X-Files ashcan) 2.50

HERO SPECIAL EDITION

Batman: From Dark Knight
    to Knightfall with ashcan 3.00
1993 The Year in Comics with 3 cards 3.00
100 Most Important Comics 3.00
Supervillains Special: The Baddest of
    the Bad 3.00
Special: Hero Guide to Science Fiction
    (with 1 of 3 movie cards) 4.00
Hero 1994 yearbook 3.00

COMIC BOOK WHO'S WHO
Special issue 3.00

INSIDE COMICS
Double Barrel Productions (1992)
1 Rob Liefeld cover 4.00
2 Wolverine 3.00
3 Infinity War 3.00
4 Jae Lee cover 3.00
5 Ghost Rider 3.00

NEW YORK COMIC ART
CONVENTION—1973
Phil Seuling 20.00

OVERSTREET COMIC BOOK
PRICE GUIDE
1 Comic logo cover (1970) 125.00
2 Comics cover 75.00
3 Comics cover 50.00
4 Justice Society 20.00
5 Edgar Rice Burroughs 22.50
6 Will Eisner 15.00
7 Porky Pig 17.50
8 B. Ward 15.00

9 Wally Wood 17.50
10 Classic Capt. America 17.50
11 . . . . 10.00
12 Mad 10.00
13 Spider-Man/Batman 10.00
14 Katy Keen 10.00
15 . . . . 15.00
16 Marvel Anniversary 15.00
17 Disney 10.00
18 Superman 10.00
19 Batman 10.00
20 Flash 10.00
21 Capt. America 10.00
22 Spider-Man 10.00
23 Flash 10.00
24 X-Men 10.00
25 Yellow Kid 10.00

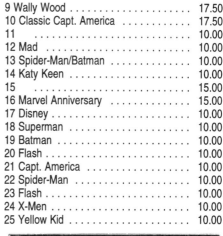

Overstreet's Price Update #12

OVERSTREET'S PRICE UPDATE
Overstreet Publications
1 to 9, each 2.00
10 Jae Lee 2.00
11 Jeff Smith's Bone 2.00
12 Ghost Rider 2.00
13 to 19, each 2.00
20 color 2.00

All prices listed are for *Near Mint* condition.

21 Andy and Adam Kubert	2.00
22	2.00
23	2.00
24	2.00
25 Barry Windsor-Smith	2.00

OVERSTREET ADVANCED COLLECTOR

1	5.00
2 Frank Frazetta cover	5.00

OVERSTREET GOLDEN AGE QUARTERLY

3 Daredevil and Claw	5.00
4 Al Williamson	5.00

Overstreet Comic Book Monthly
#15 (1994)

OVERSTREET COMIC BOOK MARKETPLACE
Overstreet (1993)
Overstreet Update merges with Comic Book Marketplace to become:

1 The Maxx	2.00
2 (Spawn card)	2.00
3 (repro of Overstreet's 1st price guide) . . .	2.00

4 (ARComics card, Plasm card)	2.00
5 (ARComics #2 card)	2.00
6 (Xenya card)	2.00

OVERSTREET COMIC BOOK MONTHLY

7 X-O Manowar versus Dinosaurs (Bartman card)	2.00
8 Hellshock (Hellshock card)	2.00
9	2.00
10 Hellshock	2.00
11	2.00
12 Daredevil	2.00
13 Starwatchers	2.00
14	2.00
15 Rob Liefeld/Extreme	2.00
15a Diamond show edition	2.50
16	2.00
17	2.00
18	2.00
19	2.00

PURE IMAGES

1 Birth of Spider-Man	5.00
2	4.00
3	4.00
4	4.00
5 Ren and Stimpy, Bill Wray cover	4.00

Triton #1 (Attic Books 1994)

TRITON: COMIC CARDS & COLLECTIBLES

1 Daredevil (3 Daredevil cards) 10.00
2 Gen-13 (Gen-13 card) 4.00
3 Star Wars (with Spider-Man nine-
    card sheet and Star Wars card which
    differs from actual card) 15.00
4 Hellshock (Hellshock card) 4.00
5 Pyramid (with one of 36 different
    Valiant promo cards and Keith
    Parkinson card) 5.00

WIZARD
Wizard Publications (1991–95)

1 Spider-Man cover 6.00
2 Ghost Rider cover 4.00
3 Wolverine cover 5.00
4 Batman cover 4.00
5 Silver Surfer cover 4.00
6 The Incredible Hulk cover 4.00
7 X-O Manowar cover 4.00
8 Bishop cover 4.00
9 Venom cover 4.00
10 Cable and Shaft (Youngblood #0 card) . 4.00
11 Spawn (Spawn card) 5.00
12 WildC.A.T.S. (Shadowhawk card) 4.00
13 Ghost Rider (Savage Dragon card) 4.00
14 X-Women (Cyber Force card) 4.00
15 Wetworks (WildC.A.T.S. card) 4.00
16 The Maxx (Wetworks card) 4.00
17 Solar and Bloodshot (Santa card) 4.00
18 Venom/Spider-Man (Pitt card) 4.00
19 Wolverine (The Maxx card) 5.00
20 The Maxx (Youngblood card) 5.00
21 Youngblood/Chapel (Stormwatch card) . 4.00
22 Deadpool/Apocalypse (Supreme card) .. 4.00
23 Deathmate (Battlestone card) 4.00
24 Acrbal/Batman (Shaman's Tears card) . 4.00
25 Deathblow (Shadowhawk card,
    25th Anniv. pog) 4.00
26 Spider-Man (Stryke Force card) 4.00
27 WildC.A.T.S. (WildStar card) 4.00
28 Bart-Man (Brigade card) 4.00
29 Spawn 4.00
30 Beavis and Butt-Head (Violator card) ... 3.00
31 Legend triple gatefold (Spawn card and
    Bone card) 3.00
32 Spawn/Batman (WildC.A.T.S. card) 4.00
33 Catwoman (Cyber Force card) 3.00
34 X-Women (Ripclaw card) 3.00
35 Prophet (Union card) 3.00

36 Spider-Man (WildStorm promo card) ... 3.00
37 Incredible Hulk (Gen-13 card) 3.00
38 Wolverine versus Sabretooth (Doom's
    IV card) 3.00

Wizard #44 (Wizard Publications 1995)

39 Spawn and Angela (Cybernary card) ... 4.00
40 Violator 3.00
41 Cyclops 5.00
42 .... 3.00
43 Warblade 3.00
44 Gen-13 (Ghost in the Shell ashcan) ... 3.00
Special Villains 3.00
Special X-Men (X-Men Turn Thirty card) .. 5.00
Special Valiant 4.00
Special Comic Con Edition + 2 cards
    (1992) 4.00
Special 100 most collectible comics
    Will Eisner cover (Spirit card) 4.00
Special Superman's Back (Superman card) 3.00
Beyond Zero Hour (DC Comics Special) .. 3.00

All prices listed are for *Near Mint* condition.

TRADING CARDS

T he vast majority of comics trading cards were issued in the last eight years, and most of those were produced in the last five years.

Superman (Gum, Inc. 1940) (reprint set)

However, the first comics trading card set was the Superman set produced by Gum, Inc. in 1940 (and reprinted in 1984). It featured comic book-style images of Superman performing various superfeats of strength, such as flying or battling tanks, etc. The art was primitive by today's standards, but the cards showed the things Superman did in the early comic books, and his exploits were treated seriously. Except for the Superman in the Jungle test set in 1968, and a few comic book cover reprints, no other card set featured serious comic book art until 1987!

There weren't any other comics cards in the 1940s or 1950s, just a few offerings based on comic strip characters. Finally, in 1966, Topps issued comics cards, but they were based on the Superman and Batman TV shows, not the comic books. The five Batman card sets from this same year were based on the campy TV show, and even though three of the sets used comic book art, all of the cards reflected the humor of that incredibly popular show.

It took more than a decade for any comic book character to be taken seriously in the aftermath of the Batman TV show. The first serious representations of a superhero on trading cards were based on the three Superman movies (1978—1983). However, these cards contained photos, not comics art. While these movies did much to erase the kid-vid image of the Batman TV show, the cards were really part of the many Topps movie and TV show cards from this era.

Batman Series #3 (Topps 1966)

The current era in comics card collecting started in 1987, but hardly anybody recognized it at the time. Comic Images was the first company to sell serious superhero art cards in anything like the current form. This was before ultraviolet coating, fancy bonus cards and other glitz, but their first card sets look remarkably modern. They started in 1987 with 90 Marvel Universe cards. This set pictured most of your favorite Marvel heroes and contained the first appearance of many on any kind of card. They followed with Colossal Conflicts (1987) and in 1988 with Wolverine, Heroic Origins and The Punisher. In 1989 they concentrated on artists cards with Excalibur (Alan Davis), Arthur Adams, The Best of John Byrne, Todd McFarlane and Mike Zeck (followed by others in 1990, including the first Jim Lee set).

Marvel Universe (Comic Images 1987); Marvel Universe I (Impel 1990); and Marvel Universe II (Impel 1991)

They helped set the stage for the 1990s but they were just a little bit early.

What really changed the landscape was Tim Burton's Batman movie in 1989. In the first Superman movie we learned to believe that "a man can fly," but in the Batman movie we finally met a comic book hero who was an adult. The Topps cards from the movie were not a departure from their movie cards from the previous 20 years and were not influential. It was the movie that woke everybody up to the possibilities of an adult, serious superhero, and it was the popularity of baseball cards that gave manufacturers the smell of money.

Comics card collecting finally took off in 1990. The trading card world changed forever with the Marvel Universe I cards from Impel. This was the first card set which combined fine comic art, good card design, quality production, bonus cards and marketing in just the right proportions. High-quality production had actually been around for a couple of years in sports cards, but it was new to what was then considered the nonsport card market.

Comics card collecting went into orbit in late 1992 when Marvel Masterpiece I came out featuring wonderful painted art by Joe Jusko. The same month DC hit it big with Doomsday: The Death of Superman cards which captured the most important comics event in 30 years and had the first (and maybe still the best) Spectra cards. The last Marvel Universe cards, X-Men II, and the second Marvel Masterpiece series kept Marvel cards on top in 1993 while 1993 DC follow-ups DC Bloodlines and The Return of Superman were both quite successful.

Comic Images continued to produce Marvel cards during this period, but they were taken from comic book pages rather than baseball card–type portraits. Still, they issued Spider-Man, Wolverine, Punisher and X-Men sets, featuring art by Todd McFarlane and other important artists. The most innovative set from Comic Images was *Conan*, the first all-chromium card set, from late 1993.

Space does not permit listing of comic book promo cards. Please see **Comic Cards and Their Prices** *by Stuart Wells III, published by Wallace-Homestead in 1994 (ISBN 0-87069-727-7).*

All prices listed are for *Near Mint* condition.

A

ACTION MASTERS TOY CARDS
Kenner/SkyBox (1994)
Cards from Kenner die-cast figures:
AM1 Batman (Animated) 1.00
AM2 Catwoman 1.00
AM3 Legends Batman 1.00

Action Masters (Kenner/SkyBox 1994)

ADAMS, ARTHUR
Comic Images (1989, Comic)
Set: 45 cards 25.00
Pack: 5 cards 1.50

ADVENTURES OF SMILIN' JACK
Samuel Eppy, Inc. (1940–41)
Set: 128 cards 150.00
Card 1.50
Card Strips of 8 .... 7.50

ALIENS/PREDATOR UNIVERSE
Topps/Dark Horse (1994, Comic)
Set: 72 cards + 15 Operation:
  Aliens cards 15.00
Pack: 9 cards 1.50
Chase cards (1:17)
  Six different, each 10.00
Promo card (Dave Dorman art) 1.00
One-card promo sheet 1.00
1 of 2 Aliens (*Hero* master-foil) 1.00
2 of 2 Predator (*Hero*
  master-foil) 1.00
P2 (Adam Hughes art) 1.00

ANIA
Comic Images (1993, Comic)
Ebony Warrior promo card ... 2.50
(*Set cancelled*)
Chromium cards, 3 diff., each 5.00
Spectrascope cards, 3 diff., ea. 5.00

ARCHIE COMIC CARDS
SkyBox (1992, Comic)
Set: 120 cards 11.00
Pack: 10 cards .... .90
Holograms, 4 diff., each 5.00
Hologram exchange card ... 12.00
B-1 The Eternal Triangle double-
  image hologram 10.00
Promos and Prototype cards
8 "A Handful" prototype 1.00
000 promo version of #8
  (*Wizard*) 1.00
37 "Sun Fun" prototype 1.00
000 promo version of #37
  (Up 'n' Coming) 2.00
62 Archie promo prototype ... 1.00

BATMAN

Batman Series #1 (Topps 1966)

BATMAN
Topps Series #1 (1966, Comic)
Set: 55 cards 150.00
Card 3-4.00
Wrapper 25.00
Topps–2nd Series (1966, Comic)
Set: 44 cards # with A 130.00
Card 3-4.00
Wrapper 20.00
Topps–3rd Series (1966, Comic)
Set: 44 cards # with B 150.00
Card 4-5.00
Wrapper 20.00
Batman Deluxe; Topps (1989)
(Reissue: Series #1, #2 & #3 cards)
Set: 143 cards, boxed 25.00

BATMAN
Topps–Series #4 (1966, TV)
Riddler Backs, Real Photos
Set: 38 cards (photos) 210.00
Card 5-6.00
Decoder 25.00
Wrapper 20.00
Topps–Series #5 (1966, TV)

"Bat Laffs, Real Photos"
Set: 55 cards (color) 165.00
Card 3.50
Pack 20.00

BATMAN: THE ANIMATED SERIES
Topps (1993, TV)
Set: 100 cards 15.00
Pack: 10 cards 1.00
Vinyl Mini-Cell (1:12)
  Six different, each 8.00
Batman Prototype card (*Advance
  #51*) 2.00
Prototype card on promo sheet 2.50
Promo card with Manbat 3.00

BATMAN: THE ANIMATED SERIES II
Topps (1994, TV)
Set: 90 cards 15.00
Pack: 8 cards 1.25
Vinyl Mini-Cels (1:18)
  Four different, each 8.00
Danny DeVito autographed
  card 100.00
Promo card sheet with Batman 2.00
Catwoman/Batman promo card 2.00

BATMAN (MOVIE)
Topps–Series #1 (1989, Movie)
Set: 132 cards/22 stickers ... 25.00
Pack: 9 cards, 1 sticker 1.00
Note: 2 different wrappers
Collector's factory set, boxed
  with 11 bonus cards 30.00
Topps–Series #2 (1989, Movie)
Set: 132 cards/22 Stickers ... 20.00
Pack: 9 cards, 1 sticker .... .90
Note: 2 different wrappers
Collector's factory set, boxed
  with 11 bonus cards 27.50

BATMAN VERSUS PREDATOR
Dark Horse (1991, Comic)
Set: 16 cards 20.00

BATMAN RETURNS
Topps (1992, Movie)
Set: 88 cards + 10 stadium
  club cards 10.00
  Spec. stadium club card, ea. . .20
Pack: 8 cards, 1 stadium club . 1.00
Promo cards
Dark Knight Returns (blue back) 4.00
Roar of the Batmobile
  (white back) 3.50
STADIUM CLUB (Topps, 1992)
Set: 100 cards 15.00
Pack: 15 cards 1.75
Promo cards
Batman (white back) 5.00

Batmobile (blue back) 4.00
Two-card promo sheet with regular
   and Stadium Club blue backs 4.00
MOVIE PHOTO STICKERS
Topps (1992)
Set: 66 Stickers 25.00
Box, unopened 40.00

BATMAN RETURNS
Zellers (Canadian 1992, Movie)
Set: 24 cards 7.00

BATMAN: SAGA OF
THE DARK KNIGHT
SkyBox (1994, Comic)
Set: 100 cards 15.00
SpectraEtch Portraits of the Batman
   Five different, each 9.00
Skydisk Hologram (1:240) . . . 70.00
Promo: Batman and Georgia Dome,
   Superbowl XXVIII 3.00
Promo: Batman and Camden Yards,
   Diamond show #11 . . . . 3.00
Prototype (Triton #4) 2.00
Promo SkyDisk, large 100.00

THE JOKER®

Legends of Batman (Kenner 1994)

[LEGENDS OF] BATMAN
TOY CARDS
Kenner (1994–95)
Cards from *Legends of Batman*
action figures, 17 diff., each . . 2-3.00

[THE ADVENTURES OF]
BATMAN & ROBIN
SkyBox (1995, TV)
Set: 90 cards+12 pop-up
   cards 17.50
Pack: 7 cards+1 pop-up 1.25
R1 thru R9, R.A.S. foils (1:11)
   untitled, each 7.50
T1 thru T3, Thermal cards (1:36)
   untitled, each 12.50
Eight-card prototype sheet 2.50

BATMAN FOREVER METAL
Fleer (1995, Movie)
Set: 100 cards 25.00
Pack: 8 cards 2.75
Jumbo pack 3.00
Double size pack: 10 cards . . . 3.50
Silver Flasher cards (1:1), each 1.00
Set: 100 cards 100.00
Gold Blaster (1:3) (1:2 double
   packs) 10 diff., each 2.00
Movie Preview (1:6)(1:5 double
   packs) 8 diff., each 4.00
Holograms (1:12) (1:10 double
   packs) 4 diff., each 8.00
Acclaim Video Game card . . 10.00
Four-card promo sheet 2.00
Metal one-card promo sheet . . 2.00

BATMAN FOREVER
Fleer Ultra (1995, Movie)
Set: 120 + 36 holograms 40.00
Pack: 8 cards + 1 hologram . . . 2.00
Chromium Animation card (1:4)
   10 diff., each 4.00
Aclaim Video Game (1:18)
   2 diff., each 4.00
Four-card promo sheet 2.00
MOVIE PHOTO STICKERS
Set: 88 stickers 12.00
Pack: 5 sticker 0.75
Chromium chase stickers (1:18)
   4 diff., each 2.50

BATMAN
TW Kids (1994)
Four card cello pack from audio tape.
1 Batman 1.00
2 Two-Face 1.00
3 The Riddler 1.00
4 Two-Face and the Riddler . . 1.00

beetle bailey

Beetle Bailey (Authentix 1995)
BEETLE BAILEY
Authentix (1995, Comic Strip)
Set: 50 cards 10.00

Pack: 6 cards 1.00
Camp Swampy, silver foil, (1:7)
   5 diff., ... 5.00
Chase Pax, gold foil (1:72),
   5 diff., ... 15.00
Jumbo cards (1:10 boxes)
   (500 made) . . . . ?
Promo #1 Beetle Bailey 1.00

BIG LITTLE BOOK SERIES
Big Little Book series, 1939–40 [R23],
   Full series: 224 cards . . . 12,000.00
   Buck Jones set: 32 cards 1,000.00
   Dan Dunn set: 32 cards 1,000.00
   G-Man set: 32 cards . . . 1,650.00
   Tom Mix set: 32 cards . 1,480.00
   Flash Gordon set: 32
      cards 3,200.00
   Popeye set: 32 cards . 1,500.00
   Dick Tracy set: 32 cards 1,500.00

BLONDIE
Authentix (1995)
Set: 50 cards 10.00
Pack: 6 cards 1.00
Silver Foil cards, 5 diff. 5.00
Chase Pax with 5 gold cards . 15.00

BLOOM COUNTY/OUTLAND
Krome Productions (1995)
Set: 100 chromium cards . . . 20.00
Pack: 7 cards + 1 sticker 2.50
Chromium Stickers
H-1 Rosebud 5.00
H-2 Bloom County Gang 5.00
H-3 Opus 5.00
H-4 Bill the Cat 5.00
Mystery card 10.00
Stickers, 90? diff., each 50
Promo cards, 3 diff., each . . . 2.00

BONE
Comic Images (1994, Comic)
Set: 90 cards 12.50
Chromium cards, 6 diff., each . 7.50
Subset cards (3:case)
   Three cards, each 15.00
Original Sketch cards (100 made)
Medallion card (2:case) 20.00
7 cards + 3 stand-ups promo set,
   (*Cards Illustrated*) 5.00
Promo card 1.50
Four-card promo sheet (D-15
   to D-18) (*Previews*) 1.50
SERIES II
Set: 90 Chromium Cards 25.00
Pack: 7 cards 2.50
MagnaChrome cards
   6 diff., each 7.00
Thorn Subset cards,
   3 diff., each 9.00
Medallion card 25.00
Jeff Smith Autograph card . . . 50.00
Mini-press sheet 15.00

Six-card uncut sheet 20.00
No# Promo card 2.00
Four-card promo sheet 3.00
Binder 19.95

BYRNE, JOHN
BEST OF BYRNE, THE
Comic Images (1989, Comic)
Set: 45 Cards + Header 15.00
Pack: 5 Cards + Header 2.00

C

CAPTAIN AMERICA
50TH ANNIVERSARY
Comic Images (1990, Comic)
Set: 45 cards 12.00
Pack: 5 cards, cello pack 1.00

COLORADO COMICS
FUTURE STARS
Dart (1994, Comic)
Set: 13 cards, plastic box, sealed
numbered, 1500 made . . . 10.00

Colossal Conflicts (Comic Images 1987)
COLOSSAL CONFLICTS
(Marvel Cards, Series 2)
Comic Images (1987, Comic)
Set: 90 cards 24.00
Pack: 4 cards + promo sticker . 1.00

COMIC BOOK HEROES
STICKERS/Brown or White Backs
Topps (1975, Comic)
Set: 40 stickers & 9 puzzle/
checklist cards 100.00
Common sticker 2.50-4.00
Ghost Rider (rookie) 11.00
Spider-Man-1 . . . . 6.00
Spider-Man-2 . . . . 6.00
Puzzle/Checklist cards (Fantastic
Four) 1 thru 9 . . . . 12.00
Pack: 4 cards + 1 puzzle 10.00

COMIC CHARACTER
CARDS
Welch's/Sugar Daddy (1953)
Type 1, Welch's [R757]
Card 4.00
Set: 50 cards 250.00
Type 2, Sugar Daddy
Card 3.50
Set: 50 cards 225.00
Note: Cards #25 (Daddy Warbucks),
#31 (Little Orphan Annie) and #36
(Sandy) are worth $15 to $20.

COMIC CHARACTER
CARDS
Lev Gleason Publication (1950s)
Set: 32 cards 200.00
Card 6.00

COMIC CHARACTER
SAFETY CARDS
Journal American (1953)
Comic Characters Safety cards
Each 3.00

COMIC COVER STICKERS
SINGLE STICKERS
Topps (1970, Comic)
Set: 44 Stickers 200.00
Batman 5.00
Other superheroes, each 4.50
Four-On-Ones, each 4.50

COMICS FUTURE
STARS '93
Majestic Entertainment (1993)
Set: 100 cards 11.00
Pack: 9 cards 1.25
Litho Foil "Hot Picks" (1:27)
"HP" Eight different, each . . 6.00
Star Players (1:27)
"SP" Five different, each . . . 5.00
"MVP" Snake 15.00
Promo cards
P1 Turbulence 2.50
P2 Treason 2.50
P3 Gai-Jin 2.50
Prototype cards
P1 Bullitt 2.00
P2 Arsenault 2.00
P3 Razer 2.00
COMICS FUTURE STARS 2
Hot Picks prototypes *(Set cancelled)*
P4 The Black Yeti 2.50
P5 Cetan 2.50
P6 Graffiti 2.50

COMICS GREATEST
WORLD
Topps (1994, Comic)
Set: 100 cards 15.00
Pack: 8 cards 1.25

Comics Greatest World (Topps 1994)
VortexMatrix cards, 6 diff.,
each 7.50
VortexMatrix promo, 2 diff.,
each 5.00
LargeMatrix cards, 6 diff., each 7.50
Promo sheet (*Previews*) 1.00
Promo card (*Advance*) 1.00

CONAN
Comic Images (1993, Comic)
Set: 90 Chromium cards
(+10 variants) 30.00
Pack: 7 cards 2.00
Prism cards (1:18), 6 diff.
each 9.00
Chromium promo card 7.50
Holochrome variations 10.00
CONAN II (1994)
Set: 90 Chromium cards
+ 6 variant cards 25.00
Pack: 7 chromium cards 2.25
Prism cards 6 diff., each . . . 10.00
Foil Subset cards (3:case)
Three cards, each 20.00
Foil Medallion card (2:case) . . 30.00
Promo card, chromium 3.50
Two-card promo strip 3.50
CONAN III (1995)
Set: 90 cards, all chromium . . 30.00
Pack: 7 cards 2.25
MagnaChrome, 6 diff., each . 10.00
Conan's Greatest Battles, subset
3 diff., each 20.00
Six-card mini-press sheet . . . 20.00
Medallion card 25.00
Holochrome variations 5.00
Promo, chromium 2.50

[THE SAVAGE SWORD OF]
CONAN THE BARBARIAN
Comic Images (1988, Covers)
Set: 50 cards 18.00
Pack: 5 cards 1.50

CRACKER-JACK
Premiums [R720]
Comic Character, embossed
1½", card 5.00

*Creators Universe
(Dynamic Entertainment 1993)*

CREATORS UNIVERSE
Dynamic Entertainment (1993)
Set: 100 cards 13.50
Pack: 6 cards 1.50
Checklists CL1–CL5, each . . . 7.50
Bonus cards (1:6)
"SD" four different, each . . . 8.00
"FF" three different, each . . 9.00
SG1 Hellshock redemption
card (1:Case) 25.00
22Kt Gold Signature card . . . 25.00
Promo cards
Stronghold promo 2.00
Redline promo 2.00
Warhorse promo 2.00
The Silencer 1.50
P1 Pheros promo 2.00
P2 Sgt. Major Acre 2.00
P3 Blitzkrieg promo 2.00
Four-card promo sheet 5.00
Three-card promo strip 5.00
X1 Bron 10.00
X2 Strangelands 10.00

CRUNCH 'N' MUNCH
Franklin (1993)
(Neal Adams/Continuity Associates art)
Storm 2.00
Wolverine 2.00
Hulk 2.00
Spider-Man 3.00
Cage 3.00
Superheroes 2.00
2nd Edition (1994)
(Tom Raney art)
Cable 2.50
Cyclops 2.50
Gambit 2.50

Spider-Man 2.50
Wolverine 2.50
Jean Grey 2.50

CYBERFORCE
Topps (1995)
Set: 72 chromium cards 15.00
Pack: 5 cards (inc. 1 chase) . . 2.50
Cyber Optics, 18 diff., each . . 3.00
Cyber Matrix, 6 diff., each . . . 2.00
Clearzone, 3 diff., each 3.00
C1 promo 1.00

D

DARK DOMINION ZERO
River Group (1993, Comic)
Set: 150 cards 12.50
Pack: 9 cards 1.00
Bonus cards, Level One (1:18)
Eight different, each 5.00
9 of 9 The Shanty (from Album) 7.00
Bonus cards, Level Two (1:72)
Three different, each 9.00
4 of 4 Michael/Lorca (tin set) . 12.00
Quantum View Lens 2.50
Album, with ashcan comic, Quantum
View lens for bonus cards . 20.00
Michael Alexander promo card 1.00
Promo sheets
Four-card, San Diego con 4.00
Four-card, Comicfest '93 . . . . . 3.50
Four-card, Diamond Dist. 3.00
Two-card, one panel 1.50
Notes: 6 different wrappers.
Plasm Level 2 #4 Bonus card (1:360)
Original art, 10 made (1:216,000)

DARK HORSE
Dark Horse (1991, Comic)
Set: 24 cards 12.00
2-card strips, 12 diff., each . . . 1.50

DC COMICS

DC BLOODLINES
SkyBox (1993, Comic)
Set: 81 cards 11.00
Pack: 8 cards 1.50
Foil-Embossed cards (1:18)
S1–S4, four different, each 15.00
S5 Redemption card (1:72) 15.00
The One True Superman . . . 30.00
Promo cards
Four images (Supermen #500) 4.00
The Man of Steel 3.00
P1 The Man of Steel 2.00
The Man of Tomorrow 3.00
P2 The Man of Tomorrow 2.00
The Last Son of Krypton 3.00
P3 The Last Son of Krypton . . 2.00
Superboy 3.00
P4 Superboy 2.00

DC COMIC BOOK FOLDEES
Topps (1966, Comic)
Set: 44 cards 150.00
Card 3-4.00

DC/NATIONAL PERIODICAL/ WARNER BROS. CARDS
Wonder Bread/Hostess (1974)
DC Heroes, with comic back
Set: 30 cards 120.00
Aquaman 4.50
Batman 5.50
Cat Woman 6.00
Clark Kent 5.00
Lois Lane 5.00
Robin 4.50
Superman 5.50
The Joker 4.50
The Penguin 4.50
The Riddler 4.50
Wonder Woman 4.50
Warner Bros., with comic back
19 different, each . . . 2.50 to 4.50

DC COMICS STICKERS
Quaker Oats (1979, Comic)
4 Sets total; each set 5.00

DC COMICS STRIP CARDS
DC (1987, Comic)
Set: 48 cards (#1–#48) 20.00
Eight-card sheet, 6 diff., each . 5.00
Series II (1989, Comic)
Set: 72 cards (#49–#120) . . . 30.00
Eight-card sheet, 9 diff., each . 4.00

DC Cosmic Cards (Impel 1992)

DC COSMIC CARDS
"INAUGURAL EDITION"
Impel (1992, Comic)
Set: 180 cards 15.00
Pack: 12 cards 1.00
DC Hologram Hall of Fame
DCH1 Clark Kent & Lois Lane . 9.00

DCH2 Darkseid 6.00
DCH3 Deathstroke the
    Terminator 7.00
DCH4 Flash 6.00
DCH5 Green Lantern 6.00
DCH6 Hawkman 6.00
DCH7 Lobo 8.00
DCH8 Superman 10.00
DCH9 Wonder Woman 6.00
DCH10 Waverider 6.00
Promos
Promo sheet: Wonder Woman, Lobo,
    Deathstroke and Superman . 7.50
Five-card promo set, in
    cello pack 12.50
    Deathstroke the Terminator . 2.00
    Flash 2.00
    Green Lantern 2.00
    Superman 3.00
    Wonder Woman 2.00
Note: 4 different wrappers
44 Deathstroke, error card 4.00

DC COSMIC TEAMS
SkyBox (1993, Comic)
Set: 150 cards 15.00
Pack: 8 cards 1.25
Holograms
DCH11 Captain Marvel 5.00
DCH12 Hawkman 5.00
DCH13 Lobo 6.00
DCH14 The Spectre 6.00
DCH15 Superman 7.00
DCH16 Swamp Thing 5.00
Promos and Prototypes
Proto cards #34–#36, set 3.00
Proto card #60 . . . . 2.00
P1 Apparition promo 2.50
0 Deathstroke promo card 2.00
00 Dragonmage promo card . . 2.00
000 Catspaw promo card 2.00
0000 Computo promo card . . . 2.00

DC LEGENDS '95
SkyBox Power Chrome (1995)
Set: 150 Chromium cards . . . 25.00
Pack: 9 Chromium cards 3.00
Hard Hitters Chromium (1:2)
    18 diff., each 1.50
Battlezone Clear Chrome(1:11)
    6 diff., each 10.00
Legacy Refractor Chrome (1:36)
    3 diff., each 20.00
Superman Prototype 1.00
Two-card promo 2.00

DC MASTER CARDS
Skybox (1994, Painted)
Set: 90 cards 25.00
Pack: 6 cards 1.25
Foil cards (1:18)
    Four different, each 10.00
Double-sided Spectra-Etch (1:36)
    Five different, each 15.00

Skydisk Redemption (1:240) . 60.00
SD2 Superman **SkyDisk** 65.00
Promo cards
P1 Doomsday promo (*Triton*) . . 2.00
C1 Doomsday (Capital City) . . 5.00
H1 Doomsday (Heroes World) . 5.00
D1 Doomsday (Diamond show) 5.00
N1 Aquaman (*Non-Sport*
    Update) 2.00
Ci1 Maxima (*Cards Illustrated*) . 2.00

DC Stars (SkyBox 1994)

DC STARS
SkyBox (1994)
Set: 45 cards + 9 puzzle cards   9.00
Foil-enhanced (1:18), 4 diff. . . 10.00
Pack: 5 cards + Puzzle card . . 1.00

DC SUPER HEROES STICKERS
Taystee/Sunbeam (1978, Comic)
Set: 30 stickers 125.00
Sticker, each 5.00

[DC] VILLAINS THE DARK JUDGMENT
SkyBox (1995)
Set: 90 cards 20.00
Pack: 7 cards 1.50
Gathering of Evil (1:7)
    9 diff, each 5.00
Villains Attack (1:30) foil embossed
    3 diff., each 15.00
Sky-Motion Redemption card
    (1:180), Two-Face 75.00
    SkyMotion promo card in pouch 50.00
    Six-card promo sheet 2.50

DC VERSUS MARVEL
SkyBox (1995)
Set: 100 cards 17.50
Pack: 8 cards + 1 ballot 2.00
Impact, 18 diff., each 4.00
Holo F/X, 12 diff., each 9.00
Lenticular, 2 diff., each 50.00

Promos
(#1) Batman (*DC Versus Marvel*
    preview comic) 1.00
(#2) Captain America 1.00

DEATHMATE
Upper Deck (1993, Comic)
Set: 110 cards 15.00
Pack: 8 cards 1.50
Transitions cards (1:12)
    "T" eight different, each 5.00
Players of Deathmate (1:18)
    "P" six different, each 8.00
Lithogram (1:90)
    "D" two different, each . . . 20.00
Promo cards
Promo card, Upper Deck 3.00
Promo card, Topps 3.00
Oversize promo card 2.50

DEATHWATCH 2000: PRELUDE
Continuity Comics (1993, Comic)
Four-card promo sheet 5.00
Cards #1 thru #11, each 3.00
12 Valeria (1:25 comics) 15.00
13 Shaman (1:50 comics) . . . 25.00
Cards #14 thru #22, each 75
Cards #23 thru #29, each 50

DEATHWATCH 2000
Classic Games (1993, Comic)
Set: 100 cards 15.00
Pack: 8 cards 1.75
Superhero cards
SS1 Shaquille O'Neal 35.00
SS2 Manon Rheaume 25.00
SS3 Ken Griffey, Jr. 20.00
Hybrid cards
"HC" seven different, each   12.00
Jacquarundi (autograph card)   50.00
Promo cards
PR1 Desperate Rescue 2.00
PR2 Escape from Death-Jaws . 2.00
PR3 Inches from Death 2.00
PR4 Lith Kasti 2.00
PR5 Valeria the She-Bat 3.00
Variation promos, foil stamped
    "May 2–5, 1993 Capital" each 5.00
Four-card promo sheet 5.00
Numbered four-card promo sheet,
    with 3 super-heroes 25.00
Jumbo Pack Prism cards
Set: 20 prism cards 40.00

DEFECTIVE COMICS
Active Marketing (1993)
Set: 50 cards, boxed 10.00
Set: 50 cards, hand assembled 7.50
Pack: 7 cards, 1 foil card 1.00
Silver Foil cards (1:1)
Set: #SF1–#SF50 . . . . 30.00
Card .50
Gold Foil card (1:10)

#GF1–#GF50, each 5.00
Autographed card (1:400) . . . 30.00
Original Sketch card (1:4,320)
Promo cards
P1 Sprain #1 . . . . 1.50
P2 Defective Comics #27 . . . . 1.50
P3 Unfazing Fantasy #15 . . . . 1.50

DEFIANT UNIVERSE
River Group (1994)
Promo cards *(Set cancelled)*
1/3 Skipper (Plasm) 2.00
2/3 Billy Ballistic (WarDancer) . 2.00
3/3 Ngu (Charlemagne) 2.00

DICK TRACY
Novel Candy Company (1950s)
Dick Tracy Package Designs
Card 7.00
Set: 12 cards 65.00

DICK TRACY
Topps (1990, Movie)
Set: 88 cards/11 stickers 16.00
Deluxe, boxed collectors
set, with 22 bonus cards . . 20.00

*Doomsday: The Death of Superman
(SkyBox 1992)*

DOOMSDAY: THE DEATH OF SUPERMAN
SkyBox (1992, Comic)
Set: 100 cards (1–90, C1–C9,
CL1) 50.00
Pack: 8 cards 4.00
Spectra cards "A Memorial Tribute"
"S" four different, each . . . 18.00
Foil-Stamped puzzle cards
"F" Two different, each . . . 17.50
Prototypes
0 Superman's Tombstone with red
inner border 2.50
00 Superman's Tombstone with yellow
inner border (Superman #75) 5.00
000 Bleeding "S" shield with silver

inner border (in *Wizard #17*) 2.50

THE EUDAEMON
Press Pass (1994)
Promos *(Set cancelled)*
Two-card promo sheet 2.00
Three-card promo sheet 3.00
P.P.2 Eudaemon (*Wizard*) 1.00
Mordare promo (*Comic Book
Collector*) 2.50
The Eudaemon promo (*Card
Collector Price Guide*) 2.00

EVIL ERNIE
Krome Productions (1993, Comic)
Set: 100 cards 12.50
Pack: 8 cards 1.25
Chromium cards (1:18)
Five different, each 8.00
Autographed cards (1:200) . 25.00
Promo card, chromium 5.00
Silver promo card, B&W 1.00
Promo card (Arena mag.) 1.00
Promo card #1 (of 2), chromium 2.50
Promo card #2 (of 2), chromium 3.00
**(SERIES II)
GLOW IN THE DARK**
Krome Productions (1995)
Set: 100 chromium cards . . . 25.00
Pack: 8 cards 2.50
State of the Art,
5 diff., each 9.00
Autograph card (1000 made) . 25.00
#1 Promo card, chromium
(*Combo #5*) 1.00

Excalibur (Comic Images 1989)

EXCALIBUR
**Comic Images (1989, Comic)
(Alan Davis art)**
Set: 45 cards + header 15.00
Pack: 5 cards + header 1.50

EXTREME
Extreme Studios (1993)
Caricatures of Extreme Studios
Personnel, 15 diff., each 50
Ten-card set from Cards Illustrated
#3 (three in each copy), set . 4.50

EXTREME SACRIFICE
Image/SkyBox (1995)
Cards from crossover comic book
series; backs form a nine card
superpanel
Set: 9 cards 10.00

FAMOUS COMIC BOOK CREATORS
Eclipse (1992, Photos)
Set: 110 cards 15.00
Silver-autographed blue back cards
Chuck Dixon 7.00
Tom Lyle 7.00
Pack: 12 cards 1.00
Promo sheet (Perez & Aragones) .50

FEM FORCE
AC Comics (1993, Comic)
Set: 14 cards & blue wrapper 15.00
Set: 2nd printing, green wrapper 9.95
Set: 2nd printing, signed &
numbered,
orange wrapper 15.00
Ms. Victory sticker (*Femforce
Up-close #6*) untitled 50

FEM FORCE II
Set: 14 cards & purple wrapper 9.95
Set: 2nd printing, signed &
numbered, green wrapper . 15.00

FEM FORCE III
Set: 14 cards & yellow wrapper 9.95
Set: 15 cards & red wrapper with #43
No-Nose Nanette card . . . 11.00

AC COMICS PROMO PACK
AC Comics (1993)
Set: 8 cards with wrapper . . . 10.00

FLAMING CARROT
Comic Images (1988, Comic)
Set: 40 cards 15.00
Pack: 5 cards, cello pack 1.50
Uncut Sheet (700 made) 35.00

FLASH GORDON
Topps (1968)
Set: 24 cards (test set) . . 2,500.00
Card (scarce) 100.00
Card (not so scarce) 75.00

FLASH GORDON SERIAL
Jasinski (1991, Movie Photos)
Set #1: 36 cards 13.00

Set #2: 36 cards 12.00
Set #3: 36 cards 11.00
5,000 numbered sets in each series.

G

GARFIELD
Skybox (1992, Comic Strip)
Set: 100 cards 17.50
Holograms, Set of 5 . . . . 15.00
Prototypes, 2 diff., each 1.00

GEN 13
Wildstorm (1995)
Set: 107 cards 25.00
Pack: 7 cards 2.25
Gen-Active Motion (1:8)
9 diff., each 12.00
Glow-in-the-Dark (1:6)
9 diff., each 9.00

GHOST RIDER
Comic Images (1990, Comic)
Set: 45 cards + header card . 12.00
Pack: 5 cards + header card . . 1.25

GHOST RIDER II
Comic Images (1992, Comic)
(Mark Texeira art)
Set: 80 cards/10 Glow-in-dark 13.00
Glow in the Dark card 80
Pack: 10 cards 1.25
Promo card 3.50

GOLDEN AGE OF COMICS
Comic Images (1995)
Set: 90 chromium cards 25.00
Pack: 7 chromium cards 2.00
Magnachrome cards
6 different, each 10.00
MagnaChrome subset
3 different, each 15.00
Medallion card, numbered . . 20.00
Autographed card, 2 diff., each 40.00
F1-F3 promos (*Fan*), each 1.00

GOOD GUYS GENESIS, THE
The River Group (1993)
Two-card promo sheet 3.50
3 of 3 Mr. Fingerman promo . . 5.00

H

HÄGAR THE HORRIBLE
Authentix (1995, Comic Strip)
Set: 50 cards 10.00
Factory Set: 10.00
Pack: 6 cards 1.00
Hagar Warfare, silver foil (1:6)
5 diff., each 5.00
Chase Pax, gold foil, (1:72)
5 diff., each 15.00

Jumbo box card (1:10 boxes)
(500 made) 30.00

Hägar the Horrible (Authentix 1995)
Autograph card (1000 made) . 40.00
Original art card
Promo #1 . . . . 1.00
Three-card mail-in set 4.95

HEROIC ORIGINS
(Marvel Cards IV)
Comic Images (1988, Comic)
Set: 90 cards 30.00
Pack: 4 cards + promo sticker . 2.00

HOWARD THE DUCK
Topps (1986, Movie)
Set: 75 cards/22 stickers 12.00
Pack: 9 cards, 1 sticker 1.50

I

IMAGE UNIVERSE
Topps (1995, Comic)
Set: 90 cards 25.00
Pack: 6 chromium cards 2.75
Clearchrome (1:11) 6 diff.,
each 15.00
Image Founders (1:14), 6 different,
i1 – i6, each 9.00
First Covers (1:14), 6 different,
d1 – d6, each 9.00
#0 chromium promo 2.00

INCREDIBLE HULK COMIC COVERS
Drakes Cakes (1978, Comic)
Set: 24 cards 90.00
Card 4.00

INCREDIBLE HULK
Topps (1979, TV)
Set: 88 cards/22 stickers 20.00
Pack: 7 cards, 1 sticker 2.50

INCREDIBLE HULK
Comic Images (1991, Comic)
Set: 90 cards (Dale Keown art) 15.00
Pack: 10 cards 1.50

J

JOE PALOOKA
Novel Candy Co.
Joe Palooka Boxing, card 8.00
Set: 8 cards 75.00

JUDGE DREDD
THE EPICS
Edge Entertainment (1995)
Set: 90 cards
(Prog #1 to Prog #90) 12.50
Pack: 8 cards 1.50
Sleep of the Just (1:4) 1.00
Legends (1:10) 13 diff., each . 3.00
EdgeTech Dark Judges (1:19) 7.00
Movie Previews (1:15),
3 diff., each 6.00
Black Death (1:350) 15.00
Promos
Four-card promo sheet 2.00
Proto1 Judge Dredd 1.00
Proto2 Judge Anderson 1.00
Proto3 Judge Death 1.00
Proto4 Mean Machine 1.00
Proto5 Chopper 1.00
Proto6 Brit-Cit Babes 1.00

JUDGE DREDD
THE MOVIE
Edge Entertainment (1995)
Set: 90 cards
(#1 to #90) 10.00
Pack: 8 cards 1.25
Sleep of the Just (1:4?) 1.00
Nine additional Sleep of the Just
cards, mail-in 10.00

JUSTICE LEAGUE OF AMERICA
Fleer (1970, Comic)
Set: 17 Tattoos 25.00

K

KIRBY, JACK UNPUBLISHED ARCHIVES
Set: 90 cards 12.50
Pack: 10 cards 1.00
Unsung Heroes chromium cards,
six different, each 7.50
Villains subset, 3 diff., each . 15.00
Medallion card 20.00
Minipress sheet 20.00
Six card uncut sheet (1:case) 20.00
Promo card 1.00

[The Comic Art Tribute to Joe Simon and]
KIRBY, JACK
21st Century Archives (1995)
Set: 50 cards 7.50
Pack: 8 cards 1.25
DiamondChrome (K1–K5) 3.00
Great Machine mail-in set
(KM1–KM5) 8.95

KITCHEN SINK CARDS
Set: 36 cards, oversized 50.00
Card 1.00

L

LADY DEATH
Krome Productions (1994, Comic)
Set: 100 chromium cards . . . 30.00
Chase cards, 5 diff., each . . 10.00
Mystery chase card 15.00
Autographed card 50.00
SERIES II (1995)
Set: 100 Chromium cards . . . 25.00
Pack: 6 cards + 1 . . . . 2.50
Chromium chase cards,
5 diff., each 10.00
Chase Tryptic, 3 diff., each . 10.00
Autograph card (500 made) . . 50.00
Promo card (*Collect 10-95*) . . . 1.50
Promo card (*Combo #10*) 1.50

LEE, JIM
Comic Images (1990, Comic)
Set: 45 cards + header 14.00
Pack: 5 cards + header 1.50

LEE, JIM II
Comic Images (1991, Comic)
Set: 45 cards + header 13.00
Pack: 5 cards + header 1.50

LEGACY #0
Majestic Entertainment (1993)
Set: 150 cards 17.50
Pack: 9 cards 1.00
Silver Binder 10.00
Gold Binder 15.00
Dyna Etch foil (1:18)
"D" nine different, each 6.00
Promo cards
Set: 9 cards, 1 thru 9 . . . . . . 10.00
Limited Prints, San Diego Comicon:
Punch-Hurt-Kill-Kill 7.00
Legacy #1 cover 7.00
Limited Print, Chicago Comicon:
Three Villains (5,000 made) . 5.00

LOIS & CLARK
SkyBox (1995, TV)
Set: 90 cards + 9 tattoos 12.50
Pack: 8 cards + shield tattoo . . 1.50
HoloChip Painted cards (1:15)

Lois & Clark (SkyBox 1995)

6 diff., each 10.00
Difuser Foil (1:7) 9 diff., each . 6.00
Pin (1:box) or mail-in 4.00
NSU1 promo (*N-S Update*) . . . 1.00
LC1 promo 1.50
L&C1 Prototype 1.00
L&C2 Prototype 1.50
L&C5 foil promo 1.00

M

McFARLANE, TODD
Comic Images (1989, Comic)
Set: 45 cards + header 20.00
Pack: 5 cards + header 1.50

McFARLANE, TODD II
Comic Images (1990, Comic)
Set: 45 cards + header 17.50
Pack: 5 cards + header 1.50

MAD MAGAZINE
Lime Rock (1992)
Series I
Set: 55 cards 7.50
Pack: 11 cards 1.00
Hologram
Vote Mad double sided, silver . 12.50
Alfred E. Newman 9.00
Mail-in Gold holo, double sided . 18.00
Promo cards, set of 6 . . . . . . 3.00
Promo 7 (*Inside Trader*) 1.00
Series II
Set: 55 cards 9.00
Pack: 11 cards 1.00
Hologram, Spy vs. Spy 7.00
Series III
Set: 55 cards 9.00
R1 & R2 Spy vs. Spy Rookie
prototype prism cards, each . 3.00

MADMAN X50
Dark Horse (1994)
Set: 50 cards, boxed 15.00

MAGNUS ROBOT FIGHTER
Valiant (1991, Comic)
Set: 24 cards (#2–#25) 6.00
Uncut sheet, with coupons . . 10.00
Redemption card (from
Magnus Robot Fighter #0) . 25.00

MARVEL

MARVEL [ANNUAL] INAUGURAL EDITION
Fleer/Flair (1994, Comic)
Set: 150 cards 75.00
Two #8 cards and no #6 card
Pack: 10 cards 5.00
Nine-card promo sheet (*Advance*
or *Previews*) 1.00
Three/Four-card promo sheet . 5.00
Powerblast (1:2)
Eighteen different, each . . . 7.00

Marvel Annual '95 (Fleer Flair 1995)

MARVEL ANNUAL '95
Fleer Flair (1995, Painted)
Set: 150 thick cards 40.00
Box (pack): 10 cards
(inc. 2 chase) 4.50
PowerBlast (1:1), 24 diff. 1.50
Chromium cards (1:2), 12 diff. . 2.00
Holoblast cards (1:3), 12 diff. . 3.00
Duoblast (1:6), 3 diff. 3.50
Four-card promo sheet 1.00

MARVEL COMICS
Sugar-Free Bubble Gum Wrappers
Topps (1978, Comic)
Set: 34 gum wrappers 50.00
Each: 2.00

MARVEL COMICS
Bubble Gum Wrappers
Topps (1979)
Set: 33 wrappers 30.00
Each: 1.00

MARVEL COMICS SUPER HEROES
RUB-A-TATTOO
Donruss (1980, Comic)
Tattoos, 44? diff., each 1.00
Pack: 1 Tattoo + instruct card . 2.00

MARVEL 1st COVERS SERIES II
Comic Images (1991, Covers)
Set: 100 cards 15.00
Pack: 10 cards 1.50

1992 Marvel Masterpieces (SkyBox 1992)

1992 MARVEL MASTERPIECES
SkyBox (1992, Painted)
(Art by Joe Jusko)
Set: 100 cards 50.00
Pack: 6 cards 4.50
Bonus cards
1-D Thing vs. Hulk 15.00
2-D Silver Surfer vs. Thanos . 17.00
3-D Wolverine vs. Sabretooth 20.00
4-D Spider-Man vs. Venom . . 19.00
5-D Captain America vs.
    Red Skull 15.00
Prototype and promo cards
Captain America, promo 4.50
Hulk, promo 3.50
Hulk, prototype 3.50
Psylocke, promo 4.50
Silver Surfer, promo 4.50
Spider-Man, promo 3.50
Spider-Man, prototype 3.50
Wolverine, promo 3.50
Wolverine, prototype 3.50
Tin set, 100 cards + 5 bonus
    cards (released Fall, 1993) 95.00
Bonus cards from tin set
LM-1 Scarlet Witch 3.00
LM-2 Feral 3.00
LM-3 Deathbird 3.00
LM-4 Typhoid Mary 3.00
LM-5 Jubilee 3.00

1993 MARVEL MASTERPIECES
"FINAL EDITION"
SkyBox (1993, Painted)
Set: 90 cards 25.00
Pack: 6 cards 1.50
X-MEN 2099 Spectra cards (1:9)
   "S" eight different, each . . . 10.00
She-Hulk prototype card 4.00
Hulk 2099 promo card 3.50
Daredevil promo card 5.00

MARVEL MASTERPIECES 1994
Marvel/Fleer (1994, Painted)
Greg & Tim Hildebrandt art
Set: 140 cards 20.00
Set: 139 signature cards . . . 100.00
Pack: 9 cards + 1 signature series
   card 1.50
Holofoil cards (1:3)
   Ten different, each 3.00
PowerBlast cards (1:6)
   Nine different, each 4.00
Eight-card promo sheet with Captain
   America back (*Previews*) . . . 1.00
Eight-card promo sheet, with Captain
   America masterprint back
   (San Diego Comic Con)
   (and media) 2.00
Eight-card promo sheet, with Venom
   masterprint back (National
   Sports Con) (and media) . . . 2.00
Four-card promo sheet 1.50

MARVEL MASTERPIECES '95
Fleer (1995)
Set: 151 cards 25.00
Pack: 2.50
Canvas (1:2)
   22 diff., each 2.00
Holoflash (1:12)
   8 diff., each 8.00
Mirage Lenticular (1:360)
   2 diff., each 50.00
Four-card promo sheet
   (*Collect 12-95*) 2.00

MARVEL METAL 1995
Fleer (1995, Painted)
Set: 138 cards 30.00
Pack: 7 cards + 1 silver flasher 1.50
Silver Flasher cards (1:1)
   137 diff., each 1.00
Metal Blaster cards (1:2)
   18 diff., each 2.00
Gold Blaster cards (1:3)
   18 diff., each 3.00
Four-card promo sheet
   (*Previews, Collect, Wizard*) . 1.00
Four different wrappers

Marvel Metal 1995 (Fleer 1995)

MARVEL 1993 ANNUALS
Marvel Comics (1993, Comic)
Set: 27 cards + checklist 20.00
Cards, each 1.00

MARVEL SUPERHEROES
Donruss (1966, Comic)
Set 66 cards 150.00
Captain America #s 1–11, each 2.00
Iron Man #s 12–22, each 2.00
Daredevil #s 23–33, each 2.50
Spider–Man #s 34–44, each . . 2.75
Hulk #s 45–55, each 2.25
Thor #s 56–66, each 2.00

MARVEL SUPERHEROES First Issue Covers
FTCC (1984, Covers)
Set: 60 cards 20.00
Set: 60 cards in factory box . . 25.00
Pack: 5 cards 1.50

MARVEL SUPER HEROES
STICKERS/White Backs
Topps (1976, Comic)
Set: 40 stickers (plus 6 caption
   variations) + 9 puzzle cards 125.00
Wrapper: 3 diff., each 4.00
Common sticker 2–4.00
Deathlok 7.50
Peter Parker 6.00
Silver Surfer 6.50
Spider-Man 4.00
The Punisher 18.50
Warlock 5.00
Puzzle/Checklist cards: Picture is
Conan the Barbarian #1 cover
1 thru 9 . . . . 10.00
Pack: 3 cards, 1 puzzle 5.00
See also: Comic Book Heroes Stickers

MARVEL UNIVERSE
(Marvel Cards I)
Comic Images (1987, Comic)
Set: 90 cards 60.00
Pack: 4 cards + promo sticker . 3.00

Marvel Universe I (Impel 1990)

MARVEL UNIVERSE I
Impel (1990, Comic)
Set: 162 cards 45.00
Pack: 12 cards 4.00
Tin box set (4,000 made) . . 200.00
Holograms
MH1 Cosmic Spider-Man . . . 15.00
MH2 Magneto 18.00
MH3 Silver Surfer 17.00
MH4 Wolverine 21.00
MH5 Spider-Man vs. Green
Goblin 17.00
Promo cards
Diamond promo packs, 5 cards
in cello pack (rare) 30.00
Promo cards say "Produced &
distributed by Impel Marketing, Inc."
above the Marvel copyright line on the
card back. Regular cards say
"Exclusively distributed by Impel
Marketing Inc." below the Marvel
copyright information.
Promo cards 5–7.00
**Diamond *Previews* uncut four-card
sheets**
Cards 57, 62, 83 & 82 . . . . . 25.00
Cards 39, 8, 3 & 32 . . . . 25.00
Cards 29, 6, 78 & 60 . . . . . . 25.00
Cards 100, 89, 96 & 87 . . . . 25.00
Cards 63, 125, 136 & 139
Existence not verified 25.00
Diamond *Previews*, cut, each . 5.00
Note: Diamond cards have a gray
diamond symbol overprinted on the
cards' backs.
Toy Biz variants, unnumbered
Nine different 1–2.00

MARVEL UNIVERSE II
Impel (1991, Comic)
Set: 162 cards 25.00
Pack 2.50
Holograms
H-1 Spider-Man 13.00
H-2 Hulk 13.00
H-3 Punisher 14.00
H-4 Dr. Doom 12.00
H-5 Fantastic Four vs. the
Mole Men 12.00
Collector's set in tin box with all
5 holograms (7,500 made) 100.00
Promo cards
Diamond Precut Set (Dealer) . 14.50
1 Spider-Man 3.00
45 Silver Surfer 3.00
51 Cyclops 3.00
57 Magneto 3.00
124 Fantastic Four vs. Doctor
Doom 3.00
Diamond *Previews* uncut insert sheet
Cards 1, 45, 51, 57 & 124 . 17.50
Diamond Inserts, cut, each . . . 2.50

Marvel Universe II (Impel 1991)

MARVEL UNIVERSE III
Impel (1992, Comic)
Set: 200 cards 20.00
Pack: 12 cards 1.50
Tin box set (10,000 made) . . 60.00
Holograms
H-1 Hulk 9.00
H-2 Thing 7.00
H-3 Wolverine 10.00
H-4 Venom 10.00
H-5 Ghost Rider 9.00
Venom promo (*Advance*) 10.00
Prototype promo cards
1 Spider-Man 3.00
34 Invisible Woman 2.50
37 Captain America 2.50
Set: 3 cards in clear cello pack 9.00
Diamond *Previews* uncut insert
sheet (Human Torch, Silver Surfer,
Spider-Man, Thanos) 10.00

Diamond Insert, cut, each 2.00
Mini Press four-card sheet 3.00

Marvel Universe IV (SkyBox 1993)

MARVEL UNIVERSE IV
SkyBox (1993, Comic)
Set: 180 cards 20.00
Marvel 2099 Foils (1:10)
Nine different, each 6.00
Hologram (1:180)
H-IV Spider-Man vs. Venom . 75.00
Promo cards
0 Deathlok promo card 4.50
Silver Sable promo 3.50
Pack: 10 cards 1.25
Note: 4 different wrappers.

MARVEL CARDS
UNIVERSE 1994
Marvel/Fleer (1994, Painted)
Set: 200 cards 30.00
Pack: 12 cards 2.50
Pack: 9 cards 1.50
Holograms (1:18)
Four different, each 12.00
Power Blast (1:4)
Nine different, each 3.00
Gold background = Walmart packs;
silver background = jumbo packs;
multicolor backgrounds = regular packs
Suspended Animation (1:6)
Ten different, each 4.00
Promo cards
Nine-card promo sheet (*Advance*
or *Previews*) 1.00
Four-card promo sheet (*Collect*) 1.00
Four-card promo sheet (*Cards
Illustrated*) 1.00

[SAM KIETH'S]
THE MAXX
Topps (1994, Comic)
Set: 90 cards 12.50
Pack: 8 cards 1.50

All prices listed are for *Near Mint* condition.   **341**

Etched Foil cards (1:18) untitled
1 (Julie Winters) 7.00
2 (Queen of the Leopard
   Women) 7.00
3 (The Maxx) 7.00
4 (The Maxx and The ISZ) . . . 7.00
5 (1:case) 35.00
6 untitled promo Etched Foil . . 2.00
Promo card 1.50
Promo sheet with card 2.00

MELTING POT
Comic Images (1993, Comic)
Set: 90 chromium cards (+10 variant
   cards: #23, 25, 28, 50, 52,
   59, 69, 73, 74 & 82) 20.00
Pack: 7 cards 2.00
Prism cards (1:12)
P1 Eastman 7.50
P2 Talbot 8.00
P3 Bisley 10.00
P4 In the Beginning 7.50
P5 Inspiration 7.50
P6 The Melting Pot 7.50
Prism promo (*Advance #58*) . . 2.00
Chromium promo card 5.00
Holochrome variations 5.00

MILESTONE:
THE DAKOTA UNIVERSE
SkyBox (1993, Comic)
Set: 100 cards 10.00
Pack: 8 cards 1.00
Foil-Embossed cards (1:36 packs)
M1 Hardware 14.00
M2 Static 14.00
Promo cards
M1 Hardware 1.00
M2 Blood Syndicate 1.00
M3 Icon & Rocket 1.00
M4 Static 1.00
M5 Hardware vs. Alva 1.00
M6 Boogieman 1.00
M7 Holocaust 1.00
Prototype cards
19 Icon & Rocket 1.00
20 Hardware 1.00
21 Static 1.00
23 Blood Syndicate 1.00
Diamond Dist. Show promos
The Admiral (David Robinson) 15.00
Magic (Johnson) 15.00

MIRAGE/
NEXT CHARACTERS
Mirage/Next (1993, Comic)
Set: 24 cards in "Secret" band 12.00

N

NEXT MEN
Dark Horse Comics (1992, Comic)
Set: 12 cards, mail-in from

Next Men #1–#6 . . . . 12.00
Bethany & Jasmine promo . . . 1.00

O

OMAHA, THE CAT DANCER
Kitchen Sink (1993, Comic)
Set: 36 cards boxed (Reed Waller)
   + 3 Cherry promo cards . . 14.00

P

PEANUTS
PREVIEW EDITION
Tuff Stuff (1992, Comic Strip)
Boxed, 33-card set 8.00

PEANUTS CLASSICS
ProSport Specialties (1992)
Set: 200 cards 25.00
Hologram Snoopy for President 7.50

The Phantom (Comic Images 1995)

THE PHANTOM
Comic Images (1995, Comic)
Set: 90 cards 12.50
Pack: 10 cards 1.00
Chromium cards, 6 diff., each 7.00
Rare Art, 3 diff., each 12.00
Medallion card 20.00
24-K gold signature card (500) 50.00
Six-card uncut sheet 15.00
Promo card 1.00
Binder 20.00

PLASM
Zero Issue Trading Cards
River Group (1993, Comic)
Set: 150 cards 12.50
Pack: 9 cards 1.50
Bonus cards, 8 diff., each . . . 8.00
9 Oob (from binder) 18.00
Level 2 Bonus cards
1 Lorca & His Enemy 15.00

2 Lorca & His Lust-Mate 15.00
3 Lorca & His Lover 15.00
4 Heroes from Earth 15.00
Raised Foil cards, each . . . 35.00
Promo Sheet 4.00
Promo–10 cards, cello pack
   for Diamond Comics 8.00
   for Heroes World 10.00
Album Binder 60.00
Album Binder, 2nd printing . . 20.00
Warriors of Plasm special edition
   tin box set with 4 bonus cards
   and Level 2 #4 raised foil . 35.00

POPEYE (BOOKLETS)
Deitz Gum (1930s)
Set: 30 booklets 1,000.00
Single booklet 35.00

POPEYE
Card-O/Whitman (1930s)
Popeye Sectional Figures, [R112-11]
   Set: 26 cards 100.00
   Each 5.00

POPEYE
Ad-Trix Cards (1950)
Set: 66 cards [R738] 250.00
Card 3.50

Popeye (Card Creations 1994)

POPEYE
Card Creations (1994, Comic Strip)
Set: 100 cards 12.50
Pack: 6 cards 1.00
Character Foil cards (1:9)
   12 different, each 6.00
Evolution Chrome cards (1:36)
   8 different, each 12.00
Power Cels (1:360)
   3 different, each 25.00
   Promos, 4 diff., each 1.00

POST CEREAL STICKERS
Post (1979)

4 Sets (Superman, Batman, Wonder
Woman, others) 10.00

Prince Valiant (Comic Images 1995)

PRINCE VALIANT
Comic Images (1995, Comic Strip)
Set: 90 cards 11.00
Pack: 10 cards 1.00
Chromium cards
Six different, each 7.00
Funny Pages subset,
three different, each 10.00
Medallion card 15.00
Signature card (500 made) .. 50.00
Six card uncut sheet 25.00
Promo card 1.00

PUNISHER
Comic Images (1988, Comic)
Set: 50 cards 17.50
Pack: 5 cards, cello pack 2.00

PUNISHER
WAR JOURNAL ENTRY
GUTS & GUNPOWDER
Comic Images (1992, Comic)
Set: 90 cards 12.00
Pack: 10 cards 1.50
Prizm promo card 5.00
Promo card 3.50
Prism cards, 3 diff., each 9.00
Scratch & Sniff, 3 diff., each .. 7.50

R

RETURN OF SUPERMAN
SkyBox (1993, Comic)
Set: 100 cards 25.00
Pack: 8 cards 1.50
Foil Enhanced Bonus cards (1:36)
SP1of4 Superman–The Man of
Steel! 15.00
SP2of4 Superman in Action! . 15.00
SP3of4 The Adventures of
Superman! 15.00

SP4of4 Superman! 18.00
0 Promo card 4.00
Complete factory set, with all
bonus cards and inc. two special
cards + double-sided binder 80.00

S

SACHS & VIOLENS
Comic Images (1993, Comic)
Set: 90 cards 8.00
Prism cards (1:16)
6 diff., each 7.00
Sachs promo card (*Triton*) 2.00
Violens promo card (*Triton*) ... 2.00
Promo card 2.50

SAD SACK
Novel Candy Company
Sad Sack Funny Money, each . 4.00
Set: 2 cards 10.00

Sandman (SkyBox 1994)

SANDMAN
SkyBox (1994, Comic)
Set: 90 cards, 4½" tall 25.00
Pack: 6 cards 2.00
Endless Gallery, Gold Foil (1:18)
I Dream 15.00
II Destiny 15.00
III Desire 17.50
IV Despair 15.00
V Delirium 15.00
VI Destruction 15.00
VII Death 17.50
3-D Stereo Hologram card (1:180)
a Morpheus 75.00
Foil-border prototypes, Silver
I Dream 30.00
II Destiny 30.00

III Desire 35.00
IV Despair 30.00
V Delirium 30.00
VI Destruction 30.00
VII Death 35.00
S1 Dolls House promo (4½" tall) 4.00
Three-card promo packs, 3 diff.
from *Cards Illustrated*, each 1.50
Four-card promo sheet 5.00
Six-card uncut sheet 5.00

SAVAGE DRAGON
Comic Images (1992, Comic)
(Erik Larsen art)
Set: 90 cards 11.00
Pack: 10 cards 1.50
Prisms (1:12)
"P" six different, each 10.00
Prizm promo card 8.00
Promo card 3.50

SHADOWHAWK
Comic Images (1992, Comic)
(Jim Valentino art)
Set: 90 cards 11.00
Pack: 10 cards 1.00
Prism cards
"P" six different, each 10.00
Promo card 4.00

IMAGES OF SHADOWHAWK
Image (1994, Comic)
Set: 100 cards 17.50
Pack: 8 cards 1.50
Holofoil cards (1:9)
"SP" seven different, each .. 7.50
Superchase card (1:12 boxes)
0: ShadowBart 50.00
Three-card promo packs, 3 different,
from *Cards Illustrated*, each 1.00
Promo sheet (*Advance*) 1.50
Promo sheet (*Previews*) 1.50

SHI
Comic Images (1995)
Set: 90 chromium cards 25.00
Pack: 7 cards 2.00
Shi Action MagnaChrome cards
6 diff., each 8.00
Crusade Subset cards,
3 diff., each 12.50
Medallion card 20.00
William Tucci Autograph cards
(500 made) 50.00
Six-card uncut strip 20.00
Chromium promo card 2.00

SILVER SURFER
Comic Images (1992, Comic)
Set: 72 cards, all prisms 40.00
Pack: 7 cards 4.00
Promo card, prism 5.00

All prices listed are for *Near Mint* condition.

SIMPSONS, THE
SkyBox (1993, Comic)
Set: 90 cards (Tattoos, Characters,
Itchy & Scratchy, Radioactive
Man) 12.50
Wiggle cards (1:4)
"W" nine different, each 3.00
Animation Cel cards (1:18)
(C1) Barber Shop background . 8.50
(C2) Barber Shop chair 7.50
(C3) Barber Shop Cat's head . 7.50
(C4) TV background 8.50
(C5) 17 characters watching TV 8.50
(C6) Maggie and TV Set 7.50

The Simpsons (SkyBox 1993)

Glow-in-the Dark (1:36)
(G1) Eyeballs (5 Simpsons) . . 12.50
(G2) Shock! (Cat & Mouse) . . 12.50
(G3) Smilin' Joe ("Nuclear
Power") 12.50
(G4) TV ("The Simpsons") . . . 12.50
Promo cards
Four-card promo sheet 2.50
18 Otto the Busdriver promo . . 1.00
P3 Itchy & Scratchy promo . . . 1.00
B1 & C1 two-part cel promo card 7.50

SIMPSONS II
SkyBox (1994, Comic)
Set: 80 cards (S1–S40, I1–I20
R1–R10, B1–B10) 15.00
Pack: 8 cards 1.00
Smell-O-Rama cards (1:3)
1 to 10, each 1.00
Wiggle cards (1:6)
W1 to W9, each 2.00
Disappearing Ink cards (1:36)
D1 to D4, each 10.00
Arty Art cards (1:180)
A1 to A4, each 30.00
Promos
P1 "Comin' at ya" promo 1.00
P2 Itchy & Scratchy promo . . . 1.00
P3 Grampa Simpson Smell-o-rama
promo 1.00
P4 Willy "The Dupe" Dipkin . . . 1.00

B4 Black Belch promo 1.00
B5 Radioactive Man/Bart
spinner 1.00
How to use spinner card promo . .50

SPAWN
Wildstorm (1995, Comic)
Set: 150 tall cards +
2 checklists 15.00
Pack: 8 cards 1.25
Painted cards (1:9)
12 diff., each 5.00
ToddToys Action Figure cards
(1:18) 6 diff., each 7.50
Todd McFarlane all-new Art (1:36)
4 diff., each 10.00
ToddChrome (1:360)
TC1 Spawn, New Costume . . 25.00
Autograph cards 50.00
Promo & Prototypes
P1 direct market promo 1.00
P2 promo (*Cards Illus.#17*) . . . 1.00
Toys "R" Us comic two-packs
Prototype 1 . . . . 2.00
Prototype 2 . . . . 2.00
Prototype 3 . . . . 2.00
Prototype 4 . . . . 2.00

SPEED RACER
Prime Time (1993, Comic)
Set: 55 cards 7.50
Set: gold foil 25.00
Pack: 7 cards + gold foil card . 1.00
Gold foil cards, each 50
Chromium cards, 6 diff., each 5.00

SPIDER-MAN
The Todd McFarlane Era
Comic Images (1992, Comic)
Set: 90 cards 15.00
Pack 10 cards 1.75
Promo card 1.50
Prism cards
"P1–P6" six different, each 15.00

SPIDER-MAN II
30th Anniversary
Comic Images (1992, Comic)
Set: 90 cards 14.00
Prizm promo card 8.00
Pack: 10 cards 1.75
Prism cards
"P7–P12" six different, each 12.00

SPIDER-MAN TEAM UP
Comic Images (1990, Comic)
Set: 45 cards + header card . 12.00
Pack: 5 cards + header 1.50

AMAZING SPIDER-MAN
Marvel/Fleer (1994, Comic)
Set: 150 cards (MBa) 20.00
Polaroid Holograms (1:18) All

packs, 4 different, each . . . 10.00
Suspended Animation (1:4) Regular

Spider-Man, The Todd McFarlane Era
(Comic Images 1992)

packs, 12 different, each . . . 4.00
Gold Web (1:7) Jumbo packs,
Six different, each 8.00
Gold Web (1:7) **11 card** Blue packs,
Six different, each 8.00
Masterprints large panels (1:case)
Nine diff., each 5.00
Promo cards and sheets
Three-card strips w/Master Prints ad
Powers strip 1.50
Venom strip 1.50
Enemies strip 1.50
Nine-card promo sheet 1.50
Nine-card promo sheet (*Triton*) 2.50
Nine-card promo sheet (*Comic
Book Collector*) 2.00
Large Web card promo 2.00
Four-card sheet (*Advance
or Collect*) 1.50
Four-card sheet (Doctor Octopus,
Vulture, Venom, Spider-Man)
(from *Spider-Man* mag. #1) . 1.50

SPIDER-MAN
Fleer Ultra (1995, Painted)
Set: 150 cards 25.00
Pack: 10 cards 2.00
Gold Foil Signature Cards: (1:Pack)
Set: 149 cards 100.00
Golden Web, Chromium (1:3)
9 diff. 2.00
Masterpieces, Chromium (1:3)
9 diff, each 2.00
ClearChrome (1:7)
10 diff., each 3.00
Holoblast (1:9) 6 diff., each . . 4.00
Nine-card promo sheet
(*Advance, Collect, Previews*) 1.00
Four-card promo sheet (*Wizard*) 1.00

All prices listed are for *Near Mint* condition.

SPIDER-MAN CEREAL
Ralston Foods (1995)
Set: 5 cards 5.00

SPIDER-MAN
Cookie Crisp (1992)
Set: 6 cards 5.00

SPIRIT
Kitchen Sink (1995, Comic)
Set: 36 in box 15.00
Promo #1 of 2 The Octopus (*Cards Illustrated #17*) 1.00
Promo #2 of 2 P'Gell 1.00

SPLATTER BOWL I
The River Group (1994)
Two-card promo sheet 2.00
Preview set: 30 cards, plus 1 foil
card, in tin box 10.00

Spoof Bogus Hero Cards (1992)

SPOOF COMICS PRESENTS
Spoof Comics (1992)
Batbabe
Set: 37 cards 13.00
Bogus Heroes
Set: 37 cards 13.00
Spider-Femme
Set: 37 cards 13.00
Spoof Comics Month
Set: 37 cards 6.00

SPY VS. SPY
Lime Rock (1993)
Set: 55 cards 7.50
Pack: 9 cards 75
Holograms
Spy vs. Spy #2 . . . . 3.50
#3 hologram 3.00

S.T.A.T. #0
Majestic Entertainment (1994)
Promo cards *(Set cancelled)*

Set: 9 cards, A-1 thru A-9 . . . 10.00

SUPERGIRL
Topps (1983, Movie)
Set: 44 sticker/cards 10.00
Pack: 6 sticker/cards 1.00

SUPER HERO STICKERS
Philadelphia Gum (1967, Comic)
Set: 55 stickers 350.00
Sticker 7.50

SUPER HERO, see DC or MARVEL

SUPERMAN
Gum, Inc. (1940) (R145)
Set: 72 cards 3,500.00
#1 Superman 50.00
#2–48, each 30.00
#49–71, rare, each 75.00
#72 Superman vs.Torpedo . 120.00
WTW Inc. (1984) Reprint
Set: 72 cards 17.00

SUPERMAN PACK DESIGN
Leader Novelty (1942)
Set: 48 cards. 1,900.00
Cards #1–#24 . . . . 30.00
Cards #25–#48 . . . . 40.00

SUPERMAN
Topps (1966, TV)
Set: 66 cards (B&W photos) 180.00
Card #1 Krypton Is Doomed . . 5.00
Card #66 Harmless Blow 5.00
Card 3.50
Wrapper 15.00
Back variations:
1. White (scarce);
2. Orange w/Copyright below text;
3. Orange w/1965 copyright on side &
"Watch Superman on T.V." on bottom

SUPERMAN IN THE JUNGLE
Topps (1968)
Set: 66 cards (test set) . . . 2,700.00
Card 40.00

SUPERMAN THE MOVIE
Topps (1978, Movie)
Series 1
Set: 77 cards/12 stickers 20.00
Pack: 10 cards, 1 sticker 2.00
Series 2
Set: 88 cards/14 stickers 25.00
Pack 1.50

SUPERMAN
Drakes Cakes (1979)
Set: 24 cards 75.00
Card 3.50

SUPERMAN II
Topps (1981, Movie)
Set: 88 cards/22 stickers 17.00
Pack: 11 cards, 1 sticker 1.50

SUPERMAN III
Topps (1983, Movie)
Set: 99 cards/22 stickers 17.00
Pack: 10 cards, 1 sticker 1.25

Superman, The Man of Steel (SkyBox 1994)

SUPERMAN THE MAN OF STEEL
SkyBox (1994, Painted)
Collector's Edition
Set: 90 tall cards 17.50
Pack: 6 cards 1.19
Spectra-Etch (1:7)
"S" six different, each 5.00
SC1 Collector's Edition promo . 2.50
Premium Edition
Set: 90 tall cards, Platinum
Series 49.95
Pack: 6 cards 4.00
SD3 Man of Steel SkyDisk . 125.00
Forged in Steel (1:18)
"FS" four different, each . . 25.00
SP1 Premium Edition promo . . 4.00

SWEET LUCY TECHNOPHILIA Set #0
Brainstorm Comics (1993)
*From Interzone #1, Sweet Lucy #1,
Interzone #2 and Technophilia #1*
Set: 20 cards + header slip . . . 8.00

T

TANK GIRL
Comic Images (1995, Movie)

Set: 90 cards 10.00
Pack: 10 cards 1.00
Magnachrome, 6 diff., each . . . 7.00
Subset: 3 cards 12.00
Promo card 1.00

Teenage Mutant Ninja Turtles–Cartoon
(Topps 1989)

TEENAGE MUTANT NINJA TURTLES–CARTOON
Topps (1989)
Set: 88 cards/11 stickers
  (Lime green border) 15.00
Super Glossy set in collector's
  box, with 22 bonus cards . 20.00
Pack: 5 cards, 1 sticker 50
Note: Four different wrappers.
Deluxe (Topps Ireland 1990)
Set: 66 cards, no stickers
  in collector box 8.00
Set: 66 cards, 11 stickers . . . 10.00
SERIES II Topps (1990)
Set: 88 cards/11 stickers . . . 9.00
Pack, 11 cards, 1 sticker 75
Note: Two different wrappers.
Holograms, set of 4 . . . . . . 10.00

TEENAGE MUTANT NINJA TURTLES–MOVIE CARDS
Topps (1990)
Set: 132 cards/11 stickers
  (film strip bottom border) . . 11.00
Pack: 9 cards, 1 sticker 75
Pack A set of 66 deluxe cards . 6.00
Pack B set of 66 deluxe cards . 6.00
Collector's Set: 132 cards
  in box 12.50

TEENAGE MUTANT NINJA TURTLES–MOVIE II
THE SECRET OF THE OOZE
Topps (1991, Movie)
Set: 99 cards/11 stickers
  (red border, green ooze) . . . 9.00
Pack: 8 cards, 1 sticker 75

TEENAGE MUTANT NINJA TURTLES–MOVIE III
Topps (1993, Movie)
Set: 88 cards, 11 stickers 7.50

TEENAGE MUTANT NINJA TURTLES TOY CARDS
Playmates (1994)
Cards from TMNT action figures,
  47 different, each 1.00

TEK WORLD
Cardz (1993, Comic)
(Lee Sullivan art,
Ron Goulart words)
Set: 100 cards 15.00
Pack: 8 cards 1.00
TekChrome cards
  "T" four different, each . . . 10.00
Lee Sullivan autographed card 30.00
William Shatner autographed
  card 60.00
Prototypes, 3 diff., each 1.00
Four-card promo sheet
  (Comicfest '93) 2.50

TICK TEST SET
NEC Press (1992, Comic)
Set: 32 cards + 4 full-color cards
  (4,000 numbered sets) . . . 12.00

TOM & JERRY
Cardz (1994, Animated)
Set: 60 cards 8.00
TekChromes, 3 diff., each . . . 7.50
Promo cards, 3 diff., each 3.00

TRADING CARD TREATS
National Safe Kids Campaign
Impel (1991, Comic & Cartoon)
Marvel Super Heroes, set of 6 4.00
Captain America 75
Ghost Rider 1.00
Hulk .75
She-Hulk 75
Spider-Man 75
Wolverine 75
Archie, set of 6 50
Came in clear cello packs of 3 cards.
Packs come in bags of 24, by set.

TRIBE: THE INTRO
Press Pass (1993, Comic)
(Larry Johnson/Todd Stroman art)
Set: 90 cards 12.50
Pack: 8 cards 1.00
Prism cards (1:12)
  "P" five different, each 7.00
Thermofoil cards (1:36)
  "T" five different, each 11.00
Tribe Comic #1 cover (5,000) . 40.00
Note: 4 different wrappers.

Promo cards, 1–4, set forms
  panel 5.00
P.P.1 Hannibal, Rosalyn, Lord Deus
  Deivirile promo card (*Wizard*) 1.00
Unnamed comic card (*Arena #9*) 1.00
Hannibal card (*Arena #10*) . . . 1.00

U

ULTRAVERSE
SkyBox (1993, Comic)
Set: 100 cards 12.50
Pack: 8 cards 1.10
Bonus Rookie cards (7:36)
  "R" nine different, each 3.00
Bonus Ultimate Rookie cards
  "S" four different, each 6.00
Bonus Ultraverse Ultra (1:36)
  "U" two different, each . . . 12.00
(Mere) promo cards!
0 The Night Man (*Comic Book
  Collector #8*) 3.00
00 Boneyard promo (*Hero #1*) . 4.00
01 Prime promo card 3.00
02 Mantra promo card 3.00
P0 Warstrike promo card
  (U logo) 1.50
P0 Warstrike (*Heroes World*) . . 4.00
P0 Warstrike (*Capital City*) . . . 3.00
P1 Prototype promo card 2.00
Promos bagged with Comic Books
C1 Prime promo (*Prime #2*) . . . 2.50
C2 Hardcase promo
  (*Hardcase #2*) 2.50
C3 Strangers promo
  (*Strangers #2*) 2.50
C4 Freex promo (in *Freex #1*) . 2.50
C5 Mantra promo (in *Mantra #1*) 2.50
Four-card front promo sheet . . 4.00
Six-card promo sheet (National
  Sports Collectors Con.) 5.00

ULTRAVERSE II: ORIGINS
SkyBox (1994, Comic)

Ultraverse II (SkyBox 1994)

Set: 90 cards 17.50
Factory Set: 90 cards, all 9 bonus
    cards, 2 new cards & album 75.00
Pack: 8 cards 1.50
Painted Bonus cards (1:10)
    "B" seven different, each . . . 8.00
Ultraverse Ultra (1:36)
UB1 Mantra 15.00
UB2 Yrial (Julie Bell art) 17.50
Autographed cards (1:3,600) . 50.00
Comic Art Exchange (1:71,000)
Four-card promo sheet 2.00
P0 Mantra promo card 1.00
P00 Sludge promo card 1.00
P1 Prime promo card (*Comic Book
    Collector #14*) 1.00
P2 Rune promo card (*Wizard*) . 1.00

ULTRAVERSE EDITION
SKYBOX MASTER SERIES
SkyBox (1994, Painted)
Dave Dorman art
Set: 90 cards 15.00
Ultra cards
    "U" five different, each 7.50
Holithograms
H1 Ultraforce flash 15.00
H2 Warstrike flash 15.00
Autographed card (2400 made) 50.00
Original artwork exchange card
Promo cards
C1 Sludge promo (*Cards
    Illustrated*) 1.00
P0 Tyrannosaur promo 1.00
P01 Book promo 1.00
P02 Heater promo 1.00
P03 Solitaire Diamond 1.00
Large promo sheet (from *Advance
    and Previews*) 1.00
P05 Yrial promo 1.00

ULTRAVERSE: RUNE
SkyBox (1993, Comic)
0 Promo card (*Hero*) 2.00
00 Promo card (*Hero*) 2.00

Unity (Comic Images 1992)

UNCANNY X-MEN, see X-MEN

UNITY
Comic Images (1992, Comic)
Set: 90 cards 18.00
Pack: 10 cards 1.75
Promo card 6.00
Chromium cards, Valiant Rookies
Bloodshot 17.00
Hotshot 16.00
Rai 16.00
Turok 19.00
Rai and the Future Force . . . 14.00
Screen 14.00

V

VALIANT ERA, THE
Upper Deck (1993, Comic)
Set: 120 cards 15.00
Pack: 8 cards 1.50
Upper Deck Logo card 15.00
SP1 The Art of Joe Quesada . 35.00
First Appearances
FA1 Shadowman 9.00
FA2 H.A.R.D.Corps 10.00
FA3 Tohru Nakadai 42nd Rai . 9.00
FA4 Tekla 9.00
FA5 Toyo Harada 10.00
FA6 Ivar, The Timewalker . . . 9.00
FA7 Turok 10.00
FA8 Master Darque 9.00
FA9 Bloodshot 9.00
Unseen Art
U3, U6, each 10.00
U1, U2, U4, U5, U7, U8, U9 6.00
Turok & X-O Manowar promo . 9.00
Promo cards, 30 diff., cards for
    ComicCon 1993, each 1.25

VALIANT ERA II
Upper Deck (1994, Comic)
Set: 140 cards 20.00
Pack: 8 cards 1.25
Promo card (*Advance*) 1.00
Promo cards, 36 diff. (*Triton #5*
    and other sources), each . . 1.00
HoloView 3-D
LE1 X-O Manowar 30.00
First Appearances (1:10)
    "FA10 to FA18" each 5.00
Promotional Art (1:10)
    "PA" nine diff., each 4.00
Oversize cards (1:Box)
    "OS" eight different, each . . 8.00

THE VALIANT FILES:
SECRETS FROM THE
HARBINGER FOUNDATION
Upper Deck (1994, Comic)
Promo card (*Advance*) 1.00

VAMPIRELLA
Topps (1994, Various)
Set: 90 cards 15.00
Pack: 10 cards + 1 gold or
    chase card 1.25
Gold cards, 90 diff., each 1.00
Horrorglow, 6 diff., each . . . 8.00
Pin-Up Gallery, 6 diff.,
    3"x5" (1:box) 7.50
00 Promo (from *Vengeance
    of Vampirella #11*) 1.00
C1 Promo (from *Combo #2*) . . 1.00
P1 Promo 1.00
P2 Photo promo (from *Vengeance of
    Vampirella #8*) 1.00
P3 promo (Listner art) 1.00

VAMPIRELLA GALLERY
Topps (1995)
Set: 72 tall cards 25.00
Pack: 7 cards, inc. 1 gold . . . 2.00
Gold foils (1:1), each 50
Set: Gold foils 40.00
Femme Fatale Chromium (1:18)
    6 diff., each 12.00
Vampirella Hologram (1:360) 50.00
One-card promo sheet
    (*Previews 10-95*) 2.00
P1 promo card (*Advance #84*) . 1.50
P6 promo card (*Bad Girls*) . . . 1.50

VERTIGO
SkyBox (1994, Comic)
Set: 90 oversized cards 25.00
Pack: 6 cards 2.50
SD4 Death SkyDisk (1:180) . . 75.00
Foil cards (1:18)
    I–VI, Six different, each . . . 12.00
Promos
SP1 Swamp Thing promo 1.00
SP2 John Constantine promo . 1.00
SP3 The Sandman promo 1.00
SC1 The books of Magic 1.00

W

WETWORKS
Wildstorm Productions (1995)
Set: 107 chromium cards . . . 25.00
Pack: 7 cards 3.25
Gold Chromium, 9 diff., each 10.00
Die-Cut chromium, 9 diff., each 5.00

WILDC.A.T.S
Topps (1993, Comic)
Set: 100 cards (no card #68, 2 diff.
    card #66) 12.50
Pack: 8 cards 1.00
Prism cards (1:18)
    Six different, each 10.00
Promo sheet ("Coming Nov.92") 5.00
Promo card (1992) 3.50
0 promo card (1993) 3.50

All prices listed are for *Near Mint* condition.

0 Red promo card 30.00

WILDC.A.T.S '94
Wildstorm Productions (1994)
Set: 96 cards, oversize,
chromium 35.00
Pack: 6 cards 2.50
Painted Refractor (1:8)
"P" Twelve different, each . 10.00
Double-Sided (1:12)
"D" Six different, each 12.50
WildDISCs (1:Box) 4½" diameter
5 different, each 5.00
Autographed cards #2, 10, 11, 15, 16,
17, 29, 33, 40, 48, 52, 62, 69, 78,
93, 96, each (1:375) 25.00
Promo cards
P1 *Diamond* 2.50
P2 (*Wizard*) 2.00

WILDC.A.T.S. (ANIMATED)
Wildstorm (1995)
Set: 135 cards 20.00
Pack: 8 cards 1.50
Animation Cels (1:12)
9 diff., each 7.00
Foil Etched (1:12)
9 diff., each 7.50
35mm Frames (1:360) . . . . . . spec.
Oversized Cards (1:box)
5 diff., each 10.00

WildC.A.T.S Toy Cards (Playmates 1995)

WILDC.A.T.S. TOY CARDS
Playmates (1995)
Cards from WildC.A.T.S action
figures, 29 diff., each 2.00

WILDSTORM ARCHIVES
Wildstorm Productions (1995)
Set: 99 Chromium cards 25.00
Pack: 6 Chromium cards 2.50
Gen[13] **Holo Foil** (1:6)
11 diff., each 10.00

WILDSTORM SET I
Wildstorm Productions (1994)
Set: 100 chromium + checklist 40.00
Refractor cards (1:24)
"C" nine different, each . . . 10.00
Autograph cards (1:86)
Mark Silvestri 50.00
Jim Lee 50.00
Others, 13 diff., each 20.00
WildC.A.T.S. promo sheet 3.00
Promo cards
WildC.A.T.S. promo 3.00
PR1 chromium promo (*Wizard*) 1.00

WILDSTORM GALLERY
Wildstorm Productions (1995)
Set: 138 tall cards 15.00
Pack: 8 painted cards 1.75
Battle cards (1:9)
12 diff., each 6.00
Reader's Choice (1:18)
6 diff., each 10.00
Promo cards:
P1(A) (Direct Market) 1.00
P1B Diamond 1.00
P2 Combo 1.00
Cards from WildStorm Rising
comic books, 11 diff., each . 1.00

WINNIE WINKLE
Novel Candy Company
Winnie Winkle 4.00
Set: 8 cards 35.00

WIZARD OF ID
Authentix (1995)
Set: 50 cards 10.00
Factory Set: 10.00
Pack: 6 cards 1.50
Silver Foils, 5 diff. 10.00
Gold card Chase Pax 15.00
Jumbo chase card redemption 25.00

WOLVERINE
(Marvel Cards III)
Comic Images (1988, Comic)
Set: 50 cards + header 25.00
Pack: 4 cards + header + promo
sticker 1.75

WOLVERINE:
FROM THEN 'TIL NOW
Comic Images (1991, Comic)
Set: 45 cards 12.00
Pack: 5 cards + header 1.25

WOLVERINE:
FROM THEN 'TIL NOW II
Comic Images (1992, Comic)
Set: 90 cards 12.00
Pack: 10 cards 1.25
Prizm promo card 5.00
Prism cards

"P" six different, each 12.00

X

X-FORCE
"THE BEGINNING OF THE END"
Comic Images (1991, Comic)
Set: 90 cards (Rob Liefeld) . . 24.00
Pack: 10 cards 1.50

X-Force (Comic Images 1991)

UNCANNY X-MEN COVERS I
Comic Images (1990, Comic)
Set: 90 cards 24.00
Pack: 5 cards 1.50

UNCANNY X-MEN COVERS II
Comic Images (1991, Comic)
Set: 45 cards 12.00
Pack: 5 cards 1.50

X-MEN
Comic Images (1991, Comic)
Set: 90 cards 15.00
Pack: 10 cards 1.00

(UNCANNY) X-MEN
Impel (1992, Comic)
Jim Lee art
Set: 100 cards 15.00
Tin box set (7,500 made) . . . 55.00
Pack: 6 cards 1.00
HOLOGRAMS
XH-1 Wolverine 10.00
XH-2 Cable 10.00
XH-3 Gambit 11.00
XH-4 Magneto 6.00
XH-5 X-Men 12.00
Magneto promo (*Advance*) . . 8.00
Jim Lee signed card w/stamp 75.00
Promo cards
Cable (Card #19 in set) 3.00
Magneto (Card #41 in set) . . . 3.00
Storm (Card #14 in set) 3.00
Wolverine (Card #2 in set) . . . 3.00

X-Men (Impel 1992); X-Men II (SkyBox 1993); Ultra X-Men (Fleer 1994).
X-Force and X-Men action figures from 1992 to 1995 have cards from these three series.

X-Men (Card #171 in set) 3.00
Note: Promo cards are almost identical
to the regular cards but have ™ in
black next to Marvel logo on back.
Regular set cards have ™ in red.
Toy Biz variants, each 1.00

X-MEN II
SkyBox (1993, Comic)
Set: 100 cards 17.50
Pack: 6 cards 1.50
Foil cards
H-1 Cable 11.00
H-2 Magneto 10.00
H-3 Storm 9.00
H-X Wolverine **3-D Hologram** 70.00
Gold Foil–Stamped: 30 Years
  "G" ninedifferent, each ... 5-7.00
Juggernaut prototype card 4.00
Juggernaut prototype (*Comic*
  Book Collector) 2.50

(ULTRA) X-MEN
Fleer (1994, Comic)
Set: 150 cards 20.00
Team Portrait cards (1:5) 10 card
  packs, 11 & 12 card WalMart packs
  (forms 3x3 Super-Panel)
  Nine different, each 6.00
Fatal Attractions "Power Blast"
  (1:11) 10-card comic shop packs
  (1:7) 14-card jumbo packs
  Six different, each 7–9.00
X-Men's Greatest Battles
  ("xxx of six") (1:3) 14-card
  jumbo packs (only)
  Six different, each 7.50
X-Men Silver X-Over foil cards
  (1:11) WalMart 12-card packs (only)
  Six different, each 15.00
Red Foil/X-Men Team Triptychs
  (1:11) in 11-card WalMart packs

(1:1) in 12-card WalMart packs
Blue Team (1–3), each 4.00
Gold Team (4–6), each 4.00
Promo cards
Nine-card promo sheet 4.50
Nine-card sheet, small
  (*Previews*) 2.50
Four-card magazine promo sheet of
  Cyclops, Storm, Gambit and
  Wolverine, with 4 football
  quarterbacks 3.00
Four-card promo sheet (Rogue,
  Wolverine vs. Spider-Man,
  Apocalypse, Jubilee)
  (*Spider-Man Magazine #1*) . 1.50
Variation Iceman card with card
  number (#98) missing 2.00

(ULTRA) X-MEN 1995
Fleer (1994, Comic)
Set: 150 cards 17.50
Pack: 10 cards 1.75
Jumbo Packs: 14 cards 2.50
Note: Four different wrappers.
Sinister Observations (1:9)
  Chromium, 10 different, each 4.00
Hunters & Stalkers (1:4) foils
  9 different, each 2.00
  Multicolor background = regular packs;
  Silver background = Jumbo packs;
  Gold background= Walmart packs
Suspended Animation (1:5)
  10 different, each 3.00
Nine-card promo sheet
  (*Advance*) 2.00

ULTRA X-MEN
Fleer (1995)
Set: 100 Chromium cards ... 25.00
Pack: 8 Chromium cards 3.00
  4 different wrappers
Gold Foil Signature Set:

100 cards 75.00
Gold Foil Signature cards (1:1) 1.00
Impact Cards (1:2), embossed
  20 diff., each 1.50
HoloFlash (1:6)
  9 diff., each 5.00
Wolverine chromium promo
  (*Advance #81*) 2.00
Cyclops chromium promo (*Cards*
  Illus.#23) 2.00

X-MEN (Oversized)
Haines (1993)
Blue Team
Cyclops 2.00
Gambit 2.00
Wolverine 2.00
Triptych
Wolverine and Marvel Girl ... 10.00
Storm, Cyclops & Professor X 10.00
Gambit and Rogue 10.00

X-MEN VIDEO
Pizza Hut (1993)
X-Men Team (Gold X) 3.00
  with Video tape & ashcan . 10.00
Professor X and Magneto
  (Silver X) 3.00
  With Video tape & ashcan . 10.00

X-MEN POCKET COMICS
ToyBiz (1994–95)
Eight different, each 2.50

X–MEN WATCH CARDS
Character Time (1993)
Cable 8.00
Cyclops 9.00
Dark Phoenix 10.00
Professor Xavier 8.00
Wolverine 9.00
X-Men 8.00

All prices listed are for *Near Mint* condition.   **349**

Y

YOUNGBLOOD
Comic Images (1992, Comic)
(Rob Liefeld art)
Set: 90 cards 13.00
Promo card (red border) 2.00
Prism cards
"P" six different, each 11.00
Comic promo cards blue border
0 Youngblood 3.50
1 Shaft 1.50
2 Bedrock 1.50
Foil comic promo 1.00
Youngblood & Cable (50,000 made)
Inside Comics promo 10.00

YOUNGBLOOD
SkyBox (1995, Comic)
Set: 90 cards + 9 stickers . . . 30.00
Pack: 8 cards + sticker (1:2) . . 4.00
Each pack has either a sticker or a
merchandise offer card
Wiggle Cards (1:8)
W1 Badrock 10.00
W2 Die Hard 10.00
W3 Kodiak 10.00
W4 Riptide 10.00
W5 Shaft 10.00
SkyDisc (1:72)
ESD1 Badrock 75.00
Large SkyDisc (1:1st
5,000 cases) 100.00
Promos
C1 Battlestone promo 1.00
P0 Shaft promo 1.00
P1 Sentinel promo 1.00
Badrock promo 1.00

Z

Mick Zeck Cards (Comic Images 1989)

ZECK, MIKE CARDS
Comic Images (1989, Comic)
Set: 45 cards + header 15.00
Pack: 5 cards + header 1.50

ALBUM STICKERS

Batman: The Animated Series (Panini 1993)

BATMAN: THE ANIMATED SERIES
Panini (1993, TV)
Set: 216 stickers+16 holograms 15.00
Album, 31 pages, inc. poster . . 1.00
Pack: 6 stickers 40

GARFIELD
Diamond Toy (1989)
Set: 180 album stickers
+ album 20.00
Pack 1.50
Album 2.50

HISTORY OF THE X–MEN
Comic Images (1987)
Set: 75 album stickers + album 40.00
Pack 3.00
Album, 24 pages 5.00

I LOVE SNOOPY
Panini (1986)
Set: 288 stickers 25.00

MARVEL'S MAGIC MOMENTS
Comic Images (1987)
Set: 80 album stickers + album 35.00
Pack 2.50
Album 3.50

MARVEL SUPER HEROES SECRET WARS
Leaf (1985, Comic)
Set: 180 album stickers
+ album 125.00
Pack 1.50
Album, 24 pages 5.00

MUTANT HALL OF FAME
Comic Images (1988)
Set: 80 album stickers + album 40.00
Pack 1.00
Album, 24 pages 2.50

OFFICIAL MARVEL UNIVERSE STICKERS
Comic Images (1986 i.e. 1987)
Set: 77 album stickers + album 50.00
Pack 1.00
Album, 24 pages 3.00

THE PUNISHER PAPERS
Comic Images (1990)
Set: 75 album stickers + album 30.00
Pack: 5 stickers (card size) . . . 1.50
Album, 24 pages 2.00

Webs (Spider-Man) (Comic Images 1991)

WEBS (Spider-Man)
Comic Images (1991)
(Todd McFarlane art)
Set: 75 album stickers + album 25.00
Pack: 5 stickers (card size) . . . 1.50
Album, 24 pages 3.00

WOLVERINE UNTAMED
Comic Images (1990)
Set: 75 album stickers + album 50.00
Pack: 5 stickers (card size) . . . 2.50
Album, 24 pages 5.00

WORLD OF SPIDER-MAN
Comic Images (1988)
Set: 50 album stickers + poster 30.00
Pack: 4 stickers 1.75
Poster 7.50
Album 15.00

X-MEN
Diamond Publishing (1993)
Set: 180 album stickers + album 20.00
Pack: 6 stickers 75
Album 2.00

POGS

I n 1992, the Hawaiian milkcap or pog craze began to register on big business radar screens. The blips on those screens looked like round trading cards to the corporate "powers that be," and so marketing plans called for all the same elements: packs with 8 or 10 pogs, foil-enhanced bonus or chase pogs and lots of promotion. No one wanted to miss this boat, so all the usual suspects got on board.

There was just one problem: no one collected them. There were too many trading cards on the market to begin with and pogs are too small to have interesting art-work. As a final insult, most of the caps came with an authentic scored groove for the tab, which would have been used to pull the cap out of a milk bottle, as if the cap had been intended to be used in a milk bottle, which it wasn't. Naturally, the groove was right in the middle of the art-work!

As a collectible, pogs were a dud in 1993, but as a game in 1994 they were a huge hit with the under-10 crowd! They are now sold by the handful from bags of 1,000 with colorful art-work of all kinds. Most cost 10¢ to 25¢, and there is no point in paying extra for one because you can get as many as you want at the local comic shop or show.

Thus, pogs aren't worth much today. But how about tomorrow? It takes demand as well as limited supply to make a collectible. Will there be a demand?

Marvel pogs (SlamCo 1993); DC promo and DC SkyCaps (SkyBox 1993)

DC SKYCAPS
SkyBox (1993)
Set: 54 caps 8.00
Foil-enhanced bonus SkyCaps
F1 Superman S-Shield logo 50
F2 The Last Son of Krypton
   S-Shield logo 50
F3 The Man of Tomorrow
   S-Shield logo 50
F4 Superboy S-Shield logo 50
F5 The Man of Steel S-Shield logo.50
F6 Batman logo 50
DC SkyCap Slammer, double-weight
   and thickness; foil-enhanced DC
   bullet on one side with SkyCap
   slammer logo on the other . . .50
Promo card with 4 pogs 1.00

BATMAN KNIGHTFALL
SkyBox (1993)
Set: 54 caps 8.00
Bonus Foil-enhanced caps (1:9)
B1 Classic Batman and Robin! . .50
B2 Arkham Asylum Breakout! . . .50

B3 The Man Who Broke Batman! .50
B4 New Batman! 50
Slammer (1:36) 50
Promo Caps
S1 The Joker 25

HERO CAPS
Marvel Action (#75011) 5.00
Spider-Man (#75011) 5.00
X-Men (#75011) 5.00

JIM LEE
SkyBox (1993)
Set: 71 caps 9.00
Bonus Foil-Stamped SkyCaps (5:36)
   5 different, each 50
Bonus Jim Lee Slammer (1:36) . .50
Promo caps
S1 Grifter 25
N2 Grifter 25

MARVEL POGS
SlamCo (1993)
Set: 20 caps 3.50

POPEYE
(1995)
Set: 60 caps 5.00

SIMPSON'S SKYCAPS
SkyBox (1995)
Set: 50 pogs 5.00

[Todd McFarlane's]
SPAWN SPOGZ
Eclipse (1993)
Set: 54 Spogz 7.50
Todd McFarlane Slammer Spog .50
Prizmspogz
   6 different, each 50
Platinumspog
M1 Spawn 75

ULTRAVERSE
SkyBox (1993)
S1 Ferret promo 25
G1 Reese promo 25
G3 Ferret promo 25
G5 Man of War promo 25

Batman Knightfall and Jim Lee pogs (SkyBox 1993); Popeye pogs (1995)

Superman Super Hero Stamps (Celebrity Stamps 1976)

PHONE CARDS

CYBERFORCE
GTS (1994)
Cyberforce #A (Team) 10.00
Cyberforce #B (Ripclaw) 10.00

DARK, THE
Peoples Telephone (1995)
The Dark (Bart Sears) 15.00
The Dark (George Perez) ... 15.00

MARVEL COMIC COVERS
GTS (1994)
Incredible Hulk #393:
  30th Anniv. 10.00
Amazing Fantasy #15: Intro
  Spider-Man 10.00
X-Men #30: Cyclops/Jean
  Grey wedding 10.00

MARVEL
Marvel Christmas set of 4,
  Logofon 10.00
Marvel Halloween set
  of 4, each 10.00

X-MEN FIRST APPEARANCES
GTS (1994)
X-Men #1: first X-Men 10.00
X-Men #50: first Polaris 10.00
X-Men #58: first Havok 10.00
X-Men #101: first Phoenix ... 10.00
Giant-Size X-Men #1: first
  New X-Men 10.00
Uncanny X-Men #282: first
  Bishop 10.00

ZEN INTERGALACTIC NINJA
Peoples Telephone (1994)
Zen #0, Jae Lee art 15.00

Zen #1, Hoang Nguyen art .. 10.00
Zen Earth Annual #1, Sam
  Keith art 10.00

BOOKMARK CARDS
Antioch Publishing (1993)
These are I.D. card size, plastic cards with color graphics on the front and B&W text on back.
X-Men, 4 diff., each 1.50
  Student Trainee, Xavier's Institute
  Staff, Xavier's Institute
  Pass, Danger Room, etc.

STAMPS & STICKERS

SUPER HERO STAMPS
Celebrity Stamps (1976)
(10 stamps in pictorial envelope 4¼"x11" plus 1 gold foil sticker)
DC1 Superman 6.00
DC2 Batman 6.00
DC3 Shazam 5.00
DC4 Wonder Woman 5.00
DC5 The Flash 5.00
DC6 Super Villains 5.00
M7 Spider-Man 6.00
M8 Hulk 5.00
M9 Thor 5.00
M10 Fantastic Four 5.00
M11 Captain America 5.00
M12 Iron Man 5.00

MAIL-IN OFFERS
Celebrity Stamps (1976)
Gold Foil Blocks of four stamps
FBDC-1 Superman 5.00
FBDC-2 Batman 5.00
FBDC-3 Shazam 5.00
FBDC-4 Wonder Woman 5.00

FBDC-5 Flash 5.00
FBDC-6 Joker 5.00
FBM-7 Spider-Man 5.00
FBM-8 Hulk 5.00
FBM-9 Thor 5.00
FBM-10 Fantastic Four 5.00
FBM-11 Captain America 5.00
FBM-12 Iron Man 5.00
Mint Sheets; 15 or 20 per sheet
MSDC-10 Superman 7.50
MSDC-11 Superman's Mission 7.50
MSDC-12 Justice League 7.50
MSDC-13 Batman 7.50
MSDC-14 Shazam 7.50
MSDC-15 Batman and Robin . 7.50
MSDC-16 WW Hall of Fame .. 7.50
MSDC-17 Diana Prince 7.50
MSM-18 Spider-Man Hall
  of Fame 7.50
MSM-19 Spider-Man senses .. 7.50
MSM-20 Spidey 7.50
MSM-21 The Hulk 7.50
MSM-22 Thor Hall of Fame ... 7.50
MSM-23 Iron Man–Sock it to 'em 7.50
MSM-24 Captain America 7.50
MSM-25 Fantastic Four vs.
  Galactus 7.50

SUPER HEROES PUFFY STICKERS
Henry Gordy (1982)
Rack packet of 6 stickers
  2 diff., each 4.00
Set: 12 stickers 7.50

STICKERS
Our Way Studios (1979)
Super-Stickers (DC), 15 stickers 5.00
Marvel-Stickers, 15 stickers ... 5.00

Super-Stickers (Our Way Studios 1979)

All prices listed are for *Near Mint* condition.

Comic Strip Classics 20-stamp sheet (United States Postal Service 1995)

The United States Postal Service issued a 20-stamp sheet honoring comic strip classics in late 1995. The stamps are worth 32¢ each until the postoffice runs out of them, but they should be collected as a complete sheet, with header strip, as shown above. The backs of the stamps have text which identifies the comic strip and artist and gives a short history. The back of the header strip has a mail-in offer for a souvenir hardcover edition of *American Comic Strip Classics*, which comes with two full sheets of the stamps for $29.95 plus $4.20 for shipping. Not a bad deal when you consider that two sheets of the stamps comes to $12.80.

20-stamp sheet (while they last) . . 6.40